ECONOMIC DEVELOPMENT
OF THE UNITED STATES

THE IRWIN SERIES IN ECONOMICS

Consulting Editor   LLOYD G. REYNOLDS   Yale University

Economic development of the United States

RALPH GRAY, Ph.D.
Professor of Economics
DePauw University

JOHN M. PETERSON, Ph.D.
Dean and Professor of Economics
College of Business Administration
Ohio University

Revised Edition • 1974

RICHARD D. IRWIN, INC.   Homewood, Illinois 60430
IRWIN-DORSEY INTERNATIONAL   London, England   WC2H 9NJ
IRWIN-DORSEY LIMITED   Georgetown, Ontario   L7G 4B3

Revised Edition

First Printing, March 1974

ISBN 0-256-01549-X
Library of Congress Catalog Card No. 73–89113

Printed in the United States of America

PREFACE

Our purpose in this revised edition of *Economic Development in the United States* is, as it was in the first edition, to present a brief version of the American economy's growth story. This new edition includes an expanded discussion of the colonies (Chapter 4) and a largely new chapter on economic growth as it relates to the quality of life (Chapter 16). The other chapters have been rearranged and revised significantly to account for new developments in the study of American economic history.

Although for the most part our account is presented in laymen's language, the point of view is very much that of the economist. This orientation emphasizes quantitative measurements and the changing geographical, technological, and institutional conditions that influence human material progress.

The remarkably different rates of growth and levels of economic attainment that we find in the world today explain the intense interest of both the economist and the layman in the subject of economic growth. Why does the United States have a standard of living so far above any other nation? How did our historically rapid rate of economic growth start? How was it sustained? Will it continue? These are some of the questions that this book introduces at the outset and keeps in focus throughout.

It is not our purpose to relate everything that occurred in the American economy between the first colonial landing and today. Rather we wish to explain how the economy grew and to demonstrate the effects of growth upon economic life. In accordance with this limited objective the text is shorter than the comprehensive textbooks on American economic history. Extensive use of graphs and tables, however, adds greatly to the information supplied in relatively few pages. We have opted for brevity in the text in order to avoid the mass of details that would cause a loss of perspective about the overall processes of growth and change in the system. Thus topics related to growth are given lengthy treatment while some standard topics in American economic history texts are omitted or given only brief mention. For example, wartime conditions, early unionism, and social reform movements are described but only as they are relevant to the growth process.

The book is divided into four parts, each dealing with a traditional period of American history. This division permits emphasis upon four phases of American development: preparation for growth, the start of rapid growth, transformation into a modern economy, and the strains of continuing rapid technological change in the contemporary economy. This organization also permits dealing with colonial origins and the between-wars years, 1860 to 1920, which are often slighted in the shorter textbooks on American economic history. Part I reviews the various economic, political, and social developments that set the stage for rapid growth in the late colonial and subsequent periods. Each of the subsequent sections begins with a summary of overall growth data, then analyzes changes by sector in the same sequence as the decades in which they were most important. This unified treatment of the economy within short periods avoids the disconnected treatment of particular sectors covering the whole length of American history—an organization common in shorter textbooks.

The framework of the text is built of the concepts of economic theory. Essential terms, therefore, are introduced gradually and are explained at their first point of use. Brief explanations of economic principles are woven into the exposition wherever necessary to focus on key relationships. Yet the emphasis is on the use of theoretical tools to tell the growth story and not on a technical discussion of the tools themselves. Several appendixes are included, not as afterthoughts, but because the material is best treated as a unit which makes review of the immediately preceding chapter and reading of subsequent chapters more meaningful. In the same spirit, we avoid preliminary definitions, argumentative digressions, and self-conscious introspection about the limitations of our present state of economic knowledge.

Economic data are presented graphically wherever possible, and the reader is instructed on how to read graphs. All graphs and tables are essential parts of the story, and the text refers directly to the specific points brought out by the graphs and tables. The visual aids along with the text headings are selected to aid the reader's grasp of the story of the text as it unfolds. Detailed facts presented in the text also are marshalled as supporting or illustrative material to the sequence of main ideas.

Varied uses of this book are possible. It was developed and tested as the sole textbook for a college of business administration course on American economic history that is required of freshmen students prior to their taking the principles course. We hope that foreign students and adults concerned with economic development problems will find it a succinct account of the American growth experience. We also hope that it can serve as a reference book for high school teachers and their students.

On the other hand, more advanced courses in American economic history can use this book as a core text, an organizing device, to be supplemented by library readings and/or research paper assignments. It has been used in this way by one of the authors. Also, several books of readings are available to supplement the text in standard upper division courses.

This text is still very much a joint product; however a shift in writing and editorial responsibilities accounts for the transposition of the authors' names on the title page of this edition. The conception of the book and its basic design are attributable to Peterson as was two thirds of the writing of the first edition. The new material included in this edition and the chapter-by-chapter revisions were Gray's responsibility. As with the first edition, this one was jointly planned and in preparing the final draft it was jointly reviewed by the authors.

The list of people we wish to thank is long. George D. Green reviewed in great and helpful detail the first edition as we prepared to revise it and then provided very useful comments on the next to last draft of this edition. Gary Walton was very helpful with Chapters 1 and 4. If there is praise for the outcome of this effort Green and Walton deserve their share, but certainly no share of the blame for errors and omissions is due them. Shepherd and Walton's *Shipping, Maritime Trade, and the Economic Development of Colonial North America* was especially useful in writing Chapter 4. Our typists were unflagging and dependable; we thank Susanne Fornaro, Sally Gray, Charity Pankratz, and LaVerne Peterson.

February, 1974

RALPH GRAY
JOHN M. PETERSON

CONTENTS

9. The transformation of the economy 312

Industrial structure: *Agricultural productivity increases. Strains of farm adjustment. Mass production and specialized suppliers. Foreign trade. Shift to an export surplus. Higher tariffs. Balance of payments.* Changes in industrial location: *Regional specialization. The heartland and the hinterlands. Regional growth and development. Urbanization.* Changes in industrial organization: *Big plants, giant businesses. Industrial concentration. Ownership, control, and financing. Professional management. Employee relations.*

10. The changing role of government 351

Changing social philosophy. Monetary and banking policy: *Civil War financing. Debt retirement and hard money. Bank regulation. Financing World War I. Money supply and prices.* Subsidies and regulation: *Development subsidies. Financing the railroads. The economics of railroads. Railroad regulation. The antitrust movement.* Public administration and services: *Rising government expenditures. Administrative problems. War mobilization.*

Part IV
ADJUSTING TO RAPID CHANGE: 1920–1970

11. Science-based growth 397

Trends since World War I: *The growth rate. Sources of growth. Income distribution.* Rapid technological change: *Diversity of innovations. Science, technology, and productivity increases since World War I. Education and the scientific age.* Shifts in industry structure. Progress and economic welfare.

12. Growth and instability 424

The cyclical record: *Prosperity decade. Depression decade. Expenditure interaction. The Great Contraction. Restrictive policies.* The New Deal: *Relief. Recovery. Reform. Recovery policy appraised.* World War II "prosperity": *Wartime stabilization policy.* Postwar stability: *Favorable postwar setting. Evolution of economic thought. Fiscal policy tools. The fiscal policy record. Monetary policy.*

13. Business and farm adaptations 462

A giant business enterprise: *Big firms in a big economy. Changes in market theory and behavior. Enterprise among giants. The quest for social control.* Agricultural adjustment: *Productivity increases. Overproduction. Price fluctuations. Basic trends. Rural poverty. Compensatory farm policy.*

14. The quest for security 503

Union bargaining: *The growth of the union movement. The bargaining process. Labor's progress.* Individual security and opportunity: *Personal*

ABBREVIATIONS

AER American Economic Review
AH Agricultural History
BHR Business History Review
BJEMS Bell Journal of Economics and Management Science
EEH Explorations in Economic History
EHR Economic History Review
EIHC Essex Institute Historical Collections
JB Journal of Business
JEH Journal of Economic History
JPE Journal of Political Economy
JSH Journal of Southern History
MLR Monthly Labor Review
MVHR Mississippi Valley Historical Review
PI The Public Interest
PP Past and Present
PSQ Political Science Quarterly
RES Review of Economics and Statistics
RRPE Review of Radical Political Economy
TAPS Transactions of the American Philosophical Society
VMHB Virginia Magazine of History and Biography

Part I

Preparing for growth:
1492–1790

1 ECONOMIC GROWTH AND THE DEVELOPMENT PROCESS

In a flicker of time the United States grew from economic insignificance to the largest economic power on earth. Over that same period, U.S. living standards raced ahead of the living standards of other nations. By the 1960s U.S. income per person was 30 percent above that of Britain, its mother country. Why?

King Cotton sparked the new Nation's growth, yet apparently left the South economically moribund. Did it? The Civil War was a needless bloodbath—by 1860 slavery was unprofitable and on its way out. Or was it?

The Civil War is often credited with stimulating a rebirth of the Industrial Revolution in America. What are the facts? In a similar vein, railroads are given credit for the American "takeoff" into sustained economic growth and for spearheading the settlement of the West. How important were they?

Did big business erode the economic welfare of the common man in the late 19th century? Or did consumers profit by the same forces that produced the Robber Barons?

Was the Great Depression inevitable given the structural faults the economy developed in the 1920s? Did New Deal policy prove or disprove the theories of John Maynard Keynes?

Was the combination of wage and price controls, heavy borrowing, and consumer rationing the only way to run the economy during World War II?

Recognize the questions? They and others like them are the subjects of this book. Our hope is to explain the dramatic development record

3

of the U.S. economy. In doing so, we want to examine rather critically the conventional wisdom of U.S. economic history, some of which is cited above. A few years ago one scholar wrote, "Even a cursory examination of accepted 'truths' of U.S. economic history suggests that many of them are inconsistent with elementary economic analysis and have never been subjected to—and would not survive—testing with statistical data."[1] A reappraisal of what we came to "know" about the American economy back in junior high school is, we think, an interesting way to review the American growth story.

INTRODUCTION

The subjects of this book are the economic growth of the United States and the underlying development process which made that growth possible. The growth of the American economy from colonial days to contemporary times constitutes a rich source of data for those who wish to learn about the development process in general as well as for those who are looking for new insights into political or social change.

The United States and the thirteen colonies that preceded nationhood have chalked up a remarkable economic growth record. In three and one-half centuries, an instant when measured against the world's history, a beleaguered handful of civilization's outposts grew and matured into the economically largest political unit in the world. The affluence of the United States not only outranks that of any other nation—it exceeds the wildest dreams of the social prophets of several centuries ago. Never before have a collection of humans had so great a material capacity to attack mankind's ills.

Our purpose is to review the course of U.S. economic history as a way of learning just how this fantastic growth record was attained as well as to scrutinize some of the usual assertions as to how it all happened. In this chapter, we shall sketch an outline of American economic development and then present some of the theoretical concepts and related definitions that are useful in analyzing the growth record of particular economies.

Before we take even one step into our economic past, a qualifying word is necessary—growth is not without its costs: development brings higher incomes, but it also produces dislocations, frictions, and strains of adjustment. Indeed, at the 20th century's three-quarter mark, many of the Nation's problems stem from its economic success and the rapid rate at which it attained that success. The threat of industrial and domestic pollution to the natural environment is a glaring example. Mechanization has displaced workers; new techniques and changes in production patterns have depressed entire regions while rendering major

---

[1] North (1963), p. 129.

industries obsolete; and the stresses of rapid urbanization followed by suburbanization have produced social time bombs.

International political competition has always complicated our attempts to deal with domestic economic problems. In the mid-1960s government programs to smooth adjustments to growth had to give way to military expenditure (and, some would say, to the space race). Spending to finance the war in Southeast Asia caused aggregate demand to outstrip increases in capacity to produce. Consequently, the unemployment ratio fell but price inflation accelerated. Now, as this is written, space and military spending have slacked off, growth has been interrupted by a recession; yet, paradoxically, price inflation continues at high rates, rates so high that President Richard Nixon has adopted a policy of continuing government controls over wages and prices.

Internationally, we find the United States in several dilemmas. First, as a political entity, the Nation has viewed itself as in a growth race with the centrally planned powers but unable and unwilling to guide the economy with as tight a rein as are Russia, China, and the East European nations. Second, U.S. foreign policy has had assistance to the less developed nations as an express goal—a goal for which we certainly have the material resources. But, unfortunately, we do not know enough about growthmanship to generate satisfactorily the kinds of advances low-income countries desire. Third, we share with the other non-Communist nations the vexations that arise from an inadequate international monetary system.

These problems as well as our successes have stimulated new interest in the growth experience of the United States. If we come to understand our own history better, we might be a little wiser in dealing with our own growth problems and assisting other nations. But this does not mean that past experience can be repeated or applied as an exact guide in the future. Nor can we transfer, unaltered, lessons from our past to nations with radically different social and economic conditions—study of just one nation's experience is not enough. Yet, as we asserted above, the past is a rich source from which we can discover the forces controlling both our growth and that of other nations.

THE COURSE OF U.S. ECONOMIC GROWTH

Primarily political events have divided American history into five periods. It is useful to look at the history of the American economy in this traditional context simply because forces which are not specifically economic have much to do with shaping economic phenomena and influencing the course of economic growth. The division we have selected is outlined below. Note that although wars set the periods apart we have used economic concepts to describe each period. Also note that the division into periods is a convenient organizational device—the similarities between periods are great, and the distinctions are the results of gradual change, measured evolution.

1. A colonial economy in a mercantilist world
2. Transitional America: foundation of national economy
   a. The Revolutionary economy, 1775–89
   b. Early nationhood, 1789–1815
3. Early growth and transition, 1815–65
   a. King Cotton
   b. Manufacturing ascent
   c. The War Between the States
4. Transformation of the economy, 1865–1914
5. Adjusting to rapid change in an affluent economy, 1914 to the present

Now let us rough in this outline so that you, the reader, have some foreknowledge of what we will investigate and, we hope, explain in subsequent chapters.

America joined what is called the civilized world by being colonized in the *mercantilist* era. This was the period in which colonization as an explicit policy of the major powers was designed to help maximize the power of the mother country. In short, the North American colonies were of mercantilist parentage. But, oddly enough, once they almost all became British colonies they were largely ignored from the standpoint of British mercantilist policy. It is only slightly overstated to say that until 1763 the American Colonies operated as if they were a group of English counties that were contiguous with England in all respects except geography.

The early years in a colony's development were years of heavy investment, and for the colonists the rewards were generally great. The towns the colonists founded, the roads they built, the ships they launched, the harbors they improved, the pastures and arable fields they carved from the wilderness, and the business and financial institutions they created became the bases for rapid economic expansion—so rapid that income per person grew modestly in an age when unchanging levels of living were the rule.[2]

Next, America entered 40 years of continual upheaval. The War of Independence was followed by a period of independent nonnationhood, initially as an economic beneficiary of the Napoleonic Wars, ultimately as a victim of those same conflicts. By the time this political-economic maelstrom had settled, the United States had achieved two highly significant victories: acceptance abroad for its claims to sovereignty and the establishment of political union at home. After a generation of struggle, the new nation was able to join as an officially recognized player in the international game of commerce.

---

[2] See chapter 4 for discussion of income data and sources.

Cotton became King Cotton in the period that began in 1815, with the end of the War of 1812. American exports, dominated by cotton, grew; the total economy expanded; and soon the market was large enough and transport efficient enough to enable domestic manufacturers to increasingly outcompete their British rivals here and, by the 1850s, abroad. It is not clear whether cotton can be considered the prime mover of the American economy in this period or one among a host of forces producing expansion and per capita income growth. However, it is clear that cotton culture influenced the *entire* antebellum economy's growth.

After the depressed decade from the late 1830s to the late 1840s, per capita income growth revived and agriculture lost ground relative to manufacturing as a development force. The evolution of economic forces with some outside pressures in the form of tariffs and related public policies laid the groundwork for a move toward national economic self-sufficiency.

Tragedy followed. The issues of slavery, international trade policy, and interregional frictions cut the Nation into a score of rival factions. Ultimately, two armies formed, one Rebel, one Yankee, the latter manned by Northerners, the former manned by Southerners, but, symptomatic of the crosscurrents of feeling at the time, both armies were supplemented by volunteers from the Border States. The economy stagnated. War meant human and material destruction, allocation of resources to wasteful ends, and interruption of normal commercial relations. Economic development paused, perhaps receded.

After the war came a resumption of growth, then an acceleration in the rate of income production in both total and per capita terms. In spite of monetary upheaval and volatile year-to-year movements, the upward trend of economic indices persisted to World War I. Efficiency both on the farm and in the factory increased markedly, while new products and better transportation facilities revolutionized life for rich and poor alike. The economy underwent a sweeping transformation in which manufacturing growth, industrial concentration, government regulation, and urbanization were key events.

By the end of this era, the Nation stopped pushing out and started to fill up. Further, the economy had become almost self-sufficient—the portion of the work force that depended upon foreign trade directly or indirectly for its livelihood declined persistently in the 19th century as growth of the domestic market and, in varying degrees, tariffs made national self-sufficiency profitable for domestic producers.

For reasons which are still not clear to historians, the United States chose in the last third of this period to push its expansion beyond the continent. The push westward had been facilitated by the seizure of Indian lands, so perhaps becoming a colonial power was a natural projection of the Nation's trajectory of expansion. The United States acquired some of Spain's overseas possessions and successfully extracted from China the trade and legal prerogatives that normally go with colonization.

World War I ended this period and ushered in an era in which the U.S. economy has become so vast that American economic movements can send shock waves around the world, whereas, paradoxically, no other nation is able to affect us in a comparable way. The first of these shock waves was the Great Depression. Our initial reaction to the Depression was to raise tariff barriers as part of a beggar-thy-neighbor strategy that threw world trade into chaos and transmitted the Depression's effects from nation to nation, round after round.

In 1933 Franklin Roosevelt launched the New Deal to cope with the mass unemployment and poverty that the Depression brought to the land. In doing so, he acknowledged that the 20th century American economy was basically different from its 19th century forebear—different enough to warrant, to urge in fact, a new economic role for government. In addition to providing a basic framework for a laissez-faire market system, government was assigned an active role in stabilizing income and employment and insuring the masses against privation. Later administrations and Congresses ratified government's enlarged role by adding to New Deal programs.

World War I marked the end of an era for the world economy—or at least for that portion of it which produced most of the output. In the 19th century Britain and its European neighbors had built an integrated international economy, one in which the United States participated in a piecemeal fashion by continuing to welcome immigrants but maintaining unfashionably high tariff barriers. Goods, services, and funds flowed almost unencumbered among these nations much as they do now among the 50 states of the United States. The Great War, as it was first named, and its Carthaginian peace all but destroyed and blocked rebuilding the community aspects of the world economy. The United States and other nations threw up new trade barriers and restricted immigration severely. The Great Depression reversed attempts to restore the old order.

Politically, the 1914–18 war had not settled anything. After a two-decade pause, war resumed. U.S. participation meant massive government spending and an end to the Great Depression. Unemployment was absorbed by the war effort and its stimulus to the civilian economy; paradoxically, the tragedy of war accelerated U.S. economic growth and raised consumer spending on goods and services.

The depression everyone expected did not follow the end of hostilities. Slightly more enlightened economic policies, continued high levels of government demand occasioned by foreign policy commitments, easy money, and a great deal of good luck produced a quarter century of reasonably high growth rates and unprecedented stability. Other industrialized nations followed suit, in no small measure because of material stimulation from U.S. imports.

Not that the Nation was without domestic economic problems—as noted above, coping with the by-products of our success has not been easy. But internally we have been very successful—family incomes are higher than at any other time in history; the poor are now near the smallest fraction of the population on record, even by drastically elevated standards; and U.S. citizens enjoy more leisure than ever. If the quality of life is not what a backward glance suggests it could be, it is not because the domestic economic system has failed in the terms in which people usually define failure.

Since World War II the United States has participated in building a new institutional basis for dividing up the world's labor and trading its output and raw materials. If the appraiser looks at trade volume only, it would seem that the architects did their work well. But the continued misery of the people of the so-called third world, the less developed countries, and recurring international financial crises suggest that progress has been very uneven. Postwar economic history suggests that the international economy will not right itself. Rather, new conventions, new institutions, and new knowledge must be brought to bear.

SCARCITY, GROWTH, AND MEASUREMENT

We have discussed economics, economic growth, and related income concepts without defining them. This we rationalize on the assumption that we have been general enough for our context to define our terms. But we shouldn't proceed further without some definitions, starting with a definition of economics.

Economics is often referred to as the science of scarcity. Man simply has more desires than his scarce, or economic, resources can accommodate—his economic problem is that his material wants exceed his capacity to produce goods and services that will satisfy those wants. *Economics is the social science that deals with man's behavior as he combats the scarcity problem,* as he organizes scarce economic resources—labor, capital, and natural resources—to produce and distribute products. And *economic growth is the result of a complicated set of processes by which economies increase their capacity to produce* so that living standards can rise.

Unfortunately, we have no direct way to measure the amount of *want satisfaction,* or *economic welfare,* any given period's production makes possible for the people of a society. However, economists have developed methods for measuring the monetary value of national production and income which give at least some notion about the volume of products produced to satisfy wants. It is these monetary measures, called the **national income accounts,** which we use to compare economies in a particular period and to chart their development over time. The national income accounts provide several different measures of total economic activity, each with a slightly different composition. Data presented in tables and graphs in this book use a number of these measures according to the availability of information and the type of analysis being presented.

Turn now to 1–1, which summarizes the U.S. national income accounts for 1970. At the extreme left we have the most familiar production measure used by economists, **gross national product,** or GNP. GNP is simply the market value of all goods and services produced in the economy in a given time period, usually a year. The gross national product is composed of goods and services purchased by consumers, government purchases, net sales to the rest of the world (exports), and purchases of productive facilities (investment). GNP can also be viewed from the standpoint of those who engage in economic activity as workers or owners of productive facilities. Looked at in this way, GNP is a measure of gross earnings arising from the time period's production for consumers, investors, governments, and the rest of the world.

When GNP is divided by population or the number of workers in the labor force, the result is a measure of output or income per person or per worker. Per capita estimates provide the most useful measures economists have for comparing the productiveness of various economies or charting the growth of an economy over time.

If you will move step by step from the GNP bar in 1–1 to the bar on the extreme right which is labeled **disposable personal income,** you will note that a series of deductions from and additions to GNP have been made. The purpose of these refinements is to produce a figure which gauges the net flow of income into households, in other words, to show the amount of income households have available to spend on consumer goods and services.

The deductions are for items that are claims on income but do not become available to households for division between personal consumption and personal saving. For our purposes, the most important item deducted is the **capital consumption** allowance, which is an estimate of the amounts of privately owned capital goods that are worn out in the process of producing the year's output. In other words, the capital consumption figure is an allowance for depreciation of the Nation's stock of plant and equipment and housing. When subtracted from investment, it reflects the net additions to the Nation's productive facilities—in 1970 net investment was $47 billion, which was composed of $135 billion investment less $88 billion capital consumption. GNP less the capital consumption allowance (CCA) yields **net national product** (NNP).

The addition to GNP shown in 1–1 is for government transfer payments which do not involve productive activity but do constitute income to households. In the United States, *transfer payments* consist chiefly

(relation of the four major measures of production and income flows)

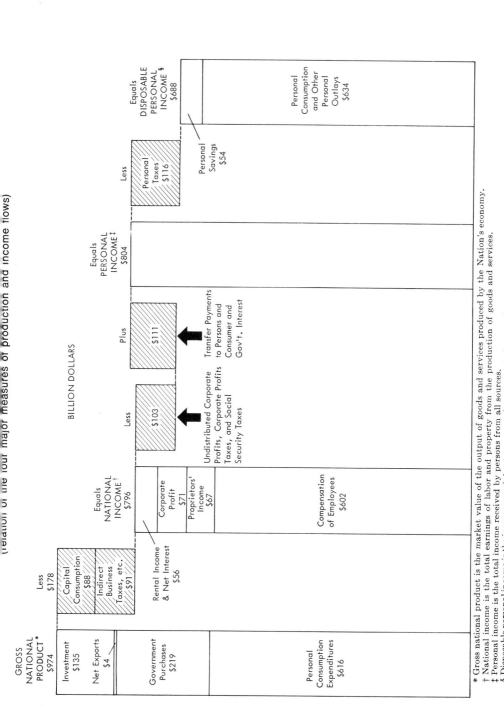

* Gross national product is the market value of the output of goods and services produced by the Nation's economy.
† National income is the total earnings of labor and property from the production of goods and services.
‡ Personal income is the total income received by persons from all sources.
§ Disposable personal income is the income remaining to persons after payment of personal taxes.
SOURCE: U.S. Department of Commerce, p. 12.

of social security payments which are part of such programs as Aid to the Aged and Aid to Dependent Children.

As you will see illustrated time and time again in later chapters, there are important reasons to qualify conclusions about growth that are based strictly upon monetary measures. At this point, several examples might help you understand why income data should be supplemented by additional figures as well as other kinds of observations.

Take two mythical kingdoms with precisely the same income per person, i.e., total income divided by total population is identical. However, in one kingdom the sovereign receives half the nation's income and his subjects divide the rest about evenly, whereas in the other kingdom the king gets a modest salary in return for serving as ruler and commander in chief while the people receive about equal shares of the nation's total income minus the monarch's paycheck. Obviously a prima facie case can be made for saying that economic welfare rather than being equal in the two states is higher in the latter than in the former. Why? Because data on the income distribution patterns serve as useful supplements to our per capita figures.

A second example is drawn from U.S. history. Recently, Stanley Engerman used per capita figures for the Nation and the South to support his assertion that the plantation economy of the slave South did not produce economic stagnation in the period 1840–60. Over those two decades the South's per capita income grew at 1.8 percent per annum while the Nation's grew at only 1.3 percent per annum.[3] But in a paper commenting on Engerman's work, Marvin Fischbaum and Julius Rubin note that "in an open economy regional differences in the rate of growth of real per capita income do not necessarily reflect differences in the rate of improvement of economic welfare."[4]

In this case, it could be that the Southerners who moved north bettered their economic positions. And we know that the North was the principal recipient of immigrants from other nations who sought among other things a higher level of living. Yet because immigrants to the North from Europe and the South were predominantly low-skill, low-wage workers, their arrival would tend to slow Northern per capita income growth rates. Thus, it could be that on the average Southerners who remained in the South did not experience as rapid growth in economic well-being as the average person who lived in the North over the entire period. Per capita growth figures suggest that Horace Greeley's advice for those times should have been "Go South, young man," whereas immigration data (and, doubtless, wage differentials) suggest that the best opportunities were in the North (including the West).

These examples demonstrate why all of us—students, teachers, schol-

---

[3] Engerman, pp. 71–97.
[4] Fischbaum and Rubin, p. 331.

ars, the public—must use income statistics with great care and with an eye toward other evidence. On the other hand, monetary measures with supplemental evidence are very useful in learning about growth and the growth process.

ECONOMIC GROWTH AND DEVELOPMENT

Why and how did a few nations in Western Europe and North America start and maintain such a rapid economic growth that their incomes far exceed any generated in other parts of the world? What are the forces that influence the starting and sustaining of rapid growth? The past is perhaps our best key to answering these and related questions.

A reinterpretation of the past

History as a field of study aims to provide a narrative record and interpretation of the more important events in human experience. While attempting to consider all important aspects of human events, written history must necessarily select from the great mass of details available. And it must always interpret what happened. Indeed, each generation of historians has interpreted past events in terms of its current understanding of relationships in nature and human society. Thus, some reinterpretation of history is made necessary by new concepts and new quantitative information about past events.

Economic history arose as one specialized kind of interpretation of facts about the past—a concentration on the economic aspects of human activities. In other words, economic historians study man's historical struggle with the scarcity problem, his attempts to get the most welfare he can with his meager resources. As historians began to try to take into account the widest possible range of political, economic, and cultural events, they relied more and more on specialized studies. Thus, economic history became a special field as economics developed as a major social science.

Over the past decade or so, what has come to be called the New Economic History has emerged as a natural reaction to the improved data and richer theory available to the student of American economic history. The U.S. Department of Commerce's *Historical Statistics of the United States: Colonial Times to 1957* marked a watershed in economic history in that it brought an unprecedented amount of data within the economic historian's grasp. And the growth and maturation of economic theory since 1920 has meant that the economic historian now has a firm intellectual base from which to analyze his new data.

The New Economic History differs from its narrative forebear in several respects. First, its methodology involves specifying an explicit hypothesis about a given historical phenomenon. Economic theory is used to construct a cause-and-effect statement about a historical event. Second, statistical data and analysis are used to test the tentative explanation for the event in question; if the data are as the theory predicts the hypothesis is not rejected, but if theory and fact do not agree a new hypothesis is sought. Third, theory is used to measure obliquely data that was not directly recorded in the past, to "produce" statistics. Of course, narrative economic history used quantitative data; but, conventionally, hypotheses were left implicit and were not systematically tested, and statistics were cited to illustrate points of argument rather than as evidence used in a theory's "trial."[5]

The study of economic growth has been the major interest of the New Economic historians. Its subject matter is ideally suited to their analytic approach. Growth studies concentrate on long-term trends, on aggregate measures, and on the interrelations of a nation's major productive sectors.

This approach to the study of the past is influenced by the economist's practice of looking at all current economic activities in a nation as one interrelated system—often referred to as the national economy. New data have been developed to extend the national income accounts to previous periods. New applications of theory have been used to demonstrate how key measures of productive activity and various forms of organization may be interrelated in a complex sequence of changes over time, i.e., to explain economic growth in cause-and-effect terms.

Growth measures and concepts

To analyze changes in productive capacity and economic welfare over time, we need to distinguish between two terms. The first is that of *economic expansion,* or *extensive growth.* This merely refers to an increase in GNP or income. The growth of other measures, such as total population, may accompany an increase in production. Since many parts of an economy may increase in unison, population changes may be used to represent the expansion of the economy when a good measure of total production is not available. Population increase, for example, has been used to estimate expansion in production in eras for which no production measures are available on the ground that population could not have grown unless the ability to produce the bare essentials grew as well.

You should note at this point that we are referring to continuing increases over long periods of time. In this kind of study, we are con-

---

[5] There is already a rich literature on methodology and the New Economic History, too vast to cite here. The interested student could start with Part I in Andreano, then work backward and forward in the literature from there.

cerned with secular trends rather than with temporary and erratic changes, such as booms or recessions.

The second term is *economic growth,* or *intensive growth.* This means an increase in production relative to population and, thus, growth in income per person, or *per capita income*—an increase in the ratio of production to population which makes possible higher living standards. When both production and population are increasing, production must increase faster in order for their ratio to increase. The term economic growth is applied to any increase in the ratio, whereas a decrease might be referred to as negative growth.

The proximate cause of sustained intensive growth is rising *productivity,* that is, increased efficiency or productiveness of inputs. Higher productivity can be thought of as making possible more output with the same quantity of inputs or attaining a given level of output with fewer inputs. At least since the Civil War, the U.S. economy has characteristically split its increases in productivity between more production and shorter working hours.

Unless we indicate otherwise, the term rate of growth refers to the percentage change in the production/population ratio, i.e., the rate of intensive growth. This provides a means of comparing the growth of nations of different size and the growth of the same nation at different periods of time. As already noted, the ratio of production to population is an indicator of average welfare in a nation, although it does not show how incomes are distributed among persons or how wisely resources are being used to serve human needs. It also reflects the average productivity of the population as a whole, although it does not indicate the proportion working or their hours and efficiency.

The significance of the distinction between extensive and intensive growth is that not all expansion involves growth in the sense of increases in per capita income levels. If population rises as fast as production, there are simply more people with the same average means of satisfying their wants. If population outruns production, there may actually be both expansion and negative economic growth. Or production might conceivably remain the same while population decreases (say, through migration), so that although there would be no expansion economic growth would occur. Economic growth has usually been accompanied by expansion and has often, as we will see, been aided by it; but one does not require the other, and the two may differ in their rates of change.

A third term should also be defined: *economic development* is the process by which changes in production methods and organization generate economic growth. It is not a measure but a historically evolving sequence of alterations in technical, economic, and social relationships that transform the structure of the economy. To use a sports analogy: economic development is the game, economic growth is the score. The study of economic development aims to identify the changing relationships associated with economic growth, to examine critically the conditions and events that seem to cause the changes, and to propose ways to influence future changes.

We can clarify the interrelationships of economic growth, economic expansion, and the development process with an analogy to living organisms. In the life of a plant or animal, growth involves more than simply getting bigger, more than expansion. The growth of living organisms involves changes in the proportions and relations of the parts to the whole while the whole expands. In fact, the sequence of changes in the parts and in their functioning within the whole permits or causes the expansion of the whole organism. Growth to maturity implies not only greater size but also greater capacity to function. Thus a man is not merely larger than a child: he is able to perform a far greater variety of tasks than a child.

The analogy of economic growth with growth in living organisms is frequently used in connection with rising production in nations. However, we must be careful not to let our choice of words dominate our thinking about this subject. We do not know whether growth ever reaches "maturity" and stops in the history of nations as it does in the lives of men. Also, we do not know whether different nations or different historical periods belong to the same species—that is, we do not know whether they will grow in the same patterns or whether their growth will be determined by the same causes. Our terminology merely helps us keep clear what changes we are referring to—changes in total production, changes in production per person, or changes in methods and organization that influence production.

Growth variables

At any given time, a nation's maximum potential output and income per head is determined by its population, its supply of inputs, current technology, the state of economic organization, and the cultural, social, and political conventions that help determine the configuration of the economic environment. In turn, intensive economic growth comes from a variety of factors in a variety of combinations. Economic growth can result from any or all of the following:

1. More material resources per person.
2. Better resources.
3. Better economic organization.

After allowances have been made for year-to-year ups and downs in economic activity, when any combination of the above generates sustained increases in productivity, economic growth is the consequence. In recent years, the U.S. economy has grown at about 2.1 percent per year, while growth rates in other industrialized nations have ranged as high as Japan's 7.7 percent. In many of the less developed nations, intensive growth rates have been zero or negative. The United States, while head and shoulders above the rest of the world in per capita income, is among the slowest growing industrialized nations in percentage terms. Yet in absolute terms, because the U.S. per capita income base is so large, its yearly increases are still above those of fastest-growing Japan.

The growth factors cited above will not appear or bear fruit unless the political and social dimensions of the economy are conducive to growth. If by design or accident attitudes and customs conflict with growth-oriented economic organization, growth won't occur. For example, in nations where population growth periodically outstrips growth in foodstuffs because folkways place a large number of children ahead of all other considerations, no amount of technical assistance or capital transfusions from developed nations will turn up the GNP/population trend line.

We have already listed the resources which are combined as inputs to produce a society's output. Let us make their implied definitions explicit, then explain their roles in generating growth.

Labor, or *human resources,* refers to people who perform productive services either as employed or self-employed workers or managers. *Capital* usually refers to the nonhuman resources which are produced so that work can be performed more efficiently—buildings, machines, and transport equipment are examples. *Natural resources* refers to arable land, minerals, and other gifts of nature which are useful in producing goods and services.

Some examples of how more resources per person could come about and contribute to economic growth might help you at this point. If a nation channels part of its income into savings, then the resources that are released from consumer goods production can be used to produce capital equipment. If the capital is designed correctly, if it is labor-saving, it can replace depreciated capital in such a way that the same national work force can operate a larger capital stock than before and thus produce more output.

If in a given economy capital investment is directed toward draining swamps and clearing trees, then access to natural resources is increased. Food production can therefore rise, and an increase in per capita income will have been recorded.

If potential workers enter the work force and find jobs, production will rise simply because employment of the labor force has expanded. Economic growth will have resulted from a rise in what is called the labor force participation rate.

Over the history of industrial economies—those with large manufacturing sectors—economic expansion has been brought about by massive increases in productive resources. Per capita income growth has usually accompanied expansion because inputs have grown faster than population. Technological innovation has made possible laborsaving machinery; capital investment has improved access to land and other natural resources; and labor force participation rates for women have increased.

As subsequent chapters will show, better or more efficient resources are even more important as a source of growth than more resources per person. Here science, technology, and education as a diffusing mechanism occupy center stage.

Let's start with technology. First, technology makes possible new and improved products so that the amount of human satisfaction that scarce inputs will yield can increase. Second, technological change increases the efficiency of productive resources so that the same amount of input produces more output, i.e., production costs per unit of product are decreased. When technological change proceeds over time, economic growth is fostered.

Technology's cost-reducing role is as varied as it is significant. As mentioned above, technological change can involve redesigning capital goods so that operators can control more energy and thus turn out more products in a given amount of time: multiple head drills, for example, allow workers to drill all the holes in a part simultaneously rather than one at a time. Economists refer to such an innovation as embodied technological change because it requires the design and production of new capital.

Technological change does not need to be embodied in all cases of increased efficiency. Resources can become better, that is, more efficient, simply because they are used more effectively. When inputs are not changed in nature but used more efficiently, productive ability rises even though technological innovation is not embodied in capital or some other resource. In factories, reorganization of the production process can make the same capital and workers more efficient. On farms, new plowing techniques, crop rotation, or different cultivation procedures can increase yields with the same land, labor, and capital inputs.

Science plays a crucial role in the process of making resources more productive. Pure scientific inquiry generates new knowledge which the inventor, often but not always a trained scientist or engineer, uses to develop a new product or production technique. After an invention has been tinkered with, ways are found to incorporate it in the actual production process of a particular firm and the invention becomes a technological innovation. Soon the innovation spreads throughout the industry and, by adaptation, to other industries. Often, diffusion of an innovation results in a feedback process by which new scientific inquiry and invention are stimulated by the advantages or shortcomings of the innovation in question.

The part played by education must be quite apparent to you by now. The more widespread knowledge is, the greater will be the rate at which scientific discovery, invention, and innovation take place and become diffused. What's more, knowledge should not be interpreted narrowly to refer to the pure sciences and the various engineering fields. The art of management and the social sciences are also vital to technological change—remember that a major contribution to increasing resource efficiency comes from organizational changes that are not embodied in capital or other inputs.

The subject of knowledge and its impact on productivity or productive efficiency is a major interest of investigators in a relatively new field in economics, the study of *human capital formation.* The field is so named because society devotes inputs to producing increases in the capacity of human resources through formal education, on-the-job training, and scientific research. As you will see in later chapters, some economists attribute as high as 40 percent of U.S. extensive growth over particular periods to improvements in human resources and the application of new knowledge.[6]

Better resources promote intensive growth along a second causal chain. Often an economy finds itself with better resources just because it has acquired more resources. It realizes *economies of scale,* or greater efficiency in resource use with larger size. Since a larger sized economy means larger industrial units can be formed, technology may permit use of larger sized equipment with lower unit costs, thus achieving internal economies of scale. More importantly, a larger sized economy means a greater number of industrial units. This permits some units to specialize in providing certain services to other units more efficiently than each can provide for itself, thus achieving external economies of scale.

The notion of synergy, of cooperating mechanisms, is useful in understanding scale economies. As an economy grows in size, it can become more diverse from an industrial standpoint. As the industry mix becomes more varied, particular industries interact to lower each other's costs or, to say the same thing in another way, raise each other's productivity.

Anyone who has observed horses standing side by side but facing in opposite directions at fly time has seen synergy in operation. Apart, two horses can only shoo away the flies around their rumps that their tails will reach, perhaps not quite a third of the flies that view them as dinner. Alongside each other, one horse can simultaneously shoo away flies from his hindquarters and his stablemate's forequarters while his

---

[6] Simon Kuznets is foremost among those who study the innovation process. For references to the burgeoning literature on human capital see the *Journal of Economic Literature* under the heading "Manpower; Labor; Population—Human Capital" and the *Index of Economic Journals* under the heading "Economic Theory . . . —Human Capital." Theodore Schultz, Gary Becker, and Burton Weisbrod are leaders in the latter field.

colleague is returning the favor. Synergy in this case means that nearly all of the flies can be shooed away by cooperative action whereas only one third can be shooed away by independent maneuvering.

For those who weren't raised in the country or in front of a TV screen, a second example of synergy might help. Large cities have advantages in treating liquid waste products that smaller community sewage treatment plants don't have. Why? Because the great variety of wastes means that particular waste products tend to offset each other—acids neutralize bases, highly dilute solutions become transport media for highly concentrated discharges, and so on.

In economies taken as a whole, external economies often arise because new industries emerge to serve the firms of long-existing industries by taking over some of the functions those firms performed. Even if the new industry uses accepted methods and traditional capital, productivity will rise because the new industry specializes. For example, the machine tool industry came into existence when it became apparent to managers of capital- and consumer-goods firms that machinery could be acquired more cheaply from a specialist than by producing it in the firm's own machine shop.[7]

A second and more specific example is provided by textiles. In the decade before the Civil War, the U.S. cotton textile industry had grown to such an extent that several textile machinery manufacturers could operate by selling at prices lower than the costs of producing textile machinery at individual mills. U.S. textile mills phased out their machinery-building function and took advantage of the external scale economy that these specialty machinery manufacturers represented.

Social overhead capital is a special source of external economies, a special kind of synergy. It is the capital that simultaneously serves many industries and lowers their costs. An initial large investment in commonly used facilities and services may be essential in the creation of certain industries. For example, construction of a dam to provide large amounts of cheap electricity is a prerequisite for building an aluminum production plant; but the dam may be larger than one plant or industry needs. Improvements in such common facilities as telephone lines, roads, warehouses, and ports may assist the growth and efficiency of many separate industries. Extensive growth of an economy makes it feasible to invest in such social overhead capital.

Historically, transportation is an excellent example. At the beginning of the 19th century there were too few farmers in Ohio, western New York, and western Pennsylvania to justify heavy transportation outlays. But when farmers grew in number, the Erie Canal became practical, and it increased the productivity of western farmers by lowering the cost of shipping out foodstuffs and shipping in capital equipment.

---

[7] On this point see George Stigler's fascinating article "The Division of Labor Is Limited by the Extent of the Market."

Better *economic organization* is often a source of economic growth. Economic organization in our context refers to the legal, social, and political institutions as well as the economic institutions which make it possible for managers to recruit productive inputs, to combine them to turn out products, and to sell products to consumers and investors. In other words, we are speaking of the man-made environment in which people buy and sell.

Russia's command system provides a useful first illustration of what is meant by organizational improvement. Russian growth has depended very heavily upon massive capital formation whose nature and volume in any given year depend upon planners' decisions and the effectiveness of the system's managers in carrying them out. Capital accumulation can be achieved at less sacrifice of consumer goods if the planning mechanism is improved so that individual producing units get better instructions, redundant functions are eliminated, and the least-cost combinations of inputs are more closely approached. Recent administrative changes in the U.S.S.R. have been designed to improve economic organization by streamlining the planning process.

In the United States most economic decisions are made in markets. Better economic organization can speed the growth of a market system in many ways. Let's look at an illustration that parallels our Russian example. Improvement of the financial markets, which convey savings of households to firms and individuals wishing to purchase capital equipment, can spur economic growth through increased capital accumulation. A wider variety of financial firms—commercial banks, savings banks, stock exchanges, bond dealers, and the like—means that savers and investors have more ways to get together which can encourage both saving and investing.

An aspect of economic organization that is very important to almost any economy is access to foreign markets. The need for particular raw materials is an obvious illustration. However, in many respects external economies that arise from foreign trade are more important than access to raw materials. When economies do not have to produce the entire array of products they wish to purchase, they can specialize in the areas of their greatest relative efficiency, a cost-reducing factor in itself. Such specialization breeds scale economies which further lower costs. Anyone familiar with Russia's agricultural problems or the relatively high cost of certain steel products in the United States is aware of the sacrifices that autarkical policies require, and thus by implication the advantages of an international division of labor should be obvious.

What this discussion of economic organization should make apparent can be summed up both positively and negatively. Innovations that increase the effectiveness of economic organization can speed a nation's growth. Put in the negative, laws, social conventions, private agreements, or foreign policies of other nations that block the most productive employment of a nation's material and human inputs will brake its economic development. To return to our sports analogy, the outcome of a Little League game will certainly be affected if on one side the manager must yield to parental pressure in deciding who plays where and how long.

By now it is probably apparent to you that there is no neat dividing line between higher productivity of specific resources and improved economic organization as sources of growth. For example, transport innovations can raise productivity in the sense that fewer of society's resources will be required to bring a given product from its raw material stage to the final customer's door. Improved transport in such a case may also make possible a different and more efficient organization of manufacturing industries—specialists in providing component parts, financial services, and/or services such as warehousing may enter the picture because transport costs are lower. In short, increased productivity of certain inputs (transport in our case) can reduce costs by reducing input requirements in general and by making possible changes in economic organization that further reduce input requirements as compared with the initial situation.

GROWTH THEORIES

How do all these growth variables fit together to produce a history of increasing per capita income? Unfortunately, we can't tell you conclusively. Economists have been unable to propound a single growth or development theory capable of giving cause-and-effect explanations for all of the growth experiences they have observed. We have instead a variety of theories, all of which involve the variables described above, but in different ways. Any one of these seems to explain satisfactorily the development of some but not all economies. By the same token, any one of our growth theories seems useful in predicting the effects of policies designed to change the development pattern of several national economies; yet no single theory is powerful enough to serve as the basis for designing development policies for all types of economies.

Things, however, are not as bleak as the above seems to indicate. On the one hand, research is providing a wealth of insight into the growth process by systematically checking growth theories (or hypotheses) against available evidence. On the other hand, our growth theories are to a degree complementary rather than competitive, which suggests that perhaps scholars are on their way to defining a truly comprehensive growth theory.

What we shall do in the next few paragraphs is to describe briefly four growth hypotheses that have proved useful. Then we shall conclude this section by again summarizing the colonial and U.S. growth experience, this time more briefly and in terms of the variables we have cited as crucial to growth and with reference to the growth theories cited below.

Four growth hypotheses

The most abstract of the four theories is the Harrod-Domar growth model, so labeled because Sir Roy Harrod and Professor Evsey Domar independently developed their hypotheses about the time of World War II. According to the Harrod-Domar model, capital and labor inputs must grow at positive and equal rates to produce stable economic expansion. Any tendency for one to grow faster than the other will generate a cyclical pattern of booms and busts—with one major exception. That exception is the case in which technological advance permits one input to grow faster than the other by redesigning the processes in which they cooperate to produce output.

A rudimentary example may help. If digging a canal is to proceed at a faster rate, more shovels will require more workers to operate them. But if the shovels are redesigned, then capital (shovels) can be increased by a larger proportion than workers. A 1 percent addition to the work force might be supplied with steam shovels whose value represents a 100 percent increase in digging capital; and the rate at which the canal is dug might approximately double. But without radically redesigned digging tools, 1 percent more workers would limit the effective growth of capital, and output, to 1 percent.

The above example applied to the entire economy suggests that intensive growth depends to a great degree upon technology making possible the growth of material inputs at a faster rate than population is growing. Unfortunately, though, beyond underscoring the vital role of technological change to per capita income growth, the Harrod-Domar analysis has not greatly helped the architects of growth policies.[8]

Colin Clark, an Australian economist, has developed a growth theory that emphasizes the importance of the structure of the economy as per capita income advances. Although it may not provide a great deal of assistance in formulating growth-inducing policies, it is useful in anticipating the pattern of development and thus in making policies designed to adjust economic life to that pattern as it unfolds.[9]

Clark and others noted that economies follow the pattern of consumers' tastes and habits as they change in response to income growth. At low income levels, productive capacity is concentrated in the *primary industries,* i.e., agriculture and the extractive industries, such as mining. As income per head rises, the industrial structure shifts in favor of the *secondary industries,* the manufacturing industries. Finally, changes in

---

[8] For an exposition of the mathematics of the Harrod-Domar growth theory and the role of technology in the model, see Dernburg and McDougall.

[9] See Clark, chap. 9.

employment and earnings are dominated by the **service**, or **tertiary, industries** as income per capita reaches levels we would describe as affluent.

Useful though Clark's thesis may be in forecasting where development might lead, it does not indicate that a developing economy's production patterns must pass through stages one and two in order to reach stage three. In our discussion of industrial development a few pages hence, you will see that foreign trade relations can make possible different growth sequences.

Professor Walt W. Rostow has proposed a second kind of stages theory of economic growth. Rostow lists his five stages very descriptively as follows: (1) the traditional society; (2) the period during which preconditions for takeoff are established; (3) the takeoff; (4) the drive to maturity; and (5) the age of high mass consumption. Rostow bases his stages upon "a dynamic theory of production" involving "leading sectors," rapidly expanding industries which dominate the economy at each stage. It is this production theory, according to Rostow, that explains why economic history is usefully thought of as a series of stages rather than a continuum.

Rostow's work has come under a good deal of attack in recent years from those who have examined the data very closely for each of the stages he has identified for various nations, including the United States. However, as a framework for discussing growth phenomena and as a way of identifying and classifying the important growth variables, Rostow's five stages can prove useful.[10]

Douglass C. North, a leader among the New Economic Historians, has adapted a fourth type of growth theory to the problems of economic history. North's thesis is that "the timing and pace of the economy's development has been determined by: (1) the success of its export sector, and (2) the characteristics of the export industry and the disposition of the income received from the export sector."[11] Unless low per capita income economies are very large in terms of population and natural resources, a nation's markets will not be large enough to support each of the various industries whose products it wishes to consume. In such instances, to consume as it chooses a nation must develop an export base by specializing in one or several types of output. Exports will be breadwinners in that they will earn the foreign exchange necessary to finance the importation of products that cannot be produced efficiently at home.

Economic growth, therefore, results from growth in the efficiency and total earnings of the export sector. In turn, the exact course of development is determined by the repercussions of the export industries

---

[10] See Rostow (1960), Rostow (1964), North (1966, 1st citation), Temin versus Rostow (1971), and Hession and Sardy, chap. 13.

[11] North (1966, 2d citation), p. 1.

upon the balance of the economy. If supplier industries are stimulated in great numbers, external economies will arise and the efficiency of the domestic economy will be enhanced. If earnings from the export base are directed into capital investment and consumption of output in a way that stimulates productivity increases, then export-base growth will stimulate intensive growth as a secondary effect. What is more, because of export-base growth a pattern of regional specialization may evolve that will further intensify per capita income growth.

North has applied his thesis to the antebellum U.S. economy; although the details of his findings have been modified as a result of subsequent statistical investigations, his analytic framework remains useful.

Industrialization and economic development

Often industrialization and economic development are equated. This is a mistake; they are not identical, though they usually go hand in hand over a rather long stretch of a nation's development.

Given the usual nature of people's tastes and habits the development process may require moving away from a predominantly agricultural economy and toward a rapidly growing manufacturing sector. This transition is what people refer to when they speak of industrialization or industrial development. And they often take it as synonymous with economic development. But the course over which an economy's maturation takes place goes much further than industrialization, and industrialization may not have to be the main thrust of development at any stage. Let's look briefly at consumers' habits to see how we might explain industrialization's role in development.

Very low income families provide themselves with food, shelter, clothing, and little else. Manufactured goods are limited to clothing and home furnishings and perhaps a very old car. If we move up a notch on the income scale and look at family budgets, we find that manufactured goods occupy a larger portion of the total budget than for the typical very low income family. When we reach that nebulously defined bracket called middle income, we find that services are of greater importance than for the lower two brackets—medical and dental care, cosmetic services, sight-seeing trips, and sports and recreation bulk larger. Finally, for the high-income brackets services are of great importance but leisure is of more significance than for lower income families. Vacations are likely to be longer, there are fewer working wives, children enter the labor force later because they study longer, and so on.

As Colin Clark has demonstrated statistically, many nations over their development course follow roughly the same expenditure patterns that can be observed in any given year in a set of households of different incomes. When agricultural productivity rises enough to yield a surplus, the average diet improves in a developing nation, but some agricultural inputs will be reallocated to urban manufacturing uses. In short, the human stomach can hold only so much. Consequently, when productivity rises beyond a certain point, resources will be directed to the next item on the economy's list of priorities; that item is usually manufactured output. Thus, an early stage of the total development process is often industrial development. Having once industrialized, a nation's growth in per capita productive capacity will be directed to satisfying other appetites—the welfare state with its great emphasis upon providing health and educational services for the masses seems to be a common postindustrialization phenomenon.

At this point, a warning: apart from light manufacturing, massive industrial development may not be an economically appropriate takeoff strategy for some nations. For certain economies the relative advantage their agricultural sector holds over other nations is great enough to warrant expanding food and fiber exports to gain growth in the consumption of manufactured goods. Industrialization might proceed, however, after a period of agricultural export growth—King Cotton in the U.S. economy is a classic example of this twist in the process of development.

Unfortunately, internal and international political considerations have motivated some of the predominantly agrarian economies to turn their backs on the agricultural sector. Instead, they have force-fed heavy industry when purely economic considerations would have dictated land reform and agrarian development as the first steps toward sustained per capita income growth.

Given this word of caution and this discussion of the impact of consumer habits upon the actual course of economic growth, we ask you to bear in mind while reading future chapters that industrial development is characteristically part of, not all of, economic development.

A second overview

Let's summarize this discussion of growth variables and theories with reference to the U.S. growth record since 1789.

The formulation of the Constitution meant true nationhood and provided a foundation for an overall economic organization that fostered growth. In this, North American attitudes favoring material progress were salutary. Export-base growth and associated rapid economic expansion yielded the scale economies, including those associated with social overhead capital, that produced intensive growth. Technological innovation, which, at many points, featured improved industrial organization and management, further intensified per capita income growth. Heavy investment in human capital, especially in the North, aided the diffusion and adaptation of knowledge that technological change requires. In turn, technological change made possible the growth of capital at a more rapid rate than labor. This capital-deepening process added to the intensive growth rate.

After an initial emphasis upon agriculture, especially cotton exports, manufacturing growth became the focus of development. At the end of the Korean War, manufacturing had reached its peak as a percentage of the work force, and agriculture had declined to less than 10 percent of the work force. On the other hand, services, which had been gaining in this respect since the turn of the century, continued to increase their share of the work force.

The notion that the United States, spurred on by railroads and manufacturing growth, "took off" in the period 1843–60, as Rostow says, has been refuted. It is clear, though, that the United States and its colonial forebear moved along a continuum in which preconditions for rapid economic progress were established, rapid income growth was realized, and, ultimately, industrialization and high mass consumption were achieved.

ECONOMIC SYSTEMS AND DEVELOPMENT

It must seem obvious that all economies, rich and poor, face the scarcity problem—our wants exceed our ability to satisfy them regardless of the existing living standard. It follows that economic growth, the process by which want-satisfying capacity is increased, is important to even the rich economies.

What may not seem so obvious is that the characteristics of economic growth and development are much the same regardless of the political-economic system in which resource allocation decisions are made—we don't have one kind of economics for so-called capitalist nations and another kind for Communist powers; scarcity is politically nonpartisan. However, the political and social conventions that determine who makes a nation's production decisions also determine the precise way in which basic economic forces influence the course of economic development and the ultimate pattern of production, consumption, and income distribution.

Broadly speaking, there are three major types of economic systems. Though conventions associated with all three may be employed in varying degrees in any one economy, we may roughly classify countries as having one or another dominant type of organizing principle.

First, there are systems that rely on *tradition* to make the basic economic decisions. Under this principle, all decisions as to methods of production, choice of products, choice of occupations, and distribution of rewards are determined by tradition; secular customs and religious beliefs and practices are shot through with economic rules and regulations. In today's primitive and old agricultural societies this principle of organization has predominated for many centuries. Past experience has been embedded in the social customs and thinking of the people, with the resulting rules handed down from parents to children. Custom dictates everything an individual is supposed to do, including his lifework. Social criticism and discipline are exercised over those who would try to change the social order. When a society must live close to the margin of starvation, experiments that fail can mean disaster, so those who stray from proven ways are severely disciplined.

Second, there is resource allocation by *command.* This is the principle of using physical force to coerce people to do what a central authority decides should be done. Whether the source of authority is military or political, the principle is one of deciding for others what shall be produced, how resources shall be employed, and how income shall be divided up. In some countries, particularly dictatorships, a large part of the productive activities of the multitude of the people may be determined by general rules or by arbitrary decisions of a few officials or a ruling class. This may be a shortcut means—as in the People's Republic of China—to make a rapid break with traditional customs and introduce new methods of production. But it also involves sacrifices of individual freedom, preferences, and standards of consumption. In some democratic societies the productive activities of the masses may be planned and directed in very general ways while leaving the individual considerable freedom and initiative to adjust to centrally determined decisions.

Third, there is guidance of economic activity by market choices—the *market system.* Decisions on production and consumption are left up to individuals who register their preferences by buying or not buying particular products. The system is described by the word market because markets are the medium through which decisions are transmitted. (The term capitalism, which is commonly used to describe the American economy, refers only to the ownership of capital and natural resources by individuals and private producer organizations. The term market capitalism is often applied to economies like that of the United States as a means of stressing that the decisions of private owners of productive imputs are constrained by the forces of the market.)

The U.S. economy is a market system. Much of the American growth story can be told in terms of the success of markets in facilitating the structural changes that development requires. When the development process called for manufacturing growth, urban wages pulled country folk away from the farm to fill urban factory jobs. Later, burgeoning markets for services absorbed workers as factories introduced laborsaving devices, reducing the need for manufacturing workers. However, it is important to remember that a prominent vein in our economic history has been the intervention of government on a continuing basis when markets actually or apparently failed to perform their functions.

CONTRASTS IN INCOME

Now let's put to work the definitions and principles we have discussed by investigating what the U.S. growth record means in comparison with that of other nations and other times. This review should serve two purposes: it will enable you to see how crucial the differences in growth variables among nations can be, and it will impart some notion of the unique aspects of our colonial and national development.

Contemporary income differences

In order to make international comparisons meaningful, let's start with family income comparisons in this country. How widely do family incomes vary within the United States? According to the 1970 population census, median family income in the United States was $9,433—that is, half of the families received more and half received less than the figure cited. The one fifth of the families with the highest ranking incomes had incomes in excess of $13,000 per year, while the one fifth of the families with the lowest ranking incomes had annual incomes of $3,500 or less.

We must turn to state averages for some figures more comparable to those of a poor nation. Because of variations in family size, a convenient single figure for purposes of comparison is provided by dividing total personal income by the population in a given area. Personal income per capita in the United States in 1970 was $3,920. The state of Connecticut had the highest per capita personal income—$5,032—about one fourth above the national average. The state of Mississippi had the lowest per capita personal income—$2,575—not quite two thirds of the national average.

How do these income differences within our country compare with international differences? For these comparisons, the more inclusive measure GNP is more readily available. In the mid-1960s, GNP per capita in the United States reached $4,000.

The United States was far above the other non-Communist industrial nations in per capita GNP. The second ranking nation was Sweden, followed by Canada, then Iceland; each of these nations reached about two thirds of our figure. Next came most of the West European nations, Australia, New Zealand, and the United Kingdom, with per capita GNP figures ranging from $2,000 to $2,600. Israel and Japan, the remaining non-Communist industrialized nations, were in the range between $1,100 and $1,500.

Among the less developed nations of the world, per capita GNP levels are below one fourth of the U.S. average. Most of the land area and the bulk of the population of the world is in these nations. Since one fourth of the national average is regarded as a poverty level within the United States, most of the world appears poor indeed. Although international GNP statistics have notorious shortcomings, apparently half of the world's population lives on less than $300 per year, or $6 per week.

Explaining income differences

How do we account for these wide differences in income? The nucleus of our explanation consists of the differences in the growth variables we discussed earlier. Further, most of these differences lie among the variables that are subject to human control.

Population density is one of the most significant growth variables open to control through conscious human effort. A high ratio of people to natural resources can inhibit achieving a high ratio of production to population. And a rapid rate of population growth can intensify the problem.

Individual worker productivity is a second vital variable. Workers who are well educated and have sophisticated equipment to operate will have high productivity levels. U.S. workers, given their skills and large stock of capital equipment, can produce more per hour than most workers elsewhere. In farming, U.S. yields per man and per acre are higher than those of all or most other nations for many crops. In manufacturing, some U.S. industries can compete successfully with foreign products made by workers paid much lower wages because far less labor time is required for each unit of output. Differences in worker quality explain a significant portion of national productivity variations. Poor health, insufficient food, and illiteracy have obvious effects upon worker skills and energy. Thus, it is not surprising that the health and literacy data in 1–2 vary among nations in a manner similar to income levels.

A second element that explains differences in worker productivity is the amount of capital each worker controls—the tools and the power the worker has to assist him are key development variables. Similarly, the amount of social overhead capital backing up the work force is important in determining productivity. GNP devoted to industrial and social overhead capital investment in the less developed nations is generally low compared with the affluent countries. (See 1–2.) Energy consumption per capita follows the same pattern as income in 1–2, which indicates that the typical worker has relatively little electrical energy to assist him in manipulating capital equipment.

A cursory glance at 1–2 reveals a closed circle of poverty for the typical nation in the two lowest income classes. Low GNP per head results from the low productivity associated with hungry and illiterate workers. Low labor productivity requires the devotion of a very high portion of the work force to agriculture. Even though what appears to be a large percentage of a low GNP is devoted to capital investment, the absolute amount per worker is small because GNP per capita is low and population increases dilute the capital-deepening effects of investment. Thus, on the next round a larger but still hungry and uneducated work force must provide for a larger population with very little more capital equipment.

1-2.   Selected measures related to GNP per capita

Selected nations	Population percent increase yearly	Infant deaths per 1,000 births	Literacy percent of adults over ten years	Percent of workers in agriculture	Gross investment as percent of GNP yearly
Over $750					
United States	1.6%	27	98%	12%	18.7%
France	1.6	42	97	36	15.5
United Kingdom	0.5	26	98	5	15.9
West Germany	NA*	43	NA*	23	26.0
$300 to $750					
Israel	14.0	39	75	15	25.3
Austria	0.4	48	97	33	23.8
Italy	0.9	53	NA*	40	21.6
Argentina	2.0	62	86	23	19.0
$150 to $300					
Turkey	3.0	NA*	35	75	12.6
Brazil	2.4	107	48	68	17.7
Philippines	1.9	109	62	71	8.4
Mexico	2.8	81	55	58	10.9
Below $150					
Egypt	2.5	127	25	75	5.0
Indonesia	1.6	200	55	71	6.0
India	1.3	119	18	70	10.0
Pakistan	1.1	125	14	80	5.1

* NA: Not Available.
SOURCE: U.S. Senate, pp. 242–43.

Differences in natural resources among nations are important but not consistent sources of income disparities. It is possible to overcome natural resource disadvantages with heavy investment in material and human capital. As inspection of 1–3 will show you, some of the continents in which low-income nations are concentrated have rich resource endowments compared with population, whereas Europe, for example, has less than its population share of all the natural resources listed.

Disparities in economic organization account for the remainder of per capita income variations among countries. There are wide differences between the high-income and low-income nations in their knowledge of production methods and their ability to organize production and exchange.

In the less developed nations much production is still conducted by obsolete methods for lack of skilled workers and engineers able to use new methods, lack of university teachers to train managers and engineers, and lack of research institutions and scientists to adapt methods to local conditions. Furthermore, few managers in these nations have experience with large-scale business organizations; and business services, financial institutions, or marketing channels are inadequate to enable large-scale production to be carried out in a modern fashion.

1-3. Natural resource potentials

	Land area (million acres)		Population (million)	Iron ore (billion metric tons)	Coal (billion metric tons)	Petroleum (million bbl.)	Waterpower (million h.p.)
	Total	Arable					
World totals	33,381	3,030	2,400	293.4	6,266	95,208	750.3
			Percent of world totals				
North America	14.0%	17.9%	6.9%	25.6%	48.9%	28.8%	13.8%
Latin America	17.2	6.9	6.7	12.4	—	12.5	11.4
Europe	3.6	12.0	16.5	8.6	10.2	0.7	11.5
U.S.S.R.	16.5	18.3	8.0	3.7	19.1	5.9	10.7
Asia	19.9	28.2	53.0	8.9	17.6	51.9	13.1
Africa	22.5	15.2	8.3	40.7	3.3	0.2	36.5
Oceania	6.3	1.5	0.5	0.1	0.9	—	2.8

SOURCE: Woytinsky and Woytinsky, p. 471.

Germany and Japan, with many of their factories destroyed during World War II, were able to reindustrialize rapidly because of their technical know-how, organizing abilities, and institutions. Yet, in contrast, many of the less developed nations are not ready for industrialization. They do not have the attitudes, knowledge, and organization needed to make full use of the financial aid and advice that have come to them from other countries.

Apart from chiefly economic institutional differences that make some nations grow while others languish, there are a host of man-made social and political differences that cause productivity to differ. Where government is looked upon as a servant of the people and the economic system in general, growth rates tend to exceed those in nations where government is regarded as an agency to be manipulated for the profit of a ruling establishment. Similarly, the attitude of those who rule, whether by majority consent or out of sheer power, has much to do with whether the economic factors we have cited above are conducive to growth. For example, in our South in the days of King Cotton the ruling class saw little reason to spend heavily in the public sector for education or other purposes. As a result, the transition to a nonagricultural economic base has been slow and painful.

SUMMARY

1. As compared with other Western developed economies the United States has grown rapidly since colonial times. In three and one-half centuries, a tiny nucleus developed into the world's largest national economy in both total and per capita terms.

2. Economics is the social science that attempts to explain how men organize to combat the scarcity problem. The scarcity problem arises because men's wants are vastly greater than the productive resources at hand to produce goods and services capable of satisfying those wants. Thus, the economist studies how societies organize the use of a fixed quantity of productive resources—labor, capital equipment, and natural resources—in attempting to produce the most output with those scarce resources. Gross national product (GNP) is the money value of all goods and services made in an economy in a given year; GNP per capita is a measure of the degree of success attained in coping with the scarcity problem.

3. Economic growth, or intensive growth, is usually defined as an increase in GNP per person in an economy. Economic expansion, or extensive growth, refers to increases in GNP without reference to population. One can take place without the other, but often intensive growth is fostered by extensive growth.

Economic development is the process, the host of structural and organizational changes, that produces growth. Economic history is a branch of economics which deals with the evolution of economies over time. One of its most important fields is the historical study of economic growth and development.

4.   Economists do not have a single growth theory capable of explaining all the national growth experiences recorded to date. However, they have been able to identify the variables that affect productivity or productive efficiency and are therefore crucial to intensive growth. They include: (1) more resources per person, (2) higher quality resources, (3) improved economic organization, and (4) a social climate that emphasizes material progress, efficiency, and endeavor.

Investment in human capital—i.e., education, skill training, medical care, and other activities that determine the productivity of workers and managers—has been found to be one of the most vital factors affecting growth rates. Technological innovation that makes possible new products and more efficient production processes is a second vital growth factor that affects both the quality of resources and the efficiency of economic organization.

5.   People often confuse industrialization and economic growth—the two are related but not identical. Industrialization, or industrial development, refers to the span in an economy's growth history over which the agricultural sector declines in relative terms and the manufacturing industries grow very rapidly both in absolute terms and in their relative contribution to GNP.

6.   Growth problems are common to various alternative economic systems because all nations are plagued with the scarcity problem. Some economies let custom and tradition dictate what products will be made and by what productive process and how production will be divided among the populace. Nations with command systems, such as the People's Republic of China and the U.S.S.R., rely upon central governmental planning to make these decisions. The U.S. economy depends primarily upon market exchanges and the movements of product prices, wages, and interest rates to determine production and consumption patterns. Thus, the U.S. economy is classified as a market system.

7.   A brief survey of current economic conditions throughout the world underscores the importance of industrial and social overhead capital accumulation and investment in human capital in explaining differences in living conditions among nations. Economic organization and cultural values are also important determinants of GNP/population differences. On the other hand, natural resource variations do not have any consistent relationship with GNP per capita.

REFERENCES

R. Andreano, ed., *New Views on American Economic Development* (Cambridge, Mass.: Schenkman Publishing Co., Inc., 1965).

C. Clark,   *The Conditions of Economic Progress,* 3d ed. (London: Macmillan and Co., Ltd., 1957).

T. F. Dernburg and D. M. McDougall,   *Macro-economics* (New York: McGraw-Hill Book Co., 1960).

S. L. Engerman,   "The Effects of Slavery upon the Southern Economy," *EEH,* Winter 1967.

M. Fischbaum and J. Rubin,   "Slavery and the Economic Development of the American South," *EEH,* Fall 1968.

C. H. Hession and H. Sardy,   *Ascent to Affluence* (Boston: Allyn and Bacon, Inc., 1969).

D. C. North,   "Quantitative Research in American Economic History," *AER,* March 1963.

———,   *Growth and Welfare in the American Past* (Englewood Cliffs, N. J.: Prentice-Hall, Inc., 1966).

———,   *The Economic Growth of the United States, 1790–1860* (W. W. Norton & Co., Inc., 1966).

W. W. Rostow,   *The Stages of Economic Growth: A Non-Communist Manifesto* (New York: Cambridge University Press, 1960).

———, ed.,   *The Economics of the Take-off into Sustained Growth* (New York: St. Martin's Press, 1964).

———,   "The Strategic Role of Theory: A Commentary," *JEH,* March 1971.

G. Stigler,   "The Division of Labor Is Limited by the Extent of the Market," *JPE,* June 1951.

P. Temin,   "General-Equilibrium Models in Economic History," *JEH,* March 1971.

U.S. Department of Commerce,   *Survey of Current Business,* July 1971.

U.S. Senate,   Document 52, *Foreign Aid Program* (Washington, D.C.: U.S. Government Printing Office, 1957).

W. S. Woytinsky and E. E. Woytinsky,   *World Population and Production* (New York: The Twentieth Century Fund, 1953).

2 THE MARKET ECONOMY EMERGES

To understand the beginnings of the American economy, it is essential to see the importance of three aspects of our European origins. First, America's eastern coast was settled initially as a series of European pioneer colonies. Second, the colonial culture and institutions were influenced by the advanced stages of European transition from the medieval traditional economy to a modern market economy. Third, national status was begun with a well-developed market economy at the start of the industrial era in world history.

The fact that today's most advanced industrial nation had a colonial origin should be of considerable interest to underdeveloped nations which have recently won their own freedom from colonial status. We must be careful, however, not to try to draw oversimplified lessons or parallels from the American experience—we started with advantages these nations may not have. The thirteen American Colonies—as well as Canada, Australia, and New Zealand—were pioneer colonies which pushed aside the small, scattered native populations. In spite of Indian wars, adjusting dual societies or transforming native cultures were not significant problems. The pioneers brought a highly developed European culture and sophisticated economic institutions with them.

Europe was in the late stages of economic transition when the American Colonies were settled. The traditional economy of medieval Europe was breaking down, and a market economy was emerging. Many of the older institutions, however, lingered on as impediments to Europe's development. By contrast, in the American Colonies most of the features of the new society were established from the start, and few of the drawbacks were inherited. There was no struggle to overthrow a ruling class or to make over outdated institutions. This new beginning was also influenced by the pioneering conditions in the colonies. The natural opportunities and obstacles attracted the most adventurous individuals and forced them to be economically, socially, and politically adaptive.

The United States began its history in 1789 with a market economy at a time when the Industrial Revolution was in its first stages. This meant that we started at an advanced stage of development with a high degree of readiness to begin our industrialization and rapid growth. Per capita income in America was already at least equal to that of England and may not have been matched elsewhere in the world. We were an agricultural nation highly specialized in export crops and a trading nation actively engaged in world commerce. We had the institutions, leadership, skills, and wealth needed to launch our own development. In short, the preconditions of rapid economic progress were virtually established.

In this chapter we shall lay the foundation for our study of colonial and national growth by discussing three major topics. First, we will describe the nature of the system that preceded the Industrial Revolution. Second, we will discuss how the American Colonies developed as part of the process by which medieval life gave way to a new order. And, third, we will sketch the operation of the market system.

The last is especially important because the market system was integral to the industrialization process—so much so that some economic historians claim that one could not have been established without the other. In turn, U.S. development was very much determined by the Nation's role in the Industrial Revolution—first as a supplier of raw cotton to Britain's vanguard industry, cotton textiles, then as a direct participant.

EUROPE'S TRADITIONAL ECONOMY

At the peak of the Roman Empire a fairly high standard of living had been achieved in the Mediterranean area and much of Europe. The Roman military presence brought with it security, order, and a legal system. Consequently, considerable cooperation through exchange flourished, although one could not argue that the Romans had pushed aside tradition and command in favor of markets as the basis of economic organization.

However, with the end of the Western Roman Empire, in 476, European society became fragmented and went into decline. The following period, referred to as the Dark Ages, Middle Ages, or medieval period, lasted about a thousand years, until about 1453, when the Eastern Roman Empire ended and Constantinople fell to Muslim armies. It was during this period that Europe first developed and then began to emerge from its traditional economy.

Medieval hierarchy, customs, and religious influence

Although medieval European society was highly fragmented politically and economically, it had common characteristics and a thread of unity in its religion and its economic and social attitudes. Western and central Europe were loosely organized into a federation that contained two rival pinnacles of power. One hierarchy was the Church, with the pope at its head. The other was the "Empire," a tradition of leadership that began in 800 when Charlemagne was crowned emperor.

The medieval political hierarchy and the military system that went with it are referred to as the feudal system. The main characteristic of the feudal system was a power structure whose key structural member was a middle layer of numerous and semi-independent lords called barons. Emperors, kings, princes, and dukes derived their power from the sworn loyalty of the barons, who were the personal leaders of small armies of knights and foot soldiers. A baron and his knights were supported by an estate or manor called a fief, which they possessed as long as they performed their feudal duties.

The baron's army was a disciplined unit of mutual defense against marauding bands or neighboring armies. This often was not true, however, of the military resources of the larger political units. Among the kings there was constant jockeying for power over territories and much forming and reforming of coalitions which made their armed might uncertain and unpredictable. The emperor seldom exercised more than nominal authority. All rulers in the upper strata were supported chiefly by their own estates and only partly by levies from their subordinate barons.

At the bottom of the feudal structure, and in many respects supporting it, were the serfs. Bound to the estate, obligated to serve the lord of the manor as laborer and soldier, the West European serf led a slavelike existence with two great exceptions. Unlike the slave, the serf could not be bought and sold as a mere chattel. Nor could he be treated arbitrarily by the lord: custom had the weight of law in defining the serf's and the lord's rights and obligations to each other, although it was the lord who adjudicated disputes between himself and the serf. The serf's "wages" were the right to work a share of the land and to huddle his family behind the castle wall while he fought to defend the manor.

It was this hierarchical structure and its relationship of land, ruler and protector, and peasant that Spanish, French. Dutch, and English colonialism attempted to transplant to America. However, the vastness of the American landmass compared with the small size of the colonial population and the safety of the colonies as compared with Europe of the Dark Ages were key distinctions. It proved impossible to bind labor to a particular estate and establish baronial control. Nevertheless, some Americans owned and collected rents from estates of thousands, even millions, of acres in the colonial period.

By the time America was opened up to English colonization, English institutions had become a mixture of feudal customs and new ways

of organizing social and economic life. It was from this transitional
society that the colonists selected their modes of institutional organization to cope with life in America. Thus, although attempts to establish
the feudalism that was already a part of the English past largely failed,
the colonists did re-create much of the contemporary English socioeconomic structure on the western shores of the Atlantic. Consequently,
we can trace a clear line of descent from feudal England to the American
Colonies. This shows up in the communal nature of the New England
towns, which were patterned on the preindustrial English villages. It
also shows up in the landholding patterns of the proprietary colonies,
which took as their models the medieval fiefdoms established on
England's Scottish and Welsh borders in the 14th century.[1]

The Catholic Church had a hierarchy of its own and asserted at
least nominal authority over the political hierarchy. Having been established as the official religion under the Roman Empire, the Church filled
a power void by assuming the authority to appoint emperors and kings.
Because of an accumulation of religious offerings and gifts by both
individuals and rulers, the Church acquired wealth and estates of its
own, controlled armies, and ruled some territories. It was frequently
involved in struggles between kings and rivaled the emperor for power.
In addition to its religious influence over the people, it was able to
wield considerable power because of the divisive conflicts between kings
and barons.

Below these two upper classes of noblemen and churchmen were
the townspeople (the burghers, or **bourgeoisie**). Like the noblemen's
castles, the towns were walled and fortified. The towns contained a
central marketplace, merchants' stores, craftsmen's shops, often a nobleman's residence, and a cathedral and other church buildings. The merchants and craftsmen were a small middle class who ranked a bit higher
in status than the soldiers and supervisors of the noblemen's estates.
In the lower classes were the apprentices, the servants, and the peasants
who made up the vast bulk of the population.

Throughout Western Europe, similar social conventions and religious
attitudes prevailed in the medieval period. Custom ruled all behavior;
production and daily living went on year after year with little or no
change. A person's social status and occupation were inherited from
his parents, who also passed on the skills and methods of the past.
Traditional ways were accepted as the best; changes were feared and
often reason for punishment. In exchange for a few privileges, persons
in a lower position in the hierarchy owed certain services, contributions
of specific goods, and obedience to persons of a higher rank. Customary
prices and wages were expected to be paid, although usually in goods
or services rather than money.

---

[1] For discussion of the continuity of the English and American socioeconomic
structure see Andrews, Berthoff, Demos, Greven, and Lockridge.

Religious attitudes toward trade and market exchange activities were ambivalent. Only customary wages and prices were sanctioned as ethical, as *fair wages* and *just prices.* However, the doctrine of just price did not call for arbitrary prices or ignore economic forces. In fact, a medieval moral philosopher using modern terms would say that a just price was the current price, the price that the interaction of supply and demand would bring about in a competitive market. An unjust price would be a higher price gained because the buyer was ignorant or was, through extenuating conditions such as monopoly, under the control of the seller. In times of general shortage, attributed to God's will as they were, the price could be elevated with impunity to equate supply with demand.[2] In short, some gains through sales were clearly moral while others were sinful; deciding which was which must have provoked great distress on certain occasions.

Religion urged charity to meet individual misfortunes and emergencies. In most cases, lending was regarded as an act of charity to tide someone over a time of personal tragedy, and the charging of interest, called usury, was regarded as a sin. But ordinary business loans weren't made to those in distressed circumstances, so such loans were exempt. However, deciding whether an element of distress entered a sale contract that included an interest charge because of deferred payment must have sent many a local cleric to his copy of Aquinas.[3]

Preoccupation with monetary gains and the accumulation of wealth, or even an emphasis on consumption and pleasure, were condemned as immoral. Thus, medieval Christianity was in some ways hostile to business and provided little encouragement for individuals to strive for greater productivity, to experiment with new methods, or to introduce change. Yet the Church condoned at least certain types of materialistic behavior, and trade was considered worthwhile, indeed necessary.

Subsistence agriculture: The manorial system

The economic organization that produced the feudal hierarchy was the manorial system. In the Middle Ages over 90 percent of the working population was engaged in agriculture. The basic unit of production organization was the manor, a self-sufficient agricultural estate. The manor was possessed and ruled by a nobleman, or lord, or by the Church. The products of the manor barely supported the lord, his servants, his soldiers, and the peasants, and the levies of the kings and the Church. Each manor or each group of manors near a town attempted to be self-sufficient. As we will see at the end of this chapter, the manor's

---

[2] Baldwin, pp. 63–80, analyzes Aquinas and others at length and finds that their main thrust justifies the merchant, exhange, and, consequently, prices on the basis of utility to society.

[3] See Baldwin's treatment of usury, especially pp. 49–50.

self-sufficiency was partly responsible for the bare-subsistence living standards of feudal times.

The typical manor was a small village in the midst of some cleared land and forests. There would be a cluster of huts, perhaps a blacksmith shop or a gristmill, and a manor house or castle for the lord or his supervisor. Attached to each hut was a small garden and perhaps a fenced yard for fowl and livestock. Stretching away from the village would be unfenced cropland. In addition, there were usually some untilled pasturelands and forested lands nearby. (See 2–1 for a schematic view of a medieval manor.)

2–1. A medieval manor

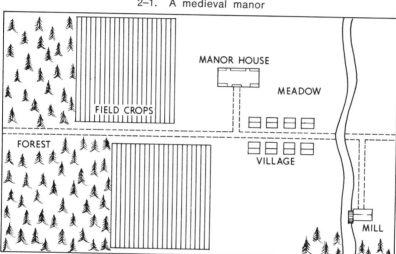

Farming methods were very primitive, so production per worker was very low. At first, a two-field rotation system was common, with one field idle or used for pasture while the other was sowed in grain. Later, considerable improvement resulted from a three-field system, with rotation of wheat or rye with barley, oats, or peas, and the third year for idleness or pasture.

The peasant's holdings were very small, with the fields divided into long, narrow strips representing what a single ox-drawn plow could cover in a single day without too many turnarounds. The peasant might hold several strips in different fields and was also responsible for working strips owned by the lord. No fertilizer was employed except inadvertently as a result of using draft animals. Horses for pulling wagons and plows became more common only after the invention of the horse collar. Cattle were turned loose in open pasture without any attempt at selective breeding. There was a shortage of hay and fodder, so most livestock was slaughtered and salted or smoked in the fall.

The manorial system and the array of feudal institutions that went with it constituted a rational response to medieval conditions. The end of the Roman Empire had left Europe, including England, depopulated. Land was abundant, compared with capital and labor. Technology was rudimentary. Productivity permitted only subsistence—a 20th century American farmhand lives a healthier, better nourished, longer, and more comfortable life than did a medieval lord. Danger lurked everywhere. A traveler risked losing his goods and perhaps his life at the hands of brigands or pirates. Settlements were threatened by Vikings, Huns, and Muslims.

Medieval man's economic problem was to get the most out of his very scarce resources under conditions of great risk and uncertainty, poor communications, and very high transportation costs. The manor evolved as a natural response to the needs and conditions of the times.

Given the sparse population density, the cheapest way to provide protection to life and property was to create enclaves of safety, the fortified and guarded manors. Individual protection was ineffective—a man's home was not yet his castle. Protection from an overlord, a king, would have required too many men, spread too thin, with no effective means of disciplining or coordinating their actions.

In those perilous times, the manor proved to be the most efficient producing and consuming unit. Specialization and trade among regions or among all but the closest manors were not advantageous. Information flowed very slowly, and the risk of loss in transit through banditry or piracy made regular shipment of goods uneconomic. The small-scale autarkical unit producing food, shelter, clothing, and protection actually maximized output per head. Alternative arrangements might have meant a higher output of agricultural and manufactured products, but these gains would have been more than offset by higher defense costs and/or higher losses to thievery and pillage.[4]

Peasants became serfs through a gradual evolution which started with the exchange of labor for protection. As the North European tribes settled down to farming, the farm worker usually fell under the protection of some lord and his soldiers in exchange for labor dues. Regulations soon bound him to the land. On the other hand, the "custom of the manor," which expressed the contractual relationship between lord and serf, delineated the serf's rights and restricted the lord's discretion. The serf was obligated to work the lord's land or to work in the manor house or mill as a servant or laborer. He also owed the Church its tithes. The lord usually monopolized and charged fees for the services of the flour mill, oven, winepress, tannery, and blacksmith shop. However, the serf usually had the right to work certain strips, to use certain tools of the lord, and to keep his own garden and household property.

---

[4] For a more extensive discussion of this view of the economics of the manorial system see North and Thomas.

Though the agriculture of the medieval period appears inefficient and unnecessarily ritualistic to us, agricultural organization in the Middle Ages served to provide a floor against famine—like the manorial system, it constituted a risk-reducing strategy. However, its communal allocation of resources hampered individual experimentation and thus slowed the growth of productivity. The lack of innovation is quite understandable. Although traditional methods were not very productive, they were consistent and dependable, whereas an experiment that failed could wipe out the narrow margin that separated the community from starvation. During the late Middle Ages, though, adaptations were gradually forced upon agricultural organization as whole regions moved away from local self-sufficiency to specialized production for commercial markets.

Handcrafts and trade

A limited amount of handcraft manufacture and trade was carried on in the walled towns. Both the craftsmen and the merchants were organized into associations called guilds. The leaders of the various guilds usually formed the town council. Political leaders often left the towns alone or even granted them self-rule and monopoly rights over their particular crafts and trades. In doing so, they sought to encourage the production and trade which yielded them additional revenues in taxes. Assistance from the towns was frequently sought to provide soldiers and to lend money to finance wars.

The master craftsmen—shoemakers, tailors, and so on—owned their own shops, tools, and materials, although they might contract for work on the buyers' materials. If their sales were large enough, they might hire one or more journeymen who had not yet saved enough money to start their own shops. Young boys also worked several years as apprentices to learn a craft. They received little more than room and board and were bound by contract to obey the master carftsman.

Other town dwellers were soldiers, servants, or casual laborers who performed menial tasks. Even for the poorest worker, however, the towns were islands of freedom; usually, a peasant who found refuge in a town for over a year became free of obligations to a manor lord.

In regulating their own trades or crafts, the guilds frequently became rather restrictive, although their regulations usually supported free market exchange, at least for their own members. Thus, restrictions were placed on the number of apprentices that could be trained and the length of their training, and shop hours were limited to prevent overproduction. There were also rules directed against harmful practices by any single guild member. Practices designed to reduce competition were forbidden. Standards of quality and fair weights were upheld by inspection. Laws of contract and credit were developed, and disputes were settled by courts.

English guild practices and feudal customs evolved through a long series of judicial rulings into the English common law. This process of evolution of course reflected the Commercial Revolution and the breakdown of the manorial system. In turn, the common law was imported by the American colonists as the legal basis for the colonial economy. Similarly, the vestiges of commercial regulation which remained in England were transported to the colonies: statutory wage and interest rates and just prices were introduced to the colonies along with the newer, more flexible business practices that were developing in England.

THE COMMERCIAL REVOLUTION

In a proximate sense, the rise of commercial activity was the main force which eroded Europe's traditional society. Behind the Commercial Revolution were generations of gradual evolution that made the manorial system obsolete.

Rise of trade and business

Trade among regions had never stopped completely in the Middle Ages, and in the 12th and 13th centuries it gradually began to flourish throughout Europe. The reduction of neighborhood warfare by the Crusades, accompanied by rising political stability and population growth, contributed to the renaissance of trade.

In fighting the Turks, the Western European nobility became acquainted with and acquired a taste for spices, silks, dyes, drugs, jewels, and other luxury goods from the Far East. Trade links to India and China were established. Soon Europe was crisscrossed with sea, inland waterway, and overland routes that connected ports and inland settlements.

To purchase luxury goods and other scarce items, people in some areas began to produce a surplus of certain types of goods for export. England had much grassland suitable for sheep grazing, so it became a major exporter of wool. The Scandinavian countries exported iron, copper, furs, timber, and naval stores. From the Baltic and North Atlantic areas came herring and salt. Various cities in France began to manufacture cloth, armor, and other handcraft articles.

The growth of trade accelerated urban growth, sparked the development of new business organizations and practices, and stimulated manufacturing activity. Annual trade fairs organized by merchants became permanent, and cities grew up around them. Port cities flourished as international marketplaces.

Some modern forms of business organization can be traced to this period. Traders jointly financed convoys, a practice that evolved into the joint-stock companies which were common in colonial times and were the forerunners of the modern corporation. In order to spread their risks, merchants invented maritime insurance: by paying a fee (the premium) to a pool, a shipper could recover all or part of his loss if his ship were lost at sea.

Double-entry bookkeeping was developed as a tool vital to business operations. Banking evolved from merely a matter of deposit accounts— or the safekeeping of gold and silver—into a lending activity. Written notes called drafts enabled agents of a merchant to withdraw money from his deposits; soon drafts enabled a seller to collect payment by drawing upon the buyer's deposit. The bill of exchange was developed as a written agreement to receive shipped goods in exchange for a promise to pay after a period of delay. Loans for business purposes ultimately became commonplace. Large wholesale merchants often extended short-term loans on goods shipped or materials furnished to small merchants and craftsmen. Deposit banks, or any businesses with large balances and diversified operations, loaned part of their reserve funds. Thus, commercial banking developed.

Breakdown of feudalism and the manorial system

In the 14th and 15th centuries, a number of troubles shook the organization of European society. In 1348, the Black Death killed many people—from one tenth to one quarter of the population in some areas. At about the same time, England and France became involved in the Hundred Years' War. The resulting manpower shortages, along with peasant rebellions, hewed away at hoary customs and ancient privileges of class. A great split occurred in the Church, followed by several reform movements. Europe had become vulnerable—in 1453, Constantinople fell to the Turks, bringing to an end the remnants of the Eastern Roman Empire. Many historians date this as the end of the Middle Ages.

These were the centuries of the Renaissance. Men of wealth supported artistic and scholarly activities. Scientific inquiry had its beginnings, as did efforts to improve the practical arts of production. The printing press, gunpowder, and new navigation instruments were among the most important inventions of the period. In a new spirit of inquiry and discovery, Europeans began to explore the oceans. Within a single generation, the Europeans had "discovered" the other continents and established colonial outposts on all of them. The 16th century also saw the beginning of the Protestant Reformation, which was to end the domination of the Church and force more changes in religious attitudes toward business.

In 1555, the existence of independent national entities was ratified by Charles V when he abdicated his throne as emperor of Europe and divided his lands between two successors. For several centuries before his abdication, various national kingdoms had gained strength—notably England, France, and Portugal. No emperor could claim to control them.

As feudalism broke down and nation-states arose, the beginnings of economic development could be observed as the preconditions for growth were gradually fulfilled. Trade among European nations, along with North Africa and Asia Minor, increased as the beginnings of national specialization got underway. In part, trade expansion was made possible by the emergence of the financial institutions that are required for a high degree of specialization and trade among nations. The newly devised commercial banks became vital links in international trade by providing for the first time many of the banking services that today's merchants take for granted.

The decline of the manorial system in England and the rest of Western Europe can be traced to the emergence of a market economy. As early as the 12th century, population expansion and the growth of towns had significantly increased specialization of manors and trade.

The higher population density made the principality or nation the most economic producer of defense. It became cheaper to patrol the roads, to seek out and imprison roving bands of brigands, and to repel invaders at the border. The manor's responsibility for defense waned, and the safety of transporting goods increased.

Trade and taxes to support a king's army required a money system, so the monetization of economic affairs naturally followed. Landlords gradually substituted fixed money payments for the labor obligations the serf owed in return for use of the land and protection.

After the Black Death, persistent labor shortages produced a rigorous competition for labor. Increasingly, heritable lifelong leases calling for fixed annual rents took the place of labor dues. Inflation steadily eroded the value of the rents until, finally, they became nominal. Then the law ratified custom by freeing serfs in name as well as fact. The manor lands were worked by free tenants or wage laborers who were free to move about in search of the best return they could get for their efforts.[5]

The economic organization that replaced the manorial system was the first stage of the market economy we know today. Land, labor, and capital emerged as separate, salable factors of production: the serfs gained their freedom, the guilds declined, the putting-out system arose as a forerunner of the factory system, and the mills that had been built adopted new techniques. Europe and its trading satellites were truly undergoing a transformation that provided the basis for an economic revolution in later years.

---

[5] For a detailed account of this process see North and Thomas, pp. 793–99.

Production for market

The discoveries and colonization of the 16th century rapidly expanded European trade. Trade, in turn, not only disrupted the political and religious order of feudal society but also began to reorganize production activity. The varied output of independent subsistence agricultural units began to be supplanted by specialized production for exchange in markets.

As trade increased, the need for monetary metals grew correspondingly. As it turned out, the Spanish colonies in South America added to the supply of monetary metals even faster than trade grew. In the century and a half after 1500, it is estimated that Spain's gold and silver imports more than tripled the total supply of money in Europe.

The increase in the money supply was accompanied by a long period of price inflation—i.e., a rise in most prices—nearly everywhere in Europe. In England, for example, it is estimated that between 1500 and 1600 the general price level more than tripled. (See 2–2.) This

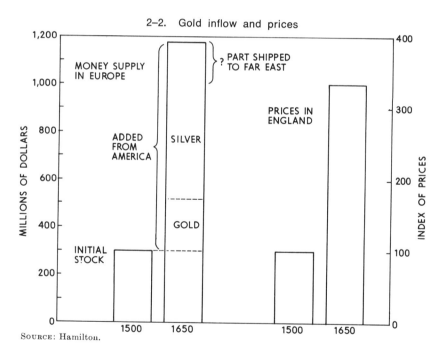

2–2. Gold inflow and prices

SOURCE: Hamilton.

represents a 2 to 3 percent annual growth rate, which was very rapid for people emerging from the Middle Ages and accustomed to long periods of stable production and prices. Continuous price increases soon confounded all of their expectations as to just prices and fair wages.

Because the money supply and, therefore, spending were increasing more rapidly than production, prices had to rise. However, this secular inflation was not the curse that some contemporary observers thought it to be. Rising prices and general trade expansion encouraged investment in manufacturing and mercantile businesses and attracted a flow of goods from ports far from Europe. Indeed, one can think of the expanding markets and monetary inflation of this period as providing a prime incentive for the Commercial Revolution. Rising prices and profits stimulated the founding of specialized producing and trading concerns which, in effect, strove to raise the flow of output to match the rate of increase in expenditures.

As production expanded, more workers were employed in the cities—a move peasants welcomed because of the greater freedom and higher incomes to be had in urban centers. The peasants who remained on farms found it easier to pay their customary rents as prices of farm products rose. The lords, on the other hand, found that rents fixed by tradition purchased fewer goods at the higher prices. They, in turn, tried to protect their incomes by increasing the portion of their acreage under cultivation and improving methods. Sometimes wealthy merchants rented idle lands and put them to use producing farm products for market.

Many improvements in production methods accompanied the rapid increase in specialized production for market. In mining and manufacturing, better machinery, organization, and products came of the desire to increase output. In agriculture, idle lands were cleared and drained, and new and old lands were enclosed by fences in order to protect crops from animals and to develop pure breeds of improved livestock. New crops were introduced, as were improved methods of crop rotation and plowing.

England's Commercial Revolution

Most scholars credit England with the Industrial Revolution, of which the Commercial Revolution was an antecedent. For this reason, and because Britain was the mother country of the American Colonies, we ought to have a look at England's experience in this period of commercial reorganization and expansion of output.

Wool exports were the basis for the early development of England's trade and for its first major manufacturing industry. A merchant class got its start handling exports of wool to the Lowlands, France, and the Baltic countries. Then some London merchants began to hire workers and produce woolen cloth. London expanded to become a major trading, shipping, and financial center. Woolen cloth and other goods were mainly produced in small craft shops, which were organized into guilds.

In the 16th century, expanding European markets and rising prices had two types of effects on England's woolen industry. First, farm production of wool was greatly expanded by devoting more pasturelands to sheep raising. Both expansion and reorganization of land use were involved. The landed gentry fenced common lands and newly cleared or drained wasteland, consolidated strip farms, and introduced new agricultural methods. These sweeping changes, called the early enclosure movement, created commercial farms in the place of subsistence feudal communities.

The second effect was that the woolen cloth merchants sought to expand woolen manufactures quickly, unhampered by the restrictions of the London guilds. They began to move their production locations into rural areas to employ farm workers and peasant families under the putting-out, or cottage, system. A clothier merchant would buy wool and send it out to neighboring cottages to be prepared and spun, mainly by women and children. Then he hired weavers to weave the yarn into cloth on his looms, either in their homes or in his shop. The finished cloth, cleaned, shrunk, and thickened at a fulling mill, was then brought to the merchant's home to be cut and stretched for market.

Since the long-haired sheep whose wool was most suitable for worsteds were raised best in northern England, worsted textile production became concentrated in that region. Gradually, the worsted merchants became more skillful in designing patterns and blending dyes. This won them an increasing share of the European markets. As demand expanded and shifted in favor of worsteds, production became even more concentrated in England's northern industrial towns.

Along with its expanding woolen exports, England was able to develop a thriving shipping industry. Some merchants carried on trading ventures with all parts of Europe; some attempted colonial ventures; and some even engaged in piracy against Spanish ships. After the defeat of the Spanish Armada in 1588, England rose to the position of a major naval power. Early in the 17th century, England began to develop colonies in North America, and the East India Company was chartered with the exclusive privilege of initiating a heavy trade with India.

Several industries arose in connection with the new consumer products made possible by colonial imports. New beverages—coffee, tea, and cocoa—soon became very popular, and with them came an increased demand for sugar. Crude sugar, or molasses, was imported from the West Indies and refined in England. Rum was also made from molasses, and it competed with brandy in European markets. In England, the main drink of the common people soon became beer brewed from locally grown hops. The British tavern became an important social institution, and, along with beer drinking, smoking became popular. This created a demand for American tobacco to be processed in England.

A rapid expansion of shipbuilding, construction in the growing cities, and the burning of firewood soon created a shortage of fuel in 17th century England. Outcroppings of coal, however, were readily available in northern England; soon over half of England's ships were engaged in coastal trade, most of them carrying coal. Not only did English consumers turn to coal for heating and cooking, but many industries began to use it as a fuel. For example, with the lumber shortage, there was a shift to the use of stone and brick in construction, and the baking of brick in kilns required coal.

The metal industries kept pace with the economy's growth. The widespread use of coal stoves required more iron for gratings. An increased need for salt by the fishing industry, as well as for preserving foods generally, led to a demand for large iron and copper kettles for evaporating seawater. The textile industry required dyes, and this led to the building of alum and copperas, i.e., ferrous sulfate, factories which used large kettles. Discoveries in England of zinc ores to alloy with copper permitted the development of brassware manufacturing. Mixing gunpowder required saltpeter mills, and cannon production called for large ironworks. A great variety of iron products was, of course, required in shipbuilding, construction, and stovemaking.

Along with the rising demand for consumer products and some heavy industrial products, more skilled crafts gradually developed. Brown wrapping paper, for example, was first produced in England. Later, with the growth of the printing industry, French methods for making fine white paper were introduced. Protestant refugees from Europe sometimes brought skills and a knowledge of special industrial techniques to England. The development of silk textiles, for example, was made possible by skilled immigrants.

Altogether, then, English manufacturing underwent a rapid and diversified development in the 16th and 17th centuries. The growth of wool exports and a concomitant increase in per capita income made possible general industrial growth and a continuous evolution away from the tradition-bound manorial system toward a market-organized economy. The period between 1540 and 1640, in fact, has been called the **earlier industrial revolution.** In this period, the North American colonies were initially settled, and the industrial structure of England left an indelible mark on the surface of American economic life.

Colonial outposts in North America

In chapter 4 we will discuss the growth and structure of the American Colonies in detail. However, because the colonial movement was a natural outgrowth of the Commercial Revolution, it seems appropriate at this juncture to discuss the formation of the colonies and the motives underlying colonization.

European explorations and colonizing efforts in the 16th and 17th centuries were motivated primarily by the desire for economic gain.

An initial objective was to find a cheap ocean route for trade with the Far East. Hopes for quick riches were stimulated by Spain's discoveries of gold and silver deposits in South America. It also appeared that new products and fertile soils provided profit opportunities through developing production in the New World.

The types of colonial settlement varied with the area and nation involved. In the Far East, trading posts were established at the ports of densely populated countries. In South America, the Spanish conquered an agricultural native population and put it to work as slave labor in mines and on plantations. In North America, where the natives were scattered and nomadic, the French established a few port cities and inland fur trading posts. Only in English colonies did large numbers of Europeans settle and simply push back the native peoples.

The earliest English colonies were established by chartered joint-stock companies in the hope of making a profit. In the 1580s, the unsuccessful attempts of Sir Humphrey Gilbert and Sir Walter Raleigh to establish colonies in Newfoundland and the Carolinas demonstrated that large and long-term financial investments and a hardy group of permanent agricultural settlers were needed. In 1607, the Virginia Company of London succeeded in establishing the first permanent colony at Jamestown. In 1620, the first New England colony was established by the Plymouth Company, which was a combined venture of merchants and a community of Puritans seeking escape from religious persecution.

In 1630, the Massachusetts Bay Company established a colony and then moved its headquarters to the colony, giving it a form of self-government. A large number of settlers then came to Massachusetts, and some of them moved on to establish colonies in neighboring Rhode Island, Connecticut, and New Hampshire. Early Dutch and Swedish companies also established colonies in New York and New Jersey, but they were not heavily settled, and later they fell under English control. In spite of success in establishing settlements, these early ventures of joint-stock companies were not profitable.

Other colonies, such as Pennsylvania and Maryland, were established by land grants from the Stuart kings to favored noblemen and upper-class commoners. In these proprietary colonies, a generally unsuccessful attempt was made to transfer the feudal estate system to the New World. The proprietors made personal investments to encourage settlement and to establish production on their own farms. They expected to profit mostly from the sale of land, rents on land granted to others (called quitrents), and duties on trade. Usually, however, the land had to be given away in order to encourage early settlers, and later the quitrents were resisted and poorly collected.

The last of the Thirteen Colonies was Georgia, established in 1732, over a century after colonizing had begun. Throughout the colonial period (until 1776), population concentrations were limited to the eastern coastal edge of the North American continent. Initial settlements were in natural harbors and along partly open river valleys. Any additional farmland required clearing heavily forested areas. Movement inland was largely determined by river transportation which ended at the fall line, where rapids or falls marked the foothills of the Appalachian Mountains, the main barrier to later penetration of the continent. Nearly all transportation and communication was by water, along the rivers to the coast and over the ocean to Europe. A heavy coastal trade occurred between the colonies, but very little road building was done to link the colonies by land. (See 2–3.)

2–3.   Colonial settled areas, 1760

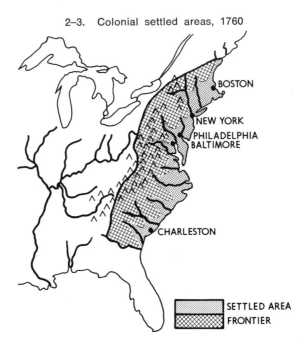

You should avoid the temptation to be provincial in your view of the Thirteen Colonies. They did not dominate the British Empire; nor were they isolated entities. Rather, as members of the British Empire, they were an integral part of a highly interdependent whole, the wealthiest, most populous colonial empire then in existence. By 1765, the American colonies of Britain also included Newfoundland, Hudson Bay, Nova Scotia, Quebec, East and West Florida, the Bahamas, Bermuda, Jamaica, Antigua, Barbados, the Leeward and Windward islands, plus Central and South American interests. In addition to Great Britain (including the kingdom of Scotland and the kingdom of Ireland), non-American components of the British Empire included outlying European islands, Gold Coast colonies, India, Ceylon, and scattered Asian islands. This vast empire was knit together by the then century-old Navigation Acts and similar regulations which protected Empire shipping, manufacturing, and agriculture from outside competition and restricted colonial trade and production to channels prescribed by Parliament.

HOW THE MARKET SYSTEM WORKS

Although the imperial system within which the American Colonies operated was tightly controlled by government regulation, in actual operation the economy that prospered within the Empire was as close to the pure form of market capitalism as you are likely to find at any point in history. Within the western portion of the Empire, colonial ships were free to call at any ports they chose, to sell what they could on whatever terms they could manage, and to take away whatever they cared to buy. Intracolonial specialization and trade flourished. At home the colonists were generally free to produce anything they pleased for their own consumption, though not for export. In general, colonial settlers were free to farm, mine, fish, or labor wherever opportunities and their preferences coincided. It's true that imperial policy spelled out economic behavior prohibited to the colonists, but such rules were largely superfluous because America's potentially most fruitful activities were in shipping and the extractive industries rather than in the manufacturing industries, which were closed to the colonists by British law.

In short, the economic environment of the workers and capitalists of colonial America was the market system, and the market system was what they opted for when independence came. Accordingly, it's useful if you understand the functions that markets perform in a market system before we take a detailed look at the colonial economy.

What is meant by a market system is often difficult for people to understand or accept. The system doesn't seem to be a system—no legal authority to enforce the rules, no legislature to change the rules, and no constituency to elect a governing body. What's more, when looked at in detail, the system seems, in fact often is, chaotic. Often onlookers, quite understandably, conclude that the system is irrational. Or, if they know a bit more about its operations, they may judge the system immoral because the selfish motives of isolated individuals provide its motive power.

At this point, you readers who haven't studied economics before need a brief digression that cuts away the vast detail market behavior involves and that presents a streamlined view of how markets work. In later chapters, we shall discuss ways in which markets fail and the government policies that have been designed to eliminate or offset market failure.

Markets as exchange places

Markets serve two main functions: they serve as exchange places and they provide an information system for making the fundamental economic decisions about production and income distribution. Let's start with the former.

Any economy characterized by specialization extending beyond the family or clan unit must have markets among its economic institutions—without markets there is no exchange; and without exchange, specialization is useless. We have already seen that in early medieval times, when the manor, little more than an extended family, was self-sufficient, going to market was a rarity. But when town guilds specialized in various manufactured and processed products and when the estates of various regions concentrated their crops in particular specialties, markets emerged. Why? Because the specialty producer requires the products of other specialty producers in order to meet his varied needs. In order to exist, he must exchange his surplus products for the surplus of specialists in other fields.

Any economic system—tradition, command, or market capitalism—must have exchange places if it is to have specialization. Though the details may vary, the Russian housewife performs precisely the same function as her American counterpart when she does her weekly marketing. What's more, even the wife of a nomadic tribesman participates in the exchange phase of the specialization-exchange cycle when she goes to the marketplace of an oasis town.

If markets are required for specialization in any system, perhaps we ought to ask, Why specialize? Why be so roundabout in organizing production? The answer is that specialization is more productive than do-it-yourself organization.

Let's look at the exchange side to begin to see why. By definition, exchange, both barter or money in trade for goods or services, is a voluntary act on the part of both parties. No one would consummate a trade unless he felt that he would benefit thereby—the essence of trading is bringing together two (or more) parties wishing to better their positions by trading something to which they hold title for something else. The alternative is to produce for oneself all one needs, an alternative that the greater part of the world, rich and poor, has generally abandoned in favor of specialization and exchange. It must be, then, that people reap benefits from specialization even after the costs of exchange are reckoned.

We should push money aside for the moment and try to get a fix on the benefits of specialization that exchange systems make possible. We ought to consider what is given and received in any trade or market exchange. Our discussion will deal chiefly with individuals, but be sure to remember that it is applicable to trade among business firms, cities, regions, and nations.

The individual gains in three ways from specializing, then trading. First, he can have goods and services he cannot produce for himself. Inventory your talents against the items you buy in any given week and ask yourself how many of them you could produce on your own and how many weeks it would take to make them. Yet, if you specialize and swap your output with that of another specialist, each of you gains something the other couldn't produce.

Second, by specializing the individual increases his productivity. Not only does practice make perfect, it reveals flaws in accepted ways of doing things. The specialist perfects his art and invents new technologies for producing. In addition, he doesn't lose time going from job to job; nor does he waste time, money, and effort in adjusting tools and storing and handling materials. And equally important, if not most important, the specialist gains economies of scale. He can divide the work between himself and capital equipment in this way and can use leverage, non-human power sources, jigs, fixtures, and dies to magnify the amount of power he brings to bear on the task at hand. If you recall the discussion in chapter 1 which dealt with economies of scale, the applicability of these principles to firms and geographic units will be apparent.

Third, if the specialist is part of a widespread system of specialization and exchange, he can pick the specialty most appropriate for him, given his abilities and the abilities of those with whom he will trade. He will be free to choose the specialty at which he is relatively most productive. For the specialist, the cost of any product he makes is the products he abandoned making in order to specialize—economists call this concept the *opportunity cost* principle. Within the confines of his tastes and interests, the individual can choose to produce the output among all things he is capable of producing that will maximize his trading power, or minimize his opportunity cost.

A man who is both highly intelligent and very good with his hands might potentially qualify as the most skillful brain surgeon in the nation, or as the best cabinetmaker. But it's unlikely that he will divide his workday between the two in spite of his superiority in both. Certainly, his talents in surgery will give him more trading power, more income, than would constructing fine furniture. He'll most likely choose medical school, knowing that this will give him more than ample income to indulge his taste for fine furniture by collecting antiques or by equipping a home workshop in which to make furniture as a hobby.

The foregoing example may seem trivial because it is so obvious; the concept illustrated is not trivial though. On an international scale, the principle called the *law of comparative advantage* states that nations, although perhaps absolutely superior in a very wide range of production, ought to narrow their specialties so as to reap the greatest relative advantage. How? By selecting specialties in which they are very productive compared with other nations and which will give them the greatest revenue, i.e., trading power, when the time comes for exchange. On the other hand, they should cast aside pursuits which will yield a lower degree of trading power even though their physical productivity per unit of input is unmatched the world over.

Looked at in the long view, a system of specialization and exchange is merely a mode of cooperation. Mankind wants a wide variety of products in quantities that exceed its production capability. Given the scarcity problem, getting the most production from inputs is imperative. The system of cooperation that points toward maximizing output from scarce inputs is specialization and exchange.

If specialization is so beneficial, why is the trade that makes it possible viewed widely with great suspicion? If an exchange is both voluntary and mutually beneficial, why do people often assume that one party to a trade is exploited? Why do students so often miss the multiple-choice question dealing with exchange whose correct answer identifies the benefits to both traders associated with specialization?

A general answer is that specialization and exchange affect not only the volume of output per capita but the distribution of income among households as well. In turn, income distribution is a subject that lies within the bounds of ethics and religion as well as economics. Moral issues are emotion-charged issues, and emotion hampers vision and distorts thinking. In the next two paragraphs we will cite several hangups which prevent objective appraisal of the benefits—and limitations—of specialization and exchange.

Often two parties to an exchange start off on an unequal footing, and after a trade they remain so. Exchange, though voluntary, doesn't correct inequalities, so the process is resented. But this is a misplaced criticism—exchange only improves the absolute position of both parties; it cannot, save in extreme cases, equalize their welfare or asset positions. Charity, progressive taxes, and expropriation are the policy tools that can equalize income and asset distributions among households. Just as specialization is part of any type of economic system—tradition, command, or market—the inherent inability of exchange to cope with problems of inequality is integral to any system of economic organization.

A second reason that exchanges are viewed with a skeptical eye is that fraud and/or monopoly are sometimes piggybacked on the exchange process. However, deceit and deceptiveness are not inherent in the exchange process, and exploitation only arises in a swap when one trader restricts the alternatives of the other or lies to him about the goods or services being exchanged. It's true that trading invites fraud just as property draws thieves, but to do away with the benefits of specialization and exchange in order to avoid fraud is a very costly alternative. A well-enforced business code and many buyers and sellers in any market—giving any single buyer or seller many alternatives—is a more judicious choice.

Do not be misled into thinking that all exchanges in which buyers and sellers are great in number and neither party commits fraud lead to increased economic welfare. Often, there are involuntary third parties to exchanges that bear heavy costs thereby. Air, water, and noise pollution are burdens borne by the general public which arise out of exchanges between auto dealers and drivers, between paper companies and newsprint dealers, and between airlines and their passengers. We will have more to say about the failures of markets in the last part of the text.

Having initially placed money outside our consideration, let's reintroduce it explicitly. Money is merely a medium of exchange in our context. Men invented money when they discovered that direct barter was too time-consuming. Two rapid transactions—wheat for money, then money for household staples—are much more efficient than searching high and low for people with surplus staples who want wheat. Money does not alter the principles of exchange, however—when the specialist trades for money he does so knowing he can then buy something which will improve his welfare as compared with his status before the initial transaction. In other words, money is merely an intermediate good, a temporary store of trading value or power. And terms of trade are much easier to compare when the exchange value of products is expressed in money prices.

Money, specialization, and exchange are the elements that are required if markets are to be convenient, fast-operating places of exchange. Without money as a medium of exchange, markets become bartering places and specialization is foregone to some degree because the time and effort required for exchange are too great.

Markets as information systems

Our discussion of markets to this point has indicated how markets serve as exchange places, a duty that markets discharge in any type of economic system. Now it is appropriate to discuss markets as information systems.

The market system is unique in the degree to which it depends on markets to distribute the information necessary to direct production and determine the distribution of income. It is also unique in that the production patterns and income distribution that result are determined by the choices of individuals rather than by tradition or centrally situated planners. In the United States, the government second-guesses a handful of the market decisions about production and income distribution, whereas in Russia the government decides in the first place what will be produced at what rates of pay, issues orders to fit the plan, and uses markets solely as exchange places.

The social cooperation that market exchanges make possible is not random, although certain markets may seem chaotic and erratic at times. The conscious choices of individuals as consumers, producers, workers, and managers when taken collectively determine output and income distribution patterns. Price and quantities exchanged are the language in which individuals communicate in the marketplace. Let's take a simple example.

If consumers as individuals decide that in total they wish to buy more lamb and less beef, what will happen? Beef sales will fall; beef producers will accept lower prices to clear out their inventories; and stockmen, noting price trends, will reduce herd sizes. Lamb shortages will develop; prices will be bid up; lamb producers will raise their slaughter rates; and stockmen, seeing high lamb prices, will expand their sheep herds. In the end, consumers will have more lamb on their tables and less beef—just what they wanted. Yet no overall planning authority had to reorder production. Consumers merely had to shift their buying habits, and production patterns shifted with them because producers received price signals that reflected the change in consumer tastes.

Now for a more comprehensive view of markets as information systems. Any economy has the scarcity problem, so any economy must make the basic decisions that taken together constitute the answer to the scarcity problem. Economies must decide:

1. How resources will be allocated—i.e., what products will be produced in what quantities while fully using all available inputs;
2. which technology will be used to produce each product; and
3. how income from participating in production will be distributed.

In the market system, prices are the signals which guide producing units, productive factors, consumers, and investors in determining the precise content of these three decisions. We should examine each in detail.

Prices show what consumers want produced. In the market system **consumer sovereignty** prevails: with certain exceptions, the consumer is king. He is presumed to know what is best for him, and he tells producers what he wants to consume by buying heavily in some markets, buying little in other markets, and not buying some products at all. In other words, the consumer determines the allocation pattern of productive resources. Further, as in our lamb-beef example, the consumer causes producers to alter their output patterns when he changes his mind about what he wants to buy.

The role of price? Remember that in the lamb-beef example reduced purchases of beef pushed beef prices down and discouraged beef production, just as increased lamb purchases pushed lamb prices up and encouraged lamb production. In the same vein, we can generalize as follows. In some markets, at prices that enable producers to cover their costs, including a return on their investment, consumer purchases will be great and vast amounts of inputs will be used in production. In other markets, at prices that cover costs, including an investment return, consumer purchases will be modest and resources devoted to production will be correspondingly small in number. It's no accident that U.S. producers made $31.5 billion worth of autos in 1970 and only $4.1 billion worth of magazines and newspapers—consumers ordered it that way.

Prices show which methods are efficient. For any product there are alternative technologies by which producers may combine inputs to get a requisite amount of output. The most efficient combination of inputs would be that combination which uses the least of society's scarce resources.

But what constitutes least? Is 3 tractors and 10 men more or less than 1 tractor and 20 men employed on a cotton plantation to produce, say, three bales to the acre? What if the planter knows that tractors cost $2,000 per year to own and operate and men must earn $3,000 per year to drive tractors and chop and pick cotton? The planter will choose 3 tractors (at $6,000) and 10 men (at $30,000) over 1 tractor (at $2,000) and 20 men (at $60,000) because the former would only cost him $36,000 and the latter would cost $62,000. Is the former, then, the least-cost combination in terms of society's scarce resources? Yes, it is!

Prices of resources (labor and capital in this case) reflect what other producers are willing to pay for those resources in other uses. In other words, input prices reflect opportunity costs. Society had to give up only $36,000 worth of other products in order to get our cotton planter's crop produced, but if the planter had opted for the larger work force and smaller capital outlay, $62,000 worth of other kinds of production would have been sacrificed in other markets.

In short, given alternative technologies, prices of productive inputs guide producers in selecting the most effective method of production. Further, when technological innovations come along, they can be expected to change the exact combination of inputs that is most efficient.

Prices determine incomes of resource owners. In our cotton plantation example, input prices were givens, or constants, for the farmer. But for entire economies, prices of productive resources are variables.

Our cotton planter faced a price for labor of $3,000 per year which he treated as a given. But that price was determined by cotton planters bidding for labor against other kinds of farmers, manufacturing firms, public utilities, and government bodies, in fact all other employers of labor. The tractor price was likewise determined by farmers, including cotton planters, bidding against all other buyers of capital equipment.

As demand for the output of various industries changes, bidding for inputs by those industries can be expected to change accordingly, and the market prices of those inputs will follow suit. Thus, the incomes flowing to productive resource owners in various industries can be expected to fluctuate as final demand for industry output varies. In a similar manner, incomes of resource owners can be expected to follow the productivity trends of particular resources.

To sum up, incomes of productive resource owners, including labor, will be determined by the quantities of resources owned and the prices the resources command in the market. Resource prices are in turn determined by the strength of demand for inputs in various markets and the productivity of those inputs.

Social control via competition

Another important aspect of market exchange is the way *competition* among a number of sellers or buyers provides the alternatives individuals can choose among. The strength of any party to a trade is largely determined by the number of alternatives he can turn to if he doesn't like the terms offered by the person he is dealing with at the moment. In fact, consumer sovereignty depends upon consumers having the opportunity to choose among alternative products and alternative suppliers of any particular product.

Without a range of potential choices the consumer is ruled rather than sovereign. By the same token, workers seeking to get the most income from their labor fare better when several employers offer alternative work opportunities. The rivalry among firms to expand their own sales and to minimize their costs in order to make a profit is what provides alternatives to consumers and resource owners alike. In this way, each firm is limited in the prices it may charge and is spurred by the actions of rival firms to seek better methods.

Unfortunately, competition is not viewed in the same light by firms as by the consumer or resource owner. The firms would simply like to make a profit and not necessarily by improving methods or expanding production. If a single firm can control the sole source of supply or if a small group of firms can agree to act jointly as one seller, *to monopolize,* larger profits can be obtained by restricting production and selling fewer goods at higher prices.

In the medieval European trade centers public regulations frequently had to be enforced to prevent a large merchant from cornering a market by entering the market and buying up large quantities for resale at higher prices (engrossing) or by purchasing the supply before it reached the market (forestalling). On the other hand, guilds frequently used public regulations to prevent the entry of new sellers and restricted production in order to hold up prices. Large merchants frequently sought to monopolize trade in a particular commodity, and kings frequently granted and enforced such monopolies. Nevertheless, with many towns and nations in rivalry, with rapidly expanding trade volume, and rapidly changing methods, it was difficult for a few suppliers to exercise complete monopoly power for very long. The point to be noted is that while ideal competitive conditions seldom existed, active rivalry among firms was an important element in the successful development of the European market economy and its transfer to the colonies.

Ultimately, the social value of a market economy depends upon maintaining competitive rivalry among firms. It is competition that forces profit-seekers to expand production in areas of expanding demand and to introduce cost-reducing methods of production. Thus, competition is the social discipline or control that is exercised over profit-seeking firms.

Free enterprise, the slogan so highly valued in America, does not refer to a divine right of businessmen to do as they please. Rather, it refers to the freedom of rival firms to enter or expand in any field of production in which they can make a go of it. But contrary to the distorted view of some, free enterprise does not mean the right to monopolize an industry or profession either through private restraints to access or by enlisting government to impede entry by new firms or individuals.

Most American legislation dealing with markets has followed the tradition of English common law with respect to monopolizing activities. One of the ways in which the U.S. government second-guesses the market is to prosecute buyers or sellers who have acted to reduce the alternatives of those with whom they trade. On the other hand, U.S. law has followed the feudal and mercantilist traditions in several respects. Public utilities are granted legal monopoly rights; various professions, such as medicine and law, are invested with guild powers over membership; and fair wages are prescribed in state and federal minimum wage laws. On the whole, the law seems ambivalent on the question of social control through competition—at times promoting it, at times obviating it.

Now let's briefly recapitulate our discussion of the role of prices and quantities exchanged in a market system.

1. Any economic system is faced with the scarcity problem, so all economic systems must decide (a) what outputs to produce, (b) how inputs will be combined in producing them, and (c) how income will be distributed.

2. The market system relies chiefly upon the price mechanism to make these three basic decisions.

3. Consumers react to product prices on the basis of their preferences by buying a great deal of some products and very little of others. Prices, in turn, reflect costs of production including a return to investors.

4. Knowing what their technological alternatives are, producers decide on the basis of input prices which combinations of natural, human, and capital resources to use. Their objective is to attain the least-cost combination of productive inputs that technology will permit given supply prices of inputs.

5. Resource prices and quantities exchanged determine the income

levels of productive resource owners. The more resources a given house-hold owns and the higher the unit price of those resources, the larger will be the household's income.

6. Changes in consumer preferences and technological innovation will lead to new patterns in resource allocation. Fluctuations in prices act as signals to producers to expand or contract production or to vary input combinations.

7. Competition, the availability of a large number of alternatives for both buyers and sellers, is a requirement in the market system; otherwise, the consumer loses his sovereignty. Where competition fails, the U.S. government may provide alternative arrangements. Or, in other instances, our government steps in to insulate buyers or sellers from competitive pressures.

SUMMARY

The above subtitle is inaccurate. We have elected to withhold chapter 2's summary statement for the end of chapter 3, where we will sum-marize the decline of the traditional economy, the rise of the market system, the political evolution that paralleled these economic changes, and the Industrial Revolution—all in terms of their importance to the American Colonies and the early days of the United States. You may want to have a peek at that summary now as preparation for reading chapter 3.

APPENDIX TO CHAPTER 2: RATIO CHARTS AND INDEX NUMBERS

The study of economic growth requires frequent reference to rates of increase in various types of data. Ratio charts and index numbers provide two of the helpful ways that a number series can be presented so that *percentage rates of change* can be observed and compared most easily. A little time invested by you in studying this appendix will prove very valuable in understanding the various comparisons and analyses of economic data series that we will present throughout the succeeding chapters.

Start by examining carefully the graph (2–4A) shown on the opposite page; it uses an *arithmetic scale* as the vertical axis. Note that as time went on, colonial population increases got larger and larger when expressed in terms of numbers of people: e.g., about 50,000 between 1670 and 1680, but about 250,000 between 1730 and 1740.

Now look at the next graph (2–4B). It presents the same data as the preceding graph but uses a *ratio scale* as the vertical measure. The usefulness of plotting data on a ratio scale graph is that the slope of the trend line automatically represents the percentage rate of change.

2–4A. Colonial population trend
(arithmetic scale)

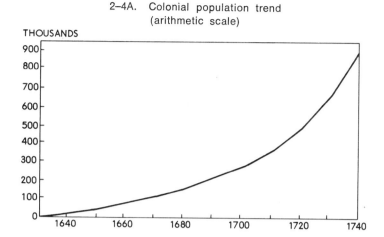

2–4B. Colonial population trend
(ratio scale)

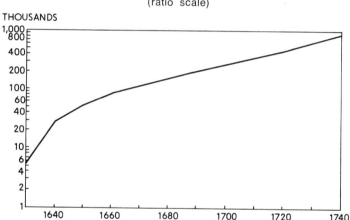

The **steeper** the trend line, the **faster** the rate of change (or the higher
the percentage increase). By comparing the slopes of the trend line
at two different periods of time, we can compare rates of change in
the different periods. Or, by comparing the slopes of two different trend
lines in the same period, we can determine which trend is faster.

On the arithmetic scale, population appears to start out with slow
increases and then to increase more rapidly. Actually, this is a half-truth.
Although, in absolute terms, the increases are small in size at first and
later get larger, the slope of the line on the ratio scale reveals that
population grew at a very rapid percentage rate between 1630 and 1640,
at a slower rate between 1640 and 1660, and at a still slower (but
steady) rate after 1660. About the same percentage rate of increase

(a doubling every 20–25 years) continued with very little change for the next two centuries—until after 1860.

The ratio scale is a logarithmic scale. The series of numbers in 2–4A could have been converted into logarithms by looking up the numbers in a logarithm table in a mathematics book. Logarithms could have then been plotted on the arithmetic (ordinary) scale in 2–4A, and the result would have been a curve identical with the one in 2–4B. The same result is achieved more easily, however, by plotting the original series of numbers on a sheet of semilog paper, graph paper which has the space intervals varied in accordance with logarithms. A ratio scale (or semilog graph) is quickly identified by the rapidly narrowing spaces between successive intervals of numbers of equal value. The spaces start wide and get narrower as the numerals go from 2 to 9. Notice, however, that the ratio chart is evenly spaced for each cycle. The cycles all begin with the numeral 1 as follows: 1, 10, 100, 1,000, and so forth. Each cycle has a different number of digits following the same numeral.

Index numbers provide another method of comparing the rates of change in a number series. Index numbers are most useful for comparing two series over the same period. In the first column of the table at the end of this appendix are presented the total colonial population figures for alternate decades. In the second column are presented the population figures for blacks (mostly imported slaves) on the same dates. The difficulty in comparing the changes in the two series is due partly to the large number of digits and partly to the difference in size of both series. Index numbers simplify the comparisons.

To convert the first column into index numbers (shown in column 3), a base year is selected, in this case 1700, and the index number 100 is assigned to this year. For any of the other years (say, 1680), the number for that year (151,507) is divided by the number for the base year (250,888) and multiplied by 100 (to move the decimal two places to the right). The result is the index number (60). This computation is repeated for every other number in the series. The same base year is used for the series on black population; and each number in that series is divided by the number in the base year (27,817). This provides the second index number series shown in the fourth column.

With both series of numbers expressed as index numbers with a common base year, it is possible to compare quickly which series grows faster between any other year and the base year. For the year 1720, the index number (159) minus the base year index (100) shows a 59 percent increase in total population since 1700 and a 147 percent increase in the black population. From 1700 to 1740, the index numbers show increases of 261 percent and 439 percent, respectively. For the two decades prior to the base year, it is quickly seen that total population increased over three times, while blacks increased almost ten times. From 1680 to 1700, the total increased by two thirds, while blacks quadrupled. It is not as easy to compare the percentage change between years not including the base year (for example, between 1720 and 1740), but even for those years it is easier to work with the index numbers than with the raw data.

2–5. Colonial population by race

Year	Number of persons		Indexes	
	Total (1)	Black (2)	Total (3)	Black (4)
1660	75,058	2,920	30	11
1680	151,507	6,971	60	25
1700	250,888	27,817	100	100
1720	466,185	68,839	159	247
1740	905,563	150,024	361	539

One final word of warning: the size of index numbers in two different series does *not* reflect their *comparative size in the original numbers.* In 1740, for example, the black population was obviously smaller than the total population. Each index number, it must be remembered, merely shows a comparison with the base year number in the same series of numbers.

REFERENCES

C. M. Andrews, *The Colonial Period in American History,* vol. 2 (New Haven, Conn.: Yale University Press, 1936).

J. W. Baldwin, "The Medieval Theories of the Just Price," *TAPS,* part IV, 1959.

R. T. Berthoff, *An Unsettled People* (New York: Harper & Row, Publishers, 1971).

J. Demos, *A Little Commonwealth: Family Life in Plymouth Colony* (New York: Oxford University Press, Galaxy Books, 1971).

P. J. Greven, Jr., *Four Generations: Population, Land, and Family in Colonial Andover, Massachusetts* (Ithaca, N.Y.: Cornell University Press, 1970).

E. J. Hamilton, *American Treasure and the Price Revolution in Spain* (Harvard University Press, 1934).

K. A. Lockridge, *A New England Town: The First Hundred Years* (New York: W. W. Norton & Co., Inc., 1970).

D. C. North and R. B. Thomas, "The Rise and Fall of the Manorial System: A Theoretical Model," *JEH,* December 1971.

3 POLITICAL EVOLUTION AND ECONOMIC REVOLUTION

The American Colonies inherited far more than the market system from England. They also inherited political conditions, institutions, and policies that favored economic growth within a market economy. In fact, some scholars argue that the Americans assumed just the better elements of the British tradition rather than importing British political economy lock, stock, and barrel.

In the colonial period, certain basic political conditions necessary to growth under any kind of economic system were present in both England and America.

1. England had developed a stable system of commercial law and courts and passed these institutions on to her colonies. Specialization and exchange are rooted in a common understanding as to rights and obligations associated with transactions. These must be enforceable or subject to adjudication if men are to be willing to make production decisions based upon contractual agreements.

2. England, the American Colonies, and, after 1815, the United States were benefited by a combination of circumstances that produced periods of security and political stability which lasted long enough to enhance foreign trade. Markets must be large enough to absorb the large surpluses generated by specialists if the advantages of specialization and exchange are to be captured. A large population and diversified resources in one political unit provide two of the conditions necessary for markets large enough to promote specialization and exchange. Both internal order and peace among nations are also required. When a political unit is too small to support a high degree of specialization, foreign markets can take the place of a large domestic market. Thus, a compara-

tively high level of international order and tranquility encouraged English and American growth.

3. The economic role of the state was gradually reduced during the colonial period. As England emerged from the medieval period, an autocratic king, a narrowly defined ruling class, and a tradition of official control of economic activity were the order of the day. What initially evolved from this starting point was a system of national political economy in which economic affairs were open to regulation in any way that might enhance the power of the sovereign. A complex system of national economic controls called *mercantilism* was enacted to take the place of feudal laws and traditions.

However, movements for constitutional reform and expanded civil liberties plus the impracticality of enforcing many of the controls over economic activity gradually eroded—not erased—the role of the state in economic affairs. As a consequence, political institutions and traditions especially favorable to a market economy were developed in England and passed on to America. Although in both places governments persisted in trying to regulate prices and wages, they did so with decreasing frequency and increasing futility. But trade flows among political units continued to be objects of regulation.

4. Finally, certain economic aspects of British colonial policy were probably helpful to growth under a market system. For one thing, economic objectives rather than missionary religious zeal were dominant in colonial policy. For another, international trade aside, only a minimum of governmental control was actually exercised over private economic activity.

By the time the American Colonies were of significant size, liberal British attitudes and shortage of administrative funds had left them largely, but not entirely, self-governing and free of government economic control. None of this is to say that there was no unrest in colonial America. The colonies were treated as vassals, with the nature of political, economic, and legal relationships between England and America being determined primarily by the British. In fact, the Stamp Act, the Tea Act, and the Townshend duties provoked violence because they were interpreted as reactionary measures designed to reimpose close British supervision. In view of this history, it is not surprising that the United States started with popular support for restriction of government's powers.

POLITICAL EVOLUTION

During the American colonial period, continental Europe was embroiled in almost constant wars over religion, national boundaries, and colonial empires. Absolute monarchy was the typical form of national government, and mercantilism the predominant economic policy of governments. These were political aspects of the transition from a traditional to a market economy, a transition in which Britain proceeded well in advance of the European continent. A chronological view of America's Old World ties with references to American events, is shown in 3–1.

3–1. A chronology of America's European background

European events	Centuries	American events
Renaissance	15th	1492 Columbus "discovers" America
1517 Reformation starts 1524 Church of England Religious wars in Europe Gold imports; inflation England expands trade; sheep raising, enclosures; textiles 1588 Spanish Armada defeated	16th	
England develops manufacturing industries		1607 Virginia Colony founded 1620 Plymouth Colony founded
1642 Civil War in England Cromwell; Navigation Acts 1660 Stuart kings restored; Whig and Tory parties 1688 Glorious Revolution, Bill of Rights, Cabinet 1689 King William's War	17th	British colonies founded in West Indies and Canada
Agricultural improvements, population rise		1713 Peace of Utrecht, France cedes Canada to Britain
1702 Queen Anne's War 1745 King George's War 1754 Seven Years' War Industrial Revolution 1776 Smith, *Wealth of Nations* 1789 French Revolution 1793 Napoleonic Wars start	18th	1732 Georgia Colony founded (last of original 13) 1754 French and Indian War 1775 War of Independence 1776 Declaration of Independence 1789 Constitution ratified
1815 Napoleonic Wars end	19th	1812 War with England

Nationalism

Several large nation-states emerged from the Middle Ages as the new form of political organization in Europe. Strong national kingdoms arose in Spain, France, Holland, Sweden, and Russia. The kings were able to suppress the power of provincial barons by using large armies of mercenaries and with the aid of a large bureaucracy of tax collectors and central government officials. For a variety of reasons, people began to become conscious of their identification with a nation.

The new nations were regarded by their kings as personal domains. Whether they were ordained by the Church or not, they justified their insistence on absolute authority as a divine right inherited by birth. Trade and industry were regarded as mere sources of tax revenues and military supplies. Colonies were sought by the kings as sources of personal riches and power.

England, as an island nation, was favored by its geographic isolation from Europe. With most of its population concentrated in the broad flatlands of the southwest, it achieved national unity more easily. Wales, Ireland, and Scotland were less populated and more rural, and they came fairly readily, if not enthusiastically, under the control of the English kings. Starting with a less rigid feudal structure and weaker provincial barons, the Tudor kings were able to establish firm control at the beginning of the 16th century. Having built a strong navy under Queen Elizabeth, England staved off the only major invasion threat by defeating the Spanish Armada. England established naval supremacy in the 17th century by a series of naval battles with the Dutch and the French. Yet it made only very limited commitments of soldiers and resources to land warfare on the European continent.

England was also favored with comparatively little religious strife. The Church of England was established to serve political purposes, not doctrinal unorthodoxy. However, as the spirit of Protestantism grew stronger in England, continual demands for reform were pressed. Then an attempt by Queen Mary to restore Catholicism produced internal controversy and civil war. But by the start of the 18th century, religious struggles and civil strife had subsided, and increasing diversity of individual beliefs was tolerated.

The material ramifications of these political developments favored British economic development. England established a series of colonies, among them North American outposts, and built up a significant world trade.

At home, productivity increased as a reflection of the greater specialization made possible by growing domestic and colonial markets, by technological innovations, and by the economic reorganization that marked the end of feudalism and the ascent of what we might call commercialism. Overseas, the American colonists, many of them lured to the New World by the abundance of land and the chance to prosper, held an enviable position. Their trade was shielded by the Royal Navy and protected (as well as circumscribed) by British commercial regulations. To a large degree, the Americans were left free to produce in their most productive specialities for an expanding British empire, and, as we will see in chapter 4, their fortunes accurately reflected their opportunities.

Representative government

For reasons in part attributable to England's insular position and its unimportance to Europeans, British governmental institutions took a decidedly more democratic direction than did those of the Continent. The power of the king to lay taxes and enact laws was challenged by the nobility in King John's reign. John was forced to sign the Magna Charta, which conferred on the nobility, and only the nobility, such privileges as trial by jury and a legislature (Parliament), whose consent was required for new tax legislation. The Magna Charta was hardly the first step on the path that led inexorably to representative democracy, but it did set a precedent in forcing the king of a united England to cede some of his power to an organized pressure group, the nobility. However, until the mid-17th century, the period of early colonization, the king retained the balance of power in government and neither the sovereign nor the landowners showed any predisposition toward popular government.

Beginning in the middle 1600s, civil war, Cromwell's dictatorship, restoration of the monarchy, and, finally, the Glorious Revolution succeeded in further restricting the powers of the king. The Bill of Rights (1689) made permanent various powers of Parliament while restricting those of the king, especially the "pretended Power of Suspending of Laws or the Execution of Laws by Regall Authoritie without Consent of Parlyament." It also established a variety of civil rights, some of which applied to citizens in general, while others applied only to Protestants or members of Parliament. Later, the king's ministers could serve only if approved by Parliament.

English constitutional reform had a long way to go at the time of the American Revolution. Only male real property owners were regarded as capable of participating in government. Thus Parliament was drawn from a small minority of the population composed of the landed aristocracy and middle-class merchants, manufacturers, and professional men who had acquired estates. Nevertheless, in winning prerogatives for the legislature at the expense of the king, the English aristocracy established Parliament as a source of political power which over the centuries was to become accessible to other strata of English society. Parliamentary reform gradually, very gradually, widened the electorate, first through inclusion of the middle class, then by extending suffrage to the working classes.

With less reason to be tradition-bound in America, the momentum of English constitutional reform was accelerated as it was swept into the tide of American political development. Colonial legislatures were patterned after Parliament, although they anticipated their English predecessor by expanding their electoral bases more rapidly than did Parliament.

Following English precedent, the colonists used their legislatures as power bases from which to challenge both the king and Parliament. As a consequence, the U.S. Constitution in its expressions and implications comprised a far more developed system of governmental checks and balances than did the government of England. The constitutional basis of the U.S. government became the most liberal ever enacted, more than anticipating the English reform bills of the early 1800s. Nevertheless, the U.S. Constitution did not eliminate all property and sex barriers to suffrage or outlaw Negro slavery.

In short, the English 17th century revolutions were certainly less sweeping in their democratizing effects than the American Revolution of the 18th century. But England did pass onto America a revolutionary precedent and a host of political ideas whose main thrusts were constitutionally limited government and a wide latitude for freedom of choice for individual citizens. If the resulting political structure didn't constitute a necessary ingredient for the persistence of a market economy, it provided at the very least a complement to the burgeoning American market system.

Mercantilism

As the Commercial Revolution elbowed feudalism aside, a new era of economic policy began. However, the feudal heritage was strong, and it was surely unthinkable that market decisions should be allowed to determine the deployment of society's scarce resources. Quite the contrary! Feudalism, a traditional system designed to ensure survival of the principality and its estates, was replaced by mercantilism, a command system whose objective was to enhance the power of the sovereign and his nation.

The varied lot of policies that constituted mercantilism cannot be fenced in meaningfully by a single definition; however, the following description may serve our purposes:

> Mercantilism was an economic policy calling for a great deal of government intervention in economic affairs; it was directed toward increasing a nation's wealth, power, and degree of self-sufficiency in a period of intense international rivalry; its principal tactic was to encourage exports with which to earn gold and silver and, thus, provide a source of tax revenues to support the military.

The main goal of mercantilism was national power. This meant primarily the power to make war. Little consideration was given to the economic welfare of the bulk of the population as individuals. The national government was not oriented toward consumer choice and individual values. When mercantilism prevailed, little thought was given to improving production methods in order to raise productivity and workers' living standards.

In a world of fixed opportunities, the way to get ahead was through seizing an increased share of available resources and wealth. Thus, the objective of national governments was economic expansion rather than economic growth, and economic expansion usually involved colonization and the acquisition of neighboring real estate through aggression.

The three main concepts of mercantilism may be summed up under the terms *bullionism, autarky,* and *colonialism.* Bullionism meant that national power and wealth depended upon the stores of *specie*—money metals—in the government treasury or in the hands of wealthy ruling classes. A well-stocked treasury could be used to buy supplies, build navies, and hire troops in time of war.

Essential to the idea of bullionism was the additional idea that money metals could be accumulated by means of a favorable balance of trade, i.e., by an excess of the value of exported goods over the value of imported goods. The difference in payments was expected to result in an inflow of specie. By selling more to other nations than it purchased from them, a nation received a greater share of the world's money. Mercantilist states therefore passed laws favoring exports and curbing imports. Of course, not all nations could simultaneously succeed in running favorable trade balances, so international rivalries sharpened and trade restrictions escalated.

Another idea subsidiary to bullionism stated that a nation which carried imported and exported goods in its own ships would avoid freight payments to other nations. Thus, shipping was regarded as an export industry, and regulations such as the British Navigation Acts were enacted to discourage the use of foreign merchant vessels.

Autarky, a policy of national economic self-sufficiency, was rationalized on the ground that it guaranteed supplies of essential materials which might be cut off in time war. The danger of being cut off from supplies when at war provides some justification for seeking autarkical restraints on trade. However, under mercantilism, self-sufficiency was viewed as nationally beneficial without considering the costs of forgoing cheaper imports or the actual degree of damage that might result from having supplies cut off. Thus, the quest for autarky meant that the state had to protect inefficient national industries from lower-cost imported goods by such measures as tariffs (taxes on imports), subsidies to home industries, or the banning of certain imports. Consumers, of course, paid higher prices for many domestically produced products that they would have imported under free trade conditions.

Colonialism required that colonial production and trade should be organized to serve the needs of the home country. Colonies were sought as sources of raw materials that were not available or were scarce within the home country's boundaries. Further, colonial trading posts were a means of ensuring a favorable balance of trade. Spain showed how colonies could be a direct source of imports of specie from South American mines; and sugar produced in the West Indies was an equally desirable source of wealth because it could be sold to other nations. The Portuguese and Dutch demonstrated the value of Far Eastern trading posts as sources of exotic goods which could be traded at high prices in Europe.

Colonies were regarded solely as instruments of national power and welfare and were not expected to have objectives of their own. Thus, they were required to confine their trade almost entirely to the mother country. In addition, lists of products which could not be produced in the colonies were specified. Characteristically, they included all but a few manufactured items. Military protection was provided to the colonies, not out of compassion, but because it was prudent to protect overseas investments.

Mercantilism tended to emphasize shipping and manufacturing as strategic to national development. The manufacture of arms, munitions, and ships was, of course, directly important to a nation's warmaking power. Manufactured goods were also viewed as the main means to increase exports and obtain a favorable balance of trade. A general improvement in agricultural productivity in the 17th century generated a considerable surplus of labor in Europe. Thus, the way to national wealth appeared to lie in using idle workers to produce more manufactured goods. Trading a surplus of labor services (embodied in manufactured goods or used in shipping) for rare raw materials and additional stores of monetary metals seemed an ideal way to build national power.

Mercantilism relied chiefly upon government command, plus various positive and negative incentives, to influence private decisions. The assumptions behind this approach seemed to be that whatever was commanded to happen would happen and that little would be accomplished in the absence of government decisions and actions. These assumptions, of course, reflected a lack of understanding of how market exchange can direct private production through price signals.

The two most direct methods of mercantilism involved (1) the establishment of government enterprises to carry out certain activities and (2) the passage of laws regulating economic behavior by specifying such things as what kinds of workers might migrate, whose ships might carry the nation's trade, and what foreign products might be excluded. Special incentives and penalties, such as export subsidies, import tariffs, and monopoly rights, were also used to further mercantilist aims.

England entered the colonial race later than the continental powers, so its options were restricted to settlement colonies for its political, religious, and economic refugees and plantation colonies that might serve as sources of raw materials. The sites for bullion colonies had already been occupied when Britain elected to become a colonial power.

The nature of the North American colonies and the shortage of administrative funds meant that actual administration of colonial regulations was liberal when not lax. Consequently, it was not until England attempted to stiffen enforcement of colonial regulations that these policies were widely criticized in England as a disservice to national interests and in the North American colonies as oppressive.

FORMATION OF A NATION

For a variety of political, social, and economic reasons that we shall explore in chapter 4, the 13 contiguous colonies of Britain's North American holdings opted for independence in 1775. Britain failed to win the Revolutionary War, and the Thirteen Colonies found themselves independent, fragmented, and outcasts among the imperial powers. Their task was to find a political form that would give them sufficient unity to make them (1) economically viable, (2) capable of remaining politically independent, and (3) acceptable on an equal footing by the nations of Europe.

Nonnationhood, 1776–89

After the outbreak of fighting in 1775 and the Declaration of Independence in 1776, a seven-year period of warfare and blockade passed before England finally recognized American independence in 1783. During the war, the thirteen states had been very loosely united. The Continental Congress served as little more than a steering committee for the war. In 1781, the separate states finally ratified the Articles of Confederation (these were drafted in 1777). After the war, a number of problems engendered by disunity plagued the Confederation. This led to the drafting of a constitution for a stronger union, in 1787.

In the period of nonnationhood, the absence of a viable system of national defense was a paramount problem. The war itself had been won in part by default: Britain had not been able to ignore dangers elsewhere and could not concentrate enough military force in America. The alliance between the colonies and France had brought decisive land and naval forces that helped the colonies to win the final victory. But the Continental Congress had had to rely upon the unequal and irregular support of the states to raise and assign militia to a national army.

The new nation continued without adequate powers to raise and support a national army and navy while the security and economic development of its western lands were threatened by European colonial powers. In the north, England refused to abandon its fur trading posts along the southern shores of the Great Lakes and encouraged Indian hostilities against American pioneer settlements.[1] Many American loyal-

---

[1] In some cases the British paid bounties to Indians for American scalps, thereby perpetuating a custom initiated earlier by the colonists.

ists had found refuge in Canada, and their hostility promoted fear of future conflicts. In the south, Spain held Florida and fomented trouble with the Indians. While Spain held the Gulf Coast and New Orleans, the export of western goods was restricted. Of most immediate importance, the Barbary pirates, who had long received tribute to let British shipping alone, began to prey upon American ships.

Congress also found it difficult to establish favorable trade agreements with European countries. The most serious problem was with England. American ships now found themselves outside the British Empire and restricted by the very enactments of British mercantilism that once protected them. Import duties and port charges hurt American exports and shipping, and a flood of postwar British imports caused considerable outflow of specie and exacerbated the shortage of coins in America. In attempts to retaliate and bring Britain to terms, the state legislatures began to place tariffs on British goods; but the different duty levels only caused British ships to seek the ports with the lowest duties.

Congress was heavily in debt and had no power beyond borrowing to raise revenues. During the Revolutionary War, the states had been reluctant to supply Congress with funds. Both Congress and the states had incurred large debts and had issued a great deal of paper money. There was little confidence in the ability of the Continental Congress to redeem its paper money, so it traded for vastly less than its face value: hence the expression "not worth a Continental."

The combination of a shortage of goods and a large supply of newly issued money caused severe inflation of the general price level during the war. Most prices, even in coin, more than doubled. (See 3–2 for

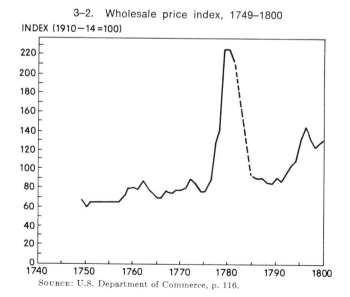

3–2.   Wholesale price index, 1749–1800

INDEX (1910–14 =100)

SOURCE: U.S. Department of Commerce, p. 116.

a graphic representation of the wartime inflation and refer to the appendix in this chapter for an explanation of price indexes.)

After the war, the economy entered a severe depression. Shipping continued to be crippled, and exports to England were low as compared with the early 1770s. Prices fell drastically. This pressed especially heavily upon people who had incurred debts during the war when prices were high. In the period's most violent reaction to hard times, discontented farmers from Massachusetts rallied around Cap. Daniel Shays in revolt against heavy taxation and attempts to foreclose mortgages and imprison debtors.

On top of these problems, the states were involved in intense commercial rivalry. They not only used a variety of devices to compete for foreign shipping, but also levied duties upon interstate shipments of goods. Fortunately, a settlement of conflicting claims to western land was reached when Maryland refused to sign the Articles of Confederation until other states agreed to cede their western lands to federal ownership. This made possible the Ordinances of 1784, 1785, and 1787 which provided for the survey and sale of western lands by the national government and for the eventual organization of new western states.

Shays' Rebellion underscored the realization that the Confederation was not the vehicle required to establish political, social, and economic nationhood to the satisfaction of either the Americans or Europeans. The Constitutional Convention, called to overhaul the Articles of Confederation, soon found itself working on a wholly new design which featured a stronger central government with powers to deal with the kinds of problems that had led to Shays' Rebellion.

Welding the thirteen separate states into one nation was of fundamental importance to later economic development. Unity made possible the creation of a large internal market, so important to specialization, large-scale production, and consequent high productivity. Therefore, one of the most important powers granted to the federal government was the power to regulate foreign and interstate commerce. Put negatively, the states lost the right to maintain the barriers to interstate and international commerce which had produced mutually destructive trade policies under the Confederation. The federal government was also given the power to control a national army and navy and to supervise foreign relations. The prerogative to levy taxes granted by the Constitution was essential to make the federal government's other powers effective.

The federal government was given several additional sources of power important to its economic functions. The right to incur debts and issue and regulate money rounded out its fiscal powers and eventually made possible a uniform and centrally controlled monetary system. Specific provisions were made for the regulation of bankruptcy, the issuance of patents, and the establishment of post offices and post roads. The "general welfare" and the "neccessary and proper" clauses were two catchalls which, together with the right to regulate interstate commerce, provided the basis for later expansion of federal economic powers.

Initial economic policies

The way the new government used its constitutional powers inevitably set precedents that influenced the later economic development of the Nation. The principal economic policies were few, and they arose out of the problems that had been experienced in establishing the United States.

1. Three sources of revenue were established.

One of the first acts of Congress was to pass the Tariff Act of 1789. It set low import duties so as to *encourage* imports and thus yield tax income. Uniform tonnage duties were passed at 50 cents per ton for foreign ships and 6 cents per ton for U.S. vessels. In traditional mercantilist fashion the rates discriminated against foreign ships to encourage U.S. shipping and to give the United States a bargaining point in negotiations over practices that discriminated against U.S. trade.

Alexander Hamilton, the first secretary of the Treasury, recommended two additional sources of federal revenues. One was the rapid sale of lands in the western territories. Unfortunately for the small settlers, the Land Ordinance of 1785 provided for the sale of land in minimum units of 640 acres, or at least 16 times the economically optimum size of a family farm in those days. This meant that many pioneers had to buy land from speculating intermediaries. However, this may have provided the most efficient way for a new government with little administrative structure to transfer land to settlers and obtain revenues.

The second source of revenue proposed by Hamilton and adopted by Congress was the levying of excise taxes on domestic production, mainly on whiskey. The whiskey excise can be regarded as a test of responsible democratic government in which Congress recognized the necessity of paying the cost of government by levying domestic taxes—it was an especially rigorous test, since it was levied upon a commodity that was held in very high esteem.

2. A uniform monetary system was enacted.

A national currency system was established by the Mint Act of 1792, which incorporated Hamilton's recommendation that both gold and silver coins be issued.

Perhaps Hamilton's major monetary proposal was the Bank of the United States, which was chartered in 1791. The bank acted as a depository for government funds and was empowered to lend to the government. The bank was also authorized to issue its own paper money, notes backed partly by gold and silver but mostly by government bonds. This established a fairly sound system of paper money at a time when monetary metals were much needed for foreign trade.

The Bank of the United States could also exercise a mild restraining influence on the issue of notes by state banks because it could refuse to accept notes of doubtful value in handling the transactions of the government. Nevertheless, prices rose considerably in the first two decades of nationhood.

3.   The federal government promised to pay all the state debts incurred during the Revolution as well as the debts incurred by the Continental Congress.

By indicating a willingness to pay all debts and by adopting an orderly application of tax revenues to this purpose, the United States won the confidence of foreign governments, foreign investors, and private citizens. This act of good faith enabled Hamilton to sell new U.S. bonds to replace the old debts and to provide for a gradual paying off of the new bond issues with tax revenues.

This kind of credit policy paved the way for large inflows of foreign financial capital that helped build the economy's industrial and social overhead capital. Federal borrowing was made easier in later years. State governments were able to establish sounder financial policies and, later, to borrow large amounts to build roads and canals. And, indirectly, foreign investors gained confidence in the environment for private business ventures in the United States.

One of Hamilton's major policy recommendations was not acted upon—the deliberate fostering of new manufacturing industries in America. Hamilton's famous *Report on Manufactures* proposed higher tariffs on imported manufactured goods and subsidies to new industries. This represented a continuation of mercantilist thinking that was common to his time. The Revenue Act of 1792, however, failed to raise import rates to the levels he recommended. Congress was apparently not willing at that time to consider any economic policies that did more than provide the minimum functions of the new central government. Patent laws aside, initially no federal programs were undertaken either to regulate the private economy or to use direct government expenditures for investment or production. For the time being, at least, the American people were wary of central government actions beyond the minimum needs of providing for defense and establishing a monetary system.

The states, on the other hand, continued and extended many of the mercantilist policies they had initiated in colonial times and during the Confederation. State governments were generally expected to be economic activists, to enhance economic development. They were charged with directly creating social overhead capital and assisting in financing private social overhead projects. Where private enterprise failed to produce a product widely demanded by the farming or business community, public enterprise was expected to fill the gap.

With modifications in form and a significant transfer of state responsibilities to the federal government, the policies we have just described continue to characterize the federal and state governments of the United States.[2]

EMERGING IDEAS

As we have stated earlier, the ideas about governmental economic policy which were widely accepted in colonial times were those of mercantilism. Nevertheless, at the time of the American Revolution, new ideas about government economic policy were emerging in France and England. These ideas were critical of mercantilism and favored less government regulation of economic activities. Note, though, that they were not widely influential in America until after the Civil War. We mentioned them here because the late 18th century was the period in which they were first widely discussed.

Laissez-faire

Beginning in the late 17th century, a number of writers in both England and France issued critiques of mercantilism. In their view, government should be liberal rather than restrictive in its economic policy. They saw that a profusion of taxes, duties, and regulations could be a hindrance to production and exchange. These criticisms of mercantilism culminated in the 1750s in a series of tracts written by Frenchmen who became known as the *Physiocrats.*

The Physiocrats popularized the policy slogan *laissez-faire*—that is, let markets alone, let buying and selling chart the course of prices and the quantities exchanged. This meant that governments should cease trying to command or direct the allocation of scarce resources. These views were based in part on a better appreciation of the workings of markets. The Physiocrats asserted that individuals unhindered by government regulations, but driven by self-interest and guided by market prices and competition, could bring about socially desirable production patterns. It was not necessary for government to command things to happen.

In 1776, the year the Declaration of Independence was written, a Scot named Adam Smith published *The Wealth of Nations*. Smith, influenced by Britain's rapid industrial growth and by Physiocratic thought, also advocated leaving the market alone. He argued that if each member of society were free to pursue his self-interest, a harmonious and socially beneficial economic order would result, as if guided by an "invisible hand." Smith stressed the importance to productivity of specialization and exchange within and among national economies and the division of labor within the individual firm. He saw the impor-

---

[2] See Lively for a review of the literature on state and federal government and economic activity, with special attention to the ideological basis of public intervention in the economy.

tance of capital in providing labor with more productive tools. In his view, capital investment raised productivity and thereby served as a source of cumulative economic growth.

Freedom of trade

Both the Physiocrats and Adam Smith argued for freedom of international trade. They rejected the mercantilist idea that national wealth consisted of money in the central government's treasury and emphasized the nation's productive capacity as the real source of wealth. To them, the objective of exporting products was to obtain useful and needed goods, not merely to obtain money which has value only if it can be exchanged for goods. They viewed international trade as a mere extension of specialization and exchange to a larger market. These notions reflect a shift in orientation in which economic activity came to be seen as directed to furthering the welfare of individuals (what Smith saw as the true "wealth of nations") rather than buttressing the power of the crown.

Following Smith, various liberal writers were influenced by the concept of comparative advantage in their advocacy of free trade among nations. They recognized that free trade would allow nations to reap the mutual benefits of specialization and exchange that are sacrificed by a policy of self-sufficiency. Smith and others also recognized that persistent attempts to sell more abroad than was purchased overseas might be self-defeating. An excess of exports could not forever bring an inflow of gold, because other nations would run out of specie.

A quantity theory of money suggested how market adjustments might be made to balance exports and imports under a free trade policy. It would come about through effects on price levels in both nations. If England had an export surplus and received gold from, say, Spain, the gold inflow would increase the money supply in England and generate higher English prices. The opposite would happen in Spain. With prices falling in Spain and rising in England, it would grow difficult for English merchants to continue selling exports to Spain, while English buyers would increase their imports from Spain. So England's export surplus would soon be wiped out by a decline in her exports and an increase in her imports.

On the other hand, the national interest, in terms of all producers and all consumers, was sacrificed by tariff policies intended to protect or favor the interests of any particular group of producers. If Spain were to raise the tariff on woolen textile imports to protect the Spanish textile industry, the results would be higher prices for Spanish consumers of woolens and hard times for resource owners, including workers, in Spanish export industries. Fewer woolen imports would reduce the ability of wool-producing nations such as England to buy Spain's output.

In the end, international specialization would be reduced and productivity would fall accordingly.

The writings of the Physiocrats and Adam Smith were confused and confusing on many points. But they were the beginnings of the application of scientific thinking to economic matters. In many respects, they were the first systematic theories about the causes and effects of economic events.

Adam Smith and the Physiocrats not only developed some useful theoretical analysis but also expressed a policy point of view about maximizing welfare. Specifically, as we noted above, they shifted the definition of economic welfare from the state to the individual.

A policy expresses value preferences about what is regarded as good. But, unfortunately, as we pointed out in chapter 1, economists are unable to unambiguously quantify and measure good, or welfare, as a particular policy defines it. Consequently, there is usually a good deal of debate over economic policy even when the disputants have a common goal.

The opposed ideas of mercantilism and laissez-faire should be understood as an aid to historical perspective. They represented distinct policy viewpoints that arose out of the conditions of particular historical periods, and they influenced the policies of governments in later periods. In fact, some elements of these ideas are essential parts of today's economic policy and will prove useful in analyzing the economic growth and development of our Nation.

ECONOMIC REVOLUTION

As we noted at the beginning of this chapter, our political inheritance from England made it possible to establish a market economy in colonial America. The development of that economy in late colonial times and the first few decades of the new nation's life prepared the United States for the importation of a second British phenomenon, the Industrial Revolution.

At this point, we are going to retrace the historical steps we have just examined. This time, however, we shall look specifically at the economic revolution whose final chapter was the Industrial Revolution.[3]

A definition seems a required first step. The term Industrial Revolution has generally been used to refer to the historical period in England when the modern industrial method was introduced and rapid economic growth first started. We shall define "modern industrial method" in detail later in the chapter; for purposes of introductory discussion, think of it as making possible mass production

The period 1750–1850 is often used to date the Industrial Revolution. However, a long sequence of discoveries and improvements preceded

---

[3] For a review of the literature on the Industrial Revolution see Hughes.

that span, and some of the discoveries of the 1750–1850 period were not widely adopted until much later. In fact, the improvements in agriculture, transportation, and other fields that preceded and accompanied innovations in manufacturing may have had greater immediate effects on output. As you can see by looking closely at 3–3, the Industrial Revo-

3–3. Historical setting of the Industrial Revolution

Century	Resources	Transportation	Manufacturing	Trade	Markets
15th		Navigation improved	Guilds, custom manufacturing, handcrafting	Rise of trade	Emergence of factor markets
				Exploration	Farm "surplus" traded in cities
16th	More wool raised Displaced farm labor	Shipbuilding	Cottage textile manufacturing	Spanish gold Increased trading	Inflation Growth of London
17th	Timber shortage Use of coal	Coastal shipping	Diversity of industries Use of water-wheels, power transmission equipment	Colonies	Income rise New products consumed
18th	Improved farming Released farm labor	Canals Roads	Coke Textile machines, better iron, tools Steam engine	India cotton goods imported American cotton	More food Population rise More cities War demands
19th	Improved extraction methods	Steam railroad Steamships	Standard parts Steel	Free trade	American expansion

lution was the culminating episode in a much longer period of economic development in which technology, economic organization, and the legal framework of economic life were revolutionized.

Preconditions

England was the first nation to undergo an industrial revolution. Yet in 1500 England was a weak and relatively backward country, whereas for the next two and a half centuries France was regarded as the most advanced manufacturing nation. It's time to list the advantages that helped England prepare for this first stage in the modern industrial age.

Of great importance, the political and intellectual climate favored enterprise, innovation, and individual initiative. Not only did England's middle class enjoy considerable personal freedom; it also possessed a large stock of intellectual capital.

Undoubtedly, England was favored in its geography and natural resources. As an island nation, its fishing and shipping industries were developed early. Coastal transportation was easily available and cheap. Much of the country was relatively flat and afforded few barriers to travel. Agriculture was prosperous enough to permit production of a wool surplus. Finally, materials of special importance to manufacturing, especially coal and iron, were available locally.

Most important, perhaps, was the commercial and industrial progress that England had achieved by the mid-17th century. Farming was highly commercialized. The middle class was large. Its extensive merchant fleet transported an active world trade. It had well-developed financial institutions and large accumulations of capital. Besides textiles as the major manufacturing enterprise, England had developed a diverse manufacturing sector. If France still was the manufacturing leader, England was a close second.

There were three features of England's industrial development which distinguished it from that of France. England's manufacturing plants were larger. Its manufacturing production was concentrated in low-cost, mass-consumption goods. And its overall technological change outpaced that of France.

Many of the new industries introduced in England early in the 16th century—paper mills, blast furnaces, sugar refining, and brass making—required heavy equipment and large numbers of workers. Because these industries required large accumulations of capital and a high degree of management skill, British entrepreneurs gained experience that proved valuable in adopting new technologies as they were developed.

France had long excelled at producing low-volume, expertly crafted luxury goods, whereas England produced cheaper goods to be consumed in huge quantities by the middle classes and higher income workers and farmers. The bias of Britain's industrial markets helped it in two ways. First, when the new, high volume modes of production were developed, the economics of market size dictated their adoption by the British. Second, the rapid expansion of population, income, and trade in Europe caused the demand for British manufactures to grow much faster than the demand for the handcrafted French luxury goods.

In part, England's more rapid rate of technological advance can be attributed to the managerial and market factors we have just cited. Experienced managers and large, specialized markets are certainly conducive to technological development. However, the most important stimulus may have come from rising costs resulting from certain resource scarcities—recall the old cliché which deals with the maternal genealogy of invention.

When particular inputs become scarce relative to their demand, their supply prices rise, stimulating a search for innovations that will economize on those inputs. Depletion of English forests in the 16th and 17th centuries produced a more than fourfold rise in lumber prices. Charcoal prices rose too, though not as dramatically. Coal and other mined minerals rose in price as outcroppings were exhausted and deep shaft mines had to be opened. Periodic shortages of labor pushed up wage rates.

As a consequence of these pressures on input prices, the 16th and 17th centuries were years of considerable technological improvement. Power-transmitting devices—shafts, pulleys, chain drives, sprockets, gears, roller bearings, and universal joints—reduced power waste, magnified the amount of power a worker could control, and permitted greater use of windmills, waterwheels, and draft animals. Mining was revolutionized by drills, geared hoists, improved pumps, and ventilation systems. Metallurgy underwent a basic change with the introduction of a crude blast furnace for smelting at the beginning of the 16th century.

Remember that agricultural development is usually a prerequisite to industrial development. On the supply side, productivity increases in agriculture release labor for work in manufacturing and social overhead industries, such as road and harbor construction, public utilities, transportation, communications, and finance. On the demand side, lower agricultural input costs mean lower food and fiber prices and a smaller portion of consumer spending devoted to food and clothing budgets; income is released to finance purchases of manufactured goods and to support social overhead capital formation through saving and taxation. (Note that it is lower food and fiber prices compared with other prices that bring supply and demand conditions back into a harmonious relationship.)

Significant productivity gains in England's agriculture date back to the so-called earlier industrial revolution which we discussed in chapter 2 in connection with the transition from feudal to modern times. By the 1600s, English agriculture was highly commercialized (a great deal of specialization and cash cropping) as compared with that of the colonies or the Continent.

The demand for wool and for food for the fast-growing urban centers provided rapidly expanding agricultural markets. Imports, land clearing, new crops, and new cultivation and breeding techniques helped bring the growth of supply into line with the expansion of demand. The period's array of innovations in agricultural practices is impressive—especially when you stop to think that the changes were primarily managerial, coming as they did before the age of agricultural mechanization.

Beginning in the 17th century, Englishmen harvested the seas at an accelerated rate, bringing cod in unprecedented lots to British tables. The colonies supplied a variety of products—chief among them were sugar, rum, indigo, rice, cotton, hides, and tobacco—to supplement British production where it was short and to provide what the British couldn't produce. Ireland provided beef and dairy products. Thanks to better methods and extensive land clearing, Britain's grain production expanded almost as fast as population.

A large number of changes raised agricultural yields and/or lowered agricultural labor requirements. New crops, such as clover as a feed and rotation crop and the potato as a cheap substitute for breadstuffs, were introduced. Crop rotation, row cropping with machinery for plowing, planting, and cultivation, and selective livestock breeding all reflected the English farmer's need to wrest more from his soil. Continued enclosure of common lands and clearing and draining increased the amount of plowland. The effectiveness of these changes can be seen in the fall in England's farm labor requirements and the growth of its population. Over the 18th century, agriculture's share of total labor inputs fell from two fifths to about one third of the work force. At the same time, population grew by 50 percent, with most of the increase concentrated in the last 60 years of the century.[4]

The colonial ramifications of the revolution in British agriculture went far beyond the colonial role in supplementing Britain's output. England showed the way to the American and other colonies: it constituted a gigantic agricultural experiment station. Late in our colonial period, new British techniques were observed, copied, and adapted to colonial conditions. This trend accelerated after the Revolution and into the 19th century.

The Industrial Revolution

Consider again the preconditions of the Industrial Revolution cited above and in chapter 2. In England, the market had emerged as an organizing force; consumption levels reached historic highs; population was increasing; per capita farm output was growing; and a wide variety of industries had been established.

The list continues: business practices suitable to widespread specialization and monetary exchange had been developed; the money supply and the variety of financial institutions had increased; workers had acquired an unprecedented range of handcraft skills; large mines and factories were in operation; and a great demand had been established for more products from nonagricultural industries.

Recent estimates of the total real output of Great Britain in the 18th

---

[4] For discussion of the nature of agricultural change and its impact on income growth see Deane and Cole, pp. 62–74.

century suggest that production rose very little up to 1740, then more than doubled between 1740 and 1800. (See 3–4.) The data in 3–4 are built up from estimates of the component sectors of the economy. The disaggregated data show that manufacturing for export was consistently

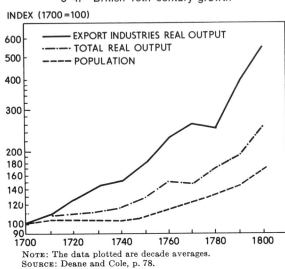

3–4.   British 18th century growth

INDEX (1700 = 100)

EXPORT INDUSTRIES REAL OUTPUT
TOTAL REAL OUTPUT
POPULATION

NOTE: The data plotted are decade averages.
SOURCE: Deane and Cole, p. 78.

the most rapidly increasing segment of the gross national product. In short, Britain's accelerated economic development in the 18th century was spearheaded by a manufacturing revolution which brought English manufactured goods into ports all over the world in unprecedented quantities. Let's look at some of the immediate factors that established Britain as the leading manufacturing nation.

Three clusters of inventions and their application in various innovations rank high among the proximate explanations of England's ascendancy in manufacturing. These were (1) inventions of machines in the cotton textile industry, (2) inventions in metals and machine tools, and (3) inventions to provide power to drive the machines.

From 1733 through 1785, cotton textile manufacturing was converted from a labor-intensive, handcraft industry to a highly mechanized, capital-intensive sector of the British economy. Spinning and weaving were mechanized and powered by waterwheels rather than human energy. Other stages of textile manufacturing were also mechanized. On the input side, Eli Whitney invented the cotton gin in 1794, and in the 20 preceding years machinery was developed to card and comb the fiber. On the output side, chlorine to bleach the cloth replaced the sun and hand printing gave way to the rotary press.

The demonstration effect of mechanizing cotton textile production was, of course, very important to the Industrial Revolution. Further, the productivity increase that came from removing cloth manufacturing from the cottage to the factory released labor resources in England. In the same manner that agricultural productivity increases made possible manufacturing expansion, the release of hands from labor-intensive textile production provided labor for other types of manufacturing activity.

Developments in metals and machine tools made possible not only textile machinery but a host of improvements and inventions in other kinds of machinery. Coke from coal replaced increasingly scarce charcoal in ironmaking. Puddling (stirring) in a reverberatory furnace eliminated much of the hammering needed to make wrought iron, and the steam hammer and rolling mill further reduced the labor requirements of wrought iron. The crucible steel method improved steel production. Between 1774 and 1800, a series of machine tool developments increased the precision and durability of machinery, thereby improving some machines and making volume production of new machines possible.

Efficient steam engines were developed to power the new machines. Improvements were centered on reducing fuel input and increasing the efficiency of power transmission from the piston so that steam power could be used elsewhere than in coal mines. By the turn of the century, steam engines powered textile machinery, air and water pumps, and huge hammers, and the adaptation of steam power to transportation was just around the corner.

The inventions and innovations cited above were applied in what we identified earlier as the *modern industrial method.* We may define the modern industrial method as:

1. The use of nonhuman power sources
2. to drive machinery
3. in the repetitive manufacture of large numbers of identical products
4. by methods involving the division of labor in the production process.

The terms mass production and factory system are often used to signify the use of the modern industrial method as distinct from handcraft methods in which hand tools are used by craftsmen with only occasional assistance from power tools. Today, automobile manufacture exemplifies the former while, sadly for low-income home buyers, conventional housing construction exemplifies the latter. Of course, large workshops and mills, machinery, and nonhuman power sources were not unknown prior to the Industrial Revolution. However, the unique aspect of the modern industrial method is the combination of these elements in mass-producing standardized products by utilizing a high degree of division of labor in parts manufacture and assembly.

The three clusters of inventions that launched textile development climaxed a long period of scientific inquiry and invention which led up to them. (Remember our discussion of the comparative manufacturing development of France and England prior to the Industrial Revolution.) Further, the modern industrial method did not become ubiquitous the moment the textile example proved itself. Other industries had to await market growth, key inventions, and/or adaptations of the principles employed in cotton textiles—in the last respect Americans made significant contributions. Also, men are slow to change operating techniques, especially when existing machinery still operates—in fact, they often improve an old process as a reaction to the advent of a new one. In cotton textiles, for example, steam power was not widespread until the 1840s.

Contributing conditions

Large and growing markets, improved transportation, highly productive resources, and highly motivated enterprisers were jointly responsible for the timing and geographic placement of the first industrial revolution.

As compared with the output potential of mass production, Britain had a large internal market made larger by an extensive overseas trade, especially within the Empire. In 1701, the population of the United Kingdom numbered 9.5 million; by 1750, it totaled 10.5 million; in 1801, 16 million.[5] As we cited above, total real GNP grew even faster than population. The demand for British goods in continental Europe and the colonies soared as their populations and incomes increased rapidly in the late 18th century.

The foreign demand for British factory-produced cloth, clothing, and household articles virtually exploded in the late 1700s. British exports, as 3–4 shows, led real income, pulled it along in fact, with cotton and worsteds spearheading the export market. The Napoleonic Wars (1793–1815) may have provided an additional impetus to industrialization, though the evidence is conflicting.

Improvements in transportation also played a major role in making mass production and larger markets possible. At the end of the 18th century, England had about half of the Western world's shipping tonnage, and the United States accounted for another fourth. Scale economies plus reduced piracy made possible larger cargoes, smaller crews per ton, and fewer days in port. As a result, ocean freight rates fell markedly in the 1700s. In American shipping, which was subject to the same forces as British shipping, productivity rose at 0.8 percent per annum in the 18th century. After 1814, technological changes in shipping accelerated productivity growth to 3.5 percent per year.[6]

---

[5] Deane and Cole, p. 6.

[6] See North, Walton (1967), and Walton (1970–71).

England's coastal harbors and rivers gave most parts of the country ready and low-cost access to world markets. Further, beginning in 1760, a network of canals was built to extend river navigation inland and interconnect navigable rivers. In turn, rails were laid for horse-drawn railways which joined mines with waterways. Internal communications and the distribution of lighter goods between cities and towns were improved by a period of rapid road building in the 1760s and 1770s. The roads that were built were innovations—they were smooth-surfaced, rock-based, and well-drained.

In sum, costs were greatly reduced and speed and safety increased in both travel and the transportation of goods. Lower transport charges and better communications made goods less costly and easier to sell. The resulting larger markets produced scale economies that further reduced costs and product prices.

All these transport improvements (and the improvements that followed) may have been as important as manufacturing inventions in making goods cheaper and expanding output. Tobacco freight and handling charges illustrate the importance of improved marketing facilities. Tobacco freight and other charges totaled 100 percent of the colonial tobacco price in 1737 and only 64 percent of the colonial price in 1774.[7]

The availability of natural resources was another condition important to England's Industrial Revolution. Discovery, invention, and innovation opened up a rich supply of raw materials to feed England's voracious industrial appetite, and without the steep rise in import costs that had hampered earlier manufacturing expansion.

The invention of coke for use in making iron released England from one of its major natural resource limitations, the shortage of forests. At the same time, it unlocked the technological door to its vast natural wealth of fuel resources in the form of coal. This permitted a great expansion in ironmaking, which, in turn, made possible the development of the steam engine as a new source of power, since steam generation required iron boilers and pistons.

The rapid expansion of the cotton textile industry was made possible by access to expanding cotton supplies in America. After the Revolution, southern planters in America shifted to the new crop and opened up an expanse of new lands in the interior Mississippi regions.

The British labor supply also increased rapidly. Population growth provided the basis for an expanded labor force. In addition, the reduction in farm labor requirements enabled manufacturing employment to grow faster than total population. The technology of the textile industry also permitted the use of more of the population in the work force. The light nature of the work enabled the textile industry to employ women and children effectively, in contrast to coal mining or ironmaking,

---

[7] Shepherd and Walton, table 4–3.

where female and child labor, though employed, were comparatively inefficient.[8]

As in the case of natural resources, industrial expansion could take place without straining the labor supply and running into steep increases in wage costs. In fact, for a while the labor supply was too plentiful. In the 1830s and 1840s, the rapid introduction of steam power in cotton textiles and the extension of machinery into woolen textiles caused problems of technological unemployment. In the late 1840s, the Irish potato famine drove more starving immigrants to English cities than could be quickly absorbed by industry.

Rapid expansion in the supply of capital—the man-made, accumulated resource—was especially vital to England's Industrial Revolution. Accelerated production requires expansion in working capital, the funds that must be advanced to purchase materials and pay for labor services before the final goods are sold. A larger stock of raw-materials, goods-in-process, and final-goods inventories must be built up. In addition, mechanized methods of production require more fixed capital in the form of buildings and the machines and tools that embody innovations. Clearly, capital inputs had to increase faster than labor inputs (but not necessarily faster than output, since technological changes could make new units of capital more productive).

Capital accumulation requires the diversion of resources from the production of consumer products to the construction of capital goods. Only if income earners are willing to abstain from consuming, i.e., to save part of their incomes, will resources be released to capital accumulation. During the 18th century, the saving-investing process was carried on, in small part, by individuals who bought securities, mostly canal and turnpike bonds. But the major source of business capital accumulation was business profits.

New manufacturing firms were usually started by one or two men already wealthy from other businesses. The rapid growth of manufacturing firms depended upon their owners' success in earning profits and reinvesting them in the business. Profits from the reduced costs associated with technological innovation were probably large enough to account for most of the rapid accumulation of capital out of profits. In addition, inflation profits during the Napoleonic Wars plus a lag in wage-rate increases supplemented productivity increases as a source of capital accumulation.

The story of the Industrial Revolution would not be complete without a consideration of the role of the key individuals who acted to bring it about—the new industrial managers. The leaders of the Industrial

---

[8] This should not be taken as saying that textile employment was humane by today's standards; in fact, by today's standards most employment in and out of manufacturing was inhumane.

Revolution usually combined many roles in one person—inventor, financier, engineer, organizer, supervisor, and salesman. The single proprietorship and partnership were the chief forms of business organization, so owners usually had to be all-around managers.

The most successful proprietors demonstrated outstanding characteristics that enabled them to see and take advantage of opportunities and to organize and expand their firms. All of them were so strongly motivated by a desire to make profits and accumulate wealth that they were willing to run great risks in investing their own capital. It is very appropriate, therefore, that they should be designated by the French term *entrepreneur,* with which daring and initiative are associated.

Here it is important to distinguish again between the terms invention and innovation, because there has been too much interpretation of the Industrial Revolution in terms of the former rather than the latter. Recall that to invent means to contrive a new product, a new device, or a new process. On the other hand, as we pointed out in chapter 1, to innovate means to apply a given invention in the production process either in the form of a new product or a new production technique. The entrepreneurs were not merely inventors; they were innovators.

England at the time of the Industrial Revolution provided a very favorable intellectual environment for both invention and innovation. The scientific age was relatively new, and the widespread philosophy of rationalism encouraged the idea that man could control and change his environment. Men were excited by the possibilities of discovering how to make material improvements in production. Even though knowledge was expanding rapidly, in those days the total stock of knowledge was small enough for an intelligent layman to be familiar with developments in a wide variety of fields. Modern science was in its early stages, and physicians and chemists were in close contact with businessmen, writers, and other educated persons. Many businessmen were fellows of the Royal Society, which was devoted to scientific studies and discussions.

Historians have noted that many of the new industrial leaders were members of minority religious sects—such as Quakers, Methodists, and Scottish Presbyterians. This has been widely interpreted as meaning that they were nonconforming individualists. Probably more relevant than their dissenting views, however, was the fact that these religious minorities came chiefly from the better educated section of the middle class.

The English entrepreneurs also had a keen sense of market opportunity. In that period of relatively low per capita income, the potential rewards were great for those who could find a way to reduce the production cost and price of consumer goods or who managed to develop new products or improve the quality of traditional goods.

EFFECTS AND CRITICISMS OF THE INDUSTRIAL REVOLUTION

Surprisingly, the first experience with industrialization is commonly regarded with disapproval as a bad example of how to bring about a revolution in living standards. The traditional interpretation of historians, reflected in much of our literature, was that, initially, progress was not shared by workers. It has long been assumed that the laboring masses, the industrial and agrarian proletariat, paid for the Industrial Revolution in terms of reduced wages and horrible living conditions.

The "evils" of industrialization

In the more lurid versions, a story was told of contented peasants being dispossessed of their lands, herded into slums devised to profit from their misery, driven at the treadmill pace of machinery by slave-master factory owners, and paid a bare subsistence wage. The dragon of the story was pictured as a brutal capitalist running rampant in a free market. The white knight in this scenario rescued the workers by impaling the capitalist with the lance of social-reform legislation and hacking away at him with the sword of government control.

More recent studies and new information have caused historians to revise this interpretation. Contrary to the traditional view, in general the workers' share in progress appears to have been rather substantial from the beginning of the Industrial Revolution.

The accounts of misery, deprivation, and arbitrary treatment suffered by industrial workers are accurate enough. What was slighted by historians was the fact that rural migrants came from conditions that by today's standards were equally brutal. Rural emigrants entered an urban-industrial environment in which life was about as cruel as it had been on the farm. Child and female labor were not innovations of the Industrial Revolution. Women and children had known the grueling conditions of farm labor long before they became industrial laborers. The Industrial Revolution raised the productivity of workers in agriculture, mining, and manufacturing. And contrary to the tradition of English agriculture, the benefits of higher productivity associated with the Industrial Revolution were shared by workers in general.

However, as with any economic transition in any kind of economic system, there were cases in which workers failed to make the necessary adjustments required by a transition from rural to urban life. In other cases, workers chose to migrate just as a depression was producing widespread unemployment in the cities. But data suggest that for the great mass of workers, the Industrial Revolution meant a rise in living standards.

British output per person rose about 60 percent during the 18th century, and fully half of this gain occurred in the last two decades of the century. The rate of growth continued to increase in the 19th century, so that per capita income nearly doubled between 1800 and 1850 and more than doubled between 1850 and 1900. (See 3–5.)

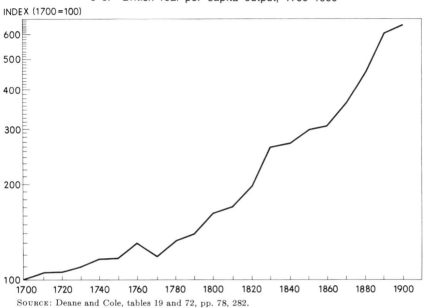

3–5. British real per capita output, 1700–1900

INDEX (1700 = 100)

SOURCE: Deane and Cole, tables 19 and 72, pp. 78, 282.

The faster rise in output than in population does not necessarily mean that the products consumed by workers increased faster than their numbers—remember that highly aggregate per capita figures can hide what happens to smaller groups. Yet, in view of the rapid total output rise, it would be surprising if the working classes did not experience some gains. The improvements in crops and the rise in population suggest that the bulk of the farm workers had improved consumption standards. After mid-century the migration of the rural population in northern England switched from a movement toward London to a movement toward the new industrial cities. We can at least speculate that this reflects the pull of employment opportunities that the workers regarded as superior. Furthermore, the expanding textile industries provided better work opportunities for women and children that added to total family income.

Some data are available that permit the construction of indexes of changes in prices and in the wage rates of employed workers. While there are serious limitations in the available figures, they indicate the broad trends. Between 1700 and 1760, both prices and money wages were fairly stable, and there was no clear or substantial change in real wages, i.e., wages after accounting for price-level changes. Between 1760 and 1790, both prices and money wages rose, but important differences in trends occurred in different regions of the country. In London, wage rates apparently rose less than prices; early historians accepted this as evidence of the depressing effect on real wages of the Industrial Revolution. However, in the northern parishes where the new industrial cities were growing, wage rates rose faster than prices. It is because northern employment was not yet as large as employment in southern England that overall average real wages appear to have declined slightly.[9] (See the appendix to this chapter for a discussion of real wages.)

The temporary inflation of the Napoleonic Wars distorted the trends. It is clear that from 1790 to 1810, prices rose faster than wage rates—the former about doubling, while wage rates increased by about three fourths. So real wages fell early in this period. But in the last few years of the Napoleonic Wars and afterward, prices fell faster than wage rates. Thus, by 1815 real wages had risen to their prewar level, and they continued to rise thereafter. While the price trend continued downward to 1850, money wage rates stabilized after 1830. Accordingly, the rise in real wages was about 25 percent from 1800 to 1825 and about 40 percent from 1825 to 1850. For the next hundred years the rise in real wages continued, with some tendency toward a reduction in the rate of increase.[10]

The Napoleonic Wars produced a series of economic dislocations that temporarily halted the improvement in working-class living conditions and created antagonism between workers and "the establishment." Repeal of the income tax after the war kindled the flames of class animosity, while the Corn Law of 1815 fueled the fire. The former measure favored the rich in general, while the latter protected landlords by blocking grain imports at times of falling grain prices.

Labor-displacing machinery, especially in textiles, periodic depressions, and the Irish potato famine all accentuated the misery of Britain's working class. To many landowners, popular agitation against high bread prices and the mechanization of textiles were only first steps toward an English version of the French Revolution. Consequently, Parliament enacted repressive measures designed to hold revolutionary tendencies in check.

The Reform Movement

A series of reform bills were passed as measures designed to widen the electorate, to relieve the oppression of the masses, and, perhaps

---

[9] Deane and Cole, p. 19.

[10] Deane and Cole's analysis of the British economy includes a detailed inquiry into British wage rate movements.

most important, to reduce food prices so that wage rates would fall, thereby improving the competitive position of British manufacturers. It is hard to characterize these measures in a general way except to indicate that they produced a legal break with the past that paralleled the severance of ties with the traditional economy that the Industrial Revolution accomplished.

Parliamentary reform was fought for by the Whigs, or liberals, as representatives of urban entrepreneurs who were underrepresented and often had no right to vote. The liberals also pressed for the repeal of mercantilist laws, especially the Corn Laws, because of their upward push upon wage rates.

On the other hand, the Tories, most of whom were landowners, opposed the Whig stands on foreign trade and parliamentary representation. What's more, the Tories incurred the wrath of Whig politicians by proposing restrictive factory legislation.

By 1848, both Whigs and Tories had gotten some of what they wanted: the first phase of parliamentary reform had been enacted, the Corn Laws had been repealed, and a pair of Factory Acts had prescribed hours and working conditions for women and children. Working-class resentment and agitation did not end, however; the Chartist movement for universal suffrage was still very much alive.

As we noted above, the main power struggle of the Reform Movement was between the wealthy landowners and the new middle class of merchants and manufacturers. While the latter worked for less government restriction and freer trade, the landowners, hostile to new manufacturing industry, sought every means to discredit industrial leaders.

The parliamentary commissions set up during the 1830s and 1840s to investigate conditions in factories and new industrial cities were frequently dominated by Tories, and the written record of their hearings reveals an unscientific crudeness in the observation and analysis of economic and social conditions. A few events and outstanding cases were taken to represent general conditions. A handful of large cotton textile factories were regarded as typical of British manufacturing at a time when the great bulk of the workers were still in small shops and cottage industries. Thus, the early legislation to control working hours and conditions for women and children singled out the large textile mills and ignored the prevalence of similar hours and conditions in small plants, in the cottages, on the farms, and in domestic service of all kinds.

Social attitudes colored the political and economic views of the middle-class reformers and intellectuals of the times. On the one hand, there was a strong Puritan disapproval of the new and pleasurable forms of consumption that higher wage rates made possible. On the other hand, there was a romantic philosophy about rural living and the ideal conditions of "natural" human behavior before it was corrupted by industrial society. Everything about lower-class living and working conditions in the cities looked especially horrible compared to the romantic conception middle-class intellectuals held of rural English living conditions.

The Reform Movement also involved an element of self-criticism by some members of the new middle classes. In the long struggle against royalty and the landowning nobility, the merchant had frequently been allied with the common people. To many merchants and manufacturers, individual liberty and democratic representation could hardly be reserved for the bourgeoisie. Some of the large factory owners, such as Robert Owen and Sir Robert Peel, were in the forefront of reform experiments and advocates of factory legislation. However, most cotton producers felt unfairly discriminated against by regulations that singled out large factories. And the opposition of other manufacturers to the Factory Acts reflected an age-old attitude of indifference toward the welfare of the masses.

The remarkable thing about the Reform Movement is that it was the first such movement in history. It occurred first during the Industrial Revolution, not because the conditions of the masses were extremely bad—they always had been—but because incomes were improving rapidly. In addition, the development of scientific knowledge popularized the idea that the social environment of man conformed to rational principles which could be discovered and used to improve human conditions. Thus, in Britain in those times, as in underdeveloped countries today, accelerating aspirations for improved living conditions for the masses fostered a great impatience to achieve new goals immediately.

In part, the Reform Movement was based upon a false premise. The reformers believed that a redistribution of the annual flow of wealth either through regulatory legislation or more radical means would raise the working classes out of their shocking misery. In fact, national income in Britain, the most materially advanced nation, was not large enough to bring about this end. Social accounting had not been developed enough for per capita income to be measured, so men and women relied upon impressions about the rate of growth in making judgments about the size of total income. What England and other nations needed was a continuation of growth so that all might enjoy higher levels of living or so that redistribution policies would have some chance for success.

As the Reform Movement progressed, liberal intellectuals became pessimistic about what could be accomplished by governmental measures. England's Rev. Thomas Malthus reasoned that population would soar because improved economic conditions would reduce death rates and encourage high birthrates. As a result, population was bound to outrun improvements in production and keep the masses at a subsistence level.

Contrary to Adam Smith, David Ricardo, a brilliant English financier, politician, and economist, could not see inevitable harmony in the economic interests of different classes. He believed that as population grew in Malthusian style and that since capital expanded while land remained fixed in quantity, rising land rents stole the benefits of progress from workers and capitalists. Further, if government welfare programs attempted to make the worker's lot better, population growth would surge ahead, exhausting the benefits of higher family incomes. Paradoxically, just as the laissez-faire notions of Adam Smith were beginning to influence legislation, economists were expressing serious doubts as to whether the working classes could ever escape poverty, regardless of the policy tack navigated by government. No wonder Thomas Carlyle called economics the dismal science!

The socialists emerged as an optimistic strand of rational thinking about the possibilities for the improvement of human welfare. The most important representative of the socialist school of thought was Karl Marx. During the European revolutions of 1848, Marx and his longtime collaborator Friedrich Engels issued their *Communist Manifesto,* urging the workers of the world to throw off their chains, to unite in "the forcible overthrow of all existing social conditions," and to establish "an association in which the free development of each is the condition for the free development of all."

In the first volume of his Brobdingnagian work *Das Kapital* (1867), Marx turned narrative accounts of the exploitation of workers during the period of the Industrial Revolution into a theory that workers would inevitably be exploited by capitalist factory owners in any and all capitalist eras. In the brief summary of Marx's theory that follows, note that Marx presents an appealing package of ideas which have a luster for poor people; it is easy to see why many less developed nations are Marxian today.

Marx reasoned as follows: labor alone was productive and labor produced a surplus above its subsistence needs; the owner of capital had the power to expropriate this surplus as profit because if a worker wouldn't work on the capitalist's terms he could be replaced; reinvestment of profits in machinery displaced workers; competition among the "army" of unemployed workers bid down wages to a subsistence level; capital accumulation made a few capitalists more and more wealthy and initiated a struggle for survival that reduced their ranks to a few great monopolists; a need for expansion of markets led to imperialism; and ultimately the masses of workers in their misery would revolt and, after a period of proletarian rule, establish a utopia free of government and private property.

In the view of orthodox economists (the present authors included), the theories of Marx have a number of flaws. Marx failed to attribute to all productive resources—natural, human, and accumulated—their contributions to production. But, perhaps his gravest theoretical error was his assumption that all invention and mechanization reduced the employment of labor. It is true that labor-displacing machinery is a common type of capital accumulation. But the labor that is conserved thereby is characteristically reemployed elsewhere, albeit after an arduous adjustment process in many cases.

The greatest historical disproof of *unrevised* Marxism has been the contradiction of Marx's predictions. Wages have not fallen. The poor have not gotten poorer. The wealthy have not decreased in number. Capitalism has not broken down from its own growth and resulted in revolution in the countries where it has existed the longest and grown the most.

SUMMARY OF CHAPTERS 2 AND 3

Over three to five centuries of European social, political, and economic development, Western civilization emerged from the static world of feudalism and ultimately embarked upon a course of industrialization. The American Colonies were founded as part of the mercantilist phase of this evolution.

A rich endowment of natural resources, strategic isolation from Europe, and the nature of political events in Europe were factors especially favorable to economic development in England's North American colonies. Early U.S. economic development was favored in a similar manner after initial handicaps were overcome. Scholars have identified six sets of forces that created the environment in which the American Colonies and the United States grew and prospered.[11]

1. The development of science and the growth of scientific inquiry led to significant achievements in transportation and communication, geographic exploration, and machinery driven by nonhuman power. These advances made possible dismantling the local self-sufficient subsistence economies of feudalism in favor of specialized production for markets in which products were exchanged against money.

2. As manorial estates, dukedoms, and principalities were breaking out of their autarkical life-styles, nation-states emerged with governments capable of protecting both internal and international trade and commerce.

3. Geographic exploration led to the discovery of new sources of monetary metals, thereby increasing the supply of money and concentrating it in relatively few hands—the rulers and merchants who were emerging as the dominant characters in the postmedieval Commercial Revolution. The spending associated with the growth of the money stock strained local sources of supply, produced significant price inflation, and stimulated the movement of goods over long distances both by

---

[11] For discussion of these factors in the context of economic growth theory, see Abramovitz, pp. 160–61.

land and by sea. The market became worldwide, with Europe as a nucleus.

4. The institutional fabric of society changed to make commerce respectable and favor its development. The attrition of the manorial system gave the serfs their freedom and lifted prohibitions against the sale of land. Private property, freedom of contract, and the emergence of land, labor, and capital as readily exchangeable productive inputs jointly marketized the economies of England and Western Europe. Concomitantly, specialization increased among local and national economies and their trade with other economies expanded.

5. Attitudes veered away from a determination to maintain essentially static subsistence economies and toward a calculated, rational pursuit of wealth. Just prices, fair wages, prohibitions against interest charges, and the notion of the illegitimacy of material progress gave ground to a materialism in which vigorous enterprise was highly regarded.

6. The growth of political freedom, the restriction of the sovereign's prerogatives, and the beginnings of representative government enhanced social mobility as rigid class distinctions and barriers between classes were eroded by the rise of a merchant class. The rewards of enterprise were no longer just economic; political power and social prestige could come as a result of commercial success.

7. The political-economic evolution that had its origins in the late Middle Ages included three discernible phases.

First, feudalism and the manorial system were interred by the joint consequences of the Commercial Revolution and the emergence of strong nation-states.

Second, commercialized nations adopted mercantilism as a national policy. The encouragement of trade, colonization, and manufacturing became objectives of a national policy whose ultimate aim was aggrandizement of the state rather than enrichment of the populace.

Third, industrialization, starting with Britain's Industrial Revolution, was built on the joint foundations of commercialization and technological development, and was reinforced by a dismantling of mercantilism in which market forces were given freer play to determine production and trading relations within and among nations. Technological development made possible the large-scale exchanges that are necessary when individual producers and geographic areas are highly specialized.

8. The British Industrial Revolution evolved on the basis of three principal developments.

First, the productivity of English agriculture was increased tremendously by technological innovation and commercialization. Greater agricultural productivity enabled the release of resources, especially labor, to produce manufactured consumer goods and social overhead capital.

Commercialization orginated in the complex set of events that gradually did away with the manorial system. Technological innovation was the result of a modest degree of mechanization combined with sweeping organizational improvements.

Second, technological development made possible the modern industrial method, i.e., invention and innovation made possible the repetitive manufacture of standardized products in large volume by means of machines powered by nonhuman labor. Steam power generation and transmission eliminated dependence upon often undependable waterpower and made mechanization of many production processes economically feasible. Better metals and machine tools made possible the large-scale construction of laborsaving, mass-production machinery. A series of inventions mechanized the cotton textile industry, demonstrating the great productivity of mass-production technology and releasing labor to other manufacturing industries.

Third, social and political developments in England before and during the Industrial Revolution led to the repeal of mercantilist legislation and the emergence of market forces—price, demand, and supply—as dominant in deciding how England's productive resources would be allocated.

9. Two opposed schools of political economy developed as the Industrial Revolution progressed: liberalism, which espoused maximum freedom for the operation of markets, and various socialist schools of which the Marxian is the most important. As a by-product of industrialization, the British Reform Movement led to a broadening of the electorate, the reduction of international trade barriers, and regulation of industrial hours and working conditions.

Colonial America imported the preconditions of industrial development from the mother country. Colonial society was comparatively democratic; colonial government was liberal as compared with government in Europe; the market was the organizer of colonial economic activity; and the colonies had commercial and intellectual links with Britain that made it possible to import British know-how when economic conditions made it appropriate to do so. After the Revolution and the War of 1812, the United States was able to capitalize on these preconditions in building an industrial economy.

APPENDIX TO CHAPTER 3: COMPOSITE PRICE INDEXES

In discussions of economic growth it is frequently useful to refer to changes in the general level of prices of all goods. It is not difficult to understand the notion of some average change in all prices, even though particular prices change in varying degrees. What is not immediately realized, however, is that the measurement of such general changes may be difficult or not very meaningful unless the relative importance of each good is specified and held constant in computing the average price change. What is required is the computation of a *weighted average* of all price changes—that is, a *composite price index.* Common examples of composite price indexes are the **Wholesale Price Index** and the **Consumer Price Index** of the U.S. Bureau of Labor Statistics.

Let us construct a hypothetical example of how a composite price index may be computed. Suppose we wished to construct a composite index of prices for American colonial exports and that there were only two goods, wheat and rum. Assume the following hypothetical price and quantity data for two periods of time:

	Year	
	1750	1760
Wheat quantity (bushels)	75,000	105,000
Wheat price	$4.55	$5.11
Rum quantity (gallons)	25,000	30,000
Rum price	$2.53	$3.54

What we are trying to do is *average the changes* in prices. We could do this using price indexes for each type of food price separately and then average the changes in their indexes. If we select 1750 as the index base year, we can set each price for that year as equal to 100. For each food, the price index for the next period is the price for that period divided by the base year price and multiplied by 100. (See the appendix to chapter 2 on ratio charts and index numbers.) This gives us these price indexes:

	Year	
	1760	1770
Wheat price index.	100	112
Rum price index	100	140

The indexes show that the wheat price has risen 12 percent while the rum price has risen 40 percent.

What is the average price change? If we total the two indexes and divide by 2, we get an average of the two indexes in 1770 equal to 126. (The base year index remains 100 regardless of method of averaging.) This is commonly called an unweighted average, but it might more accurately be referred to as an equally weighted average, for both index numbers are treated as equally important. By this average, the general price level appears to have risen 26 percent.

How do we measure the relative importance of wheat and rum in making up a composite price index? There are various alternatives, and the one we select depends largely on the particular problem we are considering. For example, we can select the total sales value of each product sold—the price times the quantity of each product. Our example indicates that in 1750 the total sales value of wheat ($4.55 × 75,000 =

$331,250) was about five times as large as the total sales value of rum ($2.53 × 25,000 = $63,250). The total value is an appropriate measure of importance when we are considering national income or consumer spending. Alternatively, we might want to use physical quantities as a measure of importance—say, when the physical cargo space is an important consideration. In our example, however, let us use total sales value as the measure of importance or weight.

How do we use the weights in making up the composite price index? We could use the sales figures, but to reduce the example to the simplest terms, let us simply use their ratio, 5 to 1. The sum of these two weights is 6. Now, a weighted average is obtained simply by multiplying each price index by its weight, summing the results, and dividing that sum by the total of the weights, as shown in the following for both years:

		Year				
	1750			*1760*		
	Weight ×	*Price index* =	*Weighted index*	*Weight* ×	*Price index* =	*Weighted index*
Wheat	5	100	500	5	112	560
Rum	1	100	100	1	140	140
	6		600 ÷ 6 = 100	6		700 ÷ 6 = 117

The result that we now have for the second period (the base period index of 100 again is not changed by averaging methods) is an index of 117, which shows that the weighted average change in prices was an increase of 17 percent.

In this example, the weighted average price change (+17 percent) is smaller than the unweighted average price change (+26 percent) simply because the price change for wheat was smaller and because wheat was five times as important in total food sales in the base year.

In order to understand the meaning of composite price indexes, we need to be aware of the following two important assumptions. First, the computation requires the selection of some measure of importance to provide the weights for the composite index. Different weights can produce quite different results. The selection involves some judgment as to the measure that is most appropriate for the particular purpose of the index. Second, the same weights are used for all years of comparison. This is because the purpose of the index is to show price changes alone. This kind of comparison, therefore, requires an assumption that the relative importance of the different foods (determined in this case, by their sales value) remains the same. Actually, we know that this assumption is seldom valid. But usually when we use price indexes, we want to compare the price changes alone with the quantity changes looked at separately. (A more serious difficulty occurs when the types of food or their quality actually changes, but this is still another problem in the measurement of economic change.)

REFERENCES

M. Abramovitz, "Economic Growth," in *A Survey of Contemporary Economics*, ed. B. F. Haley (Homewood, Ill.: Richard D. Irwin, Inc., 1952), vol. 2.

P. Deane and W. A. Cole, *British Economic Growth, 1688–1959* (New York: Cambridge University Press, 1967).

J. R. T. Hughes, *Industrialization and Economic History* (New York: McGraw-Hill Book Co. 1970).

R. A. Lively, "The American System," *BHR*, March, 1955.

D. C. North, "Sources of Productivity Change in Ocean Shipping, 1600–1850," *JPE*, September/October 1968.

J. F. Shepherd and G. M. Walton, *Shipping, Maritime Trade, and the Economic Development of Colonial America* (New York: Cambridge University Press, 1973).

U.S. Department of Commerce, *Historical Statistics of the United States* (Washington, D.C.: U.S. Government Printing Office, 1960).

G. M. Walton, "Sources of Productivity Change in American Colonial Shipping, 1675–1775," *EHR*, April 1967.

———, "Obstacles to Technical Diffusion in Ocean Shipping, 1675–1775," *EEH*, Winter 1970–71.

4 AMERICAN COLONIAL DEVELOPMENT

The thirteen original states were a product of a unique confluence of geography, economic and political evolution, and European social history.

England set about establishing a colonial empire at a late date as compared with its continental neighbors. The West Indies and the North America's eastern coast were about all that were left for colonization when England sought to establish colonies on a concerted basis.

Contrary to the hopes of the earliest English settlers, treasure colonies were out of the question. Instead, settlement and plantation colonies were established. They evolved as sources of raw and processed materials for the mother country's fast-expanding nonagricultural industries and as supplements to English agriculture. From the linked standpoints of natural resources and geographic accessibility, the production potential of the American colonies was well suited to such a relationship. In turn, the colonies became rapidly growing markets for finished products produced in or reexported by England.

England's economic, social, and political development by the 17th century was highly appropriate to this kind of colonial enterprise. The Commercial Revolution had laid the intellectual and institutional background for establishing colonies. The British economy had been marketized, albeit with significant mercantilistic modifications, and people were accustomed to responding to market stimuli in conducting their economic lives.

The success of both plantation colonies and colonies of settlement required adapting existing technology to the particular mix of production inputs available in America. The Englishmen who came to the New World had the technological know-how and ability to make such a transition.

> While the contemporary French and German peasants were still depressed by the survivals of an outworn feudalism, the English villager was ready to play an independent part in any new development . . . .

104

The medieval serf would never have planted the free and self-sufficient townships of New England . . . ; the English Colonial movement was the migration of a modern society, self-governing, half-industrial, awake to economic and intellectual change.[1]

The success of the English colonies in America is in no small part attributable to the early settlers' ability to adapt English ways of governing, producing, and buying and selling in a potentially rich but initially hostile environment.

The British bequeathed an institutional heritage which was conducive to economic growth. Rich natural resources, high-quality labor, and opportunity to import English capital goods interacted with that heritage to produce what may have been the most successful colonial venture in history.

AN OVERVIEW OF COLONIAL GROWTH

As we pointed out in chapter 2, the American colonies varied in the manner in which they were founded and governed. And, as we will see, the economic bases of the colonies varied. However, there is a common thread that runs through the history of all the colonies.

Development of the typical colony

We can think of the development of the typical colonial settlement as dominated by two successive and distinguishable themes, although not so distinguishable as to be designated as distinct stages. The first was the struggle to survive, a struggle some settlements lost. The second was rapid economic expansion, accompanied for the most part by a modest rate of economic growth.

Historians have come to refer to the early years of the Virginia Colony as the "starving time" simply because the colony was forced to cling tenuously to the edge of the precipice that divided survival from extinction.[2] To a significant degree, the other colonial settlements had the same experience when they were first established. Consequently, early colonial economic organization was determined by the inhospitable nature of the environment.

In a sense, the manorial system (without the feudal obligations that went with it in Europe) served as a model for the initial economic organization of the coloniés. Because risk minimization and physical

---

[1] G. M. Trevelyan, quoted in Hughes (1970), p. 36; see Hughes, chaps. 3 and 6, for further discussion of the strategic importance of our English origins.

[2] For discussion of the early years in the various colonies see Andrews, pp. 110–11; Bidwell and Falconer; Bruchey, chaps. 2 and 3; Gray; and Nettels, chaps. 6 and 9.

protection were the overriding considerations in economic decisions, a manorlike economy proved the most appropriate.

The early settlers formed tightly knit bands whose energies were directed at establishing a dependable source of agricultural output and a viable system of defense against the Spanish to the south, the French to the north and west, and the Indians everywhere. The result was a closely guarded, often barricaded, group, economically self-sufficient; living in tents, natural or dugout caves, or cellars, practicing a rudimentary agriculture, and, to a large degree, dependent upon game and fish as a source of protein.

Commercial contacts were infrequent and undependable, so manufactured products were generally homemade and rudimentary. Death rates were high, as harsh winters, disease, and, in some cases, starvation cut deep into the ranks of the immigrants. At worst, whole communities were wiped out; at best, settlements survived at subsistence levels. Of course, the later colonies could profit from the experiences of their predecessors; yet in all the colonies, the first agricultural ventures were carried out under very harsh conditions.

The earliest colonists brought with them a general knowledge of agricultural methods but had no knowledge of either American soil types or the crops most appropriate to the American soils and climate. Until they learned from the Indians or experience, planting often produced a harvest rich only in disappointment. Draft animals and even plows were scarce or nonexistent. Crops were planted in abandoned Indian fields, on sparsely forested riverbanks, or between the trunks of felled trees. Many of the colonists learned to hunt and fish after the realities of frontier life showed them that the forests and the streams could mean the difference between life and death.[3]

Eventually, the colonists were able to separate themselves from a wholly communal existence and to build individual homesteads. In this transition, the threat of extinction gradually lessened, and population growth and economic expansion replaced mere survival as the central tendency. The penalties associated with taking risks were reduced—the Indians had been "civilized," pacified, or banished, and storehouses contained agricultural carry-overs. But note: risks were only reduced, not eliminated! Disease, perfidious weather, Indian attacks, and colonial extensions of European wars continued as threats to existence.

Families were able to fan out to establish farms or plantations. New settlements were established within the colonies. Manorlike settlements grew into villages surrounded by an agricultural hinterland. The ports developed in very much the same way as the towns that emerged in the Commercial Revolution. They became centers of trade and hand-

---

[3] For a more extended discussion of colonial agriculture in the starving time and citations of the literature, see Gallman, pp. 17–18.

crafted manufactures. Journeymen established shops; merchants traded in agricultural exports and manufactured imports; and ships called regularly. In general, a pattern of specialization and a market mechanism grew up in place of a largely communal economy with a military civic organization. However, deep in the hinterland, farmers had only infrequent contacts with the market and continued to make their livelihood in subsistence, self-sufficient agriculture.

During the starving years, productivity was very low—in some cases, supplies from England made the difference between survival and extinction. However, over the relatively brief period in which life outside the stockade was being established, productivity probably increased very rapidly. The colonists were adapting familiar agricultural, manufacturing, and mercantile techniques to a new environment and increasing productivity thereby. But this kind of productivity gain is a one-shot phenomenon; there is no indication that productivity increased rapidly on a long-term basis once the transition from a survival to a growth orientation was completed.

When survival no longer dominated decision-making, the settlers in the typical colonial community laid the physical and institutional foundations required for continuous expansion.

First, the economy's organizational base was revamped. Institutions required to support specialization and exchange were established. Commercial law, financial institutions, credit and insurance arrangements, and marketplaces were developed. Trade and communications within the Empire and with other American settlements were established on a regular basis. The communities within a colony found their respective comparative advantages and developed an export base largely through trial and error. For an entire colony the export base was usually dominated by agriculture, and this stage of the development process involved commercializing a significant portion of the farm sector. In short, each colony repeated in miniature and over an abbreviated period England's Commercial Revolution.

Second, social overhead capital was accumulated—docks and wharves were built, harbors were improved, and warehouses and public buildings were constructed. Third, population and private capital investment grew, thereby simultaneously increasing productive capacity and the potential size of the market in each colony.

When the base of a market-organized economy was established, the colony in question was prepared to expand and raise its per capita income simultaneously. Natural population growth and immigration were matched by new farm formation, by urban capital formation, and by the growth of nonlabor inputs in general. Further, to a small degree, technological change and, to a greater extent, economies of scale raised productivity so that the colony's output grew slightly faster than its population.

Population and income growth

Two attributes of colonial population growth are outstanding: its rapidity and the dominance of natural population increases. From 1660 to 1780, population grew at about 34 percent per decade. By contrast the U.S. population has grown by less than 20 percent per decade since 1910 and by under 30 percent since 1860. Natural population increases ranged from 26 to 30 percent per decade over the 18th century and thus accounted for three fourths to almost nine tenths of each decade's total population growth.

From 1630 to 1780, colonial population increased from 4,645 to 2.8 million; the latter figure is more than one fourth the population of England in 1780. As the data plotted in 4–1 show, the population grew most rapidly in precentage terms in the 17th century and fastest in absolute terms in the 18th century (recall the explanation of ratio charts in the appendix to chapter 2). The percentage growth rate declined, then became stable, as the decades passed by—population almost doubled from 1640 to 1650, but between 1770 and 1780 the increase was only 30 percent. On the other hand, the decade-to-decade absolute increases in population rose almost without exception over the entire period—from 1630 to 1640, the increase was 22,000; from 1710 to 1720, it was 135,000; and from 1770 to 1780, the Revolutionary period, population expanded by 630,000.

Whether measured in absolute or percentage terms, the population growth rate was phenomenal by the standards of the day. The success of the economy in supporting that population is attested by the fact that in the colonized areas the settlers and their slaves outnumbered the Indians by perhaps one million people.

Taking the colonial period as a whole, native births accounted for the bulk of population growth. American rates of natural increase for this period still stand out in history as notable for their rapidity, about doubling every 25 years. However, we shouldn't dismiss the importance of immigration. The revival of colonization after 1680 and renewed migration from England were two sides of the same coin. Later, from 1730 to 1750, a flood of German and French immigrants came to the English colonies. By 1790, one fifth of the white population claimed origins other than England, Scotland, and Ireland, and blacks from Africa accounted for 20 percent of the total population.

Urbanization was not a pronounced tendency of colonial America. By the end of the colonial period, only about 5 percent of the population lived in urban places. However, the colonial cities served a trading hinterland that included a sizable if not precisely quantifiable portion of the population. The typical city's population engaged in daily market activity. The city was surrounded by farmsteads, roughly within a ten-

4–1. Colonial population, 1630–1780

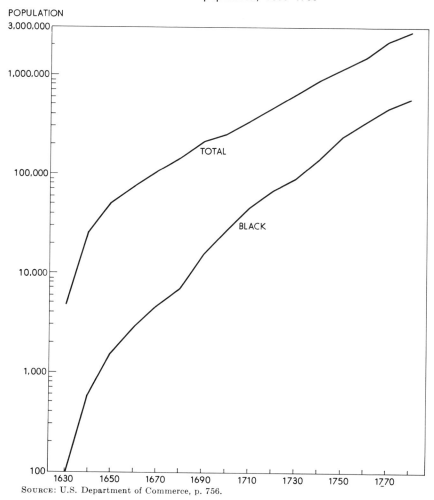

SOURCE: U.S. Department of Commerce, p. 756.

mile radius, whose families engaged in market transactions perhaps once or twice a month. A second band followed in which market activity was a monthly occasion. A series of bands continued to the frontier line. In these zones, a trip to a city or trading post was an irregular event and required hauling furs or whiskey to trade for staples and manufactured goods, especially arms and ammunition.

The hinterland was dotted with tiny settlements whose general stores bought local produce and sold what couldn't be manufactured in the home, usually on barter terms because money was scarce. The settlement stores were supplied by the export-import merchants of the ports, such as the Hancocks of Boston, who served as both wholesalers and retailers.

The foregoing should be put in the context of urbanization in the Western world at this time. In 1780 a total of 78,000 people, 3 percent of the population, lived in Philadelphia, New York, Boston, Charleston, and Baltimore. The first three of these cities ranked among the largest in the British Empire. Thus, though the colonies were not highly urbanized—England was perhaps one-fourth urban by this time—American cities on a par with European trade centers did exist.[4]

Our interest in colonial income movements arises primarily from our need for some gauge of the relative success of colonial ventures in providing opportunities for people to improve their economic welfare. The geographic and political separation of the colonies plus great disparities in their levels of development at any given time suggests that attempts to generalize about intensive growth rates for all the colonies taken together over the period 1607–1775 is rather fruitless.[5] When institutional considerations and statistical vagaries prevent income from serving as such a measure, then other avenues of analysis ought to be used.

It is useful, however, to generalize about the growth of individual colonies if the economic evolution of a typical colony that we have described is historically accurate. Our conjectures about the growth of economic welfare in the colonies are set forth below.

1. In the course of the transition from a stockade existence to a rural community surrounded by farms, or, in the South, by farms and large plantations, the per capita income of the typical colonial settlement grew rapidly. The transition was one of adapting a known agricultural technology to American conditions. As we noted above, this adaptation process meant that productivity increases could be achieved rapidly but with an upper limit set by contemporary agricultural know-how.

The occupants of family farms rose from the edge of starvation to a high-level subsistence. Many plantation owners were able to achieve a luxurious level of living, although the average standard of living of those who lived and worked on plantations was not much over subsistence.[6]

In our view, the income levels achieved put the free rural colonists on at least an even footing with their English counterparts. These conclu-

---

[4] See Bridenbaugh (1938 and 1955) for discussion of colonial cities. Ethnic data are reported in U.S. Department of Commerce, p. 756. Colonial population trends are discussed by Andreano, pp. 43–47, Taylor, p. 60, and Shepherd and Walton (1972), chap. 2.

[5] This line of reasoning has not prevented scholars from estimating colonial growth rates. Their findings indicate zero intensive growth from 1607 to 1713 (the Peace of Utrecht) and intensive growth of 0.3 to 1.0 percent per annum from 1713 to the Revolution. For an evaluation of this literature, see Shepherd and Walton (1972).

[6] In reading contemporary accounts of colonial life, remember that the word plantation usually means any farming unit, whereas in this text it refers to the large farms of the South.

sions we base on various analyses of contemporary descriptions of colonial farm-making, and plantation building.[7]

2. Once their existence as a town and port was established, the settlements that were destined to become major ports flourished. Per capita income grew rapidly to reach or nearly reach the levels enjoyed by comparable English towns and cities. Contemporary descriptions of colonial urban life by men such as Benjamin Franklin and Bridenbaugh's analysis of *Cities in the Wilderness* are our basis for these conclusions.

3. What can we say about income growth for an entire colony? We deduce that the typical colony grew very slowly in per capita terms but expanded rapidly after the greater part of its settlements had been transformed from frontier outposts to agricultural communities. A variety of studies suggest that the "mature" colony grew in per capita terms at about the same rate as England, roughly 0.3 to 0.5 percent per year over the long run. Further, at the end of the colonial period, America's economic well-being seems to have been on a par with England's.[8]

4. From our observations about the intensive growth of the typical colony a picture of economic success emerges. Per capita income did grow, albeit slowly. Over the years, new colonies were formed, based at least in part upon the success of immigrants to already established colonies. And, as we noted above, colonial population grew very rapidly by both historical and present-day standards. Over the long pull, the colonies proved themselves as places to which men could migrate for any of a variety of reasons and in which they could fare at least as well economically as the people of Britain, France, or Germany.[9]

Let's assume that we are correct in our conclusions about colonial growth. What does such a record of intensive and extensive growth mean as compared with the accomplishments of other 17th and 18th century economies and relative to the performance of economies of the 20th century?

As we noted above, in well-established colonies individual welfare appears to have grown at about the same rate and to have attained about the same level as in England. Considering that England was among the few nations to experience rising per capita income during the 18th century and that England ranked near the top in per capita income, the American experience compares very favorably with that of Europe during the 18th century.

Judged by modern standards, this growth record is topsy-turvy. The

---

[7] See the sources cited in footnotes 2 and 5 above.

[8] See Gallman, pp. 18–24, and Deane and Cole, pp. 79–81.

[9] Some scholars believe that during the 18th century population concentration in the older portions of the New England colonies eroded the economic position of the working classes and thereby created pressure to move westward; see Lockridge as an example and for citations of the relevant literature.

very rapid expansion that population growth indicates for the 17th century is half again faster than the fastest-growing nations managed over the past century. And 18th century extensive growth at least matched the U.S. expansion rates of recent years. Yet the intensive growth record of the typical colony is very poor as measured by 20th century criteria—only a few of the high-income nations we cited in chapter 1 grew at average rates of less than 1.5 percent. On the other hand, compared with today's less developed nations, the colonial growth performance is excellent.

What can we conclude from this mixed record? American colonization involved the displacement of an indigenous population by a group of people who were well equipped to teach themselves how to live in the New World and who had ready access to English markets as buyers and sellers. (Only modern-day Israel has had a similar experience, and its growth rate is unusually high by modern standards.) Yet the conditions the American colonists confronted were more difficult than those faced by most of today's less developed nations. Consequently, a positive, although modest, intensive growth rate constitutes an enviable record when viewed from a modern perspective.

OUTPUT AND TRADE PATTERNS

By the late 1600s all the colonies except Georgia had been established and had worked out the production and trade patterns that best fitted their respective endowments and world trade conditions. As we shall discuss below, the evidence assembled to date indicates that the **net** impact of the British mercantilist code was of a minor order. The actual output mix of the American Colonies differed little from what it might have been in the absence of the Navigation Acts. Although trade relations were obviously influenced by the acts, the influence was superficial in that in overall terms colonial well-being was little changed by them. To state it positively, the colonies were able to pursue their respective advantages much as if they operated in a laissez-faire international environment.

The colonial output mix, 1770

Beyond question, agriculture dominated output in the colonial economies. On the eve of the Revolution, 85 to 90 percent of the population was engaged in agriculture or closely related pursuits. Perhaps one third of the agricultural population produced food for local consumption, while the remaining two thirds produced food or agricultural raw materials for export to other colonies, England, Africa, and southern Europe.[10]

---

[10] This average varied greatly among the colonies as is shown by Shepherd and Walton's data on exports.

Other economic activity included manufacturing and the extractive industries. The local industries that characterized all the colonies included household manufacturing (mainly clothing and processed foodstuffs), manufacturing in small craft shops or by itinerant craftsmen, and the mill industries (especially flour and iron mills).

In addition to agriculture, other export industries were also widespread—shipping services, shipbuilding, the production of naval stores and other forest products, distilling, fishing, fur trapping, and iron mining abounded. However, their distribution pattern among the colonies varied greatly, determined as it was by differences in natural endowments and alternative uses of labor and capital. Even though overshadowed by agriculture, colonial output in some of the pursuits listed above became very significant in the overall world trade picture.

As you might expect, variations in the American climate and soils and other natural resources produced different output patterns among the colonial regions. Compared with total output, the South produced great quantities of rice, tobacco, indigo (for dye), wheat, and corn. Grain production exceeded local food requirements even in the tobacco colonies, where you would imagine that specialization in tobacco would preclude large-scale wheatgrowing.[11] Lumber and naval stores were also garnered from the forests of the South. And livestock, fruits and vegetables, hemp, and flax were raised, mostly for home consumption.

The most common farm unit in the South was the subsistence family farm. However, in at least Virginia and South Carolina, plantation agriculture accounted for an overwhelming portion of the output that found its way to market.

The prime mover of the Southern plantation was the West African slave. The emergence of slavery in the South can easily be explained in economic terms. In the South, through trial and error and with pressure from English investors who hoped to reap a profit, it became apparent that a plantation agriculture which produced crops for export was the most profitable use of entrepreneurial skills, capital, and natural resources.

The colonial South was characterized by a special type of labor shortage which made the establishment of slavery inexorable. Virtually free land and a distaste for plantation employment made wage labor too expensive—why work like a slave for subsistence wages when you could carve out a farmstead and slave on your own behalf? So in the early years, indentured servants—men who sold themselves into bondage for four to seven years in exchange for passage to America—were employed simply because they could be bound to a master at minimal wages paid in the form of food, shelter, and clothing plus cash severance pay.

---

[11] For a discussion of the key role of grain in the tobacco colonies, see Klingaman (June 1969), pp. 268–78.

At least by 1700, slaves had begun to displace indentured servants because the gap between the cost of indenture contracts and the price of slaves had narrowed enough for the higher acquisition price of slaves to be more than offset by their lifetime in bondage and their ability to reproduce themselves.

In brief, the institutions of slavery and indentured servitude were destined to arise given conditions in the colonial South—both institutions were legal; there existed a group of would-be agricultural entrepreneurs who wished to operate plantations; under the right labor conditions, plantation agriculture offered superior profit opportunities; and wage labor was too expensive because free workers could always establish their own farms. The only way to operate plantations at a profit was to shackle labor.[12]

The Middle Colonies had soils and climates especially suited to livestock and cereal production. The colonists of New York, Pennsylvania, New Jersey, and Delaware soon developed the capacity to feed themselves and many others as well. Although grains and livestock dominated the market sector in the Middle Colonies, wood products and shipping services were also important, especially the latter. Middle Colony grain farms tended to be large as compared with the subsistence farms at or near the frontier, but they never reached the size of the Southern plantations.

Although indentured servants were common, slavery was never significant in the Middle Colonies or New England because the growing season was too short and off-season uses of labor were too few to make slaves profitable investments given the prices established by the Southern demand for slaves. In the North, most slaves were acquired as servants and prestige symbols—or, in isolated cases, to enable a heathen savage to achieve salvation through conversion to the Christian faith on the theory that a lifetime of servitude was a small price to pay for an eternity in heaven.

New England soils tended to yield more rocks than crops, so farms were small and incapable of providing food for Boston, Newport, and other urban places. Many Yankees therefore turned to the sea for a living—as shipwrights; sailors, mates, and masters; fisherman; and international merchants. To make up for their agricultural deficits, New Englanders used their earnings at sea to import food from the South and the Middle Colonies.

Output surpluses and trade, 1770

From a development standpoint, international trade, that is, trade within the British Empire and with the world outside the Empire, was

---

[12] For a discussion of this explanation of slavery's emergence and the related evidence, see Hicks and Domar, chapter 8.

the lifeblood of the American Colonies. Commodity and other export earnings of the colonies were about 15 percent of total production on the eve of the Revolution, having grown almost as fast as the total economy over the 18th century.[13] Fifteen percent seems modest when viewed by itself—however, some additional information shows why we identify the foreign sector as the key to American colonial success.

1. *A large portion of the work force not required to provide for subsistence was involved in producing for export.* Recall that as high as 33 percent of the agricultural labor force may have been engaged in producing food for local consumption. Add to this figure workers engaged in producing foodstuffs for colonies which were not self-sufficient, chiefly the New England colonies, and the portion of the work force required to feed the colonies appears to range from 37.5 percent to 62 percent.[14] Handcraft manufacturing, the mill industries, mining and logging, construction, mercantile activities, and coastal shipping would bring the total to, let us say, 60 to 70 percent of the total work force.

In other words, in the neighborhood of two thirds of colonial workers were required to provide rudimentary levels of food, shelter, and clothing, and about one third were what we can call the discretionary work force. About half of the discretionary work force was engaged in the production of commodities for export, ship construction, shipping, and providing insurance and other services related to foreign trade.

Each of the colonies chose collectively to allocate a huge portion of its discretionary workers to export activity for very rational reasons.[15] Exporting and trade services were profitable; and they were profitable because Americans were relatively more productive in agriculture and shipping than in manufacturing. The best solution to the colonial scarcity problem called for specializing and trading rather than domestic production of the entire array of products the colonists wanted to purchase. To put it more forcefully, international trade was strategically vital to colonial well-being and growth: without imports, the colonists would have been consigned to grubbing out a mere survival-level existence under frontier conditions for generations.

2. *Colonial exports gave Americans access to capital in two forms.* First, earnings overseas meant purchasing power with which to import

---

[13] Shepherd and Walton (1972), chap. 2. The statistics cited in the next few paragraphs are from Shepherd and Walton (1972).

[14] This range is based upon Klingaman's per capita estimate of the monetary value of dietary needs and Gallman's conclusions as to the value of per capita income just before the Revolution. Klingaman provides four estimates ($4\frac{1}{2}$, $5\frac{1}{2}$, $6\frac{1}{2}$, and $7\frac{1}{2}$ pounds sterling) of food needs that rise from 37.5 percent to 62 percent of the Gallman figure for per capita income. See Klingaman (April 1971), pp. 566–69, and Gallman, p. 24.

[15] North Carolina and New Jersey were notable exceptions, owing to their poor port facilities.

manufactured and semifabricated products, especially machinery and equipment required for agriculture, shipbuilding, mining, and what little manufacturing was carried on. These were products which the colonials would have had to handcraft at great expense in the absence of export earnings. Second, exports made it possible to buy African slaves to man the South's plantations, at rates as high as 4,700 per year.

3. *Export specialization meant that the colonials could obtain consumer goods on the best possible terms, in some cases, on the only possible terms.* By specializing in staple exports and shipping services, the colonies were able to import manufactured consumer goods, especially cloth, from Britain.

4. *The export sector was a source of productivity increases.* As the volume of trade grew, scale economies were realized and the costs of moving cargoes to their ultimate markets, exchanging them for imports, and bringing imports back to America declined significantly. We will have more to say on this development shortly.

As we have mentioned, the principal recipients of the American colonies' commodity output were Great Britain, the West Indies, southern Europe, and Africa. Their importance, indicated by the order in which they were named, varied greatly—Britain outweighed the West Indies almost two to one, and exports to Africa were so small in value that they would not be mentioned except for Africa's strategic importance as a source of slave labor. The flow of goods to England was especially heavy because the colonies' legal relationship with the mother country required that most goods destined for northern Europe be shipped to England for reexport to the Continent.

The data in 4–2, 4–3, and 4–4 summarize colonial trade relationships in 1770. In the next few paragraphs we will cite the more important characteristics revealed by these tables.

In 4–2 we show merchandise export figures for all the British continental colonies, including, of course, those that were destined to join the United States. The most striking aspect of these figures is the importance of agricultural pursuits—in fact, fishing, pig iron, and distilling aside, the entire table, including the manufactured products, consists of items associated with farming and rural industry. Second, food products make up the largest single category (45 percent of the total), with tobacco in second place.

The destination of output in conjunction with origin data gives us some insight into the nature of commodity export relations of particular colonial regions with Great Britain and other areas. (See 4–3.)

The South ranked first, as both an exporter to and an importer from Great Britain. As a producer of tobacco, indigo, and naval stores, the South clearly complemented the British economy.

The Middle Colonies (especially the Delaware, Hudson, and Mohawk valleys) and the Upper South constituted a breadbasket for the West

4–2.   Merchandise exports from the British continental colonies, 1770

Export	Amount (in pounds)	Percent of total
Food products.	1,259,134	45.16
(Bread-flour and grains, except rice)	(664,011)	(23.82)
(Rice)	(266,411)	(9.55)
(Fish)	(255,501)	(9.16)
(Livestock and meat).	(73,211)	(2.63)
Tobacco	725,186	25.99
Forest products, including maritime supplies.	182,015	6.53
Furs and deerskins	167,559	6.01
Indigo	105,520	3.78
Extracted products, including whale oil and beeswax	104,130	3.73
Iron and minerals	99,302	3.56
Rum	26,901	.96
Miscellaneous	119,253	4.28
	2,788,000	100.00

SOURCES: Shepherd and U.S. Bureau of the Census, p. 761.

Indies and southern Europe. New York and neighboring colonies accounted for nearly a third of the West Indies trade and almost two fifths of the sales to southern Europe. (See 4–3.) For the Middle Colonies and New England, food for the huge sugar plantation labor forces was the most important commodity group in the array of exports to the West Indies; the comparative advantage in sugar apparently forbade the use of plantation labor to grow food or catch fish.

New England's important commodity exports were highly varied: maritime supplies, such as naval stores; various wood products in addition to maritime products; meat, fish, and other food products; whale oil; potash; iron; horses; and rum. The region's chief customers were the sugar planters of the West Indies, with the British and southern Europeans in second and third place, well behind the sugar islands. The West Indies imported fish; southern Europe, fish and rum; and England bought whale oil, potash, and miscellaneous wood products.

Shipping services and shipbuilding were important sources of income for New England and made up for the fact that in value terms New Englanders had to import more commodities than they could produce for export. (See 4–4.) About half of New England's international earnings came from ships, shipping, and related mercantile services. At the time of the Revolution, about 30 percent of British merchant ships were of colonial origin and most of them were from New England yards.

Each of the colonial economies imported a wide variety of products, especially in the 18th century, when colonial cities and plantations in-

4–3. Origin and destination of colonial exports and commodity and slave imports
(in thousands of pounds)

	Ireland and Great Britain			Southern Europe			West Indies			Africa			Total Balance (13)
	Exports (1)	Imports (2)	Balance (3)	Exports (4)	Imports (5)	Balance (6)	Exports (7)	Imports (8)	Balance (9)	Exports (10)	Imports (11)	Balance (12)	
Northern Colonies	39	-402	-363	106	-7	99	10	-7	3	0	0	0	-261
New England	125	-460	-335	62	-15	47	318	-312	6	20	0	20	-262
Middle Colonies	148	-754	-606	214	-45	169	255	-273	-18	1	-3	-2	-457
Southern Colonies	1,303	-1,435	132	183	-12	171	219	-196	23	0	-76	-76	-14
Florida, Bahamas, Bermuda	17	-61	-44	0	-1	-1	3	-4	-1	0	-6	-6	-52
Total, Number American Colonies	1,632	-3,112	-1,480	565	-80	485	805	-792	13	21	-85	-64	-1,046

SOURCE: Shepherd and Walton (1969).

4–4. Colonial overseas earnings and imports, 1770
(in thousands of pounds)

| | Commodity and slave trade | | | | Invisible items | | | | Balance |
	(1)	(2)	(3)	(4)	(5)	(6)	(7)	(8)	(9)
Northern colonies.	155	−416	0	−261	8	3	NA	11	−250
New England	525	−787	0	−262	323	100		423	161
Middle Colonies.	618	−1,072	−3	−457	188	84		272	−185
Southern colonies.	1,705	−1,621	−98	−14	95	42		137	123
Florida, Bahamas, Bermuda.	20	−65	−7	−52	1	1		2	−50
Total, North American colonies	3,023	−3,961	−108	−1,046	615	230	400	1,245	124*

(1) Exports   (5) Shipping
(2) Imports   (6) Other services†
(3) Slaves   (7) Official British expenditures‡
(4) Balance   (8) Total
NA: Not Available.
* Regional figures do not include British governmental expenditures or the cost of importing indentured servants, which averaged about £75,000 in this period according to Shepherd and Walton (1972), chap. 8.
† Includes interest, insurance, and mercantile profits from overseas transactions.
‡ Expenditures in the colonies to cover civil and customs administration and military and naval costs of the British government less customs duties; data for regions not available.
SOURCE: Shepherd and Walton (1969).

cluded a significant number of high-income families. Manufactured products were, of course, the imports of greatest value; perhaps 70 percent of colonial imports were manufactures.

As we have said, the American market was too small and its agriculture too productive to justify much manufacturing investment even if British regulations had not come to outlaw it. Britain was the chief proximate source of manufactured products, although a sizable share of such goods had been imported by Britain from Europe for reexport to her imperial holdings. Foodstuffs that could not be raised in the temperate zone and specialties of other regions were also imported, as the following selection of items illustrates: tea, salt, pigments, sugar, rum, molasses, fruits, wine, chocolate, and spices.

The slave trade was vital to southern economic development and thus was important beyond its relative numerical significance in the total trade picture (see column 3 in 4–4). Most of the slaves that were brought to the continental colonies arrived in the 18th century, perhaps as many as 300,000 between 1700 and 1790, with about 3,500 per year coming in from 1715 to 1770.[16] In value terms, slaves accounted for only $\frac{1}{40}$ of total imports in 1770. Yet without slaves, the southern colonies would not have developed their export bases to the degree that they did, given their labor-intensive plantation agriculture.

Having looked at specific trade flows, we ought to discuss total commodity exports and other sources of colonial overseas earnings in conjunction with total import data. The southern colonies accounted for almost 60 percent of total colonial exports, followed by the Middle Colonies and New England. Total colonial exports came to only three fourths of total commodity imports, which meant that a one million pound trade excess of imports over exports had to be offset by other earnings and/or made up by borrowing from overseas (see columns 2 and 3 in 4–4).

New England and the Middle Colonies accounted for all but 14,000 pounds of the trade deficit of the original Thirteen Colonies (see column 4, 4–4).[17] Trade with Britain produced the largest contribution to the trade deficit (see column 3, 4–3). Only the South was a surplus trader with Britain. In contrast, southern European trade produced a large offset to the British deficit (see 4–3, column 6). And the West Indian and African accounts nearly balanced (see 4–3, columns 9 and 12).

In 1770, shipping earnings, over half of which were accounted for by New England, produced £614,000. This made shipping second only to tobacco among individual sources of overseas income. An additional

---

[16] See Shepherd and Walton (1972), chaps. 3 and 8, for discussion of the literature on total slave imports.

[17] Imports are understated relative to the average for the period because the nonimportation agreements affected New England and Middle Colony imports during most of 1770.

£230,000 was earned through the interest payments, insurance, and mercantile profits associated with shipping and export-import trade. Colonials did not, however, carry all of their own exports and imports. Taking the Empire as a whole, the British dominated some routes, the Americans others; thus, British ships called regularly at southern colonial ports while New England ships prevailed over the West Indies route (see 4–4).

Colonial overseas earnings were rounded out by a highly significant item, namely, the net expenditures in the colonies by the British government. The British administered and protected the colonies. This required an executive establishment, a system of courts, and an army and navy. Civil and military expenditures by Britain came to £400,000 in 1770, or 10 percent of total continental American imports and 40 percent of the import-export deficit. (See 4–6.)

Overall, the data we have shown for 1770 indicate that £200,000 in excess of colonial imports was earned by the colonists through their involvement in overseas trade. This meant that, on balance, colonists did not borrow overseas to finance imports in 1770. However, if the subject is dropped at this point, you may be somewhat misled. First, although net borrowing overseas did not occur in 1770, some colonials certainly went into debt by borrowing from British merchants and otherwise, while other Americans extended credit to overseas contacts. Second, 1770 was a plus year largely because of the nonimportation agreements. But in other 18th century years, earnings from exports and the invisible items cited in 4–4 were less than import costs, leaving a negative figure at the bottom of the balance column.

Shepherd and Walton estimate that the Thirteen Colonies averaged a deficit of £50,000 to £100,000 over the period 1768–72.[18] The key fact to remember is not that a deficit existed, but rather the modest size of that deficit. One hundred thousand pounds was only 2.5 percent of total colonial imports and less than 0.25 percent of total colonial income. Overall, the colonies managed to finance most of their capital accumulation out of their own savings rather than by borrowing heavily from England and other nations to finance capital imports. On this count, the advantage of trade to the colonies was the access it gave to slaves and the British and European manufactured goods desired by savers who wished to increase their agricultural and mercantile investments.

Sea-lanes and coastal trade

Contrary to what we all learned in the eighth grade about triangular trade routes, merchantmen in the colonial period generally made bilateral, or shuttle, runs. The colonial or British shipowner's usual practice was to commission his captain to take a cargo from the home port

[18] Shepherd and Walton (1972), chap. 8, n. 43.

to a specified foreign port, unload, then obtain a return cargo which would be transported directly to the home port. This process would be repeated with little variation year after year, primarily because it constituted a profit-maximizing strategy in an uncertain world of piracy and poor communications.

Ships did sail in triangular and other multilateral shipping patterns—for example, peddler ship captains made their way from New England to West Africa with rum, iron, and pepper, which they traded for slaves, then to the West Indies to trade slaves for sugar and molasses, and from there back to New England, perhaps with a stop at New York. But such voyages contributed an insignificant portion of total colonial tonnage and were notable, it appears, because they were the principal slave trade routes and because of their romantic aura.

The high frequency of shuttle runs was a sign of market imperfection rather than its opposite. Communications were poor and piracy rampant, so risk minimization required a shipping pattern that assured the owner of a market for his cargo and a return cargo with little idle port time. Accordingly, once a dependable and protected bilateral route had been worked out and a trustworthy and aggressive business agent had been engaged at a foreign port, the owner preferred not to stray into other waters. Only if demand at a familiar port failed or if the port could not provide an appropriate return cargo would a captain choose to tramp, thereby sailing a triangular or other multilateral route.[19]

How could the colonial economies manage to specialize in their production patterns yet import manufactured goods uniformly if shipping patterns weren't multilateral? Two factors explain this paradox. First, as we have noted, England and the South were complementary in their production mixes—southern export specialties found a ready market in England and were bartered or sold to buy much-needed manufactured goods. Second, the colonials carried on a heavy waterborne trade among themselves which served two ends: (1) supplying deficit colonies with the surpluses of other colonies and (2) assembling and redeploying cargoes for or from international trade. (See 4–5.)

Business records of colonial merchants and shippers, contemporary newspaper accounts, legislative records, and descriptions of colonial life by such people as Benjamin Franklin signify a heavy coastal trade. These accounts name Charleston, Philadelphia, New York, and Boston as the **entrepôts** at which colonial cargoes were gathered for export and imports were assembled for distribution in coastal and inland waterway routes. The legislative records of New York, Massachusetts, and

---

[19] Walton (1968) summarizes an exhaustive analysis of enter and clear data, ownership patterns, and route changes for the 18th century. His work shows that predominantly bilateral shipping patterns are consistent with his risk-minimization hypothesis for that period, although earlier routes, established when colonial entrepreneurs were still exploring various alternatives in search of profit-maximizing patterns, might have been more on the tramp than the shuttle side.

4–5. Average annual coastal and overseas exports by colonial
region, 1768–72
(in thousands of pounds)

Colonies	Total	Coastal	Overseas
Northern.	222	35	187
New England	781	304	477
Middle	779	220	559
Upper South.	1,250	88	1,162
Lower South	706	103	603
Florida, Bahamas, and Bermudas	43	17	26
	3,781	767	3,014

SOURCE: Shepherd and Williamson, pp. 17, 19.

Pennsylvania suggest the importance of the entrepôt trade to these colonies. The records are studded with mercantilist proposals, some enacted into law, which were designed to attract ships at the expense of other ports.

Colonial economic geography explains the importance of coastwise shipping as a complement to international shuttle runs. In the South, only the Virginia-Maryland area comprised a sufficiently dense market to permit dealing directly with the British. Charleston served as the most important pickup and delivery point for British merchantmen serving the balance of the South.

Market size and geography were also crucial in determining northern shipping and trade patterns. Small vessels had to assemble exports at Philadelphia, New York, and Boston because producing points were too scattered to justify direct shipments to overseas ports. Further, such products as grains and raw materials had to be assembled for processing before they could enter international trade.[20]

Coastal shipping was needed for another reason. Each colony developed output specialties which complemented not only the products of overseas nations but also the products of other colonies. Consequently, even if tramping had prevailed in international trade, a large volume of colonial products would have been moved among the colonial ports.

In all this, New England fishing vessels made a glamorous contribution and perhaps even accounted for a significant portion of the trade among the colonies:

> During the winter when there was little fishing carried on, the owners of small fishing-ships [how many?] would load their craft with salt,

---

[20] For a discussion of Virginia and Massachusetts coasting, see Klingaman (forthcoming and January 1969).

rum, sugar, molasses, iron and wooden ware, hats, caps, cloth, handker-
chiefs, and stockings, which they carried to the southern colonies and
peddled from place to place, returning early in the spring with a valuable
lot [how valuable?] of pitch and tar and supplies of corn and pickled
pork.[21]

The foregoing certainly suggests that waterborne intercolonial commerce was strategic in determining colonial economic welfare. How important? Perhaps the best way to put it is to say that cessation of the
coastal and river trade after the mid-1600s would have exacted a toll
in colonial well-being sufficient to cut deeply into the average colonist's
margin above subsistence.

THE GROWTH RECORD ANALYZED

We have reviewed the structure of the colonial economy and the
growth record it chalked up over about two centuries. Now we will
analyze the development process by identifying the forces that generated
growth. The appropriate starting place is with an analysis of American
productivity with an emphasis upon the later colonial years, when GNP
per head in the colonies was roughly on a par with and growing at
the same rate as that of Great Britain.

Why were these new economies able to match their elders in productivity? The answers seem to be that the colonists were favored by especially productive resources and that in their combined effect these resources were at least as productive as those of England.

Colonial inputs and economic organization, 1770

American natural resources were abundant relative to population.
Once the colonists had learned how to extract mineral wealth, harvest
the forests, and till the American soils, the resource base produced a
high yield. Given the huge supply of land and the scarcity of labor
and capital, the colonists maximized productivity by "mining" the land,
i.e., cropping it intensively until the fertility of the topsoil was exhausted.
This they did simply because clearing new land was cheaper than devoting labor to soil-rebuilding activities. Other natural resources were used
at rapid rates for a related reason—with the exception of timber, their
exhaustion was a remote danger given the small population relative
to natural resources.

In combination with abundant natural resources, free colonial workers
were able to earn high incomes compared with workers in England
and Europe. Indentured servants and slaves were, of course, "paid" sub-

---

[21] Johnson, pp. 169–70.

sistence wages which in most cases were less than they could have earned in the free labor market or as self-employed farmers.

The return the self-employed farmer earned for his labor at least equaled that of his British or European counterparts after the long years of farm-making were over. Newspaper accounts and other contemporary records indicate that the American artisan was less skilled but perhaps more versatile than his English counterpart, a jack-of-all-trades and perhaps almost a master of a few. Yet skilled labor was so scarce compared with England that a mature apprentice could migrate to America and earn more as a wage earner or a self-employed master than his journeyman teachers who stayed in England.

Free labor found its way to the colonies in two ways. Primarily in New England, groups of settlers obtained land grants and settled in villages. Outside New England, individuals obtained land grants under the headright system, whereby a specified acreage was granted for each person who landed in the colonies. Under the headright system, would-be farmers of modest means acquired just enough land to establish family farms, whereas wealthy immigrants obtained a great deal of land by bringing servants and financing passage for others.

On the average, free laborers were perhaps intrinsically more productive than their English counterparts. Migration in the recent past has been biased in favor of the better educated. Studies of 19th century immigrants show that they were not concentrated among the landless and unsuccessful but were proportionally distributed among the various socioeconomic groups. Thus, indentured servants aside, it's not unlikely that the 17th and 18th century colonists followed the same patterns in that they were better educated and, on the average, no poorer than English or West European workingmen. Further, analysis of data on literacy in early America indicates that colonial literacy was well above that of any of today's less developed economies, 40 to 80 percent higher, in fact, and among the highest in the Western world at the time of the Revolution.[22]

As far as labor is concerned, it is probably a serious mistake to draw a parallel between today's less developed economies and any of the newly established American colonies. As we noted in the introduction to this chapter, the immigrants to colonial America came from the most highly developed economies of their time and were wise to the ways of a marketized, industrializing economy.

It is not clear that bondsmen were less efficient workers than free laborers. But let's weigh the argument against the use of bondsmen

---

[22] Kenneth Lockridge, whose work is still in preparation, is responsible for the observation on literacy; see Wolfbein, chap. 5, for a summary of current mobility patterns. Curtis demonstrates that 19th century movers were not the luckless have-nots.

and assume that the productivity of slave and indentured labor was low compared with that of free labor. We must then conclude that free labor commanded such a high wage that the productivity per pound sterling expended to employ free workers made free labor an inferior alternative. (We will discuss the economics of slavery in greater detail in chapter 6.)

We can probably safely assume that nonhuman capital was accumulated at roughly the same rate as the growth of colonial income. As we noted in the foregoing section, in at least the 18th century, the colonists provided most of the savings required by capital accumulation with very little net assistance from overseas investors. However, short-term credits advanced by English merchants doubtless grew in volume over time, and in the early days the capital supplied by colonizing ventures was all-important.

The capital brought by immigrants significantly augmented colonial savings. Wealthy Englishmen who immigrated to the South brought equipment and funds with which to build plantations and purchase slaves, and farmers who immigrated to the North brought tools and implements with them. Also craftsmen, boatbuilders, fishermen, and merchants brought capital in both coin and kind with them. We do not know how large a contribution to colonial capital growth was made by immigrants' capital; however, given the dominance of natural population increases, this source surely pales in significance beside colonial savings.

In urban areas, private savers accumulated monetary resources which they spent for ships, business buildings, workshops and boatyards, residential construction, and a wide variety of machinery and equipment. Urban social overhead capital projects, such as wharf construction, harbor improvements, sewers, and highways, were financed by fees and taxes, European investors, and associations of private citizens who recognized the direct and indirect profitability of various public projects. Boston's huge Long Wharf (1713) is a classic example of colonial social overhead capital formation.[23]

In the rural areas, private capital accumulation came chiefly from devoting labor resources to the creation of capital goods. Clearing land, constructing farm buildings, and building agricultural machinery were all jobs performed by the farm or plantation owner or his hands. Imports, financed by the sale of agricultural products or from the capital resources brought to the colonies, were crucial in establishing farms and plantations because certain materials weren't available in America or because various types of equipment could not be constructed economically at the farmsite.

---

[23] See Bridenbaugh (1938), pp. 8–25, 152–74, and 313–29 for descriptions of colonial social overhead capital formation and financing.

Public projects in rural areas were limited to roadways. These were usually financed by taxes or built with labor required of able-bodied property holders in the area. Among the chief financial sources were the port cities, which needed highroads to connect them with their back-country customers.

We have no quantitative basis for comparing the productivity per unit of American capital with that of Britain or Europe in colonial times. However, scraps of evidence gleaned from contemporary accounts give us some indications. It appears that American capital equipment when not imported from Britain or the Continent was copied from European models, then adapted to conserve labor. However, without better data than exists on interest rates, wages, and returns to landowners we cannot say anything definite about the comparative returns to capital investment in the colonies and England. It is possible, though, that returns to both labor and capital were higher in the colonies given the vast supply of natural resources; we lean toward this conclusion.

Colonial economic organization rounds out our discussion of productivity. In spite of political division, commercial rivalry, and horrendous roads, and largely because of an enterprising spirit and a huge investment in merchant ships, by 1770 colonial America had established well-defined and efficient regional production and trade relations. Investment in social overhead capital, a network of well-established business relationships, and a clearly defined system of commercial law and business practices constituted the base upon which the superstructure of colonial production and trade was erected. To put it another way, the colonial economy was both monetized and marketized, and thus its people enjoyed the benefits that come of having both a wide range of choices in buying and selling and a high degree of specialization in production. In general, overall economic organization has to be viewed as a factor which contributed to the colonies' high ranking in per capita income.

The colonial monetary system (or, better, nonsystem) constitutes a triumph of ingenuity in economic organization. Specie, that is, precious metals, was the preferred form of money in those days. But the British colonies mined no specie, and a good deal of what was earned by exporting was very soon spent overseas for much-needed manufactured goods. Consequently, the colonists always complained of a shortage of money, meaning specie.[24] However, they did admirably without. How? By printing money. By treating certain kinds of private and business debts— long-term charge accounts, promissory notes of well-reputed individuals, and bills of exchange—as if they were money. By monetizing certain high-value, easily transported commodities, such as whiskey and tobacco,

---

[24] This was not an uncommon complaint in at least the Western world in the 17th and 18th centuries. Shortages of coins, especially in small denominations, were widespread in this era of expansion without well-developed banking facilities.

or by passing warehouse receipts for such items from hand to hand. And by barter.

Bills of exchange from international transactions, usually on London merchants, served as hand money in international and domestic trade. At home, merchants extended open book credit to their customers for protracted periods, and exchanges among merchants were frequently carried out by merely adding to or crediting the buyer's account. Warehouse receipts (e.g., "tobacco money") and paper money made possible other domestic transactions. Colonial governments, public loan banks, and land banks issued notes, most of them interest bearing, which passed from hand to hand, just as Federal Reserve notes are used today.

Economic historians used to condemn as ruinous the note issues of colonial governments and land banks. They took this attitude primarily because from time to time notes were issued at a faster rate than was justified by economic activity. In such cases, the printing press became an inflation machine; the note issues of the Continental Congress during the Revolution are dramatic, but untypical, examples. Between 1775 and 1779, $241 million in Continental currency was issued, and, largely as a consequence, the price index was driven from 78 in 1775 to 2,969 in 1779. (Turn back to 3–2 in chapter 3.)

In more recent years, students of the colonial period have come to take a modified view of pre-Revolutionary note issues. The only way to import more from England than was exported as goods or services was to pay for the balance in specie earned elsewhere. Given the almost insatiable demand for imports, specie constituted a very expensive domestic medium of exchange. Therefore, substitutes for hard money were contrived to supplement specie as a circulating medium. Consequently, the need for barter was reduced and the efficiency of markets was enhanced. In short, the paper money issues and other substitutes for hard money facilitated the process of exchange over a period in which total economic activity was growing very rapidly and the market sector of the economy was growing even more rapidly.

When you consider that the wholesale price index rose from 59 in 1720 to only 78 in 1775, an increase of less than one third, you can hardly assert that the pre-Revolutionary note issues produced protracted runaway inflation. (See 4–6.) It is quite true, however, that in short periods rapid note issuance (usually during wars) produced sharp increases in price levels and, over the long pull, too much paper was issued to hold prices constant. Ideally, the stock of money should grow at the long-term rate at which the economy is capable of expanding. By this criterion, no one can assert with a straight face that the colonial note issues were well managed—note issuance fluctuated widely and erratically.[25]

---

[25] For a review of the literature and a test of the efficiency of note issues see. Weiss, pp. 770–84.

4–6.   Index of colonial wholesale prices, 1720–75

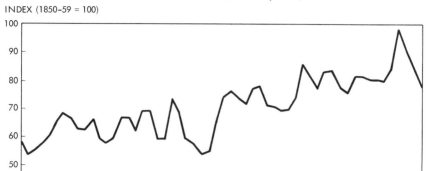

SOURCE: U.S. Department of Commerce, p. 772.

Intensive growth factors

Economic expansion in the American Colonies still stands as an un-challenged speed record. This experience can easily be explained in terms of the factors we have just cited in our discussion of productivity.

Rich yields could be obtained from an abundant landmass if labor and capital were applied with sufficient skill over a long enough time span. Thus, English, Scottish, Irish, and continental Europeans who were restless for economic, political, or social reasons were attracted to England's portion of the New World. They brought capital with them and added to it by devoting long hours of their own labor to capital projects—in a fundamental sense, the growth of population and the labor force automatically generated capital growth. Because land was virtually unlimited in supply and because the capital stock grew auto-matically as the labor force grew, the colonial economies were able to absorb new people at very rapid rates and to expand economically as population grew.

Intensive growth is a different story than expansion. Recall that al-though each colony's total economy grew very rapidly, per capita income growth was very modest, less than 0.5 percent. Let's look at the various forces that were exerting pressure for and against economic growth over the colonial period.

On the negative side we have the following:

1. As we noted earlier, *agricultural technology was largely static during the colonial period.* Though there is little evidence one way or the other, we feel that this description applies to manufacturing as well. Thus, once European methods were adapted to American farming

and manufacturing conditions, there was no year-to-year tendency for farming and manufacturing productivity to rise. Given that agriculture and rural industry claimed about 80 percent of the work force and urban manufacturing perhaps another 2½ to 5 percent, the importance of this element should be obvious. To us, it is the most important factor explaining slow intensive growth.

2. *Economic expansion exacted a toll in productivity.* After the colonists became familiar with the American soils, they settled on the best situated of the most productive lands, But as population grew, newcomers were forced to choose between relatively good soil in remote areas or poorer soils with good transport access. Both choices meant less productive farms and the need to devote scarce resources to road building.[26] Expansion raised fuel and timber costs significantly. Urban growth pushed forests farther and farther away from colonial hearths and construction projects. And, often, iron ore deposits had to be abandoned because the local firewood supply was exhausted.

We know of no quantitative estimates of the importance of these factors, but we speculate that their combined effect was minor.

3. *Colonial times were never peaceful for very long.* Scrapping among the colonial powers and with the Indians took a significant toll in man-hours, capital, and lives. War is not only hell, it's expensive too, as the colonists were periodically reminded. Just how costly we don't know, but we do know that the more peaceful conditions of the early 1700s lessened the destructive impact of war.

4. *Certain elements of British colonial policy have to be charged with some responsibility for slow colonial growth.* Even though on balance the Navigation Acts and related colonial policies probably exacted no toll in colonial economic welfare, some elements of these policies and colonial reaction to them had adverse effects, just as other elements spurred economic growth. In addition, the welfare costs of particular items in the total array of British policies reduced colonial saving-investing capacity and precluded certain activities that would have spurred intensive growth. As you will see, it is almost impossible to quantify the welfare effects of an item of colonial policy for any given year, let alone assess its impact on growth over the years; our conclusion is that the negative effects upon growth were of a minor order.

On the plus side we have the following:

1. As we have noted, *the adaptation of European agricultural methods and tools produced rapid progress in each of the colonial settlements during the period of adaptation.* But, again we stress, once this process was complete, sustained productivity increases in agriculture were not

---

[26] Agricultural innovation and productivity trends are discussed exhaustively in Bidwell and Falconer and in Gray.

characteristic of the colonial period. You can get some idea of the importance of this factor by remembering that this process brought the settlements, first, from their starving times to a subsistence-level general agriculture, then, ultimately, to a specialized agriculture that yielded the colonial farmer or planter a high level of living as compared with his counterparts in Europe.

2. *Productivity of colonial shipping and allied industries grew at about 0.8 percent per year over the period 1675–1775.* Oddly enough, technological change had little to do with this record—ships did not get faster or bigger. External economies and the Royal Navy get the credit for increasing productivity.

As markets increased in size, warehousing and other special marketing functions grew—accordingly idle port time, a very important cost element, was cut drastically. For example, ships in the tobacco trade increased their annual runs from two to three in the 18th century, largely because tobacco came to be warehoused at various entrepôts in America and, thus, awaited vessels instead of being awaited by them.

The chances that merchantmen would arrive safely at their intended port grew considerably after the pirates were bought off or driven out of American sea-lanes. Insurance rates appropriately reflected the rise in safety by coming down significantly. Sustained patrolling of the sea-lanes meant that merchantmen could carry smaller crews and eliminate guns, thus simultaneously cutting labor costs and raising payload capacity.[27]

3. Capital grew over the period; and if conclusions drawn from contemporary narratives are any guide, *capital grew faster than population.* In fact, to a large degree, students of colonial living standards base their conclusions on observed increases in capital compared with population. However, we know of no estimates of the importance of capital deepening as a growth stimulus.

Town and country houses became finer and larger. Urban business and manufacturing facilities grew. On the farm, lean-tos were replaced by sheds, excellent barns were built (some still stand today), fields were fenced, and mills were erected. The urban social overhead capital formation we described above surely made doing business more efficient and introduced considerable convenience into the everyday life of the average citizen.

4. *The labor force probably grew faster than population, and its quality increased as literacy rates rose over the 165 years of colonization.* Immigrants who came of their own will were naturally of working age, as were indentured servants. Slaves, whose number grew faster than did the number of free men, were imported at working age, may have

---

[27] See Shepherd and Walton (1972), chap. 4, for discussion of the evidence and citations of the literature dealing with productivity growth in ocean shipping.

worked longer hours than free labor, "joined" the work force earlier than free men, and probably retired later than free men. How important this factor is for growth trends, we can't say.

5. *External economies of scale and resulting improvements in economic organization were doubtless of prime importance among the forces promoting economic growth.* The growth of colonial markets made feasible improved economic organization and cost-reducing capital investments which, in turn, increased the productive capacity of the colonial economies.

We've already discussed the fact that external economies in assembling and marketing cargo enhanced shipping productivity. And the social overhead capital formation we talked about is to a very large degree a physical embodiment of external economies—after markets reach a certain critical size, transport, storage, and exchange facilities involving large amounts of capital investment can be created because they will be used very intensively with significant cost reduction for those who use them.

Further, externalities permeated the economy in other instances than the ones we've just cited. Specialist merchants and artisans set up shop as urban places and their hinterlands grew in population. In the larger places, such as Boston, Philadelphia, and New York, the number of business establishments of each type grew sufficiently to give buyers and sellers realistic alternatives in selecting customers or suppliers. More efficient business conventions, modes of extending credit, and ways of adding to the stock of money reduced wheel spinning and friction in the daily conduct of business. In short, the efficiency of buying, selling, and producing grew as colonial population, income, and expenditure grew.

Let's see if we can get some insight into the quantitative importance of external economies of scale for colonial growth. We know that efficiency in shipping grew by 0.8 percent per year; assume half of that rate of increase—0.4 percent—is attributable to inroads on piracy and half to scale economies. Agriculture and rural industry constituted 80 percent of the economy, so shipping, urban-based manufacturing, and commercial services claimed the remaining 20 percent. If external economies were limited in their impact to urban areas, and if land-based economic activity was affected by them in the same manner as ocean shipping, then intensive growth attributable to external economies of scale would have averaged .08 percent per year (20 percent of the 0.4 percent productivity increase registered by shipping). If scale economies benefited rural economic activity, i.e., if the cost reductions in urban areas spread to the countryside through urban-rural business transactions, then scale economies would have coaxed along the efficiency of the entire economy at the full 0.4 percent per year we have assigned to external economies. In our view, the truth lies between these extremes but nearer to the latter estimate.

6. Apart from changes in economic organization induced by expansion, *colonial buyers and sellers improved the efficiency of market organization simply by gaining experience.* No one can read Baxter's *House of Hancock* without gaining an appreciation of the difficulties of doing business'in a world of uncertain transport and slow communications. Nor can you read about Thomas Hancock without learning to respect the significance of innovations in trading relationships as contributions to economic growth.

Gains in organizational efficiency that come from learning by doing cannot be separated from the organizational changes made possible by expansion. Therefore, the quantitative impact of both these factors appears as part of the estimate given in number 5 above.

Looked at in the broadest terms, colonial expansion and per capita income movements were the results of a maturation process. That process started with a series of disconnected, self-sufficient English communities fighting for survival against nature, other Europeans, and the original Americans. It culminated in a federated cluster of colonies which possessed a high degree of economic sophistication: agriculture was commercialized; a coastal trade flourished among the colonies; exchange with England, southern Europe, and Africa was a source of much-needed manufactured products and slaves; per capita income provided not mere survival, but a level of living that compared favorably with that of the mother country; and the economy's capacity for expansion had supported a remarkably high population growth rate with continuing if modest gains in per capita production.

Urban growth over the first hundred years of colonial development illustrates well this process of maturation. New York, Boston, Charleston, Newport, and Philadelphia

> were primarily commercial communities seeking treasure by foreign trade, and their economic vitality and commercial demands led to their early breaking of the narrow bonds of medieval economic practice to forge ahead on uncharted but highly profitable commercial adventures. All five, during their first century, developed from simple manorial organizations, completely dependent upon European connections, into full-fledged commercial centers, only partially tied to England, and in many cases competing with British cities for a share of imperial traffic.[28]

Gallman has stated that "by 1713 the colonies had not only outgrown their origins as outposts of specific business enterprises, but had also assumed a shape which made them independent, in important ways, of the Empire . . . [though] they were perhaps not . . . capable of

---

[28] Bridenbaugh (1938), pp. 468–69.

political union."[29] By 1775, the ways in which the colonies could be independent of the Empire had multiplied so that political and economic secession from Britain and political union among the states were possible.

BRITISH COLONIAL POLICY

The historical importance of British colonial policy has been debated by generation after generation of economic historians. The issue revolves around two central questions which have often been confusingly intermingled:

1. How large were the net costs (or benefits) incurred by the colonists as a consequence of British mercantilism?
2. What role did British colonial policy play in inciting the colonists to revolt?

These questions are obviously related, but you must exercise great caution in interpreting their interrelationship. For example, even if the Navigation Acts and related imperial policies were costly to the colonists, it does *not* necessarily follow that the economic aspects of colonial policy caused the Revolution—it depends upon how the colonists viewed their situation. On the other hand, if the mercantilist policy of Britain was of net benefit to the colonies, it doesn't follow that it had no role in sparking the Revolution—it is not inconceivable that the colonists would have viewed any policy, beneficial or not, as unwelcome interference.

British mercantilism, 1775

Britain designed its colonial policy with the intent of making a maximum contribution to the mother country's economic welfare. Britain's strategy involved a series of laws and regulations passed over the course of the colonial period and designed to alter the pattern of world trade in its favor. Some of these enactments turned the terms of trade against Britain's colonial possessions. Others were designed to subsidize the colonists in order to assure Britain a source of supply of certain vital products.

Viewed from an economic standpoint, colonial policy just prior to the Revolution fell into four main categories: (1) commercial regulations, (2) regulation of colonial currency, (3) regulation of colonial population movements, and (4) protection of colonial holdings. The first category, usually referred to as the Navigation Acts, applied equally to the entire Empire, whereas the others varied within the Empire according to local conditions.

---

[29] Gallman, p. 19.

The Navigation Acts and the related Trade Acts influenced colonial commerce in four ways.

1. Ships built and manned by Englishmen, including colonists, were given a monopoly of the carrying trade both within the Empire and between the Empire and nations outside the Empire.
2. Colonial exports and imports were closely controlled. "Enumerated" articles, such as tobacco, had to be exported to England, although their ultimate destination might have been Europe. Similarly, most imports from Europe and the East Indies had to be transshipped through England or bear a very heavy duty. What's more, certain products, e.g., beaver hats, could not be exported by a colony; in turn, the colonies were granted monopolies in certain commodities, such as tobacco.
3. Import and export bounties, export taxes, rebates, and drawbacks were designed to encourage particular colonial industries that were considered vital to England. Naval stores and indigo are the most important examples.
4. The expansion or creation of production facilities in certain industries, such as finished iron products, was forbidden in the colonies in order to protect the English home market.

After 1740, Britain issued a series of restraints on colonial paper money issues by prohibiting the extension of legal tender power to colonial currencies and requiring the withdrawal of colonial legal tender currencies.[30] Two considerations explain this policy. First, British merchants claimed injury from having accepted payment in colonial notes that subsequently depreciated. Second, Britain needed to earn specie in the colonies in order to finance growing imports from the Baltic region. Consequently, Parliament was anxious to prevent currency issues that might displace specie as a means of colonial payment for English goods.[31]

The Proclamation of 1763 and the Quebec Act of 1774 restricted the settlement of colonists to the territory east of the Alleghenies (the Proclamation Line) and placed the area north of the Ohio River under the Quebec provincial government. The purpose of these measures was to reduce the possibility of warfare with the Indians and the friction among the colonists over competing land claims. The policy was very unpopular in the Thirteen Colonies because it shut down the operations of American land companies at the frontier.

The Royal Navy and tribute paid to the Barbary pirates protected American sea-lanes. Correspondingly, British troops stationed in America

---

[30] Legal tender power means that by law the currency must be accepted in payment of public or private debts or the debts are canceled.

[31] See sources in Weiss for discussion of this point.

were responsible for protecting colonial settlements from attacks by Indians and other Europeans. The four wars between France and Britain in North America between 1689 and 1763 as well as various engagements with the Indians kept British troops busy for most of the colonial period.

The costs (benefits?) of imperial policy

A realistic way to assess the impact of the economic aspects of British imperial policy is to ask the question: How would the colonies have fared had they been outside the Empire in a mercantilist world? Prior to the Treaty of Paris (1763), the French would have simply taken over the continental colonies south of Canada had Britain stepped out of the picture. Thus this question has to refer to the colonial period after the end of the French and Indian War, i.e., 1763–75.

Several scholars have attempted to quantify various aspects of British colonial policy from the standpoint of economic welfare. The most recent studies ask the question set forth above and conclude that the economic burdens were about offset by the economic gains.[32] Let's identify the ways in which imperial policy produced colonial gains and losses.

The fact that colonial exports of enumerated products to Europe had to be transshipped through England meant higher shipping costs and, therefore, lower colonial prices and higher delivered prices on the Continent. As a consequence, colonial production and income was reduced. For example, in the case of tobacco, Peter McClelland estimates that during the period 1763–75 transshipment through England raised the delivered price of tobacco 40 percent above its price in a Maryland or Virginia port. Further, McClelland believes that this ratio applies to all enumerated articles.

On the import side, transshipment through England meant higher import prices for the colonists—40 percent higher if McClelland's calculations and assumptions are correct. Thus, colonial welfare was lowered by the need to pay higher freight costs on imported products.

The combined effect of these import and export controls has been evaluated by a number of scholars using a variety of approaches. In no case do the upper-bound estimates exceed 5 percent of colonial income, and 2 percent seems the soundest estimate, according to Gary Walton's evaluation of the studies. Of course, smuggling flourished as a result of these restrictions, which means that the costs were somewhat less than they might have been had the Americans abided faithfully by British commercial law.

The restrictions on manufacturing activity were viewed as a burden

---

[32] See Walton for an evaluation of attempts to assess the burden of the Navigation Acts and a citation of the literature on the subject beginning with the 1940s. Harper's, Thomas's, and McClelland's contributions are especially important milestones on this long and tortuous academic pathway and are appraised by Walton.

by particular colonists. Yet the broader, retrospective view of the economic historian indicates that in reality the manufacturing restrictions were not harmful. First, they did not apply to products in which colonial production obviously served England well—pig iron and other primary products, rum, extracted products, forest products, and ships were all permissible colonial product lines: in fact, some of them were subsidized. Second, anecdotal evidence suggests that the prohibitions were not enforced very well, so if a colonial entrepreneur saw a chance to make a profit he invested in a forbidden field or otherwise evaded the law. The Hat Act (1732) provides the best example of evasion: because hats could not be exported from a colony, hatmakers moved from colony to colony, making hats in and for the local market, so that no finished hats had to be exported from one colony to another.

Looking at this question more generally, we can observe that the colonies had particular fields in which they enjoyed a definite comparative advantage. The British manufacturing restrictions, **in the degree that they were enforced,** did little to interfere with the colonists' pursuit of their most lucrative activities. On the other hand, British prohibitions against growing tobacco in England were doubtless redundant because English resources could be used more profitably in other fields.

Independence would have meant turning the shipping clauses of the Navigation Acts against the Americans. In fact, after the Revolution, American shipping services did decline from 59.4 to 53.2 percent of total colonial commerce. On the other hand, as we noted above, total American commerce would have been greater had the colonies been independent during the period from 1763 to 1775. As Robert Thomas's calculations work out, American ships carrying a smaller portion of a larger tonnage would have earned slightly more than the merchant fleet actually earned.

In short, according to Thomas, opposite forces acting upon the carrying trade would have changed the industry's routes and cargo composition but left earnings about the same. However, the sad state of the shipping industry after the Revolution suggests that Thomas understates the importance of British naval protection. Further, as the Americans learned after the Revolution, the loss of ship sales to England constituted an important potential loss of earnings for the New England economy from 1763 to 1775.

British subsidies, such as the bounties paid on indigo and forest products and the preferential duties extended to most enumerated articles, benefited the colonies to the extent that they accounted for colonial revenues over and above what the resources involved would have earned had the colonies been divorced from England. Thomas's figures show that these benefits of mercantilism came to £88,000 in 1770, or only 2 percent of colonial income.

The loss of British military protection within the colonies and on the high seas proved costly when independence was actually achieved. The Americans had to pay tribute to the Barbary pirates to get permission for their ships to pass—a payment the British had originally borne. An army had to be maintained and a fleet of warships constructed at the turn of the century.

Presumably, similar national defense requirements would have presented themselves had America succeeded in breaking its English ties in 1763. The costs of a military establishment would have been between 1 and 2 percent of per capita income if American expenditures after the Revolution are a guide.

The effect of the Proclamation Line is conceptually and factually difficult to deal with. Its provisions were violated, so that movement west did take place, but how much compared with what American policies would have allowed we cannot say. If migration to America was slowed by the Proclamation Line, extensive growth and the realization of scale economies may have been impeded. But, on the other hand, if migration wasn't slowed, more concentrated expansion may have produced scale economies that wouldn't have been realized otherwise. Yes, the colonial land companies lost profit opportunities, but these would have been profits earned not from production but from buying and selling an existing resource—land. It seems safest to assume that colonial costs here were limited to the effects of ill temper stirred by the British policy.

The impact of currency regulation on the colonists is also difficult to assess. We know, however, that after the Revolution the Americans had monetary difficulties attributable to the lack of a central monetary authority. And we can assume that they would have had similar problems from 1763 to 1775 had they been independent. If you agree that the actual issuance of notes was too much of a good thing—good because of the shortage of hard money, too much because some inflation did result—then you must conclude that English policy enhanced welfare because it slowed but did not prohibit the issuance of paper money.

Can we arrive at a summary judgment as to the impact of imperial policy on colonial economic welfare? Let's look at a scorecard:

Policy	Burden	Benefit	Zero net effect
Commercial controls			
Shipping monopoly.		X	
Enumeration	X		
Import restrictions	X		
Bounties.		X	
Preferential duties		X	
Military protection		X	
Proclamation Line			X
Currency regulation		X	

Both burdens and benefits appear. We can add up the various estimates of the burdens of transshipping exports and imports, then subtract the benefits of bounties, preferential duties, and military protection. This process, when performed by Thomas, yields a net burden of less than 1 percent of per capita income. Add to that a slight plus associated with currency controls, and British colonial policy seems to have left the average American unaffected—at least in the sense that, arithmetically, 1 percent is a negligible portion of income per person.

Imperial economic policy and the Revolution

Must we conclude that because the toll of British mercantilism was slight, the Revolution was fought solely for noneconomic reasons? We think not.

In the period after 1763, Parliament passed a long series of colonial acts which had economic implications but which in our view were most important in their political implications. The Townshend Acts, the Tea Act, the Stamp Act, the Sugar Act, the Proclamation Line, and the Quebec Act were all regarded as burdensome beyond their direct pecuniary implications. They were viewed as heralding a "new colonial system" after many years of virtual inattention from Westminster. To the Americans the turn in British policy suggested that the colonies were to become England's serfs.

The Nonimportation Agreements (invoked twice), the Boston Massacre, and the Boston Tea Party were all reactions far out of line with the immediate economic importance of the specific British policies that prompted them. A constitutional issue represented the axis around which these controversies whirled: Would Britain continue to dictate colonial policy and do so in response to special English interests such as the East India Company?

Those who, like Benjamin Franklin, looked toward the day when the Empire would be directed from America and those who merely wanted a laissez-faire existence within the Empire saw no assurance for their aspirations. British willingness to negotiate on a particular issue, to repeal specific taxes, such as the Townshend Acts and the Stamp Tax, in no way signified abandonment of Parliament's prerogatives. Parliamentary control was nonnegotiable, and no English consideration of concessions to the colonies ever took place except on the premise of colonial subservience.

As the colonists viewed their situation, the only thing new about the new colonial policy was its detail. In spirit, it adhered to the principle Cromwell established in 1650 when he asked for an English monopoly of shipping within the Empire: colonial policy was to be made by and for England. This the British reaffirmed, beginning in 1763. No matter how slight the narrowly defined economic costs of imperial policies, the colonists could no longer live with the principle by which they were promulgated—especially when they felt that the costs would not always be so small.[33]

SUMMARY

1. The typical American colonial community began its history as a self-sufficient, manorlike settlement wholly preoccupied with the struggle for survival. However, once the "starving time" was over, the colonial settlements and their hinterlands became marketized with a high degree of specialization in production.

Once established, the economy of the typical colony expanded at rates that were phenomenal by either contemporary or modern standards. Although per capita income grew less than 0.5 percent per year in the typical colony, this record compared favorably with that of England which was among the few nations exhibiting intensive growth in those days. At the time of the Revolution, the average American colonist appears to have enjoyed about the same level of economic welfare as his English counterpart.

2. Once established as a viable economic entity, the typical colony developed a specialized output mix and sold its surplus production to Britain, southern Europe, the West Indies, Africa, and, of course, other colonies.

Colonial exports were dominated by agricultural output, followed in importance by ships and shipping services, whereas imports consisted primarily of manufactured consumer and capital goods. Although trade with Africa was a small portion of total colonial international commerce, the importation of slaves was strategic in the development of the southern colonies.

The colonists carried on a heavy coastal trade to exchange their respective surplus outputs and to redeploy the cargo that came to such ports as Charleston, Philadelphia, New York, and Boston. Although triangular and other multilateral trade routes did characterize a portion of colonial shipping, the most common trade route was the shuttle run between two ports: poor communications made tramping from port to port a risky venture.

3. The high productivity of American inputs and a well-articulated market structure account for the high GNP per capita achieved by England's colonial outposts in North America. Land was plentiful, high-quality labor flowed to America in great streams, and the colonists were able to accumulate business and social overhead capital at rates capable of sustaining rapid extensive growth. However, although American

---

[33] On the political importance of imperial economic policy see Hughes (1969) and Hacker, pp. 88–98.

productivity was high compared with that of the rest of the world, as was the case in the rest of the world colonial productivity grew very slowly in the 17th and 18th centuries. When productivity did increase, its growth seems to have been based upon improved economic organization and/or external economies of scale rather than technological innovations.

4. In total, British colonial economic policy does not appear to have exacted more than a negligible toll in colonial economic welfare. However, imperial economic policy came to be viewed as oppressive by many colonists. When England tightened its rule after 1763, many colonists reacted with resentment to its reaffirmation of the principle that colonial economic policy was to be made by and for England.

APPENDIX TO CHAPTER 4: REAL INCOME

"Real," an innocent-looking little word that economists have a habit of inserting in their texts, has a special technical meaning. It is used when data have been adjusted to reflect changes in the general level of prices. A general increase in the prices of most goods reduces the purchasing power of the dollars of income people receive, and vice versa. That is to say, price inflation reduces the value of money, and price deflation increases the value of money. Accordingly, if we wish to measure an increase in production and income over a period of history in which we know most prices have been rising, we must adjust for the fact that the increased money income received will not be all "real" because rising prices will have diluted the purchasing power of the increase in income. By the term *real income,* then, economists mean the *quantity of purchasing power that would have been received if prices generally had not changed.* The term is used to compare changes in income at the same prices.

To compare real incomes at two different periods, we first need a composite index of general prices for the two periods. Using the hypothetical illustration from the appendix to chapter 3, let us suppose that it represents a composite price index not just of wheat and rum, but of all goods produced. Starting with an index of 100 in the base year, 1750, the composite price index rose to 117 in 1760. Let us suppose it also rose to 125 in 1770. Now, let us assume that we have data on the wages paid all employed workers in the colonies, and that we can say the average wage was $6.00 per week in 1750 and that it increased by $0.75 in each of the two following decades. What happened to labor's real income, or real wage? Did it increase at all? Did it increase by the same amount each decade?

To find out what happened to any series of money income figures (the amounts currently received in money terms), simply *divide by the indexes of composite prices* for the same years, then multiply by 100 to move the decimal:

$$\text{Real Value} = 100 \times \frac{\text{Money Value}}{\text{Price Index}}$$

In the illustration following, the money wages divided by the price index and multiplied by 100 equals the real wages. The real wages fell from 1750 to 1760 but increased from 1760 to 1770. This is because the decade-to-decade percentage increase was greater for prices in the first decade but greater for wages in the second decade. In this example, the changes in the two periods were canceling, so real wages in 1770 were at the same level as in 1750.

Year	Money wages	÷ Price index	× 100 = Real wages
1750	$6.00	100	$6.00
1760	6.75	117	5.71
1770	7.50	125	6.00

Interpretation of any real income series is complicated by the possibilities of error either in the income figures or in the price index. It should be kept in mind that either set of figures may have errors of **inclusiveness** and of **weighting.** Some of the early estimates of changes in real wages during the Industrial Revolution were based on existing data on the wage rates of construction workers in London and on the prices paid by certain institutions for selected foods. Obviously, this did not measure either the wages received by all types of workers or the prices of all goods consumed by workers. The wage series, incidentally, is not a total income series. It can only tell what the rate of pay was for one worker working full time. It cannot tell how regularly the worker worked or how much other members of the family worked. The weighting of a price index would also assume that the types and proportions of goods consumed remained constant.

The early historians' interpretations of the effects of the Industrial Revolution were based largely upon poor data. Recent studies use much more comprehensive data. While some of the weaknesses of data and indexes still remain to throw some doubt on the accuracy of estimates of real wage trends, the preponderance of ancillary evidence shows that the real income of the bulk of working people must have risen. Production rose faster than population; the bulk of the production was in goods consumed by the masses; the types and qualities of consumer goods improved; health improved (death rates fell); more family members worked as more women and children were employed; and the migration of rural population was predominantly toward the new industrial cities rather than toward London.

REFERENCES

R. L. Andreano, ed., *New Views on American Economic Development* (Cambridge, Mass.: Schenkman Publishing Co., Inc., 1965).

C. M. Andrews, *The Colonial Period in American History,* vol. 2 (New Haven, Conn.: Yale University Press, 1936).

W. T. Baxter, *The House of Hancock* (Cambridge, Mass.: Harvard University Press, 1945).

P. W. Bidwell and J. I. Falconer, *History of Agriculture in the Northern United States 1620–1860* (Washington, D.C.: Carnegie Institution, 1925).

C. Bridenbaugh, *Cities in the Wilderness* (New York: Ronald Press, 1938).

———, *Cities in Revolt* (New York: Alfred A. Knopf, 1955).

S. Bruchey, *The Roots of American Economic Growth, 1607–1861* (New York: Harper & Row, Publishers, 1968).

M. Curtis, *The Making of an American Community* (Stanford, Calif.: Stanford University Press, 1959).

P. Deane and W. A. Cole, *British Economic Growth, 1688–1959* (New York: Cambridge University Press, 1967).

E. Domar, "The Causes of Slavery or Serfdom: A Hypothesis," *JEH,* March 1970.

R. E. Gallman, "Pace and Pattern of American Economic Growth," in *American Economic Growth,* ed. L. E. Davis et al. (New York: Harper & Row, Publishers, 1972).

L. C. Gray, *History of Agriculture in the Southern United States to 1860* (Washington, D.C.: Carnegie Institution, 1933).

L. M. Hacker, "The First American Revolution," in *Issues in American Economic History,* ed. G. D. Nash (Lexington, Mass.: D. C. Heath and Co., 1964).

J. R. Hicks, *A. Theory of Economic History* (New York: Oxford University Press, 1969).

J. R. T. Hughes, "The Cost to America of British Imperial Policy, Comment," *AER,* May 1969.

———, *Industrialization and Economic History* (New York: McGraw-Hill Book Co., 1970).

E. R. Johnson et al., *History of Domestic and Foreign Commerce of the United States,* (Washington, D.C.: Carnegie Institution, 1915).

D. C. Klingaman, "The Development of the Coastwise Trade of Virginia in the Late Colonial Period," *VMHB,* January 1969.

———, "The Significance of Grain in the Development of the Tobacco Colonies," *JEH,* June 1969.

———, "Food Surpluses and Deficits in the American Colonies, 1768–72, *JEH,* April 1971.

———, "The Coastwise Trade of Colonial Massachusetts," *EIHC,* forthcoming.

K. Lockridge, "Land, Population and the Evolution of New England Society, 1630–1790," *PP,* April 1968.

D. C. North, *Growth and Welfare in the American Past* (Englewood Cliffs, N.J.: Prentice-Hall, Inc., 1966).

C. P. Nettels, *The Roots of American Civilization* (New York: Appleton-Century-Crofts, Inc., 1938).

J. F. Shepherd, "Commodity Exports from the British North American Colonies," *EEH*, Fall 1970.

J. F. Shepherd and G. M. Walton, "Estimates of 'Invisible' Earnings in the Balance of Payments of the British North American Colonies, 1768–1772," *JEH*, June 1969.

———, *Shipping, Maritime Trade and the Economic Development of Colonial North America* (New York: Cambridge University Press, 1972).

J. F. Shepherd and S. H. Williamson, "The Coastal Trade of British North American Colonies, 1768–1772" (Bureau of Business and Economic Research, University of Iowa, November 1971).

G. R. Taylor, "American Economic Growth before 1840," in Andreano, cited above.

U.S. Department of Commerce, *Historical Statistics of the United States* (Washington, D.C.: U.S. Government Printing Office, 1960).

G. M. Walton, "New Evidence on Colonial Commerce," *JEH*, September 1968.

———, "The New Economic History and the Burdens of the Navigation Acts," *EHR*, November 1971.

R. W. Weiss, "The Issue of Paper Money in the Colonies, 1720–1774," *JEH*, December 1970.

S. Wolfbein, *Work in American Society* (Glenwood, Ill.: Scott, Foresman and Co., 1971).

Part II

Early national growth:
1790–1860

5 EXPANSION THROUGH TRADE

Political independence did not bring economic independence. The U.S. economy remained predominantly agricultural and closely tied to the European market. The domestic market was small, and buyers and sellers were scattered and isolated by poor roads and hazardous coastal trade routes. Consequently, the American market was in effect smaller than its 1790 population of 3.9 million suggests. In the area of U.S. jurisdiction, population density was only 4.5 persons per square mile (versus 57 in 1970), and only 5 percent of the Americans lived in or near cities.

No wonder, then, that, as in colonial days, the chief commercial crops had to be sold abroad and most manufactured goods had to be imported. In short, the Nation's high per capita income depended on international trade, and continued economic growth hinged on its ability to maintain overseas markets.

In 1789, the American economy was not prepared to industrialize. At least a half century had to pass before it appeared that the United States might become a great industrial power. Yes, consumer incomes were high, there was an active, aggressive commercial class, political institutions favored business enterprise, and ample natural resources needed in manufacturing were either at hand or awaiting discovery inland.

However, these advantages had to be combined with an adequate supply of labor and capital and a body of entrepreneurs who understood the technology and management implications of the Industrial Revolution—these were endowments America lacked. What's more, even if America had had all the inputs required to establish a manufacturing sector, the home market would have been too small to absorb its output and England's head start and mercantilist restrictions would have shut America out of overseas markets.

The early development of the U.S. economy involved a long period of rapid and volatile extensive growth with a higher long-term growth rate of per capita GNP than characterized the 1700s. Just prior to the

Civil War, manufacturing growth accelerated sharply. But during the bulk of the period before the War Between the States, expansion depended upon agricultural, trade, and transportation improvements, with an important assist from a relative shift of labor from agriculture to manufacturing.

The sectoral developments underlying growth in the antebellum period were highly interrelated. However, the importance of each sector is great enough to warrant separate chapters on trade, agriculture, and manufacturing. In this chapter we will discuss the period of the Confederation, then summarize the trends that characterized the total economy during the period and analyze the influence of international trade upon our development pattern.

THE CONFEDERATION

We have considered the economic issues related to the Revolution and, in chapter 3, the political developments associated with early independence. Now is the time to review the course of growth and development during and after the War of Independence.

The Revolution

The Revolution appears to have significantly affected extensive and intensive growth, though we do not have precise income data to support this assertion. Extensive growth was stunted by the reduction of factor inputs associated with the war. Military action:

1. reduced voluntary immigration and the importation of slaves,
2. induced the emigration of Tories, many of whom were entrepreneurs,
3. tapped manpower in the most productive age brackets for the army, and
4. led to the destruction of farming, urban, and maritime capital.

Thus, although America's high birthrates in the 1760s meant that large numbers continued to enter the work force, the war's destruction, manpower requirements, and impact on immigration slowed expansion of the economy. Given the close connection between population size and total economic activity, the reduction of the rate of population growth probably constitutes a lower-bound estimate of the war's negative impact on expansion. Here are the changes in population growth rates for 1770–80 versus 1760–70:

	1770–80	*1760–70*
Total population growth	29%	35%
Free population growth	31	33
Slave population growth	25	41

No matter which of these dimensions of population growth we compare for the two periods, expansion was significantly reduced in the Revolutionary decade.

If per capita income actually declined during the Revolution, economic expansion would have been reduced by even more than the above figures suggest. There are several indicators that point in this direction.

Domestic and foreign trade was disrupted by the British, so Americans had to turn to inefficient domestic sources of manufactured products. The printing press—the Continental Congress substitute for taxes—produced a hyperinflation which disrupted trading patterns, forced people into barter exchanges, and turned the energies of entrepreneurs into speculative activities that were less productive than their peacetime pursuits. In addition, the manpower and other resource costs associated with the war meant reduced inputs per capita.

It seems somewhat surprising that the Revolution didn't have an even greater negative impact on economic welfare—Britain was, after all, the world's leading power. British strategy provides a partial explanation. It was so inept that the Americans could get by with fielding no more than 21,000 men at one time, although 400,000 served during the eight-years conflict. The Americans' familiarity with the terrain and Indian fighting also helped. The structure of the economy completes our explanation: a major portion of economic activity was of the nonmarket variety that the war left untouched.

Postwar adjustment

Our earlier description of the post-Revolutionary economy and the political problems of the Confederation certainly suggests an economy in dire straits. However, close inspection of the fragmentary data available for the period shows that the economy muddled through while the Founding Fathers were building a nation-state out of a loose confederation.[1]

Douglass North has summarized the data as revealing "an economy reorganizing itself, developing its own new export sector and earnings, and gradually emerging from the problems of readjustment throughout the 1780s and early 1790s."[2]

What were the forces that made this kind of summary judgment possible? The reasoning goes as follows. The largely self-sufficient farming units were barely affected by the political and economic turmoil that characterized the market sector. In the market sector, changes in exports and imports of goods and services dictated movements of total income and per capita welfare. Region by region, producers found new

---

[1] For an appraisal of the data in light of earlier and conflicting studies of the period see North (1966), 2d citation, pp. 57–63; see David also.

[2] North (1966), 2d citation, p. 63.

exports to replace those that British commercial policy ruled out, and import prices fell slightly while export prices rose significantly.[3]

Tobacco, wheat, and flour prices received by American exporters were markedly higher after the war than in the early 1770s. Americans gained from having direct access to Amsterdam's tobacco market and by the reopening of the British home market to American shipping. The West Indies food trade was reestablished, in part by smuggling, and expanded in the non-British islands. West Indies food exports were periodically supplemented by European demand in poor harvest years. On the import side, direct access to foreign sources and a slight general downtrend in prices benefited American buyers.

New England ship sales fell tremendously while the percentage of American cargo carried in U.S. ships declined. After the Peace of Paris, Britain opened its home ports but not its colonial ports to American shipping. There are no comprehensive data on shipping earnings for the period. However, North's survey of contemporary accounts reveals a badly depressed maritime sector. As you would expect, the effects of this depression were very intense in New England. On the other hand, New England's exports to Britain increased as compared with the prewar period, and the cod industry eventually grew beyond its prewar size. Nevertheless, on balance, New England had to pay for some of its imports by exporting specie.

The former Middle Colonies expanded their processing of grain products and exported some of their manufactured goods to the South, displacing English sellers. Export earnings of the Middle Atlantic states followed the ups and downs of the European cereal market. Earnings from shipping suffered because it was no longer legal to sail to the British West Indies.

The Upper South continued to expand its grain production and resumed the exportation of tobacco with general prosperity as a result. But the Lower South lost its indigo bounty. So in spite of continued rice culture and expanded tobacco planting, export earnings per capita fell precipitously as compared with prewar days.

How did these sectoral adjustments affect the overall economy? We can assume that in the nonmarket sector the pace of very gradual per capita income growth through farm-making and improvement continued. In the market sector, the growth of export earnings and declining import prices stimulated the economy, but population growth outstripped aggregate gains. At the same time, the outflow of specie produced domestic price deflation and consequent burdens on debtors who had contracted debts in the inflationary wartime years. Further, the Confederation was plagued by a variety of economic problems including its obligations to veterans, the war debt, and commercial warfare among the states.

---

[3] For a regional analysis of the foreign sector's development in the period 1784–92, see Bjork; the following analysis is a summary of Bjork's findings.

Thus, although the early adjustment to life outside the Empire was impressive in view of the odds, recovery was not so powerful that it overwhelmed the debilitating effects of political and economic disunity. There were, indeed, strong economic reasons for a constitutional convention.

OVERALL TRENDS

Rapid economic expansion was the dominant characteristic of nearly everything about the American economy in the first half of the 19th century. All the resource inputs increased rapidly—additions were made to the Nation's territory and natural resources; population continued to double every generation; and wealth in the form of capital goods of all sorts accumulated at a rapid pace. Not surprisingly, total output expanded very rapidly as well. But what is most significant is the fact that output expanded faster than inputs increased.

Output trends and fluctuations

Over the period 1790–1860 total output grew at an average compound interest rate of 4.3 percent per annum. As compared with other economies of the day, this was certainly a very respectable rate of expansion. Further, when you compare this 70-year span with the long-term expansion rate of the economy in the 20th century, it turns out to be somewhat phenomenal—fully a third higher than the 1900–1960 rate of 3.12 percent.[4]

In the first two or three decades of the period, the United States was still adjusting to existence as an independent entity. Over an expansion course that was marked by violent fluctuations caused by shifts in the winds of war, the new nation developed new exterior markets and modified its production and internal trade patterns. Over the balance of the antebellum years, rapid expansion was sustained by the continued rise of King Cotton followed by significant increases in manufacturing activity. (See 5–1.)

Per capita output also grew rapidly for the times. In 1790, output per person was about $50 in 1840 prices. By 1860, the figure had grown to $122. Although international comparisons are difficult, given the data problems, it appears that we slipped slightly compared with Britain.[5] Qualitative evidence suggests that we gained on the rest of the world.

The average growth rate implied by these figures is 1.3 percent per annum, which is only slightly off the 1.5 percent of the 1840–1860 period

---

[4] Expansion rates are for net national product and are computed from data reported in Gallman (1966, 1972) and David (1967).

[5] Gallman (1972), pp. 40–41.

5-1.   Total and per capita real income, selected years, 1710–1840
(in 1840 prices)

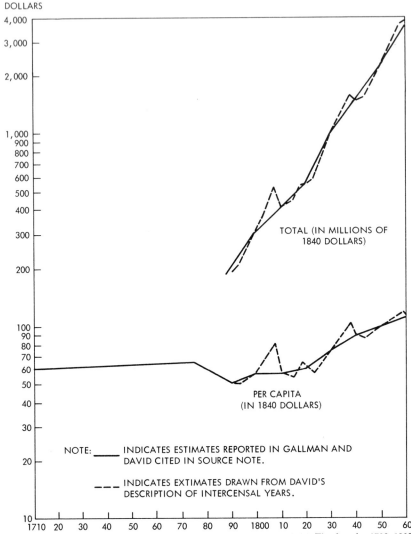

DOLLARS

TOTAL (IN MILLIONS OF
1840 DOLLARS)

PER CAPITA
(IN 1840 DOLLARS)

NOTE: ———— INDICATES ESTIMATES REPORTED IN GALLMAN AND
DAVID CITED IN SOURCE NOTE.

———— INDICATES EXTIMATES DRAWN FROM DAVID'S
DESCRIPTION OF INTERCENSAL YEARS.

1710 20   30   40   50   60   70   80   90 1800 10   20   30   40   50   60

Sources: David (1967), table 8 and n. 69; Gallman (1972), pp. 22–24. The data for 1790–1860
are net national product (= income) figures derived by applying David's indexes for gross domestic
product to Gallman's net national product/head data for 1840; and for 1710, 1774, and 1840 the
data are Gallman's estimates.

and is vastly better than the colonial performance of less than 0.5 percent. (See 5–1.)

These data at first lead you to think that much of the rapid expansion
in output per person was attributable to postwar recovery. However,
we think this overstates the importance of the war and understates the
adjustments required by having to go it alone as a new and small nation

in a mercantilist world. Recovery from war suggests restoration of an old order, but America was forced to construct a new order when independence was achieved. Within the constraints of that new order, a new export base had to be established.

Per capita income followed the fluctuations of the total economy. In 1793, shortly after the Constitution was ratified, economic growth was accelerated as the outbreak of the Napoleonic Wars increased American international trade and shipping earnings. The resulting boom peaked in 1807, when political and commercial isolation followed by the War of 1812 cut deeply into overseas earnings. A trade boom of short duration followed the end of the War of 1812 and the reopening of international trade.

In the 1820s, a second acceleration in economic growth set in. In this subperiod, America's small manufacturing sector began to recover from the depression that came with the flood of British imports after the War of 1812. Manufacturing recovery plus the revival of shipping and resumed expansion of key exports, such as cotton and foodstuffs, produced an expansion that lasted until the Panic of 1837.

A third surge in economic growth began in the late 1840s, with manufacturing for the market as the prime mover. This acceleration lost its steam in the late 1850s, and total economic activity reached a cylical peak just prior to the Civil War.

Overall, the economy transformed itself by stages—from a shipping nation looking for an export staple, to an export-oriented economy in which cotton was king, to an economy in which a burgeoning mechanized manufacturing sector demonstrated clearly that King Cotton and handcraft manufacturing were deposed.

The regional economic structure of the Nation reflected these developments. The South concentrated on cotton exports and imported manufactured goods and business services from the rest of the world. The Northeast exported manufactured goods and services to the South and the West (what we now call the Midwest). The West produced foodstuffs and shipped them chiefly to the Northeast and to a minor degree to the Mississippi Delta region in exchange for manufactured output. Clearly, U.S. development involved a regional division of labor based on the productivity advantages of the respective regions.[6]

Input growth

Over the antebellum period, total inputs grew rapidly—3.1 percent per annum—but not as rapidly as the 4.3 percent by which total output

[6] The job of linking the events of the 1790–1860 period with the income, employment, and output data that have been pieced together over the past ten years has not been completed. Thus, inconsistencies that are minor for our immediate purposes appear in the sources on which the above estimates are based; the sources are David (1967), pp. 186–88, and Gallman (1972), pp. 25–42.

expanded.[7] The gap between the two figures was filled by productivity increases from a variety of sources—shifts in the industrial allocation of labor, more efficient labor and capital, new production methods, more nonhuman inputs per worker, and improved economic organization traceable to expansion of the economy. Let's look at the forces that explain economic expansion over the period, then turn to the question of productivity increases.

The peace treaty with England established the claim of the United States to all of the western territory between the Appalachian Mountains and the Mississippi River from the Great Lakes to Florida. Compared with the initial territory of the Thirteen Colonies, the U.S. land area doubled at the close of the Revolution. Subsequent territorial additions tripled that area by the middle of the 19th century.

The resulting wide bank of territory stretching across the continent from coast to coast provided a rich natural resource potential. But natural resources do not contribute to production until people gain access to them and bring them into use. Therefore, the frontier line provides a better indication of the expanded employment of land. In 1800, the frontier line hardly extended beyond the western slopes of the Appalachian Mountains except in Kentucky and Tennessee. By 1860, it extended beyond the Mississippi, and isolated settled areas had developed on the West Coast. (See 5–2.)

The initial spread of western settlement was shaped by both geo-

5–2. Expanding land area

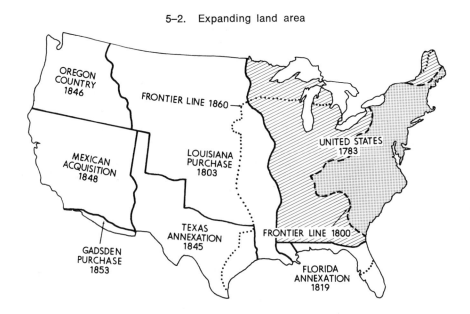

---

[7] See Gallman (1972), table 2.3, for the input growth rate (the period is actually 1805–40).

graphic and political barriers. Directly after the Revolution, Indian hostility was encouraged by the British in the Great Lakes area and by the Spanish in the regions near Florida. Early pioneers, therefore, moved over the Appalachian Mountains into the safer central regions. Some moved through the Cumberland Gap to settle along the Ohio River near Louisville and along the Cumberland River at Nashville. Others moved across near the Maryland-Pennsylvania border and settled in the Pittsburgh area.

The pioneers depended on the Mississippi River and its northern tributaries to ship their products to various markets through New Orleans. For a few years, the Spanish attempted to restrict the use of this port. But this barrier was removed by the Louisiana Purchase in 1803, shortly after the French had acquired certain Spanish colonies, including New Orleans. The War of 1812 finally ended Indian hostilities in the Great Lakes region, and shortly thereafter military action forced Spain to concede the Florida territories.

With these political barriers removed, rapid settlement occurred in both the Gulf and Great Lakes regions. The first wave of settlers came immediately after the War of 1812, between 1815 and 1819. Another surge westward occurred in the late 1820s and early 1830s. The opening of the Erie Canal in 1825 plus high wheat prices in the East induced large numbers of settlers to enter the vast grain-farming area near the Great Lakes. At the same time, high cotton prices caused a rapid expansion of cotton production in the Gulf States.

The final phase of territorial additions began with the push of a few pioneering settlers into foreign or disputed territories in the West. U.S. settlers who had established cotton farms and cattle ranches in Texas revolted against the Mexican government in 1836 and established the Republic of Texas. In 1845 Texas joined the Union as the 28th state. The northern boundary of the Oregon territory was settled by treaty with the British in 1846. Hunger for cotton land and President Polks' determination to acquire California and New Mexico brought on the Mexican War in 1846. The resulting treaty (1848) gave California to the United States just months before gold was discovered there.

Throughout the westward movement, revisions of federal land policy, as well as the relative abundance of land, made it increasingly easy for small farmers to acquire land. Some of the last vestiges of large feudal landholdings were ended by the seizure of Tory lands during the Revolution. Then, when the original states gave up their conflicting claims to the West, the federal government assumed ownership of the western territory and established a uniform policy for sale of land to individuals. The Land Ordinance of 1785 required dividing the Northwest Territory into rectangular townships of 36 square-mile (640-acre) sections. As we pointed out in chapter 3, a minimum of 640 acres had to be purchased at an auction price of not less than $1.00 an acre in cash. The Land Act of 1796 extended this system to all new territories, setting the minimum price per acre at $2.00 but allowing a year for payment.

Because it was difficult for small farmers to raise this much money, political pressure resulted in a gradual reduction of the initial cash requirement. In 1800, the minimum acreage was reduced to 320 acres, and half of the payment was to be made in cash, with the remainder due in four years. Because farmers had frequently failed to make later payments, as of 1820 full initial payment was required, but the minimum purchase was reduced to 80 acres at $1.25 an acre. In 1832 the minimum was cut to 40 acres, which meant that a man could buy a tract with as little as $50 in cash.

Part of the pressure for easier purchase came from the widespread practice of settling on land before it had been surveyed. While illegal, squatting was hard to prevent. The Preemption Act of 1841 finally gave squatters first right to purchase a quarter section of the land they occupied. The Graduation Act of 1854 also provided for a gradual lowering of the price of any land that long remained unsold. During the 1850s political agitation for making land free for small farmers increased.

Finally, the Homestead Act of 1862 provided 160 acres for a nominal fee to any adult citizen who would live on it and cultivate it for five years. Or he might purchase it immediately at $1.25 an acre. Title to such lands was, of course, frequently purchased by speculators or large farmers.

In spite of the rapid extension of territory, population and the labor force grew even faster (see 5–3, columns 3 and 6). Thus, the history of America's westward movement was also a history of increasing population density. In spite of vast additions to territory, the United States

5–3.   Population and labor force trends

Year	Land area (million square miles) (1)	Population (millions) (2)	Density (persons per square mile) (3)	Percent of population in: Non-Atlantic states (4)	Urban areas (5)	Labor force (6)
1790	0.86	3.93	4.5	4.3	5.1	NA
1800	0.86	5.30	6.1	8.7	6.1	32.2
1810	1.68	7.22	4.3	16.3	7.3	32.3
1820	1.75	9.62	5.6	24.4	7.2	32.9
1830	1.75	12.90	7.4	29.9	8.7	32.5
1840	1.75	17.12	9.8	38.7	10.8	33.3
1850	2.94	23.26	7.9	43.9	15.2	35.5
1860	2.97	31.51	10.6	50.4	19.7	35.5

NA: Not Available.
SOURCES: U.S. Dept. of Commerce, pp. 7–8, and David (1967) table 3.

increased its population per square mile from 4.5 in 1790 to 10.6 in 1860.

Despite a persistent trend of declining white birthrates, the Americans carried over their amazing fecundity from colonial days. Labor shortages, the family-farm mode of production, and the benefits of good diet and robust health produced comparatively high birthrates and survival rates among infants. Consequently, native-born population continued to grow at rates that would have doubled the population every 25 to 30 years.

Immigration gave natural population increases a healthy assist although not until the last two decades of the antebellum years, when accelerated growth in labor demand pulled the starving Irish and land-hungry (and often politically persecuted) Germans to America. The net migration rate climbed slowly from 1805, when it was one person per thousand people, to 1835, when it was 3.3/1000. Then, between 1850 and 1860, it accelerated to 9.4/1000. At its 1850–60 peak, immigration accounted for one third of net population growth. Over the period 1820–60, about 5 million people came to the United States, compared with perhaps 22 million who were born here during the same time span. Although the data are not very reliable, it appears that from 1790 to 1820 perhaps 250,000 people came to the United States.[8]

Up to 1860, the westward movement consisted primarily of settlement in the central Mississippi Basin region. The proportion of the population living west of the Atlantic coastal states rose from 4.2 percent in 1790 to 50.4 percent by 1860. Very few people, however, were beyond the frontier line just west of the Mississippi. Further, in spite of the westward movement to settle vast new farming regions, the percentage of the population living in cities increased in every decade except between 1810 and 1820, the decade of the second war with Britain. American economic development from the beginning has been characterized as much by the "great urban movement" as by the "great westward movement." (See 5–3.)

The growth of the labor force exceeded both the population and the territorial expansion rates. By 1860, the labor force participation rate was 35.5 percent, compared with 32.2 percent in 1800. The 10 percent rise in the employed portion of the population is probably chiefly attributable to immigration, which tends to be concentrated among people of working age.

Americans also carried over their capital accumulation habits from colonial times. Heavy investment of time and energy were made both on the frontier and in settled regions to build and improve farms and plantations. The slave population, treated as capital by slaveowners, continued to grow through natural increase and smuggling.[9] In the cities,

---

[8] U.S. Department of Commerce, pp. 7, 48; for purposes of comparing births with immigration, we have assumed a birthrate of 50/1,000.

[9] The Constitution forbade importation of slaves as of 1807.

social overhead capital formation and manufacturing plant and equipment investment became the bases of urban development.

For data on capital we have only estimates of the total value of "tangible, reproducible wealth" for 1805 and 1850. These figures reflect the stock of man-made economic assets—such as agricultural and manufacturing machinery, wagons, factory and farm buildings, and houses. They exclude land values, ownership claims (such as debts and patents), military equipment and facilities, and semidurable or perishable civilian goods inventories. Adjusting for price changes, they may be expressed in real values, as though all were purchased in the same year. These estimates show a tenfold increase between 1805 and 1850, whereas population increased only fourfold in the same period.

On a per capita basis, real wealth almost *tripled* according to these estimates, rising from $166 in 1805 to $441 in 1850. In comparison, real income per capita rose only a bit more than two thirds in the same period.[10]

Sources of productivity increases

We are interested in productivity growth because of its impact on the level of living that Americans experienced in the years between the ratification of the Constitution and the Civil War. At this point, though, we stress that without productivity increases the antebellum period would have been characterized by economic growth. Why? Simply because inputs grew faster than population—recall that over the period the portion of the population in the labor force rose by about 10 percent, population density grew by over 100 percent, and capital per head increased by almost 300 percent. According to Gallman's estimates, productive factors grew at 3.3 percent per year between 1774 and 1840. Consequently, inputs per person grew 0.3 percent per year over that stretch of years. Thus, if productivity of inputs had remained constant, economic growth would have averaged out at about the same rate as during the pre-Revolutionary period.[11]

We have very little data on which to base estimates of productivity increases attributable to various sources. However, we can use Gallman's estimates to get a rough notion as to what elements dominated productivity growth. We must confine most of our analysis to the years between 1810 and 1840 because of data limitations. Over that span, income per person grew from $57 to $90; and $5 of the $33 increase was attributable to the per capita increase in productive factors. The balance, $28, was generated by productivity advances. Gallman has been able to isolate the effect of two contributions to output growth during this span—move-

---

[10] For wealth estimates see Goldsmith, p. 272.

[11] See Gallman (1972), pp. 23–25, for input growth estimates.

ment to better land and the movement of workers to manufacturing jobs.

If the farm/nonfarm division of the labor force had remained constant between 1810 and 1840, while the opening of new land in the West had proceeded according to history, per capita income would have risen by $2. Western land was on the average more productive. Thus, for example, as cotton moved west into the Alabama black belt and the rich Mississippi Delta, the average farm unit became more productive in terms of output per worker.

Far more important than the regional shift of agricultural labor was the change in the proportion of workers in nonfarm occupations. In 1810 only 3.2 percent of all workers were in manufacturing, compared with 8.8 percent in 1840. Similarly, all nonfarm jobs were only 19.1 percent in 1810 and grew to 36.9 percent in 1840. Given that labor income per worker was much higher in the nonfarm sector in 1840—$267 versus $140—it is easy to see how the relative concentration of labor force growth in nonfarm occupations would increase productivity. Gallman estimates that the shift in the labor force's concentration accounted for $9 of the period's per capita income growth.[12]

So far we have accounted for $11 of the $28 advance in productivity. What of the remaining $17? We cannot express the other factors that affected productivity in precise quantitative terms. However, we can cite forces that played important roles. Remember as you read the list that follows that the various entries are not mutually exclusive—items overlap in ways that aren't easy to unravel conceptually, let alone separate quantitatively.

1.   The growth in size of the American economy opened up a variety of development options through scale economies. Certain types of social overhead capital became economic as the economy grew; e.g., roads and later canals and railroads became practical as the rise in population density guaranteed a socially profitable number of users. Reorganization of economic activity was made possible as population and national income increased the volume of transactions—specialist middlemen and new financial institutions improved the efficiency of markets and thereby lowered transaction risks and costs. The urbanization that we discussed earlier was one of the more obvious signs of scale economies at work.

Perhaps scale economies influenced manufacturing more than any other sector of the economy. As American markets grew, the potential sales volume of the textile and other manufacturing industries increased significantly. New firms were formed, and Americans found themselves buying domestically produced products at prices at least competitive with imports. This process of displacing imports with domestically produced products is known as *import substitution* and is a classic phenome-

---

[12] For discussion of Gallman's method and results, see Gallman (1972), pp. 25–29.

non in developing economies. At the same time, improved transportation knitted the isolated and growing interior markets together and made possible replacing high-cost handcraft manufactures with products produced in centralized factories using the modern industrial method. Factory employment increased 20-fold from 1810 to 1860.[13] In short, America imported the Industrial Revolution.

Scale economies did not leave farming unaffected by any stretch of the imagination. As greater numbers of farmsteads were established at the frontier and as settled areas filled up, roads, canals, and railroads were built. These enabled self-sufficient farmers to specialize increasingly in money crops that were designated for export to other regions and outside the United States. This meant that farmers could concentrate on their most productive crops and activities.

2. The economy underwent a steady process of capital deepening as is witnessed by the fact that per capita real wealth (business and private capital) grew by a factor of three, whereas income per head increased by only two thirds. In agriculture alone, capital inputs grew at 3.34 percent per year, while land under cultivation and labor increased at 2.78 and 2.37 percent, respectively. At the same time, farm output grew by 3.11 percent per year.[14] Thus, capital deepening was associated with increased output per unit of labor and land.

Technological innovation and/or the adoption of known capital-intensive techniques enabled capital to take on jobs that were performed by workers in earlier decades. The relative displacement of labor enabled total output to grow more rapidly than the labor force or the population. On the farm, capital deepening released a portion of the rural population for work in nonfarm jobs. In the factory, capital deepening supplemented natural labor force increases and migration from rural to urban areas.

3. Technological innovation improved production processes in general. Quite apart from its role in making possible capital equipment that was designed specifically to conserve labor, new technology increased the output that could be obtained from all productive resources. Interchangeable parts made possible a high degree of division of labor, thereby permitting the mechanization of certain operations and reducing waste. Consequently, the production process became more capital intensive, and all inputs were reduced for each unit of output. In farming, improved plows, better livestock breeds, and more enlightened management produced the same kinds of results.

In summary, over the antebellum years real per capita income grew from $60 to $122 because:

1. productive resources grew more rapidly than population;
2. in relative terms, labor and capital shifted from agriculture to the more productive manufacturing sector;

---

[13] Lebergott, table 1 and pp. 178–79.
[14] See Gallman (1972) for agricultural productivity estimates.

3. increasingly, farm units became specialized and manufacturing moved out of the household and the handcraft shops;
4. the distribution of farming shifted to more productive land;
5. technological innovation and scale economies raised productivity in both the farm and nonfarm sectors of the economy;
6. capital deepening increased the productivity of labor and capital; and
7. innovations in economic organization improved the efficiency of markets and lowered the costs and risks associated with transactions.

Now that we have reviewed the broad trends that characterized the economy over the 1790–1860 period, we can analyze the role of the foreign sector in the economic development of the United States.

EARLY TRADE FLUCTUATIONS, 1789–1815

In chapter 1 we discussed the importance of foreign trade in the development of an economy whose markets are small compared with the optimum production rates of various industries. Without the opportunity to specialize and trade with the rest of the world, a small economy is liable to remain in the doldrums generation after generation, eking out a hand-to-mouth existence with the agricultural sector dominant and handcraft industry as its chief source of manufactured commodities.

After the Revolution, the Americans naturally sought to return to international commerce as buyers and sellers. Individually they sought new opportunities, and in discovering them they jointly developed a new export base for the American economy. Consequently, for several generations after the Revolution, the United States was very dependent upon foreign trade and thus much affected by world trade policies and international strife.

In addition to providing development opportunities, the foreign trade sector periodically presented serious economic problems to the fledgling nation. Overall, however, the evidence suggests that trade was the key factor behind American development in most of the antebellum years. Prosperity based on trade generated the capital accumulation and changes in economic organization upon which later growth hinged.

Early trade came from serving the world as a merchant and carrier, a gigantic mercantile and shipping concern. Later trade was based on King Cotton. Perhaps a quick review of the trade structure will provide you with the reference points necessary to appreciate the significance of trade to early U.S. development.

Although the bulk of the colonial population was engaged in high-subsistence general farming, recall that a market sector did grow and prosper during colonial times. As we pointed out in chapter 4, the nature of the market economy varied in the three colonial regions according to the dictates of their respective natural resource endowments.

Remember that independence changed the ground rules of American external economic relations. As we noted in chapter 4, until the middle 1790s massive importation plus a prolonged slump in exports played hob with the American economy. In the South, British markets for tobacco, rice, indigo, and naval stores were restricted or eliminated when the sword of British mercantilism was turned against the Americans. In the North, British restrictions against exports to England and the West Indies depressed the whaling, fur, crude iron, shipping and shipbuilding, fishing, and milling industries. Increased trade with the French failed to offset the loss of British sales. What's more, the end of British protection again drew American shipping to the attention of the Barbary pirates. Before the Constitution, the attempts of individual states to retaliate against the British and to protect American manufactures with tariffs were futile at best.

Neutrality prosperity

In the 30 years after 1790, two favorable lines of economic development revived the economy and helped prepare the way for later growth. The Napoleonic Wars brought an immediate but temporary northern boom in shipping and shipbuilding. Southern agriculture was revived for a longer period by a shift to cotton which became increasingly important as time went by.

The wars between France and England began in 1793 and lasted until 1815. Since nations at war tend to purchase more supplies from other nations in order to supply their armies, build up their industries, and make up for losses, the United States enjoyed a rising world demand for both northern and southern exports. Exports of American goods doubled by 1795. While this level was not maintained in the next few years, it was achieved again after 1800.

American-owned ships benefited, of course, from the increased volume of exports but the greater part of the shipping boom was in reexports. Goods produced abroad were brought to American ports and reloaded into American ships for export to the warring European nations—Americans thus served both France and England as merchant middlemen and shippers. The ships of a neutral nation were not subject to attack by the nations at war; so both sides relied upon neutral ships to help bring supplies from their West Indies colonies into their own ports. The volume of foreign goods carried soon became much larger than the expanded volume of American goods. Total exports more than doubled by 1795; and by 1805 total exports were more than five times as large as in 1792. (See 5–4.)

Europe's ills brought the Americans prosperity. The protracted European wars provided the United States with a new export base—mercantile and shipping services—which, although temporary, proved strategic to later growth. Production and the prices of farm products rose.

5–4.   Neutrality trade boom

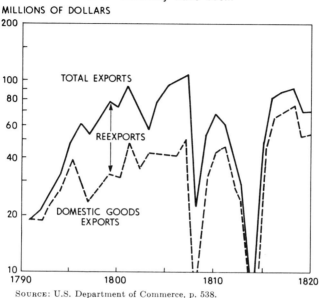

SOURCE: U.S. Department of Commerce, p. 538.

Demand for new ships increased among American as well as foreign merchants; the annual tonnage of new ships built after 1800 was five or six times as large as it had been in the good years prior to the Revolutionary War.

Most important, undoubtedly, was the income earned from shipping. Net freight earnings rose almost six times from 1792 to 1807. These earnings were quite large, amounting to about one third of the total value of exports. Why? Because they were earned by carrying imports as well as exports. Also, freight charges in early times were high in relation to the value of goods carried. In turn, shipping income was an important part of GNP, as single sources of earnings go; perhaps 4 to 6 percent of national output was accounted for by international shipping activity during these years.[15]

At the same time that the North was prospering from a boom in neutral shipping, southern agriculture began to revive with a shift to cotton as the major export crop. Georgia and South Carolina suffered most from the decline in indigo production and low prices for rice. In Virginia, low tobacco prices between 1791 and 1796 exacted a heavy economic toll. A new crop was badly needed.

Cotton showed little promise at first because of the large amount

---

[15] Computed on the basis of data reported in U.S. Department of Commerce, p. 536; North (1966), 3d citation, p. 249; and Lipsey, p. 554. See North (1966), 3d citation, chaps. 2–5, for a review of trade and the national economy over these years.

of hand labor required to remove the seeds from the lint of the short-staple variety as compared with the labor required to grow the crop. It took one person a whole day to clean one pound of cotton. Consequently, the acreage devoted to cotton was limited by the amount of cotton a slave force could clean in the winter months. However, in 1793, Eli Whitney's cotton gin removed this bottleneck. It enabled one worker to clean 50 pounds a day. The cost of American cotton was drastically reduced at the same time that demand for cotton was rising by leaps and bounds. England's textile industry, which embodied the modern industrial method, had developed a voracious demand for cotton as a result of lower prices and rising income in England and its overseas markets.

Cotton quickly became the major export crop of the South. From just a few thousand bales in 1793, production rose tenfold by 1800 and doubled again in the next decade. The value of cotton exports in 1811 was more than 50 percent larger than that of tobacco exports. (See 5–5.) On the eve of the War of 1812, about three fourths of cotton production was concentrated in Georgia and South Carolina; another 19 percent was produced in North Carolina and Virginia; and the rest, about 6 percent, was produced in middle Tennessee and the lower Mississippi Valley.

The new export crop also proved very profitable to farmers. Around 1800, cotton could be produced at a profit if the price was 12 cents a pound or more. Prices during the early years were actually very much higher, reaching a peak of 44 cents a pound in 1801 and averaging 15 to 19 cents a pound during the next two decades. Many small farmers moved up into a prospering middle class. Production, however, relied heavily upon unskilled slave labor. The price of slaves soon tripled. Therefore, only the most successful farmers and those with the best lands could afford to expand into large plantations.

The North's neutrality prosperity was short-lived. Trade slumped in 1803, when England and France were briefly at peace. Not long after the Napoleonic Wars resumed, both sides began to deny neutral ships access to enemy ports, and many American ships were seized by both France and Britain. President Jefferson attempted to retaliate through the Embargo Act (passed in December 1807), which forbade our ships to trade with Europe. This hurt our own trade so much in 1808 that it was repealed early in 1809. Conflict with England over our neutral rights, as well as trouble on our western borders, led finally to a declaration of war against England in June 1812.

Although the wartime interruption of trade caused a general depression, it provided a further stimulus to domestic manufacturing. Cut off from English textile goods and faced with a large surplus of cotton, American merchants seized the opportunity to invest their capital in cotton spinning mills. Merchants had accumulated a large stock of finan-

5–5.   Tobacco and cotton exports

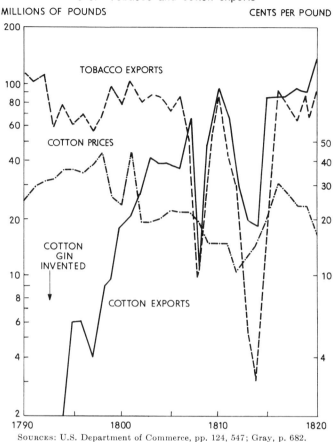

MILLIONS OF POUNDS

CENTS PER POUND

SOURCES: U.S. Department of Commerce, pp. 124, 547; Gray, p. 682.

cial capital in the lush trading years, which meant that funds to back new ventures were more plentiful. In 1807, 15 mills using copies of England's Arkwright machines were already in operation. By 1815, the number of American mills had grown to 213. In other industries, less dramatic but significant new ventures were launched. The preceding period of prosperity had increased consumer incomes and enlarged local markets. Cut off from English manufactured goods, American consumers bid up prices to levels which made production profitable for the less efficient American manufacturers.

While these beginnings in manufacturing were not quantitatively important in the national economy at first, within a few decades the new industries were to constitute a major source of national economic growth, and the experience gained in this brief period was invaluable. This is not to say, however, that cutting off the Americans from their comparative trade advantage increased economic welfare. Rather, the decline in income shown in 5–1 was not as drastic as it might have been. Imagine the consequences if no manufacturing investment had taken place to make possible the marketing of the cotton crop and the employment of hands idled by the interruption of international trade.

LATER TRADE TRENDS, 1815–60

After the war with England ended, in December 1814, a trade boom got underway that lasted until the slump of 1818–19. The boom involved an increase in both exports and imports, but the increase in imports was much larger. A pent-up wartime demand for English manufactured goods was matched by a drive by English sellers to dispose of surplus goods, restore their markets, and utilize their rapidly expanding capacity.

The import boom was also fed by loans and investments that ultimately expanded the production capacity of export crops in the South and West. High postwar cotton and wheat prices swelled farm profits. Starry-eyed settlers rushed to settle in the Mississippi and Ohio valleys. New farms needed capital for tools and for an initial consumer goods stake. Credit flowed from English merchants, American merchants in the Northeast, and the numerous new banks in the West. The purchase of goods by the new farmers at first exceeded their sale of products for export. Eventually, as supply expanded, falling prices brought a halt to farm prosperity and an increase in debts.

The Northeast did not participate in the postwar prosperity. Shipbuilding declined, and American ships again faced restrictions in trading with England and its colonies. The new manufacturing industries were even more drastically affected by the stiff competition of English imports that were lower in price and often better in quality. Transportation improvements had produced lower freight rates both internally and between the United States and its trading partners. The initial impact of lower freight rates was to intensify the British comparative advantage in manufacturing and thus bankrupt many of the American manufacturing firms that had gotten a "false start" in the period of interrupted trade.

Many cotton spinning mills closed, while the surviving mills tended to adopt the power loom and the more efficient integrated spinning and weaving operations common in England. Other industries also experienced the competition of English manufactured imports in domestic markets without a compensating enlargement of foreign markets. Only after the American market had grown significantly did American manufacturing join in the general expansion of the economy.

In this period the American economy acted out a scenario very much like that of the immediate post-Revolutionary period. In this case, instead of having to adjust to new conditions, the Americans had to resume production and trade patterns they had earlier found appropriate to life outside the British Empire. They were quite successful as you'll see.

The tariff issue

After the War of 1812, pressure for higher tariffs on imported manufactured goods produced a policy issue that was to be prominent for many decades. There were great disputes over tariffs because people with different economic interests were affected differently by tariffs.

In the Northeast, manufacturers and workers favored protection of their industries and jobs, although some northeastern merchants were more interested in handling expanded imports than in excluding them. Southern cotton and tobacco farmers were opposed to tariffs, which reduced the income they obtained from exports and raised the prices they paid on manufactured goods. Western opinion was at first on the side of higher tariffs. Many small manufacturers and craftsmen serving relatively isolated local markets in the West were under pressure from lower-priced manufactured goods being transported into their areas. Northern and western farmers were selling grain and meat products primarily in American cities; so they had an interest in any tariff measures that would increase incomes of city workers. The western clamor for cheaper land and for federal aid in building roads and canals also added political support to tariff proposals, because land sales and tariffs were the main sources of federal revenues and thus the means of financing any spending programs.

A series of tariff laws raised duties to historically high levels by the early 1830s and then progressively lowered them so that by the Civil War America was almost a free trade nation. The tariff rates passed in 1816, designed to help the new manufacturers of the beleaguered Northeast, were about double the prewar levels. The depression of 1819 stimulated political pressures for protection so that rates were again raised in 1824 and reached a new peak in 1828. The South, however, objected strenuously, and so the rates were lowered progressively, beginning in 1833. An increase in 1842 was quickly reversed in 1846, and further reductions were made in 1857. Political embarrassment over surplus government revenues aided the enactment of the last two reductions.

While the duties applied to particular types of goods varied widely, the effects of these rate changes are reflected in a rough measure of the average rates—the ratio of duties collected to the value of imported goods subject to duty. This ratio, plotted in 5–6, was between 0.45 and 0.50 in the 1820s, reached a peak of 0.62 in 1830, and fell to 0.16 in 1859. A rapid increase in the proportion of goods imported free of duty in the mid-1830s lowered the effective average rates even more rapidly during that decade.

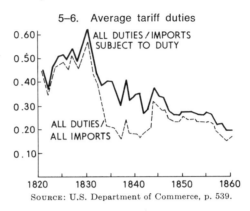

5–6.   Average tariff duties

SOURCE: U.S. Department of Commerce, p. 539.

The influence of tariffs on manufacturing industries was confined mostly to the years when new industries were getting started. High duties and falling prices after the War of 1812 tended to close out the cheapest coarse-quality cotton textile goods from England. American manufacturers were able to produce such goods for a growing domestic market while acquiring the skill and efficiency needed to produce higher quality goods. Other American industries probably benefited similarly in their early years.

Do not construe the foregoing as an argument in favor of tariffs—all we are saying is that the welfare losses associated with screening low-priced foreign goods from the American market were offset in part by the learning experience that protection made possible for faltering new industries. On the other hand, some industries may have used their tariff shields to deflect the advance of new techniques. Textiles were indeed characterized by productivity increases gained through learning by doing; yet David's exhaustive study of the textile industry led him to conclude that "the blanket subsidies provided for all domestic entrants into cotton production were—from the Tariff of 1824 onward—a largely redundant set of measures."

As the American economy grew, it was the expanding domestic market which provided new manufacturers with the opportunity and protection they needed; expanding sales provide a lot of leeway for learning from mistakes and making gradual improvements in efficiency.

As an alternative to tariff protection, in the early postwar years, a handful of government-subsidized pilot plants could have provided the necessary "laboratory course" for American entrepreneurs who wanted to operate mills using the new British techniques. On the basis of knowledge gained in pilot plants, new firms could have been formed whenever the American market grew large enough to justify more producers.[16]

---

[16] David (1970), pp. 599–600.

Expanding exports and imports

After the postwar boom and recession, trade activity reflected the accelerating expansion of the American economy. (See 5–7.) The rate

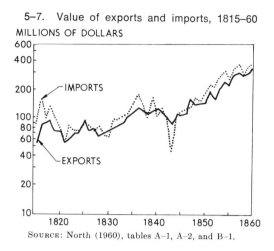

5–7. Value of exports and imports, 1815–60

MILLIONS OF DOLLARS

SOURCE: North (1960), tables A–1, A–2, and B–1.

of expansion, however, was probably steadier than the figures indicate, because prices continued their postwar decline until about the mid–1840s. If adjustment is made for declining export prices, their real value (or physical volume) appears to have increased at a steady rate between the War of 1812 and the Civil War. Overall, import prices fell faster than export prices so that the terms of trade moved in favor of America.[17]

The rapid expansion in the production and export of cotton played a major role in the rising total export trend. America had developed the export base required to replace shipping and mercantile services as an international breadwinner. As early as 1815, cotton came to about one third of the total value of exports. This share was boosted to more than half after the mid-1830s, when another great western land boom occurred. Exports of wheat and many other goods also expanded, but no other major export expanded as rapidly as cotton during the middle decades 1820 to 1840. In that period, American expansion was dominated by cotton production for export.

A three-way division of trade figures—into materials, foods, and man-ufactures—provides some indication of the changes that occurred during this long period of expansion. Among exports, materials rose in relative importance, primarily because of cotton. The relative shares of tobacco and lumber exports declined. Foods decline in importance, dragged down by the decline in the export shares of wheat and flour, rice, and fish. Meat products increased in importance but contributed only a small

[17] North (1966), pp. 91–93.

share of the total. Manufacturers declined initially, but after 1840 their percentage of export value began to increase.

Among imports, there was little change in the importance of food products. These consisted primarily of sugar, coffee, and tea. Initially, the share of materials—such as hides, iron, and chemicals—rose, while that of manufactures—especially textiles—decline but after 1840 these shares remained about the same. (See 5–8.)

5–8. Changes in composition of U.S. trade

	Exports			Imports		
	1820	1840	1860	1820	1840	1860
Distribution by type of goods:						
Materials.	61%	68%	69%	5%	12%	11%
Food.	23	18	16	30	31	30
Manufactures	16	14	15	65	57	59
Distribution by country:						
England	35	44	50	44	33	39
European	31	30	24	20	29	22
Americas	27	24	21	28	24	29
Other	7	2	5	8	14	10

SOURCE: U.S. Department of Commerce, pp. 545, 551–53.

A similar division of trade statistics by country of origin and destination shows a change in America's relations with other trading nations. England remained our largest supplier and market; but our imports from England declined in relative importance, while our exports to England increased in relative importance. As you probably anticipated, the relative increase in exports to England was largely attributable to the steady expansion of American raw cotton shipments to the English textile industry. England's relative decline as a supplier reflected the rising importance of trade with other countries on the American continent, a growth in imports from Europe, a declining dependence on English manufactured goods, and rising trade with the Far East. (See 5–8.)

The American shipbuilding industry began to thrive again during this period. The clipper ships were developed for fast travel from the Northeast around Cape Horn to the West Coast. Furs were taken from there to China, and tea, silks, and chinawares were brought back to the Northeast.

The major seaport cities also prospered from foreign trade, perhaps more than one would expect. Even though manufacturing industries were depressed immediately after the War of 1812, shipping, warehousing, transporting, and financing activities thrived. These were concentrated mainly in a few port cities—especially Boston, Baltimore, Philadelphia, and New York. The neutrality trade boom plus long colonial experience as a shipping and mercantile center had left the Northeast with a rich legacy of experience, know-how, institutions, and capital. All helped serve the region's function as a link between the English cotton mill and the southern cotton plantation.

A touch of mercantilist policy also helped the region. American laws excluding foreigners from coastal shipping among American cities encouraged foreign ships to unload at one port from which goods could be reshipped to other ports. This gave American shippers and merchants an advantage in the southern plantation areas, where northeastern merchants did much of the lending, wholesale merchandising, and cotton brokerage business. In this they displaced the British, who controlled the southern ports in colonial days.

New York developed certain advantages for shipping that soon enabled it to overtake Philadelphia as the largest American city. A regular public auction facilitated the quick disposal of cargoes not destined for particular merchants. Because of New York's central location it was also the logical terminal for the first regularly scheduled passenger-mail ships, or packets, which began operating between England and the United States in 1818. The opening of the Erie Canal in 1825 accelerated New York's growth as the terminal for the main route from the Great Lakes states to the East Coast.

How strong a monarch was King Cotton in the realm of trade? According to North, "direct income from the cotton trade was probably no more than 6 percent of any plausible estimate of national income which we might employ."[18] Yet Cotton's portion of total exports ranged from 40 to 60 percent over the period 1815–60, and exports gave us access to the rest of the world's wares. Six percent also looks quite large when well over half of an economy's resources are devoted just to keeping its people alive. But, perhaps most important, cotton determined the division of labor among regions that set the stage for the ascendancy of manufacturing. Monarchs rule—they decide the course of events; and King Cotton decided the course of America's development from the 1830s to the eve of the Civil War.

There are indications that after 1840 internal developments rather than foreign trade were becoming increasingly important in American expansion. Exports as a portion of GNP declined by about 10 percent during the three decades before the Civil War.[19] Cotton's share of exports remained about the same. As we noted earlier, the relative importance of agriculture declined, while that of manufacturing trade, and services

---

[18] North (1967), p. 69 (1966), 3d citation.
[19] Lipsey, p. 554.

increased. Given the agricultural bias of our exports, this meant that American production for domestic markets grew faster than export output. Another crude indication is the rising tonnage of domestic shipping. Coastal, river, and lake shipping quickly surpassed the tonnage of American ships in foreign trade after the mid-1830s. After the mid-1840s, foreign shipping began to catch up again, but only because the rise of railroad transportation was taking much of the domestic cargo away from inland shipping. (See 5–9.)

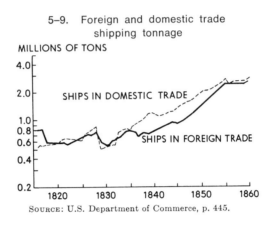

5–9. Foreign and domestic trade shipping tonnage

SOURCE: U.S. Department of Commerce, p. 445.

Paying for imports

Throughout the pre-Civil War period, the value of imports tended to exceed the value of merchandise exports in most years. Traditionally and misleadingly, this has been called an "unfavorable balance of trade." Unless some other way could be found to pay for the excess of foreign purchases over sales, shipments of specie—gold and silver—would have to pay for the difference. In the 1780s, some drain in specie from the United States did take place. But aside from the immediate post-Revolutionary years, until the California gold discovery of 1848, little specie flowed out of the United States and considerable amounts flowed in. How is this to be explained?

In our discussion of colonial external trade relations we presented informally the framework for accounting for various kinds of international transactions. At this point a digression is appropriate in order to define the elements of the *balance of payments* and to show how the accounts can be used to explain a nation's trade history. Glance first at 5–10, which gives the U.S. balance of payments with other nations for 1860, then read the explanatory paragraphs below.

To explain the total balance of payments among nations, we need a broader set of accounts than is needed to compute the *trade* balance (exports less imports of goods) or the *specie* balance (outflow less inflow of money metals). We also need to account for exports and imports

5–10.   U.S. balance of payments with other nations, 1860
(in millions of dollars)

Accounts	Receipts	Payments	Balance
Trade: goods sold and purchased	$335	$367	$–32
Invisibles: payments for services	42	67	–25
Transportation charges.	(35)	(17)	(18)
Travel and other expenditures.	(2)	(20)	(–18)
Returns on past investments.	(5)	(30)	(–25)
Specie: gold and silver shipped	66	9	57
Capital*:			1
Unilateral transfers of funds.	–	–	(8)
Changes in debts and investments*	–	–	(–7)

* Estimate (for balance only) is derived as a residual; and the sign is opposite to the net balance on other payment totals (trade, invisibles, specie).
Source: U.S. Department of Commerce, pp. 538, 563–65. (Specie flows shown on p. 538 are deducted from the merchandise figures reported on pp. 563–65.)

of services. Payments for these are called **invisible items** because they represent payments for services rather than goods. Lastly, we must account for **capital flows,** both public and private, among nations.

In short, we use four broadly defined accounts to summarize a nation's balance of payments:

1.   exports and imports of merchandise,
2.   exports and imports of services,
3.   long- and short-term capital movements, and
4.   shipments and receipts of specie.

The transactions in all four categories are overwhelmingly of private origin, although government transactions can and do appear in each of the accounts.

If we add merchandise transactions to the invisible items, we get what is often referred to as the **current account,** so called because it summarizes the results of ordinary, day-in and day-out commerce among nations. The capital and specie accounts are sometimes called **balancing items,** because they summarize the transactions that bring the flows of foreign money among nations into harmony with the flows of goods and services. For example, in 1860 Americans wanted to spend $57 million more on current account than their $377 million in overseas sales of goods and services would permit. The resulting shortage of foreign purchasing power was made up by borrowing a net $1 million overseas and, thanks to California gold, by a $56 million specie outflow, thereby bringing the nation's international payments into balance. (See 5–10.) In this case, the United States had a negative balance on current account which was offset by the positive balance for the sum of the capital and specie accounts.

Let's look at the kinds of items that appear under the invisible and capital flow headings. Freight charges and various port fees are important transactions among nations. Similarly, passengers account for a considerable flow of money among countries. Whether they travel for business or pleasure, passengers spend money for fares, food and lodging, and other services while abroad. A third type of invisible item is the payment or receipt of interest on debts or dividends on prior investments. These are payments for the services of capital; and the greater the volume of capital investment, the greater these capital charges will be.

Capital may flow between nations in the form of loans (or repayment of loans) and investments (or withdrawal of investments). It may be helpful to think of capital movements as transactions in paper claims to assets which resemble transactions in physical goods. When a New York state bond is "exported" to London in exchange for an English lender's money, we can describe this as a positive long-term capital transaction which gives rise to an inflow of funds. The transaction is negative when Americans invest or lend abroad (or pay back loans). When merchants extend short-term loans, physical goods are usually exchanged for paper claims (IOUs), and no money is exchanged. Some capital transfers are between governments, as when the United States paid for the Louisiana Territory or when the United States refinanced its national debt in the post-Revolutionary years.

We have included one-way transfers of funds among nations (gifts or unilateral transfers) because their economic effect is similar to the usual capital transfer. Some unilateral transfers are made by or between individuals, as when immigrants bring funds with them or send back money to their relatives. Others involve gifts from one government to another. (See 5–10).

People do not need to transfer physically all their payments across the seas. An importer in New York City who needs English pounds can trade his dollars through his bank with an exporter who has already received English pounds and wants them converted to dollars. At the same time, the corresponding exporters and importers in London may be trading their dollars for pounds. In modern times, payments are customarily made by check, and ownership of bank accounts in various currencies is transferred; so no currency to speak of is shipped between countries. In early American history, exchanges of businessmen's IOUs served to reduce actual shipments of money metals.

By examining just the positive and negative net balances of each of the four main types of accounts, we can gain a useful perspective on certain international aspects of national development. In addition to noting the size and type of exports and imports in relation to total national production, we can examine (with the aid of the balancing accounts) how differences in trade were paid for and the extent to which outside capital aided national growth. Very large short-term fluctuations in the various net balances are important indications of business conditions—the booms and depressions. Also, each of the four types of accounts may show a persistent tendency or trend, toward the positive or the negative side, which provides another source of insight into development patterns. Let's look at the U.S. pattern for 1815 through 1860 by examining 5–11 and 5–12.

5–11.   U.S. balances of trade and invisible items, 1815–60

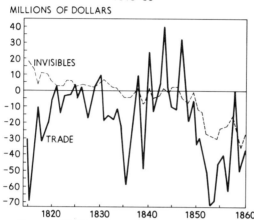

SOURCE: U.S. Department of Commerce, pp. 538, 563–65. (Specie flows shown on p. 538 are deducted from the merchandise figures reported on pp. 563–65.)

5–12.   U.S. balances of specie and capital payments, 1815–60

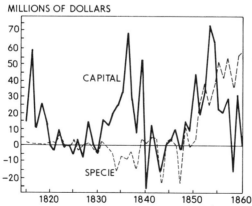

SOURCE: U.S. Department of Commerce, pp. 538, 563–65. (Specie flows shown on p. 538 are deducted from the merchandise figures reported on pp. 563–65.)

The U.S. *trade* balance was usually negative, meaning that imports usually exceeded exports. The excess of payments to other countries for imports reached large negative amounts in three different periods.

The first occurred from 1816 through 1818, when the postwar flood of English manufactures came to American shores. The years 1836 through 1839, when a western land rush occurred, were a second period of large net imports. The third period came during the mid-1850s as a result of a further boom in western land settlement and the rapid building of railroads.

The *invisible items* balance was usually positive from 1815 through 1840 and thus helped offset some of the negative trade balance. Immediately after the War of 1812, freight earnings were high, although not quite as high as during the peak of the previous neutrality period. Although freight earnings remained substantial, the ratio of American freight earnings to foreign freight earnings from U.S. trade declined significantly toward the end of the period. Various navigation laws plus sharp foreign competition came to limit American shipping to the U.S. export and import trade; gradually the U.S. ceased to be the carrier for other nations.

The balance of travel expenditures also tended to fall during the 1840s and 1850s as Americans began to travel abroad more. Most important, current payments of interest on debts and earnings on investments gradually became larger as the total of foreign lending and investment in America accumulated. The net balance of all current payments, therefore, gradually fell so that by the late 1840s it had become negative; in the 1850s the negative balance became large and persistent.

The balance of *specie* movements was usually not very large; so precious metals did not help much in offsetting the large negative trade balances of the first two boom periods. Until the 1830s, the balance was usually slightly positive, representing a small outflow of money metals to help pay for excess imports. During the 1830s and 1840s however, the balance was usually negative, meaning that money metals were being shipped in. Only in the 1850s did specie exports in large volume provide a major positive balance to offset the large negative trade balances. This was because gold itself became a major export commodity after the California gold discoveries in 1848.

Positive *capital* balances were usually required to offset excess imports. America called upon the resources of the rest of the world, especially Britain, to augment American saving and capital formation. Consequently, a significant portion of American growth can be attributed to capital inflows from other nations e.g., in 1850 foreigners' net claims on U.S. capital equaled about 10 percent of total nonfarm capital.[20]

Funds brought by the increasing number of immigrants were an important part of the growing positive capital balances of the 1850s. During all three trade booms there were especially large capital inflows. In part, they occurred because Americans went into debt to finance an excess of imports, and in part they reflected long-term British investments that

---

[20] U.S. Department of Commerce, p. 151.

helped America to expand. During the 1815–18 period, British merchants undoubtedly extended more credit to help finance the large inflow of British goods. During the boom periods of the 1830s and the 1850s, a great deal of trade credit was extended by British merchants. Also in these decades, substantial long-term investments of foreign capital funds were made to help build American canals and railroads. Most of these investments involved purchases of bonds issued by state governments and railroad companies. A large part of the dollars British merchants earned by exporting to America were in effect sold to British investors so that they might purchase American canal or rail bonds.

Persistent positive capital balances indicate a cumulative buildup of foreign-held American debt and investment. During the early decades of the century, the foreign-held debt accumulated during boom periods tended to be paid off in later years. During the 1830s and 1850s, however, the investment flows of the boom periods of canal and railroad construction were not offset by later outflows (although some debt repayment reduced the cumulative foreign holdings during the 1840s). The accumulated net balances of the capital account, therefore, tend to reflect the extent of permanent foreign capital investment which aided American growth.

The absolute rise in foreign purchases of U.S. securities was almost as great in the 1850s as in the 1830s, but the percentage increment was much greater in the 1830s. Compared to the size of total production and private investment in the economy, therefore, outside investment probably was most important during the canal-building period. (See 5–13.)

5–13.   Foreign-held debt and investments in the United States, 1800–1860

SOURCE: U.S. Department of Commerce, p. 566.

SUMMARY

1. The disruptive effects of the Revolution slowed the expansion of the American economy and probably reduced per capita GNP. However, the effects of the Revolution on the economy were limited chiefly

to the urbanized market sector, whereas much of American agriculture was left largely untouched by hostilities.

After the Revolution, the Confederation of newly freed states found itself outside the British Empire and beyond the benefits of the Navigation Acts and, thus, was forced to struggle to establish new output and trade patterns. By the time of the Constitutional Convention, the states were emerging from the problems of adjustment to life outside the Empire.

2.   Over the antebellum period, the total economy expanded rapidly in terms of both inputs and outputs. Compared with present-day figures, the expansion rate was something of a marvel.

The intensive economic growth rates of the period also compare very favorably with those of modern economies. The consequent level of per capita income, just behind that of Britain, was probably the second highest in the world.

3.   Per capita income growth can be explained by two factors: inputs expanded more rapidly than population and, most important, the productivity of all inputs increased.

4.   A host of factors explain the rise in the productivity of productive resources—review the list at the end of the subsection "Sources of productivity increases" in this chapter (p. 158).

5.   Foreign trade played a key role in the development process. After the Revolution, the economy established a new basis for its growth and its high degree of prosperity—it served as a merchant and carrier for other nations, principally France and Britain. After the War of 1812, the export base shifted away from shipping and mercantile services in favor of cotton exports. By the last 15 to 20 years of the period, the growing manufacturing sector had displaced traditional imports, especially finished cotton textiles, and the export base had become relatively less important as a determinant of growth and welfare.

6.   Perhaps the best way to conclude this chapter is to expand upon a theme that was summarized in it, namely, the relationship between the export base and economic development. According to the export-base hypothesis, the export sector determines the pace and pattern of a nation's economic development, at least as long as domestic markets remain small compared with optimum productive capacity in various industries. This is the hypothesis on which this chapter and the next two chapters rest. As applied to the U.S. economy prior to the Civil War, the details of the hypothesis are as follows.

From 1790 to 1812, the U.S. economy managed to adjust to life outside the British Empire by jointly developing its shipping and mercantile industries as an export base. In this the former colonists were quite successful. Considering their domestic and international political problems, they rebuilt the war-torn economy rapidly, and total and per capita income grew at highly acceptable rates.

True, much of the post-Revolutionary prosperity was based on the Napoleonic Wars. But the fact that the Northeasterners were able to continue their vocations as traders, shippers, and financial intermediaries and to continue to build their mercantile and shipping capital proved crucial to future development.

Cotton picked up where the carrying trade and merchant capitalism left off as the force generating expansion and growth in income per person. After the War of 1812, cotton—which had become an important crop after 1793—became our most rapidly growing source of export income.

King Cotton defined a regional specialization pattern for the United States. The Northeast responded to the expansion of cotton exports by becoming the South's fiscal agent, shipper, financier, insurer, and purchasing agent. The Northeast also added to its social overhead capital, sparked the development of inland transport facilities, invented new financial institutions, and improved ways of buying and selling. The West responded by becoming a breadbasket for the East.

American markets expanded, the Northeast accumulated social overhead capital and business acumen, and rising agricultural productivity reduced per capita farm labor requirements. Conditions became appropriate for rapid manufacturing growth. By the 1840s, as a consequence of developments which can be traced back to the coronation of cotton, rapid manufacturing growth had become the force behind economic expansion and per capita income growth.

Throughout this process of development, the export sector never exceeded 15 to 20 percent of total GNP. On the eve of the Civil War, it was only 5.6 percent of GNP. How could it serve as a prime mover? Two factors dovetail to explain the strategic role of the export base.

First, at least half of the economys' resources were involved in local production, most of it farm-related, for local consumption. A large portion of the economy's output never reached a market. These were days of poor transportation and communications. Markets were still scattered and isolated, although certainly less so at the end of the period than at the beginning. Thus, a range of 5 to 20 percent of GNP actually represented 10 to 40 percent of the resources that could be used in production for national markets or export.

Second, the development of an export base suggests that the economy in question is able to allocate its resources in the most efficient manner. If Americans had been forced to rely only on themselves for the full array of products they desired from 1783 on, manufactured products, for example, would have had to be produced at home, diverting inputs from the uses for which they were best suited. By intensifying farming, exporting cotton, and importing manufactures, we were able to increase our total output. The higher level of productivity showed up as more products produced at home—in absolute terms, the domestic sector of

GNP and total GNP became larger than they would have been otherwise. Consequently, moving resources out of domestic production into more efficient export markets raised both the numerator (exports) and the denominator (GNP) of the fraction by which we measure the size of the export sector.

REFERENCES

G. C. Bjork, "The Weaning of the American Economy," *JEH*, December 1964.

P. A. David, "The Growth of Real Product in the United States before 1840," *JEH*, June 1967.

——, "Learning by Doing and Tariff Protection," *JEH*, September 1970.

R. E. Gallman, "Gross National Product in the United States, 1834–1909," in *Output, Employment and Productivity in the United States after 1800*, ed. D. S. Brady, (Princeton, N.J.: Princeton University Press, 1966).

——, "The Pace and Pattern of American Economic Growth," in *American Economic Growth*, eds. L. E. Davis, et al., (New York: Harper & Row, Publishers, 1972).

——, "Changes in Total Agricultural Factor Productivity in the Nineteenth Century," *AH*, January 1972.

R. Goldsmith, *Income and Wealth of the United States: Trends and Structure* (London: Bowes and Bowes, 1952).

L. C. Gray, *History of Agriculture in the Southern United States to 1860* (Washington, D.C.: Carnegie Institution, 1933).

S. L. Lebergott, "Labor Force and Employment 1800–1960" in D. S. Brady, cited above.

R. E. Lipsey, "Foreign Trade," eds. L. E. Davis et al., cited above.

D. C. North, "The United States Balance of Payments, 1790–1860," in *Trends in the American Economy in the Nineteenth Century*, ed. W. N. Parker (Princeton, N.J.: Princeton University Press, 1960).

——, *Growth and Welfare in the American Past* (Englewood Cliffs, N.J.: Prentice-Hall, Inc., 1966).

——, *The Economic Growth of the United States, 1790–1860*, (New York: W. W. Norton & Co. Inc., 1966).

U.S. Department of Commerce, *Historical Statistics of the United States* (Washington, D.C.: U.S. Government Printing Office, 1960).

6 THE AGRARIAN ECONOMY

Usually the agricultural sector is a pivotal element in the development of an economy. As we demonstrated in chapters 1 and 3, if farm productivity rises in a predominantly agricultural economy, workers and purchasing power can be directed into the expansion and nonagricultural industries. As farm labor requirements are reduced, production costs fall and relative farm prices follow suit. Workers who are released from agriculture can be employed to produce goods and services that consumers wish to buy with their food budget savings.

In chapter 1 we also stressed that rising agricultural exports in conjunction with growing farm productivity can stimulate the growth of the entire economy. Recall our discussion of the export base and growth. If the value of exports grows faster than population, import growth will also outstrip population expansion. Thus a nation can gain the rewards of productivity increases through a roundabout process whereby agricultural export growth increases the number and variety of products consumers can buy overseas.

The American growth story for the antebellum period is a blend of the phenomena summarized above plus their feedback effect on manufacturing as an added, less widely recognized, element. Certainly, the economy was chiefly agricultural in the Nation's early years: 85 to 90 percent of the labor force was engaged in farm work. And as the economy evolved, productivity in food production increased significantly—between 1800 and 1860 the number of farm workers per hundred people in the population fell from 26 to 18. At the same time, we expanded our cotton output from a mere 73,000 bales to 3.8 million bales, while raising both output per acre and output per farmhand. In short, we managed to expand cotton for export and reduce our relative food input requirements simultaneously. The result was a major contribution to the rather impressive growth record summarized in chapter 5. What's more, during the early mechanization of agriculture, a very young manufacturing sector received an important stimulus to its growth, especially in the Midwest.[1]

Between 1815 and 1840, agriculture not only contributed to growth and expansion but, in our view, also dominated the growth-generating forces. Prior to 1815, shipping held center stage, and after 1840 manufacturing took over as the economy's principal actor. However, in the middle of the antebellum period cotton culture and food production played the lead development roles.

AGRICULTURAL TRANSITION

Agriculture in the United States has been characterized by three distinct but overlapping phases: westward expansion, technological improvement through mechanization, and the emergence of scientific farming.[2]

From about 1820 through 1860, westward expansion managed to offset the effects of crowding in the Northeast, where the land was all taken up, in two ways—by skimming off the excess farm population of the Northeast and by compensating for the Northeast's ever-growing food deficit. Over the same time span, the migration of cotton to the West far more than offset the burning out of Eastern soils.

By the 1830s, laborsaving mechanical devices were promising significant increases in output per farmhand. However, scientific farming was not an early 19th century characteristic—yield increases from better seeds, improved breeding, new veterinary techniques, and agricultural chemicals were negligible in the antebellum period. In fact, not until the 1940s did agriculture's scientific age arrive in any significant sense; farmers had to await key developments in chemistry, botany, and biology.

Changes in the structure of agricultural organization were superimposed on these three historical phases. On the self-sufficient subsistence farm of the early 1800s, producer and consumer were identical—some farmers would go a year without entering into a monetary transaction. As transportation improved and markets expanded, the self-sufficient farm became a commercial family farm: the farmer produced a cash crop for the urban consumer and used the cash to buy products he formerly grew or manufactured himself. This organizational structure came to dominate both northern and southern farming in the antebellum period and characterized agriculture until quite recently. Now, as a consequence of scientific farming, the farm is more like a highly mechanized processing plant in which vast amounts of material inputs are combined with comparatively little labor to produce a single output.[3]

---

[1] See David, pp. 215–17, for a discussion of the feedback effects of mechanization.

[2] For an expanded discussion of these phases, see Parker (1972), pp. 370–93.

[3] See Parker (1972), pp. 400–402 for a discussion of "vertical disintegration of farms and farming."

Improvements in transportation permitted farmers to cash in on the inherent agricultural advantages of the Northeast, the West, and the South and their subregions. When farm products could not be shipped very far, each region had to produce all the major food crops, no matter how suitable its soils and climate. But after the "transportation revolution," regions could specialize according to their natural endowments. As a consequence, regional specialization and the specialized commercial farm evolved hand in hand.

To recapitulate: In the early antebellum years, most backwoods farmers were forced into a self-sufficient output mix. Transport costs were too high to permit specializing for sale at distant markets. And farms were too scattered to permit building transportation facilities. But with the westward push and the promise of higher population density, roads, canals, and railroads were built and made self-fulfilling prophecies out of western population predictions. Farmers and regions specialized and a national division of agricultural labor emerged.

Following a pattern set in late colonial days, New England farmers produced for the urban areas of the Northeast. Middle Atlantic farmers exported grain and meat products, and southern planters exported cotton, tobacco, and rice. By 1815 cotton was the South's major crop and the Nation's largest single source of export earnings. In the Southwest the push westward was a cotton migration. In the Upper South tobacco moved west into Kentucky and spilled across the Ohio into the southern reaches of the Midwest. In the North, grain and meat production moved into western New York and Pennsylvania and on across the Great Lakes states to Missouri and Iowa.

In turn, agricultural specialization became an integral part of regional specialization throughout the economy. The Northeast became a net importer of foodstuffs as it concentrated on manufacturing and commercial and financial development. The West (today's East North Central states) started as pioneer country, sparsely populated by self-sufficient farmers. Then family farms marketing cash crops evolved in the West as the frontier line moved on. By the close of the period, manufacturing growth had become commonplace in such western cities as Cincinnati, Detroit, Cleveland, and Chicago. Throughout, the South stayed with farming; plantations and commercial family farms grew cash crops for export, while subsistence family farmers raised their own food and grew a little cotton or tobacco to finance the few things they bought for cash.[4]

SOUTHERN COTTON FARMING

Southern agriculture and the southern economy can be characterized on the basis of several linked generalizations. Southern agriculture was

---

[4] See Ransom (1964, 1971), for discussion of transportation and regional comparative advantage.

the backbone of the southern economy and was dominated by King Cotton. Cotton exports were the single most important U.S. source of export earnings in the antebellum period. At least in the short run, plantation agriculture and the slave system that went with it constituted a highly efficient allocation of southern resources. Over the long pull, it is not unlikely that a more diversified farming and industrial pattern would have generated a higher level of economic welfare for both white southerners and emancipated blacks than has actually been achieved.

Supplying world markets

The end of the Napoleonic Wars threw open the doors of world markets to the British cotton textile industry. As one of the main cotton-producing areas of the world, the South benefited from high prices and rapidly expanding demand. Britain bought as much as 60 percent of the U.S. crop, and the United States supplied as much as 80 percent of British needs in the period 1830–44. Other foreign buyers and the rapidly expanding American cotton mills purchased the balance of the crop.

Cotton was the South's major crop simply because it was the most profitable alternative. Although tobacco production was shifting westward, the exhausted fertility of overworked tobacco lands near the coast meant that the volume of tobacco exports did not expand for another two decades. While both rice and sugar were profitable export crops when raised on large plantations, their production was restricted by the limited areas of easily flooded lowlands in South Carolina and southern Louisiana. A large amount of acreage was devoted to grain and livestock, although not for export.

The South's rate of increase in cotton production was very rapid. Output grew at over 7 percent per year from 1800 to 1840, after which the expansion rate slackened. The early growth rate was about 60 percent faster than the 4.3 percent per year at which real national income grew over the period. (See 6–1).

If you just glance at 6–2, you can't help but be impressed by cotton's importance as an export. It made a huge contribution to paying for manufactured imports from England. Early in the period, the value of cotton exports quickly rose from one third to over one half of the value of all exports (excluding reexports). About three fourths of the cotton grown before 1840 was exported, and American textile manufacturers in the Northeast purchased the rest. After 1840, cotton's share of total exports declined in response to the growth of the American textile industry.

Natural resource advantages dictated that increases in cotton output be concentrated in the New South—the territories to the west and southwest of the Appalachian Mountains. While the climate was suitable

6–1. U.S. cotton production, 1800–1860

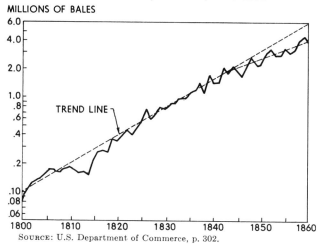

SOURCE: U.S. Department of Commerce, p. 302.

6–2. Importance of cotton exports, 1815–59

| | Cotton exports as a percent of | |
Period	Cotton production	All exports of U.S. products
1815–19 . . . . 64%		38%
1820–24 71		44
1825–29 70		58
1830–34 76		52
1835–39 71		65
1840–44 77		55
1845–49 74		45
1850–54 69		54
1855–59 67		51

SOURCE: U.S. Department of Commerce, pp. 302, 538, 547.

for cotton over the entire South, superior soils were available in certain parts of the new Gulf states and in the lower Mississippi Valley—especially the black belt soils that curved across central Mississippi and Alabama. In 1860, cotton production was still important in Georgia, but the combined output of Mississippi, Alabama, and Louisiana accounted for over half the total, and even the newest cotton producers, Texas and Arkansas, ranked ahead of South Carolina.

The New South had another natural advantage admirably suited to an export crop—easy access to ocean transportation. The Mississippi River provided a well-established transportation artery to the busy port of New Orleans. Other major rivers in Mississippi and Alabama provided barge transportation direct to the Gulf. The first settlers located along the rivers, and most other fertile lands were but a short wagon haul from the nearest barge landing. Throughout the antebellum years, most cotton made its way to market over water routes.

From the beginning of the antebellum period, the New South's transportation advantage was a persistent influence. And as the cost of ocean shipping declined, the region's transportation advantage was gradually enhanced and its comparative advantage in agriculture fortified. Freight rates on cotton shipped to England from New Orleans in the late 1850s were about half their 1820 level. Although ship speed did not increase in the 19th century, other factors raised shipping productivity by an average of 3.5 percent per year. Cargo size grew from 120 to 500 tons, or from 19 to 21 tons per crew member, and after 1840 the heavy immigrant traffic on the return voyage reduced the cost of operating packet and shuttle freighters.[5]

The growth of banking and credit facilities also enabled the cotton kingdom to grow. Plantation banks, financed in part by selling securities to British investors, provided credit facilities for the development of new land and the internal slave trade. Cotton factors proliferated to supply planters' short-term credit needs. Also, the Second Bank of the United States became an important purchaser of cotton bills; and, for a brief time after it had become the U.S. Bank of Pennsylvania (1837–41), it financed the shipment of cotton. (Unfortunately, the bank's foray into cotton speculation set in motion the processes that led to its bankruptcy in 1841.)

Although we can't give precise figures, we know that productivity in cotton production increased over the entire antebellum period for a variety of reasons. Output per acre rose as improved growing techniques were introduced, and the number of acres that each hand could cultivate increased as laborsaving innovations were introduced. Of course, the cotton gin was the most important innovation of the period— it made cotton culture profitable. However, other factors were significant. The move to the more fertile western soils raised yields per acre. Improved cultivating techniques and better seeds also added to yields. More efficient plows and the introduction of mules reduced labor requirements. And by-product uses for cottonseed were discovered, especially the use of cottonseed oil in paints, which raised the value of the harvest.[6]

Demand, supply, and price fluctuations

From a price standpoint, the cotton market was nothing if not volatile. As 6–3 indicates, the long-term trends of prices were interrupted time and again by sharp breaks—20 percent year-to-year fluctuations were common, and 40 percent changes were not unheard of. The antebellum

---

[5] North, pp. 170–71.

[6] See Gray, chap. 30, for a discussion of cotton culture innovation in the antebellum years.

6–3.   Raw cotton prices, 1800–1860

PRICE (CENTS)

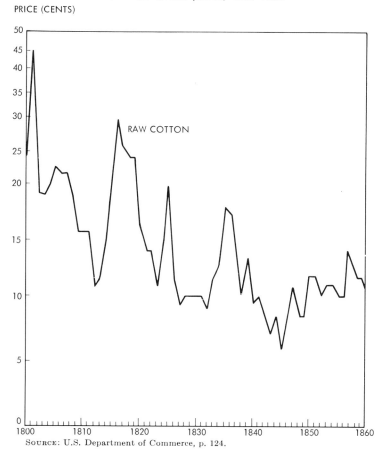

RAW COTTON

SOURCE: U.S. Department of Commerce, p. 124.

behavior of cotton prices can be explained by fluctuations in the rate at which worldwide demand for cotton textiles expanded and variations in the rate at which new cotton land was cleared.[7]

During the period 1820–60, British and American demand for cotton textiles grew tremendously as a response to total and per capita income growth. Over the same time span, other national economies grew, and their market sectors expanded, with a consequent reduction of home spinning and weaving: factory-produced cotton textiles replaced home-made fabrics and wool and linen goods. In short, economic expansion, per capita income growth, and marketization of economies the world

---

[7] Using different estimating techniques, Temin and Wright (1971) came to some-what similar conclusions. We are convinced that Wright's specification of the supply function is superior to that of Temin. Hence we report Wright's analysis in what follows, including his emphasis upon both supply and demand shifts as determinants of cotton prices.

over generated huge increases in the demand for cotton textiles and, therefore, for American cotton.

The growth of demand was met by clearing additional acreage, by raising bigger and bigger crops on more productive soils, and, to a slight degree, by using more productive methods. As the cotton industry expanded, production costs declined: hence the downward price trend. But neither demand nor supply expanded at a constant rate. Thus, year-to-year price fluctuations were necessary to bring supply and demand into equality.

On the supply side, cotton production was limited by the rate at which newly cleared land was made available. The actual cultivation of cotton acreage fluctuated with expected cotton prices and the amount of new land recently prepared for cotton. This leads to the conclusion that recent cotton prices and land sales plus, of course, weather conditions determined the actual year-to-year path of U.S. cotton expansion. For the entire period, we can assume that profits from cotton growing were high enough to produce a trend of expanding cotton output. Fluctuations around that trend were generated by the vagaries of weather, the influence of recent price experience on land clearing, and the size of the spring planting.[8]

On the demand side, gyrations in the growth path are less complicated to explain. Booms and depressions generate ups and downs in total and per capita income. In the antebellum period, cyclical income swings in British markets shifted the demand for cotton textiles—in poor times the working classes made do with mending and patching and fewer changes of clothing; in good times they enjoyed the luxury of more clothes and even some ostentatious touches. British balance of payments fluctuations also generated shifts in British demand for raw cotton.

The general story that emerges from all this is one of overall expansion and volatile price behavior in which demand and supply changed rapidly with uncoordinated ratchetlike actions. This history is aptly illustrated by the experience of the late 1830s. In 1837–38, poor British and American economic conditions coincided with the biggest American crop to that time—as compared with 1836–37, output expanded by 21 percent while the price fell by 24 percent, so that although export volume increased, export earnings declined. In the following year, British and American economic conditions revived while drought cut the cotton crop by over 30 percent; consequently, cotton prices rose by a third and the value of cotton sales held constant. Then, in 1839–40, a bumper crop again sent cotton prices earthward despite improving economic conditions.

An appendix at the end of this chapter deals at length with the

---

[8] Wright (1971) found that land sales were influenced by recent price history and that a given year's cotton production was chiefly determined by land sales two years earlier plus the New Orleans cotton price one year earlier.

process we have just described. We suggest that you finish the chapter, read the appendix, then review this section. The appendix teaches an important lesson which will be helpful in reading the balance of the text—we urge you to refer to it in connection with later chapters.

The plantation system

The way in which the South's cotton, rice, tobacco, and sugar were produced had profound effects upon all facets of southern life. Plantation agriculture shaped the balance of the southern economy and in our opinion determined until quite recently the course of southern economic development. At this point, we should specify what we mean by the plantation system, then examine its relationship with slavery, and, finally, discuss the plantation system's influence on southern economic history. (As this text is in press, Fogel and Engerman's two volume work *Time on the Cross* is being circulated for review in advance of its 1974 publication date. While the bulk of the following discussion of slavery and southern agriculture is compatible with Fogel and Engerman's work, specific points are in conflict and are noted. If you're interested in the economics of slavery, Fogel and Engermans' work is very important.)

By the term plantation system we mean a regional agricultural organization in which large commercial farms, using large labor forces and labor-intensive methods, produce cash crops. In such a system, medium and small farms coexist with the plantations and make a small contribution to the region's cash crop output. In the South during the antebellum period, the plantation labor force consisted of slaves and the cash crops were exported from the plantations. Southern plantations were family owned and operated, with huge capital investments in land and slaves. Although slaveholding was not limited to the plantations, only 7.4 percent of southern white families owned ten or more slaves, and in the Lower South, where slaveholding was most important, slaveowners never exceeded 41 percent of the free population. Cotton dominated the slave economy, but earnings from other export crops were significant.

Other than the cost of slaves, the fixed capital requirements in cotton lay somewhere between those for tobacco, on the one hand, and for rice and sugar, on the other. Tobacco required almost no equipment and a very large labor force per acre because one worker could tend only two or three acres of tobacco. Tobacco farming also demanded considerable close supervision and management skills. Rice and sugar plantations required large investments—the former, in dikes and ditches; the latter, in machinery and equipment. Cotton production required moderate acreage per worker and hardly any equipment. Since the work was simple and easily supervised, large acreages and many slaves could be managed on one cotton plantation.

The competitive advantage of large plantations was greatest for sugar and rice and smallest for tobacco. The first two were produced predominantly on plantations of 50 or more slaves, while tobacco soon became, for the most part, a product of small farmers. In cotton, medium planters (those with 10 to 50 slaves) and large planters (those with more than 50 slaves) coexisted, which suggests that the advantages of very large-scale production were not overwhelming. In fact, Fogel and Engerman found that scale economies characterized large slave plantations not large free labor operations.

The large cotton plantation, however, did tend to be more prosperous. Larger plantations achieved economies because they had a greater division of labor, used more equipment, obtained loans at lower rates of interest, and made more favorable marketing arrangements. What's more, successful small farmers enlarged their acreages and slaveholdings, often by moving to the most fertile lands, so size and success became identified with each other.

Gavin Wright's recent analysis of the 1850 and 1860 census data for the cotton South confirms "the traditional view that the social implication of the slave-cotton regime was a highly unequal distribution of wealth." Compared with the holdings of the largest 5 percent of northern farmers, the portion of total improved acreage held by the largest 5 percent of all cotton farmers was great. Further, the large planters held better land and had more slaves per acre than the small farmers of the South.[9]

Initially, high prices resulted in very favorable profits for both large and small farmers. All kinds of planters rushed to settle the new lands in the Gulf states. Small farmers hoped to get a new start and to grow larger by acquiring more land and more slaves in the Southwest. Large southeastern planters moved their operations to the richer soils of the delta and the black belt. A few large tobacco farmers converted to cotton; and even northeastern investors joined cotton plantation ventures.

However, as the supply of cotton expanded and prices fell in the 1820s, widespread high profits disappeared and the basic condition of low labor productivity held down the incomes of small farmers. Cotton was a labor-intensive crop; so at prices that were barely profitable for large plantations using slave labor, the small farmer earned a relatively low rate of pay. Because slaves were "paid" only a subsistence wage, cotton prices could fall a great deal and still remain profitable for the owners of large- and medium-sized plantations. But the small farmer with few or no slaves just didn't produce a large enough volume to stay much above subsistence.[10]

The higher incomes of the South were earned as a return from the larger amounts of capital invested in the plantations. For example, a

[9] Wright (1970).

[10] In addition to Wright (1970), see Gray, chaps. 21–23 for an extended discussion of the plantation system and slaveholding.

typical large cotton plantation of 60 hands in Mississippi in the late antebellum period required an investment of almost $100,000. About half the total was accounted for by the purchase price of slaves and the rest by the cost of land and equipment. Sugar and rice plantations required even larger capital investments. By contrast, the smallest cotton farm that could manage to survive required an investment of $15,000.[11]

The medium and small farms that coexisted with the plantations were apparently largely self-sufficient units which produced a very limited range of commodities for market. A recent analysis of the 1860 census suggests that these units produced sufficient foodstuffs to feed their inhabitants and perhaps enough surplus to supply neighboring towns and cities. Cotton output was highly concentrated among the larger plantations: the smaller half of Southern farms accounted for only 4 to 5 percent of total cotton production. These data suggest that cash crops, including cotton, were raised in order to purchase products produced outside the region.[12]

For years historians assumed that the cotton South's small farmers existed to complement the output of the staple-producing plantations. However, the 1860 census data show that the large plantations were more than self-sufficient in basic foods. Thus, food sales by small farmers to large plantation owners was not a consistent concomitant of cotton production.

According to Gallman, the reason for this may lie in the nature of cotton culture. Before the relatively recent invention of the mechanical picker, a work force could raise far more cotton than it could pick. Consequently, in the antebellum years, the harvesting ability of the slave population determined the size of the cotton crop, and leftover acreage was planted in corn, which could be harvested over a protracted period. Given that slaveholding was concentrated among the larger plantation owners, it should follow that grain production was also concentrated among the large plantations, as indeed it was.[13] Evidently, there were no economies to be gained from specializing in corn or cotton and leasing out or renting slaves to or from neighbors according to harvest demands.

Historians also long believed that a heavy trade existed between the food-producing West (today's Midwest) and the cotton-producing South. However, trade-flow data don't bear out this assumption for the 1840s and 1850s, decades in which cotton had already moved to the Southwest and therefore in which such a trade should have been heaviest.

The actual grain trade flows were as follows: the Upper South, i.e., the Border States, sent grain and other foodstuffs to the Atlantic, Missis-

---

[11] Data on capital costs are from Gray, pp. 541–42.
[12] Gallman.
[13] For more details see Gallman, pp. 22–23.

sippi, and Gulf ports, chiefly to feed the urban population of the Lower South; the Middle South was self-sufficient in part because poor transport facilities required self-sufficiency; and the Upper South exported significant quantities of corn and flour to the Northeast.[14]

Nor was the export of foodstuffs to the South crucial to the West. Prior to 1870, only a minuscule portion of northern food production made its way into the South. After 1840, when the West and Southwest had grown significantly, southern imports of western food products were less than 20 percent of total output.[15]

None of this denies a regional division of labor among the West, the South, and the Northeast. However, in relative terms, the regional specialization we discussed above did not include heavy West-to-South food shipments.

If you attended an American grade school within the last 20 years, you were probably taught that southern agriculture was inefficient. Perhaps you learned that the plantation system with its slave labor produced high-living, devil-may-care planters who were more interested in gracious living, gambling, horses, women, and whiskey than in matters of agricultural technology. Though it doesn't refute the planters' alleged Sybaritic bent, a hard look at the data on southern farming show it to have been more efficient than northern agriculture in 1860. For example, a comparative analysis of northern and southern agriculture shows that input productivity was 39 percent greater in the South than in the North.[16]

The major explanation for the productivity differential appears to be the use of slaves in the South's plantation agriculture. Slaveholders treated their slaves not as labor, but as capital—on the average, working conditions and the lengths of the workday and workweek were calculated to get the most work per man-year out of the slave force while at the same time keeping each hand alive and strong.

The slaveowner could treat his work force as if it were composed of beasts of burden who required 8 to 12 hours of idleness per day, minimal shelter, and a healthy ration to keep in shape.[17] Comparable work was performed on northern farms by family and hired workers who demanded more leisure than was usually allotted the typical slave. Also slaves were members of the labor force longer than free workers. Consequently, for each dollar spent on him, the slave laborer accomplished more in a year than his northern counterpart. Further, it appears

---

[14] See Lindstrom for analysis of trade flows culled from contemporary public records.

[15] See Danhof, pp. 11–13, for a review of the literature viewed from a northern standpoint.

[16] Fogel and Engerman, pp. 364–66.

[17] This explains the paradox of humane treatment of slaves coexisting with the inhumanity of humans owning other humans; incidentally, in no sense should the humane treatment of slaves be confused with the good life.

that the larger farm units which characterized the South permitted a more productive deployment of labor resources if they used slave labor.[18]

The economics of slavery

We have already described how slavery came to be part of southern agriculture. In labor-scarce colonial times, plantation cultivation of export crops demanded the recruitment of workers who could be paid no more than subsistence. Free workers weren't to be had on those terms, so the law obligingly made possible the importation of West African slaves.

Why slavery persisted until the Civil War brought it to an end is another question. A very weak answer is that noneconomic factors demanded the retention of the peculiar institution—indeed we know that whites feared the political and social consequences of large-scale manumission, let alone emancipation. Another way of giving this weak response is to say that no economic factors were capable of overcoming the political and social forces which "required" slavery. If the plantation system no longer required slavery or if slavery were unprofitable, then slavery's persistence could be explained wholly by the white man's fear of unleashing millions of blacks in his midst. However, if the plantation system required or was most profitable with Negro slavery, then we can say that economic forces strengthened other motives for continuing slavery.

It seems unlikely that the survival or expansion of the cotton economy and plantation culture demanded slavery in 1860. Cotton plantations are ubiquitous in the contemporary Southwest, and after the Civil War cotton acreage doubled by around 1900 and then doubled again by 1925. Cotton prices rose slightly after the war. This covered the higher labor costs associated with emancipation and enabled the cotton plantation to survive with sharecropping and tenant farming as substitutes for gang labor.[19] In short, the world needed cotton, and American planters were able to devise ways to use free labor so as to produce cotton at a profit; in effect, planters arranged for blacks to sell themselves back into slavery.[20]

Whether slavery was required to establish the cotton South is another question. Here the pivotal date and event are 1793 and the invention of the cotton gin. What if the slaves had been freed in that year? To us, it seems likely that the plantation economy based on tobacco and

---

[18] Fogel and Engerman argue persuasively that statistical analysis of southern agriculture should be southern in orientation, i.e., slaves should be viewed as capital. You can infer from this discussion that if man-hours were used instead of man-years the calculations might produce very different results.

[19] See Fogel and Engerman, p. 331, for discussion of postwar cotton prices and acreage.

[20] Parker, p. 118.

rice could and would have converted to a cotton base using free black labor in variations of the post–Civil War systems. At that time one third of the South's population was slave, so the potential labor force was certainly there, and other conditions were similar to those of the post–Civil War period. However, this question will never be pushed beyond the realm of speculation simply because we have no data with which to test the hypothetical alternative.

If slavery wasn't necessary to the survival of the cotton South, was it at least profitable enough to have survived even if no one feared emancipation on social or political grounds? In other words, would Southerners have continued to invest in slaves because the cotton plantation was most profitably operated using slave labor? The answer is yes! Yes, in spite of a long tradition in the social sciences which asserted that slavery was a moribund institution in 1860.[21]

Since 1958, a variety of studies using a wide range of data have shown that funds invested in slaves for cotton production yielded investment returns which were comparable to yields from other investment opportunities open to Southerners. For example, the data in 6–4, which

6–4. Estimated rates of return on capital investment per male slave in cotton plantations, 1830–60

Land quality	Cotton yield in bales per slave	Capital per slave*	Rate of return at farm cotton prices of		
			7 cents per pound	8 cents per pound	9 cents per pound
Poor	3	$1,250–1,300	2.2%	3.9%	5.4%
Typical	3.75	1,350–1,400	4.5	5.2	6.5
Better	4.50	1,600	5.0	7.0	8.0
Best	7	1,700	10.0	12.0	13.0

* Present value of total plantation capital outlays for 30-year life expectancy of slave.
SOURCE: Conrad and Meyer, p. 107.

summarizes potential rates of return on capital invested in slaves, is drawn from the pioneering research of Alfred Conrad and John Meyer. What's more, the proceeds from the sale of slaves were great enough to cover the cost of rearing them. Put slightly differently, price of the slaves was high enough to assure a profit from raising them, but not so high as to preclude employing slave labor at a profit.[22]

[21] See Fogel and Engerman for a review of the debate and the evidence as well as for citations of the relevant literature.

[22] Conrad and Meyer were the first to explicitly treat slave purchases as capital investments and to ask whether such investments were profitable in reference to alternative investment outlets. Dozens of articles have followed in their wake, many of which appear or are cited in Aitken, Fogel and Engerman, and the references related to plantation economies cited above.

Until recently the accepted view of the economics of slavery was as follows:

> To the leaders in the South, with their ever-present view of the possibility of negro uprisings, the regulations of slavery seemed essential for safety and prosperity. . . . Most of the later generation of ante bellum planters could not see that slaveholding was essentially burdensome. . . . In the great system of southern industry and commerce, working with seeming smoothness, the negro laborers were inefficient in spite of discipline, and slavery was an obstacle to all progress."[23]

Interestingly, the data on which this view was based are the same as those used by Conrad and Meyer to produce the figures shown in 6–4. Phillips and others noted that slave prices rose from $450 in 1800 to $1,800 in 1860 for a male fieldhand while the price of cotton fell over the same period from 30 cents to 11 cents a pound. Productivity increases were acknowledged, but the increase in slave prices was held to be "too great to be explained except by reference to the severe competition of the planters in selling cotton and in buying slaves . . . , an irresistible tendency to overvalue and overcapitalize slave labor."[24]

Phillips and others overlooked two crucial facts. First, productivity increases in cotton production did, in fact, justify the rise in slave prices. Second, after 1840 cotton prices did not trend downward but rather fluctuated around a slight upward trend.

For a slaveowner, slave productivity was determined by two factors: the ability of the slave to perform various tasks, especially field work, and the ability of the slave force to expand itself. Conrad and Meyer's pathbreaking study took both factors into account in computing the rate of return on funds invested in slave capital. Since their work was published, a stream of quantitative studies utilizing additional data sources has confirmed their findings—investments in slaves were remunerative until, of course, the Emancipation Proclamation.

Slave labor has been viewed as uneconomic because (1) slaves are inefficient and unwilling workers; (2) slaves require detailed supervision; (3) slaves must be supported before and after the working years; and (4) the purchase price of slaves represents a sum that could be earning interest. What Conrad and Meyer and others have shown is that, whatever the element of truth that exists in these assertions, the work actually performed by slaves was sufficiently valuable to offset any costs and inefficiencies peculiar to slaveholding, including interest sacrificed on the purchase price of the slaves. What's more, the data show that, when viewed in conjunction with cotton price movements, slave productivity justified, indeed generated, the historical rise in slave prices.

The latter statement applies to both males and females. Although the

---

[23] Phillips, p. 275.
[24] Phillips, p. 268.

typical male was stronger than the typical female, the productivity effects of inferior strength were partially offset by the ability of females to bear children. For example, when slaves were rented for field work, males commanded a rental fee from 1.4 to 2.3 times the fee that could be charged for a female; yet purchase price differentials were far lower, falling in a range from 0.88 to 1.09.[25] In short, the price of female slaves reflected both their ability to work and their value as child bearers.

The evidence we have just reviewed shows that southern slavery really constituted two separate production activities, and this duality plus the superiority of western cotton lands produced an intraregional division of labor. The Border States and the Southeast became slave-breeding areas simply because the demand for slaves in those states grew less rapidly than the supply. In the New South the situation was exactly opposite—demand for slaves grew at a faster pace than natural rates of increase because the New South was the center of expansion in cotton production.

Given that slave importation from abroad became illegal after 1807, the New South could only make up its deficit by importing slaves from the Old South and the Border States. For example, Conrad and Meyer report that from 1790 to 1850 the slave population of the Old South grew at only 2 percent per annum while the New South averaged an increase of 18 percent per annum. Their figures show that 742,000 slaves were exported to the buying states, chiefly to the New South.[26]

While some slave-breeding plantations may have existed in the Upper South and the Atlantic Coast states, we don't know how many there were if, indeed, there were any. It seems likely, however, that most of the slaves who were exported to the New South were brought there when eastern planters moved their entire operation west or when families whose slave holdings had outrun their needs made isolated sales.

Before moving on to consider the broader ramifications of plantation agriculture, we want to make several points about the apparently callous attitude that is suggested by computing slave productivity, especially in slave breeding. First, scholars like Conrad and Meyer, and Fogel and Engerman, approached slavery from a slaveholder's viewpoint, as if slaves were so much livestock—they asked if slaveholding was economically rational. The morality of the issue was beyond their scope of study.

Second, those who wish to study the moral or philosophical aspects of slaveholding or to learn something about slavery's impact upon the Nation's social history can't do so validly without knowing the economics of slavery. Because Charles Ramsdell misunderstood the economics of slavery, he led an entire generation to believe that the Civil War was a needless bloodbath fought to destroy (preserve) an unprofitable insti-

---

[25] See Conrad and Meyer, p. 115.

[26] Conrad and Meyer, pp. 112–13.

tution which was on its way out.[27] Certainly, the more penetrating analysis of historians like Conrad and Meyer, and Fogel and Engerman, has made possible a more accurate account.

The plantation system and southern economic development

We have already suggested that the plantation economy and cotton exports constituted an economic use of southern resources, that the region's comparative advantage came from specializing in export staples and importing manufactured products. Another way of saying this is that in any given year, or any decade for that matter, if southern investors had examined all their production alternatives, they would have chosen plantation cotton all over again because doing so would maximize their prospective incomes. (Our conclusions in this section are not in accord with those stated in Fogel and Engerman's *Time on the Cross*.)

This does not say that a single southern leader, a philosopher-king with a drawl, with the power to choose for the whole South would have elected to preserve slavery. What makes sense for single entrepreneur acting in isolation may not make sense for all such entrepreneurs acting collectively. It is conceivable that the economic welfare of the South would have been greater and grown faster over the long run had the South turned its back on the plantation system and developed a more diversified agriculture and a larger manufacturing sector. Let's see why.

Discrepancies between social and private rates of return are commonplace in development situations. For example, as we will see in the next main section of this chapter, very high rates of return to society from transport investments were often accompanied by financial losses for private investors in transportation companies. The reverse of this situation is a possibility for the South with respect to investment in plantation agriculture—private rates of return may have been higher than net social returns. Let's examine some key factors related to economic welfare from this standpoint.

First, the costs of racism are well documented.[28] We know that skilled blacks were discriminated against after the Civil War to their loss and the loss of the South as a whole—see Fogel and Engerman's *Time on the Cross* in this regard. To the degree that the plantation economy encouraged slavery and to the degree that slavery encouraged racism, southern economic welfare was impaired. However, the nature of the link between slavery and racism is not clear. Free blacks were discriminated against in the North as well as the South in the antebellum years, and nations which have never known black slavery practice ad-

---

[27] Ramsdell, p. 177.

[28] See Becker and Nicholls for discussions of racism and economic welfare.

verse racial discrimination. There is little to indicate that racism requires slavery as a precondition.

Second, plantation agriculture is frequently cited as a drag on per capita income growth. Here the data suggest the opposite. In fact, as compared with the North, the South's growth excelled, as 6–5 indicates.

6–5.   Per capita income of the free U.S. population by region, 1840 and 1860

	Per capita income (dollars)		Annual growth rate (percent)
	1840	1860	
National average.	109	144	1.3
North.	110	142	1.3
Northeast	130	183	1.7
North Central (West).	66	90	1.5
South.	105	150	1.8
South Atlantic (Old South)	96	124	1.3
Eastern South Central (New South)	92	124	1.4
Western South Central (New South)	238	274	0.7

Notes: (1) Because the figures are for the free population, they are not comparable with regional per capita income figures shown elsewhere in this text.
(2) Population shifts toward low-income areas in the North and toward high-income areas in the South explain the slower growth of the North and the faster growth of the South compared with their subregions.
SOURCE: Engerman, p. 87.

The per capita income of the free population, after adjustments for costs associated with maintaining slaves, approached or exceeded the U.S. average in both 1840 and 1860, although the long-established South Atlantic states fell far below the equally long-established Northeast.

Further, the per capita income of the free population grew at 1.8 percent annually in the South compared with 1.3 percent in the Nation as a whole. (Note that we are looking at the data from a southern standpoint and counting slaves as chattels rather than as consumers.) To say that income per capita in the South grew faster than in the Nation as a whole is not, however, the same as to say that income per capita grew at the maximum potential rate. Nevertheless, the rapid comparative rate suggests that the maximum was approached.

Third, the movement of economic welfare may very well have been at variance with per capita income movements. (Recall our discussion in chapter 1 of the usefulness of the national income accounts in charting the course of economic welfare.) Comparative population growth rates suggest that on the average individuals made greater welfare gains in the North than in the South. The North's population grew at an annual rate of 3.3 percent, whereas the South lagged at 2.4 percent.

Only in the western reaches of the New South, where new cotton plantations were most profitable, did both population growth and per capita income exceed the northern averages. The rest of the South was hardly a land of opportunity. The rapid increase of opportunities for unskilled workers in the North drew labor from the South and overseas. The resulting change in skill mix would have caused per capita income to drop in the North and to rise in the South without affecting the income or welfare of individuals already in the North and the South.

In the antebellum years, large-scale migration from Europe, of which very little was directed to the South, plus a small outward migration from poorer sections of the South, biased the per capita income growth figures against the North. Nevertheless, the Southwest aside, it was in the North that the immigrant and the poor southern migrant found his chance to better himself.[29]

A fourth way to view the consequences of the plantation economy is from the standpoint of forward and backward linkages and related feedback effects that might have made for rapid income growth in the antebellum period, yet retarded growth in subsequent decades. It has long been asserted that human and social overhead capital formation were checked by the intertwined realities of plantation economics and politics. The usual argument is that plantations did not require a large stock of social overhead or an educated laboring class and that the planters, who were also the political establishment, kept their taxes low by discouraging such projects.

On the surface, the data on this count appear conflicting. Certainly, field work didn't require skilled labor inputs to any great degree, and the facts are that human capital formation received very little encouragement in the form of expenditures on public education. The same can be said of social overhead associated with urban areas. On the other hand, the South had its share of railroad mileage by 1860, and as compared with the North it was heavily subsidized from the public purse. Apparently the establishment saw potential payoffs in better transportation, yet recognized that the prospective rate of return on public spending for human capital investment and other forms of social overhead was very low.[30] Further, plantations manifested a wide variety of skill demands in other than field work, demands that were met by training slaves.

A second linkage argument is that the South grew cotton while the North financed, transported, warehoused, merchandised, and spun it, then turned around and sold the planter whatever merchandise he

---

[29] See Fischbaum and Rubin for a fuller account of the argument against using per capita income growth as a definitive criterion of an economy's success.

[30] See Fogel and Engerman, p. 337.

needed. Consequently, the South did not build up an institutional structure that would make the region profitable ground in which to plant
other kinds of enterprises, especially manufacturing. Certainly, urbanization, commercial activity, and manufacturing—all good indicators of
this kind of social overhead—were underrepresented in the South. It
was to the southern investor's advantage to literally plough back his
earnings from cotton rather than venture into manufacturing or
commerce.

What if the South had been chiefly characterized by small commercial
family farms like those of the West? It could be that investment would
have covered a broader range and, although near-term per capita income
growth might have suffered as it did in the West, the long-term growth
rate would have been higher. The degree of truth in this we will never
know, but we do know that by the mid-19th century cotton earnings
yielded ground as a percent of total U.S. income as world demand
for cotton slowed in its rate of increase—from 1860 to 1900 the value
of cotton production rose at 1.7 percent per year, whereas U.S. population grew 2.2 percent, and the population of the South grew at 2.0
percent. Thus, by 1859 the South found itself tied to a low-growth industry, a victim of its own comparative advantage.[31]

A third linkage argument is that manufacturing was not stimulated
because the southern market was too small, that the highly unequal
distribution of income made the market for manufactured products too
thin. But admittedly scanty data show that income distribution was
no more unequal in the South than in the North. Moreover, in 1860
the southern market was large enough to support 50 cotton textile plants
and 200 footwear plants of a size comparable to that of the Massachusetts mills.[32] Again, the point is that prospective private returns
steered financial accumulation into plantation capital—comparative advantage, as a collection of individual investors determined it, dictated
cotton specialization.

So what can we say in summary about the plantation economy and
the South's development? We can't, of course, conclude definitively that
had southern leadership encouraged diversification, the South today
would be among the high-income regions of the United States. We do
think incomes in the South would be higher, however.

In our view, the social returns on manufacturing investment, human
capital formation, and other forms of social overhead would have justified steering a portion of plantation investment toward these areas and
bearing the short-term sacrifices in per capita income growth that such

---

[31] Fischbaum and Rubin present a similar argument based on the elasticity of
demand; however, their elasticity figures are short run.

[32] See Genovese for a statement of the argument and Fogel and Engerman,
pp. 336–37, for its refutation; see Engerman (1970), pp. 141–42, for income distribution analysis.

a reallocation would have entailed. It is not likely that relative attrition of the plantation economy would have brought widespread manumission—slaves worked effectively in southern factories in Charleston and elsewhere. However, factory experience would have proved valuable to former slaves after emancipation. We recognize, however, that no institutional framework for planning the region's investment pattern existed at that time, and we doubt that ending slavery even as early as 1793 would have curtailed the plantation system enough to accomplish this end.

How do we reach this conclusion? Perhaps the following comparison of the southern and northern economies will make clear the basis for our conclusion that the South's initial comparative advantage worked to the region's long-run disadvantage.

The South and the North developed along markedly different paths from basically agricultural beginnings. Both regions grew in the way they did as a result of individual decisions made by hundreds of thousands of farmers, merchants, and manufacturers operating in a free enterprise market economy. The decisions they made were rational choices designed to maximize their potential gains within the environment in which they found themselves.

In the North, considerations related to natural and human resource endowments produced an investment pattern conducive to growth. The North's export-industry mix and agricultural structure encouraged:

1. development of laborsaving farming methods and machinery;
2. industrial diversity based partially upon local processing of food products and the manufacture of farm machinery in such cities as Chicago;
3. urbanization with its attendant external economies;
4. growing local markets shielded by high transportation costs; and
5. the cultivation of energetic business leaders.

Thus, although industrial specialization is usually a source of economic strength, being forced to diversify turned out to be fortunate for the North—when the U.S. market became large enough to support a wide variety of modern manufacturing industries, the North was able to provide the required entrepreneurs, labor force, and external economies.

In the context of southern resource endowments, equally rational profit-oriented decision-making produced an agricultural export base dominated by cotton culture. What did not, could not, show up in the decision-making calculus of southern investors was that plantation agriculture resulted in a lack of favorable feedback effects through linked industries. Consequently, in the postbellum years, when southern leaders recognized that cotton would remain, at best, a feeble economic sovereign, their attempts to encourage different forms of export investment were severely restricted by the cumulative manifestations of two centuries of plantation agriculture. Predominantly rural, low-income, poorly educated societies with highly stratified social systems and a farm-oriented middle class provide very poor environments in which to situate manufacturing plants.

NORTHERN AGRICULTURE

Four key characteristics of northern agriculture are helpful in understanding its antebellum history. First, as we have already indicated, the frontier line and the geographic center of U.S. food production moved steadily westward. Second, northern farming became increasingly specialized and commercialized. Third, productivity growth in food production made possible the expansion of nonfarm industries. And, fourth, improvements in transportation divided the period into three distinct epochs.

Commercial family farms

From 1790 to about 1820 northern farming changed very little. In the Northeast, the agricultural hinterland provided food and fuel for the urban populations, which, in turn, earned their livelihood from or on the seas. In the backwoods, beyond the range in which most crops could be shipped to urban markets, basically self-sufficient farming units were arrayed around hamlets which sometimes reached a population of 2,500 but were usually smaller. In all, perhaps 80 percent of the rural North's food output was consumed by the 90 percent of the population that lived on farms or in rural villages.

In this early period, individual farmers strove to be self-sufficient in food and manufactured goods while producing a small surplus to barter for things which it was impossible to produce on the farm—for example, tobacco, coffee, tea, salt, spices, gunpowder, firearms, knives and axes. The local storekeeper served the vital role of assembling the surpluses of local farmers for sale to the 20 percent of the rural population that didn't farm—the blacksmiths, masons, shoemakers, millers, teachers, ministers, and innkeepers. The one or two stores in each village constituted the main commercial link with the outside world by shipping local surpluses of high-value produce (e.g., smoked meat and whiskey) and importing manufactured goods. In short, rural life was insular, independent, and spartan. Until transportation improvements were made, there was no economic alternative to virtual self-sufficiency.[33]

As rural and urban populations expanded and, after 1815, as steamboats and canals were introduced, the self-sufficient farm was gradually replaced by the commercial family farm, which produced a specialty

---

[33] See Danhoff, pp. 2, 3, for further discussion of this epoch and citations of the relevant literature.

crop to be sold for cash. Steamboats and canals meant lower freight rates and, thus, a wider market range for any farmer on a navigable stream, the Great Lakes, or a canal. In addition, improved water transport connected areas within the West, integrating small, isolated markets into a whole large enough to support intraregional specialization. The growth of rural and urban population meant larger markets within that range. A heavy East-West trade developed in which western foodstuffs were exchanged for manufactured goods from the East.

Gradually, farmers changed their output mixes to reflect increased contact with the market. First to go were home-crafted goods—time could be spent more profitably in producing foodstuffs for sale outside the region. Next, farmers abandoned the practice of raising almost all of their food supply in favor of more specialized output patterns. They purchased more food products and a wider range of condiments, sweeteners, and beverages. Rural life didn't take on a leisurely pace, but it did become more varied and less rigorous as the farmer and the market came together.

The villages reflected the marketization of northern farming. Increasingly, local handcraft manufacturing gave way to factory-produced products that were shipped from the developing manufacturing centers. Typical of the transition, the blacksmith became less the manufacturer of iron implements, especially plow fittings, and more the horseshoer and local repairman.

The timing of the emergence of the commercial family farm varied geographically. Near the cities of New England and the Middle Atlantic states, roadways and high population density produced a significant amount of commercialization before 1820. In the West, self-sufficiency was generally a transitional stage during the period of farm-making. The early movement west followed the navigable rivers and the later westward movement was canal-bound, so, once established, the western farmer could grow a significant cash crop for sale outside the region.

In the 19th century, the greatest difference between farming in Europe and in America was the shortage of labor here. This helps to account for America's higher farm wages. Economic analysis, of course, leads us to expect that as compared with other regions where one factor of production (land) is plentiful and demand for the product is growing, the other factors (labor and capital) will be more highly rewarded. The high rewards, then, will attract more labor and capital, and production will expand as a result. In America, when times were good and prices high, the adventurous who had a stake moved west to open new lands, producing a series of surges in western land settlement.

The first source of farm labor was the farm family itself. A high birthrate, healthy mothers, and a good diet produced many children who survived and at an early age were out to work gardening, milking, herding, churning, and fruit picking. As children grew to maturity, they gradually shared in the heavier work at home—haying, fencing, harvesting, and threshing—or were hired out to other farmers. The object of most young men was to own a farm, although many remained hired laborers. The first step to ownership might be to rent a farm and share the crop with the landowner, hoping to save enough to buy the land. Or a small stake might be saved and used to move west and buy public land to start a farm.

A second source of farm labor was the immigrant. Many immigrants had been farm tenants or farm laborers in Europe, and their object was farm ownership. Competition for such workers, however, was provided by city work and construction projects that could provide high wages and long steady periods of employment. Because many of the immigrants came with enough funds to start their own farms, it was not easy to find or hold farm workers. In general, family workers far outnumbered hired hands.

From the earliest times it was characteristic of most American farmers to hold more land than could be worked immediately and to devote much of their initial labor to building up capital improvements. Before the prairies were reached, a western farmer had to repeat the colonial farm-building cycle. He first cleared a small patch of forest for a garden and corn to feed his family and a few head of livestock; then he cleared more land for wheat and other small grains to sell for cash. From then on he steadily cleared, fenced, and expanded his holdings. His methods were crude and destructive of the fertility of the soil, but with so much land at hand he had little conservation incentive.

Like the southern planter, the northern farmer was often heavily in debt. The farmer borrowed to buy land, livestock, and tools, to build a house and barn, and to expand his operations. As long as prices held up, those loans represented an investment in future production capacity and could be repaid out of expanded output.

There is little evidence to show that debt was a crushing weight to farmers in general, although particular farmers did overextend themselves. When the farmer speculated in more land than he could work or counted too heavily on very high prices, he risked losing everything in mortgage foreclosures. The region, however, was fertile and provided profitable opportunities; the farmers were ambitious and optimistic; and owners of capital were ready to make loans at the high prevailing interest rates. So the surges of land settlement brought streams of capital as well as flows of labor to the West.

Productivity increases

Food output grew at about the same rate as total population in the antebellum period. However, American agriculture was able to keep up with an expanding demand for food while simultaneously reducing agricultural labor requirements. In other words, productivity gains were chiefly of the laborsaving variety: this means that capital equipment was substituted for labor, thereby expanding output per worker. In the North, although agricultural workers increased from 997,000 in 1820 to 3.1 million in 1870, farm workers dropped from 76 percent to 37 percent of the labor force. The real value of northern farm output per gainfully employed worker rose from $294 to $495 over the period.

The gains in food productivity were split between releasing a portion of the farm population to nonfarm work and accommodating a slightly healthier national appetite—while the farm population increased less than 3-fold from 1820 to 1870, the urban population grew 14-fold and the value of northern farm products consumed or sold rose from $51 to $59 per capita. For reasons we will suggest below, almost all the productivity gains in northern farming were achieved in the period 1850–70.[34]

Four factors are chiefly responsible for the rise in agricultural productivity: the reduction in the proportion of redundant farm workers; the increased cultivation of Western soils; improvements in farming methods and equipment; and external economies associated with general population growth and transportation changes.

Labor shortages plagued the American economy in the colonial and antebellum years. But there is some evidence to suggest that, as compared with manufacturing and other nonfarm pursuits, there were too many people engaged in farming just after the War of 1812, that some farm workers were redundant. Consequently, for the early stages of the antebellum period, farm and nonfarm productivity increases can be partially attributed to the relative reduction in agricultural employment. In other words, economic growth was generated in part because a portion of the Nation's labor resources was shifted out of farming into areas of greater productivity. Again, note that the shift was relative; in absolute terms, both farm and nonfarm employment grew throughout the period.

As the frontier moved westward, the new land brought into cultivation raised the average productivity of American land under cultivation. In the Northeast, farms were abandoned or their productivity was increased by conversion to livestock and dairy operations, while in the North Central region, new grain farms were established on superior soils. Until 1850, mechanization and changes in farming methods were only modest. Thus, a major role in explaining total factor productivity increases must be assigned to the geographic shift in northern farming. Further, input versus output measures indicate that the growth of total factor productivity in northern food production was very modest over the first half of the 19th century.

Improved farming methods and mechanization began to play a sig-

---

[34] See Danhoff, table 1, and Towne and Rasmussen, pp. 258–61.

nificant role in increasing farm efficiency in the 1850s and 60s. In fact, this 20-year period is sometimes called America's first agricultural revolution because the machinery and new methods that had been developed in the 1820s, 30s and 40s were widely adopted just before and during the Civil War. Compared with farming's almost static world history, the results of this agricultural revolution were just short of phenomenal—real output per farm worker rose from $294 to $362 in the two decades ending in 1870 and most, if not all, of this gain was concentrated in the North.[35]

Mechanization was spurred in the 1850s by high grain prices resulting from the Crimean War. For example, as wheat farmers increased production to take advantage of high world prices, they bid up farm wage rates and expanded their individual acreages to a point at which they were encouraged to substitute the mechanical reaper for harvest workers. Then, during the Civil War, when one third of the farm labor force joined up, labor shortages provided a tremendous incentive to mechanize and adopt improved techniques.

Agricultural mechanization had a long and checkered history before the period from 1850 to 1870. Farmers were always anxious to save labor and ingenious in doing so. But the underdeveloped state of the arts handicapped them. As a consequence, each of the devices that became widely used in the 50s and 60s had made its way along a tortuous route, led on by the stubborn pragmatism of the northern farmer. For example, the improvement of the plow, always an obvious candidate for redesign, was seriously impeded by knowledge barriers. In 1800, men just didn't know enough soil chemistry to specify how deep a plow should penetrate, or enough metallurgy to design a light, durable plow that would penetrate to the proper depth and turn the soil without having it stick to the moldboard. By 1840, however, enough had been learned to make a plow that was vastly superior to its 18th century counterpart.

Rather than leave farming, many northeastern farmers sought to lower costs by increasing yields and developing laborsaving devices. The farmer with an idea fashioned parts out of wood, and the local blacksmith could manufacture almost any part or fitting the farmer had in mind. Thus, as competition from new, more fertile western lands grew, the Northeast became a font of technological improvement.

As you might guess from the foregoing, the first important improvement in farm tools was a better plow. As early as 1797, Charles Newbold had patented a one-piece cast-iron plow, but it was expensive, heavy, and brittle. Between 1814 and 1819, Jethro Wood brought together a number of existing improvements to perfect a plow with three replace-

---

[35] See Towne and Rasmussen, pp. 258–61, Danhoff, and David for accounts of farm productivity changes in the period from 1850 to 1870.

able iron parts. It was simpler, lighter, and less expensive than its predecessors, and the parts could be manufactured in factories in large numbers. In 1837, John Deere developed the first successful steel plow. Steel plows were especially important in prairie farming, since the sticky soil could be pushed off the smooth, polished surface relatively easily.

In the 1830s and 1840s, other laborsaving inventions were developed. In 1833 and 1834, Obed Hussey and Cyrus McCormick patented reapers that could be pulled by a horse and could cut many times as much wheat as a man swinging a sickle or a cradle. In the late 1830s, John and Hiram Pitts combined thresher and winnowing devices and linked them to a horse-powered treadle. Later, mobile steam engines were introduced to run the threshers which contract operators moved through the wheat areas for a fee. Many other devices were developed to save labor by using horse power—for example, the mower, the hay rake, the tedder, the horse fork (to hoist hay to the loft), the grain drill, and the corn planter.

By 1851, at the World's Fair in London, American farm machinery was acclaimed as superior to that of any other nation. By that time, factories in the East and in the North Central states were mass-producing the equipment. Successful mechanization increased the output per farm worker but required the family farm to be much larger in acreage. It also increased the capital requirements of the farm, and did so in a way that required the purchase of capital equipment rather than merely allocating on-farm labor to the construction of capital goods. Farm implement and machinery investment rose from an annual rate of $2 million in 1845 to $54 million in 1875.

In the course of agricultural mechanization, an advantageous reciprocal relationship arose between the farm and the factory. Improved manufacturing methods enabled the actual production of many implements that could not have been brought beyond the idea stage in earlier decades. The farm sector, in turn, provided demand for manufactured goods and, through laborsaving mechanization, released labor to work in factories. The American consumer came off the big winner—his income bought increasingly more food and manufactured goods.

The following account from the May 1873 issue of *Scientific American* suggests the vast feedback effects that agricultural mechanization had upon manufacturing and urbanization in the antebellum period:

> The increasing tide of emigration settling toward our Western territory, together with the rapid settlement of large tracts of fertile and arable land by classes devoted to agricultural labor as a means of subsistence, has given rise to the development of an industry that has assumed proportions of almost incredible magnitude. We allude to the manufacture of agricultural implements, without the aid of which the profitable working of large farms would be a physical impossibility. Of these great works the largest and most complete are located in Chicago. The

most extensive is the manufactory of Messrs. C.H. McCormick & Brother, and it is engaged in the production of the celebrated McCormick reaper.

Farm operations also improved in ways distinct from mechanization. Recognition of the market premium that superior breeds and strains would bring for livestock and grains turned farmers toward controlled breeding and seed improvement. Commercial fertilizer sales became significant in the 1850s. Farmers took to manuring their fields on a regular basis. Lime and plaster plus rotation crops were used where the soil was depleted.

Agricultural journals, pamphlets, and papers, some of them government-sponsored, gained increased circulation as labor and market pressures plus soil exhaustion focused attention on the need for better cropping practices. People began talking seriously about experimental farms where new knowledge could be developed, and Congress passed the Morrill Act in 1862 to give federal aid to state-supported agricultural colleges.[36]

Transportation economies played a key role in enabling the farm sector to continue to feed adequately a growing and urbanizing population. As a nation grows, farm output must grow at least as fast as total population if diet is not to suffer. If urbanization is taking place at the same time, farm produce usually must be brought over increasingly greater distances to urban markets. Longer hauls in supplying food can be made possible by any combination of the following:

1. urbanites can pay higher relative food prices by spending less on nonfood items;
2. city dwellers can pay higher relative food prices by increasing their productivity and, thus, their disposable incomes;
3. farm productivity can increase, offsetting higher transportation costs; and
4. transportation productivity can increase, offsetting the costs of shipping food longer distances.

Pre–Civil War history shows that in fact all but the first of these alternatives came into play. Roads, steamboats, canals, and railroads were built and improved, which steadily increased the amount of arable land within reach of transportation facilities and reduced transportation costs between established shipping points. As agriculture pushed west, higher-yield land was put under the plow, mechanization reduced labor inputs, and improved methods and greater specialization of farms increased efficiency.

In all this, the establishment of transportation facilities, especially the steamboat and canals, must be assigned the major credit for per-

---

[36] Changes in northern farm methods are reported in detail in Danhoff, chaps. 3, 7, and 10; Towne and Rasmussen cite input expenditure figures, pp. 260–61.

mitting urban growth, at least until 1850, when agricultural mechanization probably took over as the major factor. In the absence of transportation investment and improvement, population change would have been largely limited to the growth of rural farm families working subsistence-level, self-sufficient farms in the West. Had this happened, not only would the direct gains from cheaper transportation have been lost, but in addition the gains from mechanization and output specialization, which depended upon access to markets, would have been lost as well.

BUILDING A TRANSPORTATION NETWORK

As we noted above, the history of northern agriculture is divided into three phases, marked off by two major improvements in transportation. To a large degree, this evolutionary pattern was reflected in the development of the Nation and its regional division of labor. The first phase covered the period from the end of the Revolution until 1825; in this period, transportation improvements were largely confined to providing roadways in the more densely settled areas and improving river cargo vessels. The second phase was the canal era, in which settlers moved across the Appalachians in unprecedented numbers. The third phase began with the railroads pushing into Illinois, Wisconsin, Iowa, and Missouri and accelerating the growth of midwestern population density and agricultural output.[37]

Roads and riverboats

Prior to 1800, road building had connected the major cities of the New England and Middle Atlantic states in a system of more than 20,000 miles. Later road construction was primarily confined to tollways, with the National Pike as the chief exception.

Private toll-road building in the United States was stimulated by the success of the Philadelphia and Lancaster Turnpike, which was built in 1789. During the next four decades more than 400 companies constructed several thousand miles of hard-surfaced highways in New England, New York, and Pennsylvania. However, only the shorter, heavily traveled roads near or between large cities were profitable. Stagecoach passengers, but little freight, moved over long distances. After the mid-1830s short plank roads were built for farm-to-market travel because they cost less than the macadam-topped highways.

Government involvement in road building was restricted almost entirely to the state and local levels, and even that was limited. When Ohio was admitted as a state in 1803, it was stipulated that part of the revenue from public land sales was to be used for state and federal

---

[37] In addition to the transportation references cited below see Fishlow, pp. 472–91, for discussion of antebellum transportation improvement.

road construction. After much controversy over implementing this stipulation, federal construction was authorized in 1811 for the National Pike
(or Cumberland Road), which is now U.S. 40. It was completed from
Cumberland, Maryland, to Wheeling, West Virginia, in 1818. Not until
1833 was it extended to Columbus, Ohio; and it did not reach Vandalia,
Illinois, until the mid-1850s. Other proposals to build a system of federal
roads and canals were defeated largely because of sectional rivalries.
New York and Pennsylvania were jealously vying for western routes
connected to their own port cities; the New England states had built
their own road systems; and the South, relying on river and ocean transport, preferred to minimize the need for federal revenues, largely because tariffs were the chief source of federal income.

Road building was not to prove revolutionary in any event, because
it was costly to move bulky farm products by wagon. On a trail, a
horse could carry about three 60-pound bushels of wheat. Over a road
a team might pull a wagonload of 25 bushels. On a canal barge, a
horse could pull 50 times as much weight as it could on a wagon.
It is not surprising that average freight rates in 1850 have been estimated
at around 15 cents a ton-mile by wagon and a penny a ton-mile by
water. After deducting the costs of an average wagon haul of 80 miles,
a Minnesota farmer might receive three fourths or less of the price
of his wheat delivered at the nearest port. An effective argument in
favor of the proposed Erie Canal, which was begun in 1817, was that
it would lower by one fourth to one half the transportation cost from
western New York to market. Farmers saw that this could double their
receipts if prices held.

The westward movement, confined as it was to navigable rivers in
this period, presented a transportation dilemma. The usual farm commodity route was over the Ohio and Missouri tributary systems to the
Mississippi, down the Mississippi to New Orleans, then shipment by
sailing ship to the East. Downriver shipments were comparatively easy,
but the return trip was expensive under any conditions. Flatboats could
be broken up and sold for lumber after arrival at New Orleans from,
say, Pittsburgh, but the trip home was a long one on foot or horseback.
Keelboats could manage a round trip, but rowing, pulling, and poling
upstream when the wind failed required a huge expenditure in manpower. Consequently, Fulton's demonstration in 1807 that steam power
could propel a vessel was greeted with immense enthusiasm in the West.

By 1815, the *Enterprise* had successfully steamed over the New Orleans–Pittsburgh route. This voyage portended a series of freight-rate
reductions which were even more dramatic in their effects on inland
transportation than railroad shipping cost reductions. On the New Orleans–Louisville run, upstream freight rates fell initially from $64 per
ton in 1815 to $40 per ton in 1820. Then, as the steamboat and steamboat-
ing were improved and the industry became increasingly competitive,

freight rates continued to fall, reaching $5.60 per ton in 1860. Perhaps the steamboat should be credited with starting the transportation revolution, while canals and railroads carried it on—certainly the steamboat opened up the West for market-oriented agriculture.

Flatboats remained profitable throughout the antebellum period, although their share of total freight declined in favor of steamboats. They were still inexpensive to build and operate, and the owners could book passage on a steamboat for the return trip. So flatboating remained viable. However, keelboating could not survive the incursion of the steamboat; the keelboat disappeared from the Mississippi run in the early 1820s.[38]

Road building and steamboats had quite different influences on the structure of agriculture. Even improved roads left rural areas without an economical means of transporting bulky foodstuffs to market. They did, however, reduce the cost of exporting high-value commodities, such as whiskey, hides, and smoked meats, and of importing expensive manufactured articles. Thus the farmer who lived well outside the major urban areas and far from navigable rivers had to remain largely self-sufficient until the canal-building period.

In marked contrast, farmers on navigable streams were highly favored by the advent of the steamboat and improved efficiency in steamboat and flatboat operations. Reduced freight rates increased their access to markets and, accordingly, their specialization. In turn, cities such as Pittsburgh, Louisville, Cincinnati, and St. Louis thrived as interior entrepôts linking the Midwest with New Orleans and the East.

Canals

In 1825, completion of the Erie Canal from the Hudson River at Albany to Lake Erie at Buffalo marked the beginning of a canal-building fever and a new era in transportation. Although very short canals connecting inland centers to ports had been built prior to 1800, the Erie Canal—364 miles long—was America's first major canal. It was immediately apparent that it would be a financial success. Very fertile wheatlands lay between Rochester and Buffalo, so a heavy movement of wheat over nearly the full length of the canal was assured from the start. However, the most important value of the canal was that it circumvented the Appalachian Mountain barrier to east-west travel. The Erie Canal connected two great waterways—the Great Lakes and the Atlantic Ocean—via the Hudson River. Before its completion, Niagara Falls and the rapids on the St. Lawrence River had blocked exit from the Great Lakes to the Atlantic.

A burst of canal-building activity occurred in the late 1820s and early

---

[38] For freight-rate movements see Mak and Walton (1972, 1973); Haites and Mak report on the history of flat- keel- and steamboating from 1810 to 1860.

1830s. (See 6–6.) Four western canals were built to link the Great Lakes with the Ohio and Mississippi river system (the Ohio and Erie, the

6–6.   Canals linking rivers and lakes

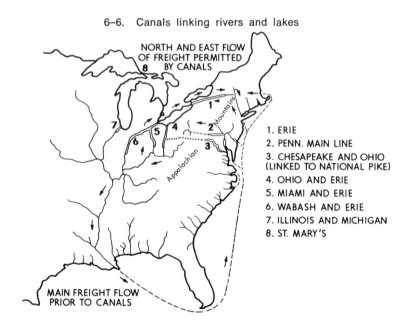

1. ERIE
2. PENN. MAIN LINE
3. CHESAPEAKE AND OHIO
(LINKED TO NATIONAL PIKE)
4. OHIO AND ERIE
5. MIAMI AND ERIE
6. WABASH AND ERIE
7. ILLINOIS AND MICHIGAN
8. ST. MARY'S

Miami and Erie, the Wabash and Erie, and the Illinois and Michigan). These routes shunted the flow of farm products from a southward to an eastward direction after the mid-1830s, and they also increased traffic on the Erie Canal. However, they were not as successful financially as the Erie.

Two other major canals were designed to compete with the Erie by crossing the Appalachian Mountains. The Pennsylvania Main Line was completed from Philadelphia to Pittsburgh. It involved an ingenious combination of canals and rails, with the barges lifted onto rail cars to be pulled over the mountains. The Chesapeake and Ohio was designed to connect the Potomac River with the Ohio but was completed only as far as Cumberland. Neither was financially successful. Compared with the Erie Canal, they were costlier to build and carried less local traffic, and, unlike the Erie, they did not connect with a vast inland lake and river system (the eastward movement on the Ohio being an upstream one).

Other useful canals were built near the eastern port cities, but the canal-building fever was quickly over. Generally, canals inspired by the Erie did not duplicate the Erie's main-line profitability—their narrow markets in the crucial early years, the depression of 1837, and the competition of railroads beginning in the 1840s all combined to discourage further building. Exceptions were the St. Mary's Canal, built in the 1850s, which opened up navigation to Lake Superior and the iron ore mines in the Upper Peninsula of Michigan, and the anthracite canals in Pennsylvania.

Specialized wheat farming received its greatest impetus from canal transportation. The Ohio River valley lost its predominance as a wheat farming area as the canals gave the midwestern prairies access to markets. The big increases in public land sales during the 1834–37 boom were in Michigan, Indiana, and Illinois. In spite of the depression following that boom, Illinois continued to have active land sales during the 1840s, when sales also began to be substantial in Iowa and Wisconsin.

The close of the canal-building period was ultimately brought about by the railroads, although the canals were important transport arteries until at least 1880. The history of the canals leaves us with a paradox: on the average they were not profitable, yet their mark on American economic history is irrefutable.

Where canals were built, freight rates fell initially from an average of 15 cents a ton-mile by road to 2.3 cents by canalboat, and by 1850 rates were around a penny a ton-mile. Freight charges were reduced so drastically that the Mississippi lost its control over the pattern of interior settlement—the entire direction of population movement and the flow of commerce shifted. The Upper Midwest became the center of settlement, and east-west trade became the predominant pattern.

Yet a look at the books of the various companies would tell you that the canals were losing propositions. Too many of the benefits of better transportation spilled over into areas which could never be tapped by toll charges; the social rate of return on canal investment exceeded by far the private rate. In other words, had the investment decision been based upon a full social-benefits calculation, there seems every reason to believe that at least the Erie and Ohio systems would have been built, even given prior knowledge of the coming railroads.

The prairies and the railroads

By the 1850s, technical and economic factors combined to produce a railroad-building boom. A generation of experience and experimentation with engine and track design, materials, and roadbeds made possible the building of a dependable national railroad system with a high load-carrying capacity. Economical employment of the horse-drawn reaper, the thresher, and the other mechanical innovations we discussed earlier required larger farms. Consequently, the high wheat prices of the 1850s touched off a new spurt of land sales which were concentrated in Illinois, Iowa, Wisconsin, and Missouri and gave the railroads someplace to go. And go they did—track mileage rose from 9,000 to 30,000 miles in the 1850s. (See 6–7.)

6–7. Main railroads, 1850 and 1860

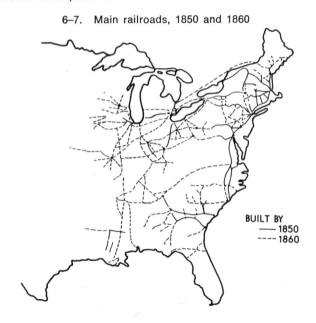

BUILT BY
—— 1850
---- 1860

Railroads also provided a new and better interregional link with the Northeast. Rail transportation was faster, less disrupted by weather, and permitted fewer transfers of cargo en route. While some railroad construction had occurred in the mid-1830s, further construction was probably delayed by the canal boom and then the depression of the late 1830s. During the 1840s, construction was generally confined to the East, linking the coastal areas from north to south. Then, in the beginning of the 1850s, several rail lines were extended across the mountains in New York and in Pennsylvania, while a line was completed across Michigan to link Chicago and Detroit.

In the North Central states a network of lines was established, connecting all of the major cities and fanning out over the prairies. Rail lines could be laid hastily and cheaply across the flatlands, and the wheat crop promised to provide a heavy freight traffic. In the South, there were fewer railroad lines and these usually connected the more isolated upland areas with a South Atlantic port. Rail connections were made with the North only at Cairo, Lexington, and Richmond. The South's river and ocean routes apparently made rail lines seem less necessary. (See 6–7.)

A peak in immigration added momentum to the railroad's penetration of the West in the 1850s. Scandinavians, other northern Europeans, and Germans began to flock to the prairie farmlands. Railroad developers helped promote farm settlement along their lines, while land companies provided credit and aided in establishing whole communities.

The railroad has been accorded a hallowed place in American economic history, often being cited as the prime mover in 19th century economic development. Reduction in freight rates and opening new land for cultivation and new markets for manufacturing industries are the broad stimuli to economic growth usually attributed to the railroads. Precisely how important the railroads were in influencing our development experience is a subject of current debate and a topic we shall take up in chapter 8, when we are prepared to consider eastern and western railroad development simultaneously.

At this point, we wish to caution you as follows: The railroads did indeed speed passenger travel, reduce freight rates, permit additional farms to enter the market economy, and buy huge amounts of goods and services from other industries; but these are very gross measures. Remember that there already existed a canal and river system when the railroads were introduced, and rates charged on that system were quite low even compared with rail rates; further, the inputs claimed by rail construction had alternative uses, so one must be able to show that rail construction was a superior use of those resources.[39]

SUMMARY

1.   The mix of labor, capital, and natural resources that characterized the United States in its early nationhood dictated specialization along agricultural lines. In turn, the Nation's farm economy sustained economic development and per capita income growth in two ways: agricultural exports permitted importation from the rest of the world, and laborsaving innovations permitted supplying workers to other industries.

2.   Given the vast size of the territory under U.S. control and the diversity of natural resources with which the U.S. economy was endowed, a pattern of regional agricultural specialization naturally evolved during the early antebellum years. Southern producers concentrated on growing cotton, tobacco, and sugar, with cotton as the predominant export crop. Northeastern farms supplied fruits, vegetables, cereals, meat, and dairy products to nearby cities. And western farmers supplied grains and livestock to eastern markets and, by the end of the period, significant amounts of wheat to European markets.

The pattern of agricultural specialization among regions fitted nicely into the Nation's overall regional division of labor. While filling its food deficit by importing from the West, the Northeast provided a wide range of commercial and financial services as well as manufactured products to the South and West. In turn, the South earned most of the Nation's supply of foreign exchange by selling a major portion of its staple production overseas, especially by exporting raw cotton to England.

---

[39] See chapter 8 for citations of the literature on the economics of American railroads.

3. Southern agriculture was dominated by family-owned plantations which employed slave labor, although families owning more than ten slaves never made up more than 10 percent of the southern population. A variety of studies indicate that on the eve of the Civil War slavery remained a viable and profitable institution and that purchase of land and slaves would yield a southern investor at least as high a return as alternative uses of his savings that were open to him. Northern agriculture was almost wholly made up of commercial family farms which employed few workers outside the family.

4. Transportation improvements made possible two important changes in northern agriculture. First, the steamboat, the canals, and, to a lesser degree, road building enabled subsistence family farms to specialize and produce for markets, that is, to become commercial family farms. Second, transport improvements enabled commercialized farming to penetrate farther and farther into the West, adding to the amount of land available to support the appetites of burgeoning eastern cities. In one sense, the improvements in waterborne commerce were even more dramatic in their effects than the railroads—the railroads filled in transportation gaps and opened up the territory west of the Great Lakes, but the initial westward movement of commercial agriculture was made possible by the steamboat and canals.

5. The secondary effects of regional farm and nonfarm production patterns became important influences upon development that persist to this day. Midway in the antebellum period it became clear that the South's continued domination by plantation agriculture was going to brake its economic growth rate as compared with that of the rest of the Nation. This occurred even though King Cotton had brought initial prosperity and purchases of land and slaves continued to be profitable for individual investors.

By contrast, the dynamics of northern agriculture forced diversification on the region. In the Northeast population growth exceeded agricultural capacity. In all of northern agriculture, laborsaving methods and machinery released larger and larger portions of each new generation to supply labor to urban-based industry. Industrialization became both the chief manifestation and the chief part of the process of sustained northern development. On the one hand, northern industrialization was abetted by comparatively heavy investments in human and social overhead capital. On the other hand, the structure of economic incentives in the plantation South militated against public education and widespread internal improvements.

APPENDIX TO CHAPTER 6: DEMAND AND SUPPLY ANALYSIS

Economic theory uses demand and supply curves as logical tools for picturing the results of the interactions between buyers and sellers in a market for a particular good. Just as an X-ray picture provides only a skeleton outline of the body, so supply and demand curves provide only a skeleton outline of market phenomena. The pictures are static snapshots showing relationships at one instant in time. By changing the positions of the curves to reflect the introduction of controlled successive changes in basic market conditions, the economist achieves something like the stop-action camera techniques now fashionable in television and the movies; he is then able to predict the results implied by changes in market conditions.

The material that follows may be somewhat difficult to comprehend upon first reading if you haven't had some introduction to economic theory elsewhere. But we do not expect you to master this analysis on the basis of these few paragraphs. What we are demonstrating is that economists have developed analytic tools that permit organizing, interpreting, and explaining the seeming chaos of price and quantity movements in real world markets. We will be gratified if you're able to gain an appreciation of the power of these analytic tools in explaining historical occurrences. More specifically, we hope that you can follow with greater insight our descriptions of particular events in U.S. markets, such as our account of the relationship between cotton prices and the expansion of capacity under the heading "Demand, supply, and price fluctuations" in this chapter.

Let us approach this by plotting theoretical demand and supply data on a graph just as the economist would do in working with an actual historical problem. (See 6–8.) Note that we show prices on the vertical axis and quantity per time period on the horizontal axis.

Demand curves are illustrations of schedules that pair various quantities that purchasers would buy at alternative prices, assuming that other factors are constant over the time period in question. In the example given in 6–8, at 10 cents per unit buyers would purchase 7,000 units per year. This you can determine from the graph by locating 10 cents on the vertical axis, moving at a right angle from that point until you reach the demand curve, then moving down parallel to the vertical axis until you strike the quantity axis at 7,000 units. If the price were lower, let us say 7 cents per unit, a greater quantity—9,000 units—would be purchased. If other conditions are held constant, the less expensive a given product, the greater will be the quantity of that product that people are willing to purchase. Thus the demand curve, which is drawn by linking the various price-quantity points, slopes downward to the right. (For now, ignore the solid dots to the right of the demand curve.)

Correspondingly, supply curves are illustrations of schedules that pair various quantities that sellers would be willing to bring to market at different prices, other factors being held constant during the period under study. The higher the price, the greater the willingness of producers to bear the higher costs per unit associated with increasing their

6–8.   Theoretical demand and supply curves

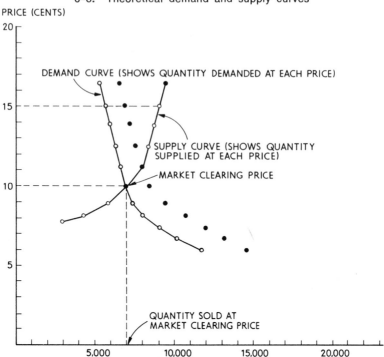

PRICE (CENTS)

DEMAND CURVE (SHOWS QUANTITY DEMANDED AT EACH PRICE)

SUPPLY CURVE (SHOWS QUANTITY
SUPPLIED AT EACH PRICE)

MARKET CLEARING PRICE

QUANTITY SOLD AT
MARKET CLEARING PRICE

QUANTITY / TIME

rates of production in order to increase the supply. Thus the supply curve we get by linking our price-quantity points slopes upward to the right.

At the price of 10 cents we have a unique price-quantity combination. Only at that point in our price-quantity space does the quantity demanded—7,000 units—equal the quantity supplied. Only at 10 cents will buyers' decisions match sellers' decisions. In other words, 10 cents in our illustration is the **equilibrium,** or **market-clearing, price.** This can be readily understood by considering buyer and seller reactions to higher or lower prices.

At a higher price, the quantity demanded is less than the quantity supplied. Suppliers will note that they are in danger of not selling all of their goods, so they will offer lower prices in order to get some buyers to increase their purchases. Consequently, the market price will fall.

At a lower price, the quantity demanded is greater than the quantity supplied. Sellers, noting that sales are unusually brisk, will raise their asking prices. As the market price floats upward, some buyers will be cut out of the market.

These opposite pressures on the price reach an equilibrium at the market-clearing price, where the quantity demanded just equals the quantity supplied. The quantity sold then clears the market, satisfying both buyers and sellers.

So far, only one static set of conditions is involved. But the usefulness of demand and supply curves lies in determining the results of a change in conditions—i.e., shifts of either demand or supply or of both. Let us consider first an increase in demand. For example, buyers' preferences could change so that at each price they would be willing to purchase a greater quantity. The solid dots plotted to the right of our original demand curve illustrate this: note that at 10 cents nearly 9,000 units would be bought and that at 7 cents more than 12,000 units would be purchased. This would shift the entire demand curve to the right, as you can see by mentally linking the new points together.

Now a new market-clearing price-quantity combination would come about. Because buyers are willing to pay more per unit, sellers are able to bear higher unit costs in bringing a larger quantity to market with the result that the price would rise to 11 cents and the quantity sold would advance to 8,000 units.

You can picture similar results on the assumption that the demand curve remains constant but that a cost-reducing innovation causes the supply curve to shift to the right. As you might guess, the market-clearing price would fall while the quantity sold would increase.

At this juncture let us add a realistic element to our analysis by turning to 6–9, which illustrates the cotton market in the antebellum years. The curves are hypothetical but are drawn so that their equilibrium points fit the actual price-output experience between 1837 and 1860. Thus they illustrate the statistical analysis that Wright performed, which we cited in reference to cotton price fluctuations.

In 1836–37, cotton sales came to 1.13 million bales at 13 cents per pound, as is illustrated by the equilibrium point of the supply and demand curves labeled with the subscript 37. In 1837–38, poor British and American economic conditions reduced the demand for textiles, shifting the raw cotton demand curve to the left, while a bumper American crop moved the supply curve to the right. As the demand and supply curves labeled 38 show, the quantity sold increased to 1.43 million bales and the market-clearing price fell to 10 cents. Then, in 1838–39, British and American economic conditions revived, shifting the demand curve to the right, while drought cut the cotton crop by over 30 percent, shifting the supply curve to the left. As the curves marked 39 show, the market-clearing price rose to 13 cents again, and the quantity exchanged fell to 1.09 million bales. The bumper crop of 1839–40 was large enough to more than offset the continued improvement in economic conditions, so cotton prices again fell precipitously (see the S and D curves labeled 40).

6-9.   Cotton prices for selected years, 1836–37 to 1859–60

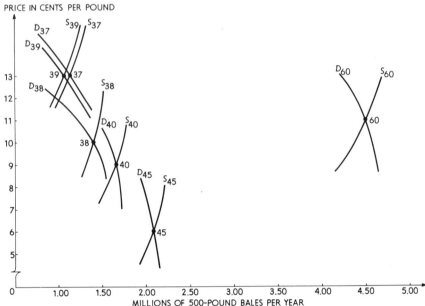

SOURCE: U.S. Department of Commerce, pp. 124, 302.

Now let's shift to 1844–45. By that season, world textile demand had grown in response to population and per capita income growth. Supply had increased as well, to 2.08 billion bales, largely in response to the long-run tendency to expand cotton cultivation as long as cotton production remained generally profitable. Note, though, that the rightward movement of the supply curve had exceeded the shift in demand so that the market price hit its antebellum low, 6 cents per pound. After this nadir, cotton prices—exemplified by the S and D curves for 1859–60—displayed an upward trend with only minor deviations until the Civil War broke out.

At this point, we can generalize on the basis of the example we have just presented. Because demand and supply conditions are constantly changing, this illustration of shifting demand and supply curves is helpful in understanding the types of price and output changes that result:

1. when demand expands faster than supply, a scarcity of goods tends to raise the price;

2. when supply expands faster than demand, a surplus of goods tends to lower the price;

3. when demand contracts while supply expands, prices tend to plunge in order to induce reluctant buyers to purchase an augmented supply; and

4. when demand expands while supply contracts, prices zoom in order to ration a restricted supply among eager buyers.

REFERENCES

H. G. J. Aitken, ed., *Did Slavery Pay?* (Boston: Houghton Mifflin Co., 1971).

G. S. Becker, *The Economics of Discrimination* (Chicago: University of Chicago Press, 1957).

A. H. Conrad and J. R. Meyer, "The Economics of Slavery in the Ante Bellum South," *JPE*, April 1958.

C. H. Danhoff, *Change in Agriculture: The Northern United States, 1820–1870* (Cambridge, Mass.: Harvard University Press, 1969).

P. A. David, "The Mechanization of Reaping in the Ante Bellum Midwest," in *The Reinterpretation of American Economic History*, eds. R. W. Fogel and S. L. Engerman (New York: Harper & Row, Publishers, 1971).

S. L. Engerman, "The Effects of Slavery upon the Southern Economy," *EEH*, Winter 1967.

M. Fischbaum and J. Rubin, "Slavery and the Economic Development of the American South," *EEH*, Fall 1968.

A. Fishlow, "Internal Transportation," eds. L. E. Davis et al. *American Economic Growth*, (New York: Harper & Row, Publishers, 1972).

R. W. Fogel and S. L. Engerman, "The Relative Efficiency of Slavery: A Comparison of Northern and Southern Agriculture in 1860," *EEH*, Spring 1971.

R. E. Gallman, "Self-Sufficiency in the Cotton Economy of the Antebellum South," *AH*, January 1970.

E. D. Genovese, "The Significance of the Slave Plantation for Southern Economic Development," *JSH*, November 1962.

L. C. Gray, *History of Agriculture in the Southern United States to 1860* (Washington, D.C.: Carnegie Institution, 1933).

E. F. Haites and J. Mak, "Ohio and Mississippi River Transportation, 1810–1860," *EEH*, Winter 1970.

D. L. Lindstrom, "Southern Dependence upon Interregional Grain Supplies," *AH*, January 1970.

J. Mak and G. M. Walton, "Steamboats and the Great Productivity Surge in River Transportation," *JEH*, September 1972.

———, "The Persistence of Old Technologies: The Case of Flatboats," *JEH*, June 1973.

W. H. Nicholls, *Southern Tradition and Regional Progress* (Chapel Hill, N.C.: University of North Carolina Press, 1960).

D. C. North, "Sources of Productivity Change in Northern Shipping," Fogel and Engerman, cited above.

W. N. Parker, "Agriculture," eds. L. E. Davis et al., cited above.

U. B. Phillips, "The Economic Cost of Slaveholding in the Cotton Belt," *PSQ*, June 1905.

C. W. Ramsdell, "The Natural Limits of Slavery Expansion," *MVHR*, September 1929.

R. Ransom, "Canals and Development: A Discussion of the Issues," *AER*, May 1964.

——, "A Closer Look at Canals and Western Manufacturing in the Canal Era," *EEH*, Summer 1971.

P. Temin, "The Causes of Cotton-Price Fluctuations in the 1830's," *RES*, November, 1967.

M. W. Towne and W. E. Rasmussen, "Farm Gross Product and Gross Investment during the Nineteenth Century," in *Trends in the American Economy in the Nineteenth Century,* ed. W. E. Parker (Princeton, N.J.: Princeton University Press, 1960).

U.S. Department of Commerce, *Historical Statistics of the United States* (Washington, D.C.: U.S. Government Printing Office, 1960).

G. Wright, "'Economic Democracy' and the Concentration of Agricultural Wealth in the Cotton South, 1850–1860," *AH*, January 1970.

——, "An Econometric Study of Cotton Production and Trade, 1830–1860, *RES*, May 1971.

7 MODERN MANUFACTURING EMERGES

In 1851 U.S. manufacturing stole the show at Great Britain's Crystal Palace Exhibition. American technology so impressed British and other observers that they termed it the *American System of Manufactures.* Manufacturing had become the prime mover of U.S. growth, and the astute observer could sense that the United States was to become the world's chief industrial power. Yet in 1790, the U.S. economy was almost wholly agricultural, dependent upon home industry, handcraft shops, and imports from English mills and factories for its manufactured products. In this chapter we will describe the emergence of modern manufacturing in the United States and offer some explanations for this remarkable record.

American manufacturing growth involved two distinct elements. First, in addition to increasing its relative and absolute size, the manufacturing sector underwent a transformation from a potpourri of handcraft shops and mills employing centuries-old processes into a series of factory industries employing the modern industrial method. In other words, the factory system landed in America. In some cases the organization of production clearly anticipated not only Henry Ford's assembly line but automation as well. On the other hand, not all manufacturing had undergone this transmutation by 1860—on the eve of the Civil War, much of America's manufactured output was made by hand and much of that in the home. The nature of the trend was unmistakable, however.

Second, *import substitution,* the process by which an economy begins to produce items which it has characteristically imported, became a dominant feature of American industrialization. Once British factory production methods were adopted in the United States, ocean freight rates became a barrier which effectively sheltered American producers. Although the textile industry provides the most dramatic case of import substitution, the process was by no means confined to textiles.

223

Data on manufacturing for the antebellum period are sketchy. Nevertheless, we can give you some idea of the absolute and relative dimensions of American industrialization. In 1820, 75,000 Americans worked in factories, 10,000 of them in textile works, whereas almost 2 million people labored on farms and plantations. The comparative factory and farm figures for 1860 were 1.5 million and 5.9 million. By 1860, manufacturing accounted for 14 percent of the labor force and farming for only 52 percent. Thus, although farm employment dominated the absolute employment changes, manufacturing employment held sway in terms of rates of growth.[1]

Note one qualification: these data do not include household and craft-shop manufacturing, but are confined to factory and mill employment; hours worked in homes and craft shops were probably greater than hours worked in mills and factories in 1810, and they increased from 1810 to 1860. Coopers, silversmiths and blacksmiths, carriage makers and cabinetmakers, cobblers and tailors were still ubiquitous in 1860. But home spinning and weaving were confined to the frontier, and factory-made furniture, clothes, and shoes were becoming increasingly common.

A variety of forces made manufacturing growth inevitable.

1. As we've noted before, agriculture released labor to other callings, including factory jobs.
2. Transportation improvements not only permitted farmers to market their crops more efficiently but also lowered the cost of importing manufactured commodities from other regions.
3. Economic expansion coupled with per capita income growth provided external economies and a burgeoning market for American manufactures—remember that after the basics are provided for, consumers want manufactured commodities.
4. And technological change produced new products and lower-cost production methods.

But just why we started on a route that permitted us to outpace Britain as an industrial nation is not clear, beyond the facts that our resource endowments, transportation facilities, and market size favored U.S. industrialization.

When Harpers Ferry came under attack, manufacturing had come to dominate American economic growth both quantitatively and qualitatively. In 1790, the U.S. economy was atomized and agrarian. In 1860, it was industrializing at a rapid pace, urbanizing with equal speed, and generating changes in business organization, finance, and govern-

---

[1] For a review of antebellum industrial composition changes in the labor force see Lebergott, pp. 188–91.

mental economic policy which were largely attributable to manufacturing growth.

THE INDUSTRIALIZATION PROCESS

Supply, demand, and manufacturing growth

If you recall our discussion of demand and supply curves in the appendix to chapter 6, you will remember that a particular industry can be pictured as in equilibrium when a market-clearing price is obtained as shown below (see 7–1A). You'll also recall that changes in

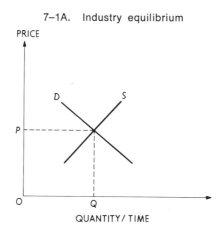

7–1A. Industry equilibrium

basic supply and demand conditions can be shown as new price-quantity relationships, i.e., as shifts in the demand and supply curves (see 7–1B).

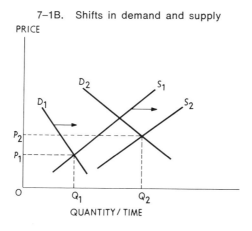

7–1B. Shifts in demand and supply

Now let's relate these principles to manufacturing growth, in particular to a given manufacturing industry.

If a given force, say growth of the total number of farms, caused demand for a certain manufactured good, say plows, to shift positively, then the price would advance and the equilibrium quantity exchanged each year would increase. Graphically, the change would look as in 7–1C. On the other hand, if the efficiency of plowmaking increased,

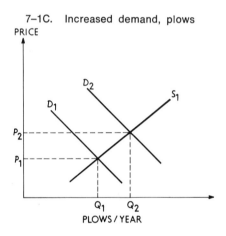

7–1C.   Increased demand, plows

the supply curve would shift to the right, reflecting the fact that lower production costs have induced new producers to enter the plow industry. Graphically, the result would look like that shown in 7–1D. Note that

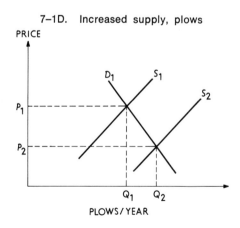

7–1D.   Increased supply, plows

in this case the quantity exchanged in equilibrium increases, **but** the price declines.

But what if new demand and new technology were to come to plowmaking simultaneously as they in fact did with the advent of the steel plow? The results would be as pictured in 7–1E. Now let's analyze the

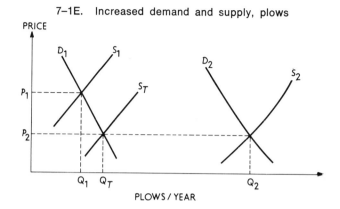

7–1E. Increased demand and supply, plows

change that took place. The industry's efficiency increased, which we can interpret as meaning that, *in the absence of an increase in demand,*

1. the supply curve would have become S_T,
2. the price would have fallen to P_2, and
3. the quantity exchanged would have increased to Q_T.

But because demand also increased, the actual quantity exchanged increased by far more, specifically by the amount from Q_T to Q_2.

Thus we can break down increases in equilibrium sales volume into quantities attributable to increases in demand and quantities attributable to increases in supply. In this case, the movement of the supply curve from S_1 to S_T was the result of greater efficiency achieved through new technology, whereas the movement of supply from S_T to S_2 was brought about by new producers entering the market. The growth in the number of farms and, therefore, the demand for plows increased profits by enough to attract new entrepreneurs and capital to the industry, thereby shifting the supply curve to the right from S_T to S_2.

Soon we will use this analytical technique to explain the expansion of the textile industry. But as a prelude to our analysis we should investigate the process which generated technological innovation in America during the antebellum period.

Technological innovation[2]

Broadly, when it comes to manufacturing, technological innovation can involve either the application of new inventions to the production

---

[2] For more extended discussions of the points covered in this subsection, see both Rosenberg and Temin (1972).

of an existing range of products or the development of new products. Often these two elements coexist in the marketplace—new products come on the market for which new production techniques have been specifically worked out, or new products are made possible subsequent to the invention of a new manufacturing technology.

The steel plow had to await metallurgical breakthroughs, whereas canned goods came to the market after the British invented canning processes to solve logistic problems during the Napoleonic Wars. In the United States, the technological innovations of the first half of the 19th century were often adaptations of European technology rather than brand-new techniques or products. In fact, before the Civil War perhaps the bulk of new products and gains in production efficiency involved importing British or Continental technology lock, stock, and barrel.

Since the early antebellum years, U.S. manufacturing growth has been characterized by the incessant development of new technologies and their application to production processes and product development. However, in the years before the Civil War the process of invention was less scientific than pragmatic. Inventors were tinkerers who got bright ideas and discovered the applicable scientific principles in the trial-and-error process of converting their brainstorms to a physical process or a product. Some succeeded and produced vast results for the economy; Eli Whitney is a titanic example. Others failed because they didn't know the physics or chemistry involved; an absurd but dramatic example is the legion of inventors who to their dying day were still trying to produce a perpetual motion machine and still ignorant of the laws of physics as they relate to friction.

One characteristic of the new products and processes that were brought forth by the American manufacturing sector prior to the Civil War was their heavy bias toward conserving labor. The reasons for this bias are not entirely clear, however.

American manufacturers had to bid labor away from agriculture in a situation in which land was very inexpensive to acquire. Accordingly, as compared with incomes from property, wages in America were higher than in Britain. Thus, whenever two production processes were already available, American manufacturers could be expected to choose the alternative that was capital- or natural resource-intensive and laborsaving. The British, on the other hand, would have a greater incentive to conserve capital and natural resources.

But why should new technologies have been predominantly laborsaving in America? Surely, manufacturers wouldn't turn their backs on other ways to reduce costs in order to continue searching for ways to conserve on labor inputs. Although we can't give you a comprehensive general explanation for the laborsaving bias of antebellum technological change, we can present some partial explanations and offer several tentative general hypotheses.

The incentive to invent and manufacture laborsaving farm equipment is easy to identify. The northern farmer in his quest for more time and a less arduous workday sought laborsaving devices. Thus he represented a rich market for manufacturers of newly developed laborsaving implements.

In other cases, the chances for substituting machine for manual operations were probably easier to see than cost-reducing innovations that conserved other inputs. For example, American woodworking, which was without a peer, employed machines and methods that, as compared with woodworking in Britain, reduced labor inputs and raised wood inputs. This was the obvious innovational route to follow in America because American forests were so plentiful.

Given the range of basic scientific information, it may be that laborsaving opportunities vastly outnumbered other ways to reduce production costs. The basis of the Industrial Revolution was the substitution of waterpower and steam power for human and animal sources of energy. Mechanization is at heart a process of designing machines that are guided by humans but are powered by nonhuman energy sources. In later decades, after science and technology had advanced well beyond their early 19th century limits, more opportunities for cost reduction by conserving raw materials and reducing capital inputs per unit of output doubtless became apparent.

It is also possible that manufacturers noted an upward trend in wage rates and thus viewed laborsaving techniques as the optimum direction of their innovational energies. However, there is no direct evidence to show that entrepreneurs consciously biased their innovations so as to hedge against rising labor costs.

American consumers were more flexible than the British in the standards they set for the products they bought. They were willing to accept standardized consumer products in order to have them at lower cost. By contrast, the British buyer just wouldn't accept reduced variety in consumer products—he wanted custom manufacturing, and this required a high labor content.

Environmental factors certainly influenced the course of technological change in the United States. Americans were utilitarian, so they kept an eagle eye on production, looking for ways to reduce input costs, and they were willing to see the final product modified if it could be made more cheaply thereby. Education in America was more democratic and more oriented toward the practical arts than education in other countries, so perhaps the potential pool of tinkerers was larger in America than elsewhere. And, of great importance, American per capita income was high and growing rapidly over much of the period, so potential returns from new products and techniques were high. In short, Americans were interested in developing new and better technologies and willing to devote resources to their development; cost reductions

obtained chiefly through laborsaving innovations and a grand variety
of new products were the results.

EARLY AMERICAN INDUSTRIALIZATION

Industrial trends

As we stated above, household manufactures, handcraft shops, local
mills, and imports were the sources of early U.S. manufactured products.
Over the antebellum period, total U.S. factory-produced output grew
faster than the total economy, displaced household manufactures, and
reduced both imports and craft-shop output to a minor portion of the
sales of manufactured goods. Early manufacturing growth was extremely
rapid in relative terms, but not until the 1840s were output and employment increases sufficiently great in absolute terms to earn manufacturing
the dominant role in the economy's development.

Although the data are sketchy, 7–2 succeeds in illustrating the growth

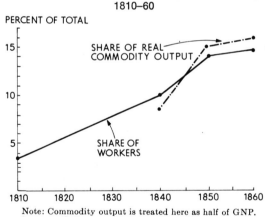

7–2. Rising importance of factory manufacturing,
1810–60

Note: Commodity output is treated here as half of GNP.
SOURCES: Gallman, p. 61; Lebergott, p. 187.

of factory manufacturing compared with that of the balance of the economy. Note that the rise in factory employment as a share of the labor
force took place when the total labor force was increasing very rapidly;
this means that the absolute increases were getting larger and larger
over the years. Note also that the very rapid increase in the factories'
share of total real commodity output between 1840 and 1850 suggests
that factory output accelerated late in the antebellum period. What's
more, the data suggest that production grew faster than employment
as a consequence of increased labor productivity.

The types of industries that were important in the rise of manufacturing are suggested by the census of 1860. (See 7–3.) Lumber and flour

7-3.   Ten leading U.S. manufacturing industries, 1860

Industry	Value added (millions)	Employees (thousands)
1. Cotton goods	$54.7	115.0
2. Lumber	53.6	75.6
3. Boots and shoes.	49.2	123.0
4. Flour and meal	40.1	27.7
5. Men's clothing.	36.7	114.8
6. Iron products	35.7	49.0
7. Machinery	32.6	41.2
8. Woolen goods	25.0	40.6
9. Carriages, wagons, carts	23.7	37.1
10. Leather.	22.8	22.7

SOURCE: U.S. Department of Commerce (1860).

mills were important from the beginning, and they were still the second and fourth ranking manufacturing industries in 1860. The first ranking industry, however, was cotton goods, while woolen goods placed eighth. Although these textile industries were virtually nonexistent in America in 1790, they constituted the first significant growth industry. Boots and shoes and men's clothing, the third and fifth ranking industries, had begun by 1860 to move from the large shop to the factory as a reaction to the commercial introduction of the sewing machine: their relative importance reflects the extent to which the making of clothing had shifted from the home to the factory. Iron products and machinery were the sixth and seventh ranking industries.

Altogether, this list suggests that, to a large degree, the rapid rise of manufacturing industries is to be explained in terms of the development and use of power-operated machinery to produce textiles, clothing, and shoes in factories rather than in the home. This was also characteristic of the Industrial Revolution in England, which was well underway by 1790. Because the American market was fragmented and smaller, that revolution did not get into full swing in America until about half a century later. The list also reflects the rapid substitution of domestic textiles for British cotton goods.

A national market

The growth of American manufacturing was shaped by transportation improvements in two ways. Better transportation lowered manufacturing input costs and increased the size of markets for manufactured commodities. The latter point requires some expansion. By welding together isolated population centers, transportation improvement created national markets where none had existed before. Consequently, wherever transport improvement pierced the hinterland, household and craft-shop manufacturing in the rural Northeast and the West gave way to factory products made in the urban Northeast (the South was always well served by river and ocean transport, so this effect was minor below the Mason-Dixon line.) Then, as the West filled up, regional manufacturing centers, such as Chicago and Cincinnati, emerged.

This effect is dramatically illustrated in 7–4, which shows the household manufacture of woolen cloth before and after the Erie Canal and its system of tributaries were completed. Note that in 1820 no counties along the Hudson River were among those having a high degree of household woolen production, while by 1845 no counties along the Erie Canal were important woolen producers. The same type of map could be drawn for craft-shop manufacturing or to reflect the conversion of the local blacksmith from custom ironwright to local horseshoer.

Transportation was not in itself a sufficient condition for the emergence of a national market. It is not enough to be able to ship goods long distances; men must be willing to do so, must feel assured that they will receive payment and can enforce the performance of contractual duties. In this, the evolution of commercial law was crucial. As Daniel Boorstin has stated it, "Without a general American legal system, technically defined and available in books, the *free commerce among our states and the industrial unity of our nation* might have been impossible."[3] [Italics supplied.]

Textiles' early lead

The textile industry provided Americans with a valuable learning experience in coping with high volume production by specialized firms that sold in national markets. The textile industry was a natural to take the lead in America's industrialization because:

1. cloth was a basic item in the household budget, which meant that the market was large;
2. the value of cloth per pound was great, which meant that it easily bore transport charges;
3. a well-developed technology for mass-producing thread existed in England;
4. Jefferson's embargo plus the War of 1812 gave the American market complete protection for a number of years.

The first successful American spinning machinery was built by an English immigrant, Samuel Slater, who smuggled the technical know-how into the country. Slater had spent six and a half years as an apprentice in the famous Strutt and Arkwright mill in England, where he had been allowed to experiment and make improvements in the machinery. He had memorized the key dimensions of the machines and

---

[3] Quoted in Higgs, p. 55; see Higgs, pp. 50–57 and 132–33, for a discussion of the role of the law and the growth of the market's geographic scope.

7–4. Household production of woolens in New York, 1820 and 1845

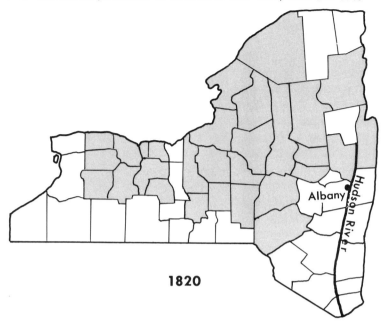

1820

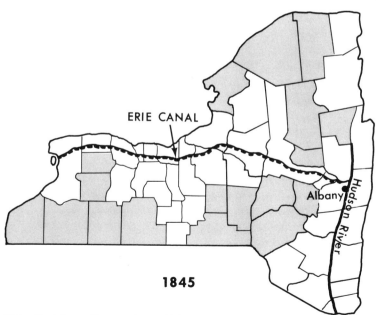

1845

Note: Shaded counties are those which account for the top 33 percent of woolen manufacturing per capita.

Source: Cole, p. 280.

was familiar with all of the parts. Knowing of the opportunities for similar factories in America, he dressed as a farm laborer and secretly sailed to New York, where he was put in touch with Moses Brown, whose firm, Almy and Brown, manufactured rough cotton goods for sale to southern plantations.

After demonstrating the success of his first machines, in December 1790, Slater became a partner with Almy and Brown and built a small factory in Pawtucket, Rhode Island. In the next few years, Slater and others who learned from him built Arkwright machines for several other factories in New England. By 1807, 15 spinning mills were operating in the United States. Between 1807 and 1815, the embargo and the War of 1812 cut off the import of British textiles, giving a great stimulus to the construction of spinning factories in America. By 1815, 213 mills were reported to be in operation.

American spinning mills made yarn and then put out their yarn to cottage workers. The cottage workers wove the yarn into cloth on hand-looms and returned the cloth to the mill for marketing. Handwoven cloth, however, could not compete with the cheaper English cotton cloth which by then was being made on power looms. Therefore, with the return of peace, cheaper British goods again flooded domestic markets and many of the American mills were forced to close.

Fortunately, another breakthrough in the acquisition of British technology had been made by an American manufacturer just before the end of the war. While traveling abroad in 1810 and 1811, Francis Cabot Lowell, a member of a wealthy Massachusetts family, learned enough about the cotton mills of Manchester to introduce power weaving to America. When he returned to America, Lowell and some business associates formed the Boston Manufacturing Company and built a mill at Waltham, Massachusetts. The Waltham mill was operating very successfully by 1814. To meet the postwar competition of British cotton goods, other American manufacturers quickly adopted the Waltham plan of combining power-driven spinning and weaving machinery in the same factory. Those that didn't failed.

At this point let's see why textiles continued to be manufactured profitably in the United States after British goods could again enter the country. In 7–5 the demand (D_1) and supply (S_1) curves for American cloth are pictured hypothetically along with the price at which British mills could deliver to the United States for the year 1816. Note that the British price was below the price ($P_{U.S.}^1$) at which American supply would meet American demand. Obviously, if this market had been left alone, Britain would have been able to undersell all but the most efficient of the new integrated spinning and weaving operations.

Americans responded to the challenge with the Tariff Act of 1816, which had the effect of raising British delivered prices enough to protect power loom firms but no handloom operations. Over the next decade

7–5. The American cloth market

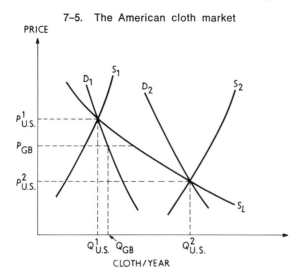

CLOTH/YEAR

or so, U.S. income and population growth stimulated domestic textile demand, and we feel that the efficiency of the industry grew with it. Our rationale for this position is simply the following: as the number of domestic producers and their combined output increased, their efficiency in getting their product into the hands of their customers probably also increased. This was a period in which warehousing, merchandising, and marketing operations in general were becoming more efficient.

Over the same period the tariff on textiles was reduced, which meant that as the industry required less protection it actually got less protection. Then, after 1825, the British government permitted exports of textile machinery to the United States, thereby making it easier to build integrated mills here. All this shows up in 7–5 as shifts in the supply and demand curves to S_2 and D_2, thus generating a lower U.S. price ($P_{\text{U.S.}}^2$). In other words, what the economists call the long-run supply curve (S_L in 7–5) was negatively sloped in this period, reflecting the fact that as the textile industry grew in size the collective efficiency of the firms in the industry increased. The data are consistent with this analysis; they show a 4-fold increase in textile imports from 1820 to 1860, compared with a more than 50-fold increase in domestic production.[4]

What the above analysis says is that if the tariff on textiles had been completely removed in the 1820s America would have continued to have a strong textile industry. Why? Because American manufacturers were by then serving a very large market, using a technology which was on a par with British production methods.

Now let's review the entire course of the textile industry's expansion in the antebellum period by summarizing a recent analysis of growth

[4] U.S. Department of Commerce (1960), p. 549.

in cotton cloth output.[5] Robert Brooke Zevin's study shows that production rose rapidly, at a compound rate of 29 percent per year, from 1815 through 1833, then increased at only 5.1 percent per year from 1833 through 1860. (See 7–6.) Although growth slowed in the latter

7–6.   Growth of the U.S. cotton industry, 1815–60
(compound annual growth rate, percent)

Period/subperiod	All cotton goods	Cloth only
1815–33	16.3	29.0
1815–24	16.1	42.1
1824–33	16.5	17.1
1833–60	5.2	5.1
1833–44	5.2	5.0
1844–50	8.0	7.8
1850–55	1.5	1.2
1855–60	6.0	6.2

SOURCE: Zevin, table 2.

period, these were very high growth rates as compared with the aggregate economy. Subperiods within these two periods show similar growth rates. Let's look at demand and supply shifts in order to explain this remarkable growth record.

On the demand side, five basic forces caused demand for cotton cloth to shift periodically over the antebellum years. Those factors and their relative importance are as follows:

1. The tariff contributed to the recovery of the industry after the War of 1812 but "made no significant contribution to the secular growth of American demand for New England mill products over the period from 1815 to 1833."[6]

2. Population can be assumed to have shifted demand for cotton cloth at about the rate of growth of the total population, i.e., at about 3 percent per year.

3. Increases in per capita income doubtless contributed to the growth of demand, but the data for the antebellum years are too poor to measure the impact of this variable.

4. Periodic improvements in the Nation's transport system permitted customers outside New England to obtain textiles at successively lower delivered prices, causing demand to grow at about 1 percent per year.

5. Increasingly, the American consumer's tastes and habits favored cotton cloth rather than woolens and cotton cloth woven at the factory rather than cotton cloth woven at home. On these counts, the demand for cotton goods shifted positively until about 1833. Zevin estimates that the shift of weaving to the mill from households

---

[5] Zevin—the discussion follows Zevin's approach closely.

[6] Zevin, p. 128.

caused mill demand for cloth to increase by about 12 percent annually up to 1833.

On the basis of Zevin's estimates of the importance of the demand factors listed above, we conclude that the demand shift alone caused sales of cotton cloth to rise at 18 to 19 percent annually up to 1833 and at 3 to 4 percent annually after 1833. These growth rates account for about 60 percent of the total growth rate of U.S. mill-woven cotton cloth in the early antebellum years and for 60 to 80 percent of the growth rate between 1833 and 1860.

On the supply side, we can similarly list a set of forces shifting supply which in turn resulted in lower prices and increased sales for cotton goods. When added to the demand factors, these supply factors complete our accounting for the total growth of cotton cloth output in the U.S. They are:

1. As demand grew, periodic bulges in profits induced new suppliers to enter the industry and existing firms to build additional mills. Even without any cost-reducing innovations, the delivery of cotton cloth to American consumers would have grown as demand shifted. Once American mills adopted the power loom, it was assured that the shifts in American demand would be accommodated by increases in American capacity.
2. The adoption of the power loom lowered the cost of weaving by 75 percent and shifted supply positively.
3. Raw cotton prices declined enough to reduce the price of cotton cloth by one sixth; and technical change enabled producers to get more than 10 percent more thread out of a pound of raw cotton.
4. Improvements in machinery and organization enabled the value of labor input per yard to decline even while real wages were rising.
5. Textile machinery prices fell over the period, reducing capital costs per yard of material.
6. To Zevin's five items we add external economies from improved marketing techniques associated with the early growth of the industry.

The technical change components that appear on the above list collectively account for over 80 percent of the decline in cotton cloth prices during the years 1815 through 1860. In turn the decline in prices which stimulated the quantity demanded accounted for about 40 percent of the increase in quantity exchanged in the period from 1815 to 1833 and perhaps a third of the total in the period from 1833 to 1860.

Graphically, we can represent the history of the industry as shown in 7–7. From 1815 to 1833, demand shifts alone would have caused cloth sales to rise to Q^D_{33} at the 1815 price. But increases in productivity plus declining raw cotton prices caused prices to decline to P_{33}, and quantity exchanged

7-7. Cotton cloth market

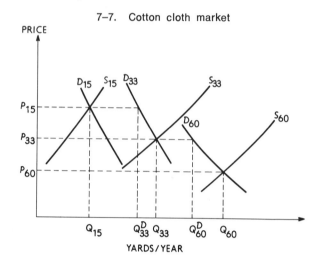

increased by the additional amount shown as the difference between Q_{33}^D and Q_{33}. Then, between 1833 and 1860, both demand and supply slackened in their rates of increase so that quantity demanded would have grown to D_{60}, and brought sales to Q_{60}^D at P_{33}. However, because the industry simultaneously grew more efficient, supply expanded beyond the requirements of the demand shift, prices fell to P_{60}, and quantity exchanged increased beyond Q_{60}^D to Q_{60}.[7]

New production processes, machinery, and tools

Much of the technology employed in America's antebellum manufacturing sector was imported from Britain—Britain pioneered in the development of steam power, in the widespread application of cheap iron, and in the substitution of machinery for hand labor. But Americans can be credited with at least two special technological innovations: continuous processing, or assembly-line production, and the assembly of products using interchangeable parts, known as the American System.

As the demand for manufactured products grew, a wide range of technological problems confronted manufacturers who sought to increase production. Basically the problems involved the design and utilization of machinery and equipment. Originally, solutions to these problems were provided by producers of consumer goods (e.g., textiles), but, ultimately, specialized capital goods firms emerged to provide the technological basis for 19th century industrialization.

The most important among these capital goods manufacturers were the machine builders and the machine-tool industry. These allied indus-

---

[7] This graphical approach was suggested by the summary of Zevin's work by Temin (1972), pp. 421–22.

tries were incessantly called upon by their customers to provide new techniques and develop new skills to solve production problems as they arose. Once solutions were worked out, the machine and machine-tool makers became a diffusion medium. By producing newly designed machines, they enabled new processes to be supplied in diverse variations to all metal-using industries. Put slightly differently, the emergence of the machine-tool and machine makers lowered the cost of innovation and spurred technological change in all metal-using industries.

A dominant trend characterized the pattern of technological innovation in the metal-using industries: the production process was increasingly subdivided, and special-purpose machinery was designed to perform single fabrication or assembly operations. In cases of mass demand and standardized products, mechanized assembly lines lowered unit costs tremendously. As the examples cited below suggest, it is no accident that the American System emerged from the firearms industry while continuous processing came from flour milling.[8] Now let's review some illustrations.

As early as 1787, a flour miller named Oliver Evans developed what may have been history's first continuous processing operation. Evans developed a system of machinery that automatically performed the sequence of heavy labor and handling operations necessary to move the grain through the mill and emerge as barrels of flour. Power from a waterwheel was geared to a whole series of devices. A shoveling device, endless belts running over rollers, and buckets on a vertical lift conveyor did the initial work of handling the grain. The grain was then allowed to fall between cracking and grinding stones, to separate the bran, and was packed into barrels by a series of chutes, valves, and rakes. Only two men were needed to operate the mill.

While Evans's system was adopted slowly and piecemeal at first, the advantages of continuous processing became so obvious that variations of automatic machinery were used nearly everywhere after 1815. The culmination of Evans's contribution is the automated assembly plant we associate with today's auto industry.

Numerous other ways were being found to use machines to perform repetitive tasks as well as in heavy work. In the 1770s, a machine was introduced that cut and headed nails. In the 1790s, woodworking machines were cutting the teeth and forming the curved parts of cards and combs for the textile industry, and a lathe was being used to turn round and oval wooden handles.

Eli Whitney, the inventor of the cotton gin, is credited with the first successful use of interchangeable parts. Having observed minting machines stamping out standard copper coins and wood-turning lathes, he decided to manufacture muskets by using a full line of guided tools.

---

[8] See Rosenberg, pp. 251–60, for an extended analysis of technological innovation; this discussion follows the outline of his argument closely.

In 1798, he obtained a contract for 4,000 muskets from the U.S. Army. To demonstrate the efficacy of his idea, he disassembled a number of guns, scrambled the parts, and reassembled them. Standard parts had advantages for the repair of products in use as well as for economy in manufacture.

Simeon North also produced arms about the same time, using even greater specialization of workers on narrow phases of the manufacturing process. The government armories at Springfield, Massachusetts, and Harpers Ferry, Virginia, also deserve special mention in connection with the beginnings and development of interchangeable parts. Later refinements in these methods enabled Samuel Colt to develop and mass-produce his revolving barrel pistol during the Mexican War.

Clockmakers soon adopted the idea of using standard parts in their industry. In 1807, Eli Terry built a large mill which used Whitney's methods of punching out and cutting standard wheels and cogs. Clocks previously selling for $25 were soon sold for $5. What's more, the substitution of metal parts for wooden parts further lowered costs and improved quality.

Interchangeable parts manufacture was aided by the development of light metals industries. Paul Revere had introduced large-scale copper rolling in order to sheathe the bottom of the *Constitution* and the dome of the Massachusetts State House. In 1802, the brass industry began to develop in Waterbury, Connecticut. While the heavy metal industries were more advanced in England, America took an early lead in mass-producing light metal products and light machinery used in mass-production factories.

If you doubt the vast impact of these technological changes, recall how manufacturing took place before the days of interchangeable parts. Even where the overall production process was divided between parts manufacture and assembly, at each stage in assembly the file was the most important tool, and its job was to make things fit so they worked. A gunsmith might spend an hour filing a hammer so that it struck in the right place. Then, the advent of standardized parts made it possible to mount the hammer in seconds by only turning a screw.

The development of specialized machine and machine-tool businesses was stimulated by and contributed to all of these developments. Evans and Whitney made their own machinery. When Slater built his first textile mill, he had the help of an ironmaster named David Wilkinson. After helping Slater build several mills, Wilkinson opened his own machine-building shop at Pawtucket in 1810, the same year Alfred Jenks started his machine shop near Philadelphia. These American machine builders independently discovered, or introduced from England and improved upon, the basic machine tools—the slide lathe, the milling machine, and gear cutters.

By 1840, a specialized machine-tool industry flourished as machine-tool manufacturers grew in number and gradually displaced many of the machine-building shops that were merely departments within textile, armament, and other types of plants. A clear line of descent can be traced from textile mills, to textile machinery makers, to manufacturers of heavy machinery and engines, including locomotive manufacturers. A similar lineage can be cited from small arms makers to manufacturers of high-precision, high-speed light machinery.

Some idea of the rise in inventive activity that came as part of American industrialization is suggested by the records of patents issued by the national government. The records suggest three periods of rapid rise in inventions—1807–14, 1825–35, and 1850–60. Each was a period of rising business activity; so you might argue that inventions were forthcoming when business opportunities were good. (See 7–8.)

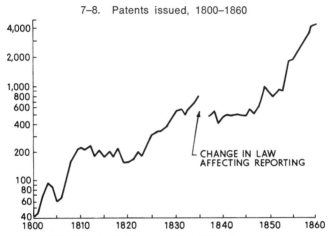

7–8. Patents issued, 1800–1860

Note: After 1830, duplications were eliminated in the reporting procedure.
SOURCE: U.S. Department of Commerce (1960), p. 608.

Most of the early inventors were businessmen, became businessmen, or were backed by businessmen. Slater was financed by Brown and became a partner in several textile firms. Evans and Whitney established their own manufacturing industries. Lowell was a man of wealth who acquired the necessary technology and started a manufacturing firm with the aid of a group of wealthy merchants.

This subsection should not close without reminding you that the history of invention is an encyclopedia of disappointments, long neglect, and business failures. A number of people, for example, experimented with the steamboat and the steam railroad before successful models were developed and successful businesses established. Seldom was it possible to exploit the monopoly rights of a patent by keeping other producers from using or closely imitating the patented idea. Both Whitney and

Evans spent a great deal of money unsuccessfully trying to protect their initial patents. Only by rapidly expanding production and improving the product did the early inventors manage to profit and stay ahead of their competitors.

Power, fuel, and iron technology

From earliest colonial times, the power to drive the machinery of mills and the bellows of furnaces was readily available from waterwheels on the numerous streams coursing down the Appalachian Mountains. Many of the early textile plants were located at the same river sites as the older mills. As these sites became crowded and more power was needed, large dams were built to provide a greater fall, use more of the water, and provide a more regular flow throughout the year. The great concentration of textile industries at Lowell, Manchester, and Lawrence, Massachusetts, was due to the development of waterworks on the Merrimack River in the 1820s.

In part, prodding from the steam engine led to attempts to improve the efficiency of the waterwheel and additional experiments with the water turbine. Practical water turbines were first used by textile mills in New England in 1843. In the next few years, Americans made important contributions to turbine technology that were widely adopted in the 1850s.

Because of the availability and cheapness of waterpower, steam engines were not rapidly applied to manufacturing. In 1804, when low-pressure steam engines were already in use, Evans obtained a patent for the high-pressure steam engine which he developed to drive his flour mill machinery. By the War of 1812, about a dozen of Evans's engines were in use, but their adoption in manufacturing was slow.

The cost of the steam engine was itself high, and, as compared with the waterwheel, its fuel intake and higher maintenance costs actually made it a labor-using rather than a laborsaving device. As late as 1840, steam power near eastern Pennsylvania coal sites was four times as expensive per horsepower as waterpower at Lowell.

Steam engines were used principally at sites where waterpower was not readily available and in furnace industries, where the heat employed could be used to generate steam. Apparently, before railroads were ubiquitous the steam engine was used as a substitute for transportation in that it made possible locating heavy power-using industries near their markets instead of at water sites.[9]

The rapid development of steam engines was due largely to their use in transportation. Steam engines were quickly demanded to operate steamboats on the western rivers and lakes. There were engine-building

[9] See Temin (1971, 2d citation) for a comparison of steam power with waterpower.

firms in Philadelphia and New York in 1803, and others were quickly started in Pittsburgh, Cincinnati, and other Ohio River cities.

After 1830, the development of steam-powered ocean vessels and steam locomotives for railroads rapidly expanded the demand for steam engine makers in the East. With the Evans high-pressure engine and the improvements in steam economy and control invented by George H. Corliss, American-built locomotives were soon among the best in the world and in the 1850s were much in demand as exports. Then, seeking to enlarge their domestic markets, American firms introduced small, standardized steam engines with interchangeable parts for use not only in small factories but also with farm machinery, pumps, and in small shops. By 1860, these small engines were sold by catalog, and steam engines in general nearly equaled waterwheels as a source of power.

Improvements in ironmaking were required by the high-pressure boiler of the steam engine, and these improvements in turn helped to rapidly reduce the cost of the steam engine and permit its wide use. In 1815, ironmaking technology in America was still about the same as it had been in the previous century. Fairly large furnaces were required to smelt iron ore into pig iron, and waterwheels were used to drive air bellows. Large forges used waterpower to drive drop hammers in making bar iron. The small-town blacksmith also operated small forges and hammered bar iron into shaped parts for farmers and local shops. Foundries usually reheated iron and poured it into molds for cast-iron pots, stove parts, and fancy ironwork. Forges hammered out sheets and frequently were connected with slitting mills that made the rods for nails.

In 1817, puddling and rolling techniques, already used for three decades in England, were introduced. The rolling mills substituted for the hammering in making wrought iron. This greatly reduced labor costs and produced a more uniform sheet iron for steam boilers. The puddling process heated the metal without direct contact with the fuel, permitting the use of coal instead of charcoal. In 1833, commercial use of the hot-blast method of smelting iron ore was introduced. This improved the puddling method by introducing a blast of hot air that had been preheated by the previously wasted heat escaping from the furnace.

The technology of steelmaking was not substantially changed until the invention of the Bessemer furnace in 1851. This process forced a blast of cold air through the molten iron to decarbonize it. However, the Bessemer process was not used for a significant volume of production until after 1860.

The use of coal as the fuel in ironmaking was limited at first to anthracite (hard) coal, which is characterized by a low sulfur content. Experiments were made prior to 1840 using coke made from the cheaper bituminous (soft) coal in smelting iron. But this method was not adopted until 1859, when the low-sulfur Connellsville bituminous was first used in a blast furnace designed specifically for it. The quality of iron made from wood charcoal was regarded as superior for such products as nails, hardware, and agricultural tools. Anthracite fuel, however, produced iron equivalent to coke iron for large-scale rolling of sheet iron and rails; consequently, the use of anthracite coal in ironmaking became important in supplying the railroad industry.[10]

The use of coal instead of wood charcoal as a fuel had important effects upon the location of the iron industry. Prior to 1830, iron smelters were widespread because of the availability in every state of small quantities of iron and the universal availability of forests to make charcoal for fuel. In many places, however, local supplies of iron ore and wood were quickly depleted. Iron ore of good quality in considerable quantities was available in the Lake Champlain area, and anthracite coal was available near water transportation in eastern Pennsylvania. The iron industry, therefore, began to concentrate in New York, New Jersey, and eastern Pennsylvania. In the 1850s, the opening of the St. Mary's Canal gave access by water to a large supply of high-quality iron ore on the shores of Lake Superior; so ironmaking began to develop at Detroit, Buffalo, and Cleveland. The supply of Great Lakes ore and the large low-sulfur bituminous coalfields of eastern Pennsylvania were destined after 1860 to concentrate the iron and steel industry in the Pittsburgh area.

The impact of these developments on overall manufacturing expansion is suggested by production trends in iron and coal. Pig iron production was set back by British imports after 1815 and in the depression of 1820, but the later census years show a steady and rapid rate of increase. Production of bituminous coal for nonmetallurgical purposes increased rapidly over the entire period. Anthracite coal had a phenomenal expansion after it began to be used in ironmaking in the 1830s, and after 1840 it achieved about the same importance as and matched the growth rate of soft coal. The railroads had profound effects upon the structure of demand in the various metal-manufacturing industries. In some industries, railroad demand accounted for 10 to 20 percent of total production. (See 7–9.)

DIFFUSION OF MANUFACTURING GROWTH

An interesting duality came to characterize manufacturing in the antebellum period. The textile industry, at the least, suggested the scale and technology we think of today when the words mass production are spoken. On the other hand, in 1860, the great bulk of manufacturing activity was just moving from craft shops into small-scale factories in which workers received considerable assistance from machinery. Such

---

[10] See Temin (1971, 1st citation) for a detailed review of these developments.

7–9.   Railroad, iron, and coal trends

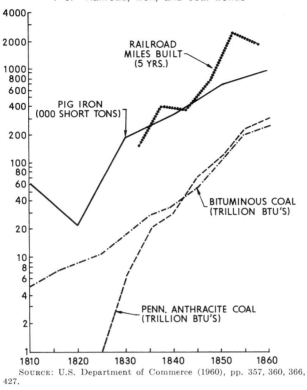

SOURCE: U.S. Department of Commerce (1960), pp. 357, 360, 366, 427.

factories were a far cry from the moving assembly line whose roots are found in Oliver Evans's "automated" flour mill.

Mass production's contemporary sense signifies automation, market concentration, ultraspecialization, and the employment of thousands in each plant. In that sense, mass production was a germ of an idea rather than a reality at mid-century. But the factory system, the modern industrial method, was rapidly diffusing itself by the 1840s. We can now turn our attention to some of the changes that came with the emergence of a national market and the simultaneous diffusion of factory manufacturing. Bear in mind, however, that most of the changes in the structure of the economy described below were just underway, so that most of their effects took hold in the post–Civil War period.

Changes in organization

The exploitation of 19th century technical and market opportunities required changes in the organization of production in manufacturing. Larger quantities of capital had to be invested in machinery; production became more specialized and standardized; more operations were coordinated in a single building or under a single management; larger numbers of more closely supervised workers were employed; and particular industries became concentrated in one or several strategic locations. Not only did the emergence of a national market make possible the diffusion of the modern industrial method, but many of the organizational changes we are about to discuss were made possible by transport improvements that knit the economy together.

The mechanization of manufacturing required large amounts of capital. First, because many of the new pieces of machinery were quite large. The smelter was bigger than ever; the iron rolling mills required huge rollers; and immense ladles and cranes were required for large foundry castings. Second, because a greater number of machines were required to perform the separate operations needed to manufacture standardized parts. Textile mills operated many spindles along with each power loom. Large buildings were required to house the machinery associated with factory production, and large sums of money were required to provide the volume of raw materials that had to be on hand.

The production of standard products in large volume also led to greater specialization by the typical manufacturing business. As machines became more specialized and capital requirements grew, the full resources of a business were absorbed in making one product or one type of product. The manufacture of iron rails became separated from rolling sheet iron, and locomotive production became a specialized type of steam engine manufacture. Machine shops that started as departments of individual textile mills soon became separate businesses, each of which concentrated on making and repairing machines for many textile mills. And individual textile mills often narrowed their range to produce only one type and quality of cloth.

At the same time, greater coordination of production operations was required. In part, this was attributable to a need for ensuring the quality of materials and accuracy of parts to meet the requirements of processing or final assembly. It was also necessary to ensure adequate and timely supply in order to maintain a steady flow of production.

Coordination of marketing and production was necessitated by production on a hitherto unknown scale. In 1803, Eli Terry would make a few clocks, then load them onto a wagon and drive to another town in order to sell them to retailers. But as production rates rose and improved transportation provided larger markets, manufacturers found it best to sell large volumes of goods to large wholesale merchants who would undertake to distribute them in distant cities.

In some industries, mass distribution came first. Large merchants anxious to sell large quantities of shoes in many distant cities would urge shoemakers to increase their output. Craftsmen in shops near the large port cities were closer to the merchants who were seeking to make large purchases. In this way, certain towns got a head start in the standardized high-volume production of particular products and became famous for their high quality and low cost.

The concentration of the production of certain products in particular towns or cities resulted both from the displacement of the craft shop by the factory and from the economies achieved by concentration in one area of many firms in the same industry. These are what we have referred to as external economies of scale—neighborhood or agglomeration effects are equivalent terms in a geographic context. Market centers always tend to form so that buyers and sellers can contact each other with a minimum expenditure of time and effort and with a maximum range of choice. Industries with many small producers, therefore, frequently tend to be attracted to some market center.

The congregation of many similar producers, moreover, tends to create a demand for specialized suppliers of materials, parts, or machinery who may produce more cheaply by concentrating on specialized operations needed by a given industry. Also, new and expanding businesses find it easier to obtain skilled workers in an area where similar businesses are already operating. Thus, producers in such a center may find that they have lower marketing, purchasing, and labor costs than more isolated producers.

When these external economies are combined with large-scale machine methods of production, one center of production may begin to supply a large share of the national consumption of a particular product. Thus, manufacturing in the Northeast began to be concentrated in a few main cities—cities noted as centers for the production of textiles, clocks, hats, shoes, rolled iron, or locomotives emerged in response to agglomeration economies. This kind of concentration was accelerated after 1840 by the introduction of the telegraph, which brought distant buyers and sellers into nearly instantaneous contact with each other.

Labor supply

The revolution in industrial production had a paradoxical relation to the labor supply. On the one hand, the economies of the factory system were so great that its products tended to supplant those produced by hand methods everywhere. However, because of economic expansion and because technological changes reduced costs and, therefore, relative prices, total production and the total quantity sold increased. Consequently, in the aggregate, the total demand for labor increased, although the composition of that demand shifted from handcrafting to machine operation.

The development and rapid expansion of concentrated factory production was made possible in the Northeast by the rapid expansion of labor available to the new factories. The rural areas of New England served as the first sources of textile mill labor. Later, immigrants arriving in the great port cities, chiefly from Ireland and Germany, found their way into the mills.

New England farm areas provided a surplus of labor supply in the late 1820s and 1830s because of the competition of cheaper wheat products from the Great Lakes region. Farmers began to seek nonfarm work to supplement their incomes or moved into the growing cities. Many New England farm families were able to add to their incomes by various forms of cottage work—at first by weaving, then by making straw hats. Since the first textile mills were located in small towns near waterfalls, workers were drawn initially from local farm families. As the textile factories expanded, farm workers had to be recruited from larger rural areas.

Two labor systems were used in the textile mills. In southern New England, the family system involved hiring whole families. Women and children could do much of the light work required in threading, watching, and operating the machines, while men repaired the machines and did the heavier work.

In northern New England, as in the first Waltham mill, the dormitory system was used. Girls from farm families were recruited to live in dormitories and work in the factories. Many of the young men were away as apprentice seamen, so this employment was attractive to girls as a temporary career and as a way to supplement the family's income. Like farm work and home manufacturing, factory work was grueling. Yet in spite of long hours, the young women in the dormitory system often received schooling or engaged in self-improvement activities under the "encouragement" of paternalistic, puritanical factory owners.

A large inflow of immigrants in the 1840s and 1850s furnished much of the labor supply for rapid manufacturing expansion in the Northeast. These workers crowded into the port cities and larger towns. A large supply of unskilled men began to supplant women and children in textile mills, and the dormitory system went by the board. In the big cities, whether in their tenement quarters or in large factory rooms, the immigrants were employed in large numbers to expand production of shoes and ready-made apparel.

Thus the migration of Europeans to America, a process which had been taking place over more than two centuries of colonial growth, began to serve a new purpose during the 1840s: the furnishing of an urban labor supply. The expansion into new farming areas west of the Appalachian Mountains continued to attract farm settlers from England and Germany. However, in the 1840s, famines in Ireland and revolutions on the Continent caused large numbers of destitute migrants to come to America. With no stake, not even travel funds to get themselves to the western farm areas, many immigrants of the 40s—and of the 50s and later decades as well—were forced to seek work as unskilled hands in urban areas.

The total number of immigrants to the United States (on which we have records only since 1820) rose rapidly with the westward expansion of the late 1820s and 1830s but was especially high in the 1840s and 1850s. Immigrants accounted for 3.9 percent of the total population increase during the 1820s, 12.7 percent in the 1830s, 23.3 percent in the 1840s, and 34.0 percent in the 1850s. (See 7–10.)

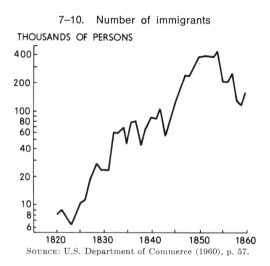

7–10. Number of immigrants

SOURCE: U.S. Department of Commerce (1960), p. 57.

As a result of the rapid expansion of the labor supply, wage rates rose very little in the antebellum period, even though manufacturing labor demand grew very rapidly. On the basis of skimpy data, the following pattern emerges: real wages in farming rose in most decades; in nonfarm employment, there was little change prior to 1830, a higher level in the 1840s, and a slight decline in the late 1850s.

As in England during the same period, however, there was considerable labor discontent. In a nation with opportunities for settling new lands, starting businesses, and achieving higher incomes, there was a spirit of optimism and high hope. Frequently, however, the urban worker felt deprived and abandoned.

The organizational changes that the modern industrial method called for inside the firm had important drawbacks. The dull routine of production-line tasks had the negative effects that Adam Smith anticipated when he observed the division of labor in a pinmaking factory—discontent and frustration came to the new factory workers who were required to work with the precision, constancy, and repetitiveness of mindless machines. Factory organization regimented the worker and, given the large work forces within a single factory, relations between worker and employer were depersonalized. For skilled workers whose crafts disappeared, the frustration was at least as great. The feeling of alienation that resulted was one of the factors that Marx felt would give rise to a revolutionary proletariat.

Urban growth and the crowding of new immigrants into big cities fostered slums. The cheaper machine methods and a large immigrant labor supply intensified competition for jobs and often put a downward pressure on wages. With fluctuations in business conditions, workers who depended solely upon urban employment suffered the hardships of prolonged unemployment. Accordingly, efforts were made to form trade unions and strike for better wages and working conditions. These efforts met with more success in skilled trades and during periods of prosperity; but, on the whole, their success was limited and short-lived prior to the Civil War.

Capital supply and business organization

As we noted above, rapid manufacturing expansion and factory production methods required large amounts of capital and new forms of business organization. Since nearly all the capital employed was accumulated within the United States, a considerable share of annual national production had to be saved, i.e., withheld from current consumption. These funds had to be invested in activities that promised to expand future production under conditions of limited information, considerable uncertainty, and grave risk of losses.

The men who became manufacturers in the early period were either merchants who saw new market opportunities or craftsmen who invented new methods. For the former group, initial capital was supplied out of funds earned in other business activities. The New England traders who had accumulated wealth in the reexport trade, the fur trade, and the China trade faced restrictions on their foreign activities during the embargo and the War of 1812. Many of them also found profit opportunities in world trade less attractive after 1815. But they had developed business management abilities and had accumulated enough wealth to finance new ventures in other industries. So they turned to manufacturing. In the South, some men of wealth also turned to manufacturing, but the opportunities in cotton plantations continued to look most promising. (Civil war always threatened but never seemed imminent.) They were not forced to look for new fields.

In addition to the assistance received from the transfer of wealth out of other industries, manufacturing gained momentum through reinvestment of the large profits that earlier investment produced. Paradoxically the innovators in some fields sometimes failed to make large profits. Yet generally even after an industry had many competing firms, annual profits of 10 to 20 percent on invested capital were fairly common. But it must not be forgotten that the risks were great and that many firms went broke. For example, remember that after the rapid construction of textile mills between 1807 and 1815 many had to close down with the return of British competition.

Most antebellum manufacturing businesses were owned by individuals or a small number of partners. Evans, Whitney, and other inventors and craftsmen built up sizable personal fortunes in their lifetimes. Slater, who came to this country penniless, left over two thirds of a million dollars in assets when he died four decades later.

On the other hand, recall that Lowell started his firm's mill by getting several other wealthy merchant families to join with him. This group of families built up several other mills and invested jointly in other industries. They became known as the Boston Associates and for a long time were prominent in the manufacturing and financial leadership of Massachusetts.

Prior to 1860, the corporation was not widely adopted as the legal form of business in manufacturing. Traditionally, the chartering of corporations by specific acts of legislatures had been used to establish monopolies in which the state and the public had a special interest. This device had been employed mainly to establish banks, public utilities, and transportation companies. However, initial steps toward a wider use of corporations were taken when Massachusetts passed a statute in 1830 giving corporate shareholders limited liability for the debts of a corporation if it went bankrupt and when Connecticut passed a sweeping act in 1837 permitting anyone to apply for incorporation. Other states soon followed these precedents. For a long time, however, public suspicion of incorporation prevailed.

Because outside loan capital was not easy to come by, the rapid expansion of manufacturing capacity was financed by plowing back profits. Bank loans were for very short terms. With little incorporation, few bonds were sold by manufacturing firms and small use was made of mortgages. Most long-term loans were made by wealthy individuals—sometimes one of the partners. In other cases, large merchant-distributors of manufactured products advanced loans to manufacturers, usually in times of stress and at high interest rates. More frequently, however, manufacturers had to advance loans to merchants because of the widespread practice of selling by shipment on consignment with payment made later.

Some of the financial institutions which later became important means of assembling the savings of individuals and making them available for investment in manufacturing did have their beginnings prior to the Civil War. Note, though, that since manufacturing businesses usually were not incorporated, and that even when incorporated their securities might be held by only a few people, they did not benefit much from the new financial institutions before 1860.

By 1860, fire and marine insurance companies had nearly $3 billion of insurance in force, and life insurance in force amounted to $160

million. The latter provided a source of savings, but perhaps more significant were the savings and loan associations, mostly in the Northeast,
whose deposits reached over $150 million.

Government bonds issued by states for development purposes provided an even more important form of personal saving and social capital
formation. They also helped accustom the public to purchasing securities
and aided in developing a private market for handling them. Prior to
the 1830s some states had run lotteries to raise money, and some of
the brokers who sold lottery tickets later dealt in bonds. Banks also
dealt in bonds. Some large investment banks specialized in handling
the initial sales of bonds, especially sales in other regions and countries.
Stock exchanges had developed in Philadelphia, New York, and Boston
prior to 1820; but most of their early transactions were in government
securities, while banks, turnpike companies, and railroads provided most
of the private securities that were widely traded.

THE ROLE OF GOVERNMENT

In the remainder of this chapter, brief consideration will be given
to the role of government in the economic development and accelerating
economic growth of the country. This review is complicated by the
variations in the behavior of governments at the state and local level
as well as at the national level. It is necessary, also, to analyze the
effects of general patterns of governmental actions without regard to
the varying and often conflicting purposes behind specific events, i.e.,
to abstract effect from intent.

Over the last century, economic historians have proved both confused
and confusing about the American public's view of the proper economic
role of government. Usually, this is because historians have been widely
influenced by the spirit and level of government involvement in the
economy at the time they were writing. The extreme points of view
that have emerged over a hundred years of analysis are alternatively:

1. that the Americans were laissez-faire minded and only very reluctantly mixed public activity and private enterprise and
2. that the Americans never abandoned mercantilism in their drive
   to conquer the continent.

From today's perspective, 19th century Americans seem to us to have
adopted the following attitude. In most cases, government intervention
is harmful or redundant, and expectations for private returns ultimately
provide the best guide to investment and output patterns. But occasions
arise in which private returns don't reflect all the social good (or ill)
that arises from a given activity, so government must step in to subsidize
(or regulate) it. Support for this point of view can be adduced from

the record of government assistance to transportation: where transport investment seemed a good idea for the aggregate economy, yet private enterprise couldn't raise the necessary capital or didn't sense high enough future returns, public aid was forthcoming. As both the canal and railroad histories suggest, when private firms could go it alone, public support dwindled accordingly.[11]

As opportunities for resource exploitation, monetary expansion, and transportation improvements appeared, a mixture of familiar mercantilist methods was frequently applied if it seemed that private initiative couldn't be counted on. In fact, government marched west with the pioneers, subsidizing their explorations and, later, their transportation improvements, aiding them in their combat with hostile Indians, and favoring them with increasingly liberal land policies by which the public domain passed into private hands.[12]

Whether it intends to or not, a government by its action and inaction influences the economy in two ways. On the one hand, it influences the environment within which private organizations and individuals make their decisions. On the other hand, it directly participates in decisions on how scarce resources are allocated among alternative products, how inputs are combined in production, and how income is distributed. The following sections deal first with matters that appear least intended to affect economic development and end with a treatment of conscious policies to direct and participate in economic decisions.

Government finance[13]

The modest role actually assigned to government before the Civil War is reflected in the small size of expenditures by all levels of government. Federal expenditures remained at between 1 and 2 percent of national income prior to 1860. According to fragmentary data, state and local expenditures combined were probably less than this until the 1850s. In 1819, for example, government expenditures on a per capita basis may be compared as follows: $2.29 federal; $0.47 for the state of New York; and $2.18 for the city of Providence. By 1860, the federal and state amounts remained about the same, while the city figures had more

---

[11] None of this should be taken as denying that some projects were aided that could have survived without aid, while others were denied government assistance when social returns would have been high. All we are saying is that in cases where aid was not forthcoming, it was held back not for philosophical reasons, but because decision-makers negatively appraised the worth of the project; and in cases where government intervention was redundant, it was given not out of conviction that all projects ought to have government support whether or not they could make it on their own, but because the level of need was miscalculated.

[12] On the evolution of government and the economy, see the review and analysis of the literature by Lively.

[13] For the classic study of 19th century fiscal policy, see Studenski and Krooss.

than tripled. Local expenditures, of course, varied widely and were much lower in rural areas.

Taxes, accordingly, were light. The main source of revenue for the federal government was the tariff on imports, while the chief secondary source was the sale of western lands. Initially, many states had no trouble meeting their needs with miscellaneous revenues (obtained, for example, from land sales, lotteries, licenses, bank taxes, and interest on federal bonds), but after the 1830s most states had to raise greater revenues and opted for property taxes—still the mainstay of local governments.

The instability of tariffs and land sales as sources of federal revenue resulted in federal budgets that gyrated from surpluses to deficits. National fiscal policy was formed primarily by the objective of rapidly paying off war debts in order to establish and protect the federal government's reputation as a borrower. During the War of 1812, this enabled the government to increase its borrowing to cover sudden increases in expenditures. Increased tariff rates and import volume accelerated the repayment of the federal debt during prosperous peacetime years. By 1835, the United States was one of the few modern nations to have completely paid off all debts. (See 7–11.)

7–11. Federal government debt, 1800–1860

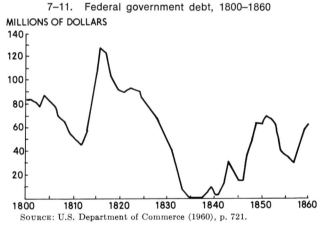

MILLIONS OF DOLLARS

Source: U.S. Department of Commerce (1960), p. 721.

During the 1820s and 1830s, the states were following an opposite debt policy. Starting with virtually no debts, the states rushed to build canals, turnpikes, and railroads, and to establish banks with money raised by selling bonds. State debts reached $66 million in 1835 and had zoomed to $174 million by 1838—adding $108 million in just three years! Compare this with the peak federal debt of $124 million in 1816. The optimistic assumption that revenues from the publicly built projects would easily cover interest and principal payments proved false in the depression following 1838. The states found themselves unprepared to suddenly raise taxes to meet their debt obligations. Consequently, nine states defaulted on some part of their payments when they fell due, and three states and one territory actually repudiated bonds totaling over $13 million. This established a bad reputation for state bonds in the minds of private investors for many decades afterward.

While the public debt was regarded as a necessary evil by government, its effects on the private economy had beneficial aspects. As already noted, the sale of government bonds helped establish the public habit of saving by buying securities, and brokerage houses and stock exchanges were started, in part, because government bonds had to be marketed. A large inflow of foreign capital into the American economy during the 1830s took place in the form of state bond purchases by private investors in London and elsewhere. Government bond ownership also provided a means of holding wealth in readily transferable form. As such, government bonds became a near-money. They were used by both individuals and governments to purchase bank stocks and thus became part of the capital reserves upon which the banks based the issue of their own notes, a form of paper money.

The power to coin money and regulate its value was given exclusively to the federal government by the Constitution. The inflation of the Revolutionary War had been attributed largely to the irresponsible issue of paper money by governments. Paradoxically, it was regarded as more sound for government to borrow (issue promises to pay with interest) than to issue paper money (issue promises to pay without interest). It was not widely recognized that bonds held by banks and used to support the issuance of more bank notes could produce an equal or more inflationary expansion in the money supply. It seems to have been assumed that bankers, as private businessmen, would issue paper notes more responsibly and conservatively than legislatures. And, of course, the requirement that interest be paid must have had some braking effect on the promises that were issued.

Given contemporary monetary knowledge, federal policy was not consistently directed toward controlling the supply and thus the value of money. One consequence was that the federal government did not provide an adequate supply of coins and paper bills to facilitate the Nation's production and exchange activities. Mintage of small coins was inadequate. Barter and commodity moneys held sway in rural areas and the western regions, which were continually short of any kind of money. Many kinds of institutions—railroads, insurance companies, and cities—issued various kinds of notes or promises to pay that had a limited circulation as money. State-chartered private banks, therefore, filled a real need by issuing notes; and the expansion of state banks, while at times inflationary, helped expand the supply of money and credit to meet the needs of an expanding economy.[14]

---

[14] For a reevaluation of the antebellum money-creating role of banks see Rockoff.

Before examining the control of bank credit, the effect on the economy of variations in government spending, taxing, and monetary management should be noted. In the early 1800s, little attention was given to the disturbances that might be caused in the private economy by the combined effect of government spending and taxes (fiscal policy) and by the way the Treasury handled its own monetary affairs (monetary policy).

A budget surplus accumulated in the Treasury produced a net reduction in private spending because government collected more in taxes than it spent, and vice versa. During the 1820s and 1830s, the federal surplus varied between a fourth and almost half of budget revenues. Quite unintentionally, however, the peacetime surpluses and deficits may have had some stabilizing influence on the private economy: during periods of prosperity and rising prices, tariff revenues automatically tended to rise and thus to reduce spending; during depressions, the opposite occurred.

The disposition of government funds also could have disturbing effects. The accumulation of a surplus by the Treasury removed money from circulation. When the surplus was deposited in private banks, it enabled those banks to increase their note issues. When the money supply increased rapidly, interest rates fell, investment and other spending accelerated, and ultimately prices rose. When the growth of the money supply slowed or the money supply contracted, the economy moved toward price deflation and unemployment.

The continued monetary and fiscal effects of government policy are dramatically illustrated by the surplus distribution of the late 1830s and land sales policy. With its own debt paid off, the federal government contributed to the boom-and-bust of 1836–37 by an act which distributed the federal surplus to the states. This not only encouraged spending on public works but precipitated a monetary crisis by transferring large amounts of cash reserves from eastern banks to western banks. The eastern banks suddenly had to restrict their loans. At about the same time, federal officials became worried about the excessive issue of bank notes and required payment in specie on sales of public land. This required western banks to draw upon their reserves in eastern banks to obtain specie for depositors who were buying western land. (These events are interpreted differently by Temin in his *The Jacksonian Economy*.)

In short, by merely running its own fiscal and monetary affairs, the federal government acted as a destabilizing influence on the economy. However, Treasury policy had matured by mid-century and the passage of the Independent Treasury Act. That act was designed to put the Treasury on a cash basis and thus to make it independent of the private financial market. But, in quite a different spirit from that in which the Independent Treasury Act was passed, Treasury policy turned toward a conscious effort to stabilize the private money market by purchasing government bonds in times when bank reserves were low and retaining surplus tax revenues when they were high. Our secretaries of the Treasury had learned something about the importance of their transactions from a half century of often heedlessly influencing the money market.

Regulating banks

Banks have a decidedly public nature in the sense that they are crucial to the orderly conduct of economic activity in a money-using society. Although the Constitution specifically indicates that the federal government is responsible for issuing money, banks through their deposit and loan functions can affect the quantity of money in the total economy. Consequently, they are perceived as "affected with the public interest" and are regulated by government.

In order to ensure the financial environment needed to encourage private production activities in the economy, governments regulate banking with three objectives in mind: first, to facilitate the expansion of private production by assuring an appropriate supply of loan funds; second, to protect depositors against losses due to bank failures or bankruptcies; third, to prevent excessive expansion or contraction of the money supply.

It is the close relationship of bank loans to the money supply and the joint relation of bank loans and the money supply to inflation and depression that make banking a matter of public interest. Rapid price inflation involves a loss of purchasing power for people receiving pensions or other fixed incomes and for people possessing cash, bonds, and savings deposits. It may also discourage accumulation and the efficient investment of funds. In depressions, rapid price declines are usually accompanied by reduction in output, unemployment, and losses from the sale at low prices of goods and other assets.

Before discussing bank operations, therefore, a brief review is needed of the historical record of instability in prices and the money supply prior to 1860. Wars have always given rise to the greatest inflations, and the War of 1812 was no exception. In the antebellum decades there were two other periods of rapid price rises, in the mid-1830s and the mid-1850s. And following each of the sudden inflations came a period of depression and sharp price deflation, during which production decreased, investment halted or slackened, and many people suffered from unemployment and losses of income and capital. (See 7–12.)

Now, it must be recognized that some variations in economic activity are unavoidable. When people rush to take advantage of new inventions or resource opportunities, they may start a rapid pace of investment that cannot be maintained indefinitely. Also, the extent of new opportunities may not be gauged correctly, and investors may become overopti-

7–12. Average wholesale prices

SOURCE: U.S. Department of Commerce (1960), p. 115.

mistic and overinvest. This may be followed by a period of losses, contraction, and some waiting for opportunities to catch up before the growth of investment is resumed. Total production is much affected by such variations in the rate of investment.

The three main depressions that occurred prior to 1860 brought the deflations we noted above. These contractions in total economic activity and the subsequent recoveries were influenced by such worldwide events as wars, bad harvests (e.g., the Irish famine), discoveries of gold, and surges of canal building and railroad building. Because world markets were interrelated by trade, migration, and foreign investments, other nations experienced business fluctuations at about the same times as did the United States.

The instability of the money supply and bank credit in the United States undoubtedly magnified price and output fluctuations. A measure of the total money supply must include not only the coins and notes issued by the federal government, but also the outstanding bank notes and deposits in banks. All three tended to expand faster than national output during the three historic boom periods and to contract faster during the ensuing depressions. (See 7–13.)

The potential power of antebellum banks to exaggerate basic economic fluctuations by expanding and contracting the money stock in the course of their normal, everyday operations arose out of a confluence of their deposit and loan roles. Deposit customers brought a given bank U.S. government currency, specie, or bank notes issued by other banks for deposit in their accounts. Loan customers borrowed money from a given bank by exchanging their IOUs for bank notes or deposits issued by it. At any time, holders of bank notes and deposits issued by a particular bank could demand specie, notes of other banks, or government currency from that bank in exchange for its notes.

Consequently, the number of notes a bank could issue in its loan-making activity was limited by its *reserves* of specie, U.S. Treasury currency,

7-13. Money supply, 1800–1860

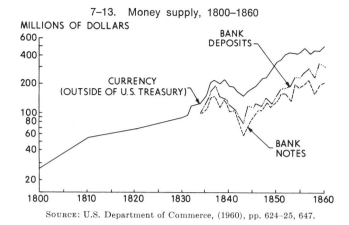

SOURCE: U.S. Department of Commerce, (1960), pp. 624–25, 647.

and notes of other banks. However, banks didn't need to hold $1 of reserves for each $1 of their own notes and deposits that they issued because noteholders and depositors didn't show up en masse to demand their total deposits. Banks, therefore, could hold a *fraction,* usually less than 50 percent, of the value of their outstanding notes as reserves. Of course, if all noteholders and deposit customers did show up at once and demand that their notes be exchanged for specie, government currency, or notes of other banks, i.e., if there were a *run* on the bank, the bank would only be able to redeem a fraction of its notes. Given this background, let's see how early 19th century banks got themselves and the economy in trouble.

One source of trouble was to overexpand loans and leave reserves too slim. During the boom of 1836, many were optimistic and wanted to expand production by borrowing capital. The banks shared their optimism, as is shown by their enthusiastic expansion of loans made by issuing notes or deposits to loan customers. Reserves became too small relative to claims.

When a fall in prices shook confidence in people's ability to pay back their loans, banks would restrict their lending. This meant that money flowed less easily and that people tried harder to get hold of cash. To get more cash, perhaps in order to pay back loans, more goods had to be sold immediately, even at low prices. With sellers suddenly outnumbering buyers, prices would begin to fall more rapidly. Banks would then call in loans, and depositors would withdraw more cash. Banks in need of currency would present the notes of other banks for repayment. Thus a cumulative panic would ensue. This is precisely what occurred in the panic that followed the boom of 1836.

Some banks which had permitted reserves to get very slim suddenly found that they could not pay all claims upon demand and had to close their doors. The closing of some banks scared depositors everywhere so that they rushed to their own banks to get their deposits out in cash. Many of the banks on which there were runs failed because their reserves weren't adequate to satisfy depositors.

A second way banks got into trouble came from the practice country banks had of depositing part of their reserves with big city banks. The big city banks treated these deposits like any others and expanded their loans, in part, on the basis of the U.S. currency or specie the country banks had left with them. However, any time demands for note redemption were unusually heavy at country banks, they drew on their city bank deposits, thereby removing essential reserves from the city banks.

In earlier decades, the federal government had made some efforts to control excess bank credit fluctuation. Recall that the first Bank of the United States was able to curb some excesses of private bank note issues by presenting promptly all such notes that fell into its hands to the issuing banks for immediate repayment in currency. It was also able to help a bank faced with a run by depositing some of its currency with that bank. But the charter of the first Bank of the United States was allowed to expire in 1811. The second Bank of the United States, established in 1816, operated similarly; but its charter, too, was allowed to expire, in 1836.

Various states also experimented with ways to control banking. The Suffolk Bank of Boston developed a private system of policing the over-issue of notes by small banks by regularly collecting all country bank notes and delivering them to the issuing banks for repayment in U.S. currency. In 1829, the state of New York enacted a safety fund system which required payments into a pooled cash reserve and regular inspection of each bank's operations.

While banks had previously been chartered by special legislative acts, in 1838 New York passed the Free Banking Act, which allowed anyone to charter a bank provided that he placed a sufficient reserve deposit of securities with a public agency. Soon Louisiana, Massachusetts, Pennsylvania, and the western states followed suit. State banking regulations, however, were not uniform, and many banks were unable to survive the crash of 1857, partly because of the practice of placing reserves on deposit in large city banks. Nevertheless, on balance free banking has been judged favorable to economic development during this period of western migration—free entry into banking permitted these important financial institutions to "follow the people" into new areas as they were opened for settlement.[15]

Overall, it was largely owing to a lack of economic sophistication plus inaction or insufficient control that the role of government in stabilizing bank credit and business fluctuations was performed poorly prior

---

[15] Rockoff, p. 420, has evaluated the comparative efficacy of charter and free banking systems and has found that free banking met the "need for an efficient mechanism to allocate [financial] capital among banks."

to the Civil War. After the war the record of government improved, but even today the public and governments are still learning how to regulate banking activity despite an additional century of legislation and experience.

On the whole, in our opinion, the monetary performance of the banking community and the Treasury in the antebellum years must be considered successful in spite of the regulatory failures that occurred. Long-term deflation was modest; the price index fell only 30 points in over 60 years; and a vast growth in GNP and related transactions was accommodated. We think it would be hard to find a contemporary scholar who would assert that monetary forces caused the economic growth rate to miss its potential maximum by a serious margin.

Regulating business

On balance, although not laissez-faire in deed or creed, the federal government did little to encourage or regulate private business activities. The most important federal action was, of course, the tariff. Although initially devised merely to raise revenues, after the War of 1812 the tariff was raised in order to protect and encourage the development of the American textile and iron industries. The patent laws were also designed to encourage the development and commercial use of inventions. In the field of foreign commerce, legislation was passed restricting intercoastal commerce to American ships, and in U.S. ports foreign ships were required to pay higher registration fees than were American ships. American ships engaged in foreign commerce were required to hire a minimum percentage of American seamen; and laws protected the conditions of seamen and immigrants on such ships. In the realm of interstate commerce, federal safety inspection was required for steamboat boilers. Federal legislation regulated trade with the Indians and prohibited the sale of alcoholic beverages to them.

Colonial Americans had little hesitancy about regulating business, and many colonial regulatory practices were carried over by state and local governments. Pennsylvania continued to inspect the quality of exported food products. Cities continued to inspect bread, and in the 1850s milk also came under their inspection. City price regulations were applied to bread, produce markets, hackneys, commercial wagons, ice, gas, and water. Provisions for the regulation of rates and operations were included in the charters of canal and railroad companies. Many of the regulated concerns functioned as local monopolies, and it was commonly assumed that restrictions should go hand in hand with monopoly privileges.

In the early decades, however, the main emphasis of government economic policy was upon conferring and granting rewards to encourage private business to undertake the kinds of production that were believed to serve the public interest. The federal government spent money on navigation aids and river and harbor improvements in order to assist shipping. In George Washington's first term, a duty was placed upon salt to finance a bounty paid to operators of cod fishing boats, and this subsidy remained in force until after the Civil War. The small arms industry was encouraged by contracts granting liberal, interest-free advances. For a few years, subsidies were granted to American companies experimenting with ocean steamships.

Much of state government legislation provided for special privileges in the charters of companies which were encouraged to furnish new services. Bounties were given to shipbuilders in southern ports and to farmers who raised silk in New England. Many states granted tax exemptions to new manufacturing firms. Industrial fairs sometimes offered prizes for product innovations.

Public enterprise and mixed investment

From the earliest times, there was an assumption that certain large-scale activities which benefited most of the public but could be performed by a single firm should be state enterprises rather than private monopolies. Further, shortly after the founding of the new nation Albert Gallatin published a discourse on the need to weigh the social costs and benefits as well as the private gains of proposed investment projects.[16]

The federal government inaugurated its postal service as a revenue-earning division of the Treasury. Other federally operated projects included the lighthouse service, the mint, armories, Indian trading posts, and hospitals for seamen. The first telegraph line from Baltimore to Washington was built with federal funds and operated by the post office. The longest and most expensive turnpike was the National Road, although Congress turned down other road-building projects.

It was at the state level that public enterprises were most prevalent. At the local government level, road building was regarded as a public function, although private monopolies were frequently chartered to build toll roads. Canal building, however, seemed far beyond the capacity of any private company of those times. Whereas the capital investment required to build a turnpike might be as little as a few hundred dollars, a canal of any considerable length seldom cost less than a million dollars. The Erie cost about $6 million, and its later branches and enlargements cost several times as much. The state of Pennsylvania spent over $60 million on its canals.

In those times, no private company had ever aggregated such large pools of capital. Obviously, a way was needed to draw upon the small

---

[16] Cited in Goodrich, p. 294.

savings of a large number of people. New York demonstrated that the sale of state bonds would accomplish this. The major trans-Appalachian and western canals were all state enterprises, but many of the smaller, privately owned canals were also heavily dependent upon public investment funds or subsidies. State and local governments made large purchases of the stocks and bonds of chartered canal companies. And the primarily private canal ventures on the East Coast received special lottery and banking privileges.

The federal government refused financial support for the Erie Canal, but it did not follow this policy consistently. It made large purchases of stocks issued by the Dismal Swamp, Chesapeake and Ohio, and Chesapeake and Delaware canal companies. Indiana and Ohio canals were also aided and encouraged by large federal land grants.

In the 1840s and 1850s, when the first wave of railroad construction was underway, the provision of transportation facilities was undertaken almost entirely by private companies, but heavy government investments and subsidies were extended to the railroad industry, continuing the government's traditional encouragement of particular types of economic activity. Some railroads had been started in the 1830s, but the existence of canals probably hindered their rapid development. Initially, some local interests and businesses with a stake in the canals opposed the railroads because they feared competition for funds and traffic. Later, the failure of many canals to make a profit created a bad reputation for state enterprises.

While the cost of all canals may have been almost $200 million, investment in railroads prior to 1860 totaled somewhat over $1 billion.[17] Many of the railroad companies, however, had relatively short lines. Such companies could be started with comparatively small stock issues. Local business leaders, anxious to obtain the advantages of railroad transportation for their communities, invested heavily themselves, but they also persuaded their municipalities to make investments, loans, and grants.

The states also made heavy investments in railroads. By 1838, the cumulative value of state railroad bonds came to two thirds of the value of state-issued canal bonds. During the 1840s and 1850s, state debts were again increased to finance railroads. It has been estimated that in the South over half the capital for railroads was provided by state and local governments, and even higher proportions were recorded for particular northern states. Perhaps 40 to 50 percent is a reasonable but rough national estimate of the share of government in railroad capital costs prior to 1860. The state charters also gave the private companies many privileges to encourage them—monopoly of routes, eminent domain, exemption from taxes, and lottery and banking privileges.

---

[17] See tables 13.2 and 13.13 in Fishlow for data on investment in canals and railroads.

Congress generally resisted the public clamor for financial aid to the railroads. But the federal government helped in other ways. Many early railroad surveys were made by federal engineers at government expense. Tariff duties on iron were reduced to help the railroads.

Finally, in 1850, political representatives from southern and western states combined forces to get an act passed to give federal land grants to the states of Illinois, Mississippi, and Alabama in order to support a north-south railroad from Chicago to Mobile. (This set a precedent for similar grants in the 1850s and after the Civil War.) Two-hundred-foot right-of-ways and alternate even sections of land six miles deep were granted to the railroad. When completed in 1857, the Illinois Central Railroad had cost over $23 million, of which stockholders contributed about one sixth while the sale of bonds secured by mortgages on federal lands raised most of the rest.

Government assistance was very important to the transportation revolution of the antebellum period. Without the agency of government to assemble private savings and to attract foreign financial capital through the sale of bonds, transportation improvements might have been delayed by several decades. In turn, as we have seen in earlier chapters, transportation improvements played an important role in reducing production costs, permitting regional specialization, creating national markets, and, consequently, raising per capita income. More generally stated, transportation facilities are important social overhead capital items which the private sector will not provide unassisted in many cases because the private returns on them are not sufficiently high even though their benefits to the community at large may constitute a high rate of return on investment.

The same can be said of the other social overhead items. The American experience reflects the recognition that in particular cases a divergence between private and social returns arises and that public intervention is needed where the divergence is important to economic welfare. Accordingly, the federal, state, and local governments applied a mixture of actions to encourage as well as regulate private enterprise.

SUMMARY

1. In 1800, farming engaged 74 percent of the working population, factory employment in the U.S. was minuscule, handcraft manufacturing in household and craft shops dominated domestic production, and imported manufactures were of huge significance. By 1860, factories employed 14 percent of the labor force, farms employed only about half the labor force, and manufactured imports had been displaced to a very large degree by domestic products.

2. American manufacturing growth before the Civil War can be characterized in three ways. First, economic expansion plus per capita

income growth increased demand for all manufactured goods—in fact, manufacturing demand grew faster than did the total economy. The growth of the economy, in turn, can be traced in no small measure to the success of agriculture. Second, the growth in the size of the market attributable to both economic expansion and transportation improvements caused a shift away from household and craft-shop production in favor of factory-made products. Third, in industry after industry the introduction of the modern industrial method put U.S. production costs on a par with British costs. Consequently, given the size of ocean freight costs, the delivered prices of American products fell significantly below import prices and purchases shifted in favor of domestic production.

Thus, the American manufacturing sector grew in the antebellum period and began changing its structure—although craft-shop production actually had increased by 1860, its relative decline was an unmistakable portent of its ultimate demise.

3.   The growth of the American manufacturing sector went hand in hand with innovations in product design and production methods and the invention of new products and machines. Although Britain was the source of most such innovation, Americans made major contributions. In general, American production methods tended to be laborsaving, although just how American labor scarcity was transmuted into a technology that conserved labor is not entirely clear.

4.   The textile industry was the first manufacturing industry to undergo the metamorphosis from handcraft to capital-intensive machinery production; and textiles provided the most notable case of import substitution. A variety of forces caused the supply of and demand for American textiles to increase at fantastic rates while imports of textiles increased only modestly. Among the more important expansive factors were the power loom, which lowered weaving costs and, therefore, prices, and economic expansion plus higher living standards, which shifted demand positively.

5.   A variety of other industries converted to the factory system, i.e., adopted the modern industrial method, during the period. The diffusion of the factory system was in no small part attributable to the emergence of the machine-building and machine-tool industries, which served both as laboratories for generating technological innovations and as media for "broadcasting" new techniques. The discovery of low-sulfur bituminous coal in western Pennsylvania and of new ironmaking techniques lowered the cost of iron products and led to the development of new iron products that made possible some of the advances achieved by the machine and machine-tool builders.

6.   The establishment of a national market was a necessary antecedent of the spread of the factory system. With a national market and the diffusion of modern manufacturing came a host of changes in eco-

nomic organization. Most notable among them were the gradual spread of corporate business enterprise, the start of a national capital market, and the growth of government influence especially as a regulator of the banking system and as a source of assistance in social overhead capital formation. Certainly, the simultaneous emergence of modern manufacturing and a national market initiated a transformation which made the economy of 1900 a vastly different organization than that of 1860.

REFERENCES

A. H. Cole,   *The American Wool Manufacture*, vol. 1 (Cambridge, Mass.: Harvard University Press, 1926).

A. Fishlow,   "Internal Transportation," in *American Economic Growth*, eds. L. E. Davis et al., (New York: Harper & Row, Publishers, 1972).

R. E. Gallman,   "Commodity Output, 1839–1899," in *Trends in the American Economy in the Nineteenth Century*, ed. W. N. Parker (Princeton, N.J.: Princeton University Press, 1960).

C. Goodrich,   "Internal Improvements Reconsidered," *JEH*, June 1970.

R. Higgs,   *Transformation of the American Economy, 1865–1914* (New York: John Wiley & Sons, Inc., 1971).

S. Lebergott,   "The American Labor Force," eds. L. E. Davis et al., cited above.

R. A. Lively,   "The American System," *BHR*, March 1955.

H. Rockoff,   "American Free Banking before the Civil War; a Re-examination," *JEH*, March 1972.

N. Rosenberg,   "Technological Change," eds. L. E. Davis et al., cited above.

P. Studenski and H. E. Krooss,   *Financial History of the United States*, 2d ed. (New York: McGraw-Hill Book Co., Inc., 1963).

P. Temin,   "A New Look at Hunter's Hypothesis about the Ante-Bellum Iron Industry," in *The Reinterpretation of American Economic History*, eds. R. W. Fogel and S. L. Engerman (New York: Harper & Row, Publishers, 1971).

———,   "Steam and Waterpower in the Early 19th Century" in R. W. Fogel and S. L. Engerman, cited above.

———,   "Manufacturing," eds. L. E. Davis et al., cited above.

———,   *The Jacksonian Economy* (New York: W. W. Norton & Company, Inc., 1969).

U.S. Department of Commerce,   *Eighth Census of the United States, Manufacturers* (1860).

———,   *Historical Statistics of the United States* (Washington, D.C.: U.S. Government Printing Office, 1960).

R. B. Zevin,   "The Growth of Cotton Textile Production after 1815," in R. W. Fogel and S. L. Engerman, cited above.

Part III

Transformation of the
economy: 1860–1920

8 THE PROCESS OF INDUSTRIALIZATION

England introduced the Industrial Revolution to the world at the end of the 18th century. In the middle of the next century America led the international race to industrialize. By 1860, the United States was the second ranking industrial nation, producing about one fifth of world output.

The rate of American expansion and the rise in productivity after the Civil War was phenomenal; and manufacturing continued to provide the main impetus to this rapid increase. Between 1860 and 1913, the U.S. share of world manufacturing production rose from 23 to 36 percent. In the same period, England's share fell from 32 to 14 percent, that of France from 10 to 6 percent. Germany's share rose from 13 to 16 percent; that of the rest of Europe, from 9 to 11 percent; the share of the rest of the world, from 13 to 17 percent. By 1913, America's manufacturing output equaled the combined output of its three nearest rivals![1]

Paradoxically, this period is often regarded as a dark chapter in American history. The gains from post–Civil War economic growth are taken for granted, whereas the associated costs are emphasized and the business leaders of the day are cited with shame as "robber barons." Economic expansion and per capita income growth brought about a sweeping transformation in the structure of the economy and engendered disruption at the same time. Business fluctuations were sharp and frequent and generated high rates of unemployment. Innovations reduced costs but cast aside those whose businesses or skills tied them to outmoded processes. Urbanization produced slums and pestilence as well as factory employment. Growth in government came as a by-product and brought with it a host of problems in public administration and policy-making.

The following two chapters will consider the growing pains of the

---

[1] League of Nations, p. 13.

rapidly industrializing economy. This chapter will consider the record of rapid growth and the ways in which that growth was achieved. Because the pace of growth was not even and automatic, attention will be given to the major innovations and waves of investment that accompanied the surges of most rapid growth.

POST–CIVIL WAR TRENDS

Growth and instability

As we noted in Part II, American manufacturing capacity began to grow rapidly around 1840. Then the Civil War took its heavy toll in economic welfare. In the postwar period the expansion and growth begun in the 1840s resumed.

During the first six decades of the 19th century, America increased its population sixfold and raised its real income at least ninefold. This resulted in a rise of income per capita of about one half. In the next six decades, population grew less than fourfold, while total production increased tenfold. The result was a threefold increase in production per person, which constituted an annual growth rate in the neighborhood of 1.5 percent. (See 8–1 and 8–2.)

8–1.   Expanding production and population, 1860–1920

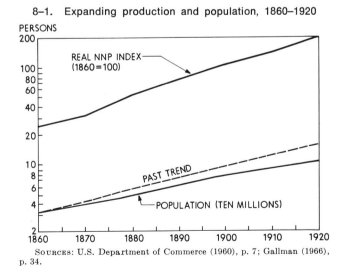

SOURCES: U.S. Department of Commerce (1960), p. 7; Gallman (1966), p. 34.

This rapid and long-sustained increase in total production was achieved in spite of a gradual slowing down of the rate of population increase. From 1830 to 1879, population increased at an average annual

8–2.   Rising production per person, 1860–1920

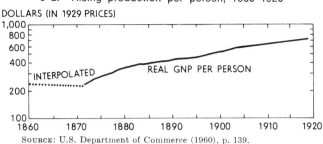

SOURCE: U.S. Department of Commerce (1960), p. 139.

8–3.   Decade rates of increase in production

*Alternative estimates
(percent changes)*

Overlapping decades	Commodity output (Gallman)	Gross national product (five-year average) (Kuznets)
1839–49	52	
1844–54	69	
1849–59	62	
1854–64		
1859–69	23	
1864–74		
1869–79	62	77*
1874–84	70	85
1879–89	63	49
1884–94	41	37
1889–99	36	47
1894–04		59
1899–09		48
1904–14		33
1909–19		29

* Less than a decade.
SOURCES: U.S. Department of Commerce (1960), p. 139; Gallman (1960), p. 16.

rate of 2.7 percent; from 1879 to 1919, the rate of increase fell to 1.9 percent.[2]

The rate of expansion and growth, however, did not occur at a steady, uniform pace. The most rapid rates of economic growth occurred just prior to and immediately following the Civil War. During the war, growth indexes hit 100-year lows. Another ten-year period of rapid increase came around the turn of the century, especially between 1897 and 1907. (See 8–3.)

The later sections of this chapter will describe the major industrial changes that accompanied the post–Civil War surges of growth.

Paradoxically, the decade of most rapid growth in our history also included the second longest depression. Each of the three decades after

___
[2] Goldsmith, p. 271.

the Civil War, in fact, had its major depression—1873–78, 1882–85, and 1892–94. Consequently, speeches, articles, and books during these decades of rapid growth were filled with critical comments about unfavorable business conditions and distress among farmers and workers. The historian with no access to data beyond those supplied by the popular press surely would record this as an era of stagnation. Why was it possible for contemporary observers to overlook the economy's trend?

A long-term decline in average prices throughout the economy was a major condition masking real growth and causing considerable distress in particular sectors of the economy. Inflation during the Civil War had doubled the index of wholesale prices, and not all of this inflation had been eliminated by the immediate postwar price decline. During the 1870s, wholesale prices fell by one third, finally reaching the prewar level by 1879. In the following decade and a half, a further decline of almost one third took place.

Essentially, what occurred was that the price rises that came with recovery from depressions failed to compensate for deflation during the depressions. Only after 1896 did prices generally begin to rise, and not until after 1910 did prices exceed the pre–Civil War level. After 1896, both prices and output were rising, and business depressions seemed shorter and milder. (See 8–4.)

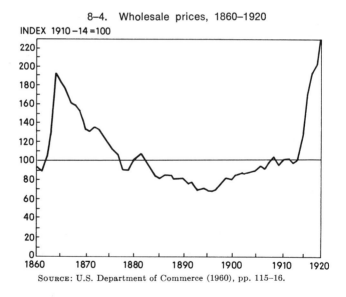

8–4. Wholesale prices, 1860–1920

INDEX 1910–14 = 100

SOURCE: U.S. Department of Commerce (1960), pp. 115–16.

The falling trend of prices caused money incomes to increase more slowly than physical production and intensified the sudden price declines in business depressions. Businessmen who purchased goods at one price and had to sell after prices had fallen took a loss on their inventories.

Farmers who borrowed to buy land and machinery when prices were high had difficulty meeting their mortgage payments when the prices of their products fell. Money wage rates failed to increase or were reduced. No wonder that discontent was abundant despite rapidly rising trends. Yet there is no clear evidence that deflation or the later price inflation hindered the long-term trend of economic growth. Nor, we should add, is there evidence to support the opposite assertion; the foregoing shouldn't be taken as an argument for chronic deflation.

Short-term fluctuations in output and prices also tended to obscure long-term trends. In a rapidly expanding economy, people are prone to take periods of increasing output for granted and to be deeply concerned about years of disappointing increases or actual decreases. Yet most periods of rapid expansion in output and rapid rises in prices have been followed by severe setbacks, such as the setbacks that occurred in 1837 and 1857 and again in 1873 and 1893. These setbacks usually started as financial crises that were referred to as panics. Later the frequency of the setbacks in output and prices became widely recognized, and the term *business cycle* came to be applied to their repeated recurrence.

While depressions were a source of severe distress for many people, their economy-wide impact should not be exaggerated. The National Bureau of Economic Research has identified 13 cyclical declines from the Civil War to World War I. In only seven of those years, however, did real GNP for an entire year actually decrease. (Monthly data would, of course, show more instances of absolute decline than annual figures.) Unemployment did exceed 10 percent of the labor force during five years of the 1870s and six years of the 1890s, but it exceeded 6 percent in perhaps only five or six other years altogether. Moreover, the most severe declines in output and employment tended to occur in the most rapidly expanding industries—construction, mining and metals, and machinery manufacturing.

We have included an appendix in this chapter that introduces business cycles and their relationship to long-term trends. That discussion provides the basis for a fuller appreciation of the preceding paragraphs. In addition, it offers helpful background information for understanding the changing structure of the economy discussed in Parts III and IV.

Impact of the Civil War

The Civil War has come to be regarded as an agency for change of unparalleled force in American economic, political, and social life. The eminent historian Charles Beard has described it as a "second American Revolution."[3] The war has been credited with the following effects.

---

[3] See Beard and Beard and Hacker for statements on the war's consequences.

1. In the absence of southern Congressmen, Yankee pressure groups pushed a brace of legislation through Congress which forever turned the tables in favor of northern, urban, and industrial interests.
2. The end of slavery provided the labor force and the economic conditions required for southern industrialization and the resumption of southern economic growth after years of stagnation.
3. The war itself stimulated economic growth via manufacturing expansion, technological innovation, accelerated adoption of the modern industrial method, agricultural mechanization, and capital accumulation.

Let's look at these assertions in the light of data that weren't available when the conventional economic history of the Civil War was written.[4]

Data on commodity output and per capita income simply do not bear out the growth stimulus thesis. According to data developed by Robert Gallman (and reported by Cochran and Engerman), the shift from agriculture to manufacturing was as rapid in the period between 1840 and 1860 as in the period between 1870 and 1900. Further, total commodity output rose annually at a rate of 4.6 percent from 1840 to 1860 and at a rate of 4.4 percent from 1870 to 1900, while the value of manufactures grew at a rate of 7.8 percent in the decades that preceded the war and at a rate of 6.0 percent in the decades that followed it.

In short, at best, industrialization and commodity output trends after the war only matched prewar trends. If the Civil War decade was *not* a turning point in economic history, we would expect the postwar percentage growth rates of the manufacturing and agricultural sectors to have been about the same as or slightly lower than those chalked up in the prewar period when factory manufacturing and the mechanization of agriculture were first becoming growth factors, i.e., from 1840 to 1860. The data in fact behave in exactly this manner.

Commodity output figures for the war decade show a marked departure *on the low side* from the 1840–1900 trend. Manufactures rose from 32 to only 33 percent of total national commodity output. What's more, this nominal gain was attributable to the war's devastation of cotton production rather than to expansion in manufacturing. Total commodity production grew by only 2 percent per year, and manufacturing expanded at a modest 2.3 percent, the low for the century. In all, the war cost the economy five years of commodity growth if prewar rates are accepted as norms.

Per capita output figures are ambiguous because slaves were considered property prior to the war. However, if we include both the free and the slave population in the prewar base, per capita commodity

---

[4] The following analysis is based primarily upon Engerman; however, Cochran can be credited with reopening the inquiry.

production plummeted by 39 percent in the South during the war, while in the North it grew at a century-low rate of less than 1 percent per year. After 1870, per capita commodity growth rates picked up. Engerman attributes this improvement to rebuilding in the South and a return to prewar performance in the North in the late 1860s and 1870s. After 1880, the expansion rate of per capita production resumed its prewar trend.

The record on capital formation also fails to bear out the growth stimulus thesis. The total stock of capital grew less rapidly after the war than before it and declined by 50 percent during the war years, although manufacturing capital formation accelerated very slightly, from 6.3 to 6.8 percent per year. New railroad track fell 4,500 miles behind its average prewar schedule. The capital creation figures are consistent with the data on income. Real wages and profits fell during the war, which in turn lowered the savings rate.

The stimulus thesis is ordinarily based on notions related to so-called war industries that experience vast increases in demand and then pull the rest of the economy along as they expand their rates of production. Any combination of three forces is capable of producing this effect. First, if the economy is in a depression at the outset of a war, war industries can, in fact, stimulate the recovery of employment and production indexes (although economic welfare would usually decline as a consequence of destruction caused by the war and concentration on war products). Second, the shift of resources toward war industries could generate economies of scale so great that nonmilitary purchases of their products would benefit. Third, wartime shortages can spur the discovery of techniques conserving labor, capital, or natural resources.

On the first count, the data deny the stimulus theory—1859–60 was a period of recovery from the Panic of 1857. The second count—the scale economies argument—fails as well, if growth rates and munitions orders are any indication. Small arms claimed only 1 percent of aggregate iron output during the war. Some of the consumer goods industries that supplied the army registered absolute declines rather than expansion. Boot and shoe manufacturers gained army contracts but lost the southern market. The output of woolen textiles increased but was more than offset by the vast decline of cotton textiles. Agriculture expanded in some areas at unprecedented rates, but growth in foreign demand can be cited as the cause. On the third count, the mechanization of agriculture did accelerate during the period 1850–70, but the war years were a time of soft demand for reaper and mower producers. To our knowledge, the technological effects of the war in other industries have not yet been studied, but they ought to be.

Let's summarize what the data mean as related to the growth stimulus thesis. The Civil War required the diversion of resources from peacetime, welfare-increasing production to war purposes. In this, the emphasis was on personnel—the Civil War was very labor intensive as compared, say, with World War II. Among the sacrificed items of production were capital goods, invention and innovation, and education, all of which are growth-inducing activities. The direct economic costs of the war were chiefly the loss of labor and damage to property, the latter concentrated in the South. If the growth stimulus thesis were valid, the sources of stimulation that we have discussed above would have more than offset the direct cost and other sacrifices connected with the war. The record of reduced industrial growth—of declining production in some instances—and only very modest stimulation strongly suggests that the damage and loss of life of the war were not offset through contemporary or subsequent acceleration of growth.

What of the southern industrialization thesis as it is related to emancipation? We have already discussed data that show one of its assumptions to be false. The southern economy was not stagnant before the war; rather, the South grew at least as quickly as the rest of the Nation in per capita (free) terms, although the North presented superior opportunities for individuals seeking to better their lot.

Second, the South went back to plantation agriculture after the war, and although rapid manufacturing growth eventually came about, this is no reason to believe that slaves couldn't have been employed in factory jobs; in fact, they were in the antebellum years.

Third, the Civil War, emancipation of the slaves with no recompense to those who had invested in them, and Reconstruction were very costly. How costly? If in the absence of the war southern income had continued at its prewar per capita growth rate, in 1870 the South's per capita income would have been nearly twice its actual level. As Robert Higgs has put it,

> the relative poverty of the South in the post-Civil War era . . . is therefore entirely attributable to (1) the existence of the slave system and (2) the abolition of that system through destructive civil war and haphazard emancipation . . . . How ironic that the Great Emancipation should have engineered a policy that has kept Southerners, black and white alike, relatively poor for over a century . . . . Had Americans been able in 1860 to foresee the future, it seems likely that a fully compensated, carefully organized emancipation would have appealed more strongly to both Northerners and Southerners.[5]

And what of wartime legislation? Studies of the tariff show its effects to have been ambiguous. The Union Pacific was successful, but it hardly affected GNP, let alone resulted in the perpetual consolidation of northern economic power. We know little of the growth effects of the other acts, but there seems no reason to believe that they placed the South

---

[5] Higgs, p. 114. Goldin has estimated the costs of a fully compensated emancipation and found that the costs would have been far below those associated with the war.

at a great disadvantage—if they induced growth in the North, then Southerners found better customers for their cotton and wood products in the postwar period. The war was the great source of loss to the South, not northern growth.

Overall, what can we say? If the 19th century economic history of the United States had a turning point, circa 1840 seems a better date for it than 1860–65. It was in the 1840s that manufacturing started to replace agriculture as the chief force moving the economy along its long-term per capita income growth trend of 1.4 percent per year. It was then that the transformation of the economy that came with industrialization got underway. (Don't confuse this with Rostow's "take-off" argument!)

End of the frontier

To account for post–Civil War growth, we first turn to changes in resource inputs over the period 1870–1920. To be sure, all of the inputs—natural resources, labor, and physical capital—were expanding. Yet there are three aspects of their growth which deserve special attention. First, the rate of increase slowed down for all three of the inputs. Second, the average rate of expansion in natural resources was the slowest, while the rate of expansion in capital was the fastest. Third, while the rate of growth of output also slowed down somewhat, it continued to rise faster than any of the inputs. This suggests the important role played by improvements in methods, organization, and capital equipment as well as increases in human capital.

Natural resources are difficult to measure as an input factor. In a sense, the natural resources were all there to begin with and remained as a fixed quantity. The continental territory of the 48 states had been acquired by the Nation prior to 1860. The history of development after the Civil War was one of settling the virgin territories and raising the average density of population, from 10.6 persons per square mile in 1860 to 35.6 in 1920, as total population more than tripled. However, the utilization of natural resources did continue to undergo an upward trend as more farmland was placed under cultivation and more mineral deposits were discovered and mined. In short, better transportation and changes in landholding patterns increased our access to a fixed quantity of natural resources.

In just three decades after the Civil War, total farmland in the Nation doubled. This means that as much land was settled in those three decades as had been settled in almost three centuries of prior history. This suggests, in turn, that heavy capital investments were made in clearing and draining land. The rate of settlement, however, merely kept pace with population growth, which about doubled in the same period. After 1900, the increase in farm acreage almost came to a halt. Large tracts of remote and otherwise uneconomic unoccupied public lands remained, but the frontier line of settlement had disappeared. No longer could the American people move westward to settle vast new territories. Further land use was a matter of filling in the gaps of less desirable or less accessible land that was still idle. Because of this slowdown, total farm acreage in 1920 reached only about 2.3 times its 1860 expanse, while population climbed to 3.6 times its 1860 level. (See 8–5.)

8–5.   Slowdown in expanded use of natural resources

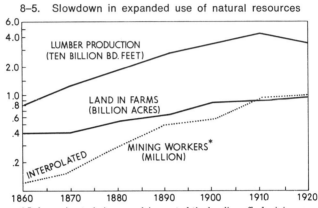

* Laborsaving techniques explain most of the leveling off of mining employment after 1910.
SOURCE: U.S. Department of Commerce (1960), pp. 278, 312, 349.

The discovery and use of timber and mineral resources also underwent a rapid burst followed by a slowdown after the turn of the century. The centers of lumber production moved west and south as the older areas were cut over and the best tree stands were exhausted. Mineral recovery rates doubled from 1900 to 1920 after having tripled in the two previous decades. The continued growth of mineral recovery rates was mostly due to the increased importance of mineral fuels; bituminous coal output tripled between 1900 and 1920 while petroleum output increased six times. After 1900, the growth of metal mining slowed down the most.

Labor inputs maintained the steadiest rate of increase. Between 1860 and 1920, the labor force grew even faster than population, almost quadrupling during the period. This is largely accounted for by the increase in median age of the population from 19.4 years in 1860 to 25.3 years in 1920. The number of children below 10 years of age fell from 14 to 11 percent of the population. This reflected some decline in birthrates as the population became more urbanized, but it was due chiefly to the large inflow of immigrants, most of whom were young adults.

In the early 1870s the peak number of immigrants arriving yearly in this country exceeded 400,000 as it had in the early 1850s. After 1900, the number again rose, reaching annual peaks of over 1 million in 1905–7, 1910, and 1913–14, although the net gain was less than that because some people also left the country. Elizabeth Gilboy and Edgar Hoover have estimated that during the decades 1880–90 and 1900–1910 net immigration accounted for about one third of the population increase measured in the respective preceding decades, and for about one fifth during the other decades. (See 8–6.)[6] The peaks and troughs in immigration are largely attributable to depressions in which job opportunities dried up and relatives were less able to provide passage and help to immigrants.

8–6. Immigrants arriving in the United States, 1860–1920

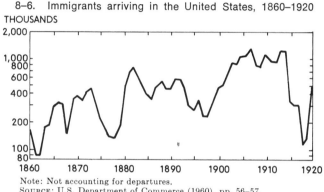

Note: Not accounting for departures.
SOURCE: U.S. Department of Commerce (1960), pp. 56–57.

Total man-hours increased at a somewhat slower pace than the labor force because the workday declined. In 1860, the usual workday for nonfarm workers was over 10 hours and the workweek was six days. By 1920, the average weekly hours for nonfarm workers had fallen to about 50. Taking into account the number of days of idleness during the year and including farm and government workers, the average workweek for the total labor force was a little less than 60 hours in 1869 and declined by about 9 percent between 1869 and 1919. (See 8–7.)

8–7. Measures of change in labor input, 1869–1919

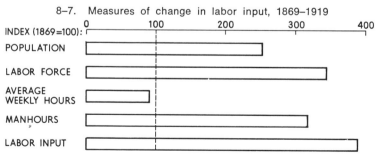

SOURCES: U.S. Department of Commerce (1960), p. 7; Kendrick, tables A VII, A IX, A XI, and A XIII.

---

[6] Gilboy and Hoover, pp. 266–67.

During this period, there was a shift toward a greater proportion of skilled workers. The overall skill index rose because of a shift from farm to nonfarm jobs which had higher output per worker ratios and because the labor forces of the growth industries had high skill indexes. Using average annual earnings in different industries as an indication of skill levels, with adjustments for increased capital per worker, it has been estimated that the real value of total labor inputs increased somewhat faster than the number of workers, even after allowing for the reduction in average hours worked. (That's why the labor input bar at the bottom of 8–7 is longer than the others.)

The input of capital increased almost as fast as output. While no figures are available for 1860, the real capital stock rose from $27 billion in 1869 to $227 billion in 1919 (both in 1929 prices). These estimates are for the value of reproducible tangible property, including buildings, machinery, inventories, and money metals, but excluding the value of land and consumer durables (such as furniture). The figures reflect deductions for depreciation and retirement from service of different types of property. These data show that the average American worker in 1919 had almost two and one-half times as much capital equipment to work with as in 1869. (See 8–8.)

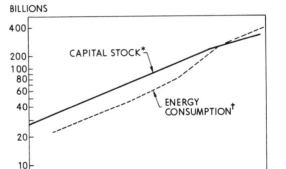

8–8. Expanded use of capital and energy, 1870–1920

* In dollars of 1929 purchasing power.
† Horsepower-hours for work; starting with 1870–80 decade average.
SOURCES: Kuznets (1961), table 3; Dewhurst, table L.

It is significant that energy consumption rose at the same pace as capital stock prior to 1900 and then rose even faster in the following two decades. Recall that the revolution in industrial methods involved the application of nonhuman energy to run machinery to make standard products. So naturally the rapid pace of industrialization in America was marked by the use of more machinery and more fuel for power. After the turn of the century, the widespread adoption of electric motors and diesel and gasoline engines rapidly expanded the use of various forms of energy, both for production and for direct consumption purposes. The American worker was given fingertip control over tremendous amounts of power that both lightened his work and vastly increased his productivity.

Productivity increases

Output per head not only increased in the post–Civil War period but grew faster than a weighted measure of combined inputs as well. In other words, productivity advanced over the period. If we shift our base and terminal year to 1840 and 1900, respectively, we can use Gallman's data to understand the details of American growth over the period under study.[7]

As column 1 in 8–9 shows, real Net National Product (NNP) grew at an annual rate of 3.98 percent per year, while labor grew at 2.77

8–9.   Growth of inputs and their contributions to output, 1840–1900

Input of NNP	*1* *Input growth rate (percent per year)*	*2* *Contribution to output (percent per year)*	*3* *Contribution weight (percent)*	*4* *Contribution to growth (percent)*
Labor*	2.77	1.88	68	48
Natural resources	2.83	0.38	13	9
Capital	5.40	1.03	19	26
Sum of inputs	–	3.29	100	83
Productivity	–	0.69	–	17
Total real NNP growth rate†		3.98		100

* No adjustment has been made for changes in the length of the workweek; therefore, the productivity measure is understated.
† 1860 prices.
Source: Gallman (1972), tables 2.10, 2.12.

percent, land at 2.83 percent, and capital at 5.40 percent. Perhaps this array of numbers leads you to the conclusion that output grew faster than population and labor input because land grew a bit faster and capital grew very much faster. This observation is true but not a complete explanation. If it were complete, we would find that the contribution of labor, natural resources, and capital to increased output summed to exactly 3.98 percent per year. In fact, if you look at column 2, 4th line in 8–9, you'll find that they sum to only 3.29 percent and that what is labeled productivity accounts for 0.69 percent.

---

[7] Gallman (1972), pp. 35–42. Data for 1889–1919 give the same impression; see Kendrick, tables I and A XXII.

In other words, if natural resources, labor, and capital had just increased in quantity without becoming more productive, then NNP would have grown at 3.29 percent per year, and output per worker and per capital unit would have grown solely because workers had more natural resources and capital to work with. Actually, however, the quality of labor and capital plus natural resources improved, and they interacted in a more productive environment. We'll say more about these sources of productivity increase in a moment; now let's explain how column 2 in 8–9 was computed.

In a market economy, NNP is divided among workers and owners of natural resources and capital roughly according to their respective contributions to production.[8] Consequently, if we know how NNP is divided among labor and other input owners, we have weights to convert a given input's growth rate to an output growth rate which is attributable to the growth of that input. For example, labor's share of NNP was 68 percent so that a labor-input growth rate of 2.77 percent converts to an output growth rate of 1.88 percent and indicates that 48 percent of NNP growth was attributable to an increased quantity of labor (see the labor line in columns 1 through 4 in 8–9).

A productivity increase of 0.69 percent per year out of a total NNP growth rate of 3.98 percent indicates that 17 percent of total growth between 1840 and 1900 is attributable to better inputs and better economic organization. Although we can't neatly divide this component of the growth rate the way we did the total growth rate, we can identify its components.[9]

Technological innovation characterized manufacturing, transportation and communications, and agriculture during the period. The machine and machine-tool builders continued to find ways to harness nonhuman power so as to mechanize additional manufacturing industries, and steelmaking improved enough to make the widespread displacement of iron feasible. Railroads became safer, used fuels more efficiently, and improved their load factor. The telephone took its place alongside the telegraph.

In agriculture, mechanization continued while selective breeding and other changes in farming techniques and farm management began to be adopted on an important scale. Better management techniques were introduced in the other broad industry groups as well. For example, steel plants were rearranged to facilitate continuous processing, and railroads standardized gauges. Thus, innovations that were embodied in new kinds of capital plus new methods of organizing production both contributed to productivity increases.

---

[8] Recall that NNP = GNP − CCA, i.e., GNP less allowances for worn-out capital equipment and housing (the capital consumption allowance) gives NNP.

[9] See Higgs pp. 34–57 for an extended discussion of the productivity factors cited below.

Human capital accumulation accelerated over this period. The Nation poured increasing amounts of resources into formal education—high school graduates as a portion of 17-year-olds increased fivefold, and B.A.'s increased fourfold. On-the-job training became important in building skilled labor pools. At the end of the century, death rates from disease were cut drastically by newly developed public health measures based upon Pasteur's and Koch's findings. In general, the ability of the average worker increased during the era as a reflection of increased formal and informal education and better health. Better economic organization, including external economies of scale, also contributed to growth.

As scholars have increasingly come to recognize, the development of American commercial law played a major role in abetting growth. Specifying property rights and assuring that the property of individuals and enterprises was secure against unlawful seizure by private persons and the state enhanced the willingness of men to do business at a distance on the basis of promises to pay, to deliver, or to produce. Thus the law assisted in establishing a truly national market, which, in turn, produced a host of external economies and opportunities for farmers and producers to reap the benefits of specialization.

The law assisted in a second way. Prior to the Civil War, the corporate form of business enterprise was sanctioned for almost anyone who could pay an incorporation fee. In the post–Civil War era, firms incorporated increasingly. This gave them easier access to financial capital markets than they could have had as partnerships or sole proprietorships—large blocks of stocks or bonds could be sold to hundreds or thousands of people and, thereby, huge amounts of funds could be raised for financing the machines and large plants required by the modern industrial method.

Urbanization continued and with it the growth of the scale economies that came from the synergistic relationship of improved transport, the modern industrial method, and urban agglomeration. The disappearance of the craft shop began in earnest after the Civil War. The cost reductions attributable to machine operations and the geographic concentration of production in urban areas overwhelmed made-to-order and small-volume production in industry after industry.

The growth of cities and the communications systems that tied them together also facilitated the building of a nationwide financial capital market. New York City emerged as the center of financial transactions, but funds flowed from region to region only because of decisions made throughout the country and communicated through New York brokerage and investment banking houses.

Capital formation

Because of the importance of capital accumulation in achieving higher productivity, and thus higher consumption levels per person, we should consider where the increased capital came from. How was it accumulated? Data on gross national product provide some general information on this. They also provide additional evidence confirming our assertion that the rising trend in output brought widespread benefits to consumers.

Remember that not all of GNP goes to consumers to be used up in current consumption each year. Some output consists of new capital goods—buildings, machinery and equipment, and government capital goods and inventories. And some current production—the capital consumption allowance (CCA)—is needed to replace capital goods that wear out or lose their value from obsolescence each year. It is the net additions to the capital stock over and above replacement needs that are important to keep GNP growing. Net additions to the capital stock are referred to as *net capital formation,* and the total of nonconsumed goods—capital consumption plus net capital formation—is called *gross capital formation.*

In the years 1917–21, the annual gross capital formation was still about one fourth of GNP, as it had been in 1869–73. Capital consumption, however, required an increasing share of GNP. This probably reflected the increased importance of durable goods in the capital stock (and the reduced importance of inventories), a shorter useful life of capital goods because of rapid obsolescence generated by technological change, and some slowing down in the rate of growth of GNP itself. In any event, net capital formation absorbed a declining share of GNP; and the growth of GNP was slowing down partly because a smaller share of the total output was being reinvested to expand capital stock and thus raise future output. (See 8–10.)

8–10. Changing components of GNP

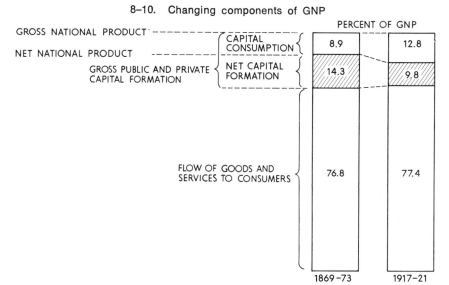

Source: U.S. Department of Commerce (1960), p. 144.

Business firms were the chief users of capital goods, taking initially almost three quarters of the total, while households at first took over a fifth. Early in the period governments absorbed a small share, but their share, especially that of local governments, increased rapidly. Personal savings of individuals, including farmers and proprietors of unincorporated firms, provided almost two thirds of total savings; corporations provided over a fourth; and foreign investors, chiefly the British, provided the balance.

These long-run trends fluctuated somewhat with the rate of increase in gross national product. When output growth was slowest, during the depressions following 1873 and 1893, the flow of capital goods required the highest share of output (in the five-year periods 1874–78 and 1894–98). The subsequent rapid growth of output reduced the percentage share of output in the form of capital goods. (See 8–11.)

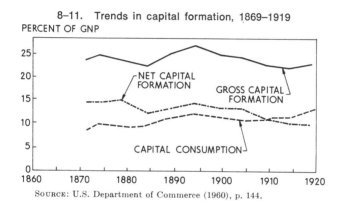

8–11.   Trends in capital formation, 1869–1919

SOURCE: U.S. Department of Commerce (1960), p. 144.

Note in 8–10 that as total output expanded, the production of consumer goods expanded in about the same proportion. This means that the gains of increased output were shared proportionately by consumers. In absolute terms, they did not have to tighten their belts and sacrifice in the present in order to build up capital for expanding output in the future. In fact, after allowances for capital consumption had been deducted, the net capital formation rate, which approximates the savings rate out of total incomes, fell to about 10 percent of GNP, while gross capital formation (gross savings) remained at about 23 percent of GNP.

In other words, about the same ratio of total output was consigned to the sum of replacing worn-out capital and providing new capital in the two time segments represented in 8–10. As our capital stock grew, the absolute amount of capital consumed in the production process grew also. To replace ever-increasing amounts of worn-out capital, we chose to reduce our new capital formation as a percent of GNP rather than reduce consumption as a portion of total output.

Emergence of a national capital market

One of the chief elements of the economy's post–Civil War transformation was the creation of a truly national financial capital market—a long and arduous process during which savers and investors groped their way and which was not completed until sometime between 1900 and 1920.

The modest scale of most antebellum business enterprises meant that a relatively underdeveloped capital market did not serve as a serious impediment to investment. However, as the scale of manufacturing firms and railroads grew, a variety of financial intermediaries had to be innovated to facilitate the flow of long-term credit to capital-hungry businesses. The result, of course, was the establishment of a national capital market.

The savings-investment process takes two forms: first, savers may invest directly by investing in their own enterprise or by financing the purchase of their own housing, or, second, savers may rely upon financial intermediation. The latter consists of buying securities issued by or making deposits at a financial firm which makes funds available to finance either the operations of business firms or the housing purchases of individuals.

Financial intermediaries include mutual savings banks, commercial banks, savings and loan associations, mutual life insurance companies, and credit unions. During the post–Civil War period, life insurance companies became the most important of the intermediaries supplying long-term credit. Commercial banks grew in number and importance throughout the period. They also shifted their portfolio policies away from long-term loans, which left them illiquid during panics, in favor of short-term farm and business loans.

Prior to the Civil War, investments were made primarily by individual savers who invested directly in their own business firms or farms or in the firms or farms of people familiar to them. Apart from social overhead projects, the corporation was almost unknown, as was the sale of stocks or bonds to anonymous savers who knew the operating firm by reputation rather than by close observation and personal contact with its management. Even when Andrew Carnegie and John D. Rockefeller built their empires, it was their personal contacts that put money within their reach; today, when U.S. Steel and Standard Oil want additional funds, they merely offer securities to the highest bidders in a market involving millions of savers and thousands of financial intermediaries whose identities are unknown to the issuing corporations.[10]

The increased use of the corporate form and the growth of savings and business investment made possible a national market for stocks

---

[10] Davis (1963) has documented the thesis that the so-called robber barons owed much of their success to their mastery of finance.

and bonds after the Civil War. As a national securities market came into being, investment banking firms—financial wholesalers—were developed. Firms such as J. P. Morgan's house, to name the best known, specialized in underwriting, i.e., in buying newly issued corporate stocks and bonds, then reselling them at a profit to the public and institutional investors. Often syndicates of several investment banking houses would form to underwrite very large issues.

In a less developed fashion than the stock market and investment banking houses, the agricultural credit market also became national in scope. Banks moved west with the farmer and brought eastern money with them. And farm mortgage agents representing eastern savers traveled westward with the settlers.

A market for commercial paper—short-term IOUs issued by business firms—appeared even before the stock market was anything more than a local phenomenon. Firms which specialized in buying commercial paper in regions where interest rates were high and reselling it at a profit in areas where interest rates were low emerged as part of the commercial paper market.

The effects of establishing a national capital market were salutary for the savings-investment process. Net interest rates were reduced to borrowers but raised for savers because the costs involved in bringing savers and investors together were reduced. Both savers and investors benefited from the use of intermediaries because intermediaries could issue securities more to the liking of savers while investors could issue securities more to their own liking and distribute them through intermediaries. Regional differences in interest rates were also reduced. A national market meant that regions which tended to save beyond local investor demand could buy the securities of firms in regions in which investor demand for savings exceeded supply.

The above suggests that the introduction of financial intermediaries and the growth of a national capital market stimulated both saving and investment by reducing the costs associated with bringing saver and investor together. In turn, economic growth was enhanced. Further, there was a tendency, as we will see, for a national securities market to eliminate financial advantages as a source of monopoly power. On the other hand, it is possible that the national capital market contributed to the economy's year-to-year instability even while it aided its growth.[11]

Income distribution

Who got the increases in income associated with contributions to the growth of output? Conventional history often assumes that the

---

[11] For a more extensive treatment of the process of capital formation and the role of financial institutions plus citations from the literature, see Davis (1972); the above discussion follows Davis closely.

Gilded Age, as the post–Civil War period has been tagged, was one of exploitation of the masses. Profits grew, it is said, because productivity increases were directed to property owners (Marx's capitalists), while the workers (Marx's producers), rather than sharing in the fruits of progress, found their real wages actually reduced.

The data contradict this indictment. In the period from 1840 to 1900, the division of national income between labor and property owners (capital and natural resource suppliers) remained in a 70–30 ratio. Over the same time span, both capital and developed natural resources increased faster than the labor force.[12] This means that labor incomes per unit of labor input rose compared with profits and interest per unit of property input.

Studies have also sought to estimate the average wage rates and annual earnings of workers. The general declines in prices were accompanied at times by a general erosion of wages, and for a while it was thought that there may have been a long-term decline in real wages prior to 1914.[13] Recent studies, however, have provided more comprehensive wage and price data that show a gentle upward trend in real wages from the end of the Civil War to World War I. (See 8–12.)

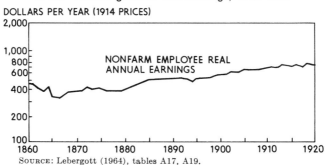

8–12. Worker gains in real earnings, 1860–1920

DOLLARS PER YEAR (1914 PRICES)

NONFARM EMPLOYEE REAL ANNUAL EARNINGS

SOURCE: Lebergott (1964), tables A17, A19.

This does not mean that all individuals shared equally in the gains in real income. Undoubtedly, this was a period when a few families became enormously wealthy, and the contrast (or spread) between the incomes of the poor cotton sharecroppers and the very rich must have increased. But is there evidence of substantially greater inequality of income distribution during this period?

Unfortunately, there are no adequate data on individual incomes prior to the start of the federal income tax in 1914. After 1914, the shares of total income going to the top 1 percent and the top 5 percent of families remained fairly constant for two decades and then declined

---

[12] Gallman (1972), p. 37.

[13] Lebergott (1972), pp. 205–13; also compare Douglas and Rees on this issue.

somewhat. Income tax data from the Civil War years and the years immediately following the war are inconclusive but suggest little difference between the top group's share in 1869 and in 1920.[14] Analysis of income tax data also suggests that inequality among the top income earners declined slightly between the Civil War and World War I.[15]

The process of industrialization and urbanization undoubtedly increased the relative size of the middle classes. The proportion of workers in nonfarm jobs and in the higher skill-index industries also increased. Thus, the distribution of incomes may have shifted in favor of middle and upper middle incomes and away from the very lowest income groups. But this does not necessarily mean that any group was worse off in absolute terms.

The conclusion must be drawn, therefore, that the benefits from this period of rapid economic growth and early industrialization were shared by workers generally and thus were widespread throughout the economy. The relative price of labor and labor's total real income rose and probably rose faster than the average price or total rewards of capital. In addition, workers benefited from less strenuous job assignments and more leisure time, while consumers enjoyed better quality and a greater variety of goods, gains not reflected in data on output and incomes.

THE RAILROAD AGE

In the two decades prior to the Civil War, national economic growth had begun to accelerate largely because of the rapid expansion of manufacturing. This trend had started slowly with the early establishment of one major mass-production industry, cotton textiles. At the same time, a diversity of innovations had laid the basis for a spread of mass-production methods to other industries. Then the rapid construction of steamboats, canals, and railroads provided cheaper transportation to tie the regions together, expand agricultural production, and, ultimately, to provide mass markets for the newly mechanized industries.

The Civil War was an interlude of retarded growth, and the South suffered property losses and drastic production cuts in the war. Immediately after the war, the rapid pace of national expansion was resumed, manufacturing and railroad construction again spurted ahead, and even in the South both farm and factory production soon recovered and grew.

Production methods and market size

We have already developed the idea that specialization among firms and the division of labor within firms raises productivity. Specialists,

[14] Kuznets (1952), table 29 and p. 144.
[15] Soltow, p. 286.

you will recall, produce more efficiently because they become more proficient, waste less time, and can utilize laborsaving, mass-production machinery. However, the capital goods used in mass production are lumpy in the sense that each unit built is very large (size being measured in terms of the minimum level of daily output when the equipment is fully manned). And each unit is very costly.

What this means is that modern industrial production requires a mass market so as to spread the cost of huge capital investments over as many units of output as possible. Otherwise, unit costs of production would be prohibitively high by other than labor-intensive production methods. Imagine how high automobile manufacturing costs would be if today's annual market were only, say, 1 million units rather than 9 to 10 million units. With today's plant and equipment, annual production could then be produced in about 40 days, leaving auto plants idle for the balance of the year and producing a ninefold increase in annual capital costs per unit. In lesser dimensions, exactly this situation threatened the potential American manufacturer in the early 19th century.

As we can see from the above, rapid manufacturing growth in the United States could not be initiated by inventions, innovations, and enterprising spirit alone. Although the period was the dawn of mass production, as long as the American market was small and scattered, it was cheaper to import manufactured goods from nations such as England that had large, concentrated markets and thus could use modern production techniques.

On the other hand, once income and population growth had increased the market, and transportation improvements had welded together a national market, the manufacturing sector was poised for a takeoff. The first signs of that takeoff can be dated at about 1840, although textile production soared in the 1820s. In the post–Civil War era, natural population increases, augmented somewhat by immigration, and the rise in total income attributable to the extensive growth of output carried more and more manufacturing industries over the cost threshold that made domestic production possible. Thus we have here an example of the principle we cited in chapter 1: namely, that economic expansion—extensive growth—can aid economic, or intensive, growth.

Completing a railroad network

Although the post–Civil War rate of increase in railroad mileage never quite reached the prewar rate, track mileage doubled in the first 8 postwar years and doubled again in the next 14 years. After this, construction slowed down, with a little more than 50 percent added in the next three decades combined. (See 8–13.)

The most dramatic part of postwar railroad construction was the spanning of the western plains and mountains to reach the Pacific Coast.

8–13.   Railroad mileage and traffic, 1860–1920

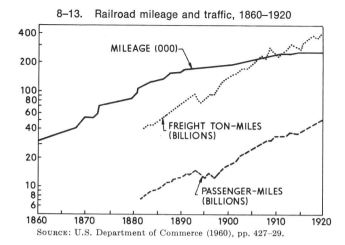

SOURCE: U.S. Department of Commerce (1960), pp. 427–29.

After having authorized engineering surveys of several routes in 1853, Congress passed the Pacific Railway Act of 1862, authorizing the Union Pacific and Central Pacific railroads to build toward each other from Omaha and Sacramento. The linkup was made in 1869 just west of Ogden, Utah. Not until 1883 was another link provided by the Northern Pacific, but by 1893 the Great Northern and Southern Pacific had added two additional routes.

The largest concentration of new track was laid in the Great Plains states. Chicago became the primary focus of a network of railroads, called the granger roads, that fanned out westward over the plains and interlaced vast new farming areas. From Chicago eastward, five major systems were built up during the 1860s and 1870s. These railroads (called the trunk lines) filled in gaps, built feeder lines, and provided multiple connections between major cities. A number of smaller railroad companies (the coal roads) connected the Appalachian coal mines with the East Coast and the Ohio Valley. Construction lagged for about a decade in the South, but by 1900 the national railroad network was virtually completed in every region and state.

Along with the increased mileage came rapid improvements in methods that helped lower costs and improve service. In the first decade of building, the improved interconnection of rail lines itself brought a big improvement and bridges crossed many rivers for the first time. This greatly reduced the need for unloading and reloading freight.

The same problem had to be overcome in moving freight over different companies' lines and equipment. In 1871, 23 different track gauges were in use. However, by 1880, four fifths of the mileage had been reduced to one standard gauge, and in 1886 the southern lines finally converted to the standard gauge.

With standardization of cars, and especially of their coupling devices, freight could move over different lines in the same car without reloading. Special freight-handling companies organized fast freight service over the roads of several companies. Standard bills of lading and uniform classifications of products were developed; and, in order to standardize time schedules, agreement was reached on four time zones covering the country.

Improvements in materials and equipment also began to increase speed and carrying capacity. A big factor was the early introduction of steel rails which were longer and heavier than their iron forerunners. This permitted a smoother and faster ride and carrying heavier, more powerful engines which pulled more and heavier cars. Immediately after the Civil War, engines had only four driving wheels, but that number was soon increased three and a half times, and pulling power increased ten times.

Because of the long distances that bulky goods were transported, American railroads were built with much larger cars than were used in Europe. Coal cars, for example, carried about 10 tons just after the Civil War, but up to 100 tons by 1920. The faster speeds made safety devices increasingly important; the automatic coupler and air brake were both introduced in 1887, and later came the electric block signal system.

These technological innovations plus various managerial improvements all contributed to lowering freight rates. Larger cars and more cars per train pulled by more powerful engines, more trains per time period, and more mileage all reduced unit costs. In turn, the forces of competition translated lower costs into lower prices.

Increased traffic on any given line tended to lower costs and rates. When a rail line was first built, there was seldom enough traffic to make full use of its capacity. As traffic grew, more trains and longer trains could be run over the same rails and use the same terminals. Later, double tracks could be laid on the same roadbed, and improved equipment carried more traffic faster on the same mileage. The initial costs of building the lines were financed by bonded debt, on which annual interest payments had to be made. As traffic and efficiency increased, these fixed costs could be spread over more units of sales and thus resulted in lower costs per unit.

During the 1870s, the rate of increase in freight and passenger traffic barely kept pace with the rapid construction of new rail mileage. But during the following decades, traffic continued to grow rapidly while new construction slowed down. (Refer again to 8–13.)

Improved communications developed parallel to improved rail transportation. The first transcontinental telegraph line, in fact, was completed in 1861, nearly a decade earlier than the first transcontinental railroad. This meant that messages previously requiring weeks to deliver could be communicated in hours or even minutes.

A successful transatlantic cable was laid in 1866. The basic patents on the telephone were filed in 1876, and during the 1880s telephone lines were strung across the country and covered cities with a maze of poles and wires. Experiments in radio were begun in the 1890s, but by World War I radio was still used mainly in shipping.

Other transportation and communications industries should be mentioned at this point. Because of greater speed, more direct routes, and year-round operation, railroads greatly reduced transportation on the rivers and canals. Only the traffic on the Great Lakes increased, largely because of the iron ore carried from Lake Superior in large lake boats. On the oceans, American shipping also declined as iron hulls and steam engines took over from wooden sailing ships. American construction and labor costs were high compared to those of European shipbuilders. Foreign ships carried nearly all of American international trade, but American shipping did increase in the protected coastal trade.

Railroads and economic welfare

The traditional interpretation of the transportation industry's impact upon American growth is highly impressionistic in attributing revolutionary effects to railroad development. Early writers viewed the railroad as crucial to the opening of the West and as the prime force behind 19th century economic growth. According to Rostow and other recent investigators, the railroads were the vanguard industry that launched the Nation's "takeoff stage" by providing major manufacturing markets in the period 1843–60. Such interpretations imply that in the absence of the railroads extensive and per capita growth would have been stalemated. In other words the railroad is held to have been indispensable to American economic development. Let's examine this axiom of indispensability in terms of the evidence available.[16]

The economic effects of railroad service fall into four broad categories: (1) cost reduction through lower passenger and freight rates, a direct benefit; (2) relocation of economic activity, a forward linkage; (3) stimulus to supplier industries, backward linkages; and (4) development of the new business and managerial techniques required to operate large-scale business organizations.

By 1890 rail freight outweighed waterborne internal transit five to one, which would seem to suggest that because rail transport was the preferred mode its benefits were overwhelming.[17] However, the direct benefits of railroads have to be computed in the light of existing alternative modes and routes of transport. When the railroads were first built, the United States already had an extensive road, river, and canal

---

[16] See Fishlow (1965); Fishlow (1972), pp. 513–31; Fogel; Rostow, p. 55; and Boyd and Walton.

[17] See Fogel, p. 5, for a comparison of rail versus waterway traffic.

system. Thus the railroads' conservation of inputs is determined by subtracting railroad carriage costs from water and highway transport costs. Although railroad freight rates never fell as low as water rates, the railroads' reduction in transshipment costs, hauling costs to shipping points, and damage resulted in a net reduction in shipping costs. This reduction, coupled with the vast increase in freight volume made possible by building railroads where water routes were absent, make it clear that railroads produced an important social saving through direct benefits.

Fishlow estimates that by the 1850s the social savings attributable to rail freight transit surpassed those attributable to the canals and that by 1890 they exceeded 10 percent of national income. Using a different estimating procedure, Fogel arrives at a 5 percent social saving. And Boyd and Walton have computed passenger social savings as 2.6 percent of GNP in 1890.[18] Most of these gains came from pushing railroads into interior western areas where water transport did not exist. However, note "that in the absence of railroads, extensions of canals and improvements in major roads would have kept in use all but 4 percent of the land actually worked in 1890."[19]

Opening the Far West permitted a regional reallocation of resources to take place that enabled crops to be grown in the areas most appropriate for their cultivation. As compared with the cost of raising 1910's wheat, oat, and corn crops within reach of canal routes, railroads made possible gains of $521 million, which represented a 10 to 20 percent saving of the 1839 cost of raising these crops.[20]

The backward linkages of railroads constituted demand for engineering services, steam engines, iron and steel rails, machinery and machine shop labor, construction workers, and operating labor. In the 1880s the sum of railroad construction and equipment purchases reached its peak. At that time the railroads accounted for 18 percent of gross capital formation. This represents an important reallocation of capital resources to the railroads. Whether that reallocation contributed to or detracted from economic development depends on what scale economies were gained and lost thereby.

If the expansion of a particular manufacturing industry to supply railroad demand lowered that industry's cost structure then all its customers would have gained thereby. But in a growth context, the expansion of a given industry means the relative contraction of another industry, so scale economies might be lost there. For rail demands to have had an important effect on total income two factors had to be present. First, *net* scale economies had to be significant and much larger than

---

[18] Fishlow (1971), p. 520; Fogel, chap. 6; Boyd and Walton, p. 290.

[19] Fogel, p. 227.

[20] Fishlow (1972), pp. 527–28.

those that would have been realized from the growth of the canal and road building that would have taken place in the absence of the railroad. Second, railroad demands had to be large.

We have no measure of the actual scale economies gained or lost by railroad expansion. We do know that steel rails took a huge portion of total Bessemer supply, 80 percent in 1880, while canals and roadways were not heavy steel users. And we know that in the late 19th century, more efficient organization of steel plants was made possible by the growth in their rates of production. So we can conclude that at least in the steel industry railroad demand probably gave rise to a social saving. But we don't have information as good as this for other industries.

Let's try another tack. The limit on reduced unit cost that higher rates of production could bring about was a reduction in cost per unit so large that the higher volumes required by railroad demand could be produced at just barely above the same total cost as before railroads came into the picture. Let's take a hypothetical example. Assume that railroads began to place steel orders on a continuing basis that resulted in a 10 percent increase in total yearly steel production. Assume further that expansion of steel capacity to accommodate the extra railroad demand lowered the cost per ton of steelmaking. The result would have been that railroads and all other steel consumers could purchase steel at lower unit prices. In monetary terms, the limit on cost reduction would have been the value of steel sales to the railroads—i.e., the limit that cost reduction could approach but never reach would have been a unit cost saving so great that the 10 percent increase in output could be produced at no increase in total cost.

In 1890, railroads accounted for less than 5 percent of total manufacturing demand, and manufacturing came to 19 percent of GNP. On the assumption that railroads did account for a full 5 percent of total manufacturing demand and that scale economies achieved thereby were equal to 5 percent of demand, then the maximum social saving that railroad-induced scale economies could approach would have been 0.95 percent of GNP (i.e., 5 percent of 19 percent). Thus, even on the *most generous* assumption, scale economies from railroads would have yielded a social saving of less than 1 percent.

What does the foregoing say about Rostow's takeoff thesis? Rostow asserts that rapid economic growth requires "the development of one or more substantial manufacturing sectors, with a high rate of growth."[21] And in Rostow's view the railroads provided the necessary stimulus to the manufacturing sector.[22] As we see it, scale economies are all that Rostow can have in mind—surely he doesn't think that without the railroads no manufacturing sector would have existed—and scale

[21] Rostow, p. 39.
[22] Rostow, p. 38.

economies, as we've shown, could hardly have had a revolutionary impact on total GNP.

When it comes to developing techniques for running large-scale enterprises, quantification doesn't help us. What we need to know is whether, in the absence of the railroad, firms in other industries could have grown large. If no railroad men had come along to show the way, would growth-industry firms have balked at the chance to expand? It's hard to conceive of Andrew Carnegie or John D. Rockefeller shying away from bigness because it was unprecedented. It also is not clear that the shenanigans of the so-called robber barons depended on the railroad experience, but it is clear that the disruption caused by those who manipulated railroad finances was costly.[23]

On balance, what can we say about the indispensability axiom? The total efficiency effects of having railroads amounted to roughly 9 to 14 percent of GNP in 1890. In other words, in the absence of the railroads the use of alternative but inferior transportation facilities would have forced a different deployment of people and production facilities. At the most, the consequence would have been the loss of not quite four years' growth given the fact that the economy actually expanded at about 4 percent per year in the post-Civil War period. Certainly, 14 percent, or four years' growth, does not make a strong case for indispensability. Yet, it's hard to think of any other single industry that had so great and protracted an effect on the economy. Put slightly differently, analysis of the railroad confirms the thesis that economic growth is generated by a host of interacting forces none of which is indispensable because each has its alternatives!

MANUFACTURING GROWTH

Developing metal and fuel industries

Along with rapid expansion of the internal transportation network came rapid improvements and cost reductions in basic metals and the power sources that were essential to mechanized mass production. Iron and machinery industries had developed along with the leading industries, textiles and railroads, prior to the Civil War. After the war, rapid mechanization of manufacturing industries plus railroad construction required an accelerated growth of metal and machinery production. The increased use of power-driven machinery also accelerated the demand for fuels.

Ironmaking underwent a rapid cost reduction through the introduction of coke as a fuel and the building of larger blast furnaces. Coke

---

[23] See North, pp. 114–15.

making was developed especially in southwestern Pennsylvania, where large quantities of soft coal were readily available at low cost. A large supply of iron was also available in this region because of cheap water transportation up the Ohio River from Missouri mines and down the Great Lakes from mines in upper Michigan and Wisconsin. The efficiency of the blast furnace was increased by building it on a larger scale with higher blast pressures and temperatures. Weekly furnace output was raised from 300 tons to 600 tons in the decade after the Civil War; and the capacity of furnaces was raised another six times in the next two decades. Thus, both concentrated sources of fuel and mineral supplies and the great size of furnaces led to concentration of iron production in a few industrial areas.

At the same time, the steel age was made possible by the Bessemer converter furnace. Though the furnace was invented in the 1850s, the first commercial production of Bessemer steel in this country came after the Civil War. Bessemer steel was not as hard as tool steel, but it was much harder and stronger than wrought iron. Although more expensive per ton at first, it was more economical than iron for rails and so was immediately favored by the railroads. Later improvements were worked out in the process of achieving large-volume production, and as the cost of Bessemer steel fell it was substituted for wrought iron in a wider variety of uses.

Production of all steel expanded ten times during the decade of the 1870s alone, and by the mid-1880s virtually all rails were being made from steel. Meanwhile, the open-hearth furnace had been improved and was rapidly being introduced. The open-hearth furnace had the advantage of being able to utilize scrap metal along with some types of iron that could not be used in the Bessemer converter; it also permitted greater control over the type and quality of steel produced. By 1908, steel production from open-hearth furnaces exceeded that from Bessemer converters and total steel output had again increased more than tenfold. (See 8–14.)

Along with the steel furnaces, large rolling mills were needed to produce rails. The same techniques and facilities permitted the production of structural steel for bridges and, by the 1890s, skyscrapers. In the 1880s a naval expansion program called for armor plate and sheet steel for ship hulls. Rolled steel plates were used in boilers, and various types and sizes of steel pipe were employed to transport oil and gas and for hydraulic mining and irrigation in the West. Steel began to replace iron in a grand variety of products, including wire and nails.

New types of heavy machinery were developed on the basis of the lower costs and improved qualities of iron and steel—among them were dredging and excavating equipment; conveying and elevating machinery; and mining, well-drilling, and refining equipment. Production of farm machinery and locomotives continued to expand. Railroad cars increas-

8-14.   Output of iron, steel, and rails

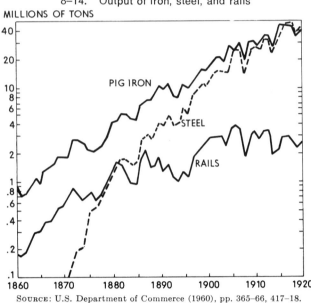

SOURCE: U.S. Department of Commerce (1960), pp. 365–66, 417–18.

ingly were made of steel. The machine-tool industry benefited tremendously from the development of high-speed cutting tools.

Improved metals and improved methods of cutting and shaping metals
were key factors in achieving better performance from engines and other
machinery. The steam engine was used more and more in factories,
and it came to surpass water as a direct source of power very early
in the period. Boilers were improved and made safer by the use of
banks of tubes instead of one large water cylinder; and fuel economy
was raised by means of mechanical stokers, forced-draft systems, and
superheaters. Engines were improved with new-type valves and gears,
as both larger engines and small, compact types were developed.

The expansion of metal and engine production required acceleration
in the output of a prior stage of production—the mining of metallic
ores and fuels. Rapid development of American industry was greatly
aided by the early discovery of large bodies of high-grade ores in convenient geographic locations and often near the surface. The discovery
of ores was aided in the 1850s by systematic geological surveys by
state governments and universities in the East and, in the 1860s, by
the federal government in the West.

For ores found at the surface, open-pit mining techniques were
rapidly developed, using huge shovels and other earth-moving equipment operated by steam engines. For shaft mines, however, the steam
engine was limited to operating hoists, air and water pumps, and venti-

lating equipment. At the end of the Civil War, underground mining was still a pick-and-shovel operation. However, during the 1870s compressed air drills and blasting powder reduced labor requirements. But further mechanization had to await the development of the electric motor. Above the surface, new equipment had to be invented to crush rock and separate ores, and new processes had to be developed to utilize low-grade ores.

Iron mining was expanded in three main locations after the Civil War: northern Michigan, Wisconsin, and Minnesota; southeastern Missouri; and northeastern Alabama. Technology, however, favored the northern mines; the mines near St. Louis played out in the late 1880s, and the Alabama ores were of a type that was unusable in the Bessemer steel process. In the late 1880s, Minnesota's Mesabi ore field was opened and mined with open-pit techniques.

Some shifts in location occurred in the mining of other metals. At first, copper was mined in northern Michigan; then, in the 1870s and 1880s, large mines were opened in Montana and Arizona. The early zinc and lead mines were located in southwestern Missouri, but later production was located in Nevada, Utah, Colorado, and Idaho.

Petroleum was first discovered in Pennsylvania before the Civil War, where it was close to convenient transportation and markets. The supply of whale oil was limited, and the demands for lamp and machine oils were rising rapidly. Kerosene was the first main petroleum product, although by the 1890s fuel oil was used increasingly in steam engines, especially in the western states. In 1893, Ohio forged ahead as the major well-producing state; it was succeeded in 1903 by California, which was displaced shortly thereafter by Texas. Up to World War I, a simple distillation process was used, until the rising demand for gasoline brought a shift to a thermal conversion process called cracking.

Mass-producing consumer goods

With post–Civil War improvements in both transportation and machinery, mass production and marketing were made possible for a whole range of consumer products. In a nation with a rapidly expanding population and rising per capita income, the opportunities for starting and expanding new businesses seemed to be unlimited. The history of consumer goods industries, however, shows that the path for individual businesses was precarious. The process of mechanization usually led to a smaller number of firms of larger size. New products and qualities frequently meant a shift of consumption patterns away from older products. Many industries that had become localized in one area underwent a shift in market or producing centers to other regions.

These trends are illustrated by textiles, which was the oldest mass-production industry and in 1919 was still the largest employer among the major industry groups. In cotton goods, the ring frame increased the speed of spinning, and the automatic loom tripled the number of machines one worker could tend. The result was that between 1870 and 1890 the number of cotton factories declined by 50 percent while employment increased by 64 percent. Spindle machinery increased 100 percent, and raw materials processed increased 200 percent. Much of the increase in production occurred in the South, as the regional pattern of location in the industry began to shift.

In woolen textiles, the major change was a shift in types of fabrics. Between 1869 and 1909, the value of nonworsted woolen output declined by a fourth, while it increased 14-fold for worsteds. Worsted factories also tended to be larger. Even so, woolen textiles lost first place in value of output to cotton goods; and new branches of the industry—knit goods and silk goods—gained on the rest.

Neither the apparel industry nor the shoe industry went very far in the trend toward large factories. After the introduction of the sewing machine in the 1850s, many specialized powered machines were developed to perform particular tasks—buttonhole making and sewing, cloth cutting, and steam pressing. But the equipment remained small; piecework could be contracted out to small shops, often in slum tenement buildings; and style variation and specialties tended to preserve the small producer. Because of rapid style changes, women's wear concentrated in New York, but men's garments were made in most of the major cities.

After specialized sewing machines for shoes were introduced in the 1860s, factory-produced shoes became commonplace. By 1895, the labor cost of making a pair of shoes had been reduced to one ninth what it had been in 1865. The sewing could be done in relatively small shops, with the material buying, cutting, and final selling done by larger firms. Consequently, the number of firms in the industry remained large while the typical firm was small. The location of the shoe industry, however, did undergo a shift from the region around Boston, where foreign hides had been imported, to St. Louis, Milwaukee, and Chicago, where domestic hides from the meat-packing industry were available.

The development of the meat-packing industry helped to maintain the food products industry group among the first ranking industry groups. (See 8–15.) The diffusion of refrigerated rail cars caused meat slaughtering to be concentrated in a few big firms located in a few large cities, such as Minneapolis, St. Louis, and Chicago. And because refrigeration and canning provided new ways to preserve beef, consumption shifted from pork toward beef. The growth of canning created additional demand for the tin can and glass jar industries. Very large flour mills were concentrated in Minneapolis, although mills continued to operate in many other cities. Breweries and distilleries were

8–15. Size of manufacturing industry groups, 1904 and 1919

	Value added (millions)		Wage earners (thousands)	
	1904	1919	1904	1919
1. Iron and steel and their products	$1,009	$ 4,588	868	1,586
2. Textiles and their products	908	3,834	1,163	1,611
3. Lumber and its remanufacture	702	1,710	734	839
4. Paper and printing	550	1,706	351	510
5. Food and kindred products	539	2,327	354	684
6. Miscellaneous	491	3,313	408	1,227
7. Chemicals and allied products.	442	1,863	227	442
8. Liquors and beverages	361	381	68	55
9. Stone, clay and glass products.	268	677	285	299
10. Metals and metal products (other than steel)	263	850	199	339
11. Leather and leather products	244	896	264	349
12. Tobacco manufactures	205	529	159	157
13. Railroad repair shops.	167	807	248	516
14. Vehicles for land transport.	143	1,561	137	496
Totals	$6,294	$25,042	5,468	9,096

SOURCE: U.S. Department of Commerce (1909, 1921).

also widely distributed, but a few grain centers, such as Milwaukee and St. Louis, became notable for their concentrations.

Lumber and wood products continued trends developed before the war. Lumber mills began to mechanize and become larger with the use of band saws and gang saws and the mechanical handling of materials; however, giant firms did not come to dominate the industry. The lumber industry also shifted its regional concentration. Although lumber production reached a peak in the Great Lakes states by 1890, it continued to build up rapidly in the South. Furniture making began moving toward the Great Lakes region from New England and New York.

The antebellum trend toward geographic concentration of industries continued after the war. For example, early historical concentration of production had identified hatmaking with Danbury, gloves with Gloversville, knit goods with the Mohawk Valley, clocks with Bristol, buttons with Waterbury, guns with Hartford, sewing machines with Bridgeport, cameras with Rochester, and cigarettes with Durham. Historical accident or the enterprise of a local firm explained initial production in these towns, but sometimes the advantages of locating other firms near the same suppliers, a skilled labor supply, and market headquarters tended to attract a concentration of similar firms. Nevertheless, initial concentration did not protect areas from declining sales if new resource discoveries or innovations shifted the advantage to other producing areas or if consumer tastes and markets shifted elsewhere.

Electric power

The Industrial Revolution introduced the use of massive sources of power as substitutes for human and animal muscle power. In the United States, the ready availability of waterpower and large coalbeds proved vital to early industrial development. Later, the introduction of electrical generation and transmission provided a very flexible means of transmitting power over long distances and subdividing it into small units.

The waterpower sites that could be economically harnessed for industry were few and often poorly located for the transportation of materials. As we've noted, the steam engine was not a cheaper source of power, but it enlarged the power supply and provided greater mobility in factory location. The transmission of either steam power or waterpower within a factory involved the use of complicated, awkward, and expensive systems of shafts, gears, and pulleys. Electricity permitted great flexibility in the location of the factory and in the internal arrangement of machinery. It also made possible precise regulation of the speed and timing of operations either by fingertip or automatic controls.

The transmission of electricity for nonpower uses antedated the development of large-scale generating equipment. The telegraph, the telephone, and electric lighting were developed in a 30-year period around the time of the Civil War. Arc lights were used in Wanamaker's department store in Philadelphia and also at the Paris Exhibition in 1878. In 1880, Edison's incandescent light bulb provided a means of using very low current for lighting. The idea of ladder circuits indicated the feasibility of providing current to a large system which could be turned on and off for particular local uses. In 1882, Edison designed and built a central power generating plant and distribution system for providing electric lighting to New York City stores. In the late 1880s, many cities developed electric companies and adopted street lighting plans.

The possibility that electric power could displace local steam, cable, and horse railways was apparent by the 1880s. In 1887, an electric street railway was operating in Richmond, Virginia. In 1890, electricity was being used on 1,262 miles of the 7,082 miles of street railway track in operations. By 1902, 21,902 miles of electrically operated street railway existed, and only 676 miles of other systems remained. And by 1918, street railway track mileage reached its peak of 44,949 miles. In addition, electric railways were extended outside the city to provide frequent and fast transportation to suburban towns and to connect nearby cities. By 1914, it was possible to travel from Portland, Maine, to New York City and from there to Chicago by a combination of electric interurban trains and electric street railways.

The very efficient, high-capacity generating stations depended upon the development of a more efficient, constant-speed steam engine. In England the design of the water turbine was copied in developing a steam turbine in 1884, but it was not until 1896 that Westinghouse bought the rights and began large-scale turbine production. At about the same time, in 1895, the first large-scale use of water to produce electricity was begun with the installation of water turbines and electric generators at Niagara Falls.

The rapid expansion of electric utility companies and electric railways in the 1890s and 1900s required a large volume of capital investment. Just as the construction of railroads was tapering off, these new industries came along to provide another major spurt of capital formation. Between 1900 and 1910, the combined investment in street railways, electric light and power, and telephones about equaled that in railroads and all regulated industries (including railroads) absorbed about one fifth of the gross capital formation that took place during that time.

Factories had hardly begun to use electric motors to operate machinery in 1900, but by 1920 over half of all power applied in factories involved electric motors. Most of the electricity was generated initially by the factories' own steam engines; however, by 1920, over two thirds of total electrical generation was purchased from the central stations of electric utility companies. Shortly thereafter, utilities surpassed factories in primary power production of all kinds. (See 8–16.)

The development of large sources of electricity made possible new processes and new industries. The introduction of the Solvay process in

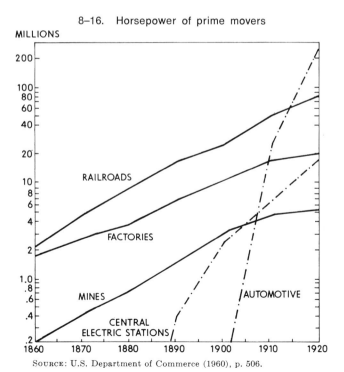

8–16.   Horsepower of prime movers

the 1890s and of the electrolytic process in the early 1900s was responsible for the development of a large-scale chemical industry in the United States prior to World War I. An electrolytic process was also used in refining both copper and aluminum. Some iron ore was smelted with electric furnaces, but this method was used mostly for refining high-grade steels.

The internal-combustion engine

The internal-combustion engine, using gasoline as fuel, was first used to operate a motor vehicle in Europe in 1885 and in the United States in 1893. The gasoline engine soon gained in favor over steam and electric power because of its efficiency and high power as compared with its size. A large number of gasoline engine improvements were devised very rapidly; four- and six-cylinder engines and the self-starter are outstanding examples.

One of the remarkable things about the automobile industry was its skyrocketing production volume. In 1899, the U.S. Census reported production of 3,700 motor vehicles, only some of which used gasoline engines. In 1908, the year the Model-T Ford was introduced, the industry produced 65,000 gasoline motor vehicles. The next year output doubled, and it doubled every two years thereafter to reach 1,746,000 in 1917. Output slackened during World War I, but another doubling had occurred by 1923, after which the growth of output leveled off. Nevertheless, by 1929 motor vehicles had become the first ranking manufacturing industry in value-added terms.

Auto production quickly became an industry of large mass-production firms. Ransom Olds produced 600 cars in 1901 and had increased this to 5,000 by 1904, thus demonstrating early that quantity production of a standard product was possible. Henry Ford led the way in further demonstrating the possibilities of mass-production methods by introducing the moving assembly line and developing mass markets on the basis of a low price. General Motors initially reflected a strategy of growth by merging a number of companies. About four fifths of the auto producers had gone out of business by the mid-1920s, but the remainder showed promise of outgrowing the railroads.

From the beginning, auto making was largely an assembly operation. So after a few shakedown years, the industry consisted of a few large producers and many small-parts makers, specialty suppliers, and toolmakers. Some major industries have grown up as specialty suppliers— rubber tires and flat glass are good examples. Other industries received significant stimulus from the expansion of automobile production. The chemical industry supplied paints, lacquers, and plastics. The primary metal producers supplied steel and aluminum. Petroleum refining expanded into a major industry to supply the users of motor vehicles.

A new life-style for consumers produced the auto industry's major effect on the economy. The rapid rise in the use of automobiles led to a demand for massive highway construction which got underway after World War I. For good or for ill, the freedom of movement afforded to the auto owner led to a decentralizing movement of city dwellers to the suburbs and to the small family residence, which stimulated a construction boom. So, while the electric railways and elevators helped build up the central city, the auto age spread out city users.

SUMMARY

1. Manufacturing had emerged as the economy's prime mover shortly before the Civil War. After the end of the war, the economy resumed its rapid growth, and manufacturing remained at the helm.

Although the percentage rate of population growth decreased somewhat, total and per capita income growth assumed rates slightly in excess of those that characterized the period from 1800 to 1860.

The post–Civil War period was one of marked instability. The recurrent business cycles of the period are usually attributed to investment booms associated with railroad building and the introduction of new techniques and products.

2. Contrary to conventional impressions, the Civil War was not a boon to industrialization and the northern economy, nor did it ultimately lift the South out of stagnation. Rather, the evidence suggests the opposite. Commodity output data indicate that the war reduced the national economy's extensive and intensive growth rates. There are no indications that suggest that emancipation contributed to southern industrialization and development. In fact, per capita income figures show that the South was not economically stagnant before the war, and there is good reason to believe that the war, the mode of emancipation, and Reconstruction were very costly for the South. Also, there is little support for the argument that Congress passed development legislation that favored the North at the expense of the South during the time in which southern congressmen were away from Washington.

3. During the period, input growth slowed down; however, productivity increases played a compensating role. Sources of productivity increases were (a) technological innovation on farms and in factories, (b) human capital formation, (c) innovations in commercial law, (d) economies of agglomeration associated with urbanization, and (e) creation of a national capital market.

4. Although the industrialization process exacted a heavy toll from workers who couldn't adjust to changing conditions, workers in general benefited from economic growth during the period. Real wages rose and, on a per unit of input basis, relative returns shifted away from capital and natural resources in favor of labor.

5. In the post–Civil War period, the eastern rail network was completed and standardized and the western railroads were pushed to the Pacific Coast. This made the continent smaller and the national market larger, thus producing gains in economic welfare through consequent cost and rate reductions.

However, the railroad building of the post–Civil War era was not indispensable to continued economic growth or industrialization. The data do indicate, though, that the efficiency effects of railroads were important sources of economic welfare, accounting for somewhere between 9 and 14 percent of GNP in 1890.

6. A host of improvements in basic metals, power production, and machinery made mechanized mass-production facilities possible in manufacturing. The result was the emergence of a large number of mass-production consumer goods industries which ultimately changed the lifestyle of the average American consumer. Breakthroughs in electrical power generation and internal-combustion engines were major innovations which had vast direct and indirect influences upon production methods and the variety of products manufactured.

APPENDIX: BUSINESS CYCLES AND TRENDS IN ECONOMIC ACTIVITY

In chapter 8 we referred to this appendix as providing a basis for understanding the deviations from our long-term growth trend known as business cycles. The subject is presented at this point because in the post–Civil War period fluctuations in economic activity became more severe and prompted various governmental actions which we shall discuss, especially currency and banking reform. In chapter 12, we will dwell on business cycles in the context of an actual historical event, the Great Depression.

In markets where individuals and firms are free to make choices, there is a great deal of variability in economic activity over short time periods. Daily quotations of stock market prices jump up and down erratically. Clearings of bank checks vary widely from week to week. Monthly new housing starts will vary seasonally, but no one year's season is exactly like another.

The longer the period of time considered, the more these variations will offset each other and average out to a smoother trend line. But different types of economic activity do not necessarily offset each other. A great number of economic measures move more or less together in expansion and contraction phases which extend beyond purely seasonal changes. The recurrence of these short swings in general economic activity led to their being called business cycles.

The behavior of GNP over a full business cycle and its variation around a long-run trend line is shown in 8–17. For observation we can

8–17.   GNP and the business cycle

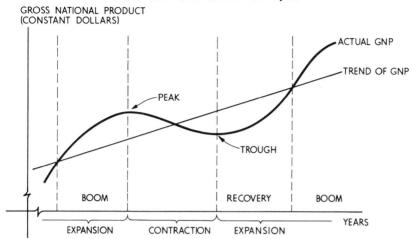

interrupt the cycle as GNP has climbed above its long-term trend and is expanding very rapidly under what are often called *boom* conditions.

At some point, the forces producing expansion play out and the cycle reaches its *peak;* thereafter, the economy enters a *contraction* phase, called a *recession* or a *depression.* When the trough of the contraction is reached, the economy is ready to turn around and enter an *expansion* phase. The early stages of expansion, known as *recovery,* blossom into a full-fledged *boom* as GNP crosses its trend line. The boom continues until the contraction phase of the next cycle gets underway.

In real terms, 19th century business cycles would not look as extreme as the raw data would show. In other words, prices and production both varied over the business cycle, so any movement of real GNP would fluctuate less than GNP in current prices. For example, a 15 percent increase in GNP might reflect a 10 percent rise in production and a 5 percent increase in prices; in the 19th century, fluctuations in GNP were primarily attributable to price movements. In the 20th century, prices have tended to fluctuate less than output over the course of any given cycle; in fact, prices have been quite sticky on the downside, although on the upside they have tended to increase. The difference between 19th and 20th century price behavior is attributed to the growth of industrial concentration which, in turn, is related to changes in the structure of costs and the greater ability of 20th century firms to vary production rates as demand changes.[24]

Studies of business cycles have not found them to be as regular in duration or severity as pictured above. In spite of much advance in economic knowledge and the statistical arts of forecasting, they are still

---

[24] Temin, pp. 63–70, discusses this question.

not very predictable. Only the severity of the swings seems to be subject to control and moderation by deliberate government monetary and fiscal policies. Studies of business cycles which occurred over more than a century, however, have shown that they average about four years in length from peak to peak, with about a year and a half of contraction and about two and a half years of expansion. Yet they have varied from as short as two and one-half years to as long as eight and one-fourth years. Because of their short and irregular length, they are usually measured on a monthly basis rather than annually.

Charts of business cycles are sometimes shown in measures of deviations from a long-term line—in fact, we present such a chart in chapter 12. In this form, the data appear to rise and fall around a constant level of GNP. Historical movements in American GNP, however, have been fluctuations around a rising long-term trend. Some of the mild downswings, therefore, have not involved absolute declines in the annual averages. The larger increases in some months offset the decreases in others, so that GNP for the year may merely fail to increase, or may increase almost as rapidly as in the preceding year. (See 8–18.)

8–18.   Yearly variations in rising trend of GNP, 1869–1918

SOURCE: Kuznets, tables R22 and R23, using moving averages in R25 and R26 to obtain implied annual estimates prior to 1889.

Business cycles are not measured solely in terms of real GNP. Many different types of economic activity also tend to rise and fall at the same time. Thus, even without an accurate measure of total output in the early years of our history, it has been possible to identify the peak and trough turning points of past business cycles by the consensus of turning points among a large number of different data series.

The term trend refers to a basic tendency to increase or decrease over a long period of time. The increase may be at a fairly steady rate, such as the growth in population in America prior to 1860; or the rate of change may be gradually speeding up or slowing down, as was the case after 1860. The trend may also reflect some average rate of change over a long period. When the average rates of change for successive long periods are sharply different, or even in opposite directions (as in the case of wholesale prices before and after 1896), they are not regarded as being a part of the same trend.

In the study of economic growth, attention is given to long-term trends and to changes in trends. For example, around 1900 there appeared to be some slowing down in the rate of GNP growth. The average rates of change for some decades also were noticeably faster or slower than those for others. Some economists have suggested that these variations in trends are part of a repetitive pattern and have labeled them long cycles.

The study of trends and changes in trends requires some sort of averaging. One method is to compare changes from peak to peak (or trough to trough) of the business cycle. This is similar to comparing monthly data with data for the same months in previous years in order to avoid the influence of purely seasonal changes. Another method is to average periods long enough to offset short fluctuations. Business cycles, however, are not as regular in duration as seasons. Because most business cycles last for less than five years, five-year moving averages provide one simple way of smoothing out the cyclical fluctuations in data in order to observe the trends and long-term swings. Five-year averages of real GNP between the Civil War and World War I, for example, show two surges in expansion. Referring back to the annual data, and using the cyclical turning points, these can be pinpointed between 1867 and 1882, and between 1897 and 1907.

The causes of business cycles and of long cycles are not fully understood. Some of the recurring aspects of business cycles are related to adjustments in business inventories. As production expands, inventories must also be expanded to handle the larger sales; so, for a time output must expand faster than sales. Once inventories are large enough, production will be cut back. This slowdown may cause some investors to be more pessimistic; their future is quite uncertain, and slight changes may be viewed as an early warning of trouble. A slowdown in investment spending, then, may cause a sharp decline in output and in prices. When inventories get low and producers realize that expansion will continue, output may increase more rapidly again.

Some of the longer swings in GNP and the more severe depressions are related to changes in population growth, changes in construction, and changes in investment in new plants and machinery. To some extent, such slowdowns are an inevitable consequence of prior periods of rapid expansion. A new invention may set off a wave of increased production to take advantage of the demand for the new product. At some point, the opportunity for rapid expansion along the same line diminishes, and this source of expansion slows down. For example, when streetcars were introduced, there was a period of rapid construction until most large cities had built the main lines they most needed; then the rate at which new streetcars and streetcar lines were built had to slow down.

Both business cycles and the long swings are believed to be affected by events that occur "outside" the economy, such as bad weather which reduces harvests and wars which destroy property and redirect production. The economic organization of society and government economic policies may also affect the nature of business cycles and long swings. Economists study fluctuations in economic activity in the hope that a better understanding will lead to policies that speed adjustments to unpredictable changes and moderate the magnitude of disturbances.

REFERENCES

C. A. Beard and M. R. Beard, *The Rise of American Civilization* (New York: Macmillan Co., 1930).

J. H. Boyd and G. M. Walton, "The Social Savings from Nineteenth-Century Rail Passenger Services," *EEH*, Spring 1972.

T. C. Cochran, "Did the Civil War Retard Industrialization?" *MVHR*, September 1961.

L. E. Davis, "Capital Immobilities and Finance Capitalism 1820–1920," *EEH*, Fall 1963.

————, et al., eds. "Savings Sources and Utilization," in *American Economic Growth* (New York: Harper & Row, Publishers, 1972).

J. F. Dewhurst, *America's Needs and Resources: A New Survey* (New York: The Twentieth Century Fund, 1955).

P. H. Douglas, *Real Wages in the United States, 1890–1926* (Boston: Houghton Mifflin Co., 1930).

S. L. Engerman, "The Economic Impact of the Civil War" in *The Reinterpretation of American History*, eds. R. W. Fogel and S. L. Engerman (New York: Harper & Row, Publishers, 1971).

R. W. Fogel, *Railroads and American Economic Growth* (Baltimore: Johns Hopkins University Press, 1964).

A. Fishlow, *American Railroads and Transformation of the Ante-Bellum Economy* (Harvard University Press, 1965).

————, "Internal Transportation," eds. L. E. Davis et al., cited above.

R. E. Gallman, "Commodity Output, 1839–1899" in *Trends in the American Economy in the Nineteenth Century*, ed. W. N. Parker (Princeton, N.J.: Princeton University Press, 1960).

————, "Gross National Product in the United States, 1834–1909," in *Output, Employment, and Productivity in the United States After 1800*, ed. D. S. Brady (Princeton, N.J.: Princeton University Press, 1966).

————, "The Pace and Pattern of American Economic Growth," eds. L. E. Davis et al., cited above.

E. W. Gilboy and E. M. Hoover, "Population and Immigration," in *American Economic History*, ed. S. E. Harris (New York: McGraw-Hill Book Co. 1961).

C. D. Goldin, "The Economics of Emancipation," *JEH*, March 1973.

R. W. Goldsmith, Testimony before U.S. Joint Economic Committee, *Employment Growth and Price Levels: Hearings*, Part 2, A 59 (Washington, D.C.: U.S. Government Printing Office, 1959).

L. M. Hacker, *The Triumph of American Capitalism* (New York: Columbia University Press, 1940).

R. Higgs, *Transformation of the American Economy, 1865–1914* (New York: John Wiley & Sons, Inc., 1971).

J. W. Kendrick, *Productivity Trends in the United States* (Princeton, N.J.: Princeton University Press, 1961).

S. Kuznets, *Capital in the American Economy* (Princeton, N.J.: Princeton University Press, 1961).

League of Nations, *Industrialization and Foreign Trade* (Geneva, 1945).

S. Lebergott, "The American Labor Force," eds. L. E. Davis et al., cited above.

———, *Manpower in Economic Growth* (New York: McGraw-Hill Book Co., 1964).

D. C. North, *Growth and Welfare in the American Past* (Englewood Cliffs, N.J.: Prentice-Hall, Inc., 1966).

A. Rees, *Real Wages in Manufacturing, 1890–1914* (Princeton, N.J.: Princeton University Press, 1961).

W. W. Rostow, *The Stages of Economic Growth* (New York: Cambridge University Press, 1960); see also 2d ed., 1971.

L. Soltow, "Evidence on Income Inequality in the United States, 1866–1965," *JEH*, June 1969.

P. Temin, "General Equilibrium Models in Economic History," *JEH*, March 1971.

U.S. Department of Commerce, *Historical Statistics of the United States* (Washington, D.C.: U.S. Government Printing Office, 1960).

———, *Statistical Abstract of the United States* (Washington, D.C.: U.S. Government Printing Office, 1909, 1921).

9 THE TRANSFORMATION OF THE ECONOMY

In its post–Civil War expansion, the economy did not merely become a magnified version of its mid-century self. The expansion was the result of economic development—a cumulative process of change in production methods and organization. It involved a complete *transformation* of the economy and the tripling of per capita income during this period was only one result of that transformation.

The elements of transformation will look familiar to you. For the most part, they date back to the dawn of the Industrial Revolution. What, then, is their significance? It arises from the fact that during the second half of the 19th century embryonic trends that had developed before the Civil War became dominant forces. Consequently, the economy of 1920 was a vastly different institution than that which existed at the time of the Civil War. In brief, here are the structural and organizational changes that transformed the economy:

1. The industrial distribution of additional workers and output shifted drastically in favor of manufacturing and other nonfarm activities and away from agriculture.
2. The geographic concentration of manufacturing stretched westward toward Chicago in a long belt, while the South and the West developed as raw material suppliers.
3. Urban places and urban life became the focal points of the Nation's economic growth and development.
4. Production in manufacturing and public utilities became concentrated in larger firms and larger individual production units managed by administrative specialists.
5. As a corollary to the emergence of a highly organized national financial capital market, financial leaders came to share key policy decisions with the operating managers of manufacturing and utility companies.

6. International trade declined in importance as the national economy grew.
7. Governments assumed new and expanded roles in determining the course of economic development.

In chapter 8 we discussed post–Civil War manufacturing in detail. In this chapter we will discuss the first six elements of transformation cited above. Then we will conclude Part III with an entire chapter on the evolution of government's economic role.

INDUSTRIAL STRUCTURE

As you recall, the Nation got its start as an agricultural economy producing a surplus for export and depending upon imports for most of its manufactured goods. During the middle of the 19th century, however, the rapid rise of manufacturing production, which we described in chapter 8, began to alter this pattern. Net manufacturing output first exceeded the value of agricultural commodities in the mid-1880s; and by 1920 the number of workers occupied in manufacturing almost equaled the number in agriculture. Also, the number of workers in other nonfarm activities expanded almost parallel with the rise in manufacturing. (See 9–1.)

9–1. Industrial distribution of gainful workers,
1870–1920

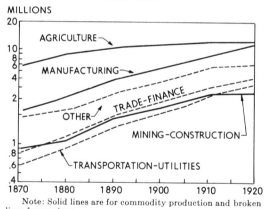

Note: Solid lines are for commodity production and broken lines for services.
SOURCE: U.S. Department of Commerce, p. 74.

Agricultural productivity increases

The rise in agricultural output was quite rapid prior to 1900. Farm output expanded faster than population. Food was produced in surplus and, following a trend established in the 1850s, continued to be an important export. Over the entire 1860–1920 period, gross farm output rose about 3¾ times while population rose only 3½ times.

By 1880 total crop and livestock production had reached twice the 1860 level. Then from 1880 to 1900 it increased by only 50 percent, and from 1900 to 1920 the increment was only 25 percent. The effects of the Civil War drastically curtailed cotton production until the early 1870s. Thereafter, both cotton and corn output had a rapid and steady increase until the 1890s, when the trend abated. Wheat production had been maintained during the Civil War despite the military drain on farm manpower. Then, when the railroad expansion came, a very rapid increase in wheat acreage and output followed. The increase in the last four years of the 1860s alone brought the decade's rate of growth to the level of the 1850s, and this rate of growth was matched in the 1870s. The growth in wheat production began to decelerate in the 1880s, a little earlier than other major cash crops

A large part of the increase in farm output came from the increased farm acreage that resulted from the settling of the West. Yet much of it was due to rising productivity resulting from both mechanization and improved methods. Grain production especially benefited from mechanization.

While 70 percent of the wheat in the North Central states already was cut by the reaper in 1860, continual improvements were made in the reaper and its use was extended in subsequent years. The Marsh brothers' harvester was widely adopted late in the 1870s. In 1878, the Appleby twine binder was invented. It enabled one man to cut and bind eight acres of wheat a day—a task previously requiring three men using a harvester or eight men using a hand cradle. The chilled iron plow was widely adopted in the 1870s, the disk harrow in the 1890s. In this last decade mechanization was also extended to corn production, with the wide adoption of the corn binder.

The overall trend of mechanization is shown by estimates of the rate of real investment in machinery and implements prior to 1900 as reflected in the manufacturing output of such equipment. Similarly, the expanded use of farm work animals shows the early substitution of animal power for human energy. (See 9–2.)

The gains in mechanization were mostly laborsaving, not increases in yield per acre. Wheat yields, for example, averaged only 13.9 bushels to the acre in 1900 compared to about 15 in 1840, while man-hours required to produce a bushel fell from 2.33 to 1.08. Similarly, corn yields averaged only 25.9 bushels per acre in 1900 compared with 25.0 in 1840, while man-hours per bushel had fallen from 2.76 to 1.47. The yield per acre figures would have been even less impressive if the increase in fertilization had not partially offset the effects of soil depletion and movement to areas in which optimum farming techniques called for increased acreage per unit of output.

Cotton, on the other hand, did not benefit from mechanization; yet, partly because of the continued movement to more fertile new lands in the Southwest and partly because of the increased use of fertilizer,

9-2.   Selected farm inputs, 1860–1920

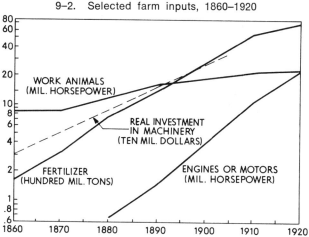

SOURCES: U.S. Department of Commerce, pp. 284–85, 506. Machinery real investment estimates by decades (in 1910–14 prices) from Towne and Rasmussen, p. 276.

the yield rose from 147 pounds of lint per acre in 1840 to 191 in 1900. With less than a one-fifth reduction in man-hours per acre, the man-hour requirements per bale fell over one third—from 4.39 to 2.80.

John W. Kendrick's estimates of output per unit of combined inputs show about the same increase in farming as in manufacturing from 1869 to 1899—about a 50 percent increase in productivity. In terms of labor inputs only, agriculture outpaced manufacturing in productivity gains in the 1870s, but the tables were turned in the 1890s, and manufacturing registered greater overall laborsaving from 1869 to 1899. In the two decades following 1900, farming showed no gain in productivity, while efficiency continued to grow in manufacturing and elsewhere in the economy.[1]

Wheat, oats, and corn, which accounted for the bulk of crop output, illustrate the importance of productivity increases as a portion of the total rise in production in this period.[2] Parker, using data for 1840 and 1910, has been able to distinguish productivity increases for the three crops as follows:

	Total increase (percent)	Increase attributable to productivity growth (percent)
Wheat	653	417
Oats	690	363
Corn	695	365

[1] See Kendrick, appendixes B and D.
[2] See Parker, tables 1 and 2.

His analysis for the period shows that output per man-hour rose primarily because of mechanization, with the shift to western soils and better methods tied for second place.

The gains in farm productivity brought about a problem that was not common in most other industries—a problem of surplus production owing to a slow rise in demand. As we pointed out in chapter 1, it is a characteristic of human consumption that the desire for additional food becomes less urgent as higher income levels are reached. Thus, the demand for food grows less rapidly than per capita income. Economists refer to this characteristic as low *income elasticity* of demand— percentage increases in food purchases are characteristically smaller than percentage increases in income. (We will explain this principle in greater detail in a later chapter.)

Studies of how city workers spend their incomes show that in a given year higher income workers spend a smaller percentage of their family budgets on food than do their lower income counterparts. Over time, as all worker incomes increased, even the lowest income families came to spend proportionately less for food. In the middle 1870s, low-income city workers spent about 64 percent of their incomes on food, while by 1919 they devoted only about 46 percent of their incomes to food. (See 9–3.)

9–3.   Percentage of city worker budget spent on food

	Low income	Average income	High income
1874–75	64%	58%	51%
1901	51	43	37
1917–19	46	41	37

SOURCE: U.S. Department of Commerce, p. 181.

Recall that the development role of agriculture is to reduce the use of labor in providing essential food and materials so that labor and other resources can be released for other types of productive activities. The resulting shift in the concentration of productive activity depends, first, on the rise in productivity in farming itself and, second, on the low income elasticity of demand for food and fibers as compared with other products.

In the United States, during the three decades after the Civil War, farm output grew faster than population and created a domestic food surplus. In 1865, per capita consumption of food already was high in the United States, and it did not increase much thereafter. Fortunately, until the early 1880s, when European tariffs rose, exports of wheat and livestock increased rapidly enough to absorb most of the surplus. But at the turn of the century it became increasingly difficult for demand to soak up a rapidly rising output. Productivity growth at rates faster than the growth of demand automatically meant less need for labor in agricultural production. Gradually, an increasing share of the national work force entered nonfarm activities—more second sons went to the city instead of to farm-making. Agriculture's proportion of all gainfully employed workers fell from 55 percent in 1860 to 37 percent in 1900 and to 27 percent in 1920. And by 1920, the total number of farm workers had begun to decrease.

Strains of farm adjustment

A random sample of contemporary accounts of farm life will yield an old but unanimous conclusion: the farmer, in spite of serving as the Nation's great provider, was allocated an ever-decreasing share of a rapidly growing national output. Discontent among farmers, especially midwestern farmers, was so great that the **Populists** emerged as a powerful political force, directed in part at ending the abuses to which the farmer was subjected. Yet, a close look at the statistics that describe the farm and nonfarm sectors of the economy suggest a farm sector that at the least held its own, and perhaps one that gained on the economy. Actually, these two extreme pictures can be reconciled by identifying the underlying forces that determined the course of farm adjustment to productivity growth in and out of agriculture.[3]

The process by which farmers left farming was not always a smooth transition in which recognition of superior opportunities drew a young man to the city. Frequently, a farmer sold out because he faced ruin, because declining prices, droughts, disease, or insects had reduced him to bankruptcy or brought him to the edge of starvation. Other times, farmers trying to establish themselves in new territory failed because they didn't have a sufficient stake, or because solutions to the unique problems of farm-making in their region hadn't been worked out yet. Others endured year in and year out, never accumulating the wealth they sought or making the transition from tenant to owner-operator, because they had never had enough good land or capital, or because they didn't have the talent the job demanded.

In short, in a period in which the basic tendency was for the growth of supply to outstrip demand, the number of farm operators and workers had to decline. Often, those who left farming were people who saw the opportunity for a better life in the city, a chance for higher income, closer neighbors, better schools, and a richer variety of social and intellectual offerings. But just as often those who left farming were driven off because in the presence of a downward trend in prices they couldn't

---

[3] See Higgs, chap. 4, for expanded treatment of post-Civil War farm adjustment and bibliographical citations; what follows leans heavily on his analysis.

keep afloat financially. And although many who remained in farming prospered, many others barely managed to stay alive.

What was the plight of the farmer, at least as he himself saw it? In his analysis of the post–Civil War economy, Robert Higgs has summarized the perceptions that generated agrarian radicalism. According to contemporary views:

> The American farmer received less than his "fair share" of the national product . . . . Railroads charged the farmer rates that were "too high"; "speculators" and "land monopolists" engrossed the best of public lands . . . ; pernicious land-tenure systems, especially in the South, shackled the farmers and resulted in rapacious "mining" of the soil . . . ; money lenders charged interest rates that were "too high"; a falling price level increased the real burden of [mortgage] debt . . . ; and farmers sold in competitive markets but purchased from "monopolists."[4]

Although railroad rates fell over the period, farm prices fell at about the same rate until 1897, when they reversed their downward trend. Consequently, for a large part of the so-called Gilded Age, farmers received no net advantage from rail rate decreases.

The usual identity of the land speculator is of great interest, given the conventional wisdom on the subject. It turns out that he was often a farmer who farmed the land while "holding for a rise," with every expectation of selling out at a fat capital gain. The financial manipulator who, living by his wits, bought and sold deeds is more a mythical folk antihero than a historical figure.

The extent of land tenancy has been overstated; even in the South, only 38 percent of farms were rented, and the U.S. average was only 28 percent. Many renters were young people who hoped to buy farms, whereas others chose tenancy over urban relocation. In the South, the terms of tenancy and the planter-storekeeper's policies that kept blacks in dire poverty were a reflection of a plantation system that depended upon subsistence wage rates for its survival. The rental contract was merely a way of stipulating the wage rate, so the blame should be laid on the introduction of slavery or plantation agriculture, not on tenancy per se. Various studies show that contract terms were set by competitive market forces rather than by landlords who wielded monopoly power and dictated lease and share agreements. Further, the terms of tenancy tended to reward building up the soil in areas where such investment would prove profitable for owner-operators or owner-landlords and vice versa; i.e., tenancy and mining the soil were not uniquely correlated or causally related.

The pressures of mortgage debt and interest payments appear to have been far smaller than casual observation would suggest. Mortgages

---

[4] Higgs, pp. 86–87.

were contracted for brief time periods, on the average 3.6 to 4.5 years in the West.[5] Accordingly, as interest rates fell in response to a fall in the general price level and an increase in competition among lenders, farmers were able to obtain money at lower rates within a few years. Further, cases in which farmers had to sell out at capital losses to pay off mortgages were negligible in number—rising land prices hedged against bankruptcy. Thus, declining farm prices in conjunction with mortgage indebtedness did not impose a lifetime of increasing real burden upon the farmer. Note, though, that cursory examination of the evidence shows that the Populists drew their greatest strength in the new farm areas where farms were mortgaged most heavily and where the highest percentage of farms were mortgaged. What's more, the Populists themselves were more heavily in debt than their less radical counterparts.[6]

Farm prices and their relation to nonfarm prices and farm incomes present a mixed picture. If you examine 9–4, you can see that the ratio

9–4.   Ratio of farm prices to all commodity wholesale prices, 1860–1920

RATIO: FARM/ALL GOODS
(INDEXES: 1910–14 =100)

Source: U.S. Department of Commerce, pp. 116–17.

of farm prices to prices in general fell until the early 1870s, then rose gently until the late 1890s when all prices rose, with farm prices leading the pack. Thus, from the standpoint of prices alone, the post-1875 farmer had no bona fide basis for complaint.

On the other hand, productivity changes caused income ratios to behave somewhat differently from the price ratio. Recall that from 1869 to 1896 farm labor productivity did not advance as rapidly as nonfarm productivity, i.e., what the farmer raised to sell didn't increase as fast as did nonfarm output, although farm prices declined less rapidly than did other prices. The net effect of these opposing forces was that gross farm receipts per farm worker did not advance as rapidly as the comparable nonfarm index for this subperiod.

In the years from 1896 to 1920, increases in farm output per worker

[5] These are Bureau of the Census data cited in North, p. 141.
[6] See Higgs, pp. 97–99.

almost halted, while nonfarm productivity continued to grow. Consequently, although farm prices increased faster than nonfarm prices, it is not clear that farm incomes grew as rapidly as nonfarm incomes in the early 20th century. For all farming, the data indicate that gross farm income per farm fell in money terms—but they suggest that at least in Populism's heartland, the Midwest, real gross farm income per farm actually rose.[7]

The farmer's impressions of how he was faring over this period were clear, however: he saw himself as denied his "fair share" until the turn of the century and thereafter thought he was gaining on the balance of the economy. In fact, the last 20 years of the period came to be called Agriculture's Golden Age because of their sharp contrast with the prior 40 years, a contrast that may have been more imagined than real. Populism waxed and waned accordingly.

If you look back on the array of items that generated agrarian discontent, the overall impression is that they didn't amount to much, that they were normal risks associated with playing the rural game, and that they had their urban counterparts. Why, then, did the midwestern farmer describe his plight in such dire terms? Why Populism?

One answer is that farmers didn't appraise their position in the same way that the economist or statistician does—disagreements between referees and players are common simply because the referees have no stakes to risk. A second answer is that some farmers had to leave agriculture, and certainly the forces that pushed them off the farm didn't originate overnight or go unnoticed by their similarly situated neighbors. A third answer arises from the sharp fluctuations in prices and yields that took place on a year-to-year basis. A year of drought at home and a bumper wheat crop abroad left many a Nebraska farmer with both a meager harvest and the lowest grain prices in history. A fourth explanation arises from the fact that Populism wasn't a purely economic phenomenon—the rural life-style was isolated and rough, in spite of a great deal of contrary mythology. Any objective comparison of western Kansas with the Garden of Eden would be highly unfavorable to Kansas.[8]

A fifth reason lies in the commercialization of farming. Unlike the days when most of his labor went to produce things he consumed directly himself, in this period the fate of the midwestern farmer depended increasingly upon prices, still another factor he couldn't control or predict. "The farmer protested about his 'deteriorating' economic position because he was locked into a system where, even if he was a 'good farmer' in pre-1860 terms, he might fail because he was a 'bad business man' in the late nineteenth-century terms."[9]

---

[7] Mayhew, p. 466.
[8] See Higgs, pp. 101–2.
[9] Mayhew, p. 475.

Mass production and specialized suppliers

As American manufacturing capacity was transformed from production by local craft shops to production by firms which marketed their products over whole regions or the entire Nation, new marketing institutions had to be developed.

The typical craft-shop entrepreneur produced almost every product within a given broad industry category. What's more, he depended upon outside suppliers to only a modest degree. He purchased raw materials, a portion of his capital equipment, labor, and financial services. If he wasn't involved in international trade, he probably didn't carry any kind of insurance. He generally retailed and delivered most of his output himself and depended upon peddlers to purchase the rest of the product if it was very valuable compared with its bulk and weight. He even financed his customers' purchases in many cases.

If he chose to expand, he depended in large measure on his own savings to finance purchases of capital goods and probably constructed a portion of his new facilities with his own and his employees' labor. Throughout, he was his own marketing, financial, and production adviser as well as his own management consultant. In brief, the craft-shop firm was a do-it-yourself establishment manufacturing a broad array of related products, each in small quantities, for a very limited market area.

As the craft shop began to mechanize its operations, as its potential volume grew and its market radius stretched out, managing such a wide range of product lines and performing many highly diverse functions got out of hand. Wise proprietors recognized their limitations. Accordingly, they reduced the array of products they supplied and sought ways to lay off functions on specialty producers. Unwise proprietors tried to play the new game with their old strategy and ended up as employees of their more farsighted colleagues.

The textile industry provides the earliest major example of specialization and division of functions among firms in a given industry, one which we cited in chapter 1. With the advent of the power loom, textile firms grew in number and size. Most mills stopped making their own machinery, while a few mills which were especially adept at machinery manufacture abandoned the spinning and weaving functions to become machine builders. Similarly, specialized cotton and wool middlemen emerged to provide various financial and marketing services at both the raw material and finished product stages of manufacture and distribution.

The evolution of the blacksmith shop, a second example cited earlier, illustrates how product lines narrowed as mechanization proceeded. The local blacksmith became the area's horseshoer and repairman. His other product lines—parts for farm machinery, household iron products, nails, and hand tools—came to be manufactured by specialized industries whose products were delivered nationally over the vast canal, river, and railway systems.

Manufacturing industries generally followed the textile example as their firms became mass-production operations over the post–Civil War years. Every year, highly specialized firms were organized to provide goods or services that the commodity manufacturer preferred to purchase rather than to produce himself. At the same time, higher per capita income stimulated the growth of consumer service industries and new manufacturing industries producing newly invented products. The consumer's greater mobility gave him more shopping discretion and generated intense competition in terms of quality, convenience, consistency, variety, and service as well as in price. Paradoxically, the Industrial Revolution, a revolution in production methods, transformed the emphasis of business from production to selling, and the economy became consumer oriented.

The emergence of a truly national market also made change the order of the day. The organization of manufacturing and distribution functions changed with the advent of a national transport system. It continued to change with new technology and as population density, purchasing power, and urbanization increased throughout the market. In some industries, functions that had been shed by manufacturers a generation before the Civil War were assumed again as the individual firms and their markets grew. Consequently, over the entire 19th century, the structure of manufacturing and its related marketing and physical distribution activities displayed trends that initially produced specialization, then integration. In the extreme examples, local multiproduct manufacturers who performed almost every function required from raw material acquisition to retail sale became national, single-stage, single-product manufacturers, then evolved as multiproduct, multistage producers serving national markets.

The specialization of farm areas in producing for national and international markets led to the emergence of specialized *middlemen* connected with financing, insuring, storing, transporting, and exchanging commodities in central auction markets. The increased processing, packaging, refrigeration, and precooking of foods placed a new group of manufacturers between the farmer and the consumer.

Two levels of middlemen distributed manufactured goods in 1860. In the northeastern manufacturing centers and port cities, large commission merchants advanced credit to manufacturers and undertook to handle the distribution of factory output to wholesalers in major cities throughout the Nation. *Wholesalers,* in turn, distributed to retail stores in a local region. In doing this, they performed for retailers the traditional roles of the import trader—the advantageous purchase of a variety of goods from far-flung sources, the handling of bulk shipments, the storage and prompt delivery of goods locally, and the advance of credit to the retailer. The prominence of the wholesalers probably reached its peak in 1880. By that time, however, changes in technology had already begun to eliminate the need for these middlemen, and both the manufacturer and the retailer began to seek to deal directly with each other.

Immediately after the Civil War, manufacturers began to handle more of their own distribution. Competition among large producers intensified. Credit became less critical as successful manufacturers reinvested profits in their own businesses and as specialized financing institutions developed. With their capacity to produce increasing faster than sales, manufacturers became impatient with the passive order-taking practices of wholesalers and hired their own regional agents and traveling salesmen to promote sales through direct contact with retailers. In the case of large durable goods or where single-line specialty stores existed (such as those for sewing machines and shoes), some manufacturers found it advantageous to develop their own direct sales agents and retail stores.

Methods of selling as well as distributing manufactured products were changing drastically. Products were no longer simple, familiar objects whose quality could be judged by inspection or touch. Farm machinery, the sewing machine, and other durable goods involved technical features and new uses that had to be explained. The quality and durability of new products might become evident only after long use. An increasing variety of foods and other products could be preweighed, counted, and handled more conveniently in packages that prevented tasting, handling, or visual inspection. Increased processing, refrigeration, and precooking of foods required close quality control and sanitary packaging. As in the case of drugs, these products required consumer trust in the reputation of the manufacturer. Nationwide distribution of some products also presented the consumer with a bewildering variety of choices. Therefore, a reputation for quality, special guarantees, and recognizable brand names all became important factors in the selection of goods by consumers.

Under these conditions, *advertising* began to assume a new character, and advertising expenditures soared rapidly in the 1890s. The function of early advertising was primarily to let the purchaser know the producer's address. But as national markets evolved, advertising aimed increasingly at making consumers desire the product in the first place.

While consumer satisfaction and repeat sales were essential, the initial buildup of a large volume of national sales depended heavily upon getting consumer recognition and initial selection of the product. The manufacturer, therefore, began to compete for a greater share of the national market by advertising his brand name and product advantages (both real and illusory) in newspapers and magazines and on billboards. It was no longer enough to simply announce the manufacturer's location, products, and terms. It became necessary to educate the consumer about the product and its uses and to convince him that the product's quality and satisfactions would be superior to those of other products. (A brief perusal of your local library's turn-of-the-century magazines will convey a vivid impression of the amount of hokum and pseudoscience involved in the consumer's education.)

In cases in which different manufacturers actually had virtually identical products, advertising, of course, served mostly to stabilize consumer purchasing habits and to concentrate sales on a few widely known brands. The initial advertiser gained an increased share of the market, but there was little advantage to each manufacturer when all manufacturers advertised. Yet for some products, especially new products, such as for cigarettes prior to World War I, competitive advertising increased the size of the entire market.

During the same period, *retailing* also changed markedly. For a long while after the Civil War, the country general store continued to dominate in the rural West and South. It handled all types of goods and served as a social center. It often accepted local food products for resale or as payment for debts. In the South, the post–Civil War lien laws formalized the storekeeper's claim on crops as security for credit, and the general store became the chief consumer credit institution for the poor southern sharecropper. The retailer, in turn, relied heavily upon wholesalers for credit.

The chief retail innovation in the rural areas was the introduction of the *mail-order* business. While some specialty mail-order firms existed in 1860, the first large general mail-order firm was established by Aaron Montgomery Ward in 1872. Low prices were made possible by large bulk purchases made directly from manufacturers, by skipping the middleman and the retail store, and by use of the low-cost delivery services of the federal postal system. Catalogs provided a much wider range of choices than was available in the country store.

In cities, the general store had given way by 1860 to numerous *specialty stores*—groceries, dry goods, shoes, hardware, and so forth. The introduction of the soda fountain in the apothecary's shop was one example of a continuing adaptation of retail stores to consumer needs and habits. One major retail change that developed from the trend toward specialization was the *chain store.* In the late 1870s, the Great Atlantic & Pacific Tea Company had been converted from a small chain of tea shops to a major chain of "economy" grocery stores. Again, low costs were achieved by buying in large quantities directly from food processors and skipping the middleman. In addition, a cash-and-carry policy cut out the costs of consumer credit. Similar principles were applied at about the same time by F. W. Woolworth's five-and-ten variety stores.

The large city *department store* represented a different trend in retailing—a trend away from specialization. Its emphasis was upon offering a full range of shopping opportunities at one location convenient to concentrated transportation facilities in the downtown center. Each department could compete with specialty stores in the variety of choices offered. The department store could make large-quantity purchases directly from manufacturers, eliminating the costs of middlemen. It could also extend a single line of credit to cover a whole range of purchases. Catering especially to women, the department store attempted to gain favor through offering deliveries, refunds upon the return of unsatisfactory goods, and other special customer services.

The interdependent evolution of mass production and mass distribution produced conflicting trends in the components of retail prices. On the one hand, in, nearly every type of store the *distribution margin* tended to rise—that is, as the manufacturing cost of goods tended to fall, the costs of wholesale and retail distribution as a percentage of final retail prices tended to rise. At the same time, new types of large retailing organizations tended to have lower margins. The distribution margin, therefore, rose moderately. Employment followed suit; commodity distribution's share of total employees rose from 6 to 10 percent of the labor force between 1870 and 1920. Throughout this period and later, however, a diversity of marketing methods persisted. The independent store did not tend to disappear, nor did the low-margin, cut-rate store attract all the customers away from the full-line, multiservices store. (See 9–5.)

9–5. Distribution spread by type of store

	Percent of retail price		
	1869	*1899*	*1919*
Grocery, independent	27.3%	28.3%	29.7%
chain	–	19.0	20.7
Shoes, independent	27.3	33.5	37.6
chain	–	33.5	32.0
Dry goods	31.5	36.7	44.9
department	–	29.4	35.6
Furniture, independent	37.3	39.0	46.4
chain	–	44.0	44.0
Drugs	39.8	46.7	51.1
Jewelry	46.9	46.5	51.7
All groups	32.7	35.4	36.5

SOURCE: Barger, selected from table 26, p. 92.

Foreign trade

As the national market grew and it became economic to produce a growing number of items for ourselves and for export, our dependence on overseas suppliers and overseas markets declined. Imports as a portion of GNP fell from 7.9 percent in 1869–73 to 4.4 percent in 1907–11, and the relative decrease in exports was almost as great.

In spite of the relative decline of trade, absolute trade volume expanded rapidly. The value of exports tripled from 1860 to 1880 and tripled again by 1915. By 1920, export revenues had more than doubled again, although much of this rise was due to general price inflation. As in other areas, the most rapid expansion took place in the decade and a half after the Civil War. Another surge of growth occurred around 1900.

In addition to the declining relative importance of trade, the most significant aspects of this portion of our trade history are the shifts that took place in the balance of trade, the types of goods exchanged, and the countries dealt with.

Shift to an export surplus

Throughout its early growth, the American economy had been heavily dependent upon its imports. In nearly every year, imports of goods exceeded merchandise exports. The difference had been made up by performing shipping services for other nations and attracting foreign capital investments. After the mid-1870s, however, the balance of trade shifted the other way. In nearly every year, exports were larger in value than imports. The United States became one of the major exporting nations of the world as it became the leading industrial nation. (See 9–6.)

The massive shift toward manufacturing in the American economy was reflected in the types of goods most important to its foreign trade. Between 1860 and 1880, exports of crude materials, dominated by cotton,

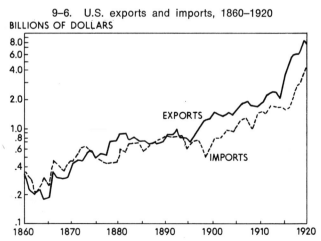

9–6.   U.S. exports and imports, 1860–1920

SOURCE: U.S. Department of Commerce, pp. 537–38, 562–63 (excluding specie).

had given way to foodstuffs, mostly wheat and flour. Manufactured exports, which had long contributed about 15 percent of the value of total exports, began to increase rapidly in the late 1890s and by 1920 totaled half of all exports. Imports shifted just as drastically. Manufacturers fell from nearly three fifths of imports in 1860 to about a third in 1920. Crude materials rose from about a tenth to roughly a third, as rubber, copper, tin, and various other materials were imported to meet the needs of expanding industry. (See 9–7.)

9–7. Percentage composition of trade, 1860–1920

	Exports				Imports			
	1860	*1880*	*1900*	*1920*	*1860*	*1880*	*1900*	*192*
stribution by type of goods (%):								
Materials	69	29	25	23	11	21	33	34
Food	16	56	40	25	30	33	27	34
Manufactures	15	15	35	52	59	46	40	32
stribution by foreign areas (%):								
England	50	54	38	22	39	32	19	10
Europe	24	32	37	32	22	24	33	13
Americas	21	11	16	31	29	32	26	46
Other	5	3	9	15	10	13	22	31

SOURCE: U.S. Department of Commerce, pp. 544–45, 550–53.

A shift in the roles of trading partners followed naturally from changes in import and export composition. England, which still furnished two fifths of our imports and took half of our exports in 1860, supplied only a tenth of our imports and took only a fifth of our exports in 1920. The rest of Europe followed at a somewhat slower pace. The big share of our import increases came from the Americas and Asia, which supplied raw materials and foods (mainly sugar and coffee).

Higher tariffs

A big shift also occurred in national tariff policy. The Republicans came to power in 1861, committed to raising duties to protect American manufacturers even though manufacturing had flourished for the two previous decades, a period in which tariffs averaged well below 20 percent of dutiable imports. The absence of southern congressmen made it possible to raise duties twice during the 1860s. By 1867, average rates were 47 percent of imports. A 10 percent reduction in rates in 1870 was reversed again in 1875; but because the number of goods on the duty list had been reduced, duties as a percentage of all imports remained considerably lower than in 1867. The Democrats continually campaigned against the tariff and during the second Cleveland administration managed to lower rates temporarily in the mid-1890s. The increasing importance of materials imports which were subject to very low or no duties caused most of the decline in duties compared with all imports after 1900. (See 9-8.)

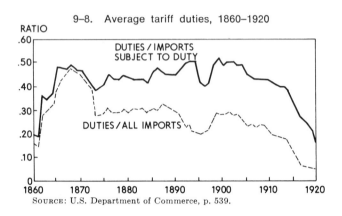

9-8. Average tariff duties, 1860–1920

SOURCE: U.S. Department of Commerce, p. 539.

Balance of payments

The composition of the balance of payments also changed to accommodate the shifts in trade emphasis. Net shipments of gold and silver fluctuated only moderately and played little role in the balance of payments. But the negative balance of invisible items, which dated back to the 1840s, became progressively larger. In part, this reflected rising interest and dividend payments on the growing stock of foreign capital which had been invested in this country. In the post–Civil War period, Europeans had continued to buy American securities. The remainder of the invisibles deficit was accounted for by shipping charges on freight, which was increasingly carried by foreign ships, the remittances by immigrants to their relatives, and increasing travel abroad by Americans. (See 9-9 and 9-10.)

Reversals in the flow of capital movements were the major source of offsets to the wide swings in the balance of trade. In the early post–Civil War years, when imports exceeded exports, and between 1882 and 1895, when merchandise trade was nearly balanced, foreign capital continued to flow into this country. Foreign savers helped to finance construction of the western railroads and, later, the electric utility industry.

When manufacturing exports boomed and the trade balance soared after 1895, it was the large outward flow of American capital that helped

9–9.   Balances of trade and specie, 1860–1914

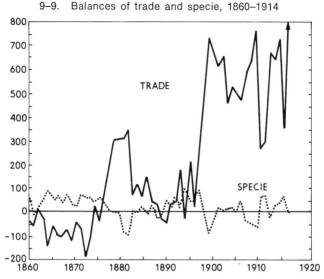

SOURCE: U.S. Department of Commerce, pp. 537–38, 563–64.

9–10.   Balances of invisible items and capital, 1860–1914

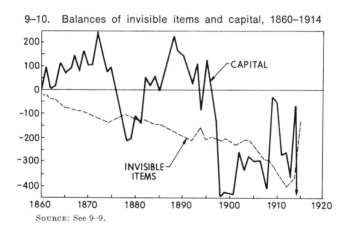

SOURCE: See 9–9.

to finance the excess of exports. In this the United States was acting much as England had earlier: rising trade with South America and Asia involved extension of credit with the sale of manufactured goods and overseas investment in mines, plantations, and transportation facilities. Even before World War I, the United States was on the way to leaving its status as a debtor nation and becoming a creditor nation. The war speeded this process. (Since the whole scale of payments balances was magnified several times by the war and inflation, discussion and graphic representation of this experience is postponed to Part IV.)

CHANGES IN INDUSTRIAL LOCATION

Continued population growth plus the transformation from an agricultural to an industrial economy had, of course, geographic ramifications. Cities grew much faster than rural areas; the population center continued moving west; and new regional patterns of specialization emerged.

Regional specialization

Think back to our discussion of export-base theory in chapter 1 and to the economic relationship of the North, the South, and the West in the antebellum economy. Perhaps you'll recall that often economic growth results from a process by which a region (or a nation, or a city) develops an export specialty. Development of an export base enables a region to take optimum advantage of its resource endowment and to achieve scale economies in the industries in which it specializes. The larger the export base, the greater will be the volume of imports the region can purchase from other specialized regional economies. In turn, the fate of the export base is reflected in the industries that serve the region in question rather than producing exports; these are the *residentiary* industries, such as construction, retail stores, consumer services, and manufacturing for local markets.

Although a regional division of labor was established in the antebellum years, the development of manufacturing and the completion of the rail system produced a transformation in that pattern. In the presence of industrialization, differences in *resource advantages* and *transport access to markets* determined the comparative evolution of the Nation's regional economies. The vast fertile areas of the Mississippi–Ohio River watershed plus the access to river transportation established the mid-continent's agricultural specialization well before the railroad. Similarly, once a national market was established, New England and the Middle Atlantic states were ideally situated to specialize in manufacturing for export to other regions. They had ports, connections to inland markets, waterpower, iron ore, coal, and timber.

In the pre–Civil War years, the manufacturing advantages of the Northeast were fortified by manufacturing growth itself. First, as the technology of various industries evolved, the production rate of the most efficient factory increased—internal economies of scale were developed. Given good transportation links with other markets, employment in thousands of northeastern manufacturing plants grew as a natural consequence of technological development and positive shifts in market demand.

Second, the external economies achieved from the clustering of similar firms in subregions or cities within the Northeast automatically favored expansion at northeastern sites over expansion in areas without industrial activity. As manufacturing firms discarded functions and specialty firms emerged to fill them, the economies of agglomeration became an even stronger concentrating force.

Third, the Northeast's high population concentration put regional manufacturers at most of their customers' doorsteps, which meant huge transportation advantages for products that were bulky or heavy compared with their value. The Northeast's initial advantages for specialization in manufacturing meant that for any particular industry advantages peculiar to some other region had to be very strong to offset the pull of northeastern sites—note that in the first half of the 1800s, food processing and farm implement production marched west with agriculture, whereas other machinery manufacturing remained in the East. In other words, the Nation's industrial heartland was well established by 1865.

The heartland and hinterlands

Following the Civil War, the most important change in the Nation's economic geography was the westward extension of the industrial heartland to become a manufacturing belt. Strong pulls overcoming Atlantic Coast locations were developed, so the geographical concentration of manufacturing activity moved west as far as St. Louis, and Chicago became an industrial city. (See 9–11.)

9–11. Regional specialization of production, 1900

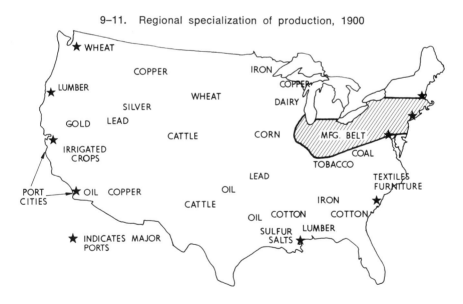

The technology of the steel industry played a large role in the westward shift of industry. Cheap water transportation brought the Great Lakes iron supplies into close contact with the coalfields of western

Pennsylvania. Initially because transportation costs in steel production were minimized by locating at the coal mine, the early steel industry concentrated in the Pittsburgh area near Connellsville, the coke-making center. Later, as improvements in steel furnaces economized on fuel consumption, newer steel mills were located on the shores of the Great Lakes at Cleveland, Gary, and Chicago.

Other conditions influencing the creation of the industrial belt were related to the Midwest's agricultural specialties. Wheat farming on the Great Lakes prairies led to the early construction of an east-west railroad network and the concentration of the meat-packing, flour-milling, and farm machinery industries in this region. Consequently, urban growth and industrial diversity gave the area advantages for subsequent manufacturing investment. Because of these advantages plus access to a national rail network permitting distribution to the rest of the Nation, most new factories were built in the eastern portion of the Midwest. For example, a significant portion of the early auto industry, a heavy steel user, concentrated in Detroit, and its location in turn influenced the location of the rubber and glass industries.

The industrial heartland that resulted from these post–Civil War trends included the East North Central, Middle Atlantic, and New England states, with the exception of most of Maine, New Hampshire, and Vermont. By 1870, 72 percent of total manufacturing employment was located in the manufacturing belt. Even though the spread westward of the national economy stimulated residentiary manufacturing growth elsewhere, the area's share of total manufacturing employees had dropped by only six percentage points by 1920.

The rest of the country continued to specialize primarily in agriculture and the extractive industries—mining, forestry, and fishing. East of the Rocky Mountains a semicircle of raw material hinterlands bordered the industrial heartland, while isolated valleys and cities in the Far West were like distant colonies.

West of the Mississippi, highly specialized farming and a few mining and lumber centers developed. Wheat production moved westward across the plains, crowding cattle ranges into the more arid and mountainous lands. Corn production was found to be more advantageous in the prairies nearer the Great Lakes, as was dairy farming. Accordingly, hog production and cattle feeding concentrated in the corn belt, and the meat-packing centers followed suit. Irrigated farming flourished in the river valleys of California and the Southwest, and cotton grew in importance. Mining and lumber production were concentrated at scattered points, and several major port cities arose on the Pacific Coast.

The South also continued to concentrate in agricultural activity, with cotton and tobacco still the major crops. Loss of slaves hampered production until sharecropping tenancy was established to redeploy the workers who had been transformed from capital to labor by emancipation. Since this system was heavily financed by seasonal short-term credits extended by merchants, such great emphasis was placed upon cash crops that corn and cattle production were neglected, and the region was no longer self-sufficient in food.

Beginning in the 1880s, the South began to expand its manufacturing activities, based partly on its raw material resources and partly on its large surplus of low-income workers. Textile factories drawn by low labor costs began to be built in the southern Piedmont area (the eastern slopes of the Appalachian Mountains between Virginia and Georgia). Between 1880 and 1900, cotton spindles increased eight times in the South, and by 1912 southern textiles were using more than half of the cotton consumed by the industry. A little later, furniture industries began to flourish in Southern Appalachia, partly due to the rapid expansion of lumber production. By 1890 the older forests in the Great Lakes region were nearing exhaustion, and production shifted primarily to the South and the Pacific Northwest. A great boom in southern lumber production occurred between 1890 and 1910.

Mineral extraction also began to grow rapidly in certain areas. Coal production expanded with the extension of railroads into West Virginia and Kentucky. Southern iron production accounted for about one fourth of national output in 1890 in spite of the unsuitability of the southern ores for Bessemer furnaces. With the increased use of the open hearth, Alabama's steel industry expanded significantly after 1900. In the early 20th century, the Texas and Louisiana area had chemical and petroleum booms. Large underground sulfur beds overlying salt domes were discovered; these were important in making a great variety of products including various chemicals, insecticides, explosives, rubber, and paper. Rich oil and gas fields discovered in eastern Texas in 1901 soon propelled the Lone Star State past California as the leading petroleum producer.

Regional growth and development

In the westward march of the American people, each region has gone through successive stages of being a frontier outpost, a specialized raw-material producer, and a more diversified and urbanized economy. The process of early rapid expansion and later slowdown as some degree of maturity was reached is reflected in the census data on population trends by region. The New England, Middle Atlantic, and South Atlantic regions displayed population trends between 1860 and 1920 that resembled the national trends of later decades. If these trends are taken as an indicator of maturity, both the East North Central and the East South Central regions had reached maturity between 1860 and 1880. The West North Central region reached its maturity in 1890 and then began to recede somewhat from the national rate of population increase.

The West South Central region achieved maturity about 1920. Only the Mountain and Pacific regions were still expanding rapidly at the end of this period. (See 9–12.)

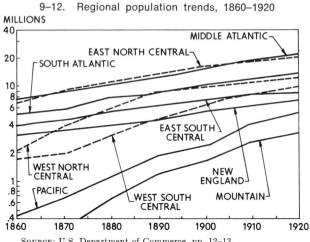

9–12. Regional population trends, 1860–1920

SOURCE: U.S. Department of Commerce, pp. 12–13.

The rate of population expansion alone, however, is at best a rough guide to economic growth and development. The pioneer subsistence farming areas were those of lowest per capita income in 1840, yet showed the highest population growth rates. Once good transportation access has been opened up to a region, however, resource advantages may create profitable opportunities that attract capital and labor resources, boomtowns with their astronomical wages and bonanza profits sprout up, and, consequently, income growth will spurt far ahead of population growth and the region can be thought of as truly developing. Thus, relatively high incomes are experienced in rapidly expanding areas. But later the expansion rate slows down as basic resource opportunities approach full exploitation. As it grew, each region tended to mature in the sense that it developed the residentiary industries appropriate to the level of incomes generated by its export base.

Post–Civil War regional trends in per capita income reflected both high-income opportunities in the Far West and the relatively low incomes in purely farm areas. The highest per capita incomes were in the Pacific and Mountain regions, the second highest in the urban-industrial areas. The predominantly farming regions of the Plains and the South had the lowest incomes. (See 9–13.)

The spread between the highest and lowest incomes was much wider in 1880—from 204 to 45 percent of the national average—than it had been in 1860—from 143 to 65 percent. This reflected both the new income opportunities of the Far West and the sad state of the southern

9–13. Personal income per capita by region, 1860–1920

Regions	Percent of U.S. average			
	1860	1880	1900	1920
Northeast				
New England	143	141	134	124
Middle Atlantic	137	141	139	134
North Central				
East North Central	69	102	106	108
West North Central	66	90	97	87
South				
South Atlantic	65	45	45	59
East South Central	68	51	49	52
West South Central	115	60	61	72
West				
Mountain	–	168	139	100
Pacific	–	204	163	135

SOURCE: Easterlin, p. 528.

economy after the Civil War. The spread in income levels began to lessen thereafter—a trend that has continued in recent decades. This partly reflected the recently gained maturity of the newer regions.

The widening and then narrowing of the spread of regional incomes also reflected the simultaneous influence of forces of *change* and *adjustment*. Areas with relatively high incomes and rapid expansion trends may be viewed as benefiting from changes in technology and demand. A discovery of resources, an invention, an improvement in transportation, or a positive shift in market demand created favorable economic opportunities. It then took a period of time for these opportunities to be fully exploited. Other areas, conversely, suffered exhaustion of resources, new competition from other areas, or some reduction in consumer demand for their products. In American history, many local areas experienced setbacks in major industries—eastern wheat farming, New England shipbuilding, lumber in New England and the Great Lakes, New England textiles and shoes, southeastern cotton, and western wheat are all examples.

In cases of both rapid expansion and relative decline, massive adjustments in resource supply were often necessary. Labor and capital resources were needed in newly expanding areas, and high-income opportunities provided an incentive for them to move to where they were most demanded and in shortest supply. At the same time, where an oversupply of resources developed in a given region, mobility of resources among regions helped equalize conditions.

Thus, in the post–Civil War period, the South found itself short of capital and with a surplus of labor. Gradually, northern capital investment flowed into the South to help develop its industry and resources. Concurrently, population out-migration from the South—both westward and northward—helped reduce the surplus of labor. On the other hand, farm areas throughout the Nation were forced to make most of their adjustments through labor migration because the growth of demand for agricultural products was slowing down and the opportunities for investment in rural areas were limited.

Urbanization

Urbanization is the demographic counterpart of the growth of manufacturing output, and the expansion of trade, service, finance, and government activities, and the emergence of a national market made up of specialized regional economies. From the beginning of the Nation, the rate of expansion in total population has been exceeded by the rate of expansion in urban population. However, it was not until the end of World War I that urban population finally came to exceed rural population. (See 9–14.)

9–14.   Growth of cities, 1860–1920

	1860	1870	1880	1890	1900	1910	1920
Population (millions):							
Rural.	25.2	28.7	36.0	40.8	45.8	50.0	51.6
Urban	6.2	9.9	14.1	22.1	30.2	42.0	54.2
Number of cities*							
Under 10,000							
population	299	495	716	994	1,297	1,665	1,970
10,000–100,000	84	154	203	326	402	547	684
Over 100,000	9	14	20	28	38	50	68

* Places with population of 2,500 or more.
SOURCE: U.S. Department of Commerce, p. 14.

The building of a late 19th century city was an enormous undertaking in social overhead capital formation. Financial capital, materials, and labor, especially construction workers, were required in huge amounts. Building material requirements, especially for steel and lumber, stimulated demand throughout the Midwest, the principal supplier region. Paving material demands were heavy in any region in which cities were burgeoning. Electrical utilities had to be built to supply industry and residents.

Modern technology made the manufacturing metropolis a reality. Structural steel and elevators made skyscrapers possible. Skyscrapers plus street cars made concentrated central cities feasible. The streetcar, and later the automobile, also made factory areas employing thousands of workers practical. Water and sewer systems plus great advances in public health practices made high urban densities safe, albeit after recurrent typhoid epidemics.

Two kinds of urbanization characterized the period—the establishment and growth of vast numbers of *commercial centers* and the emergence of *industrial* cities.[10] As long as families are not completely self-sufficient, a central place will arise at which people congregate to make exchanges, i.e., commercial centers are formed. In agricultural economies, the smallest and most numerous commercial centers are what we think of as farm towns. These serve as exchange places for agricultural specialties and markets for imported manufactured goods.

There is a hierarchy among commercial centers that arises from the fact that some transactions are made only infrequently, so that areas much larger than the hinterland of a farm town must be served. Economies of agglomeration cause commercial places that serve more than the immediate hinterland to be larger than farm towns—in short, specialized suppliers congregate. Such transactions are illustrated by borrowing from a bank, contacting a broker, buying a buggy, contracting for legal services, going to an opera, paying taxes, lobbying for certain kinds of legislation, visiting medical specialists, and going to a big league baseball game. Those who travel to enter into such transactions are from rural areas and smaller commercial centers. Consequently, in the 19th century, as today and earlier, commercial centers ranged in population size from a handful of people to towns, to cities, to metropolises. The underlying organizing principle of commercial center hierarchies is simple: the larger the commercial center, the greater the range of goods and services represented.

As the national market for farm products was knit together, quite independent of manufacturing and population growth, central places grew in size as surrounding farmers specialized and the number of transactions they made increased correspondingly. Rural population increases intensified the growth of central places and added to their number, as you can see by glancing at 9–14.

Industrialization added a second dimension to urbanization—a second kind of urban place came into being, the industrial or manufacturing city. Recall our earlier discussion of the growth of manufacturing at centralized locations. The external economies of scale from urban agglomeration and close proximity to suppliers and similar producers proved invaluable to the manufacturer in pre-auto America even after the telegraph and telephone were invented.

Consequently, with the growth of a truly national economy plus industrialization, urbanization became widespread throughout the country. Each region developed its own hierarchy of commercial centers. Chicago,

---

[10] See Higgs, pp. 58–67.

Detroit, Cleveland, St. Louis, Pittsburgh, and Cincinnati became manu-facturing cities. New York became the Nation's commercial and financial capital and a manufacturing center. Columbus, Atlanta, New Orleans, Los Angeles, and Denver, to name a few at random, grew as commercial centers.

Some towns disappeared as their hinterlands declined; many more emerged as their hinterlands flourished. The number of medium-sized cities of 10,000 to 100,000 population increased somewhat faster than cities in other size classes between 1860 and 1920—they expanded 8-fold compared with about 7½-fold for larger cities and 6½-fold for smaller ones. The fastest growth in both number of cities and urban population occurred during the 1880s, when the number of cities with over 1 million in population rose from one to three. But the basic changes in utilities, buildings, and transportation which gave cities their modern appearance and urban life characteristics didn't come until the turn of the century.

CHANGES IN INDUSTRIAL ORGANIZATION

Two major organizational changes affecting production contributed to the transformation of the American economy after the Civil War: the number of firms serving national markets began to decline as the size of individual firms grew, and drastic changes took place in the ways in which new methods of finance and management were devised.

Big plants, giant businesses

Even before 1860, the railroads and a few manufacturing firms found themselves coping with the problems of directing large numbers of workers. The Pepperell textile mills averaged about 800 workers during the 1850s, and the New York and Erie Railroad employed more than 4,000 by the mid-1850s. These, however, were exceptions. Most business firms required much smaller work forces at a single location. (Note that we are talking about numbers employed at plants—individual oper-ating units—not numbers employed by firms which might operate several plants.)

However, by 1920, plants the size of the Pepperell mills had become quite common. There were 10,000 manufacturing establishments with annual sales of more than $1 million and averaging 500 workers, *and they accounted for more than two thirds of manufacturing output.*

Employment statistics hide more than they show for this period. In 9–15, data for years prior to 1900 include "hand and neighborhood indus-tries," which were the very small craft shops in the industries whose production processes had not been mechanized. Consequently, employ-ment per manufacturing establishment shows no trend for the period

9-15.   Average size of manufacturing plants

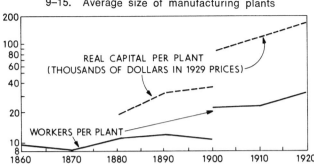

Note: Data are for wage earners and fixed plus working capital. Prior to 1900 worker averages are held low by inclusion of numerous small "hand and neighborhood industries."
SOURCE: U.S. Department of Commerce, pp. 409–10.

1860–1900—what is masked by the figures is a progressive increase in the portions of manufacturing sales and value-added accounted for by the 20 percent of all manufacturing firms that had the largest work forces. Starting with 1900, the hand and neighborhood industry figures can be purged from the data. The resulting figures give a rough view of the number of employees per manufacturing plant for industries in which the typical plant produced for a national or regional market, although not all local market producers are eliminated.

Between 1900 and 1920, workers per plant increased by about 50 percent. This increase is really quite significant when you consider that it took place over a span in which all commercial centers were increasing in size—what it says is that production in large plants for national and regional markets grew much faster than production in small plants for local markets even at a time when urbanization was stimulating local market demands.

In view of the growth of laborsaving capital investment, the increase in the size of the average plant is more accurately shown by real capital figures. Real capital invested per plant doubled from 1880 to 1900 and doubled again by 1920. Given that output grew faster than either capital or labor inputs, these figures indicate that sales per firm rose by more than 50 percent per decade from 1880 to 1920.

In railroads, the increase in size came earlier and was clearly related to technical operating needs. The large trunk-line systems in the Northeast were formed by linking up smaller lines and adding feeder routes. By the late 1880s, the Pennsylvania Railroad employed close to 50,000 employees. These workers were spread over hundreds of miles and were engaged in a wide variety of activities—construction, maintenance, repair, freight handling, warehousing, train operations, and selling.

In manufacturing, the biggest part of the expansion in size of firms was not so much in the size of the plant (i.e., the single production unit) as in the number of plants directed by one firm. As we will discuss in a few paragraphs, when individual firms expanded their plants to put new technologies to work, they were forced to invade each other's markets to gain sufficient volume. This *overcapacity* problem was solved through *horizontal combinations* in which competing firms merged and, thus, created multiplant operations.

The big change in plants per firm came around 1900, when the first big merger movement took place. John Moody reported that in 1904 the 318 most important manufacturing firms had 5,288 plants, or an average of 17 each. U.S. Steel alone controlled 785 plants. Consolidations of firms were equally common among public utilities and railroads.

Industrial concentration

Pre–World War I trends in industrial concentration were conflicting. On the one hand, as markets in various industries evolved from highly localized geographic coverage to national scope, the number of sellers in each market increased. For example, the farmer who depended solely on the local blacksmith in 1840 found that he had a host of farm machinery manufacturers to choose from in 1870. In short, the markets of local monopolies gave way to competitive national firms with the advent of mass production and mass marketing.

On the other hand, once national markets were established, we hypothesize that the dynamics of technological change and mass marketing tended to reduce the number of firms in each industry and thereby to produce a high degree of *industrial concentration.* At the same time, the forces generating concentration tended to be eroded in their effects by the growth in the national market. On balance, however, the data suggest that concentration in national markets increased over the post–Civil War period. Let's examine the role of technological change in producing industrial concentration.

Once changes in production techniques had made high-volume, mechanized output possible in a given industry, technological change became an ongoing process. Typically, the costs of production per unit of output were reduced while the size of the most efficient plant and firm increased. In other words, technical considerations associated with cost reduction dictated increases in the number of plants operated by the typical firm and in the size of each plant.

While technological innovations are being introduced, quantity demanded can be expected to increase on two counts: economic growth stimulates demand, and price reductions attributable to lower unit costs induce people to increase their purchases. Graphically, this phenomenon looks as shown in 9–16. Cost reduction will push the price down from P_1 to P_2, and economic growth will shift demand from D_1 to D_2; there-

9–16. Increases in quantity demanded

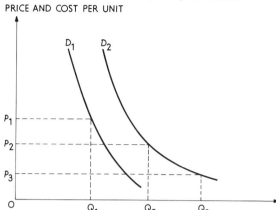

PRICE AND COST PER UNIT

fore, quantity exchanged would increase from Q_1 to Q_2. Overall, economic welfare would increase because consumers could purchase the
product at a lower price attributable to technological innovation.

Apparently, in a good many late 19th century cases, the increase
in total capacity to produce was so great that instead of price falling
to a level such as P_2, at which all firms would remain profitable, the
increase in production might be of such magnitude that only a ruinous
price, such as P_3, would clear the market. This would constitute an
overcapacity situation. In such an event, two reactions would typically
ensue. First, some firms would go into bankruptcy because their losses
would be too heavy to sustain. Second, many of the remaining firms
would enter into an agreement of some kind designed to give them
concerted, direct control over how much was produced for the market
as a whole or the price each would charge. Their goal would be to
preserve the profitability of each of the remaining firms by achieving
a price-output combination at least as favorable as $P_2 - Q_2$.

Such tactics were not always successful. Where the number of firms
was small, it seems that honor among monopolizers was as fragile as
honor among thieves, and price wars often resulted. Where the number
of firms was large, it was usually impossible to obtain agreement among
enough firms to administer market-wide price or output policies. However, when erstwhile competing firms were consolidated under one
policy-making group (trust agreements) or grouped together under one
ownership (horizontal mergers), a high degree of industrial concentration resulted and monopoly pricing practices were successful.

Data to be cited later suggest that although scale economies might
generate a move toward consolidation, concentration proceeded farther

than necessary to preserve the life of the individual firms involved. Once the number of firms became small enough to permit communication among managers, the possibilities of restricting the number of firms in the industry so as to generate monopoly prices and profits surely became apparent. And the imperfections of the capital market, which denied equal access to financing for all those firms that were potentially viable, became a decisive force in intensifying concentration.[11] *Note, however,* that although no precise measures have been made, broad trends suggest that in many cases *even with monopoly pricing technological change reduced relative prices* to below their 1870 levels, i.e., to a price such as would lie between P_1 and P_2 in 9–16.

One source of ambiguity in measuring the economic-welfare effects of increased industrial concentration is the emergence of mass-marketing techniques. In many instances, innovations in selling and distribution dictated that a firm became much larger than the optimum size of a given plant would require, i.e., that the typical firm become a giant, multi-plant operation. In some of these cases, the adoption of mass-marketing techniques was followed by lower prices *and* increased industrial concentration.

Where the uncertainty about the net effect on consumer welfare arises is in connection with promotional advertising and product innovation. Unfortunately, it is difficult to look at the turn of the century data so as to distinguish between cases in which high concentration emerged from bona fide marketing economies and cases in which advertising and product differentiation made rival firms' products appear inferior when, in fact, all the products in question were basically uniform in their capacity to yield consumer satisfaction. In the latter situation, observed price cuts may have been attributable to economies of scale in marketing which could have been realized by all firms with far less concentration among sellers.

In the period 1898–1902, a wave of mergers swept American industry.[12] The precise timing of this wave has not been satisfactorily explained; however, we do know that it came soon after the Supreme Court defined the Sherman Anti-Trust Act so as to make trust agreements illegal but to allow mergers. Further, Nelson discovered that the "newly achieved development of a broadened, strong capital market, and the existence of institutions which enabled the organization of mergers to utilize this market [plus] the generally favorable condition of business, and a rising,

---

[11] See Davis (1963) for an analysis of capital immobility as a source of economic rent to those with the right contacts.

[12] See Nelson, chap. 3, for discussion of mergers from 1895 to 1920 and their causes, and Andreano, pp. 15–19, for an evaluation of Nelson's study. Also, see Scherer, chaps. 3 and 4, for a discussion of concentration and citations of the literature.

buoyant, securities market made profitable larger and larger units of business enterprise."[13]

No one has directly tested the hypothesis that the dynamics of technological change created overcapacity because even flourishing demand did not grow as fast as capacity expanded. However, Nelson's findings are not inconsistent with this hypothesis.

Once the number of firms in a given industry had become small enough so that a change in price or output policy by one would affect the others noticeably, *administered pricing* became the dominant pattern. Agreements to maintain price or consistently following the price policy of a leading firm served to avoid the price wars that all recognized as mutually devastating. Rivalry among firms continued, of course, but weapons other than price were used—advertising, sales promotion, and product variations. Rivalry among industries became an important factor during this period in cases where different products served the same purposes; an example is competition among the steel, lumber, and concrete industries for the overlapping portions of the building materials market.

After 1902, the merger movement slowed down, in part owing to antitrust action. In addition, growth of the market made it possible for the number of firms in most industries to increase in spite of the output effects of technological change. And improved organization of the capital market meant that financial resources were available to far more of the firms which could show promise of a profit, not just the few with good connections.

Data for the 1950s suggest that concentration extended beyond the degree required for maximum efficiency in the production and distribution of products. Joe Bain's study of 20 manufacturing industries in the early 1950s revealed that in only 5 of the industries studied would economies of scale require a degree of concentration great enough to yield monopoly control through collusive action. In the other 15 industries, the dictates of technology indicated that it would be possible for all plants to attain the most efficient size and still not exceed a concentration such that the four largest firms accounted for 30 percent of total sales. Yet in 13 out of 20 cases the share of the four largest firms actually exceeded 60 percent of sales.[14]

Knowing that concentration has changed very little in manufacturing since 1902, can we assume that Bain's findings would be the same if he had had data for the turn of the century? Markets were smaller in those days, to be sure. But, certainly, the optimum-size firms and

---

[13] Nelson, p. 6; Andreano cites the possibility that the merger wave precipitated the growth of the capital market.

[14] Bain's voluminous work is reported and analyzed on this count in Weiss, pp. 511–14.

plants were smaller too. So it does seem reasonable to conclude that the level of concentration in manufacturing that existed in 1902 was greater than scale economies required.

Whether this degree of concentration resulted in excessive profits is, of course, another question, a question whose answer varies with the industry under examination. Even in highly concentrated industries, if entry by new producers is easy to gain, prices will tend to be very near competitive levels, and vice versa. Unfortunately, no systematic study of the period using price and profit figures has been made.

Concentration was negligible in 1870 when viewed from a national standpoint. Of course, where local production for local markets still prevailed, concentration must have been quite high in and around small- and medium-sized cities. But, led by manufacturing and, to a lesser degree, railroads, overall concentration increased rapidly. Even though Bain's analysis shows that by 1905 manufacturing concentration had reached a plateau, overall concentration was still increasing at the turn of the century. In 1905, the largest 200 nonfinancial business firms controlled about 18 percent of all business assets, whereas by 1929 their ratio of control had risen to about one third. By 1920 Big Business, as concentrated industry had come to be called, was composed chiefly of manufacturing firms. Next in line came the railroads and, to a smaller but increasing degree, public utilities, with mass-retail chains beginning to produce a trend toward concentration in the distributive trades.

The reasons for the trend toward overall concentration in national markets are easy to see. Over this period, agriculture, a highly atomized industry, declined in its share of the economy. In 1870, public utilities other than railroads were almost nonexistent and certainly localized. At the time of the Civil War, manufacturing had not undergone its shift toward bigger and fewer firms and accounted for a much smaller share of total GNP than was later to be the case. Wholesaling and retailing were still localized in 1870. And railroads were smaller and greater in number before their expansion in the West than at the turn of the century. In short, growth was centered in industries that were destined to become concentrated, so the overall industrial structure tended toward increasing concentration.[15]

Ownership, control, and financing

Manufacturing was slower to adopt the corporate form of business organization than the railroads. For one thing, the canals and railroads had been chartered by individual legislative acts as franchised monopolies vested with a public interest. For another, they required huge sums of capital from the start, and many small investors were solicited for

---

[15] See Bain, pp. 191–98.

funds amid considerable publicity. Manufacturing firms were usually built from small beginnings, with an inventor or resourceful businessman seizing a profitable opportunity and then plowing back his profits to expand. Bank loans and merchant credit were the most important outside sources of funds at first.

In the rapid mid-century industrial expansion, many individual manufacturers were swept upward to great wealth. As individual proprietors, partners, or owners of family businesses, they had managed to finance most of their own expansion. In the depression of the 1870s, however, the need to expand and mechanize in the face of stiff competition and falling prices caused many such manufacturers to incorporate and to take in other wealthy persons as shareholders. In most cases, the early manufacturing corporations remained closely held, and their stocks were not offered for public sale. In the late 1880s, only one manufacturing company's stock was listed on the New York Stock Exchange. But in the merger movement of the late 1890s, many major manufacturing corporations began to list their stocks for public sale. Soon such manufacturing corporations had many thousands of stockowners, very few of whom owned a large share of the companies.

At this point, the separation of ownership and control became important in manufacturing, as it already had in railroads. Even in the closely held corporation, not all investors could follow all affairs of the business, so they delegated the running of the business to the largest owner or the officers of the corporation. Thousands of small stockholders had even less chance of an effective voice in management. The board of directors, accordingly, became largely self-perpetuating and dominated by the officers, who might hold only a small share of the total stock.

Investment bankers also began to play a key role as directors of railroads and manufacturing firms. Investment bankers first became corporate directors when many railroads went bankrupt in the depressions of the 1870s and 1890s. While the stock market manipulations of individual officers and wealthy investors created scandals, the investment bankers tended to be a stabilizing influence protecting the interests of investors. Both wealthy investors and financial institutions relied on their advice about the soundness of the management of firms. So, when bankruptcy occurred, before more funds could be loaned or invested, an investment banker was called in to see that the firm was properly reorganized. To make sure the reorganized firm would continue to be well managed, often the investment banker was placed on the board of directors.

Investment bankers also tended to hold stock and directorships in large commercial banks and insurance companies which had large blocks of funds to invest. Thus they acted as go-betweens for large institutional investors and big industrial firms. The resulting widespread financial interrelations tended to be pragmatic alliances that depended for their continuance upon trust, successful service, and the mutual advantage of all parties, factors that restricted the economic power of the so-called financial magnates. In addition, investment banking was characterized by relative ease of entry, which further restricted the power of financiers.[16]

Professional management

With the disappearance around 1900 of the so-called industrial capitalists, and with the rise of so-called financial capitalists who were interested primarily in finance rather than operations, it fell to a new group, the professional managers, to run the businesses. The hired managers generally were men with middle-class family backgrounds and better-than-average educations who had risen to officer rank in the course of long experience in a business or who had been specialized advisers to firms.

By trial and error, and beginning primarily in the railroads, modern practices of management evolved. Better methods of accounting and improved flows of routine information were the first needs of the far-flung railroad operations. Accounting consultants and a separate controller's staff usually were introduced as early steps. Then, departmental responsibilities were delegated for different phases of the operation—construction, operations, maintenance, selling, and so on. As the railroads were consolidated into large systems, and as the manufacturing firms were combined through mergers, authority had to be delegated to regional divisions and subsidiary officers. The central office management group and its staff then tended to confine itself to a policy-setting and supervisory role.

One consequence of the large scale of corporations and the new bases of competition was the development of specialized research laboratories. Taking their cue from universities, technical schools, and government agricultural research centers, the major companies began to realize the importance of systematic search for improved methods, materials, and products. For the large manufacturing firms, expensive laboratories cost only a small fraction of current sales. Further, with increasingly diversified operations, some of the firms, in chemicals and drugs especially, could make use of unexpected findings in a wide variety of fields.

In 1920–21, a National Research Council survey identified 525 operating industrial research laboratories. American industry was starting to formally adopt the scientific method in place of the pragmatic tinkering that characterized early technological innovation. In no small part, credit for this must go to the European and American scientific communities,

---

[16] See Josephson versus Davis (1963) for contrasting views of the "financial capitalists."

which had developed physics and chemistry to a level that permitted their systematic application to industrial problems.

Another development in methods was referred to as scientific management. Around the turn of the century, Frederick W. Taylor and others were making systematic studies of the detailed operations of the factory—the effectiveness of cutting tools, the movements made by workers in doing their jobs, factory organization, and cost records. Their investigations became the basis for generalized principles of production management and the increased utilization of worker incentive systems, especially piece rates.

One notable improvement in mass production methods was the perfection of the *moving,* or *continuous, assembly line,* which consisted of a moving belt passing in front of specialized workers who completed their operations in turn until the finished product emerged at the end of the line. This was primarily an innovation in management methods. When Henry Ford came on the scene, all of the technical elements required were at hand—standardized products, interchangeable parts, precision tools, scientific work-study methods, continuous belts, and highly specialized definitions of each worker's job. In fact, Oliver Evans's flour mill and mid-19th century slaughterhouses served as models. Ford's contribution was the application of these elements to the production of a fabricated product. The assembly line itself was a marvel of layout design, and backing it up was a wonder of organization and planning which achieved on schedule the purchase, fabrication, and movement of thousands of components, then provided for their mass sale and distribution.

Employee relations

The transformation of production organization also changed the nature of work for the individual laborer. In the first place, very few persons still worked for themselves. America became a nation of employees in the last half of the 19th century. Farmers, self-employed shopkeepers, and independent craftsmen all declined as a percent of the labor force. If you compare the growth rate of the labor force with the growth of nonfarm employees in 9–17, you'll note that nonfarm employees increased in number more rapidly than the labor force as a whole, showing that the proportion of the self-employed—farm and nonfarm—declined from 1900 to 1920.

Organizational changes also transformed the nature of the relations between worker and employer. No longer was work performed individually or in small informal groups. Meaningful communications, let alone personal contacts, were lost between top management and the lowest worker as the numbers of employees and the layers of supervision were multiplied in the giant business organization. The possibilities for mis-

9–17. Rise of employee status and union membership,
1860–1920

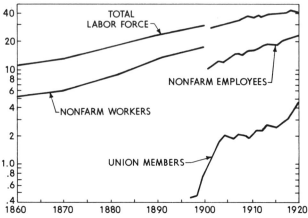

SOURCES: U.S. Department of Commerce, p. 97; Lebergott, pp. 510–13.

understandings and human grievances were also multiplied. Furthermore, the morale and cooperativeness of workers were lowered by the
depersonalized conditions of modern technology. The worker became
alienated. The factory subjected the worker to the discipline of the
clock and the machine; the process was too vast for the worker to see
the consequences of his efforts; and the repetitiveness of his tasks produced boredom and frustration. Of all these elements the monotony
of the job was perhaps the most debilitating—yet repetitiveness and
narrow definition of jobs are crucial to high productivity on the moving
assembly line.

If these frustrations were not enough, the worker also had economic
incentives to organize to serve his own interests. The American worker
was just as pragmatic as businessmen, farmers, and other producers
in seeking group organization to solve his economic problems. Generally,
it was the most skilled and highest paid workers, the scarcest workers,
who succeeded in organizing first. In times of rising demand for scarce
workers, they had the best opportunity to bargain for higher wage rates.
In times of depression and in the face of floods of unskilled immigrant
workers, they tried to protect their jobs and privileged positions by
restricting the entry and training of new workers and blocking the hiring
of nonmembers.

No attempt is made here to recount the history of unionism, but
it is important to note at this point that the transformation of the American economy included a sudden rise of worker organization around
1900, at the same time that business mergers were occurring. While
the railroad brotherhoods and building craft unions led the way in union
organization, during World War I industrial unions began to gain consid-

erable strength. Still, in 1920, only about 12 percent of the labor force and about 22 percent of nonfarm employees were union members. We will look at the history of unionism in depth in Part IV.

SUMMARY

We will not summarize the transformation of the economy at this point. Rather, we will do so after a discussion of the changing size and scope of the public sector in chapter 10.

REFERENCES

R. Andreano, ed., *New Views on American Economic Development* (Cambridge, Mass.: Schenkman Publishing Co., Inc., 1965).

J. S. Bain, *Industrial Organization* (New York: John Wiley & Sons, Inc., 1959).

H. Barger, *Distribution's Place in the American Economy Since 1869* (Princeton, N.J.: Princeton University Press, 1955).

L. E. Davis, "Capital Immobilities and Finance Capitalism," *EEH*, Fall 1963.

———, "Savings Sources and Utilization" in *American Economic Growth*, eds. L. E. Davis et al. (New York: Harper & Row, Publishers, 1972).

R. A. Easterlin, "Regional Income Trends, 1840–1950," in *American Economic History*, ed. S. E. Harris (New York: McGraw-Hill Book Co., 1961).

R. Higgs. *Transformation of the American Economy, 1865–1914* (New York: John Wiley & Sons, Inc., 1971).

M. Josephson, *Robber Barons: The Great American Capitalists, 1861–1901* (New York: Harcourt, Brace & World, Inc., 1934).

J. W. Kendrick, *Productivity Trends in the United States* (Princeton, N.J.: Princeton University Press, 1961).

S. Lebergott, *Manpower in Economic Growth* (New York: McGraw-Hill Book Co., 1964).

A. Mayhew, "A Reappraisal of the Causes of Farm Protest in the United States, 1870–1900," *JEH*, June 1972.

R. L. Nelson, *Merger Movements in American Industry, 1895–1956* (Princeton, N.J.: Princeton University Press, 1959).

D. C. North, *Growth and Welfare in the American Past* (Englewood Cliffs, N.J.: Prentice-Hall, Inc., 1966).

W. N. Parker, "Productivity Growth in American Grain Farming," in *The Reinterpretation of American Economic History*, eds. R. W. Fogel and S. L. Engerman (New York: Harper & Row, Publishers, 1971).

F. M. Scherer, *Industrial Market Structure and Economic Performance* (Chicago: Rand McNally & Co. 1971).

M. W. Towne and W. D. Rasmussen, *Trends in the American Economy in the Nineteenth Century* (Princeton, N.J.: Princeton University Press, 1960).

U.S. Department of Commerce, *Historical Statistics of the United States* (Washington, D.C.: U.S. Government Printing Office, 1960).

L. W. Weiss, *Economics and American Industry* (New York: John Wiley & Sons, Inc., 1961).

10 THE CHANGING ROLE OF GOVERNMENT

The public sector was pulled into the same current of change that transformed the private sector after the Civil War. Government policies and organization that had sufficed for a small agricultural nation were not adequate for a large nation with a modern industrial complex.

Think back on our description of the transformation of the private sector. Change constituted an evolution rather than a dramatic break with the past. Similarly, government assumed its new character in a piecemeal and hesitant fashion, often too long after proponents of new policies saw the need for change. Nor did changes in government policy and organization come about smoothly and painlessly. Adjustments were made by a trial and error learning process. Learning took place slowly, and errors were often repeated. Public understanding lagged far behind the changes in economic conditions and in spite of our wealth, experience, and individual economic sophistication many of the problems of the total economy in a modern, urban industrial setting were not adequately understood or adjusted to.[1]

Three major trends enlarged the role of government during the six decades from 1860 to 1920.

First, federal powers were used more frequently to influence economic affairs. Although the nation had been formed in an atmosphere of popular suspicion of government, as the economy became more marketized and complex, the public agitated for action by the federal government, especially to guarantee the proper functioning of the national economy.

Second, the emphasis of governmental economic policy shifted from development to regulation. Beyond providing a legal framework in which to conduct business, the chief economic role assigned to government after the Revolution was to assist in the creation of social overhead capital, chiefly transportation facilities. However, the main focus of

---

[1] For a historical treatment of the public and private institutional changes that economic growth and development generate see Davis and North.

governmental economic policy became restraint and regulation as the development process produced groups that saw themselves as victims of change.

Third, administrative machinery expanded at all levels of government. At the federal level, the growth of the nation plus increased military and international commitments required larger civil and military bureaucracies. At the state and local levels, a rapidly rising demand for public services arose in response to the complexities of an urban industrial society.

Throughout this period of swift change, a tumult of controversy and protest swirled around government policy questions. Contemporary attitudes and opinions have tended to confuse later historical interpretation of the general economic conditions of the period—the "plight of the farmer" is an excellent case in point. Considerable enlightenment can result, however, from reversing this process and using our improved information on economic conditions to better understand the political controversies. The task of this chapter is to describe the changes in the public sector brought about by the transformation of the private economy and to indicate why public policy issues stirred up such great controversy.

CHANGING SOCIAL PHILOSOPHY

The furor over economic policy took place in a controversial intellectual setting. On one side, the laissez-faire teachings of Adam Smith and later British and American economists received considerable support and amplification from a school of thought labeled by intellectual historians as *Social Darwinism.* This philosophy was first articulated in detail by Herbert Spencer, the British philosopher who coined the term survival of the fittest.

Essentially, Social Darwinism, which came into vogue shortly after the Civil War, involved a wholesale transfer of Darwin's theory of natural selection to the realm of social philosophy, including economics. Human perfection in both a biological and social sense was held to be inevitable through the operation of natural evolutionary processes. The good life would emerge naturally via technological improvements, and the actions of individuals in trying to maximize their self-interest would promote social welfare. As applied to economics, Social Darwinism constituted an overboard version of Adam Smith's *Wealth of Nations.*

For the Social Darwinists the state had only a minimal role to play in the affairs of man. Governmental attempts to steer society in the direction of improvement were misguided. If they were effective in any way, it would only be for ill, resulting in maladjustment of nature's carefully engineered machine for progress. For example, legislation designed to increase the income of the poor would only trip off a Malthusian mechanism by which higher birth and survival rates would flood the labor market, depress wages, and defeat the intent of the law. Society existed for the benefit of its component individuals and had no identity or consciousness apart from that of its individual members. Consequently, the state per se could have no goals, another basis for restricting government activity.

It is only fair to Spencer to add that the popular conception of Social Darwinism represented a gross oversimplification of his philosophy. He was not nearly as optimistic in his predictions for mankind as were his interpreters. Andrew Carnegie, certainly one of the fittest among the survivors, summarized this oversimplified, popularized view of Spencer and used it to rationalize income inequality and business concentration. Carnegie asserted in his *Gospel of Wealth* that

> the price which society pays for the law of competition . . . is . . . great; but the advantages of this law are . . . greater still . . . . But, whether the law be benign or not, we must say of it: . . . It is here; we cannot evade it; no substitutes for it have been found; and while the law may be sometimes hard for the individual, it is best for the race, because *it insures the survival of the fittest* in every department. We accept and welcome, therefore, as conditions to which we must accommodate ourselves, *great inequality* of environment, the concentration of business, industrial and commercial, in the hands of a few, and the law of competition between these, as being not only beneficial, but *essential for the future progress of the race*. [Italics supplied.]

In opposition to the Social Darwinists were those who advocated extensive reform. While accepting the evolutionary nature of society in principle, the reformers did not equate evolution and progress. Rather, they felt that individual actions left unfettered couldn't produce widespread participation in the benefits of economic progress.

This vein of intellectual development can be thought of as starting with the philosopher-economist John Stuart Mill. Near the end of his long career, Mill broke intellectually with his fellow classical-liberal economists, whose tradition stemmed from the contributions of Adam Smith. Mill did so by declaring that the laws of production may be natural but that the laws of income distribution were *man-made*, decisions for society to make through conscious deliberation.

From Mill's time on, the social reform movement was atomized, a vast and disparate collection of advocates of state control often sharing only one principle, a lack of faith in laissez-faire economics. At one extreme were the Marxists with their advocacy of the violent overthrow of bourgeois society. At the other were those who felt that the state could modify man-made social institutions in a way that would force the economy to operate as the Social Darwinists insisted it would operate automatically if left alone.

Paradoxically, the formation of the various social reform movements emanated from the scientific approach to society that fostered Social Darwinism. The growth of those diverse minorities was encouraged by the economic changes that had made the material aspects of life more rewarding, but more complex and subject to sharp variations and risk. The actual changes in government policy that came about were less dramatic than one would suppose. In the Gilded Age, various dissident minorities agitated loud and long about both real and imagined grievances suffered at the hands of an impersonal market mechanism or powerful interest groups. Out of this political tug-of-war came the Greenback movement, Populism, Progressivism, the muckrakers, and perhaps a half-dozen minor isms concerned with a narrow range of reforms. Eventually, minority opinion became majority opinion, and social welfare and regulatory laws were enacted.

Now that we have reviewed the intellectual background of government's changing role over the five decades after the Civil War, let us consider the political climate of the times. This can perhaps best be done by noting the political alignment of major economic interest groups. At the start of the Civil War, the Republican party (GOP) had come into power, and it dominated the federal government for most of the next five decades. Since industrial and financial leaders were strongly allied with the GOP, there was a shift away from the agricultural viewpoint which had dominated during the first half of the century. Because the following decades constituted a period in which great changes occurred in the size of businesses and in the conditions of farming, much of the minority political protest was from farmers, workers, and small businessmen vying against Big Business.

The ideas of Marx and other socialists, while never widely and rigidly held in America, were used by agrarian radicals and left-wing workingmen's associations to prove that farmers and workers were oppressed by an inherently greedy class of giant capitalists. Government regulations and reforms, therefore, were sought as ways to restrain the exploiter and help the oppressed. Social Darwinism was used by right-wing spokesmen to establish the superiority of an economy run by private business entirely free of interference and regulation by government.

Neither of these extremes of oversimplified ideology, however, was very useful in understanding the major changes taking place in the economy. Nor were they useful in designing adaptations of actual government policy. Further, a good deal of posturing occurred among those who claimed to be of one school of thought or another, yet used government solely to further their personal ends.

Even if the federal, state, and local governments had been operated by solid Social Darwinists, they would have been hard pressed to resist the growth of government expenditure and the government's assumption of regulatory and control functions. Three factors support this assertion.

First, if you recall our discussion of Colin Clark's growth theory, you'll remember that people's preferences are such that economic growth generates new patterns of demand that in turn produce shifts in the structure of the economy. Areas of demand that have high income elasticities grow faster than the national economy, and vice versa. As per capita income grows, one area that tends to expand faster than GNP is public-sector output—a variety of national economies displayed this trend, called *Wagner's Law,* in the 19th century.

Second, industrialization, including its effects on urbanization, produced a host of new needs that called for increased governmental activity. Third, industrialization and the emergence of a national economy required innovations in economic organization, especially in the monetary system, for which government was called upon.

Fourth, this was a railroad-building era, and government assistance to transportation was traditionally accepted as necessary and justified.

Of course, as the history of this period actually unfolded, these basic economic forces were supplemented by strategic shifts of political power. Change produced wounds and left farmers, workers, merchants, and consumers feeling victimized. By the turn of the century, broadening of the electorate plus growth in the ranks of the dissident minorities produced a "progressive" coalition which, though loose, won "reform" legislation.

MONETARY AND BANKING POLICY

The monetary sector was one of the first fields in which the shift of powers from states to the federal government took place.

Monetary policy represents an area in which there might have been the least question about the constitutional basis for federal intervention. Precedent and need seem abundant. The first Bank of the United States had been chartered in 1791. And the federal government's own financial affairs were tied to and, in turn, affected the aggregate monetary sector. Yet, oddly enough, our steps to regulate banks and the money supply were hesitant. The Independent Treasury Act (1846) is a classic illustration of this hesitancy. Although the act became the legal basis for Treasury intervention in the private money market, it was the intent of Congress to keep the Treasury aloof from the private money market, unrealistic as that goal may have been.

Civil War financing

The Civil War created money problems which plagued the federal government for the rest of the century. At the start of the war, tariff duties provided nearly the only source of revenue, and the budget had been in deficit since the recession of 1857. From $35 million in 1861, military expenditures alone jumped to $431 million in 1862, and by the end of the war they had reached the awesome peak of $1.15 billion.

Civil War finance started out somewhat cautiously and unrealistically, with the federal government expecting to raise taxes only moderately and pay for the war by borrowing. However, its initial efforts to sell bonds to the public were not very successful. Union losses early in the war caused a loss of confidence, and people began to hoard gold. At the end of 1861, the banks had to suspend payment of specie on their notes and checks. Early in 1862, the government was forced to issue non-interest-bearing Treasury notes that were also not redeemable in specie. These notes, popularly called *greenbacks,* were made legal tender for all private and public debts except customs duties and interest on U.S. bonds and notes. The greenbacks were the first real paper money issued by the United States, and it was not until 1869 that the Supreme Court settled the issue of their constitutionality.

While an omnibus revenue bill had been passed in mid-1861, it was not vigorously administered until the following year, when a more thoroughgoing tax bill added to the types and rates of taxes. It took time, however, to organize a staff of tax collectors; and the policy of relying upon almost every conceivable type of tax rather than upon high rates for a very few levies made administration more cumbersome. By the end of the war, half of the federal government's revenues were derived from excise taxes, the largest sources being taxes on manufactures, whiskey, and tobacco. The rest of its revenue came primarily from higher tariffs and from a new federal tax on personal incomes. While revenues rose slowly, they did reach almost one fourth of total expenditures by the end of the war. Altogether, the tax burden was rather regressive—that is, it took a larger proportion of the incomes of low-income families than of high-income families.

By 1863, $450 million in greenbacks had been issued, which amounted to almost half of the currency in circulation at the time. On the private market a premium was demanded for gold, and in 1865 more than $2 in greenbacks was required in exchange for $1 in gold. Small silver coins also disappeared from circulation, and for a while postage stamps had to be used in place of coins until fractional paper notes were issued. Prices rose rapidly because of shortages of goods as well as an increase in the money supply. The Treasury, refusing to recognize its own part in the inflation, tended to blame private speculators for bidding up gold prices and state banks for excessive note issues.

Since the greenbacks were initially convertible to bonds (a provision removed in 1863) and since depreciation of greenbacks made the interest payment in gold very attractive, the market for bonds began to brighten late in 1862. Having failed to sell its bonds very well, the Treasury contracted with a private banker, Jay Cooke, to act as its general agent in selling bonds for a commission of ½ of 1 percent. By hiring a large crew of salesmen and by extensively advertising throughout the country, Cooke sold the bonds very quickly, a feat he repeated later in the war. The Civil War bonds are credited with introducing the public to the practice of buying bonds as a form of personal saving. Most of the Civil War bonds, however, were purchased in financial centers and held by banks.

It was largely to help the Treasury in its financing problems that the National Banking Act was passed in 1863. This act gave national charters to groups of individuals forming banks and required them to purchase U.S. bonds, place them on deposit with the Treasury, and receive national bank notes in their place. The objective was to help the Treasury sell its bonds as well as to introduce more uniformity in bank notes. The number of new banks, however, was disappointingly small until 1865, when a 10 percent tax was placed on notes issued by state banks. This quickly eliminated the issue of state bank notes and caused many state banks to acquire national charters.

Debt retirement and hard money

After the Civil War, Republican party leaders were anxious to return to "sound finance." It was regarded as prudent, indeed moral, to pay off the debt, reduce taxes, and restore the former gold value of the dollar.

Federal expenditures were cut to one third of their wartime peak by 1867, but hopes of bringing them nearer the prewar levels were not realizable, in part because of the heavy interest burdens. The occupation costs in the South and continued skirmishes with the Indians in the West arrested the decline in military outlays, so that by 1873 defense expenditures leveled off at about double their prewar level. In 1873, pensions were more than 20 times higher than they had been before the war. Costs of tax collection, other administrative expenditures, and public works outlays were also much higher than they had been in prewar days. Nevertheless, total federal expenditures in 1873 totaled only about 4 percent of GNP, and the rapid growth of the economy was shaving this ratio.

Taxes were drastically cut or eliminated, but revenues fell somewhat less rapidly because expanding production and imports yielded more revenue than anticipated. Most taxes on business and manufacturing were lifted, but excise taxes on liquor and tobacco were continued at substantial levels, as were tariffs. The income tax was reduced in 1867 and eliminated in 1872. The controversy generated by this form of taxation culminated in an 1880 Supreme Court decision that it was unconstitutional.

Because expenditures fell faster than receipts, a surplus resulted; and the Treasury used this to pay off its debt. The short-term debt was reduced first, and every effort was made to refund the debt with longer term issues and at lower interest rates. A brief effort was also made to repurchase and retire greenbacks, but political protest quickly brought a halt to this practice after less than a third of the outstanding supply had been withdrawn. (See 10–1.)

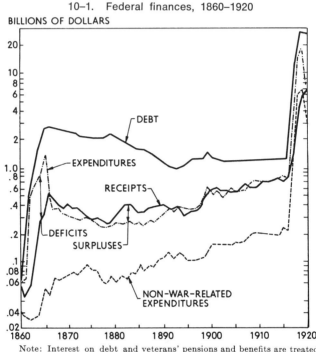

10–1. Federal finances, 1860–1920

BILLIONS OF DOLLARS

Note: Interest on debt and veterans' pensions and benefits are treated as war-related.
SOURCE: U.S. Department of Commerce, pp. 711, 718.

The continued postwar decline in prices provoked a great deal of political controversy over the financial policies of the Republicans. After the Panic of 1873, a prolonged depression intensified the popular demand, especially among farmers, for an easy-money policy. Since price inflation had accompanied the flood of paper money during the war, a cry went up for more greenbacks to raise prices. A National Greenback party even ran a candidate for president in 1876. Business recovery helped stay these political pressures, and a favorable balance of trade dating from 1876 helped bring an inflow of gold. Consequently, the Treasury was able to acquire an adequate gold reserve by the sale of bonds at more favorable interest rates than prevailed in most European countries. This series of events restored the prewar price of gold by 1879, and the Treasury resumed the redemption of greenbacks with specie upon demand. Thus, the Nation returned to a metallic currency standard after having had an irredeemable paper currency for 17 years.

Thereafter, the political protests against declining price levels shifted to a demand for an increased issue of money in the form of silver coins or silver-backed certificates. During the 1870s, great new silver mines in the Rocky Mountains began to pour out huge quantities of silver. At that time world demand for silver was not expanding: in fact, most nations were already on a gold standard and some were switching from silver to gold. And at home the "Crime of 1873" terminated Treasury purchases of silver for monetary purposes. This caused a fall in the price of silver. Popular demand to expand the money supply was therefore combined with an appeal to aid the western mining industry by Treasury purchases of silver at prices well above the market.

A compromise was reached in 1878, when the Bland-Allison Act obligated the Treasury to purchase between $2 and $4 million in silver a month at above-market prices for coins or to back newly issued silver certificates. Later, the Sherman Silver Purchase Act of 1890 required the Treasury to purchase silver and to issue Treasury notes redeemable in either silver or gold.

Shortly afterward, however, the Panic of 1893 led to a run on the Treasury by holders of Treasury notes and greenbacks who wanted gold, and in the midst of a worldwide depression gold flowed out of the United States. The Sherman Silver Purchase Act was repealed in order to stanch the flow of gold from the Treasury. Then, in the presidential election of 1896, William Jennings Bryan proposed a silver money standard as his major campaign issue. His decisive defeat by William McKinley, who advocated retention of the gold standard, was the first step in settling the issue politically.

A change in economic conditions in the mid-1890s helped bring a decisive end to the political controversy over the Nation's monetary standard. During the 1890s, new discoveries of gold were made in Africa, Australia, and Alaska. The introduction of the cyanide extraction process also increased output. World gold production rose from 5.7 million ounces in 1890 to 13.9 million ounces in 1898. A favorable balance of trade brought an inflow of gold to the United States. Between 1896 and 1898, the Nation's gold stock increased 40 percent. (See 10–2.) With rapid business recovery in the late 1890s, the general price level also began to rise. Thus, the economic basis of the political controversy had been removed when the Gold Standard Act of 1900 finally defined the value of the dollar solely in terms of gold.

Bank regulation

Going on the gold standard did not settle all money supply questions; commercial banks had come to be responsible for a large and growing

10-2.   Currency in circulation, by type, 1860–1920

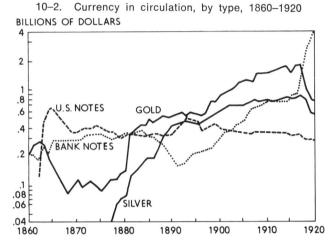

Note: Bank notes include state bank notes prior to 1879 and Federal Reserve notes and Federal Reserve Bank notes after 1915. Minor coins are included in silver. Fractional currency, Treasury notes of 1890, and other U.S. currency are included in U.S. notes.
Source: U.S. Department of Commerce, pp. 648–49.

part of the money supply through their issues of bank notes and demand deposits (checkbook money). During the next decade public discontent with the inflexibility of the banking system during business fluctuations was to result in further banking reform legislation.

The National Banking Act had been a Civil War measure designed to help the Treasury sell its bonds and issue a more respectable type of paper money. Since the national banks could issue notes in exchange for Treasury bonds, issues of national bank notes were potentially just as inflationary as the Treasury's greenbacks. However, the increase in national bank notes were largely offset by the elimination of state bank notes. During the 1880s, the use of budget surpluses to retire debt tended to aggravate the general monetary contraction because there was a reduction in national bank notes when the bonds the national banks held were retired. Not until after 1900, when there was a generally expanding demand for currency of all types and an expanding gold stock, did the value of national bank note issues grow substantially.

The slow growth rate of bank notes is in part attributable to the declining importance of currency in the total money supply. In urban areas, where transactions were growing faster than in rural areas, the use of checking accounts was rapidly replacing currency for all but minor expenditures. By 1870, demand deposits in banks exceeded the total currency in circulation; and thereafter, deposits continued to grow more rapidly than currency.

As a means of creating uniform bank note issues, the national banking system was successful. The 10 percent tax succeeded in driving state bank notes out of existence. The number of state banks dwindled until it became apparent that banks did not need to issue notes in order to make loans. Creating a bank deposit for a borrower was just as effective as issuing notes. Because most of the state regulations on bank reserves were less restrictive than the national regulations, state charters again became very popular. Look at 10–3 to see a dramatic reversal:

10–3. Growth of national and state banks

Year	Number of banks		Assets (millions of dollars)	
	National	State	National	State
1860	–	1,562	–	1,000
1870	1,612	325	1,566	215
1880	2,076	1,279	2,036	1,364
1890	3,484	4,717	3,062	3,296
1900	3,731	9,322	4,944	6,444
1910	7,138	18,013	9,892	13,030
1920	8,024	22,885	23,267	29,827

SOURCE: U.S. Department of Commerce, pp. 626, 628.

assets of state banks declined by 80 percent from 1860 to 1870; then, from 1870 to 1920, state bank assets increased 140-fold, whereas national bank assets grew only 16-fold.

While national banks were subject to greater precautionary restrictions, it soon became apparent that the system was not much help in preventing recurrent bank crises. Numerous national banks failed during each of the post–Civil War depressions. The comptroller of the currency had powers of inspection and supervision over individual banks but no control over the system's influence on the money supply. The national banking law itself had encouraged a pyramiding of bank reserves without providing any kind of buffer for emergencies.

If you remember our discussion of banks in chapter 7, you'll recall that when a run on a 19th century bank developed, it had to draw upon the reserves it had deposited in other banks. Similarly, with a fixed volume of reserves in the entire banking system, if the public increased its demand for currency all banks would have to draw on their reserves simultaneously. Any major increase in the public's desire to hold currency might outstrip reserves and force some banks to suspend payments, to stop honoring their deposit customers' demands for currency.

Thus, any increase in demand for currency in the Nation as a whole was likely to cause a crisis in banking and financial circles. This experience was repeated regularly in the panics of 1873, 1884, 1893, and 1907.

The Panic of 1907 made popular demand for banking reform irresistible. In addition, New York had become an international banking center, and international bankers had grown impatient with the weakness of the U.S. banking system. In 1908, the Aldrich-Vreeland Act provided as a temporary measure that groups of banks could form associations that could borrow from the Treasury in an emergency. Meanwhile, a national Monetary Commission was appointed to study the banking system and make reform recommendations. The results of its studies began to be publicized in 1911, and the debates over various alternative legislative proposals began. Finally, the Federal Reserve Act was passed in December 1913.

The Federal Reserve Act did not create a strong central bank, such as many European nations have, but it did correct some of the weaknesses of the previous national bank system.[2] Twelve reserve bank districts were created, with national banks as members participating in the election of boards of directors for the Federal Reserve Bank in each district. A central Board of Governors of the Federal Reserve System, appointed by the president, was given supervisory powers. One function of the Reserve banks was to liquidate the old national bank notes and issue new Federal Reserve notes. This new issue was to be limited by a 40 percent gold reserve requirement imposed on the Reserve banks themselves. Member banks were required to keep specified reserve percentages on deposit in the Reserve banks. The Reserve banks were to act as a clearing system for checks drawn on member banks; and the member banks were able to borrow reserves from the Reserve banks in their respective districts.

The flexibility to create more money was inherent in the power of Reserve banks to make open-market purchases of government bonds and short-term commercial paper. The excessive issue of bank credit in boom times could be restrained by raising the *rediscount rate* (the interest rate charged on the loans of Reserve banks to member banks) and by setting higher *reserve requirements* (the legal reserves which banks had to hold against their demand deposit liabilities).

Financing World War I

Even before America's entry into World War I, the war had a disturbing effect on the American economy. Initially, the outbreak of aggression had caused a panic sale of securities, including sales by many foreign investors, which, in turn, caused an outflow of gold and a consequent reduction in bank reserves. Since the Federal Reserve System was not yet in operation, the Treasury used the powers of the Aldrich-Vreeland Act to lend emergency currency to banks, and more of the

---

[2] For a dissenting view on some counts, see Friedman (1962).

Treasury's own cash was deposited with banks. Still, a rapid contraction of economic activity occurred, and widespread unemployment resulted.

In 1915, business conditions were reversed by a rapid rise in exports as European nations placed heavy orders in America for war munitions and supplies. In three years, exports increased sixfold, and the real gross national product increased 20 percent. Since imports did not rise as much, the net export balance tripled, and the total balance in these three years was almost as large as the total of all previous export balances in American history. To settle this balance, foreign nations liquidated about half of their American securities and sold about $2.7 billion in government bonds to Americans. Shipping services and gold flows each brought in another billion. These gold imports were the largest in history, and the American gold stock became the largest any nation had ever held. The record gold inflows greatly expanded bank reserves and enabled credit to expand to handle increased business activity. Bank deposits (adjusted for interbank holdings) increased 30 percent; and the new Federal Reserve System encouraged credit expansion by lowering rediscount rates.

In mid-1916, federal military expenditures began to increase. In this period of preparedness, tax rates were raised. A 1913 constitutional amendment enabled restoration of the federal income tax, which helped to provide more revenues. Also, the Treasury was authorized to begin emergency short-term borrowing.

With the declaration of war, in April 1917, federal outlays shot up much faster than revenues. Expenditures tripled in 1917 and had risen ninefold by 1919. Revenues fell from 60 percent of expenditures in 1917 to 26 percent in 1919. About 30 percent of the war costs were paid by taxes; the remainder had to be raised by borrowing.

After having passed an emergency tax increase in March 1917, Congress was slow to raise tax rates further. However, it finally did so in October 1917, and again in February 1919. Many persons regarded the rates as confiscatory. The basic tax on personal income was set at 12 percent, with a maximum surtax of 65 percent. Corporations also paid a 12 percent tax plus excess profits taxes of 65 percent. Excise taxes were increased much less, and tariffs weren't raised at all. In this war, therefore, the tax burden was progressive, falling proportionately more on higher income families.

Borrowing to fill the tax-expenditure gap could have been noninflationary if the funds had been supplied by the business and consuming public and if each dollar lent reduced private-sector expenditure by a dollar. However, about one fifth of the money raised was borrowed directly from banks. The Treasury also urged people to borrow in order to buy bonds on the installment plan, which had the same effect as direct Treasury borrowing from the banking system. The Federal Reserve System, through its own policy and through legislative amendments, greatly expanded the money supply to enable banks and individuals to borrow to buy bonds and to finance increased private spending. Between 1916 and 1919, deposits of member banks doubled (this was offset slightly because deposits of nonmember banks actually declined a bit). The supply of Federal Reserve notes also expanded. So, while the government did not appear to be printing money to finance the war in an inflationary manner, the same effect was achieved through using the Federal Reserve System to rapidly expand bank deposit money.

Money supply and prices

In the two wars of this period, the government in handling its own finances had a strong disturbing effect on the economy which took the form of rapid price inflation. Unwillingness to raise taxes and thus reduce civilian outlays meant that the Treasury had to resort to printing money or borrowing from banks in a way that expanded note issues or deposits. In other words, inflation became the tax on the civilian economy that enabled the military to expand its output. Furthermore, in attempting to put its house in order after the Civil War, the government also disrupted price levels, this time by provoking deflation by policies that contracted or retarded the growth of the stock of money while production was expanding rapidly.

Most generally, however, it can be said that the major weaknesses in government policy were attributable to inaction. Treasury policies which resulted in a contraction in the money supply resulted from a failure on the part of the national government to take charge of the total economy's money system. The Treasury failed to make itself responsible for letting the money stock grow as capacity to produce grew. It also failed to adopt policies that would prevent a cascading contraction of the money supply in depressions.

The *quantity theory of money* provides a way to analyze how a grand variety of forces transmitted through the money stock influence the general price level. Let's start from the simple definition that a price is the ratio of the amount of money exchanged for a quantity of goods divided by that quantity of goods. Given this definition, net national product valued at current prices (NNP) will be equal to the price level (P) times the quantity of output (Y). The quantity theory defines P times Y as equal to the money stock (M) times its velocity of circulation (V). That is: $NNP = PY = MV$. If we rewrite the above definition as $P = MV/Y$, you can see that the price level is defined as the ratio of money exchanged (MV) for goods exchanged or production (Y).

The quantity theory of money asserts that if the velocity (or rate at which the money stock changes hands in producing the annual in-

10–4. Currency, deposits and money stock, 1867–1920

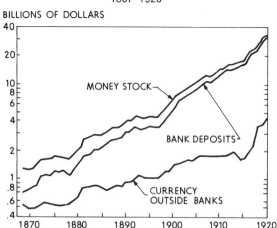

BILLIONS OF DOLLARS

Note: Includes time and demand deposits.
SOURCE: U.S. Department of Commerce, pp. 646–47.

come) is fairly stable, then faster (or slower) changes in the money stock than in production are likely to result in increases (or decreases) in the general price level. Many things, of course, affect velocity, especially in short periods of time; so it should not be assumed that prices are influenced only by the money stock. Yet, the availability of money has been important historically in influencing wartime price inflations, depression price declines, and long-term price trends. In this connection Friedman and Schwartz's *A Monetary History of the United States* is an extremely important study.

Again we stress that there is not a simple mechanical relationship between the quantity of money and the price level. Rather, a host of economic forces influence the quantity of money, which, in turn, influences spending and thereby affects price levels. The precise nature of these interrelations is still hotly debated by economists, especially as far as short-run problems are concerned. We, however, are interested in longer time periods over which money stock and price-level changes are useful sources of insight.

We can use 10–5 to trace the relationship of these variables over our study period. National output (Y) rose very rapidly immediately after the Civil War, and the money stock (M) rose also, i.e., MV increased as did PY because M and Y were increasing. However, M did not rise as rapidly as Y, so prices (P) declined. As the postwar period continued, the money stock increased but, until the mid-1890s, at rates less than the growth of capacity as measured by real NNP. Further, for reasons that economists have yet to explain satisfactorily, the velocity

10–5.   National production, money stock, and prices,
1870–1920

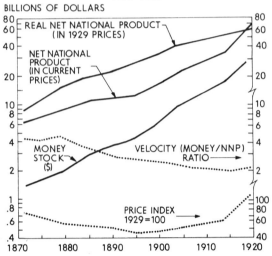

Note: The implicit price index for adjusting real net national
product is used, and it is shown in five-year averages on a ratio
scale; so it looks different from the wholesale price indexes
previously shown.
    SOURCE: U.S. Department of Commerce, pp. 139, 144, 646–
47.

of money (V) declined over almost the entire period.[3] Consequently,
as production rose, monetary forces (M and V) pushed the price index
downward until almost 1900. After 1896 and virtually until World War
I, the money stock rose much faster than NNP and more than offset
the continued downward trend of velocity. The long-term price trend,
in turn, was rising during this period. During World War I, an even
more rapid rise in the money stock was again accompanied by a rapid
inflation in prices.

It is not necessary for the money stock to have been the sole influence
on prices for this analysis to be relevant. The point is that the money
stock was one of the major influences on price levels, and the federal
government had the constitutional powers to control the money supply.
At times, it exercised its powers in such a way as to account for a
large part of the wide fluctuations in price levels—especially in wartime
and during the post–Civil War effort to get on the gold standard. At
other times, especially during depressions, it permitted price fluctuations
to occur from other causes without making adequate efforts to offset
them. If it had not been for the expansion in state bank deposits, the

[3] As real income per person rose, people may have opted for the luxury of
holding larger balances in checkbook money and pocket money, and the volume
of monetary transactions might have risen faster than Y as the economy became
more marketized and less rural; on the other hand, improvements in communications
and transport increased the physical ability to circulate the money stock.

lack of a federal effort to provide an expanding money supply for a growing economy might have brought even worse price declines. And if it had not been for the rise in world gold production, there might not have been an upward trend in prices after the mid-1890s.

Recall from our discussion in chapter 7 that price fluctuations and long-term inflations or deflations would be no source of worry except that they affect productivity and the distribution of income among households. In brief, monetary disturbances can wreak havoc throughout the private economy. Rapid price inflation can cause a wasteful diversion of capital funds into inventory speculation and hoarding of gold and land instead of into productive investments. Inflation hurts people who depend upon relatively fixed money incomes—whether they be in the form of salaries, rents, interest, or pensions. Falling price trends, on the other hand, hurt people who have borrowed money, invested in productive equipment, or are holding inventories. Particular farmers, small businessmen, and manufacturers were all hurt by falling prices in the three decades after the Civil War. And bankruptcies were intensified in railroads, in which fixed capital costs were important.

In the midst of monetary disturbances, the private market and individual businessmen tend to get blamed for the difficulties everyone is experiencing. People are quick to seize the notion that some type of government interference with the private market is needed to reform the private economy. The extent to which government policy itself is at fault may be overlooked. This was often the case over the period 1860–1920. In other words, where reform was needed was in government policy, which had too often exacerbated the instability of the private economy.

SUBSIDIES AND REGULATION

In the introduction to this chapter we pointed out to you that government's economic policy shifted away from stimulation of economic activity in favor of regulation of the private sector. If we view government's economic role as falling into three broad categories, we can see why such a shift occurred. First, government provides products that wouldn't or couldn't be produced in appropriate quantities by the private sector—protection and a system of commercial law are two examples. Second, government provides for cases in which total social benefits (or costs) exceed those received by private decision-makers—transportation and social overhead capital in general dominate this category. Third, government enacts laws that redistribute income—tariffs and the regulation of producer groups are historically important examples.

In the post–Civil War period, the activities of government were increasingly of the third variety. One major explanation for this is the growth of the density of the national market and the scale economies that came with it. As consumers grew in number and income per head increased, an increasing number of projects that originally were not privately profitable but were socially remunerative became privately profitable. For example, canals were heavily subsidized by state and local governments, but, with the exception of the South, where the market was thin, the emphasis in railroad financing was private. In the post–Civil War period, the first western roads received heavy subsidies, yet the later western railroad construction projects received little or no government aid. In both cases, the market had grown sufficiently to promise a high enough volume of traffic to assure or nearly assure private profit from private investment.

The second major explanation also arises from the growth of the market. As the agrarian sector declined in relative terms, as economic life became increasingly specialized and marketized, and as transportation and communication became speedier, producer groups found it feasible and remunerative to politicize themselves, to become "passionate minorities" and attempt to enlist the coercive powers of government to redistribute income in their favor. For example, federal regulation of railroads represents attempts by farmers to get an increased share of the pie by reducing "monopoly power" and, paradoxically, by the railroads, which viewed state regulation as all too effective in giving the farm groups what they sought.[4]

In what follows we shall concentrate our attention chiefly upon the federal government. As economic life became increasingly national in character, the economic policy of the national government consistently increased in importance.

Development subsidies

It was primarily through the exercise of its powers to set tariffs and sell public lands that the federal government initially tried to stimulate, support, and protect the productive activities of individuals in developing the country. Rather than spend public funds, the federal government followed the course of the traditionally hard-pressed English kings. Economic development was encouraged by granting special privileges and protection to spur the rapid exploitation of the Nation's natural resources.

Controversies over the tariff played a part in post–Civil War politics which was almost as important as the money issue. The Republican party had come into power in 1861 dedicated to a high-tariff policy, whereas the Democratic party tried to lower tariffs during the Cleveland and Wilson administrations. Since the Republicans were identified with business leaders, the high-tariff policy frequently has been cited as serving the class interests of manufacturers and demonstrating the domina-

---

[4] For extended discussion of this way of looking at government's changing economic role see Davis and North.

tion of government by Big Business. This is a gross oversimplification that ignores the diversity of interests among business groups, the support of tariffs by some farm and worker interests, and the importance attached to tariffs as a source of revenue.

To put it differently, those who actually benefited from high tariffs and those who suffered therefrom were related in far more complex ways than a simple business (Republican)–consumer (Democrat) dichotomy can express. Don't interpret the foregoing as denying the efficacy of special-interest groups in obtaining protective tariffs, however. We are only asserting that the web of influence followed a complicated pattern.

The complex nature of interest groups and tariffs can be seen by briefly reviewing the post–Civil War tariff history. In the antebellum period, when national manufacturing industries came into being, trade associations were frequently formed for the purpose of sharing technical information. Lobbying was a natural second step, and pressuring for tariffs to protect manufacturing markets against "cheap foreign goods" was a profitable way to use resources allocated to lobbying activities. The Senate, which was not elected directly prior to 1913, was especially vulnerable to the pressure of lobbyists, or accommodating to manufacturing interests, if you prefer. However, after 1913, senators were elected directly and economic conditions had changed. Antitariff manufacturers had emerged and organized and, in spite of their vast numbers, farmers had organized as well. "As a result, the high-tariff lobbies were forced to compete with equally vocal and well-financed low-tariff lobbies whose activities were underwritten by equally strong trade associations, and who were supported by the national farm organizations." Duties were lowered during the Wilson administration, although this turned out to be a temporary remission in a period of high and rising tariffs.[5]

The railroads favored low rates on steel, the steel companies wanted low rates on iron and coal, the woolen manufacturers sought low rates on wool, exporters of machinery favored low-tariff reciprocity, and merchants usually favored free trade. On the other hand, farm groups wanted higher rates on wool and sugar. Workers in manufacturing industries generally feared the competition of foreign imports because of the lower wages in most European countries; and during depressions the competition of imports threatened employment as well as wage rates. Further, pressures for tariff legislation fluctuated with the business cycle. It was during the depressions of the 1870s and 1890s that rates were raised, while during prosperous periods there were efforts to lower the rates.

Throughout the post–Civil War decades, the main justification publicly offered for the high tariff was the need of the federal government for

---

[5] See Davis and North, pp. 178–82, for an expansion of the account summarized above.

revenues to pay off its debts and support higher expenditures. Nevertheless, the high-tariff policy of the federal government must be regarded as a form of privilege and protection for certain producing groups. Such groups found it judicious to support a policy that would yield high tax revenues.

Government policy on the sale of public lands was a compromise between the desire for revenues and the desire to help farmers. During the Civil War, the latter motive became dominant. In 1862, several measures were passed that were designed to aid farmers. The Homestead Act removed the price on public lands (except for a nominal filing fee) for the small farmer. At the same time, the Pacific Railway Act was designed to encourage the building of railroads to open up new farmlands in the West, as well as to provide a connection with the West Coast.

Also in 1862, the Morrill Land Grant College Act was passed, and the Department of Agriculture was established. These measures aimed to raise farm productivity and incomes by encouraging research and the dissemination of new knowledge. While the Morrill Act involved only grants of federal lands, in 1887 appropriations began to be made for grants-in-aid to states in support of research at agricultural experiment stations. In 1906, a federal program was undertaken to stop the spread of the boll weevil on southern cotton farms. In 1908, Congress doubled the support to agricultural colleges; and in 1914, the Smith-Lever Act provided federal funds to finance an agricultural extension service. The expenditures of the Department of Agriculture were $3.6 million in 1900, reached $22.2 million in 1914, and rose to $66.6 million in 1920.

The disposal of western lands to business interests followed roughly the same policy lines as land sales to farmers except that a bit more effort was made to raise revenues. Beginning in the late 1840s, Congress had sold mineral lands at higher prices than those for agricultural lands. Legislation after the Civil War set similar prices for mineral lands in the West with the hope of bringing in additional revenues to reduce the national debt. Congress, however, frequently passed special measures exempting particular areas. Also, the administration of the land offices was lax until the end of the 1880s. Just as pioneer farmers had squatted on public lands, many of the early timber cutters did not always bother to legally acquire the lands they cut. The early cattlemen also grazed their cattle on public lands. The poor enforcement of the Homestead Act enabled large holdings of timber, mining, and grazing lands to be assembled by paying small farmers to "settle" the land and then buying their claims. Nevertheless, most of the timber and mining lands were purchased under laws established for this purpose.

Late in the 19th century, some public figures began to express concern over the dwindling of public lands and the need to conserve natural resources. Easterners were well aware of soil depletion in farming, exhaustion of mines, and cutover forest lands. So it was natural that they advocated setting aside public lands in the West. Western merchants frequently opposed this policy as tending to slow down the economic development of their areas.[6] Ultimately, Congress authorized setting aside public lands as national forests and the creation of national parks. On the other hand, western settlement was enhanced by the misnamed Reclamation Act (1902), which provided for using the proceeds from the sale of public lands for the construction of irrigation systems in the dry regions of the West. On balance, however, federal land policy shifted from a giveaway emphasis designed to stimulate rapid development to a more restrictive conservation orientation.

Federal river and harbor outlays rose significantly over the period. While the traffic on canals and rivers had been greatly reduced by the competition of the railroads, there were continual pressures on the federal government to subsidize improvements in waterways, partly in order to force lower rates on competing railroads and partly to aid communities on the rivers and coasts. River and harbor expenditures increased during the depressions of the 1870s and 1890s. By 1914, annual outlays for waterway improvements totaled $48 million, larger than for any yearly construction figure on the Panama Canal.

Financing the railroads

Land grants to aid in constructing western railroads constitute the largest single development effort of the federal government in our history. In 1862, Congress adopted legislation designed to encourage building a rail link with the West Coast. It did so in the belief that a subsidy of some nature was necessary and justifiable.

Although not well articulated, the underlying rationale for subsidizing the railroads was a recognition of the difference between private and social returns to transportation facilities, a notion we have discussed in earlier chapters. Turnpike, canal, and eastern railroad projects had demonstrated that transportation improvements produce broadly used benefits which are not reflected in the revenue figures of the transport firms. Thus, a project with a very high rate of return might not generate sufficient prospective profits to induce private investment in it without public assistance.

In the case of the western roads, it was widely, and perhaps incorrectly, believed that the tracks had to be laid ahead of demand, i.e., that western settlement would take place on a large enough scale to justify rail transit only if people were induced to go west by having the railroads built in advance of settlement. Consequently, a subsidy

---

[6] Their successors are very hard at work today, pushing local and regional development and opposing policies that would restrict expansion.

was considered necessary to tide the western roads over the lean years. Further, the potential costs were uncertain, especially in regard to construction in the mountains, and the capital market was too unsophisticated to facilitate privately amassing the savings required to finance construction.

The federal government was elected as the subsidizer for special reasons. Since the western territories were only sparsely populated, no state or local governments or citizens groups could raise the necessary funds. Consequently, following the precedent established in the 1850s, when the Illinois Central was built, grants of federal land were made to the Union and Central Pacific railway companies.

For a government engaged in financing a war largely through loans, the land grant scheme ranked second only to finding the goose that laid the golden egg. With no Treasury outlay, the railroads could be given a source of funds simply by conveying title to lands which the railroads could use as security for bonds sold to the general public. Eventual sale of the land, as land prices rose along the railroad line, was expected to provide funds to pay off the bonds. Under the 1864 version of the law, both the Union Pacific and the Central Pacific were to receive a 400-foot right-of-way, ten alternate sections of land per mile on each side of the tracks (or 12,800 acres per mile of track), and government loans ranging from $16,000 to $48,000 per mile, depending on the difficulty of construction. The government loans were secured by second mortgages on the land, and the railroads pledged toward bond retirement 5 percent of their net revenues and one half of any revenues for the movement of troops or government freight.

During the next seven years, federal land grants were also extended to other western railroads. Over the period 1850 to 1871, 175 million acres were granted by Congress, although 35 million acres were forfeited and returned when some of the construction contracts were not fulfilled. It has been estimated that one fourth of the land in Minnesota and Washington and from one fifth to one eighth of the land in other western states was in railroad grants. In addition, the states added about 48 million acres in land grants of their own. Only six of the railroads received government loans, but the total amounted to over $64 million. Virtually all of the loans were repaid in full with 6 percent interest by 1899.

Historians have long been interested in whether the land-grant subsidy was justified. They have come to accept the notion that if the government was repaid in the form of freight reductions, then the subsidy was a sound "investment." This is a misleading criterion of justification. Instead, you should ask whether *total benefits* constituted an acceptable rate of return on the *total investment,* then ask whether the contemporary view that a subsidy was crucial to success of the railroad projects was correct.

Fogel, whose work we discussed earlier, clearly establishes an affirmative answer to the first question insofar as the Union Pacific is concerned. The social rate of return attributable to the Union Pacific was on the order of 30 percent per year over the period 1870–79. Lloyd Mercer's more comprehensive study shows the same social rate of return for the Central Pacific System.[7]

Whether the subsidy was actually required, as contemporary decision-makers felt, is a question that can have only ambiguous answers. Would investors have recognized the potential profitability of the western roads? Would the settlers have come if the companies had just started laying track without a guarantee that the road would reach the Pacific? As the tracks moved west, would settlement and traffic have reached sufficient volume to persuade investors to buy railroad bonds as the need for cash evolved? Because federal intervention gave settlers and bond buyers a degree of assurance that the roads would be completed, we can't know how they would have reacted in the absence of the federal grants; so we can't cite the actual settlement and freight history as data signifying that the land grants were not needed. We do know, though, that the Great Northern System was built without subsidy through the uninhabited wilds and generated a huge traffic volume before completion.[8]

A public outcry arose over financial manipulations associated with the financing and construction of the railroads. In 1873, a congressional investigating committee reported the grossest example. The actual construction costs of the Union Pacific were no greater than the government loan and the amount of first mortgage bonds issued by the company; yet the construction firm, the Crédit Mobilier, had received much more. About 48 percent of the construction costs were its profit. This construction firm turned out to be owned by a group of the railroad's directors and officers; so, they had overpaid themselves for the construction at the expense of stockowners and bondholders in the railroad.

This type of maneuver by railroad promoters was not unusual, and it was one of the ways by which railroad companies became overcapitalized—or their stock became "watered"—a condition in which the value of the property is worth much less than the face value of the bonds and stocks issued.[9] Sometimes new stocks were issued as dividends to create a misleading impression of profits and expansion. In the late 1860s and early 1870s, a few unscrupulous men—such as Jim Fisk, Jay Gould, and Dan Drew—milked their firms dry of funds and manipulated stocks to make fortunes in the stock market. Usually these maneuvers were not clearly illegal, but in a few cases they constituted outright

---

[7] Fogel, table 3; Mercer, table 1.

[8] Fogel.

[9] The term was originally applied to cattle which had been "fattened" by being permitted to drink just before they were displayed to prospective purchasers.

frauds (such as when the president of one railroad issued unauthorized stock for sale and then left the country with the funds). However, we should note that in some cases what appeared to be overpricing of railroad stocks and bonds only reflected the high risks borne by the construction companies when they agreed to take payment in securities of the railroad, paper they might not be able to dispose of except at a considerable discount.

The popular concern these scandals provoked was not so much directed at the alleged excessiveness of federal subsidies as at the financial losses that investors suffered. It was during the depression of the 1870s that public disillusionment with railroad financing set in and also that agitation for state regulation began. Bonds and stocks of railroads had been widely purchased by many thousands of small businessmen and farmers. As particular railroads lost money or went bankrupt, many people incurred losses on their investments. Similarly, the farmers' complaints about high freight rates were aggravated by a belief that "insiders" had overloaded the capital costs and were making fortunes at their expense.

The economics of railroads

It was at this point in American history that we first faced highly concentrated business conditions on a national scale. Thus, the public was slow to understand the nature of the problem. Given identical cost conditions, a monopoly producer will sell at a higher price than would prevail if the market were supplied by competitive producers. On a state and local level, therefore, it had long been accepted that any unavoidable monopoly required public regulation of prices. In colonial times, grain mills, for example, were regulated. And in the early years of the Nation, state incorporation of a bank, canal company, or railroad was assumed to involve the granting of a monopoly privilege which was then hedged with restrictions, such as rate limits. Later, however, the popular desire to promote railroad development caused considerations of rate regulation to be neglected—the public gains from any railroad service were expected to be large, while the prospects for railroad profits seemed to be limited.

Railroad regulation was inaugurated for a variety of reasons. Farmers saw themselves as unfairly treated. The railroads eventually leaned in favor of regulation as a way of solving problems arising out of the structure of the industry. And the public sympathized with regulation when the Crédit Mobilier was exposed and when it got wind of similar financial manipulations.

The structure of the post–Civil War railroad industry presents a conflicting and confusing array of market forces which, nevertheless, aid in explaining why regulation was enacted. The customers along a trunk line that connected two major terminals or on a connecting route that joined a minor shipping point with a trunk line were forced to purchase rail service from a monopolist. Yet, shippers at major terminals essentially purchased transportation services from competitive firms—duplicate rail facilities served major terminals, and water transport was an alternative in many cases.

Looked at from the point of view of a particular rail line, a profit-maximizing strategy called for selling transportation services at prices established by the market in cases of shipments between major cities. But for shipments where customers had only very limited or no alternative shipping facilities, the same railroad management could set its own rates. The result was that competitive prices permitting only a "normal" return on invested capital were charged for so-called long hauls, while highly profitable monopoly prices were charged for short hauls. In other words, **rate discrimination** came to characterize the railroad industry, with higher rates per ton-mile being charged for short hauls.

A similar discrimination pattern characterized rates applied to different kinds of shippers and different classes of goods. Wherever the railroad found itself with monopoly power, a profit-maximizing strategy called for charging rates according to the different responsiveness of demand exhibited by various shippers.

The picture presented below (10–6) illustrates this principle: two shippers with two different demand curves could be charged rates A

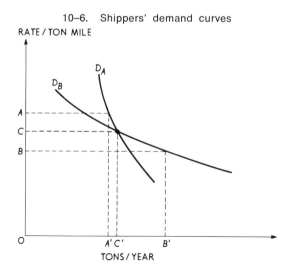

10–6.   Shippers' demand curves

and B, respectively, at a higher profit to the railroad than could be obtained by charging both the intermediate rate C. You can verify this by noting that the total revenue areas $A \times A'$ and $B \times B'$ are both greater than $C \times C'$, which is the total revenue that would be collected from each shipper if a uniform rate were charged. Price discrimination will be the profitable alternative as long as costs per ton-mile are less than B and constant for the relevant tonnage range. The economic welfare effects are a transfer of income to the railroad's owners and to the shippers with the flatter demand curve and away from the shippers with the steeper demand curve.

As an added dimension in the pricing picture, rate wars were chronic among competing trunk lines. Recognizing that an agreement among companies on any long-haul route could establish a monopoly price, competing railroads formed *cartel* agreements, or *pools*. These were elaborate monopoly agreements that established a uniform rate structure and arranged for a division of the shipping business among members of the cartel. The rate structure was set high enough to maximize profits for each of the pool members.

The cartels were inherently unstable. By secretly charging particular long-haul shippers lower than published rates, a given railroad could add to its revenues by expanding its share of the market. Even if most members of a cartel eschewed such a tactic, large shippers, such as Rockefeller, could force a secret price concession from several of them. Such secrets were badly kept. Once the cheater's tactic became public, other shippers demanded similar treatment from each member of the cartel. A rate war would break out that might last several years. Then, when the combatants were sufficiently battle weary, they would form a new pooling agreement just as unstable as its predecessor.

For the most part, shippers, who were numerically dominated by farmers, viewed rate discrimination and price wars as evils of Big Business. The isolated farmer who paid "exorbitant" rates to get his crop to market and never benefited from rate wars felt preyed upon. Even in those cases in which price differentials were more attributable to the high cost of serving a thin market than to monopoly "gouging," the lonely farmer viewed himself as a victim of extortion. For the farmer on the main line, the ups and downs of prices that came with price wars and the breakdown and re-forming of cartels introduced an additional element of uncertainty in an already uncertain life. And the long-haul shippers who didn't get concessions felt cheated. To most shippers, regulation seemed the best way to curb the power of the railroads, and the public eventually agreed.

The railroads advocated regulation as well, but for different reasons. They saw federal regulation of long-haul routes as a way to stabilize their cartels and to avoid rate wars. Further, by 1887 they welcomed federal regulation as an alternative to tougher state regulations. In fact, a railroad lawyer wrote one of the federal regulatory bills, which, not surprisingly, did not include any prohibition of pooling.

Because there was a great deal of public scrapping over the details of regulation, especially with respect to pooling, it has been said that the railroads had regulation forced on them much against their will. In fact, they had a great deal to gain from regulation if it imposed rules that prevented price cutting and didn't prevent pooling agreements.[10]

Considerable conviction that railroad rates were too high, quite apart from rate discrimination, added pressure for regulation. This view had frequently been expressed at the local level, and in 1874 a congressional committee argued the case nationally. During the Civil War, increased taxes and higher prices had forced railroads to raise their rates. After the war, taxes were reduced and all prices were falling; but it was charged that railroad rates had not fallen as much as agricultural prices. The multitude of different rates between particular places, however, made evaluation of this charge very difficult.

Actually, there appears to be little basis for the common belief that railroad rates generally were too high or too slow in falling. Average rates for all American railroads can be estimated by comparing total revenues with the total freight tonnage carried and the miles it was transported. These estimates clearly show that average revenues per ton-mile were falling during most of the period from 1867 to 1879 and were falling as fast as general wholesale prices. Furthermore, average railroad revenues per ton-mile continued to fall at about the same rate as wholesale prices, dropping from 1.92 cents in 1867 to 0.73 cents in 1900. Thereafter, rail rates rose less rapidly than wholesale prices. Accordingly, the real rates (computed as the ratio of average rates to the wholesale price index) were approximately constant until 1900 and declining thereafter. (See 10–7.)

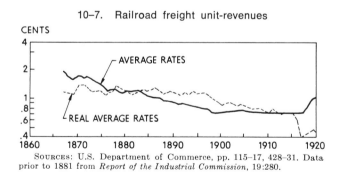

10–7.   Railroad freight unit-revenues

SOURCES: U.S. Department of Commerce, pp. 115–17, 428–31. Data prior to 1881 from *Report of the Industrial Commission,* 19:280.

Railroad regulation

The farmers in the western plains provided the initial post–Civil War demand for regulation, and this regulation came at the state level. In the 1870s, a series of granger laws were passed in Illinois, Iowa, Wiscon-

[10] MacAvoy presents this hypothesis along with confirming data and analysis.

sin, and Minnesota. These regulatory laws were named after the Granges, the social units into which the western farmers had formed themselves after the Civil War, and which had assumed a political orientation. (Earlier regulation had, of course, been practiced in New England, and many of the initial railroad charters had incorporated rate limits; but the rapidly falling prices and rates in the post–Civil War period made these limitations ineffective.)

State railway commissions were established to set rates and determine services and safety practices. State regulatory performance was not outstanding, however. Rate-setting is a complicated matter; if flat rates are arbitrarily set for all railroads, regardless of differing conditions, one road might prosper while another went bankrupt. The attitudes of state legislatures in the western farm states tended to be unsympathetic toward railroads controlled by eastern investors, which added another dimension to rate-setting.

The railroad companies fought back by using funds to bribe or politically support sympathetic legislators and to challenge legislation in the courts. In 1886, the Supreme Court severely limited state regulation by a ruling in the *Wabash* case that an Illinois law prohibiting short-haul versus long-haul discrimination was an enroachment on the federal power to regulate interstate commerce.

The moment at which the Interstate Commerce Act of 1887 was passed appears to have been decided by the Court's limitation of state regulatory powers. Congress had actually been debating regulatory legislation for several years, and both houses had approved different versions of a regulatory measure prior to the Supreme Court decision in 1886. In addition, there was some sympathy for the view that state regulation was not fully effective against large railroad networks operating across numerous states.

Eastern merchants and oil producers especially played a leading role in demanding federal regulation of railroads because they feared that rate-cutting by rival railroad trunk lines was hurting their interests, and the trunk lines were beyond the control of any one state. In 1881, the New York Central had initiated a particularly severe eastern rate war, claiming that lower rates to Baltimore and Philadelphia had diverted to those cities much of the east-west traffic and import-export business that would have gone to New York City over the New York Central's tracks. Independent oil producers claimed that Standard Oil had favored the Erie and victimized the Pennsylvania and other railroads.

The legislative compromise in the wording of the Interstate Commerce Act resulted in a vaguely phrased law to be administered at the discretion of the Interstate Commerce Commission (ICC). With the appointment of commissioners identified with railroad interests, the result was largely a regulative failure from the shippers' point of view. Exceptions were allowed for certain forms of pooling. Shippers had to take the initiative of complaining and had to bear the burden of proof. The ICC made it clear that it was chiefly concerned with avoiding unreasonably low rates that would hurt investors and might impair service.

Predictably, railroad rate wars all but ended. Long-haul rates rose, though short-haul rates declined by 15 to 30 percent. On balance, economic welfare was reduced in the eyes of Spann and Erickson, whose study concludes that "on this score, ICC regulation was a fiasco."[11]

During the late 1890s, the Supreme Court made a series of decisions that limited the discretion of the commission and denied it the power to regulate rates. Pooling also was declared a violation of antimonopoly laws. This returned the railroads to a chaotic condition of competitive instability. Thus, between 1898 and 1903 the railroads participated, along with other businesses, in the merger movement, which may be interpreted as another attempt to escape the dangers of rate-cutting. However, railroad consolidations were not complete enough to include all competitors in a region, and the large networks were still plagued with small independents who would cut rates.

During the next few years a series of laws were passed that strengthened the powers of the ICC. Ironically, these laws provided the protection against competitive rate-cutting that the railroads desired, but they were interpreted by the public and by later historians as restrictions imposed on railroads against their will.[12] The Elkins Act, (1903), which was drafted and supported by railroad men, outlawed rebating and in effect restricted secret rate-cutting. In 1906, the Hepburn Act required railroads to publish their rates, gave the ICC power to set and enforce maximum rates, and put the burden of proof on the railroads in appealing to the courts against the commission's decisions.

In 1910, the Mann-Elkins Act gave the commission power to suspend a railroad's new rate until it had been investigated, and the Commission's power to determine exceptions to the prohibition against higher rates for short hauls was restored. The act also eliminiated the right of individual roads to define long- and short-haul distinctions as they chose. While these powers could be used against the railroads, the policy of the ICC continued to be favorable to the railroads; and in 1914 a general rate increase was granted on the principle of allowing a fair return on investment. In 1913 and 1914, the Supreme Court supported the supremacy of federal regulations over state regulations.[13]

---

[11] Spann and Erickson, p. 242; see also MacAvoy, chaps. 5 and 6.

[12] The traditional interpretation by historians resulted from a concentration on the views of farmers, shippers, and politicians as revealed in newspapers, hearings, and legislative debates. What the railroad leaders were saying and writing in their trade journals, however, has been skillfully analyzed by Kolko in a study that was awarded the Transportation History Prize by the Mississippi Valley Historical Association.

[13] See Davis and North, pp. 157–62, for an expanded discussion of the railroad's influence on federal regulation.

The antitrust movement

Federal railroad legislation set the precedent for the regulation of business monopolies generally. In fact, there was a direct political continuity connecting railroad regulation with the antitrust movement. As in the case of the railroads, there was a background of state action. By 1890, 14 states had prohibitions aimed at curbing monopoly and practices in restraint of trade in their constitutions, and 13 had specific laws on the subject. In the presidential campaign of 1888, both parties advocated federal antitrust legislation. When the **Sherman Anti-Trust Act** was introduced, it was passed without hearings and with little debate or amendment.

The initial regulatory effort was feeble. The Sherman Act was sweeping yet vague. It outlawed "every contract, combination in the form of trust, or otherwise, or conspiracy in restraint of trade" and prescribed light fines or punishment for persons violating the law. Enforcement efforts were also limited. Only five cases were filed in court during Benjamin Harrison's administration, seven during Cleveland's second term, and five under McKinley. A glance at the popular press of the time shows that the public viewed itself as oppressed by Big Business, which suggests that either the public was badly misled or the Justice Department reacted to another constituency.

The initial interpretation of the Sherman Act by the Supreme Court was probably a strong stimulus to the merger movement, although this effect was directly opposite to the intention of the law. In 1895, the Court ruled in the **E. C. Knight** case that a merger of several companies into the American Sugar Refining Company, increasing its control from 65 to 98 percent of the Nation's production, did not constitute a violation of the law. Since the Court consistently held in other cases in the late 1890s that agreements between two or more businesses affecting prices or markets were illegal, the obvious message was that agreements were illegal but merger was not. Not until the **Northern Securities** case 1904 did the Court declare that a merger that could destroy competition was illegal.

A huge number of business mergers occurred between 1895 and 1904. Although other forces favorable to mergers were at work during these years, the timing of the first Great Merger Movement suggests that it resulted from the Sherman Act and the **E. C. Knight** case.

The public reacted with alarm to the Great Merger Movement. The **Northern Securities** case was initiated in 1902, and in 1903 Congress passed the Expediting Act giving preference in the courts to railroad and antitrust cases. A federal Department of Commerce and Labor was created with a subsidiary Bureau of Corporations which, purely as a research agency, began investigations of the Standard Oil and American Tobacco companies. President Theodore Roosevelt in the 1904 campaign promised vigorous antitrust prosecution, and 42 antitrust cases were begun during his administration. Fifty-two cases were started under Taft, and 95 under Wilson. Although Wilson's prosecution score was higher than his predecessors' he had less faith in "trust-busting" as a way of dealing with "bad" business combinations than Taft or Roosevelt. Rather, he looked upon the restoration of competitive markets through strict enforcement of trade regulations by the Federal Trade Commission as a resolution of problems arising from great industrial concentration.

Supreme Court decisions in 1911 ordered the dissolution of both the Standard Oil Company and the American Tobacco Company. The Court, however, based its action on a **rule of reason** whereby combinations might be lawful as long as the restraint on competition was not unreasonable. In these two cases, the Court considered it significant that the past history of the firms showed an intent to monopolize and that they had used predatory practices to this end—namely, discriminatory freight rebates and price wars to drive rivals out of business.

Two decisions at the end of World War I further limited the application of the law against Big Business. In the **United Shoe Machinery Company** case, the mergers were not declared illegal because the component companies had not been direct competitors. In the **United States Steel Corporation** case, it was found that the company did not possess the power of complete monopoly and did not evidence the predatory practices that would indicate an intent to monopolize. The Court held that "the law does not make mere size or . . . the existence of unexerted power an offense."

In 1914, Congress passed the Clayton and Federal Trade Commission acts. The Clayton Act forbade particular business practices that had been observed as crucial to establishing monopolies. However, the Federal Trade Commission learned that these provisions were difficult to enforce. The Clayton Act also excluded union and farm organizations from the legal definition of "restraint of trade." The Federal Trade Commission was created to enforce the Clayton Act, using the Interstate Commerce Commission as its model. It was given powers to investigate, to hold hearings, to issue "cease and desist" orders, and to initiate appeals to federal courts for enforcement.

The post–Civil War experience with business concentration suggests that most cartel arrangements are not viable because any single signatory could gain by shaving prices in secret. This suggests in turn that the emphasis of antitrust laws should be placed upon the prevention of mergers and other arrangements that make it possible to enforce an industry-wide monopoly pricing policy. To a large degree, the actual record shows that these principles were never applied.

On balance, the period's antitrust legislation was neither severe nor very effective. The Sherman Act was unspecific, and the Clayton Act added provisions that were difficult to interpret and enforce. The Court vacillated on mergers. Its "rule of reason" and "mere size" principles seemed to legalize the status quo for any consolidation that had not been achieved by specifically disapproved practices.

Up to 1905, the Sherman Act probably reduced the economic welfare of the pressure groups that sought its passage. After 1905, the record is ambiguous. There was no clear definition of just what a monopoly was and exactly what business practices might be illegal. And from a politically responsive Justice Department there was little inclination toward vigorous prosecution under the antitrust laws. The high points of business mergers and industry manufacturing concentration were reached in 1904. Thereafter, the extent of concentration in manufacturing remained about the same. The antitrust laws may have had some dissuading value, but the growth of the economy and the vigor of competition from other growing firms also restrained the power of individual companies in most industries.

Several broad conclusions are possible with respect to the history of post–Civil War regulation of the economy. Regulation was sought because political groups had been formed to represent the interests of specific minorities which felt cheated by the operation of the economic system. That such groups could be formed and that they felt economically alienated are attributable to the growth of the national economy. Regulatory attempts were not very successful in redistributing income in favor of "oppressed" groups. Railroad regulation made cartelization of the long-haul roads possible, whereas in the absence of a regulatory authority cartels contained the seeds of their own destruction. The antitrust laws provoked an anticompetitive response, the first Great Merger Movement, and where they appear to have been effective they may well have been redundant.

The foregoing analysis is based on the assumption that regulation of private industry is designed to curb the economic power of particular groups in order to favor other groups. The definition of economic power implied thereby is quite narrow, referring as it does to prices, incomes, and production efficiency.

None of the preceding discussion is meant to deny that in a democratic society, the electorate might legitimately choose to constrain economic power—"bigness"—for purely political and social reasons quite apart from any impact the constraints have on specific prices or proximate income flows. In other words, a public may still want legal curbs on the concentration of an industry although it can be demonstrated that prices might be lower with increased concentration. Why? In a contemporary context, because the electorate may feel that giant firms might have too much influence over foreign policy or domestic legislation. Historically, the fact that prior to 1913 the U.S. Senate was closely tied to business interests—run for profit, some said—might have been a far more important explanation for the regulation of business than any projected impact on prices.

PUBLIC ADMINISTRATION AND SERVICES

For government, running its own affairs became increasingly complex and expensive, and the size of government operations gained a larger share of total economic activity because demands for government services were stimulated to a greater degree by economic growth than many private-sector demands. The history of expanding governmental activity after the Civil War is one of learning by doing. With little by way of precedent, government officials had to learn to cope with administrative problems of almost unique complexity and scale, especially in government's urban dimensions. At the same time, the electorate and its representatives had to attempt to fashion a political system capable of fostering bureaucracies that would operate in the public interest instead of for private gain.

Rising government expenditures

As we have seen, government outlays tended to rise largely because of military expenditures which remained higher after each war. Yet in comparison to the growing national output, 19th century government expenditures were quite small and usually declining during peacetime. In 1860, total government expenditures at all levels were around 6 percent of GNP. In 1870, they were nearly 15 percent, but growth in national output had reduced this to about 8 percent by 1890. Thereafter, government outlays about kept pace with the expansion in production. Then, by 1920, after postwar demobilization, the value of government resource allocation came to about 11 percent of gross national product.

Except for the war-related expenditures, neither the largest outlays nor the greatest increases in expenditures were at the federal level. In 1860 and in 1913, before each major war, expenditures at the local levels of government exceeded federal expenditures. On a per capita basis, local governments were spending about $7.27 in 1860 compared outlays of only $2.26 by the federal government and a mere $0.43 at the state level. In 1913, the corresponding amounts were: local, $15.02; federal, $7.01; and state, $3.89. In peacetime, local government expenditures rose especially rapidly right after the Civil War and again around the turn of the century. However, over the whole period, it was the state government expenditures that rose the most rapidly. (See 10–8.)

The military aside, the growth in government expenditure after the Civil War is largely attributable to the growth of local school district expenditures. (See 10–9.) First, education displays a high income elasticity in general. Second, industrialization raised education requirements for the work force. And third, education was recognized as having spillover benefits that brought total returns above those directly received by students, so government provision of a free education was selected as a way to encourage schooling.

10-8.   Per capita government expenditures

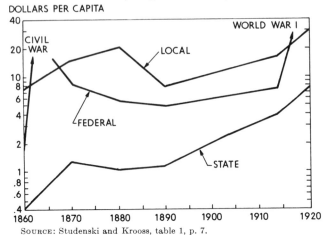

SOURCE: Studenski and Krooss, table 1, p. 7.

State governments contributed materially to the military costs of the Civil War, and after the war they provided large sums for veterans' bonuses and pensions. In the South, reconstruction costs were very heavy. In a great many states, aid to railroads and highway construction were important state-level expenditures in the immediate postwar years. The states incurred heavy debts to finance these rapid increases in outlays.

Perhaps one of the most accurate indexes of urbanization is the growth rate of city budgets—the growth of private economic activity in the cities required large outlays for social overhead capital, outlays for items that rural life didn't require. Between 1866 and 1873, American cities stepped up their expenditures to provide for their burgeoning populations. Rapid urban growth required enlarged waterworks and sewer systems. City streets were paved, first with bricks and after 1870 with asphalt. Bridges were built and gas pipes were laid. Police and fire stations had to be added, and imposing city halls and courthouses were built. Museums, zoos, and parks were created. A great expansion in public education required the construction of schools and colleges. Cities also lent their credit freely to railroads; and New York City started construction of an elevated steam railway.

With the depression of the 1870s, revenues of both states and cities dropped precipitously, so both were forced to sharply curtail their spending. Some states and cities defaulted on their debt payments, and most were hard pressed to keep their payments current.

In the 1880s and 1890s, there were new booms in urban government construction. Along with extensions of waterworks, sewers, and streets, a surge of public utility construction provided gas pipes and electric streetlights. An electric streetcar system was rapidly built in most major cities, and suburban lines were extended beyond the city limits.

By World War I a rising demand for paved highways to accommodate the automobile put pressure on state and county budgets. State governments increased expenditures on highways, education, and public welfare, and both federal and state governments provided aid to lower levels of government for these purposes. (See 10–9.)

10–9. Government expenditures by function
(in millions)

	Federal		State		Local	
	1902	1922	1902	1922	1902	1922
Totals	$572	$3,763	$188	$1,397	$959	$4,567
Defense, foreign, veterans	306	1,300	–	80	–	–
Interest.	29	988	10	45	58	337
Intergovernment	7	118	52	312	–	–
General.	34	126	23	69	118	244
Postal and utility services	126	553	–	–	131	548
Transportation	22	308	4	303	171	991
Education	3	8	17	164	238	1,541
Police, fire, correction	–	14	14	68	90	344
Health, hospitals, welfare.	7	103	42	163	55	214
Resources, parks, recreation	8	79	9	61	29	85
Other.	30	156	17	78	69	242
Insurance trust	–	9	–	54	–	21

SOURCE: U.S. Department of Commerce, pp. 725–30.

In 1902, the most important federal revenue sources were selective sales taxes (commodity excises and customs duties), land sales, and postal charges. The reintroduction of corporate and individual income taxes just before World War I shifted the burden of taxes toward the higher income groups. By 1922, state governments, which had the most diversified sources of taxes, had increased their use of sales taxes and introduced income taxes as well. Local governments continued to rely heavily upon property taxes, although revenues from various local utility services were an important source of increased revenue. Because of the limitations that states usually placed on the types of taxes that could be levied by local governments, a heavy transfer of funds from state to local governments was used to supplement local tax revenues and utility charges. The federal government began to provide more aid to state governments for highway, education, and welfare programs. (See 10–10.)

10–10. Government revenues by source
(in millions)

	Federal		State		Local	
	1902	1922	1902	1922	1902	1922
Totals	$653	$4,261	$192	$1,360	$914	$4,148
Intergovernment	–	–	9	126	56	321
Taxes:						
Property	–	–	82	348	624	2,973
Sales	487	1,152	28	134	–	20
Income	–	1,939	–	101	–	–
Other.	26	281	46	364	80	76
Charges and other						
revenues	140	850	27	181	154	742
Insurance trust	–	40	–	106	–	16

SOURCE: U.S. Department of Commerce, pp. 724, 727–29.

Administrative problems

The increasing scale of expenditures and services created administrative problems within government. Previously, American politics had been encouraged by the simplicity and small scale of government to use a patronage system for filling government jobs. It was assumed that anyone could run for office and that any supporter of an elected candidate could perform the duties required in government jobs. As the size and complexity of government agencies increased, the incompetence and corruption that accompanied this system became less tolerable. In the process of providing for new and growing service demands, the electorate, legislative bodies, and various administrators tried to fashion responsible and responsive agencies at all three levels of government. Although the results didn't yield textbook examples of good government—corruption in high places is still with us—significant reforms were enacted.

Even before the Civil War, the rise in expenditures in large cities had created administrative problems and yielded rich opportunities for politicians to divert funds to their own uses. As cities were acquiring more taxing and borrowing powers from legislatures, reforms were attempted which would give mayors more centralized administrative control. City council members, however, continued to meddle in administration and divide responsibility and spoils. For example, in New York City the city council came to be called "the Forty Thieves."

Boss Tweed's political machine long ruled New York City for its own profit. In 1869–71, when it controlled both the city council and the New York state legislature, it reached the zenith of its power. An investigating committee estimated that a private business could have run the city government for one tenth the cost, and half of the city's debt was said to represent politicians' plunder. In Philadelphia, another corrupt group was entrenched in a city-owned gas company run by trustees appointed by the city council. It employed 15 percent more workers than necessary and neglected repairs and maintenance until service broke down.

Various reform movements were started to curb corruption and wasteful spending in state and local government. Reform charters were adopted in New York City in 1873, in Boston in 1885, and in Baltimore in 1898. Reforms centralized administrative power in the mayor, gave budget-making and fiscal powers to a small financial board, and made the school board independent.

In the depression of the 1870s many local governments defaulted on their debts. State legislatures reacted by curtailing the "home rule" powers of local governments, severely limiting their authority to tax, borrow, and spend. An unfortunate side effect of restrictions on local government prerogatives was that municipal and county governments lost much of their ability to respond to growth in demand.

At the state level, a direct attack on the patronage system was launched. State constitutions were wholly revised or heavily amended to create numerous appointed commissions whose members' terms were staggered so that no one governor controlled the commissions. As it turned out, the commissions were a step in the wrong direction—on a day-to-day basis they were responsible to no one. What's more, when they were given regulatory or revenue powers, the opportunities for graft and corruption and general civic mischief were great and the chances of getting caught slim.

In spite of previous experience with governmental corruption and mismanagement and in spite of the ability of private firms to perform the desired functions, municipally owned public utility services became more prevalent. In 1900, virtually all city sewer systems and about half of the city waterworks were publicly owned. The gasworks and the street railways were almost all private enterprises, but the electric light companies, which started later, were affected by the trend to municipal ownership and were about 15 percent publicly owned.

Part of the reason for the popularity of government ownership of the "natural" monopolies is to be found in the disappointing experience with regulatory commissions. They had to deal with complicated and detailed matters for which their staff support was inadequate. Emphasis upon reports, publicity, and complaint procedures did little good if the public was not actively interested. The men appointed to the commissions tended to be drawn from the ranks of those being regulated or were susceptible to their influence.

In the 1880s, a reform movement was launched in the federal government. After the Civil War, Congress had wielded a great deal of power over the executive offices; and the legislators had been able to maintain their political organizations in their own states by appointing many workers to jobs in customhouses, post offices, and various bureaus. Special legislation was passed to provide patronage and pensions as well as special business privileges. Corruption was revealed in Grant's administration, and scandal touched various members of Congress. So demand began to grow for reform in the federal government. In 1883, Congress passed the Pendleton Act setting up a Civil Service Commission and providing for competitive examinations as a basis for filling certain classified jobs. The merit system was designed to strike at the heart of patronage corruption.

President Cleveland tried to further improve the federal administration. The Navy and Interior departments were reorganized. Greater independence from congressional interference was asserted by the president in making appointments. Studies of the Treasury resulted in some improvements in fiscal procedures. But for many years the division of responsibility for appointments among many committees of Congress prevented any unified budget decisions. President Roosevelt made efforts to have the organization and methods of the federal government studied and improved; but no centralized budget-making procedures or powers were developed.

The federal government tried to copy business organization in operating some agencies that sold services, but there was little uniformity in the way they were organized or administratively supervised. The postal service was operated as a separate entity, and only its operating deficits or surpluses were counted in the budget. The Panama Canal, the Alaska Railroad, the Reclamation Service, and Inland Waterways were operated as subsidiaries of major departments; but their expenses were listed as a part of departmental appropriations, while their receipts were shown as miscellaneous receipts of the Treasury.

In general, reform stressed honesty and equated businesslike operations with the notion of minimizing the cost of whatever tasks were assigned; and each administrative and legislative reform was naively viewed as a panacea. No machinery or procedures were set up to force a rational, explicit approach to the questions of what functions government ought to perform, at what level they should be performed, and who should pay for them. Planning remained an undeveloped art.

War mobilization

World War I threw a tremendous burden of administration on the federal government, an increase in responsibility for which it was badly prepared. The rapid establishment of a selective service system enabled large numbers of men to be drafted, but there were delays in training and equipping them for a mechanized, modern war. If it were not for the Allies' provision of transportation, American troops might not have gotten to the battlefields before the war was over. When they got there, they fought with French and British cannon. Logistic support was so poor that American production of ships and arms was just beginning to reach its peak when the armistice was declared.

World War I was the first war in American history for which the entire economy needed to be organized: over 20 percent of the Nation's production needed to be shifted to wartime needs. A War Industries Board was organized purely by administrative directives from the president, and, for the most part, its staff consisted of volunteer workers from industry who received only the nominal pay of one dollar per year. These so-called dollar-a-year men operated in industry sections to allocate scarce materials, set priorities, and fix prices.

A Food Administration was set up to persuade the public to reduce its consumption of scarce foods and to stimulate production. For the latter purpose, the Food Administration established the U.S. Grain Corporation to serve as a centralized purchasing agent on all purchases of grain for the U.S. government, the Allies, and the Red Cross. The Sugar Equalization Board similarly purchased all the U.S. and Cuban sugar crops and sold them to refineries. The U.S. Fuel Administration was established to encourage production, conserve supplies, rationalize distribution, and fix coal and other fuel prices.

A Railroad War Board of railway executives was established to facilitate shipments to the East Coast; but because of a jam of boxcars in eastern freight yards, the president ordered an emergency seizure of the railroads to put them under direct government operation. The jam was broken, but the subsequent efficiency of government operation is a matter of dispute. A Shipping Board was established to build merchant ships, and an Emergency Fleet Corporation was set up as a subsidiary to operate the ships.

A War Labor Board was established by administrative order but with no legal authority, so it was forced to rely on persuasion and public opinion to settle disputes between workers and management. For the emergency period, the union representatives on that board won the right of workers to join unions and not to be discharged for union activity.

All in all, this first great war mobilization effort was a mixed experience. Its mark on history comes from the many precedents it set and the rethinking of government administration it stirred up. The National Defense Act of 1920 authorized peacetime planning for industrial mobilization; and later an Army-Navy Munitions Board and an Army Industrial College were formed to study procedures and train personnel for future war mobilization needs. Reform of government fiscal procedures was also stimulated, and the Budget and Accounting Act of 1921 established both the Bureau of the Budget and the independent General Accounting Office. The rapid establishment of large new federal agencies and independent corporations to undertake emergency tasks was to influence public proposals for governmental action in the Great Depression of the 1930s.

The wartime experience confirmed the American people's distrust of the market system and failure to understand its operation. When it came to a matter of life or death, the public, the Congress, and the administration were unwilling to rely on the price system plus taxes to reallocate inputs in favor of military output. Perhaps this is the most historically significant aspect of our administrative experience during the Great War.

SUMMARY

As we indicated at the end of chapter 9, we will summarize both chapter 9 and chapter 10 at this point.

The transformation of the economy that took place after the Civil War was a gradual process, a continuation of antebellum trends that ultimately left no sectors untouched.

1.   In relative terms, employment and output shifted away from agriculture toward manufacturing and other nonfarm industries. Laborsaving productivity increases in agriculture were responsible for releasing workers for nonfarm employment. Although in the aggregate this transition was effected smoothly, those who left farming often did so under duress and those who remained continued to operate under conditions of great uncertainty associated with fluctuations in demand and growing conditions—hence the agrarian unrest of the period.

2.   The modern industrial method spread from its start in textiles and flour milling to include almost the entire array of manufacturing industries, especially industries which supplied mass consumer markets, such as the markets for shoes and clothing. Initially, in order to survive, manufacturers had to become specialists producing a narrow range of items for a national market as they mechanized their production processes. Later, as the markets for particular products became larger, manufacturing firms added new plants to produce additional but related products.

A national market required a nationwide system for the marketing and physical distribution of products. Wholesalers, full-line mail-order houses, chain stores, department stores, and specialty stores virtually displaced the general store, which was directly supplied by a local manufacturer. Massive promotional advertising was a by-product of the shift to national distribution.

3.   As the national market grew, it became economical to produce a growing number of items in the United States. Thus, although foreign trade expanded as the economy got larger, it grew less rapidly than GNP. As a result, the Nation shifted to an export surplus, which, after

1900, was offset by capital outflows and interest and dividend payments on foreign-held U.S. securities. The Nation's import and export mixes shifted, with manufactures declining in relation to total imports and rising as a proportion of total exports.

In spite of the rapid manufacturing growth that accompanied the low tariffs of the 1840s and 1850s, tariffs were elevated from less than 20 percent in the antebellum period to 47 percent of dutiable imports in the early postbellum period. The relative decline in customs collections after 1900 was chiefly attributable to the shift in the structure of imports away from finished manufactured products in favor of raw materials that bore low duties.

4. The establishment of a national transportation system made possible a more efficient geographic distribution of economic activity based upon regional specialization. Manufacturing activity spread westward, forming a belt that stretched from the East Coast across the Midwest and reached as far as Chicago and St. Louis. The balance of the Nation acted as a supplier of raw materials and foodstuffs for the manufacturing belt.

Per capita incomes in the Nation's regions reflected the changes in economic opportunities associated with the geographic shifts that were underway: the urban-industrial areas and the rapidly expanding western states were the affluent regions, whereas the South had the lowest income per head.

Throughout the period, urbanization outpaced population growth as manufacturing centers blossomed and commercial centers grew in response to the expansion of purchasing power in the hinterlands.

5. Technological changes in manufacturing production and marketing resulted in the operation of larger plants by larger firms which had become multiplant organizations. The growth of manufacturing concentration and of monopoly agreements among producers were the results of scale economies in production and marketing which reduced the number of firms that could operate profitably in particular markets. At the turn of the century, when the Sherman Anti-Trust Act outlawed agreements in restraint of trade but exempted mergers, a wave of business consolidations swept over the economy. In addition to mergers, the rapid growth of the more concentrated industries (manufacturing, railroads, and public utilities) compared with the atomized industries, such as agriculture, explains the overall increase in concentration during the period.

Larger firms required the corporate form of ownership. When the number of owners of the typical corporation became large, stockholders delegated management duties to hired professionals. Eventually, leading figures from the newly established national capital market gained powerful positions on the boards of directors of large operating corporations. The emergence of the large corporation presented a host of personnel problems, many of which were attributable to the impersonal nature of corporate organization and the monotony of assembly-line job assignments.

6. In spite of the Social Darwinism preached by such people as Andrew Carnegie, American governments were forced to respond to pressures for more services, subsidies, and regulation of the private sector.

Urbanization required expanded city budgets. Industrialization and rising per capita income generated new demands for government services. Industrial concentration required offsetting government action to avoid the welfare costs of monopoly. A national economy required a national banking system and a carefully controlled money supply. Geographic expansion required railroads, and railroads were viewed as requiring subsidies.

In responding to the need for more services, subsidies, and regulation, governments were less than spectacularly successful. Graft, corruption, and inept administration grew at least as rapidly as governmental budgets until the close of the 19th century, when various reform movements began to have some effect. Only with the passage of the Federal Reserve Act at the end of the period was the federal government in a position to control the supply of money so as to avoid aggravating the economy's fluctuations, and even then the available powers weren't well understood or manipulated. Although most people predicted otherwise, the western railroads would have been profitable even without subsidies; thus, in one sense, the subsidies were unnecessary. Federal railroad regulation, which pushed state regulation aside, proved to be counterproductive in that ICC policy actually provided the basis for enforcing monopoly agreements among competing roads. And the antitrust movement initially stimulated the growth of industrial concentration.

REFERENCES

L. E. Davis and D. C. North, *Institutional Change and American Economic Growth* (New York: Cambridge University Press, 1971).

R. W. Fogel, *The Union Pacific Railroad: A Case in Premature Enterprise* (Baltimore: John Hopkins University Press, 1960).

M. Friedman, "A Program for Monetary Stability" in *Conference on Savings and Residential Financing, 1962 Proceedings* (Chicago: United States Savings and Loan League, 1962).

M. Friedman and A. J. Schwartz, *A Monetary History of the United States* (Princeton, N.J.: Princeton University Press, 1963).

G. Kolko, *Railroads and Regulation, 1877–1916* (Princeton, N.J.: Princeton University Press, 1965).

P. W. MacAvoy, *The Economic Effects of Regulation* (Cambridge, Mass.: The M.I.T. Press, 1965).

L. S. Mercer, "Land-Grants to American Railroads: Social Cost or Social Benefit?" *BHR*, Summer 1969. *Report of the Industrial Commission,* vol. 19 (Washington, D.C.: U.S. Government Printing Office, 1920).

R. Spann and E. Erickson, "The Economics of Railroading: The Beginning of Cartelization and Regulation," *BJEMS*, Autumn 1970.

P. Studenski and H. E. Krooss, *Financial History of the United States* (New York: McGraw-Hill Book Co., 1965).

U.S. Department of Commerce, *Historical Statistics of the United States* (Washington, D.C.: U.S. Government Printing Office, 1960).

Part IV

Adjusting to rapid change:
1920–1970

11 SCIENCE-BASED GROWTH

Historians have found it useful to apply the term Commercial Revolution to the transformation of a feudal traditional economy into a market economy. The term Industrial Revolution has been applied to the transformation of production methods through the use of machinery and power to mass-produce standardized goods. Perhaps it is most useful to refer to recent decades as the period of the *Scientific Revolution.* The chief characteristic of the contemporary economy and the basis for its continued growth is the extent to which the systematic effort to discover and disseminate new knowledge is changing not only productive activity but also consumption and social patterns.

Technology's transformation of society has produced a sweeping disruption of previous patterns, and such broad social change is seldom smooth and easy; it requires massive adjustments that affect workers, farmers, urban dwellers, governments, and the business community. Thus the rapid growth of the American economy is not entirely a success story. The record is one of problems, solved and unsolved, as well as achievements. The changes that brought growth have introduced strains in social relations. New conditions have required new forms of organization, and attitudes and policies have been slow to adjust to new conditions.

As we all recognize, the periodic wars and continual international hostility among nations that have characterized modern history have introduced stresses and the need for readjustments in our economy. But even without the influence of international competition for political power, the technological changes that have given our growth a new basis would have produced significant adjustment problems. What is more, the limitation of the Scientific Revolution to only that part of the world which we call developed has constituted a basis of international tensions.

The story of recent economic development, therefore, is a story of continuing rapid change with attendant adjustment problems. This chapter begins with a survey of trends which is followed by an analysis of the nature of technological change; it concludes by discussing the shifts in industrial structure that have occurred since the end of World War I. Later chapters take up instability, group and individual insecurity, the problem of increased size of business organizations, and national and international adjustment problems.

TRENDS SINCE WORLD WAR I

The growth rate

By World War I, the United States had become the greatest industrial nation in the world. But could it continue its rapid pace of growth?

This question might have been suggested by the experience of other nations. The growth of the first industrial nation, Great Britain, had slowed in the 19th century. In 1913, the newer industrial nations Germany and Japan were growing at a faster rate than the United States.

During the booming 1920s there were few who doubted that America's capacity for continued rapid progress was unlimited. Then the Great Depression of the 1930s struck. Unemployment was more severe and prolonged than in any prior depression. Recovery was so slow that it was a decade of depression. The blow to American optimism was shattering.

The question then was raised publicly: Has long-term growth leveled off? Must a mature economy stagnate? This question was so heretical that it wasn't uttered before the 1930s. But conditions were different when Alvin Hansen made it the subject of his presidential address before the American Economic Association in 1938. The Great Depression had so shaken public confidence that Hansen's stagnation thesis touched off a public controversy as well as a long academic debate. To Hansen, three main conditions seemed to provide bases for a gloomy outlook.

The first basis for fear of stagnation was the slowdown in the rate of population increase. In the United States and the European industrial nations birthrates were declining while the death rate had leveled off. Therefore, the natural increase in population (births minus deaths) was slowing down in modern societies. In addition, migration to this country had been drastically curtailed by laws passed in 1921 and 1924. Whereas immigration had provided almost half of our population increase in the first decade of this century, it accounted for only one fourth in the 1920s and less than one tenth thereafter. While total population increased 21 percent from 1900 to 1910, it increased 15 percent per decade over the next 20 years and only 7 percent in the 1930s. And over the long sweep of American history, the rate of increase in population had gradually slowed.

The second basis for fear of stagnation was the limitation of natural resources. The continental territory of the United States had been established in 1853, and the westward movement to settle this territory had been completed around the turn of the century. In a sense, natural resources were fixed, and only more intensive utilization was possible. Between 1870 and 1900 land in farms doubled, thereafter the expansion rate dropped. Also, very little virgin timberland outside of national forests remained. The reserves of minerals were still being explored, but much of what was discovered was found at greater depths or in lower grade concentrations. In each of the major extractive industries—agriculture, timber, and minerals—output increased at a slower rate than total national output. By the 1920s, the U.S. economy was well on its way to becoming a net importer in the three major extractive industries.

The third basis for the fear of stagnation was uncertainty about the continued pace of technological change. Previous periods of rapid economic growth had been associated with major technological breakthroughs that had led to rapid investment in new industries. But no such industries appeared to be waiting in the wings in the 1930s. Early in the 19th century, the cotton gin and farm machinery had stimulated rapid expansion of farm exports. Also, innovations in machinery, metals, and steam power had started the industrialization process. In the middle of the 19th century, heavy investment in railroads had stimulated investment spending. Around the turn of the century, capital accumulation in electric power and street railways had taken up where the transcontinental railroads had left off. The auto industry provided a major stimulus to investment and growth just before and after World War I; but expansion in automobile manufacturing had slowed after a few decades of rapid investment.

Stagnation predictions have not been confirmed by the record of the postdepression decades. National economic growth has remained rapid despite the long interruption of the Great Depression. To be sure, some slowdown did occur in the trend of total output along with the slowdown in population increase. The average annual rates of increase of real GNP were 4.3 percent and 3.7 percent during the two 40-year periods 1839–79 and 1879–1919, whereas, the growth rate was about 3.0 percent during 1919–59. Yet, the output slowdown was not as great as the reduction in population growth, so the growth rate of GNP per person was maintained. The average annual rate of increase in GNP per person had been 1.55 percent in 1839–79 and 1.76 percent in 1879–1919, whereas during 1919–70, it was 1.85. (See 11–1 and 11–2.)

Real fluctuations around this trend were magnified by price changes. World War I inflation suddenly raised the level of national output in dollar values, and there was little postwar rollback in prices. During the 1920s the long-term GNP trend was resumed. The Great Depression, however, brought a severe decline in price levels as well as a reduction

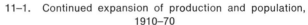

11–1.   Continued expansion of production and population,
1910–70

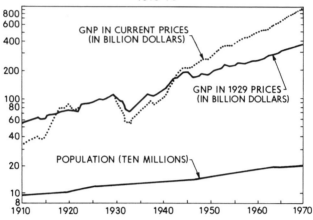

SOURCES: U.S. Department of Commerce (1960), pp. 7, 139; data
after 1954 from *Economic Report of the President.*

11–2.   Rising trend of production per person, 1910–70

in real output. Another period of rapid inflation along with rising output occurred during World War II. Accelerated inflation after the war disguised a setback in real output that was not fully overcome until the Korean War. The continued rapid growth of output with stable prices from 1955 to 1965, however, reestablished the long-term GNP trend with only minor price inflation. But the pattern was again broken when, following tradition, we attempted to fight the Vietnam War without sufficient tax increases.

Sources of growth

What explains this record of continued rapid intensive growth in spite of a slowdown in the rate of expansion? As with earlier periods, we can respond by citing capital accumulation and technological change. Yet this question cannot be answered in exactly the same manner as for previous periods because the end of the frontier limited the rate of expansion of natural resource inputs.

Scarcity of natural resources might be expected to raise the cost of output in terms of the increased labor and capital inputs required to recover more remote natural inputs. Nevertheless, rising output per worker might still be maintained if capital inputs were increased faster than labor and/or technological change raised productivity. In fact, the proportions of factor inputs did shift, and output gains continued to be rapid in the face of a slowdown in all inputs. Let's look at the input record.

While the growth of natural resource inputs slowed the most, there is little indication that scarcity was a seriously limiting factor. Instead of the costs of labor and capital rising, the extractive industries (agriculture, timber, and mineral products) generally had faster productivity gains than did all other industries. In addition, since the income elasticity of natural resource demand is low, people did not consume more raw materials as income and consumption levels rose. Instead, they demanded an increase in commodity processing (both farm and industrial) and more services. As a result, with the exception of fuel inputs, the extractive industries experienced a decline in their portion of total employment. (See 11–3.)

11–3. Resource trends, 1920–54

	1920	1954
Prices relative to all wholesale prices (index, 1947–49 = 100):		
All extractive industries	83	90
Agriculture	78	82
Timber products	62	104
Minerals	105	107
Output as percent of GNP (1954 prices):		
All extractive industries	21	12
Agriculture	14	8
Timber products	2	0.69
Minerals	4.9	3.3
Employment as percent of total employment:		
All extractive industries	28.5	11.8
Agriculture	25.2	10.1
Timber products	0.4	0.3*
Minerals	2.7	1.2

* Data for 1950.
SOURCE: Fisher and Boorstein, p. 43.

At the same time, labor input growth slowed in several ways. The restriction of immigration beginning in the 1920s limited the proportion of young adults entering the labor force. While the median age of the population continued to rise (from 25 in 1920 to 30 in 1960), this was not due to a *decrease* in the proportion of children but to an *increase* in the proportion of persons over 65. (Since 1960 this trend has been reversed, and the median age is now 28.) The total labor force, therefore, increased at a slightly less rapid rate than did population after 1920, and no longer were gains in output per capita aided by a greater proportion of the population being in the labor force. At the same time, average hours worked continued to fall so that total man-hours worked did not increase as rapidly as the labor force. (The resulting increase in leisure time, of course, was one of the intangible benefits of progress that are not recorded in the measure of increased output.)

Offsetting these trends retarding the increase in labor input was the continued shift in the distribution of workers toward the more productive industries and skills. This increased effectiveness of man-hours is crudely reflected in the labor input measure by means of weighting man-hours by the average annual earnings in each industry. The resulting measure of total labor inputs shows a somewhat larger increase than the increase in man-hours but a smaller increase than the increase in population; so, labor input did not contribute to the gains in output per capita in this period. (See 11–4.)

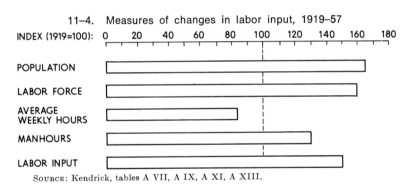

11–4.   Measures of changes in labor input, 1919–57

SOURCE: Kendrick, tables A VII, A IX, A XI, A XIII.

Net capital accumulation also slowed down. Gross capital formation continued at about the same proportion of gross national product—it accounted for about 20 percent of GNP in both the 1946–55 and the 1909–18 decades. But because the capital stock grew larger, capital consumption absorbed a rising proportion of GNP—15 percent as compared with the earlier 11 percent. As a result, net capital formation slowed—from 10 percent to 5 percent of gross national product. Further, during the depression and war decades net capital formation was severely restricted, so the increase in capital stock over the whole period was greatly retarded.

John Kendrick has devised a measure he calls the *margin for economic progress* which is useful in judging the effect of current resource allocation upon the future growth of the economy. For a given year, Kendrick deducts from GNP the level of production required to: (1) maintain current consumption, (2) hold the stock of capital constant, and (3) provide for national security. The remainder is the "margin over maintenance of population and security." Next, he deducts a provision for capital and consumer output implied by the trend of population growth. The result is the margin for economic progress, which is split between increases in the capital stock and additions to consumption per household.

Kendrick's data in 11–5 show the key role that military commitments have come to play in reducing the margin for economic progress in post-

11–5. The margin for economic progress, 1889–1959

	1889-1918	1948-53	1954-59
GNP	100.0%	100.0%	100.0%
Less: Maintenance of current population	84.2	83.4	84.1
Less: maintenance of national security	1.9	9.2	9.7
Margin over maintenance of population and security	13.9	7.4	6.2
Less: provision for growth of population	6.4	4.5	4.3
Margin for economic progress	7.5	2.9	1.9
Margin for increased consumption	1.4	0.9	1.2
Margin for increased capital	6.1	2.0	0.7

SOURCE: Kendrick, p. 100.

war years. Note that during 1889–1918 national security claimed only 1.9 percent of GNP, whereas in the post–World War II periods 1948–53 and 1954–59 it garnered 9.2 and 9.7 percent of GNP. Consequently, the margin over maintenance of population and security dropped to 7.4 and 6.2 percent, respectively, from 13.9 percent. Even with the smaller claims on GNP by future population resulting from reduced population growth rates, the margin for economic progress dropped to 4.5 and 4.3 percent in the post–World War II periods. Of the margin for progress, expanding capital per person dropped to 2.0 and 0.7 percent from 6.1 percent, while the margin for increased consumption rose toward the 1889–1918 figure. As we remarked earlier, war is a costly form of perdition.

Nevertheless, capital input continued to grow faster than labor input. Between 1919 and 1957, the capital stock of the private domestic economy almost doubled, while labor input increased by little more than a third. The result was continued capital deepening, i.e., persistent growth in the ratio of capital to workers. This meant that workers had more and more assistance in their labors—more machinery, buildings, and inventories to work with. (Further increases in fuel and power per worker also reduced the muscle power required on the job.) A higher ratio of capital to labor again helped raise the productivity of workers and thus contributed to maintaining the intensive growth rate.

However, only a small part of the period's growth can be explained by increased capital per worker. Several economists have independently estimated that only 10 to 15 percent of the growth in output per capita could have resulted from capital deepening alone. This leaves a large unexplained residual which we label productivity increases.[2]

The most outstanding fact about the continued rate of rapid growth in recent decades has been the upturn in the rate of productivity increase as measured by the ratio of output to total inputs. (Note that although the rates we are about to quote vary in a narrow range, they vary by large amounts in relative terms, which for growth rates is very significant.) The annual rate of productivity increase was 1.2 percent over the 1889–1919 period, but during 1919–57 it was 2.1 percent. A similar rise occurred in the productivity ratios for each productive factor taken separately because output increased faster than any major input. The annual rates of increase for the two periods were 1.6 percent and 2.3 percent, respectively, for output per unit of labor and 0.5 percent and 1.3 percent for output per unit of capital. (See 11–6.)

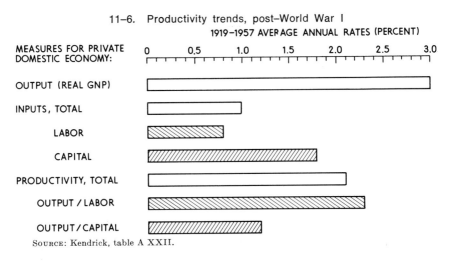

11–6. Productivity trends, post–World War I
1919–1957 AVERAGE ANNUAL RATES (PERCENT)

SOURCE: Kendrick, table A XXII.

What are the components of productivity increases over this period? We can't precisely apportion the total productivity changes among the various responsible factors, but we can identify them. (Later on, we'll present the results of one attempt to put numbers on the various sources of productivity increases.)

Technological innovation certainly ranks high, if not first, among the sources of productivity increases. Mechanization—the substitution of

---

[2] See the introductory chapters in both Denison and Kendrick for extended discussion of the problems of productivity measurements.

a machine for human or animal power in various processes—continued, perhaps accelerated, during this period. The post–World War II period has been dubbed the age of automation. However, many innovations were not embodied in capital through mechanization. Organizational improvements in which machinery was incidental may have taken on a new importance since World War I—improved factory layout and better marketing procedures are good examples.

Innovations in overall economic organization are certainly important sources of productivity increases. The environment in which buying, selling, and producing takes place has been substantially improved by better communications and various institutional changes that reduce risk and increase the speed and accuracy of decision-making.

Qualitative changes in factor inputs are quite important in explaining productivity increases. Rightfully, our estimates of input increases should reflect the higher productivity of each unit of capital and each hour of labor. However, we do not have adequate procedures for distinguishing these sources of productivity from others—when a worker who is more skilled than his counterpart of an earlier generation works with a better machine in a factory which has superior work-flow patterns and is part of an organizationally improved economy, how much of the resulting increase in output per man-hour is attributable to each of these sources of productivity?

Capital investment that does not get recorded as such is an alternative way to cite qualitative increases in the factors of production. Recall that the investment or capital accumulation process is conceptually defined as diverting inputs from production for current consumption in favor of activities that increase future output flows, that boost future GNP. Because of data problems, the rules for assembling the national income accounts limit the definition of capital accumulation to investment in buildings, machinery and equipment, and inventories. This definition misses current outlays for scientific inquiry and human capital formation (formal education and worker training) which bear fruit in later years as better production methods and more productive workers. In the contemporary era, various scraps of evidence show that the growth rate of unrecorded capital accumuulation has increased and, consequently, is a partial explanation for the acceleration of productivity growth.

Income distribution

In view of these shifts in the importance of various sources of productivity growth, how were the rewards of progress distributed? This is a key question for any historical period because income distribution is an emotionally charged issue with great political ramifications. For many, economic growth does not allay fears that progress will be achieved at the expense of workers, that property owners will take a larger share of the pie, and that household incomes will be distributed more unequally.

In spite of the faster rise in capital inputs, labor's share of national income payments increased after 1920. Wage and salary compensation averaged around 60 percent of national income during the 1920s and had increased to 70 percent by 1957. In part, of course, this was due to the decline in self-employment and in the number of proprietors of unincorporated small businesses (mostly in farming). Incomes of proprietors and the self-employed fell from 17 to 12 percent of national income. Incomes in the form of rent, interest, and corporate profit, however, also declined, from 23 percent to 18 percent. After adjusting incomes of the self-employed to reflect the portion that constituted wages, Kendrick estimated that labor's total share of income rose from 72 percent in 1919 to 81 percent in 1957, while capital's share fell from 28 percent to 19 percent.

Because productivity increased generally, real income per unit of input increased for both labor and capital. Kendrick has estimated that real income per unit of capital rose at an annual rate of 0.3 percent. Real earnings per unit of labor, on the other hand, increased at an annual rate of 2.7 percent, which is faster than the increase in labor productivity of 2.3 percent per year. The conclusion Kendrick reached is that labor absorbed nearly all of the increase in total productivity.[3]

Kendrick's findings are confirmed by other attempts to estimate labor productivity and real average hourly earnings, both for manufacturing alone and for the whole nonfarm sector of the private economy. Comparisons of productivity and wage indexes show that real hourly earnings at least kept pace with output per man-hour when measured over long periods of time. (See 11–7.) Again, this does not mean that all individuals

11–7. Nonfarm labor productivity and earnings,
1910–64

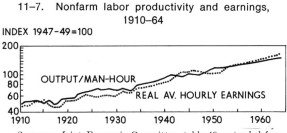

INDEX 1947–49=100

SOURCES: Joint Economic Committee, table 49; extended from
U.S. Department of Commerce (1965), table 317.

shared equally in the gains in real income. Some individuals received very large salaries which are included in the labor earnings; others belonged to labor unions that have won monopoly gains for their members; and relatively few people were owners of the lion's share of the wealth which provides rent, interest, and profit incomes.

---

[3] Kendrick, chap. 5.

Unfortunately, historical data on income distribution among households are poor. Only since the start of the federal income tax in 1914 have statistics on individual incomes been available, and in the early decades of the income tax only the upper income groups had to report incomes for tax purposes.

The top 5 percent of all income recipients received around 25 percent of incomes from 1917 until the late 1920s, but less than 20 percent in the 1960s. The share of the top 5 percent was reduced sharply during World War II, when income tax rates were hiked, and to a lesser degree during the Great Depression of the 30s. Data for the post–World War II period suggest a gentle downtrend in the share claimed by the wealthy. (See 11–8.)

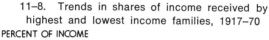

11–8. Trends in shares of income received by highest and lowest income families, 1917–70

PERCENT OF INCOME

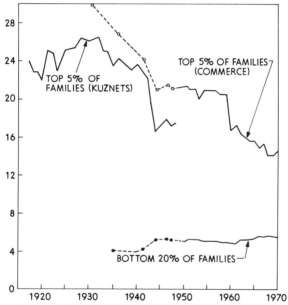

SOURCES: U.S. Department of Commerce (1960), pp. 166–67, (1972), p. 324; Kuznets's data 1917–47; Department of Commerce data 1950 on, with earlier comparable estimates.

The share of the lowest 20 percent of income receivers does not show a definite trend. It was about 4 percent during the 1930s and rose to 5 percent during World War II. But this gain was eroded during the late 1950s and early 1960s, then more than restored in the late 1960s. (See 11–8.)

A more detailed picture of the long-term changes in income distribution can be gained by comparing incomes in 1935–36 and 1962 for each fifth of the families ranked by income after taxes (similar data for 1970 yield the same relationships). Two main facts should be noted from this comparison. First, as the Nation progressed and the average real income of all families rose 98 percent, all groups of income receivers shared in the absolute gains. Second, although the income distribution pattern was far from equalized, it was the lower three fifths of the families that made the greatest percentage gains. The only group increasing less rapidly than the national average was the top income group, and the next highest income group had the next lowest percentage gains.[4] (See 11–9).

11–9. Average real income by income groups, 1935–36 and 1962

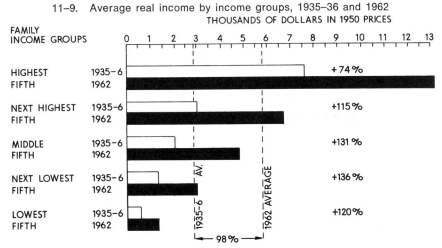

SOURCE: U.S. Department of Commerce (1966), p. 340.

These comparisons are seen even more clearly in terms of shares of total income. Only the highest income group received a smaller share

[4] As a statistical footnote, it may be noted that there is much confusion over the appropriate measures to use when comparing income gains among high- and low-income receivers. This is because the absolute gains are larger for those who start at a higher level. The top group, for example, started with an average income of $7,591 and increased its average to $13,236, a gain of $5,645, while the average of the bottom group increased from $2,937 to $5,824, a gain of only $2,887. Of course, the bottom group ended with two and one-fifth times more than at the start, while the top group ended with only one and three-quarter times more. Yet many people distrust comparisons of percentage gains. It is numerically true that percentage increases from small initial figures can look amazingly large. For example, an increase of 10 from 1 to 11 is a 1,000 percent increase, while the same absolute increase when added to an initial 100 is only a 10 percent increase. On the other hand, it is not reasonable to assume that a gain of 10 pounds in weight is equivalent for a 240-pound wrestler and a 120-pound secretary. While it is true that percentage gains from small initial figures can look unrealistically large, there is nothing misleading about the ranking of comparative increases by percentage measures—that is, a 1,000 percent increase is a larger relative gain than a 10 percent increase, even though the contrast seems extreme. The most

of national income, and it alone had a smaller percentage increase in real income than the national percentage increase. All other income groups not only shared in the absolute gains in real income but also increased their shares of national income. (See 11–10.)

11–10. Percent shares of income by income groups, 1935–36 and 1962

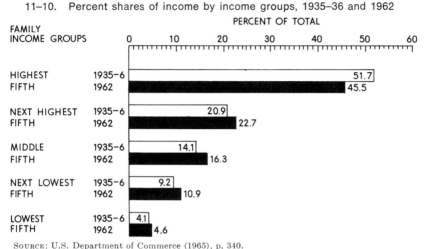

SOURCE: U.S. Department of Commerce (1965), p. 340.

RAPID TECHNOLOGICAL CHANGE

The overall record of increased productivity, which maintained its high pace of growth in spite of a slowdown in all inputs, underscores the importance of technological change in the modern period. A more detailed examination of industries and products reveals two important characteristics of modern technological change. First, it has been widespread throughout the economy. In contrast, previous surges in American growth were spurred by a few major innovations backed up by a host of lesser inventions and innovations. Second, technological change has arisen increasingly from advances in scientific knowledge. We seem to have institutionalized the process of bringing about change on a continuous basis through organized research and widespread education.

Diversity of innovations

We can't stress too much the importance of the scientific basis of modern technological change. Literally most of the 20th century's tech-

---

convincing argument in favor of the validity of the use of percentages to compare gains, however, can be made in terms of shares. Whenever one group has a larger percentage increase than the total percentage increase for all groups, it has necessarily increased its share, or percent, of the total.

nological progress could not have been made by using the trial and error inventive techniques of earlier centuries. Without this century's breakthroughs in chemistry, physics, biology, and botany, the engineering and the various applied sciences that produce technological innovations would have been stopped in their tracks. A few examples should illustrate our point and highlight the diversity of the impact of scientific advances on technological innovation.[5]

1. Advances in polymer chemistry have enabled the synthesis of a vast array of materials—both man-made substitutes for natural resources and wholly new materials have been made possible by modern chemistry.

2. Developments in ferrous metallurgy have made possible the design of a different steel for almost any set of requirements.

3. Quantum mechanics and sophisticated instrumentation have made possible advances in electronics which have revolutionized manufacturing processes and paved the way for a host of new consumer products.

4. Basic research in biology, botany, and biochemistry has produced the scientific age in farming, the age of the feed-seed-breed revolution. Crops can be tailored to local growing conditions, altered to make mechanical harvesting easier, and bred to higher yields. Fertilizers and insecticides have raised yields and cut losses. Livestock have been bred up by scientific design rather than by the casual crossbreeding of the 19th century.

5. The steam turbine and the fractional horsepower motor have increased the application of electrical energy in industry and the household. Nuclear energy may prove itself as a pollution-reducing and coal-conserving power source.

6. Computers, made possible by tying 20th century electronics to 19th century conceptions, have introduced lightning speed to research and record keeping and have made possible elaborate feedback mechanisms for controlling production processes.

7. Medicine is perhaps the example par excellence of the application of basic research results in a host of fields to solve specific problems.

8. The aircraft and airline industries represent a confluence of different lines of scientific inquiry that have made possible the engineering of the modern jet airplane and the jet age in transportation.

The culmination of these science-based innovations has been a fantastic array of new and improved consumer products as well as dramatic improvements in production processes that go well beyond mechanization in their scope.

Modern-day technological innovation has a very special quality because it is the application of basic scientific research, because it stems

---

[5] See Rosenberg, pp. 260–69, for extended discussion of the following examples.

from recent discoveries of fundamental chemical, physical, and biological processes. Thus, any given modern technological innovation has a much greater possibility of adaptation and diffusion than techniques developed pragmatically, with little understanding of their scientific bases. This accounts for the great diversity of technological innovation in the past several generations.

Rather than confront you with a long but incomplete list illustrating the new consumer products attributable to the scientific age, we suggest an alternative line of attack. Buy a Sears, Roebuck catalog of the mid-1920s (it is available in a reprint edition) and obtain a recent Sears catalog from your local catalog sales office. Compare the two, category by category. In case after case, you'll see products that mechanization alone could not have made possible. In case after case, you'll see fibers and other materials that weren't known to man during World War I. What's more, new products will dominate every broad category—household appliances, apparel, furniture, transportation accessories, leisure-time products, hardware, and house construction materials.

The tremendous scope of innovation in consumer goods has had its concomitant effects on industrial structure. Manufacturing industries that were almost nonexistent in 1918 are giants today—petrochemicals, for example. Manufacturing industries that were solidly entrenched then, or so it seemed, have all but vanished—buggy making, for example, has been reduced to a minor leisure-time industry and a supplier to motion-picture producers.

Production processes have been improved across a wider continuum than characterized 19th century innovation. For convenience, draw the line separating the Scientific Age and the Industrial Revolution at the moving assembly line and consider Henry Ford's achievements the innovational climax of the Industrial Revolution. Before Ford, the emphasis of innovation was decidedly but not solely on the mechanization of particular processes. That emphasis has been displaced in two respects.

First, today's new materials rather than mechanization are more likely to be at the heart of a production cost reduction, and chemical engineering rather than the machine-tool industry is more likely to be the source of the reduction. Second, cost reductions are highly likely to result from the diffusion of automation and cybernation. Both of these processes are lineal descendants of mechanization plus the moving assembly line, but they differ in focus. Automation involves the integration of mechanized processes, thus eliminating hand manipulation between machine operations. In its ultimate form, machines designed for specific purposes related to specific products are fed an instruction format and material on which to work; when the operations on one machine are completed, automatic work transfer and positioning devices transfer the material to the next machine. Cybernation uses electronic instruments and computers to monitor an automated process and adjust it when it gets out of control, using feedback systems of the same kind as the thermostatic control on the household furnace.[6]

As production labor was reduced and organizations became larger, the paper work and clerical tasks mounted until they too could be automated. Tape recording and copying devices have reduced secretarial operations. Electric adding and calculating machines, accounting machines, and punched cards made great strides in recording and handling figures but these are being supplanted rapidly by sensitized inks, magnetic tapes, and electronic computers.

Even selling labors are being reduced while convenience to the customer is enhanced. Self-service and the check-out counter are being used more widely in stores. Automatic vending machines provide convenience items whenever and wherever the customer chooses to obtain them. Coin machines collect fares and tolls. Dry cleaning, car washing, and various other labor services are being mechanically provided on a self-service basis.

Science, technology, and productivity increases since World War I

Since World War I, technological change, the addition to man's stock of knowledge about the industrial arts, has resulted from "the organized application of science and technology."[7] The 20th century has become the R&D era, the era in which research and development expenditures by industry and government have played a larger and larger role in determining the pace and configuration of productivity growth.

In the early 1920s, R&D expenditures constituted far less than 1 percent of GNP; in the 1960s they were about 2 percent. (See 11–11.) Private industry performs about two thirds of all R&D activity, while government and university laboratories account for the balance. Government, however, supplies about two thirds of the funds which support military and civilian R&D projects.

The chemical and drug industries set the R&D precedent around World War I, when they established research laboratories and experimental teams. The success of research leaders, such as Bell Laboratories and Du Pont, plus the government-sponsored research of World War II, encouraged the establishment of R&D departments throughout industry.

As we have already noted, research expenditures certainly qualify as capital investments since they involve the current use of resources to expand future productive capacity. Industry apparently shares this

---

[6] Some authors will not distinguish between automation and cybernation and thereby implicitly view mechanization, automation, and cybernation as positions on a laborsaving continuum. Disagreements about definitions in this area arise essentially over whether one wishes to emphasize similarities or differences among processes.

[7] Mansfield (1968, 1st citation), p. 96.

11–11.   Industrial research and development
expenditures, 1920–69

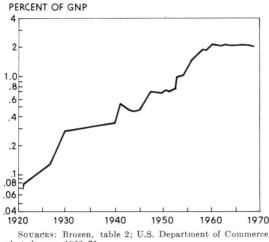

SOURCES: Brozen, table 2; U.S. Department of Commerce selected years, 1966–71.

view in the sense that there seems to be a marked tendency to substitute R&D expenditures for outlays on physical capital.

What R&D connotes is the systematic use of scientific findings to solve production problems and invent new processes or products. R&D often begins with basic research in one or several scientific areas to discover principles useful in inventing a new process or product. After the research phase comes the development stage. Then innovation takes over, and the invention becomes part of productive technology or a widely marketed new product. The diffusion of new techniques is often very slow, and it sometimes takes as much as 20 years before a new idea is adopted by all the major firms in an industry. (Xerography dates back to the 1930s, but its diffusion did not take place until the 1960s.) Involving team research carried on by highly trained scientists and technicians in well-stocked, well-financed laboratories, present-day R&D activities seem about as closely related to the methods of the 19th century tinkerers as to those of the medieval alchemists.

It only slightly exaggerates the case to say that in the 19th century new technologies appeared at random whereas today they can be created as the need arises. The production of new properties and processes on demand is aptly illustrated by the story of the glass company executive who called his research staff together, announced to them that glass was an admirable product—transparent, able to take on many shapes and colors, capable of withstanding erosion—but, he said, as he dropped a pane which shattered when it hit the floor, breakable. He concluded by requesting that they do something about the last property—which they did, to the horror of many burglars and the delight of people who like glass-topped tables.

Don't be misled by the above examples into believing that research activity inevitably leads to invention and innovation. Probable success rates are not fixed with great accuracy when projects are initiated, and quite a few development efforts prove to be flops even where the prerequisite basic knowledge is great. A British chemical firm, for example, tired of buying Teflon from Du Pont, has spent a small fortune trying to invent it on its own with no success as yet. On the other hand, fortunate accidents still account for their share of new discoveries.[8]

As you might guess, the profit margin guides the private sector in planning its R&D expenditures. The higher the amounts firms spend on R&D, the higher are the yields in terms of new inventions. In turn, rates of return on both privately financed and government-sponsored industrial research projects are high compared with alternative uses of funds. Mansfield's studies showed rates of 15 percent or more in such staid and established industries as food, clothing, and furniture. Griliches found that the rate of return to society on hybrid corn research was 700 percent per year in the late 1950s, and Shultz shows that government-financed agricultural research yields about 30 percent per annum.[9] Further, Mansfield's study shows that the successful innovators in various industries grew faster than their competitors.

Apart from agriculture, most R&D expenditure is privately financed or specifically attuned to the space program or military needs. Consequently, projects with high social rates of return but low yields in terms of private payoffs, national prestige, or defense have often been shunted aside. Transportation, housing, and ecology are examples often cited.[10]

In spite of the financial commitments associated with R&D, inventiveness has not become the sole province of the huge firm. "Despite the growth of industrial laboratories, the independent inventor continues to contribute a great deal to technology, particularly in areas where the costs of inventing are low, and time and ingenuity can be substituted for expensive equipment." In fact, according to Mansfield, the big firms may be the font of improvements, whereas "really major inventions" come from outside the R&D departments of large firms. In general, Mansfield's data show that highly concentrated industries are not more fecund than industries composed of more and smaller firms and that the biggest firms in various industries are not the most productive in terms of R&D output.[11]

Education and the scientific age

Although the independent inventor is still alive and well in the Scientific Age, the unlettered tinkerer has become a historical curiosity. A

---

[8] See Nelson for a review of the literature on invention.

[9] Mansfield (1968, 2d citation), chap. 4; Griliches, p. 425; Shultz, chap. 7.

[10] Mansfield (1968, 1st citation), pp. 228–30.

[11] Mansfield (1968, 1st citation), pp. 98, 245.

scientific or engineering education is a requirement for success in industrial research at both the invention and innovation stages. What's more,
those who manage mass production and marketing increasingly require
professional training in engineering and/or business administration. In
short, modern industry requires high levels of education and skills from
both its research personnel and its operations managers.

A similar upgrading of skill requirements has come to characterize
production jobs—the Scientific Age has shifted the emphasis from brawn
to brain. In automated plants, machinery and material-handling equipment now do the muscle work, and the routine decisions are made
by control instruments. Increasingly, the worker is limited to making
the more complex decisions, to planning, and to repairing the machines
and equipment.

The shift to higher skill demands can be seen in the distribution
of the labor force by occupation. Between 1920 and 1970, the total
labor force expanded about 90 percent. The number of farmers and
farm laborers declined absolutely, as did the number of nonfarm manual
laborers. Over the five decades, however, managers, clerical workers,
and service workers more than tripled, while professional and technical
workers increased almost fivefold! (See 11–12.)

11–12.   Distribution of occupations, 1920 and 1970
(in thousands)

	1920	*1970*
White-collar workers		
Professional and technical	2,283	11,140
Managers and proprietors	2,803	8,289
Clerical.	3,385	13,714
Sales	2,058	4,854
Manual and service workers		
Craftsmen and foremen	5,482	10,158
Operatives	6,587	13,909
Laborers	4,905	3,724
Service workers	3,312	9,712
Farm workers	11,390	3,126
Total.	42,206	78,627

SOURCES: U.S. Department of Commerce (1960), p. 74; (1973),
p. 230.

Our economy has been able to meet the skill requirements of modern
technology because of the rising supply of better educated workers. As
incomes have risen, Americans have been able to give more financial
support to public school systems, and a greater proportion of young
people has completed high school and gone to college. Not only has
the legal school-leaving age been increased, but students have sacrificed
earnings in the short term to remain in school until high school graduation and to go to college.

Gradually, the work force has gained a higher average level of education. This can be seen in the average number of years of schooling that each age group in the population had in 1969. Those who were in their late 50s and early 60s, having started working around 1930, had a median of school years completed of only 10.5. Those in their late 20s had a median of 12.6 years. The other age groups ranked successively between these two. (See 11–13.)

11–13.   The rising level of education
by age groups

Age groups in 1969	Median years of schooling
25–29	12.6
30–34	12.5
35–44	12.3
45–54	12.2
55–64	10.5
65 and over	8.7

Source: U.S. Department of Commerce (1970), p. 111.

Education certainly qualifies as capital accumulation under the conceptual definition we used earlier in this chapter. It requires a large saving flow, that is, a major diversion of resources from the production of consumer and government products to educational ends. That flow is made up of current earnings sacrificed on the part of students, outlays for instructors and equipment, and charges for maintenance of the Nation's educational plant less some allowance for the consumption aspects of education. To give you a rough idea of the magnitude of this commitment—almost an eighth of all government outlays in recent years were for educational purposes (this figure does not include sacrificed earnings or private educational outlays, but it also fails to recognize the current consumption aspect of education).

Various studies have shown that the high initial costs associated with education are justified. During 1968, for example, the average income of men with 12 or more years of education was more than three times as large as that of men with less than 8 years of education. (See 11–14.)

11–14.   Relation of education level to
income, 1968

Years of education completed	Average 1968 income, males over 24
Less than 8	$ 3,981
8	5,476
9 to 11	6,769
12	8,148
13 to 15	9,397
12 or more	12,938

Source: U.S. Department of Commerce (1970), p. 111.

Elaborate studies that account for a variety of factors relevant to education and earning power show that investment in education yields a rate of return about equal to that on investment in physical capital.[12]

SHIFTS IN INDUSTRY STRUCTURE

Although technological changes were widespread throughout the economy, they were not distributed uniformly among the various industries. As a result, widely differing rates of change in productivity among industries have characterized recent economic history. Similarly, output among industries did not increase at the same rate because the new products that won consumer acceptance were not distributed evenly among them. These changes in output and productivity brought considerable shifts in the distribution of employment among industries.

Among the major sectors of the economy, two of the extractive industries—mining and agriculture—had the slowest increases in output. Yet this was not due to any lack of progressiveness in these industries. On the contrary, the annual rate of increase in productivity for mining exceeded the national rate during the 1919–29 and 1929–38 periods. For agriculture, it exceeded the national rate from 1937 to 1953. Since 1953, agriculture has continued to achieve productivity gains exceeding those of manufacturing or the other nonfarm sectors combined. As already noted, a virtual revolution in farming technology has occurred since 1938. Yet, as a result of the slow expansion in sales compared with the expansion in productivity, the labor requirements in both mining and agriculture fell absolutely. Transportation was the only other major sector to experience employment cutbacks.

The fastest increases in output were in manufacturing and the communications and public utilities sectors. Manufacturing had an annual rate of increase in productivity exceeding the national average during the 1919–29 decade. Communications and public utilities had a faster than average productivity growth rate during the first three decades after World War I with some acceleration in its gains to 1948. Since World War II, however, the productivity gains in these sectors have been about average. (See 11–15.)

Within manufacturing, the industry groups that had the slowest gains in output were based on extractive activities and traditional labor skills. These were leather, lumber, textiles, tobacco, food, and apparel. Productivity gains also were relatively modest in most of these industries. Where demand and output grew slower than productivity—in lumber, leather, and textiles—there was an absolute decline in employment.

The fastest gains in output were in chemicals, electrical machinery, transportation equipment, petroleum products, paper, and instruments.

---

[12] See Becker as an example.

11–15. Output and employment changes, by sector, 1919–53

Broad sectors, private economy	1953 indexes (1919 = 100)	
	Output	Employment
Agriculture	138	67
Mining	200	76
Construction	307	256
Manufacturing	399	165
Wholesale-retail trade	294	222
Transportation	278	89
Communications and utilities	734	223
Finance, insurance, real estate	227	259
Service		180

SOURCE: Kendrick, tables A IV, A VII.

These were the industries in which technological changes combined to bring about new materials, new processes, and new products. These also were and are the research-oriented industries. During 1969, for example, the largest industry expenditures on R&D were as follows: aircraft, $5,801 million; electrical equipment, $4,294 million; chemicals, $1,752 million; machinery, $1,746 million; autos and other transportation equipment, $1,647 million; instruments, $664 million; and petroleum products, $572 million.[3] The productivity gains in most of these industries also were so high that the differences in employment gains between these and the slow-growth industries were not dramatic. Employment grew at more than twice the all-manufacturing rate only in electrical machinery. Paper, chemicals, fabricated metals, and machinery expanded employment at about two times the all-manufacturing rate. (See 11–16.)

Essentially, the contemporary economy still reflects the shifts that the output and employment indexes shown in 11–15 summarize. Agriculture, which was ranked just above manufacturing as the largest employer group, now ranks below all but one industry in employment and at the bottom in national income terms (see 11–17). Manufacturing accounts for slightly less than one fourth of the labor force, whereas in 1920 it was a bit greater than one fourth; this reflects both the productivity increases in manufacturing, the general tendency to shift increases in expenditures away from manufacturing and agriculture as income increases, and the increased size of the armed forces.

PROGRESS AND ECONOMIC WELFARE

In spite of great strides, the Scientific Age has not produced the good life for all Americans, let alone the rest of the world's population. Some obstacles have been overcome by affluence, but some old problems have worsened.

[13] U.S. Department of Commerce (1971), p. 511.

11–16. Changes in output and employment of manufacturing industries, 1919–57

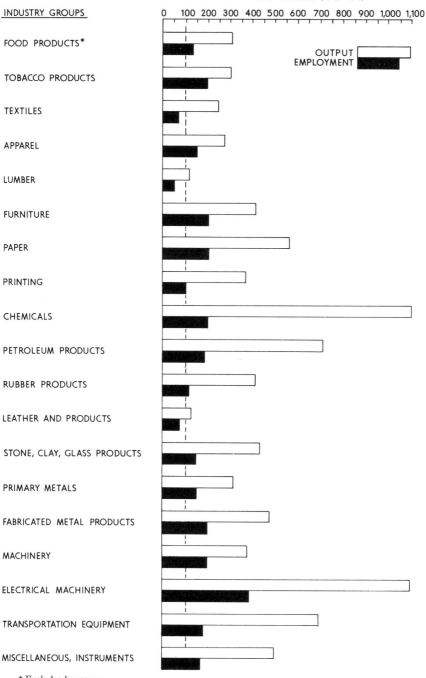

1957 INDEXES (1919=100)

* Excludes beverages.
SOURCE: Kendrick, tables A IV, A VII.

11–17.   National income and labor force, by industry, 1920 and 1970

Industry sectors or groups	1970 national income (billions)	Labor force (thousands) 1920	Labor force (thousands) 1970
Totals.	$800.8	41,610	85,903
Agriculture, forestry, fisheries.	24.6	11,400	3,462
Mining and construction	49.5	3,400	3,969
Manufacturing.	221.0	10,880	19,393
Transportation, communications, utilities	61.3	4,190	4,498
Wholesale and retail trade	121.8	4,060	14,950
Finance, insurance, real estate	88.5	800	3,679
Services	104.4	5,580	11,577
Government	125.2	920	12,597
International sources	4.5	–	–
Other*	–	380	11,878

* Includes military personnel, unemployed, self-employed, family workers, and domestic help not distributed by sector. Except for "other" and agriculture, the number of "employees" is shown by industry sector.

Sources: U.S. Department of Commerce (1960), p. 73; (1972), pp. 225, 314.

In spite of much nostalgic talk to the contrary, our cities are more livable than they were 100 years ago, but we do have menacing urban problems. Progress means more production, but it also means more waste products and environmental pollution. At this point, pollution levels are so great in some locations that we are fast approaching the absorption limits of the local environment. Highly productive giant firms have meant mass-produced affluence, but high industrial concentration and sheer bigness have had negative implications for economic welfare and political democracy.

Labor productivity has increased markedly, but at a heavy cost in worker alienation. Further, the fruits of productivity increases haven't been distributed evenly—a large segment of the labor force still falls within society's definition of the poor, whereas portions of the unionized sector enjoy monopoly incomes. Despite the growth of economic opportunity for most Americans, a great proportion of blacks, Spanish-speaking Americans, and American Indians are still "outside the system," and women point to countless situations in which their productivity exceeds their remuneration.

As productivity has increased our discretionary incomes, we have had difficulty in maintaining what many consider an optimum balance between the public and private sectors of the economy. In the eyes of many observers, we have treated ourselves to private splendor and public paucity. At the same time, federal budgets reflect extremely high military outlays and underscore the impossibility of managing an operation as large as the Defense Department with efficiency given the present state of the administrative arts.

Two products of the Scientific Age, television and the automobile, have added enormously to our comfort and convenience, yet have, in the eyes of many, assaulted us at the same time. The automobile has come around to shaping our life-styles, dominating the way we use space, and distorting resource allocation. Television has become a mind-bending machine and is regarded by many as the tool by which the trivial and luxurious uses of resources gain ascendancy over more meritorious ends, such as public education and redistribution of income in favor of the poor.

Productivity growth, economic progress, and technological change involve structural shifts and stresses within the economy. Industries and skill demands disappear as changes in technology make them unnecessary. Depressed farming and manufacturing areas, low-income regions, chronically unemployed workers, and bankruptcies are unavoidable by-products of change. Long depressions are probably a thing of the past, yet instability is not, especially insofar as inflationary pressures are concerned.

We do not hold the opinion advanced by quite a few economists and other observers of the contemporary scene that a growing GNP is an illusory measure which actually masks a serious deterioration in the quality of life.[14] At a minimum, a growing GNP indicates an increased capacity to do something about our problems. But we do believe, correctly, we think, that the world faces some traditional problems at levels of intensity unknown in the past. The sheer size of the world's population, the interrelatedness that rapid transportation and communication have produced, and the inability to fence in and localize pollutants are to a large degree responsible for this intensity—isolated acts with no side effects are becoming rare phenomena. What's more, in a world in which some nations progress while only aspirations grow in other nations, economic growth itself becomes a source of political instability. In the chapters that conclude this text we will discuss the problems we have just cited in the context of adjusting to economic growth.

SUMMARY

Nobel laureate Simon Kuznets defines economic growth as ". . . a long-term rise in [a nation's] capacity to supply increasingly diverse economic goods to its population, this growing capacity *based on advancing technology* and the *institutional and ideological adjustments* that it demands."[15] [Italics supplied.]

---

[14] For a jaundiced view of "economic progress" see Mishan and the various publications of the Union of Radical Political Economists, especially Hardesty, Clement, and Jencks; a more relaxed view of growth's negative effects is taken by Kuznets, pp. 253–54, 257–58.

[15] Kuznets, p. 247.

Certainly American economic growth since World War I conforms to Kuznet's paradigm. Advancing technology based on the results of systematic, intensive scientific inquiry has become the prime determinant of U.S. productivity increases in the 20th century. In turn, economic growth has produced a host of changes in the fabric of society and generated an equally large number of adjustment problems.

1. In spite of fears of stagnation aroused by the Great Depression, economic growth has proceeded at a long-term annual rate of 1.85 percent since 1920, which represents a slight acceleration compared with the late 19th century. An increased rate of productivity growth plus capital deepening explain the continuation of intensive growth in the modern period. Unfortunately, military commitments have grown at a faster rate than the economy, lowering the portion of GNP gains that can be channeled into capital investment and increased per capita consumption.

2. Economic growth has not come close to equalizing incomes, yet it has raised the entire array of income recipients to higher income levels with some erosion of the share of income that flows to the upper 5 percent of income recipients.

3. The acceleration in productivity growth is largely attributable to technological change. Innovations in production methods and the development of new products have left no industries untouched.

In general, technological breakthroughs have been products of the systematic application of new scientific knowledge, a far cry from the approach of the pragmatic, iconoclastic tinkerers who produced many of the 19th century's major inventions. R&D expenditures now constitute about 2 percent of GNP, which represents a vast increase in such outlays since the 1920s.

The shift to science-based growth has been made possible in part by the large investments in human capital that Americans have made over generations of economic growth. In turn, the highly technical, scientific orientation of contemporary production processes has increased the skill requirements of both managerial employees and production workers.

4. The Nation's industrial structure has undergone a major realignment since 1920. In relative terms, output and employment have shifted away from agriculture and mining in favor of manufacturing and public utilities. In recent years, productivity increases and an increased emphasis on services have eroded manufacturing's share of total employment although per capita manufacturing output has continued to expand.

5. The growth of GNP is an indication of the increased ability of Americans to cope with age-old economic problems, such as poverty. Yet, a larger, more urban population annually consuming vastly greater amounts of output than in the 1920s is not an unmixed blessing. Affluence has produced a greater intensity in a variety of problems that are inevitable elements in any growing industrial economy.

REFERENCES

G. Becker, "Underinvestment in College Education?" *AER*, May 1960.

Y. Brozen, "The Future of Industrial Research," *JB*, October 1961.

E. F. Denison, *The Sources of Economic Growth in the United States and the Alternatives Before Us* (New York: Committee for Economic Development, 1962).

Economic Report of the President (Washington, D.C.: U.S. Government Printing Office, 1972).

J. L. Fisher and E. Boorstein, Study Paper No. 13 in *Employment, Growth, and Price Levels,* Joint Economic Committee, 86th Cong., 1st sess. (Washington, D.C.: U.S. Government Printing Office, 1959).

Z. Griliches, "Research Costs and Social Returns: Hybrid Corn and Related Innovation," *JPE*, October 1958.

J. Hardesty, N. Clement, and C. Jencks, "The Political Economy of Environmental Destruction," *RRPE*, Fall/Winter 1971.

Joint Economic Committee, *Productivity, Prices, and Income: Materials Prepared by Staff*, 85th Cong., 1st sess. (Washington, D.C.: U.S. Government Printing Office, 1957).

J. W. Kendrick, *Productivity Trends in the United States* (Princeton, N.J.: Princeton University Press, 1961).

S. Kuznets, "Modern Economic Growth: Findings and Reflections," *AER*, June 1973.

E. Mansfield, *The Economics of Technical Change* (New York: W. W. Norton & Co., Inc., 1968).

———, *Industrial Research and Technological Innovation* (New York: W. W. Norton & Co., Inc., 1968).

E. J. Mishan, *21 Popular Economic Fallacies* (New York: Praeger Publishers Inc., 1970).

R. E. Nelson, "The Economics of Invention: A Survey of the Literature," *JB*, April 1959.

N. Rosenberg, "Technological Change," in *American Economic Growth*, eds. L. E. Davis et al. (New York: Harper & Row, Publishers, 1972).

T. W. Shultz, *Economic Organization of Agriculture* (New York: McGraw-Hill Book Co., 1953).

U.S. Department of Commerce, *Historical Statistics of the United States* (Washington, D.C.: U.S. Government Printing Office, 1960).

———, *Statistical Abstract of the United States* (Washington, D.C.: U.S. Government Printing Office, 1965–72).

12 GROWTH AND INSTABILITY

The Great Contraction of 1929–33 served as a dramatic reminder that economic life is often highly unstable. In an economy in which growth and change are central themes, variations in total economic activity are part of the fabric of economic life. The pattern that 12–1 shows is typical of the ups and downs of a market-oriented growth economy.

In the underdeveloped economy, growth is measured over centuries rather than decades. Very few major innovations, the prime generators of growth, come along to produce massive shifts in total spending patterns. But the rapidly growing economy is quite different in this respect. When new inventions create new products, better methods of production, or improve access to productive resources, people rush into the affected fields to expand production. When the initial surge of expansion plays out because supply catches up with demand, investment opportunities all but disappear. Because new inventions do not occur continuously, predictably, or controllably, new fields of expansion are not always at hand to replace those that are petering out. As a consequence, the developed economy often responds to its growth stimuli in a staccato fashion. Periods of very rapid expansion (booms) are followed by periods of slowdown or contraction (recessions or depressions). What is more, the growth economy's stability problems are intensified by the same things that devastate other economies—wars, crop failures, and natural disasters.

The relationship of growth and instability does not stop with the destabilizing impact of innovations. The cumulative gains of growth tend to make economies more vulnerable to various shocks. Growth is associated with—indeed, speeded by—the expansion of the market sector. And the higher income levels that growth produces mean that capital goods and durable consumer gods—items which are easily post-

12–1. American business activity since 1790, plotted as deviations from trend

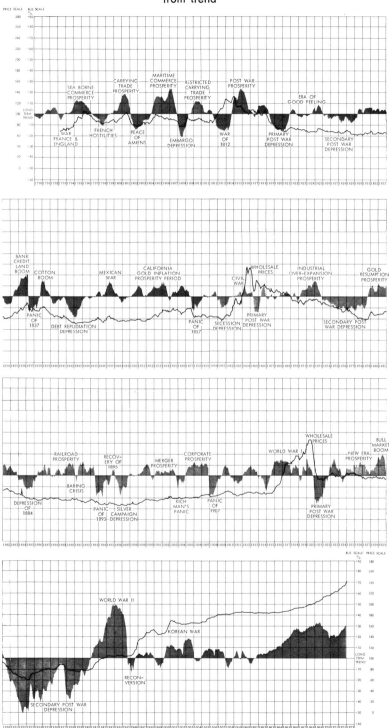

poned in the face of uncertainty about the economic future—take up a large portion of the national budget.

In the late 18th century economy, British depressions spread to the American Colonies. But because the market sector was small and most expenditures were for immediate necessities, the effects were relatively mild and mostly concentrated in the trading centers of the East Coast. The subsistence farmer was all but untouched by market events in those days. However, by the late 19th century, the market sector had grown dominant and people's economic lives had become intricately interwoven. Over the same period, productivity increases had magnified the importance of postponable expenditures. Consequently, the effects of a crisis that struck a major industry were rapidly transmitted throughout the economy, and if no offsetting surge of growth occurred in some other sector the economy would plunge into depression.

Before condemning booms as the harbingers, if not the causes, of busts, we should remember just what the forces are that produce booms. Innovations, jumps in the birthrate, new foreign markets, and waves of immigration create new demands. The fact that supply catches up with demand is not evidence of chronic overproduction or inability to consume what a market-organized society produces. Rather, it is simply evidence of the successful completion of a rush job. Over the years, the booms and busts average out to a growth trend that enables people to attain higher living standards. This suggests that the major policy task with respect to stability is to control booms and countervail depression forces, not, as some have naively argued, to do away with those sources of economic progress which are also sources of instability.

Over the 19th century, Americans had become aware that growing urban industrial economies are at bottom unstable. However, it took the Great Depression to force an explicit and thorough reevaluation of what was then called business cycle theory; people found this reappraisal especially agonizing with respect to the role of government spending and taxing. What has come of this experience? The so-called *New Economics* and the Employment Act of 1946 are major examples. The former is a theory of aggregate income and employment which designates a major role for government in stabilizing the economy. The latter expressly charges the federal government with performing in that role.

In this chapter we will review the business cycle history of the U.S. economy over the period since World War I. Our attention will be focused upon the business cycles themselves, the economic theory that developed as students groped to better understand economic fluctuations, and the governmental institutions and policies that were developed over this 50-year span. At this point, it might be useful for you to review the section in chapter 1 on the national income accounts and the appendix to chapter 8, which discusses business cycles in general.

THE CYCLICAL RECORD

Prosperity decade

The 1920s were generally prosperous years. Employment, income, production, and worker productivity all advanced with a minimum of interruption for business recessions. We had fought "a war to end war" and had entered, in the opinion of many, a period of "normalcy" in which growth and prosperity were considered the normal course of events.

At the end of World War I, the economy quickly returned to a peacetime status, but with a continuation of the high-income and -employment levels that had characterized the wartime period. Government expenditures remained high; in 1919, spending was $13 billion higher than taxes, while building construction, automobile manufacturing, and increased exports filled the gaps left by reduced armament expenditures. In general, after a few hesitant months in 1918, the U.S. experienced boom conditions until the depression of 1921.

The postwar depression set records both for the rapidity of the 1921 contraction and for the abrupt reversal of economic activity and the rapid climb back to prosperity in 1922. Exports were cut almost in half from 1920 to 1921 as Europeans who had increased their own production bought less from us, especially from our farmers. Further, discontinued government loans abroad and curtailed domestic government expenditure pushed the Treasury into a surplus position so that it was reducing rather than adding to purchasing power in the economy. However, by 1922, changes in private domestic spending turned the economy around again, and economic growth was resumed.

The recovery of 1922 initiated a period of expansion that led many scholars and most laymen to conclude that a new era had dawned in which the business cycles of the past would be replaced by a "permanent plain of prosperity." Purchases of new consumer durables, such as refrigerators, radios, and mass-produced automobiles, were made easier through innovations in consumer credit. The new consumer goods plus expanded sales of investment goods more than offset the fall in government expenditures and exports that had precipitated the 1921 contraction.

Signs of indefinite prosperity seemed to be at every corner. By 1929, industrial production had reached an unprecedented height after following an expansion course marked by only a few minor interruptions. Gross national product, expressed in 1963 dollars, rose from slightly over $100 billion per year in 1922 to over $125 billion per year in 1929, while real income per person rose from $938 to $1,041 in the same period.

However, to the worker, the executive, the shopkeeper, the industrialist, and the public servant, the most convincing evidence of prosperity was the stock market boom. By 1927, Dow Jones and Company had become a household term, and the stock prices index that bore its name reached dizzying heights as people from all walks of life poured money into the market. The Dow Jones Industrial Average moved from 153 in January 1927 to 381 in September 1929. In less than two years, speculation in the bull market had more than doubled the price of stocks. We know now with the insight that comes with hindsight that the bull market was covering up signs of trouble in the economy. When the stock market crashed in October 1929, the problems of the economy were not only revealed, they were intensified.

Depression decade

The stock market crash of October 1929 heralded a depression which in fact was already on the stage and was to become the most severe business depression in U.S. history. From August 1929 to the low point of the cycle in March 1933, the economy established new records for contraction. Real net national product, wholesale prices, and the money supply all declined by more than one third. Unemployment rose from 3.2 percent to 25 percent of the labor force. As you can see in 12–2, by 1933 the economy had literally been set back more than a decade—in 1933, real gross national product was about 5 percent less than its 1922 level. By June 1932, the Dow Jones average had toppled from its lofty 1929 height of 381 to 41, barely more than 10 percent of its bull market peak.

Nor did the economy recover rapidly. As 12–1 shows, the Great Depression was the longest on record. In fact, it was so long that, as we noted in chapter 11, people questioned whether we had entered upon an era of stagnation. Not until 1939 and the stimulus provided by the preparations for World War II did GNP surpass its 1929 peak, and not until 1943, well after Pearl Harbor, did unemployment fall below the 3.2 percent rate of 1929.

The data in 12–2 show the huge cost of the Great Depression and the impetus to recovery provided by World War II. Note the dashed line that is extended from the 1929 GNP peak to the GNP level achieved between 1940 and 1941. This line can be thought of as ceiling output under peacetime conditions. It is essentially a hypothetical extension of GNP at its long-term growth rate, using 1929's record output as a starting point. As such, it illustrates what we could have produced each year in the absence of any cyclical downturn. What we actually produced is, of course, shown by the line labeled "Total GNP." Now note that the dashed ceiling line is also extended back in time to the World War I period. Again we can see the contrast between actual GNP and maximum possible output.

12–2.   Real gross national product by expenditures

SOURCE: U.S. Department of Commerce, appendix 3.

Just a quick glance at 12–2 from the late teens to the early forties shows the vast difference in economic performance before and after 1929. In the 1920s, the toll taken by depression was relatively modest in both percentage and absolute terms. In sharp contrast, the lost production of the 1930s was astronomical by either relative or absolute standards. One additional statistical observation may help you to grasp the magnitude of the Great Depression: the production lost through idle capacity was about equal to our share of the cost of World War II, the worst war in history.

These data give some notion of the severity and persistence of the Great Depression. The figures also imply what a tragic period it was in American economic history. Historically, in the developed economy, figures on unemployment and income contraction tell about the same human story as famine statistics tell in the underdeveloped economy. Misery and waste are synonymous with the word depression. What is more, the pervasiveness of the Great Depression can only be appreciated when the viewer realizes that unemployment figures relate to a particular point in time during a year and that the number of people who experience unemployment over the entire course of a year is much larger. For example, in 1933, when unemployment averaged 25 percent of the labor force, over half of the work force had been laid off for some period during the year.

In the paragraphs that follow we are going to attempt answers to four key questions about the Great Depression: Why did it strike? Why was it so deep? Why did it last so long? What brought it to a close?

Expenditure interaction

Perhaps economists will never agree on a precise explanation for the Great Depression—the data for the period are just not good enough—but in a broad sense there is agreement on the kinds of variables that were at work toward the end of the 1920s. To get some insight into the operation of these forces, let's summarize the interrelationship of the various expenditure sectors of the economy.

12–3 is a variation of the description of the national accounts presented

12–3.   National income and product

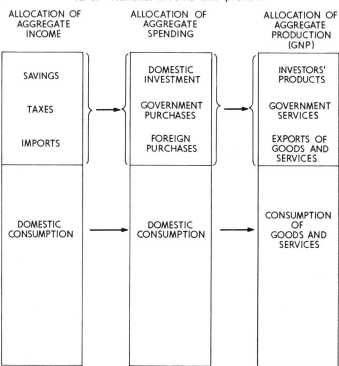

in chapter 1. The first thing to notice is that it reflects the fact that by definition the economy's total income is equal to its total output. Second, notice that the bars summarize the relationship between income, spending, and production. The left-hand bar shows that income not allocated to the consumption of domestic production is either saved, paid in taxes, or used to finance imports. The middle bar shows that the spending offsets to the nonconsumption allocations of income are domestic investment, government purchases, and foreign purchases. The right-hand bar shows the components of total production associated with the division of spending shown in the center bar.

The information summarized in 12–3, plus a general knowledge of the economy, are enough to permit some deductions about the operating relationships of income, spending, production, and employment. First, we can see that spending is the vital link that joins income and production—as long as total income is spent, the entire GNP will be cleared from the market, given that total income equals total output. Second, if the output level reflects production at full employment of available human and material resources, full employment will be maintained as long as total income is spent. Third, it follows that to maintain full employment, if any combination of spending sectors reduces its purchases, some combination of the remaining sectors must compensate by expanding expenditures by a like amount. Otherwise, total sales will decline, production and employment will, therefore, be reduced, and a downturn will ensue.

Further, the initial contraction will breed additional contraction. As furloughed workers reduce their consumption expenditures, sales will fall further, inducing more layoffs and additional cuts in consumption until a full-fledged depression is underway. This cumulative effect of an initial expenditure change is referred to by economists as a *multiplier* reaction: an initial change in investment spending sets off a chain reaction in which income, employment, and total consumption spending change further. The cumulative total change in spending becomes some multiple of the initial change.

Between the boom year of 1929 and the depression year of 1930, GNP fell by about 15 percent, a drop of $19 billion expressed in 1963 prices. Consumer purchases dropped by $9 billion, investment fell $13 billion, while government expenditures rose slightly, and net sales abroad remained about the same. The key question is, What caused investment to decline by almost one fourth and consumption to fall by about 5 percent? The answer to this question lies in the behavior of economic activity at the end of the 1920s.

We have already mentioned two complementary innovations that had an important impact on consumer purchases during the 1920s. New consumer durable goods which were mass-produced and sold at prices the man in the street could afford added a new dimension to the market. And innovations in consumer credit, especially in installment sales, made it possible to sell the new products on terms that made it easy to fit them into the workingman's budget.

However, these innovations had what one might term a single-shot effect upon the trend of consumer expenditures. New products and new financing devices gave a lift to consumption in the early 20s; then, in the late 20s, consumption slowed in its rate of increase as it resumed its long-term growth rate. In short, on the average, consumption grew in the 1920s, but its growth rate was considerably slower late in the decade. This, in turn, was echoed in a magnified way by business outlays for machinery, equipment, and new plant construction.

When a change in total consumption patterns takes place, producers must retool, build new plants, and in general expand purchases of capital equipment. This leads to a sharp rise in investment spending in the total economy. But once the capital demands of the affected consumer goods industries are satisfied, investment spending declines to levels sufficient for replacement and long-term growth. Thus, a 10 percent bulge in consumer spending could cause a 100 percent increase in investment, followed by an equally precipitous decline as consumption resumed its normal growth rate.

Economists call this process an *accelerator* reaction: changes in the rate at which consumption expenditure grows can induce absolute increases or decreases in investment spending. Thus, investment expenditure declined in 1929 because the rate at which consumer purchases grew slowed in the late 1920s as the dramatic effect of introducing new products and financing methods waned.

Investment in residential construction also declined in the last part of the decade. By 1925, the postwar housing boom had reached its peak. Thereafter, new housing starts declined every year. After 1929, the other components of investment that had offset the housing decline gave way to the accelerator effect we outlined above. The result was the cutback in investment and the related multiplier reaction that came at the turn of the decade.

The Great Contraction

By September 1929, the economy had turned around. The downslide that followed is the most often cited example of the multiplier at work. By 1933, the gap between full employment and actual performance had widened to a point at which total production was almost 40 percent less than potential GNP. As a result of the multiple contraction of the economy, 75 percent of the work force were producing only 62 percent of potential output—the inefficiency of depression had pulled real per capita GNP down by 31 percent by 1933.

The traditional explanation of the economy's breakdown, formed during the 1930s, was that the economy had severe structural faults that made the depression inevitable. Monopoly, maldistribution of income, the bull market, and chronic depression on the farm, according to the structuralist view, made history's severest contraction unavoidable. To the structuralists, 1929 was the year in which it all came to a head—the Great Crash set off a multiplier reaction which, given the inherent faults of the economy, had to produce a Great Depression.

However, economists are increasingly coming to believe that a contraction as great as that of 1929–33 was too monumental to assign solely to the multiplier operating in a flawed economic environment. The structural faults of the economy go back to at least the immediate post–Civil War period, yet none of the earlier post–Civil War panics tripped off a Great Contraction. The alternative view is that financial and monetary events as well as errors in fiscal and monetary policy intensified the effect of the multiplier and thus turned a commonplace recession phase of the business cycle into an unprecedentedly sudden and severe reduction in economic activity.[1]

The most important financial and monetary forces which reinforced the 1929 decline and explain why this depression was so deep were:

1. The stock market crash of October 1929, which occurred almost two months after the economy had turned down and was inevitable at some point given existing conditions in the market.
2. Three waves of bank failures, which were attributable to a combination of poor loans and investments and, especially, restrictive monetary policy.
3. Britain's departure from the gold standard, which promoted the expectation that the U.S. would follow suit and caused foreign holders of U.S. securities and bank accounts to cash them in for gold.
4. Restrictive monetary and fiscal policy, which intensified the ills of the business community.

Just why the market crashed when it did we do not know, but it is obvious that it had to collapse. Prices had been pumped up almost solely on the expectation that it did not matter at what price you bought because the Bull Market would pull your stock up and you could always sell at a profit. Stock prices grew to magnitudes that bore no realistic relationship to the factors which are usually crucial to a buyer's decisions—current and prospective dividends and profits, value of physical plant and equipment, and the quality of company management. The source of profit to the share buyer became the next owner of the stock rather than the company.

No market can persist by feeding on itself in this way. At some point, a wave of "profit taking" (selling out to cash in accrued appreciation) will depress prices enough so that a wave of scare selling will start a snowball effect. In 1929, securities buyers financed their purchases with loans for which their stock was collateral. When the market broke, the banks wanted their cash back, so people had to sell.

The crash exacerbated an already bad situation in a number of ways. Low stock prices meant that business firms now had to issue more shares

---

[1] See Friedman and Schwartz for a discussion of the role of the Federal Reserve System in this period; see Galbraith (1955), Soule, chap. 15, and Burck and Silberman for the "structuralist" statement of causes.

or turn to bonds to finance a given amount of additional plant and equipment. This naturally discouraged investment. The crash also ended the willingness of banks to finance stock purchases on what amounted to a low-down-payment plan, so a source of funds to finance plant and equipment dried up. And we should not neglect the psychological impact of the crash—many business managers who were charged with investment decisions were traumatized by their personal losses in the market and retrenched in their business decisions. Unfortunately, we don't know enough about the period to be able to ascertain just how important these factors were individually or in total.

The crash came early in the Great Contraction but was probably not as important as the successive waves of bank failures. The first wave came in October 1930, the second in March 1931, and the third started in the last quarter of 1932 and continued until Franklin Roosevelt declared a nationwide bank holiday on March 6, 1933. In each banking panic, poor business conditions bred fright in depositors. They feared that their banks would soon become insolvent, so they all rushed to convert their deposits into currency. Because banks did not (and do not now) keep 100 percent currency reserves against deposits, they had to sell other assets, principally bonds, to get cash for depositors. The more depositors panicked and demanded currency, the more bonds and other assets were sold, and the lower the prices of those securities fell. Soon many banks found that their securities were worth less in the market than the accounts they owed depositors. These banks failed and wiped out many depositors in the process. Further, many nonfinancial business firms and individuals were forced under as a part of the banks' death throes. In their fight for liquidity, banks demanded payment of loans, and when business borrowers couldn't pay they were forced to declare bankruptcy.

Doubtless, each of the banks that failed, and many that did not, had made loans in the late 1920s which were fundamentally unsound even for a boom. But today many economists believe that even if every loan had been sound by very conservative criteria most of the bank failures would have occurred anyway. Why? Primarily because a falling bond market was wiping out the assets of bank after bank in this period. Even a bank without a single commercial loan in default would have found it difficult to pass an examiner's test in those dark days. And why was the bond market falling? It is too easy to say that in bad times the bond market falls—rather, the Federal Reserve System simply failed to purchase bonds in amounts great enough to offset the forces that were pushing bond prices down. The system had the statutory power to take the necessary steps, but lacked either the will or the understanding to do so.[2]

---

[2] See Friedman and Schwartz, pp. 111–12; Wicker, p. 195.

What effect did the bank failures and the collapse of the bond market have on the economy? We only have to review the comparable paragraph dealing with the stock market to answer this question. In addition to personal and business bankruptcies, widespread bank failures constrict the flow of credit and alarm both consumers and those who must make capital spending decisions.

When Britain went off the gold standard in September 1931, foreign holders of bank accounts and securities that were payable in dollars cashed in those assets for gold. The run on U.S. gold meant that the basis of the domestic monetary stock declined, which, in turn, restricted the ability of banks to supply money and credit.

Each of the factors cited above operated to cut back spending and reinforce the multiplier in a variety of ways—in sum, they led to a contraction of the money supply, higher interest rates, reduced availability of credit, bankruptcies, and lack of confidence in the economic future. In turn, both investment and consumption were discouraged. While lack of confidence reduced the propensity to spend, high interest rates, credit shortages, and bankruptcies choked off some of the spending that would have taken place in spite of poor expectations.[3] In short, what might have been a mild downturn as a reaction to a change in housing activity and a slackened rate of growth in consumption was turned into the deepest depression in history through policy errors.

Restrictive policies

The U.S. was certainly subject to a paradoxical set of forces in 1929. In the midst of a recession, monetary policy makers produced a reduction rather than an increase in the supply of money and credit—a course of treatment about like prescribing hot baths for a patient in fever.

Just why our monetary policy was so restrictive is still a matter for debate that would justify an entire study in itself. However, students of the period now feel that monetary policy that would have braked the contraction was possible. The decision-makers had adequate knowledge of the operation of the banking system and the relationship of monetary controls to the business cycle. The fact remains that, in spite of their knowledge, those who made Federal Reserve policy preferred to open an economic vein and place the leech of monetary restriction upon it.

Fiscal policy was no better than monetary policy in this period. Herbert Hoover, who had become president at nearly the peak of the boom,

---

[3] There are two schools of thought among economists as to the relative importance of monetary factors compared with expenditure shifts in this and any fluctuation in economic activity; both schools agree, however, that expenditure shifts and restrictive monetary forces were mutually reinforcing in turning the recession of 1929 into the Great Contraction.

was presented with a situation for which there were few precedents. Further, many of his advisers, especially Secretary of the Treasury Andrew Mellon, were unyielding and doctrinaire in their approach to the situation—Hoover named them the "leave-it-alone liquidationists." Mellon saw only one alternative:

> Liquidate labor, liquidate stocks, liquidate the farmers, liquidate real estate. . . . It will purge the rottenness out of the system. . . . People will work harder, live a more moral life. Values will be adjusted, and enterprising people will pick up the wrecks from less competent people.

Hoover and some of his advisers were not so hidebound. Although much vilified for his policies, the president did take a number of steps aimed at ending the contraction and speeding recovery.

At Hoover's urging, a number of antidepression policies were enacted. Despite protests from thousands of economists, the Hawley-Smoot Act raised tariffs to reduce imports and favor American business. The Reconstruction Finance Corporation was formed to make loans to crisis-wracked railroads, financial institutions, and state governments. Other domestic antidepression moves included additional public works projects, expansion of the federal employment service, a variety of alterations in the banking system, Federal Farm Board purchases of wheat and cotton to support their prices, and establishment of the Federal Home Loan Bank to act as the Federal Reserve System of the home mortgage market. Internationally, immigration was restricted, a moratorium on war debt payments was declared, and a world economic conference was organized to work for reciprocal tariff reduction.

Perhaps Hoover's principal antidepression tactic was to attempt to restore confidence in the economy so that the business community would feel secure in resuming precrash levels of activity. To that end he held a series of White House conferences, established various economic commissions, and joined his Cabinet members in making reassuring statements to the public. Above all, the administration attempted to set a good example by balancing the federal budget. Thus, taxes were raised in 1932 and expenditures were reduced in a number of areas.

In sum, Hoover's attempts to end the depression were a contradictory mixture of expansive and restrictive policies. Raising taxes cut private expenditures and fortified the contraction. The hike in tariffs invited reprisals that reduced our sales abroad. On the other hand, other policies were expansionary, but these were too modest to accomplish their overall objective.

Such an assessment of Hoover's fiscal policies is clearly dictated given present-day knowledge of the economy. But, unlike the makers of monetary policy, authors of fiscal policy operated in a virtual knowledge vacuum in those days. Statistics were fragmentary—gross national product was a term known only to a few scholars who were designing a system of national income accounts, and labor force data were so bad that the level of unemployment was a matter for speculation and debate. The quality of business cycle theory was about on a par with that of the available statistical information. Generally, it was felt that the economic laws governing the total economy made for a long-run trend of near-full employment and that cyclical departures from this trend were self-correcting. Consequently, no set of rules of fiscal policy to stabilize the economy had been formulated or tested.

THE NEW DEAL

The third of our questions about the depression is, Why was it so protracted? This question cannot be answered without examining the New Deal in some detail. The Great Depression so permeated the fabric of American life that the New Deal and the Great Depression are bound up inextricably with each other. Our economic woes became the focal point for both domestic and foreign policy. The energies of Roosevelt and his Cabinet were almost solely consumed by attempts to restore prosperity.

New Deal legislation was so extensive a reaction to the depression that it changed markedly the institutional framework of the American economy. These changes created a much modified environment for economic growth and, therefore, provide a second important reason for studying the economics of the New Deal.

Roosevelt's antidepression policies were logical deductions from his conception of the Great Depression. For him, the depression was a result of a collection of economic maladjustments that happened to come along at the same time. Consequently, he amassed a series of programs to deal with the causes and effects of the depression as he saw them. He approached the formulation of policy in a highly pragmatic manner. If one solution did not work, another was tried. Advice from all corners was accepted. Often, particular problems were treated by the consecutive application of mutually exclusive formulas.

The Great Depression was not seen as a truly *national* phenomenon. As with Hoover's advisers, New Dealers failed to recognize that it resulted from the way in which a very large high-income market system operates as a unit. Rather, legislation was enacted to offset what was regarded as the failure of elements within the system—failures of state and local governments, failures of the business community, and failures of particular institutions, such as the banking system. From this experience we learned that the federal government must have a national economic policy dealing with the economy as a whole, rather than relying upon instinct and, as it often happened, uncoordinated and contradictory policies dealing with each of the separate segments of the total economy. As the economist would put it, we needed a *macro*economic policy as well as a refurbishing of our *micro*economic policies. We shall discuss that policy and the theory underlying it in the following section. At this point, our task is to trace the attempts of Roosevelt and his advisers to deal with the depression as they diagnosed it.

Relief

Historians have found it convenient to classify New Deal economic policy under three headings—relief, recovery, and reform. Relief where the tragic effects of the depression were concentrated. Recovery measures designed to restore income and employment. And reform to eliminate the social ills that to FDR and his advisers bred depression. Let us look at some major examples in each classification.

Work relief began in May 1933 with the formation of the Federal Emergency Relief Administration (FERA), which made grants to state and local governments for both direct relief payments and public works projects. A little later the Civil Works Administration (CWA) expanded the scope of FERA projects; then, in 1935, the Works Progress Administration (WPA) was formed to employ a wide array of people from musicians to ditchdiggers in their respective occupations. At its peak the WPA, which lasted until 1942, employed as many as 3.3 million workers, or 6 percent of the labor force.

A second type of relief was furnished to the financial community. A bank holiday was declared by Executive Order on March 6, 1933. The holiday, which was extended by Congress lasted until mid-March. It was designed to end banking failures by giving federal and state banking authorities a chance to examine banks and license the reopening of the sound ones. At the same time, FDR suspended gold redemption and shipments to foreigners in order to end gold hoarding and outward gold flows. When the sound banks reopened, the U.S. was off the gold standard and thus insulated from a principal source of monetary restriction.

There were, of course, many other relief measures—the "First Hundred Days" were punctuated with bills whose titles began with "emergency." Those discussed above were the most significant because they were the most sweeping. They also typified FDR's approach to the economy. We had an employment problem and a money problem, and until the causes of each could be rooted out and dealt with, symptomatic relief had to be obtained.

Recovery

To FDR, recovery required a scatter-gun approach. Consequently, off the White House desk and through the Congress came PWA, AAA,

TVA, and NRA. The Public Works Administration (PWA) was designed to stimulate recovery by employing the Nation's contractors to build dams, highways, and public buildings. The Agricultural Adjustment Administration (AAA) was formed to create scarcity and, thus, raise farm income and prices artificially by restricting the acreage under cultivation. The Tennessee Valley Authority (TVA) established a federal corporation which was charged with the development of the economy of the long-impoverished, highly rural Tennessee River watershed through the construction of multiple-purpose dams and opening the river and its tributaries for navigation.

The National Industrial Recovery Act (NIRA) was passed to make capitalism rational by having labor, capital, and the consumer prepare codes of "fair practice" which would set minimum prices and wages, regulate output, and set maximum hours of work. The idea was to achieve higher prices (then called *reflation*), spread work among more workers, and raise wages. If the vicissitudes for which the market was infamous had brought on the depression, the substitution of planning for the apparent chaos of the market seemed the thing to do.

A second approach to reflation came in our gold policy. In the period after the bank holiday, the price of gold was gradually raised to $35 per ounce. Roosevelt believed that raising the price at which the Treasury bought gold would cause other prices to rise and thus restore prosperity. The gold purchase program was based on the following reasoning: depression is essentially a problem of prices being too low; recovery, therefore, can be achieved through price inflation; since the price of gold and commodity prices are positively correlated, it follows that prosperity can be restored by government purchases of gold at higher prices.

Prices did rise slightly after the price of gold was raised, but the Federal Reserve System had instituted an easy-money policy at about the same time; so the data aren't convincing either way, and by modern standards the theory is woefully inadequate. Perhaps the most telling criticism of New Deal gold policy was contemporary. John Maynard Keynes,[4] the famous British monetary economist, wrote President Roosevelt that "the recent gyrations of the dollar have looked to me . . . like a gold standard on the booze." To Keynes the whole idea smacked of "trying to get fat by buying a larger belt," because he regarded price rises as an effect of expansion, not a cause of recovery.

These were the most significant recovery measures employed by FDR. Taken together, they exemplify the New Deal's analysis of the depression. Bad times emanated from a series of economic disorders in the Nation. Because there were so many simultaneously active sources of distress, the depression was "Great." Each of these sources required a specific remedy—hence the wide variety of recovery programs.

---

[4] Keynes is pronounced to rhyme with rains, not teens.

Reform

FDR was convinced early in the depression that reform was necessary if lasting recovery was to be achieved. He felt that the nation was on the road to "economic oligarchy," with a huge, perhaps overbuilt, industrial plant squeezing out the small businessman and displacing workers with laborsaving machinery. In times past, the western frontier provided a safety valve, but in Roosevelt's view the frontier had been pushed to the sea. Government, he felt, should provide the "maintenance of balance" as a compensation for the closing of the frontier.

Specifically, government's tasks were to assure lifelong economic security for the individual; to establish a monetary and financial system that would not permit the excesses of the precrash days; to provide an environment in which labor could organize and bargain collectively; and to conduct a program which would harness or atomize the power of the economic oligarchs.

The social security system, the maximum standard workweek, the minimum wage law, and unemployment compensation were aimed at providing economic security at a "living wage" and "decent hours" throughout the worker's years in the labor force, then a retirement income until death.

The monetary and financial reform legislation of the New Deal comprises a list too lengthy to enumerate here. However, we can get an idea of the reform philosophy of the New Deal by briefly surveying the general areas in which bills were passed. Legislation was enacted to provide a continuing government oversight of the stock market and investment banking through the Securities and Exchange Commission (SEC) and the Federal Reserve System. The latter was given the power to set the minimum down payment for stock purchases (called the margin requirement). One of the most vulnerable areas of the economy in the 1920s, public utility financing, was given a set of federal procedural and organizational ground rules.

Agricultural credit facilities were reorganized. Federal bank deposit insurance was instituted to avoid a recurrence of the tragedies of 1929–33 in which bank failures wiped out many depositors. The Federal Housing Administration (FHA) was organized to insure lenders in home mortgage contracts, and the amortized mortgage was substituted for the 5- and 10-year "sudden death" mortgages whose terms had not only provided the crisis in hundreds of showboat melodramas but in thousands of real-life situations as well. The Federal Reserve Act was amended several times to centralize control of the system and shift the balance of that control away from the commercial banks and to the presidentially appointed Board of Governors. This shift was especially important with regard to the system's open-market purchases and sales of securities because they control the volume of bank reserves in the country and, therefore, influence the quantity of money in the economy.

Reformation was extended to labor and capital. In Section 7-A of the National Industrial Recovery Act, labor was given the right to organize and bargain collectively. After the NIRA was set aside as unconstitutional, the Wagner Act—"Labor's Magna Charta"—was passed, reestablishing that privilege and setting up the National Labor Relations Board (NLRB) to enforce the act's prohibitions against certain "unfair labor practices" on the part of management. The Norris–La Guardia Act was a major factor in reducing violence in the union movement. It had been passed in the dog days of the Hoover administration, and after 1937, when the Supreme Court held it constitutional, it was effective in eliminating the more flagrant antiorganization tactics of management.

The NIRA suspended the antitrust laws and, in effect, gave business the right to form cartels to control prices and output, industry by industry. But this awesome delegation of power was to be offset by multiparty industry policy-making. Broad management policy was to be forged jointly by representatives of management, labor, and the consumer. In fact, labor and the consumer seldom got to the conference table, so Roosevelt's design to institutionalize a system of economic checks and balances never came to fruition.

Soon after the Supreme Court turned thumbs down on the NIRA, Thurmond Arnold, the Attorney General, launched an attack against the oligarchs whom FDR had renamed the "Economic Royalists" in the 1936 campaign. The "central planners" had failed in their attempts to influence policy in favor of a new NRA, and the "atomizers" had come to the fore. The idea was to splinter economic power so as to protect the system from its own force. A truly vigorous antitrust policy under the Sherman Act was begun in 1937 and was carried over, with occasional lapses, into subsequent administrations.

The foregoing makes clear that FDR's notion of reform did not mean radical social reorganization by which civil servants would replace bankers and businessmen. Rather, the decision-makers of the private economy were to be boxed in by the law so that within its confines their individual profit-maximizing decisions would help maximize national welfare as well. Reform to FDR meant "government acceptance of responsibility to save business, to save the American system of private enterprise and economic democracy."

What of the results of Roosevelt's experiments? Did they shorten or prolong the Great Depression?

The recovery and reform aspects of his programs get good and bad marks. The gold purchases were economic folly, as Keynes pointed out. The Wagner Act and trust-busting probably scared business as much as the earlier NIRA had encouraged it. Centralization of the Federal Reserve System probably enhanced the quality of monetary policy, or, as some would say, lessened its ineptitude. The financial control acts definitely discouraged businessmen if their protests are criteria, but private securities sales did continue to rise even after these acts were passed.

The public works projects, TVA, and AAA all increased aggregate spending. The NIRA's reflation strategy, according to most students of the era, met with little success—what recovery was achieved in the period before it was held unconstitutional has been attributed to other factors.

It appears that one way to summarize the New Deal is to say that its policies were a mixed bag of tricks whose contents appeared to offset one another. In other words, Roosevelt's policy, although more vigorous than that of Hoover, was also contradictory. These observations give us one explanation for the protracted duration of the Great Depression—the net effect of federal antidepression policy under both presidents appears to have been at best neutral, the good offsetting the bad. However, before we settle for this judgment of Hoover and FDR, perhaps we should look at the entire depression period in fiscal and monetary policy terms. Then we can again investigate the reasons for the depression's extreme length.

Recovery policy appraised

In discussing the factors that produced the 1929 contraction, we used 12–3 to depict the relationship between income, spending, production, and resource employment. In that discussion we pointed out that full resource employment can be maintained as long as total spending equals full employment output. We also noted that if any combination of spending sectors reduces its outlays, some other combination must expand purchases by an equal amount if full employment is to be maintained.

Thus, if government spending minus taxes had been increased so as to offset the decline in business and consumer spending that took place during the Great Contraction, income, output, and employment would have been pumped up to ceiling levels again. In short, an expansive fiscal policy—some combination of lower taxes and greater government spending—could have filled the expenditure gap. In the period we are reviewing, this policy would have called for increasing federal budget deficits by increasing federal expenditures and decreasing tax rates. Further, the easier the Federal Reserve System's monetary policy, the lower interest rates would have been and accordingly the higher private investment would have been. In other words an easy-money policy can reduce the size of the job assigned to fiscal policy, and vice versa.

Given the monetary policy of the period, just how big a fiscal policy task this was can be seen by comparing a few figures. We can trace the course of fiscal events between 1929 and 1930 by looking at Department of Commerce estimates of the main components of expenditure expressed in terms of 1958 purchasing power. As the figures cited below show, GNP fell by over $20 billion between 1929 and 1930 (see 12–4). Assuming that all changes in consumption were induced by movements in income, this change in income was generated by the $13.1 billion decline in investment and net exports, which was offset to only a modest degree, $2.3 billion, by a rise in government expenditure.

12–4. Expenditure changes, 1929 to 1930

	Amount, 1929*	Change, 1929 to 1930*
Gross national product.	203.6	−20.1
Consumption	139.6	− 9.2
Investment.	40.4	−13.0 ⎫
Government.	22.0	+ 2.3 ⎬ −10.8
Exports less imports	1.5	− 0.1 ⎭

* In billions of 1958 dollars.

Fiscal policy would have had to raise nonconsumption spending by $10.8 billion to maintain income at its 1929 level—truly a Herculean task when you consider that total government spending in 1929 was only $22 billion. Some combination of increased government outlays plus increases in consumption and other outlays induced by tax reductions would have had to fill a spending gap equal to 50 percent of the 1929 level of government spending.

The actual fiscal policy record was just the opposite of expansive. In 1929, government collected slightly more in taxes than it spent. Thereafter, in every year but two over the entire 1930–39 period, all governments taken together had a more restrictive effect on the economy than they had in 1929. Only in 1931 and 1936 did fiscal policy push the economy toward recovery.[5]

Of course, taxes did decline and government spending did rise on the average from 1929–39, yet taxes fell as a response to falling income rather than rate reductions—in fact, rates were raised—and spending fell by 8 percent from 1931 to 1933. The important point to note here is that the deficits incurred were chiefly the **result** of low incomes that produced low tax *yields* rather than of tax cuts and massive increases in government spending.

We have already seen that monetary contraction was permitted to intensify the business contraction of 1929–33. Thereafter, monetary policy was for the most part easier. However, many assign a significant role to the monetary restraint of 1936 in explaining the recession which, as a glance at 12–1 will show, occurred in 1937.

Thus, when viewed from the standpoint of the spending relationships

[5] Brown (1956).

we have just reviewed, the Hoover and Roosevelt policies failed to effectively combat the Great Depression: tax policy was contractionary while spending was only mildly expansionary; monetary policy was perverse in the early phases and only modestly easy-to-perverse in the later phases.

Any appraisal of the policies of either Hoover or Roosevelt must be made with reference to the fact that each of these men had to make decisions in a political context. Therefore, the area of applicable economic theory as they separately conceived of it was narrowed for each by what was politically acceptable in their respective views. Further, not only did their economic theory differ, but their political environments were markedly unalike—Roosevelt had a mandate to experiment, while Hoover was under pressure to retrench.

As we have seen, Hoover believed that a balanced budget was a prerequisite of recovery, especially in view of the clamor for fiscal prudence. It is almost inconceivable that the same public which pressed Mr. Hoover for balanced budgets—pressed him so hard that Mr. Roosevelt felt he had to promise to maintain them—would have permitted tax cuts and spending increases of sufficient magnitude to restore full employment.

Given the pressure for fiscal orthodoxy, it should come as no surprise that higher tax rates were legislated at all levels of government. The question is, Why was there no grasp in the years of decline of the rather simple elements we are working with here? The answer probably is that what men knew, and knew correctly, blinded them to other knowledge. Deficits did cause, as Hoover and Roosevelt predicted, unrest and lack of confidence and thus adversely affected the economy. Further, since household and business deficits could be ruinous, the people and businessmen believed that the ability to avoid deficits was a criterion of the performance of government. What is more, the accepted economic theory of the day backed up this view. Thus, both presidents failed to see the following: if done on a sufficiently grand scale, taking less from the people in taxes than is paid out as spending and relief can stimulate business sufficiently to offset the adverse psychological effects of a deficit.

At this point, we can again venture a judgment as to why the depression was so prolonged. In 1929, the economy went into one of its many recessions. Complicating factors, including restrictive monetary and fiscal policies, made the downturn more pronounced than it might have been otherwise. During the recovery phase of the cycle, after 1933, fiscal and monetary policies slowed the economy's expansion.

While the economy lingered at far less than full employment, making its plodding recovery, pessimism about the economic future reinforced the system's hesitancy. The birthrate dropped as marriages and children were postponed. The business and financial communities as well as many academicians began to accept the stagnation notion we sketched earlier in the text. For many, this view was verified when the 1937 recession followed the relatively prosperous, although not full-employment, conditions of 1936. In 1938, the economy turned up again, but this recovery was incomplete until defense and war spending provided their tremendous stimuli.

In short, then, policy errors were to a very large degree responsible for the longevity of the Great Depression. Let us now address our fourth question: What restored full employment?

WORLD WAR II "PROSPERITY"

Paradoxically, war, the most wasteful of society's institutions, was responsible for lifting millions of Americans from privation and providing them with employment and economic security. As the German military machine was rebuilt in the late 1930's, then displayed in Czechoslovakia in March 1939, U.S. foreign policy shifted from one of isolation to one of international involvement. Government expenditure expanded accordingly—first, with our efforts to assist Britain, then through our own rearmament. After Pearl Harbor (December 7, 1941), we began a massive reemployment and reallocation of resources into wartime outputs. War production became a forced-draft effort to prepare for offensive warfare while stretching a desperately small stock of military supplies and equipment over months of retreat in the Far Eastern Theater.

Starting as we did from 15 percent unemployment, we were able to more than triple government purchases from 1940 to 1942, while consumption, rather than declining, actually increased by 5 percent. As unemployment and underemployment declined in the face of military demand, a 60 percent increase in total industrial production made possible expansion in both the public and private economies.

However, we soon bumped against the ceiling of our capacity as a revitalized civilian economy added its new demands to the growth in government demand. Consequently, from late 1942 until the end of hostilities in 1945, it was necessary to both expand our total capacity and severely restrict the expansion of civilian production.

Capacity was stretched in a variety of ways. Working hours increased, especially in the direct production of war material. The portion of the population that was in the work force rose, especially among women. And some resources were rechanneled from the production of replacement capital to the production of war-related products. Cutbacks were concentrated in the consumer goods industries whose resources or outputs were vital to the war effort, in state and local government purchases, and in nonwar exports of all kinds. 12–5 graphically portrays this history. Total output (GNP) rose; labor input increased; consumption increased, then declined as new tax laws took hold; and exports and state and

12–5.   U.S. data related to the wartime economy

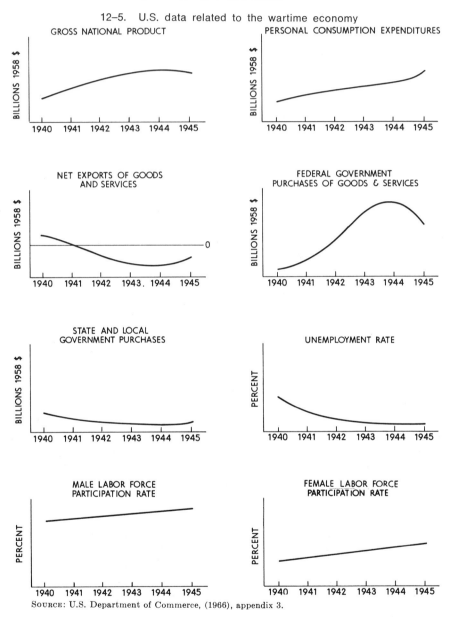

SOURCE: U.S. Department of Commerce, (1966), appendix 3.

local government purchases decreased—all to accommodate a vast expansion in federal purchases. (Note also that these indexes turned around late in the war as federal purchases were reduced.)

Wartime stabilization policy

A reallocation of resources as vast as that required by World War II cannot be accomplished without inflationary pressures. Once full employment is achieved, government must raise the prices it is willing to pay in order to induce suppliers to convert to war production. And war material producers, in turn, must raise the prices they offer workers and other resource suppliers.

The inflationary forces that come with large-scale wars can be dealt with by a system of high taxation and tight money. The price mechanism will automatically respond to a fall in demand for peacetime goods and a rise in demand for war goods and, thus, the necessary reallocation will be achieved. Price increases will be moderate, limited to what is described by economists as *structural inflation.* In turn, the precise magnitude of structural inflation will depend upon the volume of military goods required and the rate at which military spending must displace civilian spending. The larger and the faster the conversion, the greater the inflationary pressure.

In every war situation, there are those who argue for spreading the cost over several generations by long-term Treasury borrowing to finance the war. Note, though that unless a nation can be supplied by foreign powers and pay for those supplies with IOUs, wars must be fought with a nation's currently produced output, requiring current sacrifice of civilian products—there is no way to reach into future generations for guns, tanks, airplanes, and fighting personnel.[6] However, this generalization does not bar a nation from financing a war through debt issue—in other words, the resource requirements of a war effort and the financial arrangements that make it possible to reallocate resources in favor of the war effort are two different considerations.

It is entirely possible to finance government war outlays by selling bonds to the public and using the proceeds to buy materials and meet military payrolls. This means that in future generations taxpayers will bear the cost of debt service to bondholders. To restate the principle, we cannot get around sacrificing current peace goods to supply a war effort by government borrowing, but government borrowing can be used to finance purchases of war goods.[7]

Further, as our review of Civil War finance revealed, government can print money to finance a war. It need only print enough money to bid up prices in the war industries sufficiently to bring about and maintain the necessary reallocation of productive effort. With this statement of operating principles, let us see how we did finance World War II.

As it happened, we did not choose to finance our battles with Germany, Japan, and Italy on a current basis. Taxes were raised; but, as 12–6 shows, although Treasury cash receipts rose very rapidly, the federal

---

[6] Physical and human capital formation are exceptions to this rule: if capital accumulation is reduced, future generations will have fewer resources than in the absence of war and thus will be less productive, but the rate of nonmilitary capital formation is not determined by the way in which the war is financed.

[7] For a review of the debate on this issue and a last word see Mishan.

12–6.   Cash income and outgo of U.S. Treasury

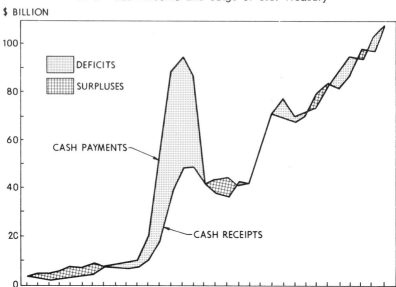

SOURCE: Council of Economic Advisers, p. 269.

deficit grew tremendously during the war. And much of that deficit was, in effect, the result of printing money; the federal government sold large bond issues to the Federal Reserve System which created new money in the form of credits to the government's checking account to pay for the bonds. From 1940 to 1946 the money supply almost tripled.

At this point, it is logical to ask why we chose to utilize all three financing alternatives open to us—taxes, borrowing, and money creation. No satisfactory answer can be given beyond saying that the public will demanded it. Some doubtless thought that the real costs could be spread over several generations through debt issues. Others preferred bonds to tax receipts. And, of course, taxes are unpopular per se.

Regardless of motivations, we ended up with what John Kenneth Galbraith has named the *disequilibrium system,* which, retrospectively, gives a title to the form of muddling through we backed into.[8] Expenditures by government were sufficiently large compared with taxation so that the total of private plus public spending would have far outstripped our ability to produce unless some brake was put on the private economy—instead of rationing private consumption by limiting purchasing

---

[8] See Galbraith's journal account (1947), but bear in mind that he was one of the Office of Price Administration's heads and that the account is not a proof, only a hypothesis.

power through taxation, we preferred to directly ration private sales of consumer goods.

The Office of Price Administration (OPA) was established to place ceiling prices on almost everything in the household budget, and ration coupons and tokens were issued to the people according to need. To buy almost anything, a consumer needed two kinds of money: the usual kind and OPA money. Similarly, workers and materials were allocated by priority classification among producers, with military priorities having the greatest weight. This combination was designed to assure that very scarce vital peacetime goods were allocated equitably rather than according to income distribution patterns.

Public spending was vastly in excess of taxes, and, consequently, private incomes were much higher than peacetime goods available at ceiling prices. Thus, the people had no choice but to save at unprecedented rates by purchasing bonds—$54 billion in bonds, over one fourth the increment in the federal debt, to be exact.

Until price controls, were lifted a few months after the war ended, the system's disequilibrium was contained by the system of price controls and ration coupons. But does this make sense? Or is it pure folly involving a rationing system which is more complex and less efficient than prices and taxes? Several telling points stand in favor of our rather pragmatic solution to World War II financing.

First, work incentives might have been damaged by higher tax rates, with harsh results for the war effort. In some industries people were asked to work 12-hour days and 7-day weeks, and some never took a vacation through the entire war. The question is, Would they have been willing to put forth so much sustained effort if their gross pay had been split, say, 50–50 between tax receipts and cash? Under the disequilibrium system, people found their gross split between cash, tax receipts, and bonds. The bonds, many economists feel, represented future purchases to their holders and kept incentives intact.

Second, bonds were cashed and spent when civilian goods were again plentiful. Thus, in periods of potentially weak demand after the war, the disequilibrium system served to support stability in the postwar economy.

POSTWAR STABILITY

At this point, we might consider how well our economy has done in regard to business fluctuations since World War II. There have been six minor dips—in 1946, 1949, 1954, 1957, 1960, and 1969. From 1961 to 1969, expansion proceeded almost unabated. Throughout the postwar period we have had a general tendency toward mild price inflation punctuated by accelerated price increases right after World War II and during the Korean and Vietnam wars. In the early 1970s, price inflation resumed rates as high as those that came after World War II when price controls were lifted.

Since 1945, consumer prices have increased at an average rate of 3.1 percent per year, but half of the increase is attributable to war. The price index rose from 53.9 to 121.3 over the period 1945–71. Within that period, the immediate post–World War II months, the first years of the Korean War, and the last four years of the Vietnam War—a total of six years—accounted for 34.6 index points of the total 67.4 point gain in the Consumer Price Index. In other words, about half of the inflation since 1945 is attributable to six years in which the economy reflected war-related pressures on prices; excluding those years, the long-term inflation rate was only 2.3 percent per year.

No other period in our history has had such a long span of growth with such mild fluctuations. However, we should note that each cycle has ended with a higher unemployment rate than the previous cycle—or did so until the 1964 tax cut plus the war in Vietnam prolonged the post-1960 recovery and pushed the unemployment rate lower than it had been in 12 years.

Favorable postwar setting

A certain amount of groundwork should precede an evaluation of our post–World War II record. First, we should look at the basic economic setting into which we stepped at the close of the war. Second, we should trace the metamorphosis of business cycle theory as it evolved into a comprehensive theory of aggregate income and employment determination.

As the close of the war approached, many scholars and lay people fully expected a return to depression conditions. This expectation was rooted in Hansen's stagnation thesis, which we discussed in the brief review of the past 50 years in chapter 12. Stagnation, you will recall, was said to result from the general maturity of the economy, especially the decline in the birthrate, the closing of the frontier, and the changing nature of capital. All these factors reduced the productivity of new capital investment. Given the high incomes and therefore the high savings levels associated with maturity, the laissez-faire economy chronically tended to generate higher levels of savings than the low productivity of new capital could justify in the way of investment. Now the question to ask is, Did the postwar economy offer the same threat of stagnation that the 1930s seemed to pose?

After the war, instead of plunging into recession the economy took up the task of doing over the Nation's plant and equipment for peacetime pursuits. The economic effects of the bulge in unemployment that came directly after the end of the fighting were partially checked by the unemployment compensation program inaugurated after 1936. And the short period of high unemployment was attributable only to the time required to convert plants. Consumers had been starved for durables over the lean depression and war years; and they had war bonds ready to cash and finance automobiles, appliances, and house repairs. In 1946, sales of consumer durables continued at high levels as the tax reductions of 1945 took effect.

Prolonged high employment accelerated the birthrate and with it investment in housing, facilitated to a large degree by the insured mortgages of the New Deal's Federal Housing Administration. A backlog of depression-spiked construction projects led to a rapid increase in state and local government spending. Soon after, the war babies descended upon the Nation's school systems and fortified local government demand. Spurred on by low interest rates and easy money, state and local government deficits soon outweighed the combined deficits of the 1930s. And the AAA put a floor under farm incomes when European production shut out a large portion of U.S. farm exports. By 1948, the Cold War generated large increases in the defense budget.

The economy emerged from the war and the New Deal quite a changed system. With all its ills and privations, World War II was for many Americans an exhilarating experience which affected postwar thinking—in spite of stagnation talk, investors and consumers entered the years after 1945 with a freewheeling optimism. The various Hoover and Roosevelt reforms added stability to the economic environment. Expansion was enhanced by the continuing deficits of the state and local governments and by the stimulating, albeit wasteful, effect of military outlays.

Evolution of economic thought

The postwar experience certainly made a poor prediction of Hansen's stagnation thesis. But what of its theoretical basis? Was the theory in error, or did policy produce full employment and growth in an economy that would have stagnated in the absence of governmental intervention? The answer lies between the extremes implied by these alternatives.

Hansen overlooked technological innovation as the kind of stimulant to growth that the frontier had constituted; in fact, he thought technological change would depress investment, whereas the opposite has proved true. Second, although American fertility has declined over the long run, fertility was abnormally low in the 1930s because economic conditions were depressed, not the other way around. Third, Hansen's assumption about savings rates doesn't square with the facts—there is no tendency for growth in per capita income to generate higher savings rates—savings continue to average about 10 percent of income. Thus, Hansen's assumptions, in part, don't match reality.

On the other hand, policy has played a significant role in stabilizing the postwar economy. However, before dealing specifically with the policy record of the past 30 years, we should review the changes in economic thought that provide the basis for both our analysis and the policy tools that have been forged since 1945.

In 1936, John Maynard Keynes, whom we have already cited as a famous monetary economist, published his *General Theory of Employment, Interest and Money*. This book, whose contents are still hotly debated in academia and condemned in some lay circles, has already made as great a mark on economic life as Adam Smith's *Wealth of Nations*. Keynes presented to a stunned and mystified world an explanation for the longest depression in history.

The *General Theory* is more than 300 pages long, and this is not the appropriate place to review it in detail. For our purposes Keynes's message can be summed up by three statements:

1. The mature, Western market economy is basically unstable.

2. In the operation of the total economy, the movement of prices and the forces of supply and demand in individual markets do not collectively constitute an inherent tendency toward full resource employment without inflation—an economy could, in fact, stagnate at less than full employment.

3. In such an economy, fiscal and monetary policy can be designed to achieve relatively full employment and price stability with only mild cyclical swings.

These three statements represent Keynes's contribution to what policy-makers and the popular press refer to today as the New Economics. Actually, the New Economics is more than 30 years old and represents a synthesis in which the monetary theory of the 1920s was blended with extensions of Keynes's work to produce what economists call modern macroeconomic theory—especially in its monetary and fiscal policy applications. Yet people refer to the New Economics as the result of the Keynesian Revolution. To see why this evolution in thought is treated as a revolution, it is necessary to review briefly the predecessor of modern macroeconomic theory.

In the early 1800s, **Say's Law of Markets** was articulated by several economists, including J. B. Say, the theory's namesake. It can be briefly summarized as follows:

1. In the aggregate economy, supply creates its own demand because the production of any one firm gives rise to income which is spent for other producers' output. (Recall the national accounts relationships of income and production.)

2. Depression and inflation are momentary, self-correcting disturbances—international gold movements, plus the ability of prices to fluctuate in individual markets in order to equate supply and demand, guarantee the automatic restoration of prosperity and price stability.

3. Any governmental action to restore stability is at best redundant and at worst destabilizing.

Again we stress that the New Economics evolved over a long period. Thus one should not infer that the theory presented immediately above in its most abstract form was universally held without modification until 1936, when the Keynesian Revolution imposed itself. Rather, the New Economics should be thought of as a revolution in the sense that in one generation economists and policy-makers reversed their position with respect to government's role in determining the level of total spending output and employment. That revolution was sparked by the depth and length of the Great Depression.

As the corpus of modern income and employment theory developed, the law followed, although somewhat reluctantly. The most significant of the legal developments was the Employment Act of 1946, which established the President's Council of Economic Advisers and Joint Committee on the Economic Report and announced this policy:

> The Congress hereby declares that it is the continuing policy and responsibility of the Federal Government to use all practicable means consistent with its needs and obligations and other essential considerations of national policy, with assistance and cooperation of industry, agriculture, labor and State and local governments, to coordinate and utilize all its plans, functions, and resources for the purposes of creating and maintaining, in a manner calculated to foster and promote free competitive enterprise and the general welfare, conditions under which there will be afforded useful employment opportunities, including self-employment, for those able, willing, and seeking to work and *to promote maximum employment, production, and purchasing power.* [Italics supplied.]

The Employment Act is actually a much weakened version of the original proposal, which was more specific in charging particular public officials with definite responsibilities related to maintaining stability. The act as actually passed forced little immediate change in fiscal or monetary policy. It did, though, provide for continuous surveillance of the economy by Congress and the Chief Executive, and, gradually, over the past quarter century, presidents, congresses, Republicans, and Democrats have grown in their willingness to use fiscal policies to combat recession and inflation. Let's look at the fiscal and monetary powers that constitute our stabilization tools.[9]

Fiscal policy tools

Stabilizing changes in federal tax collections and expenditures occur automatically when the economy starts to take a swing toward inflation or depression. These nondiscretionary fiscal policies which result directly from changes in the GNP are usually referred to as the *built-in stabilizers.* Ironically, although they are products of New Deal reforms, they

---

[9] For an account of the legislative history of the Employment Act see Bailey.

were proposed and enacted for their proximate results—equity or economic security for target groups. Since the 1930s, lawmakers have come to recognize their aggregate stabilizing influence.

When GNP and employment fall, income tax receipts fall even faster than income (because of the tax's progressive structure), and government payments for unemployment compensation and relief, and often farm subsidies, automatically rise. Consequently, under current conditions, a fall in GNP of, say, 10 percent might result in a decrease in consumer disposable income of only 5 percent. This, in turn, brakes the contraction of consumption and thus *reduces the multiplier* reaction we discussed earlier.

For example, a $10 billion initial decline in GNP would yield only a $5 billion decrease in disposable income; and, if consumers reduce their spending by 80 cents of each dollar by which their incomes fall, the $10 billion decline of GNP will result in only a $4 billion decline in consumption. It is easy to see how much smaller the *multiplier* would be in such a case as contrasted with a similar situation in which there are no taxes or transfer payments, such as unemployment compensation, to drive a wedge between the decline in GNP and the decline in disposable income: in our example, if capital consumption allowances were, say, $1 billion, then the resulting decline in disposable income would be $9 billion and consumption would fall by $7.2 billion (0.8 × $9 billion). What is more, the stabilizers work in reverse—in this example, a rise of $10 billion in GNP would produce only a $4 billion increase in consumption, not a $7.2 billion rise.

Do the stabilizers do their job well? While they do not fully iron out the business cycle, several careful studies of their effects report that they have been significant in stabilizing the postwar economy. In fact, we have learned that they can produce a *fiscal drag.* In other words, they may do their work too well in periods of postrecession expansion by checking recovery before full employment is reached, and thus some compensatory discretionary policies may be required.[10]

Stabilizing policies which require an act of Congress or an Executive Order are classed as discretionary fiscal policies. We have already seen how tax cuts and/or expenditure increases operate to check recessions and speed recovery. The principle, you will recall, is simply that the full-employment level of savings, taxes, and imports must be fully offset by private investment, exports, and government expenditure. Fiscal policy may bring this about by some combination of lower tax rates, higher expenditures for goods and services, and/or higher payment schedules for programs such as relief and unemployment compensation. Thus, during recessions, federal expansion and/or tax cuts should be the order of the day, and the opposite should be the case during inflation.

---

[10] See Eilbott for the most recent assessment of the net effects of the stabilizers and Heller for a discussion of the fiscal drag.

In any given recession or inflation, the appropriate tax-spending policy mix is an important question. On the one hand, the question is what a nation needs most at the time—more government programs, more private products (tax cuts), or more of both. Only existing conditions and the public will can answer this question. On the other hand, the problem is strategic. Recent experience has suggested that public investment projects—such as the construction of dams and highways—take a long time to get under way, so they are not very flexible in the timing of expenditures. Tax cuts can be voted quickly and take effect immediately; but Congress usually does not act quickly on tax measures. The last is especially true when tax cuts are necessary to compensate for the fiscal drag.

A reversal of antirecession policy is what is required to combat inflation—public and private spending must be reduced to full-employment levels. The problems of implementation are much the same as those of antidepression policy. Public works are hard to stop midway to completion, and tax increases are both slow to get through the Congress and politically unattractive.

The fiscal policy record

How good has our discretionary fiscal policy record been? On the inflation side, relatively good until recently. Recessions? If measured by intentions, performance has been bad; but if we consider the fortuitous tax cuts which were legislated for other reasons in the late 1940s and 1950s, the record has been fairly good. The following paragraph summarizes Professor E. C. Brown's evaluation of discretionary action from the end of World War II to 1960.[11]

Discretionary policy was mixed in its effects and underlying motivations and thus cannot be assigned much credit for the stability of the 15-year period. The tax cuts of 1945 were made too early. In 1948, taxes were cut for "precisely the wrong reasons." In the 1949 recession, policy was mildly expansionary, but fortuitously so, since it was adopted for "other reasons." During the Korean War, we moved decisively and effectively against inflation, but in the recession that followed our withdrawal from Korea, fiscal policy was deflationary. In the 1955–57 inflation, we did nothing to alter our fiscal posture. Finally, the antirecession movements of 1957–58 were modest compared with the task. However, Brown asserts, "This is too harsh a judgment. There was less moving in the wrong direction and more understanding was acquired." However, the judgment stands that in the 1940s and the 1950s the actual fiscal posture of the federal government was more stabilizing than we can assume it would have been in the absence of "wrong" and "other" reasons.

---

[11] See Brown (1960), pp. 185–86.

After 1960, policy improved markedly. Politically, the New Economics had arrived.

To boost the recovery from the 1960–61 recession, depreciation rules for tax purposes were relaxed, and a tax credit based on new investment activity was enacted. Then, in February 1964, corporate and individual taxes were cut. This action marked a watershed, the first tax reduction undertaken *explicitly* to spur a recovery and head off another recession. In February 1966, unemployment at 3.7 percent was lower than it had been since the July 1953 peak of the 1953–58 cycle. This record is to a large degree accounted for by these tax cuts.

When American intervention in Vietnam reached a serious scale, the economy still had slack in it which was attributable to the 1960 downturn. However, that slack was soon exhausted, and military expenditures pushed us into inflation. The rate of price increases almost doubled in 1966, and inflation accelerated thereafter. Taxes were raised in 1968, well after the rate of inflation suggested the restriction of private expenditure. Then, at the end of the decade, while inflation proceeded unabated, unemployment began to rise and industrial production fell in response to a variety of factors, including a reduction in the U.S. effort in Vietnam.[12]

On August 15, 1971, President Nixon, facing the dilemma of 6 percent unemployment accompanied by price inflation at more than 5 percent per annum, declared a 90-day wage-price freeze. In his freeze message, the president asked for and subsequently got a batch of special tax reductions designed to spur employment and production. After the 90-day freeze, inflation was to be checked by a "comprehensive, mandatory system of controls . . . under the direction of citizens on the Price Commission and Pay Board."[13]

The forces that prompted Nixon's action are easy to identify. Inflation had proceeded so long prior to the 1968 tax hike that annual price increases of much more than 2.0 to 2.5 percent were expected by decision-makers. Accordingly, producers, organized labor, job-seekers, moneylenders, in fact, sellers of all kinds, geared their supply prices to hedge an inflation rate in the neighborhood of 6 percent. Of course, the result was price rises at an annual rate of about 6 percent prior to the freeze—inflation had become a self-fulfilling prophecy in spite of slack in the economy.

The logical question to address at this point is, Why wasn't our postwar fiscal policy record better? The answer seems to be that public, congressional, and executive attitudes persisted in the balanced budget orthodoxy of the 1920s. Recall that even after a calamity like the Great Depression, the Employment Act of 1946 was passed as a much

---

[12] See Stein for evaluation of fiscal policy beyond Brown's period of analysis.

[13] See Miller and Williams for an evaluation of these policies.

watered-down version of the original draft; and it had great difficulty getting passed. For many years, a high historical regard for laissez-faire, as a corollary to individualism, and a penchant for drawing invalid analogies between household and public budgets overwhelmed the desire to make the economy more stable.

On the other hand, since the passage of the Employment Act of 1946, administration and congressional leaders of both parties have shown a growing readiness to seek governmental action when a recession occurs. Why is this?

For one thing, people now realize that only the federal government can take responsibility for the behavior of the economic system as a whole. In an individualistic economy, what is nobody's business in particular must be everybody's business in general. For example, when everyone is trying to protect himself by getting hold of cash, only the government can step in and make sure that enough cash is available to restore public confidence. And when state and local or private expenditure flows slacken, only the federal government can assume the responsibility of keeping everyone employed. This need not mean that the national government plans and directs private actions in the economy but that it may need to encourage or restrict total private activity to keep spending at full-employment levels.

In addition, people have a greater appreciation for the fact that idleness of men and plant capacity are both wasteful and a source of great individual suffering. The American people appear determined not to have another depression like the one of the 1930s. The liquidationist notion is no longer either economic or moral orthodoxy. Unfortunately, it is not clear that Americans have shifted their mental gears when contemplating policies to head off inflation—witness the reticence to raise taxes to finance the Vietnam War.

Monetary policy

The monetary weapons at the disposal of the Federal Reserve System (the Fed) have also been revolutionized since 1929. Hoover's and Roosevelt's monetary legislation vastly changed the nature of the financial sector. Prior to reform, the financial system was a destabilizing force, whereas today, given its new structure, it provides an excellent environment for countercyclical policy.

The tools of monetary policy are readily understood. As we said in chapter 10, the Fed was established to control the volume of money and credit in the system by changing the reserve requirements of member banks and altering the interest rate at which it would loan reserves to member banks. Since 1913, the system's power to buy and sell securities in the open market has been significantly expanded, and it is now the most formidable countercyclical monetary tool.

In general, monetary policy stimulates a flagging economy by increasing the availability of reserves to the banking system, and it combats inflation by restricting reserves. Because commercial bank reserve accounts at the Fed are the basis for the money-creating activities of the banks, the expansion or contraction of reserves produces like movements in the money supply.

If unemployment and deflation were the problems of the day, the Federal Reserve System would lower discount rates and buy bonds in the open market. Member banks would then find it cheaper to borrow reserves. And banks in general would discover that the bonds in their portfolios could be sold at a profit since the system's purchases had pushed up their prices. Consequently, banks would be more willing to increase their borrowing of reserves from the Fed, and banks in general would sell bonds in the open market. These moves would increase bank reserves and thus the ability of banks to make loans to customers. What's more, given their increased reserves banks would have an incentive to make more loans at even lower interest rates; so they would lower interest charges and encourage heavier borrowing. The individuals and firms that borrowed additional amounts would increase their expenditures, and the whole multiplier process would go into action. (If the Fed were dealing with an especially deep recession, it might also lower the reserve requirements of member banks, which, of course, would automatically raise their ability to lend.)

Inflation is dealt with in reverse fashion—the discount rate would be raised, and bonds would be sold at lower prices in the open market. Banks would be discouraged from borrowing reserves and would reduce their loan activity in favor of purchasing bonds selling at bargain prices and, therefore, at higher yields than previously. Thus, spending would contract, and inflationary forces would diminish.

Let's review our monetary policy record. During the World War II period to 1951, the Fed was denied its most powerful weapon, open-market policy. It had agreed to sacrifice countercyclical goals in order to stabilize the bond market at very low rates of interest, thus minimizing carrying charges on the war debt. Money was tightened on the average after 1951, with some easing during the 1953–54 recession. Since 1957, the Fed has permitted the monetary stock to grow, but usually less rapidly than the economy as a whole. This policy, which amounts to a tight-money policy, came in the face of the secular rise in unemployment we mentioned earlier in this section. Very recently, the Fed has been more inclined to use its powers to stimulate the economy when appropriate as well as to restrain it.

Most economists will agree that on many occasions fiscal and monetary policy have been at odds, most often with fiscal moves to prod expansion being accompanied by a monetary policy which brakes the economy. In an administrative sense, this can occur because the Federal

Reserve System is now organizationally centralized *but* very much independent of presidential control. From a more fundamental standpoint, the tug-of-war between fiscal and monetary policy arises because the goals of the Employment Act are mutually exclusive at close to full employment.

When an economy is in deep depression, the goals of "maximum employment, production, and purchasing power" are compatible. Deficit government spending plus an easy-money policy can promote higher employment and expanded output with no significant advance in prices. But when the economy is near full employment—say, 4 percent or less of the labor force unemployed—any advance in spending from any quarter will not only increase employment and production but will push prices upward as well. In short, there is a tradeoff relationship between price inflation and the reduction of unemployment when the economy is near full employment.

No economist can dictate the right amount of employment and, correspondingly, the right degree of price inflation—that is a value judgment. But economic policy-makers cannot dodge the issue: they must make a choice. As it happens, Federal Reserve officials who make monetary policy decisions become more exercised over the unwholesome results of inflation than do congressmen and presidents, and vice versa with respect to the ills associated with unemployment. Thus, the chairman of the Fed, on the one hand, and the president and the Joint Economic Committee of the Congress, on the other hand, often find themselves at loggerheads. They both operate in the context of the New Economics, yet advocate almost opposite policies. However, we should not despair that we are as vulnerable as in the 1920s because the policy-makers cannot get together. Rather, it is only on this fuzzy borderline between inflation and unemployment that coordination suffers—and we have the built-in stabilizers.

In sum, why has our postwar record been so stable? Certainly, discretionary monetary and fiscal policy deserve a large part of the credit, even if the right things were often done for the wrong reasons. Second, the postwar years have been Cold War years with huge military expenditures. Third, the stagnation thesis, which suggested chronic instability, was faulty in some of its assumptions. And fourth, the built-in stabilizers have reduced the economy's inherent instability. Thus, a basically more stable economy has been given even more stability by improvements in countercyclical monetary and fiscal policy.

SUMMARY

The Great Contraction and the Great Depression that followed jointly constitute a watershed in American economic history. Together they demonstrated that high-income, industrialized economies which are inherently unstable can be driven deep into depression if policy errors are allowed to compound the effects of an otherwise unspectacular recession. In a positive vein, the lessons learned the hard way in the 1930s showed that judicious national policy could be used to contain and modify the effects of booms and recessions.

1. Why the Great Depression? The worst depression in history started with a general downturn in economic activity in mid-to-late 1929. The 1929 recession seems to have been in no way unusual in its initial severity. It was generated by a decline in the growth rate of consumption and a drop in residential construction, changes which were in no way without precedent. Investment in capital goods tailed off in 1929 as the capital stock of the consumer goods industries reached the levels required to adjust to an earlier spurt in consumer demand. Residential construction fell as the housing stock reached the level required by the current population and per capita income.

Allegations that the Great Depression was generated by unusual structural flaws in the economy appear unfounded. The problems of the 1920s had their counterparts in earlier decades, yet recurrent panics did not produce any downturn like that of the 1930s.

2. Why so severe? The Fed permitted the money supply to contract sharply (by 25 to 30 percent), which intensified the contraction and pushed the economy from a mild recession into the Great Contraction. In turn, the severity of the Great Contraction was increased by federal income tax increases and the Hawley-Smoot tariff.

3. Why did the Great Depression last for at least a decade? The depth of the Great Contraction meant a long climb back, and public policy, although aimed in the right direction, was, on balance, only moderately expansionary. The huge federal deficits associated with World War II escalated the economy to full employment.

4. What did we learn? The book was rewritten on business cycle theory, especially in relation to monetary and fiscal policy—it is now recognized that government policy can fashion a more stable aggregate economy (the built-in stabilizers) and can take specific fiscal and monetary actions to offset the multiplier in both inflation and depression.

5. In view of our knowledge, what is our stabilization record? Scholars are divided as to whether ignorance or ineptitude explains the perversity of pre-1933 monetary policy. A lack of knowledge explains the feebleness of policy after 1933.

In World War II, we turned our backs on what we had learned and adopted a disequilibrium system held in check by central controls over prices and resource allocation. For reasons of political expediency, ignorance, and respect for tradition, we abandoned the price system and countercyclical monetary and fiscal policy in favor of central planning.

Since 1945, the trend of policy seems to have favored enlightenment, and the economy has been remarkably stable. But often the right policies were legislated for the wrong reasons. The 1964 income tax cut, the 1968 income tax increase, and the 1971–72 income and excise tax reductions were exceptions in that they were major tax changes enacted specifically to affect the aggregate economy. On the other hand, we felt compelled to adopt wage-price controls in 1971 because we were unwilling to raise taxes early enough in the Vietnam conflict to avoid high inflation rates.

REFERENCES

S. K. Bailey, *Congress Makes a Law* (New York: Columbia University Press, 1950).

E. C. Brown, "Federal Fiscal Policy in the Postwar Period," in *Postwar Economic Trends in the United States,* ed. R. E. Freeman (New York: Harper & Row, Publishers, 1960).

———, "Fiscal Policy in the 'Thirties': A Reappraisal," *AER,* December 1956.

G. Burck and C. Silberman, "What Caused the Great Depression?" in *Business Fluctuations, Growth and Economic Stabilization,* eds. J. J. Clark and M. Cohen (New York: Random House, 1963).

Council of Economic Advisers, *The Annual Report of the Council of Economic Advisers, 1971* (Washington, D.C.: U.S. Government Printing Office, 1972).

P. Eilbott, "The Effectiveness of the Automatic Stabilizers," *AER,* June 1966.

M. Friedman and A. J. Schwartz, *The Great Contraction* (Princeton, N.J.: Princeton University Press, 1965).

J. K. Galbraith, "The Disequilibrium System," *AER,* June 1947.

———, *The Great Crash, 1929* (Boston: Houghton Mifflin Co., 1955).

W. W. Heller, *New Dimensions of Political Economy* (New York: W. W. Norton & Co., Inc., 1967).

R. L. Miller and R. M. Williams, *The New Economics of Richard Nixon* (San Francisco: Canfield Press, 1972).

E. J. Mishan, "How to Make a Burden of the Public Debt," *JPE,* December 1963.

G. H. Soule, *Prosperity Decade* (New York: Rinehart & Co., Inc., 1947).

H. Stein, *The Fiscal Revolution in America* (Chicago: University of Chicago Press, 1969).

U.S. Department of Commerce, *Long-Term Economic Growth, 1860–1965* (Washington, D.C.: U.S. Government Printing Office, 1966).

E. R. Wicker, *Federal Reserve Monetary Policy, 1917–1933* (New York: Random House, 1966).

13 BUSINESS AND FARM ADAPTATIONS

We have noted several times that economic growth is associated with changes in the structure of the economy. Some of the changes are causes of growth whereas others are the result of higher incomes or the pace of growth. Some are costs, unfortunate side effects and dislocations, while others are the gains which make the pursuit of growth worthwhile. In this chapter we shall survey such developments in the business and agriculture sectors of the economy. The household, labor, government, and foreign sectors are discussed in the remaining chapters.

Taken together, the characteristics of these six sectors constitute the structure of the economy, and the changes that are part of the growth process alter that structure. Throughout, it is important to remember that the sectors are not mutually exclusive segments but are instead overlapping and interdependent categories. In sum, they constitute the medium through which the causes and effects of economic development are transmitted.

A GIANT BUSINESS ENTERPRISE

By World War I, the United States had become the leading industrial economy and had achieved a standard of living that was the envy of the world. Yet Americans remained very self-conscious and critical about their problems. They were particularly embarrassed and uneasy about the extent to which giant business organizations had grown up with mass production and mass distribution.

Americans held three types of fears concerning bigness in business. Each of these fears concerned erosion of one of the useful functions of competition in a market economy.

First, they feared the loss of the *regulating force* of competition. The antitrust movement of the last century and the prewar reform movement continued to be political forces. Competition was valued as a means of ensuring that business was efficient in serving consumers and that it did not have arbitrary powers to raise prices and restrict output. The giant corporation was frequently suspected of possessing and using monopoly powers.

Second, the public feared the loss of *incentives* to improve. During the Great Depression, charges were made that giant businesses had rigidly administered prices that weakened the flexibility of the market economy and that the enterprising spirit was dying out in the bureaucracy of large-scale business organization. Competition, in contrast, was valued as a means of motivating business leaders to make rapid adjustments and to strive to improve production and introduce new methods and products.

Third, Americans feared the loss of *individualism and democracy.* Competition was valued as a means of providing alternative opportunities to the individual and keeping economic and political power dispersed. After World War II, there was increasing concern over the plight of the "organization man" and the possible disappearance of small business. Individuals felt an increasing helplessness in a complex world in which issues seemed to be decided by the leaders of Big Business, Big Labor, and Big Government. More recently, the late 19th century fear of infiltration of government and the political process by large business firms has been revived, especially with the apparent growth of what President Eisenhower referred to as the *military-industrial complex.*

Big firms in a big economy

The American economy has grown very large. Within this economy both the number of giant firms and the absolute size of such firms have increased.[1] In 1901, U.S. Steel became the first corporation with over $1 billion in assets. In 1962, 1,533 corporations had over $1 billion in assets, and 638 had over $2.5 billion—which, given long-term price rises, was more comparable to $1 billion in 1901.

In 1962, of 1.3 million corporations, the 638 largest had 27.7 percent of all sales. Corporations, in turn, accounted for roughly two thirds of the gross output produced by the Nation's 5 million business firms. This means that, in recent times, about $\frac{1}{100}$ of 1 percent of America's business firms provided almost 20 percent of business production. Contrast that statistic with the fact that the top 5 percent of family income recipients received about 20 percent of total personal income.

Of what significance is this? It is difficult to determine. The prediction of Karl Marx, of course, was that capital ownership inevitably tends to concentrate a monopoly of economic power in fewer and fewer hands. And 19th century liberals preached against monopoly as the enemy of economic efficiency and political freedom. However, as we will discuss in

---

[1] For a survey of studies of the size, structure, and concentration of U. S. industry, see Scherer, chap. 3.

detail below, there is little evidence to indicate that giant firms dominate the contemporary American economy in the classic pattern that Marx and 19th century liberals had in mind. Further, using standard indexes of industrial concentration, the data show that there is no trend toward greater monopoly in today's economy.[2]

However, many economists and observers of the political scene feel that the vast resources that giant firms control enable them to obtain many of the strategic advantages that monopoly would entail without actually having monopoly power in the traditional sense. For example, corporate giants could spend almost unlimited funds to influence their chances of getting lucrative defense contracts. The same observation applies to their ability to influence international trade policy and governmental regulation of public utilities.

Since the early 1930s, when the first studies of concentration were made, a numbers game has been used to create the impression—or at least illustrate the potentialities—of concentrated power. Whenever there is a wide dispersion of sizes for any type of data, some small number will have some disproportionate share of the total. By selecting the right number in the top group, an impressively large percentage share— say 50 percent—can be obtained. By eliminating banks, insurance companies, and other financial corporations—on the doubtful argument that they merely hold the money and securities of the really productive corporations—the number of giants can be reduced. For example, returning to the 1962 data and eliminating financial firms, only 293 giants had 25.9 percent of the nonfinancial corporate sales. And by eliminating the separate reporting subsidiaries of holding companies, the number of giants can be further reduced: in 1933, this process adjusted the magic number from 375 to 200.

Speaking in terms of assets—rather than sales or employees—makes the share of the giants look even larger, because it is the capital-intensive technology of some modern industries that brought the giant firms into being. In 1962, the 293 giants had 44.5 percent of the nonfinancial corporation assets. In 1933, the adjusted number of 200 giants had 55 percent of the nonfinancial corporate assets.

By referring to specific sectors—those that are most concentrated and most highly capital intensive—an even smaller number of firms and even higher percentages can be obtained. In 1962, 118 of the giant corporations held 75 percent of the assets in all transportation and public utility corporations; and 141 giants held 48.6 percent of the assets of all manufacturing corporations. By implication, these are the "key" sectors of a modern industrial economy, so a few firms in these key sectors are assumed to dominate the whole economy. Further, by redirecting the focus from production to individual ownership, it can be pointed

---

[2] See Sherman for a contrary interpretation of the data and for citations of the radical literature on the subject.

out that the key giant corporations are financially controlled by a relatively small number of financial corporations, wealthy families, or company officials who, by extension of the key sector argument, can be
seen as running the economy.

It is on the basis of this type of study, plus the literature of the
early antitrust and reform movements, that much of the rest of the
world gained its impression that the American economy is dominated
by a few giant capitalists. When a group of leading Russian economists
visited this country in 1960, for example, they seriously asked executives
of large manufacturing corporations about their "orders" from Wall
Street bankers. The Harrimans, Rockefellers, and Fords are regarded
by many as behind-the-scenes rulers of our country.

Of course, the numbers game can be played in reverse. There are
5 million business decision-makers and 1.3 million corporations. Each
year there are a greater number of small businesses; and each year
opportunities abound for other new businesses to start. The figures we
presented above also mean that the nongiants control a little over 80
percent of business sales. The few giant corporations are not free to
make any decisions they please, unless it could be shown (which it
rarely can) that they have exclusive areas of decision-making as a result
of secure monopoly positions.

The relevant number at which decision-making power becomes concentrated is an important question that no one has been able to answer.
Experience with pools and collusion, for example, suggests that the harmony of business interests is seldom so great or group discipline so
strong that 20 or even 10 firms can act together for long—recall our
discussion of 19th century railroad cartels. If the top 10 or 20 firms
were spotlighted, the percentage shares of sales in the economy would
not be so impressive. On the other hand, by selecting a high percentage,
an initial impression of concentration is created without regard to
whether the number of firms is 500, 200, or 100.

The word control is also highly ambiguous, both in terms of the
consequences of percentage shares and the meaning of various types
of linkages. How much power can be exercised over other firms or
price when one firm has 10 or even 50 percent of the output of a product?
While it may be conceded that a small percentage of stockholders may
provide leadership to a large corporation with tens of thousands of passive owners, to what extent can control be exercised contrary to the
interests of the majority of stockholders? To what extent can company
officers stay in their positions if their profit-making performance is poor?
Are widespread security holdings by a particular corporation evidence
of far-reaching control for power purposes or of prudent diversification
of investments?

The historical sources of business concentration, moreover, are technology and market size rather than ownership. Until recent years, large

corporations resulted from mass-production and mass-distribution technology; and concentration was greatest where capital-intensive methods were required.[3] About the same technology and scale of organization has been adopted in all modern nations. Consequently, most modern industrial nations have greater industrial concentration than does the United States, because the U.S. market is so large and because many nations have deliberately encouraged cartels.

It's important to remember that the greatest industrial concentration is in sectors where it is technically unavoidable or socially desirable and where public regulation is exercised—that is, in transportation, public utilities, and finance. The transportation and public utility industries have long been recognized as having technical conditions requiring exclusive service facilities or as achieving economies by operating large single units in a particular market area. Historically, these *natural monopolies* have been publicly regulated by special charter conditions or supervisory commissions.

Financial institutions have the social function of collecting large aggregations of savings to provide the capital for small- and large-scale production units. Large financial institutions provide specialized analysts, diversify their investments, and handle large blocks of security issues on behalf of large and small corporations. Because financial markets are often very thin and because many of the parties dealing in securities are naive or inexperienced, public regulation is exercised in both securities markets and banking.

When economic power is measured in terms of industrial concentration, i.e., by the percentage of sales, employees, or assets of, say, the four largest firms in an industry, there is no evidence of ever-increasing concentration of economic might in the modern economy. Little information is available on how much concentration existed in earlier times on a smaller and more local scale. The early manufacturer and banker frequently had a monopoly or near monopoly in his local community; and a small group of wealthy merchants were prominent in the early textile industry.

Between the Civil War and World War I, however, when the basic industrialization of the economy occurred, it seems likely that business concentration increased when measured on a national scale. Recall, for example, the Great Merger Movement which took place around 1900, when large corporations were formed as horizontal integrations of many plants of the same type.

Concentration probably increased modestly between 1920 and the mid-1930s, when a second wave of mergers swept across the industrial landscape. In this period, major new industries took shape, many corporations integrated vertically (to control their own supply and market-

---

[3] Over the last 20 years conglomerate mergers, which we'll discuss later, have been the chief way in which new corporate giants have come into being.

ing operations), and holding companies spread in the public utility industries. But at the same time, the growth of the total economy tended to offset the concentrating effects of mergers.

Since the 1930s, no clear-cut concentration trend has appeared. Expansion of the total economy has been rapid, and additional large firms have risen to share the position of previous leaders.

A new wave of mergers has swept over the corporate sector since World War II. The average annual number of mergers among all manufacturing and mining firms from mid-1950 to mid-1960 more than matched the high level of the 1920s, and in 1968 and 1969 the merger rate was more than twice the average annual rate for the 1950s and 1960s. (See 13–1.) However, these were conglomerate mergers, which

13–1. Mergers in manufacturing and mining industries

1895–99 1,649	1920–24 2,235	1945–49 1,505
1900–04 1,363	1925–29 4,583	1950–54 1,424
1905–09 440	1930–34 1,687	1955–59 3,365
1910–14 451	1935–39 577	1960–64 4,366
1915–19 625	1940–44 906	1965–69 8,213

Sources: U.S. Department of Commerce (1960), p. 572; (1971), p. 474.

are distinctly different in type and effect from earlier mergers. Smaller firms from a variety of industries have been acquired by corporations for tax purposes, to increase financial liquidity, or to diversify operations rather than to extend their market share or to integrate related operations within the same industry. For example, in 1965 the *Annual Report of the Council of Economic Advisers* stated that the 100 largest manufacturing firms had increased their share of all manufacturing assets and value-added from 1947 to 1962, but that "concentration within specific industries has shown no significant trend."[4] (See 13–1).

In addition to the lack of a distinct trend in concentration within industries, the modern period has evidenced a rapid turnover in the identity of the biggest corporations. This is because the major technological changes of the modern period have shifted the relative importance of various industries—whole new fields (such as aircraft and electronics) have risen to prominence, while others (such as coal, shipping, and leather) have stagnated. Of the 100 largest industrial firms in 1909 (omitting transportation, utility, and financial firms), only 59 were still among the 100 largest in 1919, only 31 in 1960. Of the 100 largest firms in 1935, only 65 were still among the 100 largest in 1960.[5] Some corporations (such as U.S. Steel and Standard Oil of New Jersey) have expanded and stayed among the 100 largest but have been reduced to a smaller share of the output in their own industry group. Some corporations (such as S. S. Kresge, National Biscuit, and Wheeling Steel) have

---

[4] Council of Economic Advisors, p. 132.

[5] Kaplan, p. 136.

dropped out of the top 100, while others in their industry group (such as J. C. Penney, General Foods, and Kaiser Steel) have entered the top 100.

Aside from the attention devoted to concentration in the regulated utilities and financial concerns, the most attention has been focused on concentration in manufacturing. The market power of a manufacturing corporation depends primarily upon its share of sales in specific subindustries or product markets rather than on its size ranking among all industrial giants. The studies of corporate concentration in the 1930s have led to government-compiled *concentration ratios*—statistics on the shares of assets, employment, and sales of the firms in each subindustry which enable the measuring of market concentration.

In the auto industry, for example, in 1954 the four largest companies had 71 percent of the assets, 69 percent of the employment, and 75 percent of the value of shipments. Some experiments with concentration ratios for the single largest, 4 largest, 8 largest, and 20 largest firms show that these measures vary little in the way in which the ranking of different subindustries turns out. Any of the concentration ratios shows that some industries—such as aluminum, tin cans, motor vehicles, or cigarettes—are highly concentrated, while other industries—such as woolen and worsted goods or drugs and medicines—are not.

These indexes of concentration show that surprisingly few of the manufacturing subindustries are very concentrated. In 1954, only 40 out of 434 subindustries had concentrations of sales of over 75 percent among the four largest firms. In only a third of all subindustries was concentration above 50 percent. Some subindustries were, of course, much larger than others. Still, only one fourth of all manufacturing sales were in industries with concentrations of over 50 percent of the sales in the four largest firms. Since 1954, no signs have appeared to suggest that there is a trend toward more concentration than the pattern summarized in 13–2.[6]

13–2.   Distribution of concentration in manufacturing
industries, 1954

Industries in which the share of sales by the four largest firms was	Number of industries	Percent of total sales
75 to 100%	40	7.8%
50 to 74	101	16.7
25 to 49	157	35.3
0 to 24	136	40.2
Total	434	100.0%

SOURCE: U.S. Senate Committee on the Judiciary, Subcommittee on Antitrust and Monopoly, table 17.

---

[6] Adelman, p. 121.

Also, manufacturing concentration ratios show a long-term trend toward less concentration. A study compiling the top-four-firm concentration ratios for manufacturing subindustries in 1901 showed that 32.9 percent, or one third, of value-added in all manufacturing came from industries with concentrations above 50 percent.[7] The comparable figure in 1947 was 24.0 percent, or *one fourth*. Since then there has been little change. According to the Council of Economic Advisers, the comparable figure for 1958 was 23 percent, in spite of the postwar merger movement's increase of the share of sales accounted for by the larger firms.

The question of bigness and its relation to concentration must be viewed in the context of the total economy's growth. While the average corporation has grown larger, the economy has also expanded; consequently, whether a company is huge or not provides little insight about concentration in its markets, little knowledge about the influence it might have over the price and output decisions of other firms in the industry, and no guide to determining the precise boundaries of the industry.[8] For example, today the steel industry is far more competitive than it was at the time of U.S. Steel's birth, when its formation set the pace for the Great Merger Movement. Yet in absolute terms, U.S. Steel is much larger, not smaller, than it was at the turn of the century. Domestic and foreign markets for steel have grown so much over this period that now several dozen giants compete in markets in which 20 years ago only several producers operated. And U.S. Steel and other steelmakers must compete with rival materials for the manufacturer's and the builder's dollar.

This example is not meant to suggest that the structure of 20th century industry is typified by a situation in which the bigness of individual firms is dwarfed by the total size of the market. Rather, it is meant to suggest that the extensive and intensive growth of the national market, economic growth abroad, and the continued reduction of trade barriers have importantly multiplied the examples in which bigness doesn't connote monopoly power. In turn, the absence of a clear trend toward increased concentration is explained by overall market growth and the room it creates at the bottom.

Changes in market theory and behavior

In response to changes in market structure and conduct, economists have developed more sophisticated tools for analyzing market structure and new ways of viewing industrial behavior. In the 1930s, new ideas about competition began to appear in the corner of economic theory

---

[7] See Nutter for a survey of concentration for the period 1899–1939.

[8] See Adelman for an evaluation of the evidence on concentration as it relates to large corporations.

known as *microeconomics,* the theory that explains household, firm, and industry behavior. The idea of a simple dichotomy between monopoly and competition—which assumed that if an industry was not a monopoly (single seller), it must be competitive—was replaced with more complex concepts.

Monopoly power began to be considered as a matter of degree with more than one dimension to consider in measuring that power. In theory, the conditions for pure competition came to be defined in rather severe terms. In turn, *monopolistic competition* (many sellers of differentiated products) and *oligopoly* (few sellers in a given market) were conceived to fill the space between pure competition and monopoly. These new tools increased the ability of economists to explain and evaluate actual market behavior. Consequently, contemporary theory takes into account the many factors in addition to concentration which determine whether the useful functions of competition are performed.

The theory of monopolistic competition made it possible to explain the results of advertising and product differentiation, by which each manufacturing firm in an industry of many firms created a special demand for its own output. Increasingly, firms found that sales could be expanded by product changes and sales promotion as well as by cost reductions and price cuts. The preference of some customers for a given firm's product gave that firm discretion to charge a significantly higher price than some of its competitors, while losing only a minor percentage of its customers.

Oligopoly theory made it possible to understand the implications of recognition by a few large firms that they were mutually interdependent. As a consequence of the late 19th century merger waves, situations became common in which one firm's demand depended on other firms' reactions. If one firm alone cut its price, it might gain a large increase in sales volume from customers who shifted from competitors' products. Yet, if other firms reacted by cutting their prices too, each of the firms might gain only a very small increase in sales—reflecting the extent to which total customer sales would increase with a general lowering of price. In extreme cases, price wars broke out in which all firms experienced drastic price cuts with only modest increases in physical volume.

As you can conclude from the foregoing, whenever there was a small number of firms (or a high concentration among a few firms), each firm became very conscious of the potential reactions of its rivals. Business, therefore, became much like a poker game—in fact, economic theory began to explore the "theory of games." Unlike poker, however, the games often resulted in losses for all players. Consequently, incentives were great for oligopolistic firms to collude, either overtly or tacitly, to maintain price stability and to compete only in terms of product variation and advertising.

Rapid technological change was still another condition requiring changes in the theory of market structure and performance. This added a dynamic dimension to competition. Over the past several generations, how many firms there were or which had the largest share of sales came to have less importance than which firm first introduced a new or improved product. The 20th century consumer has demonstrated remarkable quickness in changing habits to take advantage of new product and service opportunities. Mass-production and mass-distribution techniques are capable of putting a new product on the market and very quickly capturing a large share of consumer purchases in an industry. Consumer habits and trust in recognized, well-established brands, then, make it difficult for another firm to recapture the market without a superior product. The few large firms in an industry, therefore, cannot rest easily on their share of the market and a willingness to follow the leader in price setting. The new forms of nonprice competition— product variation, advertising, and sales promotion—potentially provide a very active form of competition.

Unfortunately, however, advertising, sales promotion, and product variation also require vast numbers of bright, imaginative people whose talents could be used in pursuits more useful to society than persuading people that they really need some new product. Of course, genuine product innovations and the advertising that is necessary to acquaint people with them account for bona fide additions to economic welfare. But when changes in products don't really add to their usefulness and when purely promotional advertising produces a barrage of claims and counterclaims, but little genuine information about the ability of a product to serve the consumer, the new forms of competition waste capital, materials, and labor.

Industry classifications present only a very crude idea of the markets within which a firm must compete and can give rise to misleading conclusions regarding the degree of competition in an industry. Some products are sold by thousands of firms nationally, but individual firms in the industry operate in highly localized markets because high transportation costs reduce the penetration of firms from outside the region to forays into the market's fringe.

On the other hand, some products that just a few firms distribute nationwide have to compete with similar products from other industries. Up until World War II, for example, aluminum was produced by a single firm; and now it is produced by only a few large firms. Yet aluminum firms have to compete with producers of other metals and materials in many different markets. Aluminum competes with steel for use in auto parts and containers, with lumber for use in house siding, with copper for use in wire, and with plastics for use in many light household objects and automobile trim.

Finally, in spite of tariffs, nationally distributed products also have to compete with imported products regardless of the degree of concentration found in their respective industries at home. At the same time, large firms and concentrated industries face worldwide competition in their export markets.

John Kenneth Galbraith has suggested an additional way in which to view the structure of markets. In his *American Capitalism* he shows that checks on industrial concentration and economic power instead of just coming from competitors may emanate from customers as well. One illustration which he provides of his "theory of countervailing power" is Sears, Roebuck and Company. Sears, according to Galbraith, can use its power as a very large customer to obtain tires from the highly concentrated tire producers at very considerable savings; these are then passed on to consumers in the form of lower prices. His general conclusion is that unless the economy is under severe inflationary pressure, when two industrial giants oppose each other as buyer and seller, the consumer comes away the victor. Of course, if inflation is the order of the day, then incentives exist to encourage buyer and seller to make a compact which passes higher supply prices on to the consumer.

Since writing *American Capitalism,* Galbraith has written *The Affluent Society* and *The New Industrial State.* Taken as a unified statement, these three works indicate that the American consumer has lost his control over the market to corporate giants. Knowing that advertising can lure the consumer into buying anything, the corporation plans his shopping-center fare for him, including an excess of private goods at the expense of much-needed public production, while government serves to stabilize aggregate demand and foots the bill for the scientific inquiry required to keep innovations coming out of the corporate think tanks. What's more, according to Galbraith, corporate America strives not to maximize profits, but to survive, or, more accurately, to maintain the survival of its bureaucracy.

As has been the case with almost everything he's done, Galbraith's work on industrial organization has drawn a good deal of fire. Many economists feel that promotional advertising is self-canceling, as well as wasteful, and that there is a good deal of evidence to support assertions that the profit motive is alive and well in the American economy. Galbraith is also criticized for repeating his assumptions where evidence is called for and for neglecting the 55 percent of economic activity (as measured by GNP) that takes place outside corporations. In short, Galbraith has chastised contemporary economic theory for failing to adequately come to terms with the modern corporation, yet his colleagues, though they admire his ambition, feel that he too has failed to fill the void.

Changing economic conditions have enriched our theories of market behavior. Instead of the two rather clear-cut and simple models, competition and monopoly, we have additional and more complicated analytic devices. Yet, as both Galbraith and his critics will testify and as the next few paragraphs illustrate, economic theory has not caught up completely with economic events. Economists would like to know a lot more about the operation of various markets and the economic welfare effects of modern industrial organization.

Enterprise among giants

During World War II, the giant corporations played an important role in helping to organize a production miracle. While a large government regulatory bureaucracy was set up, production could not have gotten underway as quickly as it did if large corporations had not taken on the mass production of weapons and coordinated the activities of many small firms working on subcontracts for parts. This war record and the long postwar prosperity have helped restore public confidence in business, confidence that was destroyed during the Great Depression. In the 1950s, many business leaders and journalists took the initiative in defending corporations against the charge of excessive power. In fact, some writers seemed to worship bigness uncritically. The giant firms, it was claimed, were more efficient because of the economies of large scale, an assertion that slights the possibility that bigness was achieved in order to exert enough market power to earn monopoly profits. Also, large firms were claimed to be more innovative because they alone could afford large research laboratories.

That bigness is not a reliable indicator of lower costs, however, is suggested by the few studies that have been made of efficiency in large and small firms. Comparisons of costs and profits among firms have suggested that medium-sized firms do as well or better than the very largest firms in most industries. The continued coexistence of corporate giants and many smaller firms in the same industries also attests to the limited difference in efficiency due solely to size. In some industries, the size of modern plants is very similar even though the size of firms varies widely. Larger plant size is usually associated with lower costs only up to some minimum optimum size. The operation of multiple plants also has been estimated to provide very little savings in production costs. The efficiencies of large firm size, therefore, must come primarily from large-scale marketing, large financial resources, and capable overall management.[9]

There is little reason to suppose that the particular size of giant firms was due solely to technological advantages that yielded economies of scale. Firms have become large as a result of a variety of causes and motives. Some firms may have grown partly from desires to gain market power—through horizontal integration to gain a larger share of the market, vertical mergers to gain some independent control of strategic re-

---

[9] See Temporary National Economic Committee; J. L. McConnell; J. S. Bain, pp. 346–52.

sources, and acquisition of patents to exclude potential new competitors.

Perhaps you recall the study of manufacturing concentration by J. S. Bain that we cited in Part III. In that study, Bain examined the 20 manufacturing industries that had the highest concentration ratios and accounted for 20 percent of net manufacturing output. He found that the four largest firms in each case had larger market shares than were required by economies of scale in plant size. For example, in 1951, automobile production, with an actual concentration ratio of 98 percent, could have had a 40 percent concentration ratio if all plant complexes were no larger than required to just reach production efficiency. What's more, building a plant of only half the size of the most efficient plant would have resulted in a more than 5 percent elevation of costs in only 5 of the 20 industries.[10]

Nor is size a reliable indicator of innovation. As already noted, the process of invention is uncertain and unpredictable. Most inventions are still the work of individuals, and often the major breakthroughs come from outside an industry. It is mainly in the development stage that a giant firm with a large research laboratory has an advantage. The giant firms are also in a better position to mass-produce and mass-distribute new products. There must be strong rivalry and competitive pressures on a firm, however, to ensure that it will promote a new product or process whose acceptance might involve some losses for its old products and plants.

Changes in technology have brought some new firms into existence and enabled them to grow rapidly. Two recent examples are the Xerox Corporation and Texas Instruments. In an economy with giant firms, therefore, it has still been possible not only for some small firms to persist with costs little different from those of the giants, but also for newly-formed small firms to innovate very successfully and grow rapidly. The turnover in rank of the 100 largest industrial firms likewise suggests that initial size is no protection against the need to be enterprising in a changing world.

On the other hand, some writers have bemoaned the decline of enterprising spirit that is assumed to result from the bureaucratic tendencies of large organizations. The era of the entrepreneur may be over in terms of the individual owner-manager who single-handedly built up a large firm. However, to cite only one case, the founder of the Xerox Corporation would greet such news with unbelieving surprise. Yet it is true that the close-knit family or the close-knit group of independent business associates no longer provides imaginative direction and able management for large firms.

Nevertheless, enterprise and the entrepreneurial functions still survive

---

[10] Bain's work, which was published in stages as it proceeded, is reviewed and appraised in Scherer, pp. 83–86.

in the giant corporation. They have merely taken different forms in the structure of management. The railroad and the multiplant manufacturing corporations required that management organization be split into two levels—top management and division management. Separate, but similar, divisions had to have operating managers. The top executive, or even a team of top executives, continued to make policy and coordinate the operations of all divisions and plants. Within this coordinating group, functional specialties were developed to direct sales, production, and financial operations.

The modern trend of corporate expansion into diverse industries, e.g., through conglomerate mergers, has created a third level or type of management—a level which specializes in the more enterprising aspects of management. As operations have become more diverse within the conglomerates, coordinating responsibility has been delegated to operating divisions that are essentially subsidiary companies, usually organized along industry lines. Each subsidiary unit has an executive or executive team that must coordinate many production units. The subsidiary unit has its own functional managers of sales and production. The top level of managers, or the parent corporation's board of directors, confines itself primarily to major financial decisions, the selection of top executives, and the planning of future strategies of product development and expansion. If there is a research laboratory, it may be attached to the parent corporation. It is primarily at the top of the management structure that the vision, the planning, the initiative, and the risk-taking now must take place.

Whether conglomerates provide the ideal organizational framework for establishing and nurturing corporate entrepreneurship where individual entrepreneurship no longer can survive is not clear. The performance of the conglomerates was rated as astonishingly high until the 1970 recession brought about some spectacular reversals. Only additional experience will make possible a definitive judgment on this question.

There are indications that giant corporations may be as sensitive to changing economic conditions and to stockholder interests as were the owner-managers in former times—or more so. Top executives constantly study the profit performance of subsidiary corporations and divisional executives. Banks, large financial institutions, and individual investors also study carefully the performance of the large corporations. Whereas, in the short run, an owner-manager could stick to his opinions and to old methods regardless of current reverses or the criticisms of minority stockholders, the boards of giant corporations are sensitive to changing conditions and to the general opinion of investors about their success. Outside sources of financing and the price of securities can change; stockholder representatives on boards can change; and the top executives of giant corporations can be reshuffled—all within a brief period.

The quest for social control

At one time it seemed that a concerted attack on concentration through antimerger legislation and vigorous prosecution under the Sherman Act promised an end to our problems related to industrial structure. But, as various studies have shown, although the growth of concentration has been checked, we still have corporate giants that possess economic, social, and political power which in some cases matches that of entire nations. Adding to our uneasiness about bigness, the antitrust case law that has been built up over the years has left the Justice Department powerless to deal with bigness except where it's related to a high degree of concentration.

The history of antitrust legislation consists of a highly uneven pattern of evolution. As already noted, the merger movement around 1900 was partly encouraged by the Supreme Court's interpretation of the Sherman Act as prohibiting collusion but not merger. The merger wave set off a political reaction that led to increased enforcement and new legislation before World War I. In the **United States Steel Corporation** case in 1920, the Court again applied the **rule of reason** and refused to see mere size as an offense in the absence of clear evidence of abuse of power. Perhaps as a consequence, a new wave of mergers occurred during the late 1920s.

The unsettled world conditions after World War I and the depression of the 1930s brought policy measures that departed from reliance on competitive markets. Higher tariffs and the actions of trade associations were designed to prevent competitive pressures for price reductions. In the Great Depression, the federal government was called upon to protect industry against competitive price-cutting—through the trade association codes approved by the National Industrial Recovery Administration (the NIRA). The Robinson-Patman Act (1936) outlawed discriminatory or temporary price-cutting intended to eliminate small competitors, but for good reason it was popularly referred to as an anti-chain-store act. The next year the Miller-Tydings amendment provided an exemption from the Sherman Act for contract agreements by retailers to charge no less than the manufacturer's list price in states with "fair trade" laws. Other legislative efforts in agriculture, bituminous coal, and crude oil sought to provide government protection to producer groups against competitive price reductions.

Greater regulation of business went along with reduced reliance upon the regulatory effects of competition. In the 1930s, Congress passed the Securities Exchange Act (1934), the Communications Act (1934), the Public Utility Holding Company Act (1935), the Federal Power Act (1935), the Motor Carrier Act (1935), the National Gas Act (1938), and the Civil Aeronautics Act (1938). Thus, in the fields where natural monopoly was regarded as inevitable, public regulation was extended.

Also, late in the 1930s, an effort was made to step up the enforcement activity of the Department of Justice and the Federal Trade Commission, and Congress established the Temporary National Economic Committee to make a study of monopoly conditions.

Although World War II interrupted these enforcement efforts, they were resumed and intensified in the postwar period. In 1945, the Alcoa decision appeared to reverse the Court's narrow interpretation of the rule of reason in favor of a strong presumption that bigness and high concentration imply market power; however, this decision has not been treated as a broadly applicable precedent. After the war, an effort was made under the Surplus Property Act to dispose of plants built by the government in wartime in such a way as to encourage competition.

In 1950, the Celler-Kefauver amendment to the Clayton Act extended antimerger provisions to include the purchase of assets as well as stock. In the 1950s, the Supreme Court made several key interpretations—in the **United Shoe Machinery** case (1953), the **Du Pont Company** case (1957), and the **Brown Shoe Company** case (1962)—that tended to limit the kind of merger permitted under the laws. Some economists and lawyers now feel that insofar as vertical and horizontal mergers are concerned, whenever the parties involved have a significant share of the market, the merger will be ruled illegal.[11] Further, virtually any conglomerate merger will attract attention in Washington if such a merger is likely to generate predatory pricing or remove an element of potential competition, or if the units within the conglomerate engage in reciprocal dealing whereby purchases from outside firms are barred by company policy.

The evolution of interpretation by the Supreme Court has been away from reliance solely upon overt collusive or restrictive actions as evidence of monopoly practices. The trend has been toward recognition of large relative size of a firm within a particular market as creating a strong presumption that monopoly power exists. Evidence of concentration over, say, 50 percent of the industry does not automatically convict a large firm, but it weakens somewhat the prosecution's burden of proof that certain actions reflect abuse of market power.

The last landmark decision dealing with concentration was the **Du Pont Cellophane** case (1956), in which the court agreed with Du Pont that the competition Du Pont encountered from other flexible wrapping materials reduced its market share to 18 percent. Since then, antimonopoly suits have been settled largely by negotiation with no new case law being established thereby. At this point, although high concentration per se is viewed as an evidence of monopoly power, the definition of an industry can be so broad that most concentration ratios would appear very low.

Historically, business spokesmen have complained of the uncertainty

---

[11] For example see Scherer, pp. 480–82.

forced upon normal business decisions by what they feel is an unpredictable course being steered by the courts in their interpretations. Yet the basic difficulty lies in the inadequacies of our existing theories and knowledge about market power and how to control it. While some writers argue that the good performance of giant corporations should be the primary criterion of the legality of their size and practices, no one has proposed acceptable objective measures of performance by which the good monopolies could be distinguished from the bad.

The very sensitivity of business leaders to court interpretations is evidence that the antitrust laws may have had some effect in deterring monopolistic practices. There is clearly less concentration in the American economy than among most other industrial nations, where antitrust policy has been less pronounced. Also, the merger movement of the late 1950s and early 1960s has been in the direction of greater industry diversity resulting from conglomerate mergers rather than greater industry concentration—a trend that monopoly laws and court interpretations may have influenced.

Business leaders have also been sensitive to the public's reaction against abuse of market power if corporate preaching about the need for greater corporate *social responsibility* is any sign. Social responsibility, of course, is an admirable virtue on the part of any individual or group. The question is, Why should this virtue have to be displayed by the business community? The very intensity of the discussions of social responsibility by business leaders acknowledges their possession of power and shows that they are only incompletely controlled by external market forces. Without power to control, there would be no issue of responsibility.

The moral pep talks to which businessmen regularly subject each other, however, are poor substitutes for external restraints—the public is furnished no guarantee that social responsibility will always be considered. The logic of interdependence in an oligopolistic industry provides powerful social pressures toward monopolistic behavior—to wit, in 1961 highly placed executives in the electrical equipment industry were found guilty of criminal conspiracy in rigging bids on power generation equipment and were sent to prison. Since nearly all major corporations have been involved in antitrust cases of one sort or another in recent decades, pleas for social responsibility do not seem to promise a solution to the problem of market power.

Recognition of the modern limitations on market power, on the other hand, has helped to popularize optimistic interpretations of the salutary effects of scale economies, technological innovation, interindustry competition, nonprice competition, social responsibility, and countervailing power. In fact, there has been very little study which would lead to the conclusion that big business creates its own checks and balances.

In other words, Galbraith has only posed a hypothesis; no one has furnished the supporting evidence.

If we grant the most optimistic arguments to the effect that high industrial concentration is offset by various countervailing tendencies, the problem of bigness per se remains. Too often bigness and concentration seem to be confused, so that proof that concentration is not growing is taken as evidence that all is well with our industrial structure. However, as we noted above, the industrial giants of the post–World War II period may pose real threats to economic and political freedom in this Nation. And the conglomerate firm may represent the most dangerous threat, especially when almost every unit under the corporate umbrella is a defense contractor or subcontractor.

Yet, we have no rules against bigness per se, only against concentration, and no rules to regulate the conduct of gigantic firms unless they monopolize in the traditional sense. What's more, the case law developed on conglomerate mergers in recent years is aimed only at anticompetitive mergers and ignores completely the immense economic gains that can accrue to giants because of the political power that bigness permits.

Concentration is not so great as to constitute a monopoly situation in all but a few subindustries. But the evidence shows that concentration is greater than necessary to achieve efficiency in production. This suggests that firms like AT&T, ITT, General Motors, IBM, and U.S. Steel could be broken up with no loss in operating efficiency. Perhaps no great gains in the way of lower consumer prices would result from expanding the number of firms in each industry. But the resulting reduction in economic, social, and political concentration could generate considerable increases in the welfare of the American people if contemporary critics of the American socio-political-economic scene are correct. However, so far the antitrust statutes and case law have not developed beyond the point at which high concentration justifies presuming monopoly control of price and output in the market. The law does not call for halting the growth of a firm at the point at which mass-production efficiencies are first achieved, i.e., at the rate of output at which cost per unit is initially minimized.

AGRICULTURAL ADJUSTMENT

As you recall from our earlier discussion of agriculture, a prerequisite of economic growth is an agricultural sector in which productivity is growing very rapidly—so rapidly that it outstrips food and fiber demands and thus releases workers and capital to support the growth of other sectors of the economy. The decline of America's farm population from 30 percent of the total population in 1920 to 5 percent in 1970 certainly attests to the success of agriculture in this respect.

Productivity increases

Recall from our earlier discussions that prodictivity changes in agriculture have stemmed from four main sources: (1) transportation improvements that permitted farmers an increased degree of specialization and lowered commodity shipping costs, (2) improved land that came from opening up the West, (3) mechanization, and (4) the biochemical and biological inventions and managerial innovations that came with scientific agriculture. As we discussed earlier, the push westward in the 19th century was facilitated by transportation improvements and gave access to better land. Mechanization dates from the Civil War as an important source of productivity change. From 1910 to 1940, after a lull in mechanization, cotton and corn harvesters, small combines, and gasoline- and diesel-powered tractors became ubiquitous in American agriculture, simultaneously reducing labor requirements and increasing the land available for cash crops. Finally, in the period after World War II, scientific agriculture brought better management techniques, hybrid seeds, better feeds, improved breeds, pesticides, herbicides, and mass-produced fertilizers.[12]

In productivity terms, the consequences of 20th century improvements in farming methods and inputs have been vast, to say the least. In the period from 1920 to 1970, total farm output only doubled, largely in response to population, which almost doubled in the same time span. But farm output per man-hour increased four times over the 1920–70 period. The data in 13–3 and 13–4 summarize productivity trends for the postwar periods 1950–71 and 1961–71, respectively—they illustrate the kinds of agricultural productivity changes that have characterized the entire period since 1920:

1.   Farm population has declined and the number of farms in the United States has decreased steadily since the mid-1930s, as has the total land in farms since the mid-1950s.

2.   Average farm size has climbed, as have output per acre and per man-hour, and total farm labor input has declined.

3.   As the average farm's size has grown, so has the volume of capital per farm, especially machinery and equipment; in fact, while all other agricultural inputs have started to decline at some point since 1920, farm capital has grown persistently.

What the foregoing adds up to is simply this: by increasing farm capital and raising the productivity of all inputs through technological innovation, 5 million fewer farmers on 3.5 million fewer but much larger farms, controlling vastly more capital equipment, produce more than twice the output they produced in 1920. This is a record that has to

---

[12] The chemicals that have benefited the American consumer of food and fiber are not without their drawbacks; as we stress in chap. 16, the water pollution that results from fertilizer and pesticide runoff is not inconsequential.

13–3. Farm population, farms, and farm size: 1950–71

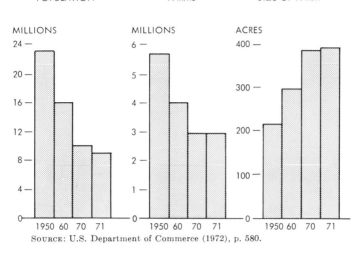

Source: U.S. Department of Commerce (1972), p. 580.

13–4. Farm production indexes: 1961–71

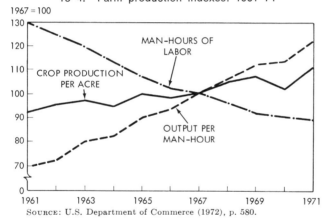

Source: U.S. Department of Commerce (1972), p. 580.

be called phenomenal—it also represents a series of adjustment problems that are of equally colossal proportions and that have generated national policy reactions.

Since 1920, U.S. farm policy has undergone significant modification. Recall that early farm policy consisted of making greater amounts of land available for the expansion of American agriculture as the total population grew. After the Civil War, and especially in the early 20th century, the emphasis of policy shifted to assisting the farmer in raising his productivity—in no small part, federally sponsored agricultural research and extension services are responsible for today's scientific farming.

Then, starting in the late 1920s, as the adjustment problems that productivity growth brought with it became evident, compensatory farm policies were formulated.

The problem that the national government was called upon to confront was simply this: productivity increases in agriculture were causing agricultural output to grow faster than food and fiber demand, which pushed down farm prices and reduced the demand for farm proprietors and workers. The paradox of the situation was that government policy was to a large degree responsible for the very high growth rate of farm productivity, the very source of farm adjustment problems. The justification for government action implicit in the situation was essentially as follows: if the American consumer was to benefit from farm policies that yielded better and more food and fiber at lower relative prices, then some of the consumer's tax dollars ought to be directed toward compensating the farmer for the income loss he suffered in the process of adjustment.

Throughout the text, we have spoken in a rather relaxed manner of releasing labor from farming. Yet this can be a very painful process for the farmers involved. It means abandoning a lifework and a way of life and learning, or trying to learn, new skills suitable for a new occupation. For farmers beyond their early years, the adjustment process has usually been too formidable to attempt, so, in the main, rural America has lost young people. One reason the federal government has been called upon to interfere so extensively in agricultural markets is the enormity of the adjustments that farmers have had to make since the 1920s.[13]

Talk abounds about "the farm problem," but historically there have been two major farm problems—chronic overproduction and rural poverty. And both problems can be linked to the process of adjusting agriculture to changing productivity. The first problem, in turn, breaks down into a wheat problem, a feed grain problem, a cotton problem, and so on. The second, similarly, comprises the problems of the small tenant or sharecropper, the hardscrabble freeholder, and the itinerant picker.

Confusing as this array must seem, there are common denominators to each of these broad categories which permit us to analyze them meaningfully. Let us begin with overproduction.

Overproduction

As we've noted, chronic overproduction in agriculture arises primarily because productivity increases cause the supply of farm commodities to grow faster than demand grows in response to population increases. The symptoms of the overproduction problem are farm prices which

---

[13] See Heady, chap. 3, for an excellent review of productivity-increasing and compensatory federal farm policy.

fall in comparison to nonfarm product prices. Starting in the 1930s, farmers who found it difficult to leave farming in response to low prices and declining profits as well as city people in agricultural states argued for and got federal programs to control these symptoms of agricultural maladjustment. Historically, price-support programs have been enacted which required the federal government to acquire enough commodities to maintain prices at levels that were defined as fair, that is, that corresponded to price levels before productivity increases flooded farm markets and depressed prices.

If you look at the feed corn example illustrated in the graph 13–5, you'll begin to see why we failed to solve the problem when we dealt

13–5. Hypothetical feed corn market

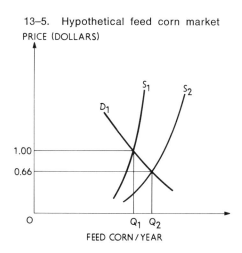

only with the symptoms of overproduction—low prices. In most of the post-World War II years, when productivity increases shifted the feed corn supply curve to the right, without government intervention the price would have plummeted to a price in the neighborhood of $0.66 so as to clear the market. Had that happened, farmers would have found their gross receipts falling below their production costs. But government did intervene by buying up the difference between Q_1 and Q_2 and reducing the supply available to the free market to Q_1, thus holding the price at $1.00.

The feed corn experience of 1960 provides a good example of the results of this kind of policy: 3.9 billion bushels were harvested, and the federal government was obliged to spend $361 million dollars to acquire a sufficient amount of corn to support the market price at almost $1.00 per bushel. This brought the total value of feed corn stored by the government to $1.7 billion. In quantity terms, by the end of 1960, the government held 1.1 billion bushels of feed corn, which was equal to about 30 percent of the 1960 crop and 60 percent of that year's corn requirement.

Prices were held at artificially high levels for corn, wheat, sorghum, and cotton during most of the 1950s and 1960s. Consequently, farmers who might otherwise have left agriculture remained on the farm, contributing to the surplus commodities that the government was forced to purchase in order to support prices. In recent years, policy changes and the growth of demand have meant that commodity carry-overs have generally declined to levels that are felt necessary to hedge against a poor crop year. In fact, compared with demand, reduced supply in feed grains has exhausted carry-overs and generated sharp price increases. However, farm economists agree that optimum carry-overs don't necessarily mean that the existing number of farmers and farm units can be maintained—farm productivity is projected to continue growing faster than demand.

If the behavior of prices is only a symptom of farm adjustment problems, why haven't the basic causes been dealt with? Why the preoccupation with prices? Before we analyze the basic long-run trends of U.S. agriculture in the 20th century, the volatility of farm prices is worth investigating in order to understand why prices have been the focus of agricultural discontent and the prime target of policies to allay that discontent.

Price fluctuations

Early in the 1920s, when prices in general were falling, farmers complained of the greater decline in the prices of farm products than in the prices they paid for machinery, farm supplies, and consumption items. Later, in the 1930s, they protested that while farm prices were more flexible than farm output, industrial output was more flexible than industrial prices. This they attributed to monopoly in the nonfarm economy and the ability of big business to administer prices, whereas agricultural markets remained out of the farmer's control. While there is an element of truth in this argument, it is oversimplified because it does not take into consideration the differences in basic economic conditions affecting supply and demand in different industries.

13–6 shows the trend of farm output and prices over most of this century. Output has expanded fairly slowly and has been rather stable except for a sharp decline during the depression of the 1930s. Prices, on the other hand, have been highly unstable, zooming upward during war booms and postwar inflations and downward during depressions, Let's review some historical instances of farm price volatility.

13–7 and 13–8 are hypothetical demand and supply curve situations. First, what happens when demand increases rapidly while supply conditions remain the same or only increase slightly? In 13–7 the demand

13-6. Farm output and prices, 1910–71

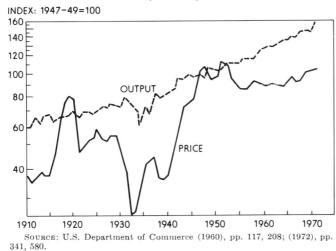

SOURCE: U.S. Department of Commerce (1960), pp. 117, 208; (1972), pp. 341, 580.

13-7. Increase in demand

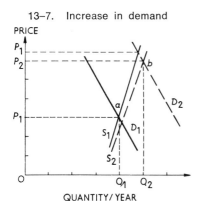

13-8. Increase in supply

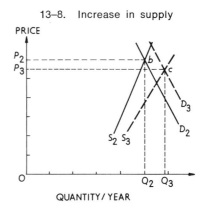

curve shifts to the right (from D_1 to D_2). At the initial price (P_1), D_2 suggests that almost 50 percent more output might be purchased; but the supply conditions indicated by S_1 show that producers can achieve only relatively modest increases in production and that they will do so only with the incentive of higher prices.

The shortage of supply relative to demand is, therefore, adjusted to both by the increase in quantity supplied which is induced by the higher price P_1' and by the restriction in the quantities demanded as a rising price makes the product more expensive and squeezes out some buyers. Even with a slight shift in supply conditions to S_2 (due to technological improvements), the resulting price (P_2) is 100 percent greater than P_1, whereas Q_2 is only about 20 percent greater than Q_1.

This diagram reflects approximately what happened during World

War I and between 1940 and 1950 under the pressure of increased food demands for domestic consumers, the armed forces, and allied countries—shifts in demand outstripped increases in output made possible by productivity increases, so prices rose to eliminate the shortage. Of course, general price inflation exacerbated this tendency to higher prices. In 1972–73 about the same situation prevailed.

13–8 shows what happens when supply increases substantially while demand remains the same or increases only slightly. In the diagram, the supply curve has shifted to the right (S_2 to S_3) to reflect substantial increases in productivity. That is, costs to produce the same quantity as initially (Q_2) are about one third less. Suppliers, therefore, would like to produce a much larger quantity at P_2—over 20 percent more. Consumers, however, will purchase increased quantities only at lower prices. Even if demand gradually expands through extensive growth, say, to D_3, the quantity demanded may not increase enough to maintain the initial price. Thus, the result is an increase in quantity (Q_3), but a reduction in price (to P_3).

This diagram reflects approximately the conditions of change between 1950 and 1960, when productivity increased supply faster than demand. It suggests a very important principle: technological change makes it possible to profitably produce greater quantities at a lower price because unit cost is lowered, **but** there is no guarantee that a price decrease equal to the reduction in unit cost will stimulate demand enough to clear the increment in production.

Note that an increase in demand (a shift in the demand curve) **increases both** the price and the quantity, while an increase in supply (a shift in the supply curve) **increases** output but **lowers** price. The opposite direction of shifts would reverse the effects. Thus, for example, in 13–7 a negative shift in demand from D_2 back to D_1 would reduce both quantity and price. Since supply conditions are rather inelastic (the curve is relatively steep), price falls by a larger percentage than does quantity exchanged.

During the Great Depression, negative shifts in demand attributable to reduced consumer incomes produced the kind of results illustrated by a shift in demand from D_2 to D_1, and during World War II the sharp climb in consumer incomes caused an equally sharp increase in demand (like the shift from D_1 to D_2 in 13–7).

The record of major demand factors summarized in 13–9 helps explain the price fluctuations of the 1930–45 period. Population has increased fairly slowly and steadily during the 20th century (this growth rate has, you recall, corresponded closely to farm output growth). And per capita consumption has not changed very much in the long run, but it did dip substantially during the depressed 1930s, and it rose most rapidly during the 1940s. At the same time, exports of farm products fell during the 1930s and recovered during the late 1940s. A good deal

13–9.   Major demand influences, 1910–60

INDEX (OR %): 1947–49=100

SOURCE: U.S. Department of Commerce (1960), pp. 7, 185, 281.

of the dip of both output and prices in the 1930s and of their rapid expansion in the 1940s, therefore, can be explained in terms of demand for food and fiber. The amount of land harvested changed only insignificantly, since most farms were kept in production in good times and bad, and the efficiency of the farm sector grew slowly, increasing only by one third from 1930 to 1945. Consequently, most of the year-to-year price and income movements in agriculture were attributable to gyrations in demand generated by the Great Depression and World War II.

Supply factors were chiefly responsible for the downward push on farm prices in the 1920s and in the 1950s and 1960s. 13–10 shows that while crop acreage was fairly stable until recently, supply was augmented by two major changes. The record of the 1920s was especially affected by the introduction of tractors and thus the decreased number of acres needed to provide feed for horses and mules. This trend continued to release acreage and increase food supply for several decades, but after 1950 the amount of change was very small. In the 1940s and 1950s, crop yield per acre began to increase rapidly. This reflected the rapid increase in productivity associated with scientific agriculture. Especially in the latter part of the 1950s, this tended to shift supply curves to the right and thus to reduce price while increasing output, just as illustrated in our feed corn example. Since consumer demand is not very responsive to price changes in agriculture, the free market price decreases might have been larger if it had not been for the gradual demand shift caused by rising population during the 1950s.

13–10.   Major supply influences, 1910–60

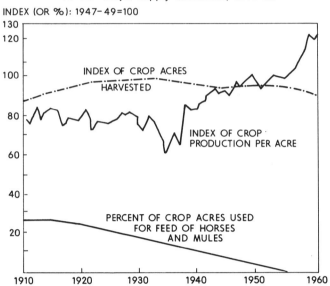

INDEX (OR %): 1947–49=100

SOURCE: U.S. Department of Commerce (1960), p. 281.

Our analysis so far has enabled us to explain the long cycles in agricultural prices, the protracted booms and busts. We must now turn our attention to the long-run trend that explains the chronic tendency toward agricultural overproduction—it is on this trend that cycles of boom-and-bust in agriculture have been superimposed.

Basic trends

On the demand side, population almost doubled while per capita income increased steadily—thus, one can conclude, the demand curve shifted positively by a factor of two since 1920. On the supply side, productivity increases have been so great that output per unit of input doubled over the last 50 years. But what's more important, the technological changes that raised productivity did so by shifting farm inputs in favor of capital. As a consequence, output per man-hour increased to more than four times the 1920 level. This means that half of the farmers who were farming in 1920 would have had to leave agriculture in order to increase farm production by just the same amount as—but no more than—the growth in demand. This is just about what happened between 1920 and 1970.

In order to get a feel for the adjustment process that was required, let's see what conditions would have been like if government policy called for freezing farm prices, at, say, their 1920 levels. Yearly increases in productivity would have lowered costs each year and, given 1920 prices, producers would have had an incentive to increase production by expanding acreage and farming more intensively—the basic trend of output would have been to increase in parallel with productivity increases as long as acreage could be expanded. On the demand side, at 1920 prices, the quantity demanded would have increased in reflection of population growth plus rising family incomes. The basic trend of demand would have been to rise at a slightly higher rate than population.

Plotting and comparing these two basic trends on a ratio chart would reveal that production rose much faster than demand. Had the policy aim been to freeze prices at their 1920 levels over the years, it would have been necessary for the government to buy and store ever-increasing amounts that demanders would refuse at 1920 prices. We would have been swamped by our commodity carry-overs.

Alternatively, how could the forces underlying these divergent trends have been reconciled? What if farm prices had been left free of government interference? Because the trend was for supply to outpace demand, prices would have fallen over the years. Farmers would have responded by decreasing output—cutting back acreage, selling or abandoning their farms. As farm prices fell compared with nonfarm prices, consumers would have responded by slightly increasing their consumption of food and fiber products. If prices had fallen sufficiently each year, the trend of actual production would have been lowered and that of consumption raised so that the two would have been identical—the market would have cleared each year and no stocks would have had to be consigned to storage.

Our knowledge of consumer reactions to lower farm product prices tells us that the bulk of the adjustment task would have fallen upon producers—currently, estimates are that a 1 percent increase in farm output would require a 4.5 percent decrease in prices to clear the market. Even a large percentage reduction in farm prices would produce only a minor increase in the quantity demanded but would prove disastrous for farmers' profits. This, in turn, suggests that when potential demand shifts slowly compared with potential supply, a very large percentage of farm operators have to leave agriculture. The surviving producers would operate profitably over the years, but many producers would be forced out by heavy losses.

In sum, what the foregoing illustrates is that productivity increases make it possible for efficient farmers to operate profitably at lower prices and higher levels of output, to the benefit of consumers. But under typical demand conditions in agriculture, price reductions which are equal to unit cost reductions will not stimulate demand sufficiently for the market to absorb the associated increases in output. Therefore, in such cases, some producers must leave the industry before supply will again equal demand at a price that permits profitable operation.

Of course, the market has *not* in fact operated in the manner described for this example. We actually attempted something like freezing prices at their 1920 levels. Therefore, government had to stockpile farm products for many years. And many unprofitable producers hung on year after year because they did not have or did not recognize alternative opportunities. Thus we had a chronic overproduction problem and huge stockpiles because prices were not left free to do their job. Actual farm policy was not as inflexible as set forth in our hypothetical example. Relative farm prices were allowed to drift down, especially in recent years, so many farmers have left agriculture and consumption has been stimulated—but the adjustment process has not been completed.

Two sets of data demonstrate the magnitude of the adjustment problem in agriculture and the influence that government policy has had on farm problems. If the federal price support program had been eliminated in 1960, by 1965 farm prices would have fallen by 15 percent, gross farm receipts would have declined by 4 percent, and farm profits would have been slashed by 34 percent.[14] Currently, if all farm output were produced on just those commercial farms large enough to generate $20,000 per year in gross receipts, only 750,000 farm units would be required, rather than the nearly 3 million we actually have.[15]

Rural poverty

The above analysis implies that the heart of the overproduction problem is the immobility of farm resources. The most acute income problem is not the volatility of prices but the historical persistence of lower incomes in farming as compared with other industries. As technological innovation, especially mechanization, raised the size of the optimum farm unit, some farmers were able to expand and take advantage of various cost-reducing options. Other farmers couldn't or wouldn't amass the capital to expand their land and machinery holdings and, thereby, slipped below the poverty line as relative farm prices fell while their productivity stood still. In spite of their reduced circumstances, many small farmers have hung on because they won't or can't find better alternatives. On the other hand, had smaller farmers found it possible to leave the land as rapidly as productivity made possible their release, overproduction would not have generated rural poverty.

Agriculture has long been characterized as having a smaller share of GNP than of national employment. Farmers and farm managers earn just over half the median income of male employed citizens. And itinerant farm workers are probably our society's most poorly situated group. 13–11 shows that incomes are lower in farm residences than in urban

---

[14] This estimate was made in a study by James Herendon; it and similar studies are reported in Tweeten.

[15] See Ruttan, pp. 16–19, for data on the productivity increases that could be achieved in agriculture with massive reorganization.

13–11.   Median family incomes, 1960

(THOUSANDS OF DOLLARS)

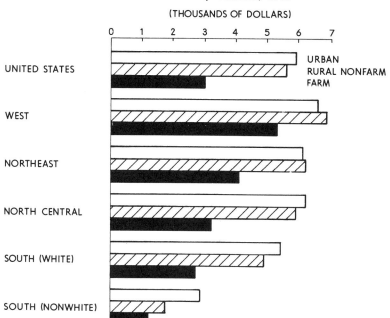

Note: Related data for 1970 indicate that the relationships shown above are representative of current conditions.
SOURCE: Fox, Ruttan, and Witt, p. 80.

or rural nonfarm residences in all parts of the country. What's more,
farm incomes are lowest in predominantly farming regions—note that
farm incomes are highest in the West and Northeast and lowest in the
Midwest and South, especially among Negro operators.

In short, poverty and rural life go hand in hand. Although only 7.5
percent of the population lives on farms, the farm poor account for
9 percent of all people below the poverty line as defined by the Social
Security Administration. Eighteen percent of white farm families and 67
percent of black farm families are below the poverty line as compared
with 14 percent of the total population, 10 percent of nonfarm whites,
and 33 percent of nonfarm blacks. Why? The answer lies in the amount
of land and capital the rural poor have to work with and the education
and skill disadvantages that are statistically linked to their residence
in the case of whites and to residence and race in the case of blacks.

13–12 shows that individual farms differ widely in income levels and
size. Farms with over $20,000 in annual sales are substantial businesses
and cannot be regarded as constituting a low-income problem. They
are not, however, in the big business category, and, like other small
businesses, they face competition from other products and producers,
have a cost squeeze problem, and are constantly trying to adopt improved methods to lower their costs. As 13–12 shows, the number of

13–12.   Number of farms and income by sales class, 1959 and 1969

	1959 farms (1,000)	1969 farms (1,000)	Income per farm 1970 ($)	
			Total	Off-farm earnings
All farms.	3,705	2,728	11,207	5,833
Farms with sales of:				
$40,000 or more	102	222	31,467	5,803
$20,000 to $39,999	210	331	13,465	3,508
$10,000 to $19,999	483	395	9,660	3,452
$5,000 to $9,999	654	390	8,476	4,984
$2,500 to $4,999	618	395	7,514	5,465
$50 to $2,499	349	193	9,013	7,954
Part-time.	885	575	NA	NA
Part-retirement	404	227	NA	NA

NA: Not Available.
Source: U.S. Department of Commerce (1972), pp. 587–88.

these larger farms is increasing, although most of the increase under the commercial farm heading is still in the family farm category rather than in the large corporate farm category.

Apart from itinerant workers, who are landless, farms that are small and inefficient in size are the sites of chronic low-income problems in agriculture. Although they constitute about 50 percent of all farms, they produce only 15 percent of total farm output on 30 percent of the acreage. In the absence of off-farm income, such units generally yield incomes well below the poverty line. No wonder, then, that the number of these farms is decreasing rapidly due to the pressures of falling prices and rising costs. Modern-day technology requires more capital and the purchase of adjoining land in order to take advantage of its cost-reduction opportunities—options usually not open to the small farmer. Thus, small- and medium-sized farmers are turning increasingly to off-farm work to supplement their farm incomes. Note the inverse relationship between farm sales class and off-farm earnings.

Frequently, a factory job will turn a small freeholder into a sundown farmer with about the same farm output and income as before. Also, a working wife can supplement the budget and help add to savings that may go to improving and expanding farm output. Studies have demonstrated nationally that counties with the most urban and industrial employment also tend to have higher farm incomes, and the reason appears to lie in the labor market. Competition for labor raises farm wages, and off-farm work supplements farm family incomes.

This brings us to the problem of the migration of farm population. Migration from farm areas has been highly selective with respect to age, farm-income potential, and education. Successful farmers over 35 have had little reason to leave farming and generally have had no desire to abandon what they view as a superior life-style. Farmers over 35 whose sole source of income has come from trying to glean a living from a hillside, postage stamp of a farm usually have had no nonfarm skills. Theirs has been a hard choice. Typically, they have had to choose between remaining in a life of rural poverty and migrating to a city to work at a dead-end job at a wage that wouldn't carry them over the poverty line.

Rural residents under 30 have been more inclined to migrate if they were from low- or medium-productivity farms. Even though such farm operators may have had poor immediate prospects for nonfarm employment, they were young enough to tough it through some bad years while they acquired a skill. Generally, the better educated among the younger rural residents in a given sex or race category have been more inclined to migrate to a metropolitan area.

Cutting across these categories have been those who had no choice but to leave. They were farm tenants who lost their leases as acreages were consolidated, poor farmers who went bankrupt, and sons and daughters of successful farmers who weren't needed on the family farm.

What the foregoing should make extremely clear is that migration from rural areas has been heavily weighted in favor of the young and the better educated. On the other hand, those who have remained in rural areas have been disproportionately over 35 (87 percent of all farm operators were 35 or older in 1969) and poorly educated. Recognition of these migration patterns has generated political support for rural development that would build up the nonfarm economy in the countryside.

In most farm regions today, people are hoping that industrial development in rural areas will solve their labor adjustment problems. They hope that factories will move near so they will not have to move away from their farms. Unfortunately, only a few farm areas will be able to solve their adjustment problem in this manner, because there are not enough new plants and new jobs to blanket the countryside. Also, remember that the amount of labor adjustment needed in farming is very great. Farm employment fell from 9.9 million to 3.8 million from 1950 to 1970. But the adjustment has not been completed. The 750,000 farm units we cited as minimally necessary to produce the Nation's farm output would require fewer than 2 million workers.

The farm labor adjustment problem is easier not only when industry moves into the rural area but when it is less difficult for labor to move because jobs are plentiful in urban areas. 13–13 shows that net migration of the farm population was very low in the depression of the 1930s. Other data show that recessions check rural out-migration, whereas recoveries and booms stimulate rural-urban movement.

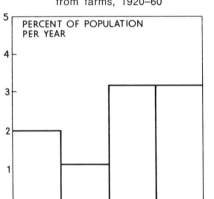

13–13.   Annual average net migration
from farms, 1920–60

SOURCE: Research and Policy Committee of the
Committee for Economic Development, p. 19.

As we have noted, it is easier for young farm people to move and to find urban work when they have received a high level of education and training. Unfortunately, a low level of education and training is characteristic of low-income farming areas, especially in the predominantly black or all-black schools of the South and the Border States. Also, young people in rural areas who are out of touch with urban America need more counseling and public employment information services to help them determine what types of jobs are available and where. Currently, little assistance is being offered to help people relocate. In spite of recent experiments to the contrary, our employment offices are designed to help local employers find workers and to issue unemployment compensation—in no meaningful sense do we have a **national** employment service.

A last note with respect to migration: even a massive migration of low-income farmers probably would not solve the oversupply problem that affects the incomes of the larger farm units. The very small units do not collectively account for enough production to dent the surplus problem. To have equilibrium in agriculture, some of the medium-sized units will have to leave the market as well. And this is where one of the greatest difficulties lies: how do you convince a man with a section of Mississippi Delta land with topsoil three feet deep that he is a submarginal farmer?

Compensatory farm policy

In 1973, farm prices climbed sharply, reaching all-time highs as compared with nonfarm prices. Record exports, especially to the Soviet

Union, and domestic affluence had pumped up demand, while two years of corn blight followed by a soggy harvest season that stranded corn, soybeans, and sorghum in the fields had restricted supply. One reaction to this essentially short-term price fluctuation was reconsideration of the long-term aspects of our basic farm legislation. Government programs to encourage the growth of farm productivity had been continued all through the years of farm surpluses and were unlikely to be terminated. But it was expected that the programs designed to compensate farmers for the side effects of rapid productivity growth would be closely scrutinized. In 1973, 14 major farm laws were to expire, which provided wide latitude for restructuring farm policy. The one-man, one-vote ruling of the Supreme Court had cut down the rural bias of the Congress and thus raised the likelihood that government subsidies to agriculture would be reduced.

Apparently, many in Congress and the administration believed that American farming could adjust to productivity increases with less federal assistance. In short, some felt that enough farmers had left farming to turn chronic surpluses into potential food and fiber deficits, thus making farm programs at best redundant. Whether this conviction was correct is not clear at this point, but why people were convinced of its accuracy is clear. In 1972–73, when the Agriculture Department spent $4 billion on agricultural subsidies, farm prices hit historic highs. In view of the recent behavior of prices, it was difficult for many to see why agricultural incomes should be bolstered from the federal treasury.

At this turn, we should review compensatory U.S. farm policy since 1920. We hope that several key factors will become apparent from our survey—because of confusion over the basic causes of the farm problem, agricultural legislation does not meet head on either the overproduction or the low-income problem; and, generally, legislation has compromised the economics of the situation to meet political requirements.

Federal policies designed to compensate the farmer for the side effects of rapid productivity increases have been aimed at maintaining the farmer in a *parity* relationship with nonfarm producers. To accomplish this aim, input and output restrictions, government purchases and storage of commodities, and subsidies paid directly to farmers when prices sag have been used in various combinations. In addition, legislation to help the rural poor has been part of the War on Poverty. By no elaborate argument or inference can you find in farm legislation per se any element that is aimed at speeding the departure of farmers from farms or even assisting them in moving to urban areas.

In the period 1921–32, farm policy proposals largely ignored the long-run tendencies of agriculture and centered instead upon the cyclical sources of farm depression. Early in the decade, low prices were recognized as effects of the 1920–21 recession and the decline in exports resulting from the postwar expansion of European agriculture. Yet, since these causes were beyond the policy-makers' scope, proposals were made to maintain parity between prices received and prices paid by farmers. After the McNary-Haugen bill, which embodied this notion, was twice vetoed by President Coolidge, the Agricultural Marketing Act of 1929 was passed and signed by President Hoover. It established the Federal Farm Board, which was to found stabilizing corporations to be owned by cooperative marketing associations.

The corporations were to use a $500 million fund to purchase farm commodities in the market to support their prices. The basic idea was summed up by the phrase *ever-normal granary,* coined in 1922 by Henry A. Wallace, who a decade later became Roosevelt's Secretary of Agriculture. Prices were to be stabilized through the purchase and storage of commodities when demand was weak and sales from stocks when demand was strong. (Turn back to 13–5 to visualize how government buying in good crop years would hold up prices and vice versa.) The crash of prices in the recession phase of the Great Depression swamped all Farm Board efforts. Other stabilizing attempts of the decade included tariff barriers and improved credit facilities.

From the above you can see that the implications of productivity increases were not apparent to policy-makers. It just did not occur to them that a growing number of Americans would require fewer *not* more farmers each decade. Thus, farm problems were attributed to business depressions and the weather—cyclical factors. People did not see that cost reductions would require a downward relative price trend and the exodus of farmers if chronic overproduction and low farm incomes were to be avoided.

During the Great Depression, the parity price support concept was extended under the Agricultural Adjustment Act of 1933 and subsequent legislation. The goal was to maintain farm incomes by pegging the ratio of prices received to prices paid at the average that prevailed over 1910–14, the so-called golden age of agriculture. On the demand side of the market, federally supported food distribution to the needy and the school lunch program were inaugurated.

For some crops, total acreage allotments were designed to reduce production and thus enhance prices. (Refer again to 13–5; an acreage allotment program that reduces the quantity harvested will have the same effect on the supply curve, i.e., move it from S_2 to S_1, as will government purchases and storage.) Cooperating farmers were also paid a subsidy based on their output. Later in the New Deal, government loans were made to farmers on their crops by the Commodity Credit Corporation (CCC) at stated percentages of parity. Whenever market prices fell below loan values, farmers had the option of defaulting on their loans and letting the CCC take title to and store their output. Starting with 1939, wheat, corn, cotton, and tobacco were stockpiled in large quantities. For crops that were not easily stored, a system of marketing agreements was established by the Secretary of Agriculture as a way of limiting output.

The farm programs of the 1930s also failed to deal with agriculture's basic problems. The marketing agreements, acreage restrictions, and marketing quotas did limit market supply and thus pushed up relative prices. But these plans were instituted by prorating production or acreage among producers according to acreage or past output records rather than the productivity of producers. To do otherwise would have been politically impossible. This meant that high-cost, inefficient farming units received allotments right along with the best farmers in the business. Further, pressure has always been applied to design the programs so that prices are high enough to make low-efficiency units profitable. By contrast, uninhibited market forces tend to push prices low enough to purge the least efficient producers, resulting in lower prices to consumers and profitable conditions for the remaining producers.

The parity concept is also basically fallacious. It implies that prices paid by farmers reflect costs and that a policy maintaining a constant ratio between prices paid by farmers and the prices at which they sell would guarantee them a constant real income. Here is where the error lies: one of the parity notion's implicit assumptions is that productivity increases will not come along to lower costs. Actually, improved farming methods could and did more than offset higher prices paid by farmers. Real unit costs declined as compared with 1910–14, with the consequence that the parity price contained an ever-increasing profit margin for the most efficient producers and enabled many of the less efficient to survive. Thus, under the parity concept some farmers have had the incentive to stay in farming when under free market conditions they would have left the industry.

During World War II, ceiling prices were placed on most nonperishable agricultural commodities. With the surge in demand, sales rose, prices hit the ceilings, and output was supplemented from government inventories. But after Europe resumed production in the postwar period, surpluses again mounted. By 1960, government stocks had hit the $6 billion mark.

Legislative innovations were proposed and enacted. They included the Soil Bank (1956) for long-term retirement of acreage, direct payments to wool producers to close the gap between free market and support prices, assistance to farmers selling crops overseas, and sliding scale price supports in place of support at a fixed percent of parity. However, in the 1950s no change in the broad framework of farm programs was made that acknowledged the root causes of agriculture's ills.

In spite of improved understanding of the problem, politicians feel they must continue to pledge the salvation of the family farm. Consequently, no concerted effort has been put forth to ease the movement of those high-cost, low-income, small-acreage farmers who constitute 80 percent of all farmers and yet benefit little or not at all from current programs. Further, under current conditions, producers of some crops have successfully campaigned against production limitations—for example, President Kennedy's marketing quota proposal was killed at the committee stage in Congress. Instead, farmers have gained a system of acreage restrictions that permit them to farm their remaining acreage more intensively and thus undermine the entire program while benefiting from price supports.

In the 1960s, only token changes in the general approach to compensatory policy were made. The small, inefficient farmer continued to bear the burden of adjustment without meaningful assistance. Congress enacted various public facility assistance programs for rural communities which were designed to help small towns attract industrial investment. Farmers who sought off-farm work were eligible for Office of Economic Opportunity training and assistance programs as long as they fell within the categories defined by the program guidelines. But no other efforts of significance were made to ease the transition for those who wanted to pack up and go to the city. For those small farm operators who chose to remain on the farm, the various price support programs were of little aid. For example, in 1964, government payments per farm in the class of farms which sold between $2,000 and $5,000 worth of products averaged only $173 and amounted to less than 9 percent of net income per farm.

In the 1960s, however, the overproduction problem did abate and CCC stocks did decline. (See 13–14.) Agricultural exports increased

13–14. Value of commodity credit corporation stocks, selected years, 1950–70

(in millions of dollars)

1950	2,624
1955	4,972
1960	6,021
1965	3,892
1970	1,858

SOURCES: U.S. Department of Commerce (1962), p. 633; (1972), p. 597.

by 10 percent during the decade. Population growth, growing exports, and rising per capita income also bolstered demand. The number of farms decreased from 4 million to 2.9 million and total acreage harvested fell almost 6 percent. In short, acreage reductions just offset productivity increases during the decade, and stockpiled commodities declined primarily through various government export programs and the increased demand associated with the growth of population.

This does not mean that chronic overproduction is no longer a basic tendency in American agriculture. As long as low per capita income prevents Asia, Africa, and South America from, in effect, harvesting our bounty, productivity increases will tend to outdistance the growth of American food and fiber demand in the foreseeable future. For the near future, no one expects the number of farm units to decline to the technically feasible 750,000 units we cited earlier, but there is still a reservoir of farms that account for a small portion of production yet comprise a majority of farm units.

Some idea of the potential for off-farm migration can be obtained by comparing the productivity of commercial farms above and below $10,000 in value of sales. If farms in the over-$10,000 category were to increase production by 20 percent, they could supply our total farm output requirements; such an increase in output is well within the potential capacity of these farms.

The history of farm policy since the 1930s clearly illustrates the futility of dealing only with price symptoms as a way of curing basic farm ills. Not until long-term acreage reduction programs were inaugurated in the late 1960s did agriculture show any tendency to reduce its potential for overproduction. Today, the farm problem is still what it has been for the past half century. Not until we show a resolve to adopt policies that will speed the flow of resources out of farming while easing the burden of those who must make the transition will the related problems of rural poverty and potential overproduction be eliminated.

Even if a basic balance between output potential and demand is struck, farming will still be subject to the sharp yearly fluctuations in net income we described above. Thus we can expect farm policy to continue to include provisions to keep the volatility of prices within legislated limits, especially on the downside. Similarly, we can expect to find government continuing to provide the same stimulus to technological innovation in farming that giant nonfarm corporations are able to provide for themselves.

SUMMARY

Giant business firms wielding unprecedented amounts of economic power have become corollaries of the mass production and distribution of nonfarm commodities. Such firms have been able to exercise an element of control over their markets and have thereby avoided sharp price fluctuations and long-term overcapacity. But in the agricultural sector, farms have remained small enterprises which are exposed to violent swings in price and the depressing effects of chronic overproduction.

1. Although many manufacturing firms and most public utilities have reached gigantic proportions, the precise impact of such scale is not clear. As firms have grown in size, the national economy has also grown,

so no distinct trend in industrial concentration has asserted itself since 1920. Further, measures of industrial concentration are ambiguous indicators of market power.

2.   Changes in market structure and conduct have led to the development of theories of oligopoly and monopolistic competition to analyze the behavior of firms operating in markets which are not characterized by either monopoly or competition. These theoretical developments have thrown new light on the relationship of advertising and product differentiation to market structure. However, in spite of theoretical breakthroughs, there is much that is not understood about the economic welfare effects of contemporary market structures; it does seem clear though that a good portion of advertising and product differentiation constitutes a waste of scarce resources.

3.   Bigness has resulted from a variety of factors in addition to economies of scale, among them the quest for market power. Nor has bigness been uniquely associated with product or production innovation. However, it does not appear that the advent of the corporate giant has put an end to enterprising management. Though differently organized and managed than the small firms of the 19th century, large firms appear sensitive to changing economic conditions and stockholder interests.

4.   Antitrust legislation and enforcement have had a checkered history since 1920. In spite of the Clayton Act (1914), a wave of mergers took place in the 1920s and the Supreme Court reaffirmed the rule of reason. The 1930s were characterized by additional regulation of business and vigorous antitrust action. Since the end of World War II, the courts and the law have leaned toward the presumption that horizontal and vertical mergers involving significant market shares are illegal. The same is true of some conglomerate mergers. Thus, the law has drifted toward recognizing that the size of a firm measured in relation to the market is a criterion of monopoly power. But as yet the law does not require halting the growth of firms at the point at which unit costs are minimized.

We have no rules against bigness per se, only against bigness that generates high levels of concentration. Thus, the social and political power that can be exercised by giant corporations can't be subjected to prior restraint by forcing dissolution unless high concentration can be demonstrated.

5.   Productivity increases in agriculture have tended to expand agricultural capacity faster than increasing population and per capita income have expanded demand. Consequently, many farmers have had to leave farming since 1920, and farm acreage has actually declined in recent years.

6.   The departure of farmers from agriculture has not proceeded rapidly enough to avoid chronic overproduction. Because farm prices have been highly volatile, government farm policy has chiefly consisted

of measures to stabilize prices. One effect of such measures has been to slow the agricultural adjustment process—relatively inefficient farmers have been able to remain in farming because government policy has maintained prices above long-term market-clearing levels.

7. Rural poverty has been a by-product of rapid productivity increases; rural areas, especially in the South and Midwest, account for more than their population share of poverty. Small farmers in their middle years with little capital and poor educations have been unable to expand their farms to take full advantage of new technologies. At the same time, their lack of skills and their age have restricted their potential opportunities in the city. Consequently, they have remained on their tiny, capital-poor farms under poverty conditions. By contrast, young rural people with adequate or good educations have either migrated to urban areas or have been able to profitably expand and modernize their farming operations.

8. Government assistance to farmers has been of two broad types: federally sponsored research and extension services to aid the farmer in increasing his productivity and compensatory policies aimed at reducing the amplitude of price swings. Unfortunately, compensatory policies have dealt only with the price symptoms of agriculture's adjustment problems, rather than assisting inefficient farmers in making the transition to a new way of life. Thus, instead of helping to bring the divergent trends of output and demand together, federal policy has actually slowed the process of adaptation to productivity increases.

REFERENCES

M. A. Adelman, "The Two Faces of Economic Concentration," *PI,* Fall 1970.

J. S. Bain, *Industrial Organization* (New York: John Wiley & Sons, Inc., 1959).

Committee for Economic Development, Research and Policy Committee, *An Adaptive Program for Agriculture* (New York: Committee for Economic Development, 1962).

Council of Economic Advisers, "Annual Report of the Council of Economic Advisers" in *Economic Report of the President* (Washington: U.S. Government Printing Office, 1965).

K. Fox, V. W. Ruttan, and L. W. Witt, *Farming, Farmers and Markets for Farm Goods*, Supplementary Paper No. 15 (New York: Committee for Economic Development, 1962).

J. K. Galbraith, *The Affluent Society* (Boston: Houghton Mifflin Co., 1958).

———, *American Capitalism: The Concept of Countervailing Power,* rev. ed. (Boston: Houghton Mifflin Co. 1956).

———, *The New Industrial State* (Boston: Houghton Mifflin Co., 1967).

E. O. Heady, *A Primer on Food, Agriculture and Public Policy* (New York: Random House, 1967).

A. D. H. Kaplan, *Big Enterprise in a Competitive System* (Washington, D.C.: Brookings Institution, 1964).

J. L. McConnell, "Corporate Earnings by Size of Firm," *Survey of Current Business,* May 1945.

G. W. Nutter, *A Quantitative Study of the Extent of Enterprise Monopoly in the United States, 1899–1939* (Chicago: University of Chicago Press, 1951).

V. W. Ruttan, "Agricultural Policy in an Affluent Society," in *Agricultural Policy in an Affluent Society,* eds. V. W. Ruttan et al. (New York: W. W. Norton & Co., Inc., 1969).

F. M. Scherer, *Industrial Market Structure and Economic Performance* (Chicago: Rand McNally & Co., 1970).

H. Sherman, *Radical Political Economy* (New York: Basic Books, Inc., 1972).

Temporary National Economic Committee, Monograph 13, 77th Cong., 1st sess. (Washington, D.C.: U.S. Government Printing Office, 1941).

L. G. Tweeten, "Commodity Programs for Agriculture," in *Agricultural Policy: A Review and Needs,* Technical Papers, vol. 5, National Advisory Commission on Food and Fiber, August 1967.

U.S. Department of Commerce, *Historical Statistics of the United States* (Washington, D.C.: U.S. Government Printing Office, 1960).

———, *Statistical Abstract of the United States* (Washington, D.C.: U.S. Government Printing Office, 1962, 1965, 1971, 1972).

U.S. Senate Committee on the Judiciary, Subcommittee on Antitrust and Monopoly, *Concentration in American Industry,* 85th Cong., 1st sess. (Washington, D.C.: U.S. Government Printing Office, 1957).

14 THE QUEST FOR SECURITY

Two related by-products of economic development are the threat to the economic security of some individuals and the reduction in the range of their economic opportunities. Indeed, even when growth produces affluence for most members of a society, individual members of that society may be pauperized in the process. Recall from chapter 13 the lot of the farmers who have been forced out of farming as labor requirements have been reduced. The farm problem amply illustrates this paradox of plenty in which the burdens of adjusting to more productive methods are heavily concentrated upon a small group of individuals.

American workers have reacted to threats to their security and constricted economic opportunity in several general ways. On the one hand, they have organized. In the 19th century, the Populist party was formed to represent the interests of farmers and industrial workers in the political arena against the power of Big Business. Workers have also formed economic coalitions of which the union movement is the most important example. The principal aim of unions has been to gain security and a larger share of the pie by capturing some of the employer's economic prerogatives.

On the other hand, many Americans have not been able to choose a strategy involving group action and have, therefore, faced economic adversity, or its possibility, as isolated individuals. In this latter group are those who through foresight and/or chance have avoided or minimized economic hardships—they constitute what Americans call the middle class. Unfortunately, there are and have been large numbers of Americans who have not been able to adequately safeguard themselves against hard times; often they are born in adverse economic and social circumstances and remain there all their lives—they are America's poor.

In this chapter we will review the union movement as a quest for group security that, in turn, yields individual security. Then we will focus our attention on those for whom security seems to be primarily an individual matter in order to learn, among other things, what the role of government has been in shaping the environment in which individuals seek economic security.

UNION BARGAINING

Union organization reflects the efforts of a producer group to influence the price of its members' services and, thereby, to increase their real incomes. In addition, unions are special kinds of political organizations composed of people who are trying to obtain some voice in determining the working conditions affecting their lives.

To a large extent, unions are protest organizations that look after the interests of individual workers in the giant, impersonal corporations of modern industry. Some writers have referred to collective bargaining as a form of industrial democracy in which the workers' representatives participate in making rules regarding working conditions. The arbitration procedures for settling grievances have been referred to as a form of industrial jurisprudence, settling a worker's claims to job rights and protecting him from the arbitrary exercise of supervisory authority. Many an employer has discovered the hard way that human attitudes and emotions cannot be ignored in running a business, that a smooth grievance and arbitration procedure and effective collective bargaining may avoid unnecessary strikes and slowdowns in productivity.

The growth of the union movement

14-1 shows that the growth of the union movement has been uneven and has leveled off in recent years. Prior to 1900, the union movement was of negligible importance from a numerical standpoint. Then, in the early years of this century, a burst of organizing activity on the part of the American Federation of Labor (AFL) brought union membership to over 2 million workers. Afterward membership growth was very slow until World War I produced a tremendous increase in the demand for labor. As part of the defense effort, cooperative union-management relations were encouraged, so union membership almost doubled between 1915 and 1920.

After the war, unions lost ground until the mid-1930s, when protective legislation gave them a boost. World War II further spurred membership as the organized industries expanded. Frequently, in cases of *closed shop* agreements between the union and management, new workers were required to join the union as a condition of employment.

In the 19th century and the first three decades of the 20th century, the growth of union organization occurred in a hostile political and legal environment. Social Darwinism and its economic corollary, laissez-

14–1.   Union membership, 1896–1970

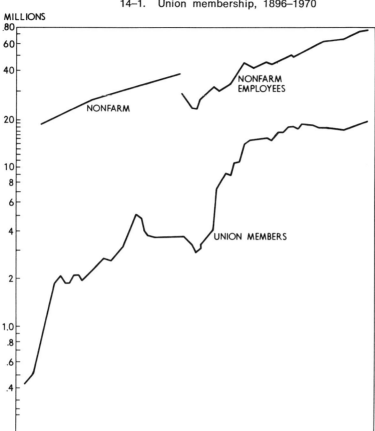

SOURCES: U.S. Department of Commerce (1960), p. 98; U.S. Department of Labor (1972), pp. 26, 333.

faire, were interpreted to mean that organization of workers to influence wages, hours, or working conditions was morally and economically wrong. And the power of the state was invoked to give effect to this conviction.

Management employed a wide variety of devices to hinder unionization: "agitators" were discharged and blacklisted by employers; employers, in effect, went on strike by locking workers out; "scabs" were employed to replace striking workers, while private detective firms supplied men to harass pickets; yellow-dog contracts (agreements not to join a union) were widespread prerequisites of employment; paternalism toward employees was designed to kill the unionization urge with kindness; and management-dominated employee associations, so-called company unions, were established to head off genuine unions. Violence and bloodshed were commonplace as both sides resorted to extralegal tactics.

For their part, the courts backed up such management practices. In the early 1800s, attempts to organize and bargain collectively were interpreted as "criminal conspiracy." After the overthrow of the conspiracy doctrine, the courts continued to rule against strikes, picketing, and boycotts. Then the Sherman Anti-trust Act was interpreted to include unions as "conspiracies in restraint of trade." In 1914 the Clayton Act exempted unions from the application of the Sherman Act, but until the Norris–La Guardia Act was passed in 1932, the yellow-dog contract was enforced by the courts, and injunctions against union activities were granted freely.

Largely in reaction to the Great Depression, the Norris–La Guardia and Wagner acts, as we have seen, gave carte blanche to unions by legally establishing the right to organize and bargain collectively and outlawing the "unfair labor practices" enumerated above. Union membership bounced back from its early depression low and grew at unprecedented rates.

By the 1930s, the American labor movement had clearly established its character, which was in large part implanted by its dominant organization, the AFL. The AFL's philosophy was essentially bread-and-butter unionism, political neutrality, and craft-by-craft organization.

Attempts of the various socialist and communist organizations to make unions an agent of the class struggle failed even in the distraught years of the Great Depression. The melting pot nature of America, the Nation's upward social mobility, and the identification of journeymen workers with their employers, themselves usually former journeymen, all militated against class consciousness. Uninterested in political control, laboring men reacted positively to a philosophy or organization that was economic in character. Labor wanted "more," as AFL President Samuel Gompers, a former radical, put it, and was determined to get more by organizing the crafts.

This organizing philosophy has remained basically intact with one major exception: the union movement was extended to include industrial workers outside the crafts. There had long been attempts to form organizations that included all workers regardless of craft who were employed in a particular industry, such as the steel industry. But except for isolated instances, such as the United Mine Workers, industrial unionism was unsuccessful until the labor legislation of the 1930s cleared the way for organization along industrial as well as craft lines. In 1936, the Congress of Industrial Organizations (CIO) was formed. The CIO's goal was to enlist in one union all the blue-collar workers in a particular industry, with no exceptions. The growth of the Steelworkers and the Automobile Workers goes a long way toward explaining the surge in union membership in the 1930s.

In the postwar period, however, union growth again slowed. Thus, starting in the mid-1930s with only 7 percent of the labor force and 11 percent of nonfarm employees, by the late 1950s union membership had risen to 23 percent of the labor force and 32 percent of nonfarm employees. Since then, union membership has grown slowly in absolute terms and receded to less than 30 percent of the labor force.

During the postwar period, two important labor acts were passed which regulated the activities of unions. The Taft-Hartley Act of 1947 defined "unfair labor practices" of unions—"featherbedding" is an example—to go along with the unfair management practices outlawed by the Wagner Act; laid down rules of conduct, especially financial, for union leaders; precluded certain provisions of collective bargaining agreements, such as the closed shop; and established a procedure for avoiding strikes that might paralyze the Nation, e.g., a nationwide rail strike.

The Landrum-Griffin Act of 1959 extended government regulation of union management in order to protect rank and file members from abuse at the hands of union leaders. It was largely a response to the congressional labor-racketeering investigations of the late 1950s, which spotlighted the alleged illegal conduct of the Teamsters Union leadership and led to criminal trials and prison sentences for several very highly placed Teamsters officers.

With notable exceptions, which we'll cite below, it appears that unions have about reached their saturation point. They have organized about all of the groups that are easy to organize and in which they have the greatest potentials for seizing a portion of management's monopoly power. The industries most highly organized tend to be the skilled crafts of the construction industry, the various transportation and utility industries, and the most highly capitalized and concentrated of the manufacturing industries. The unions are especially well organized in large plants and giant companies because they can mobilize worker protests where organizations are large and human relations most difficult. On the other hand, the atomized, highly competitive industries in manufacturing and agriculture, such as textiles and lumber, are the least organized (see 14–2); and white-collar workers in general remain unorganized.

In spite of much talk about "drives" to organize the South, unions have had only limited success below the Mason-Dixon line. On explanation for this is easily verified: it is the South's industrial structure, as 14–2 shows. When highly unionized industries open plants in the South, they tend to get organized; but the South has a higher proportion of its jobs in the less unionized industries. The importance of other factors in explaining the degree of unionization in the South is not readily assessed. Smaller plants, smaller cities, and the attitudes of workers (affected by job scarcity and individualism in a rural culture) tend to make union organization more difficult. So do *right-to-work* laws and the harassment of union organizers and employers by local law enforce-

14–2. Extent of union bargaining in manufacturing, 1958*

Industry	Workers in plants covered by bargaining		Employment in industry group	
	U.S.	South	U.S.	South
Highly unionized:			21%	18%
Petroleum refining	90%	88%		
Primary metals	89	95		
Transportation equipment	87	86		
Ordnance	84	NA†		
Rubber	81	NA		
Substantially unionized:			47	36
Stone-clay-glass	78	65		
Paper	76	79		
Electrical machinery	73	NA		
Fabricated metals	71	54		
Food products	68	41		
Machinery	68	63		
Chemicals	65	62		
Printing	65	61		
Moderately unionized:			17	16
Tobacco	63	72		
Apparel	60	30		
Miscellaneous	54	NA		
Instruments	52	35		
Furniture	50	28		
Lightly unionized:			15	30
Leather	49	32		
Lumber	44	27		
Textiles	30	14		
All manufacturing	67	46	100	100

* As late as 1968, these data on the South were verified as "still true today" (see Marshall, p. 66);
and as late as 1962, the national ratios were substantially the same as in 1958 (see Strasser, p. 165).
† NA: Not Available.
SOURCE: Douty.

ment officials whose conduct in office is determined by the resident power structure. The former prevents bargaining contracts which require employees to join the union as a condition of continued employment; the latter has obvious effects on the effectiveness of organizing campaigns. As a result of these diverse factors, in most types of industries the South has a smaller proportion of its workers in plants covered by collective bargaining. (See 14–2.)

Unions also experience difficulty in trying to organize most sales, clerical, and professional employees; such employees work in fields that are characterized by a large number of employers who often employ relatively few people. This is especially significant because these types of workers are becoming a larger part of the labor force.

On the other hand, sectors of collective bargaining are emerging that seem to foreshadow the union movement's future. The target groups in which union organization has been growing of late are white-collar workers in all industries, who now makeup more than half of the work force; service industry workers, who comprise two thirds of the work force; public employees, especially schoolteachers, policemen, and firemen; and agricultural laborers.

Collectively, these occupations have been all but free of union organization, characterized by low rates of pay, and account for a disproportionate number of blacks, Spanish-Americans, and women. In recent years, the rapid growth in demand in most of these labor markets, the militancy that came with the civil rights movement (women's lib included), President Kennedy's Executive Order facilitating the unionization of federal employees, and permissive state laws have combined to make these occupations and industries emergent sectors of union organization.

If you glance at 14–3, you'll see that, despite the recent gains in union organization, agriculture and industries made up disproportion-

14–3. Union organization by major industry group, 1970

	Percent of all union members	Percent of total employment
Organized above all-industry ratio		
Manufacturing.	44.5	26.2
Mining	1.8	0.9
Contract construction	12.5	4.7
Transportation, communications,		
public utilities.	15.9	6.4
Organized below all-industry ratio		
Wholesale and retail trade	7.5	20.1
Finance, insurance, and real estate	0.3	5.2
Other service industries	6.2	16.0
Agriculture and fishing.	0.1	3.2
Government (including public		
education).	11.2	17.3

SOURCE: U.S. Department of Commerce (1972), pp. 225, 241.

ately of white-collar and service workers generally fall well below their share of union members. Although these sectors account for virtually all of the growth in total union membership since 1955, that growth has been very modest. What's more, the competitive nature of many of the affected labor markets plus the public interest nature of such occupations as policeman and fireman suggests that organizing efforts will continue to be difficult. In short, the future of the union movement seems to be one of pushing against its "natural" limits.[1]

---

[1] For a sector-by-sector analysis of collective bargaining in the relatively unorganized industries and occupations see Wolfbein.

The bargaining process

The primary purpose of collective bargaining is to further the economic interests of union members. The prime means of achieving this end is to obtain a monopoly of the labor supply of a particular employer or in a particular trade. This involves organizing all the workers, getting the employer's agreement to hire only union members or to require that workers, once employed, join the union, or pressuring nonunion workers to stay away. Second, it means having the power (and occasionally using it) to shut down a plant by striking. This is intended to hurt the profits of a company so that the company will be "persuaded" to seek an agreement, or contract, favorable to the union members.

Once established, unions attempt to influence the level of wages in three ways—by raising worker productivity; by restricting the number of workers who enter the market (so-called exclusive unionism); and by negotiating collective bargaining agreements in which management is left free to decide how many workers will be hired but pledges itself to pay a prescribed minimum wage rate. The only important example of the first is provided by the garment workers, who have cooperated in, often initiated, studies aimed at increasing productivity. The craft unions have long practiced the second tactic as a way of putting teeth in their wage demands. And the last is the stock-in-trade of the industrial union which uses an all-or-nothing tactic, work or strike, as a bargaining lever.

Essentially, then, the bargaining process involves a lot of the tactics of a poker game and the use (or threat) of the strike weapon. Public policy has grown to essentially permit a certain kind of legalized monopoly and a certain kind of industrial warfare in order to let the parties to a dispute settle it among themselves.

In practice, very few strikes occur. Since 1929, the first year for which data are available, there has been only one year—1946—in which strikes accounted for more than 1 percent of the potential man-hours of all industry.

However, there are a number of unsolved policy problems. One involves the rights of a minority of workers who do not wish to join the union or pay dues. Another concerns the public interest in maintaining production in key public utilities and in government bodies where workers are organized. A third problem is the extent to which wage bargains may cause inflation.

Recognition of the high costs of strikes to workers, management, and the public, especially in situations in which foreign producers can easily fill voids created by strikes in the United States, may lead to compulsory arbitration as a substitute for strikes. Under a plan pioneered in the steel industry, labor and management agree to ban nationwide strikes and industry shutdowns over issues disputed in the course of negotiating a union-management work contract. Instead, when negotiation fails to settle a dispute, it is referred to an arbitration panel of outside experts whose decision will be binding on both parties. If both parties are satisfied with the plan's trial in the steel, maritime, and railroad industries, it might be adopted nationwide.

Perhaps the greatest policy problem on the labor front concerns discrimination against minority groups. A practice as old as exclusive unionism is to single out ethnic and racial groups who are or aren't eligible to lay brick, finish cement, or fly airplanes. Women have been treated similarly. Further, historical data on the sex, race, and ethnic makeup of law, dental, and medical schools suggest that the professions are not against keeping their rates of pay above free market levels by excluding particular groups.

Labor's progress

What have unions been able to accomplish for their members in terms of wage gains and improvements in working conditions? And to what degree have union activities affected nonunion workers?

Wage increases are not always clearly attributable to union power. Historically, some of the wage gains might have occurred anyway, especially in times of inflation or when the affected companies were expanding and needed to recruit more workers. From the mid-1930s to the end of the Korean War, when unions gained most of their strength and experience, there was an almost continuous rapid rise in prices and expansion of output in the country. Employers either wanted to give wage increases or put up little resistance to them. So-called pattern bargaining, by which wage increases and additional fringe benefits were transmitted to one industry after another, gave an impression of tremendous union power over wages in this country.

Some economists, however, question how much of these increases was attributable to union power. Compared with organized industries, a number of unorganized industries had faster wage increases during the 1940s and 1960s; and study of World War I shows many examples of rapid patterned wage increases at a time when unions weren't numerous enough to be a significant power.

If unions had been a major force in determining wages, you would expect wage rates to have followed the historical pattern of union growth. Although union activity has increased in fits and starts over the 20th century, it is productivity and price indexes rather than unionization that wage rates have followed very closely. 14–4 shows that for more than half a century real wages in manufacturing kept pace with the general rising trend in productivity. 14–5 shows that since 1920 wage costs per unit in manufacturing have corresponded fairly closely to the changes in the wholesale prices of finished goods. Compared to the

14–4.   Manufacturing wages and productivity, 1890–1957

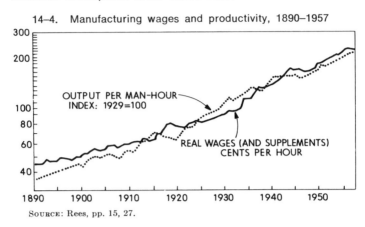

SOURCE: Rees, pp. 15, 27.

14–5.   Manufacturing wage costs and prices, 1920–57

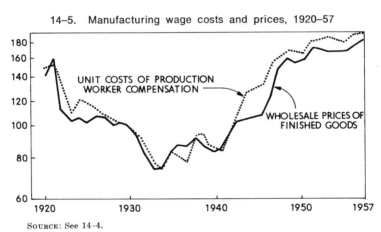

SOURCE: See 14–4.

base year, 1929, wage costs have risen a little more than wholesale prices. This may be because material costs rose a little less rapidly and wages of nonproduction workers may not have grown as rapidly as those of production workers. Also, the spread of skill differentials has narrowed with the general rise in educational levels.

Other data discount unionization's influence on wages. Economists have noted that labor's share of the national income has remained fairly stable during comparable periods in the business cycle. During depressions the profit share falls more, and during business booms profits rise more. Similarly, during booms organized labor loses ground to unorganized workers, but during recessions unorganized workers bear a disproportionate share of the burden on wages. Further, labor force and national income data show that the long-term growth of labor's share of the national income is attributable to the decline in the number of self-employed persons, especially farmers, rather than the influence of unions.

If on a per worker basis labor's percentage of the total output has not increased, it follows that union activity has not redistributed income to labor over the years.[2] Further, if, as we have seen, unit wage costs in manufacturing have not increased at the expense of profits, it follows that union wage gains resulted in either price hikes or dampened price reductions, which, in turn, reduced production and employment or dampened increases in output and employment.

Thus, if the latter observation applies to all heavily unionized industries, we cannot escape the conclusion that unions, having failed to raise the share of the pie going to all workers, have increased the share going to union members. It follows from this that these policies have retarded the growth of organized industries and produced labor surpluses in unorganized industries, such as farming, household services, retailing, and wholesaling.

In short, very high wages may cause more people to seek certain jobs but mean fewer opportunities to obtain them. This conclusion seems paradoxical at first when one considers that union growth was often most rapid in the rapidly expanding industries. However, it is important to bear in mind the fact that this deduction only states that growth rates are *retarded,* not turned into rates of decline, by union activity. It's worth adding that precisely the same conclusions can be said to apply to the output and employment effects of minimum wage legislation.

This analysis also suggests that constant pressure for wage increases may provide a *cost-push* force which generates inflation. If unions do succeed in getting higher wage gains in the fastest growing industries with the greatest productivity gains, innovation as well as expansion in those industries could be retarded. Featherbedding (insisting that obsolete or unnecessary jobs be filled) and other attempts by unions to protect their jobs in the face of new methods of production may also thwart the introduction of improvements.

In sum, in the case of unions, as in the case of farmers and business firms, we face the same long-run problem: the methods used by sellers to protect their interests may hinder the adjustments that are necessary parts of the growth process and slow the overall growth of the economy.

What can we say by way of summarizing labor's progress over the period since 1920? In spite of four wars and a devastating depression, the American economy has achieved growth records and a level of living which only the science fiction of Jules Verne anticipated in the last century. The data show that from an income standpoint labor has progressed in parallel with this growth. In nonincome terms, the gains

---

[2] That union activity prevented a worsening of the worker's relative position is unlikely—in spite of recurrent depressions, this economy has historically been one of labor scarcity in which the drift of wages was upward well before unions had control over a significant portion of the labor force. (See 15–4.)

are even more impressive: hours of work have been reduced from an average of 47.4 per week in 1920 to 39.7 in 1960; physical working conditions have improved tremendously; and the average employees are now treated as human beings rather than as glorified beasts of burden, with the exception of those who hold the high-speed, repetitive production-line jobs.

The workingman's lot today is at a vast remove from the wage-slave days when a man could be prosecuted for quitting his job. The conditions which Marx and Engles described quite accurately are no longer typical, simply because economic growth has carried the *entire* economy to higher levels of material well-being. But while the average has moved up, the itinerant farm worker, the Southern sharecropper, the unskilled urban laborer, the hard-scrabble farmer, and the Appalachian who toils at the face of a "scab" mine are not much better off than their counterparts of several generations back. Certainly, compared with that of other workers, their lot has worsened.

What role did unions play in this change? From a wage standpoint, we have seen that both union activity and minimum wage legislation have actually exacerbated the problems of the groups referred to above while improving the position of the union membership and those who retained their jobs after minimum wages were raised. Yet, in a larger sense, the union movement through direct action and by influencing legislation may have been responsible for most of the nonwage gains that labor has made since 1920—growth made them possible, but unions may have caused them to spill over to labor in general, although the bulk of nonwage benefits still resides with organized labor.

In spite of all the gains made by labor in recent generations, manufacturing workers have consistently lost ground in one important respect. Following the trend established in the 19th century, as manufacturing processes have become more and more mechanized, the growth of assembly-line mass production has steadily lowered skill requirements but raised the degree of pressure felt on the job by the average production worker. As a corollary, the boredom, tension, and feeling of alienation of the typical worker have increased. This is especially true of young workers, whose negative reaction to the production line is much more explicit and intense than their fathers'. Far from taking pride in the products they help to produce, some workers give vent to their frustrations by sabotaging products on the line. Others drink, pop pills, or shoot dope on the job and/or become chronic absentees. For many firms, the installation of ultra-high-speed production lines in recently built plants has proved counterproductive because of the negative impact on worker performance.

The reaction of some employers has been to adopt job enrichment programs (in the United States, Ralston Purina has been a pathbreaker). Production workers have been divided into teams which set output quotas, rotate the jobs within the team, and divide incentive pay among the team members. In some cases, the teams have the ultimate decision in hiring and firing their members. In most cases, the worker performs more than one task at each station.

Job enrichment has proved successful in most applications, although it is far from a widespread phenomenon. The auto industry, the most notorious for low worker morale, absenteeism, and worker sabotage, is currently trying several job enrichment techniques. Here the cue has been taken from German and Swedish car makers. The auto producers are probably providing the acid test for job enrichment, given the demands the auto assembly line makes on workers and the inflexibility inherent in the automated plant.

It remains to be seen what union leaders will make of job enrichment. The hierarchy of the AFL-CIO is top-heavy with old men who may come to view job enrichment as just another speedup by management. At any rate, the paramount issue affecting the work force in the 1970s appears to be the quality of the job rather than union organization, wages, or fringe benefits. For good or for ill, unions can be expected to play the dominant role in shaping the configuration of tomorrow's production-line tasks.

INDIVIDUAL SECURITY AND OPPORTUNITY

Over most of the post-World War II period, public celebration of our affluent society served to sweep the notion of poverty under the carpet—at least for 80 percent of the population. But beginning in the late 1950s, Americans began to ask themselves about the quality of life in the affluent society. Their investigations led them to the rediscovery of poverty—poverty in urban ghettos, in mountain hamlets, in depressed areas, in the rural South. Writers such as Michael Harrington spotlighted this sloppy housekeeping by pointing to the lump in the rug, by reminding the 80 percent who had it made of the 20 percent who lived in *The Other America*—the "invisible poor" tucked out of sight in the "invisible land" well away from suburbia and well off the commuter's, the shopper's, or the vacationer's pathways.[3]

The process of economic growth produces threats to individual security and opportunity and, consequently, poverty for particular segments of the population. However, for others the growth process reinforces security and widens the range of economic opportunity and thereby produces affluence. And the fruits of growth include the ability to do something about problems of security and opportunity. The increased public concern about poverty that dates from the mid-1960s

---

[3] Harrington, pp. 9–12; Harrington inspired much of the "conventional wisdom" on poverty which, in turn, has been effectively challenged by Gallaway.

reflects our realization that we have achieved a greater economic ability to deal with these problems.

At this point in history, our national disagreements about fighting poverty seems less related to such questions as who will pay for the ammunition and can we afford it than has been the case in the past. The current backlash against antipoverty programs seems more related to a conviction, whether accurate or not, that the War on Poverty hasn't been based on an effective strategy. In the 1960s we thought our affluence could buy us almost anything, even an end to want. In the 1970s, we are having to face the reality that our economic ability may not be matched with sufficient organizational and political skill to execute what we can afford.

Personal income distribution

We can perhaps best appreciate who the poor are and why they are poor if we bear in mind what is implied by the term *personal income distribution*. Personal income distribution simply refers to the division of aggregate personal income among consumer units, i.e., among households. Underlying the personal distribution of income is *factor income distribution*, which refers to the distribution of income to labor and owners of capital and land. From this we can see that personal income distribution depends upon the distribution of the productive factors among households. Put another way, the more and better the land and the human and physical capital controlled by a given household, the more affluent that household will be, and vice versa.

What besides the luck of the draw determines the quality of the productive factors in a given household? Native abilities and the demand for those abilities, education and training, age, race, location, and market power all combine to determine the incomes that will flow into a household.

14–6 shows that the distribution of income became slightly more equal over the period 1929 to 1935–36, then accelerated its tendency toward

14–6. Percentage distribution of family personal income, selected years, 1929–70

Quintile	1929	1935–36	1944	1950	1960	1965	1970	Change, 1929–70
Lowest fifth	3.5	4.1	4.9	4.5	4.9	5.3	5.5	+2.0
Second fifth	9.0	9.2	10.9	12.0	12.0	12.1	12.0	+3.0
Third fifth	13.8	14.1	16.2	17.4	17.6	17.7	17.4	+3.6
Fourth fifth	19.3	20.9	22.2	23.5	23.6	23.7	23.5	+4.2
Highest fifth	54.4	51.7	45.8	42.6	42.0	41.2	41.6	−12.8
Total	100.0	100.0	100.0	100.0	100.0	100.0	100.0	
Top twentieth	30.0	26.5	20.7	17.0	16.8	15.8	14.4	−16.6

SOURCE: U.S. Department of Commerce (1972), p. 324.

equality from 1935–36 to 1944, and has changed only slightly since 1944. Further, it shows that the greatest part of the change in distribution from 1929 to 1970 came from the redirection of the top fifth's reduced share to each of the four lower fifths in such a way that the highest of the four got the largest gain in percentage points, the next highest got the next largest gain, and so on. Thus, over the past four decades earnings have been redistributed toward the lower income groups but *not* radically so, even though the incomes of the lowest groups have grown the fastest. From this we can conclude that the distribution of the factors of production has been similarly modified. Since we know that labor's share of the total pie has increased only very slightly, we can reason that the ownership of the other factors of production has been redistributed only moderately in favor of the lower income classes.

However, it is important to note that the entire distribution structure moved upward in this period—annual real per capita disposable income rose from $1,236 in 1929 to $2,660 in 1971. Over the period 1947 through 1970, the portion of white families with less than $3,000 income fell from 28 percent to 11 percent of the white population, and the portion of nonwhites fell from 66 percent to 28 percent. (Note that although nonwhites still rank below whites, their rate of income growth has been faster than that of white families.) In other words, even if there had been no downward redistribution the lot of the average man in the lowest fifth of the population would still have improved markedly.

Similarly, during the 1960s the portion of the population in poverty as defined by the Social Security Administration fell from a high of more than 20 percent to a low of less than 12 percent, in 1969, then rose slightly. This record followed closely the cyclical behavior of the economy, showing that cyclical expansions have the same impact upon poverty as long-term growth. It also demonstrates that recessions can reverse, at least temporarily, progress in eliminating poverty—the 1969–70 downturn in economic activity and the rise in the incidence in poverty exactly coincided.

Concern about poverty

The fact remains, though, that we as a nation are unhappy to note that the lowest 20 percent of consumer units receive less than 5 percent of total income. Why? First, poverty is expensive; the incidence of crime is concentrated among the poor, as are the special social services that are provided by government, and the low productivity of the poor exacts its toll in lost GNP. Second, as the absolute level of incomes has risen, our standards as to what constitutes poverty and what is equitable have risen too.

Why is it that society considers today's low incomes inadequate when they are, in fact, equal to yesterday's middle incomes and are well above yesterday's poverty line? Why, in other words, have our standards escalated along with our incomes? Why have we raised the absolute line that determines the portion of society that is viewed as poor? We can only attempt a superficial explanation here.

By a generally accepted definition, poverty is the inability to purchase necessities. We have traditionally had public and private agencies which disbursed assistance of one kind or another to those who met the agencies' respective definitions of poverty.

The poverty criteria of social welfare agencies have been drawn up by compiling the budgets necessary to provide a family with at least a minimum level of subsistence. Over the years, the dollar value of these budgets has been raised over and above adjustments for price changes as the responsible officials revamped their conception of an acceptable minimum. These officials, drawn from the American middle classes and subject to the same forces that shape the general public's attitudes, institutionalized changing notions about adequacy. However, it is noteworthy that in spite of upward revisions of the subsistence budgets, they remain within a range that most of us would consider very rudimentary, i.e., food, shelter, and clothing are still defined in a minimal way, and medical services, entertainment, and reading material are scantily represented. Our rising standards have not altered our definition of necessities to include contemporary luxuries.

It appears that the greatest influence that economic growth has had upon the formulation of standards is through the impact of growth upon the wage level and budget of the "workingman." 14-7 shows the historical

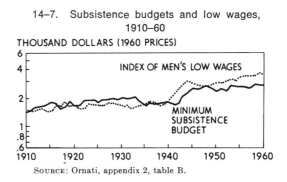

14-7. Subsistence budgets and low wages,
1910–60

SOURCE: Ornati, appendix 2, table B.

movement of real wages earned by low-paid male workers and the real value of the minimum subsistence budgets which were defined in each of the years from 1910 through 1960. Two characteristics command attention. First, the wage index and the budget values were very close in value over the period in spite of becoming inverted in their relative positions. And second, the direction of movement of the two series was very closely associated until the 1950s.

What constitutes being poor in America in the 1970s? According to the guidelines of the Social Security Administration, individuals who earn less than $1,800 per year and four-member families that earn less than $3,000 per year are considered poor.[4] 14–8 summarizes poverty lines for various types of families.

14–8.   Selected nonfarm* poverty lines by size of family and sex of head, 1970
(in dollars)

Number in family	Male head	Female head
Two members		
Head under 65 years	2,619	2,522
Head 65 and older	2,349	2,336
Four members.	3,970	3,948
Seven or more members	6,486	6,317

* Farm poverty lines are 85 percent of the nonfarm figures.
SOURCE: U.S. Department of Commerce (1972), p. 329.

Who are the poor? If you are an elderly nonwhite or Chicano female head of household, living in the rural South, in poor health, unemployed, and with less than eight years of education, the "probability" that you are *not* in poverty is less than 1 percent. The data in 14–9 summarize the characteristics of poor and nonpoor households. The percentage of low-income persons with a particular characteristic (in the shaded bar) is compared with the percentage of all persons in the total population with the same characteristic (in the light bar).

Lack of more than an eighth-grade education is a handicap of 13 percent of the population, but it is an especially common trait of low-income family heads, 23 percent of whom are so limited. What's more, evidence indicates that educational opportunities are inferior in low-income school districts, especially districts comprising black, Spanish-American, and Indian neighborhoods, if educational expenditures are any guide to educational quality.

One fifth of the heads of low-income families are persons over 65 years of age, compared with 10 percent or less in the total population. Most people who are poor were born poor. The exceptions are men and women over 65 who were not poverty-stricken during their working years but never amassed sufficient assets to have more than social security payments in their old age.

Associated with sex and race may be certain traits that limit productivity and income-earning power; but discrimination by employers also limits the opportunities of these groups. This explains why nonwhite

---

[4] There is much quibbling about where and how to draw the poverty line simply because such judgments are subjective in nature. The vital point is that a large segment of the American public—whether it is 10 percent, as some hold, or 30 percent, as others say—live in circumstances that the balance of the population considers poor enough to warrant concern and effort.

14–9.   Characteristics of low-income families, 1970

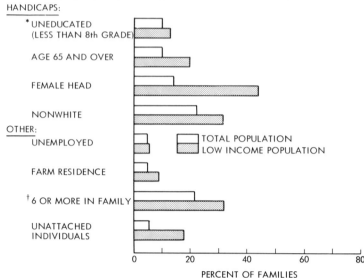

* Based on families that received less than $3,000 income in 1970.
† 1957 data.
    Sources: Lampman; U.S. Department of Commerce (1972), pp. 325–34; Bloom and Northrup, pp. 448–53.

and female family heads bulk twice as large in the poor population as in the general population. Traditionally, certain jobs have been barred to women and certain racial and ethnic minorities quite apart from considerations of ability. Usually, these have been the higher paying jobs or the jobs that are stepping-stones to higher positions.

Adverse racial and ethnic discrimination has worked against the interests of particular minorities in two ways—poor schools have restricted their development, and job discrimination has reduced their choices in the labor market. Thus families headed by blacks, Chicanos, Indians, and women tend to be low-income families in which, characteristically, health, education, and goals are at lower levels than in higher income families. The result is that poverty is self-perpetuating along lines of race, sex, and ethnic origin.

Low income is associated with the unemployment of the family head in poor times, but not particularly so in good times. This explains the dramatic reduction in the incidence of poverty in the 1960s, when unemployment levels fell from 6.7 percent to 3.4 percent of the labor force. On the other hand, underemployment has a very high incidence among poor families. In the late 1960s, nearly 70 percent of all poor families had at least one member in the labor force, but in less than half of those families was the member of the labor force a year-round, full-time worker; the balance were employed part-time or seasonally.

Incomplete adjustment to reduced farm labor requirements has generated pools of surplus labor in rural areas and has held down average farm incomes. Consequently, although farm families comprise only 5 percent of the population, farm families accounted for 9 percent of the poor at the end of the 1960s. Note that although unemployment and rural residence are important poverty characteristics, many of those who reside in cities and people who work in low-skill, low-wage jobs everywhere fall in the poverty class as well. Finally, large family size is associated with an income level that is low relative to per capita needs.

Now let's consider specifically the hazards of age and illness. One of the benefits of our rising income levels and advances in science is that people are healthier and live longer. This gain, however, is not without its costs. The older worker reaches a point where his capacity for work diminishes, and he may be discharged. Even before this time, older workers laid off for any other reason may find it difficult to get work again. Also, while medical science has brought better health, the costs of healing may come very high. Treatment for major illnesses can run into thousands of dollars. Thus the average person who lives longer may expect to incur increasing medical expenses.

At the same time that we are living longer, we are also abandoning the security of multigeneration households, and we have all but lost the neighborliness that came with small rural communities and close-knit urban neighborhoods. Fifty or a hundred years ago, the people who lived to an old age could usually count on the younger members of a family group to support them and care for them. On a farm there was usually some work they could do that was helpful to the family. Today, however, less and less productive activity—the manufacture of homemade articles and the performance of do-it-yourself services—occurs in the home. Also, the average number of persons per household has long been declining—in large part because fewer relatives live with the family. Further, in the postwar years fewer married couples have been without a household of their own. Thus, individuals must rely increasingly on themselves and less on family or neighbors when sick or when too old to work.

The War on Poverty

We have noted that poverty is socially defined and that economic growth has pulled a significant portion of the population out of poverty. From this we can infer that if economic growth proceeds as in prior decades and if we were to freeze our definition of what constitutes a state of poverty, economic growth would eradicate poverty. But the process would be a long and hesitant evolution.

What's more, it's extremely unlikely that poverty will ever come to be defined in terms of some fixed absolute income or budget—the definition of poverty has always moved with long-term income gains. Consequently, the only way to raise all families above the poverty line is by redistributing income downward, taxing the upper income brackets and directing the proceeds to the poor.

The magnitude of such a redistribution appears small as compared with aggregate personal income. A variety of studies have shown that the poverty gap can be closed by transferring 5 percent of personal income from the rich to the poor over and above what is now given to the poor in welfare payments. But such a transfer appears massive compared with federal resources; e.g., it would require raising federal personal income taxes by almost 60 percent. Nothing in our history suggests that the haves of this nation are of a mind to redirect income to the have-nots on such a scale.

Redistribution of income in favor of the poor constitutes a frontal attack on poverty, a strategy that the body politic has eschewed. As one perceptive observer of the contemporary scene has put it, "The middle class knows that the economists are right when they say that poverty could be eliminated if only we will it; they simply do not will it."[5] Yet the haves were and are unhappy about poverty in the midst of their opulence. And they were not patient enough to relax and let economic growth pull the poor over the poverty line. So the **War on Poverty** was declared in 1964.

The War on Poverty legislation constituted a potpourri of programs to be administered by a newly created Office of Economic Opportunity (OEO) with the cooperation of other federal agencies, such as the Department of Health, Education, and Welfare and the Labor Department. Diverse as the package was, a central theme held together many of the programs. Either directly or indirectly, the programs were designed to help the poor help themselves by raising their potential or actual productivity. The programs were aimed chiefly at those who were considered potential workers but were out of the labor market and at those who held low-pay, dead-end jobs.

Antipoverty programs enacted since 1964 include: a wide variety of training programs for the unskilled; basic education for functional illiterates; day care centers for the children of working mothers; payroll subsidies to encourage firms to hire and train low-productivity individuals; Head Start programs to help disadvantaged children perform better when they enter school and, consequently, in the world of work; and various youth-oriented programs designed to get dropouts back in school, prepare the unemployed for work, and provide loans and work opportunities for college students.

Participation in the programs usually required being classified as poor, and the programs entitled participants to subsistence payments when

---

[5] Adam Walinsky, quoted in Heilbroner.

full-time participation in a program prevented them from working. Other programs, most of them administered by the Department of Health, Education, and Welfare, were inaugurated primarily to raise the income levels of the poor. Examples are housing subsidies, increased public assistance payments, Medicaid (health care for the poor), and Medicare (health care for social security recipients).

14–10 summarizes OEO and other federal antipoverty outlays. Note that the amounts shown are only for those who remained poor even after participation in the program and, therefore, that actual expenditures for most programs were larger than those shown by amounts that affected the nonpoor and those whom the programs pulled across the poverty line.

OEO appropriations characteristically totaled less than 10 percent of the amount that outright distribution of income to the poor would entail: e.g., in 1965–66, a year of large OEO appropriations, closing the poverty gap would have required $30 billion in transfers from rich to poor, whereas OEO spending authority (including grants to other agencies) was less than $2.5 billion.[6]

In budgetary terms, the War on Poverty was a skirmish at best. Yet in spite of its modest scale—at its peak OEO claimed less than 2 percent of yearly federal outlays—it became unpopular. The reasons for OEO's fall from grace are varied: old-line bureaucrats resented the establishment of a new agency in their territory; OEO's legal aid program (LSO) incurred the wrath of local and state law enforcement officials, including the governor of California; giving the poor considerable program foundation powers alienated members of the middle class who felt that the needy should be ministered to but feared and/or resented a politicized underclass; and cases of mismanagement of hastily enacted programs gave taxpayers and lawgivers serious reasons for second thoughts about the War on Poverty.

Now, less than ten years after its declaration, the War on Poverty is being wound down; the OEO and its programs are being dismantled. The reason offered by President Nixon is that the benefits of the various OEO undertakings flowed chiefly to the OEO bureaucracy rather than to the poor. Whether the War on Poverty could have been, or was, a success is not clear at this juncture. What is clear is that the War on Poverty couldn't pass political muster.

The War on Poverty was certainly not the first antipoverty legislation—in fact, programs that date back to the 1930s account for about 60 percent of the outlays shown in 14–10. Nearly $60 billion in the 1970 federal budget consisted of transfer payments from taxpayers to various categories of recipients, with $36 billion accounted for by social

---

[6] See Batchelder, p. 225, for a discussion of the transfers required to eradicate poverty; and U.S. Department of Commerce (1970), p. 331, for summaries of OEO spending.

14-10.   Federal outlays benefiting persons with low income: 1968 and 1971*
(in billions of dollars)

	1968	1971
Total.	15.9	25.5
Human investment†	3.1	4.2
Maintenance‡	12.8	21.3
By program:		
Income security, cash	9.0	13.2
Social security and railroad retirement.	5.8	7.7
Public assistance payments	2.0	3.8
Veterans pensions	0.8	0.9
Unemployment benefits.	0.2	0.6
Other	0.1	0.2
Income security, in kind.	0.4	2.4
Food stamps	0.1	1.4
Commodity distribution, excluding schools.	0.1	0.3
Child nutrition, including commodities for schools	0.1	0.4
Housing subsidy payments	0.1	0.3
Education	1.1	1.5
Early childhood	0.4	0.3
Elementary and secondary	0.4	0.6
Higher education	0.2	0.3
Other	0.1	0.2
Health	3.1	5.0
Medicaid	1.1	2.3
Medicare	1.4	1.9
Other	0.5	0.9
Manpower§	1.4	1.9
Skill training	0.7	1.1
Work support.	0.6	0.6
Other§	0.9	1.5
Community action, model cities	0.5	0.7
By agency:		
Health, Education, and Welfare.	11.7	18.1
Department of Agriculture	0.3	2.2
Department of Labor	0.6	1.7
Office of Economic Opportunity.	1.8	1.4
Veterans Administration	1.0	1.3
All other‖	0.6	0.9

* For years ending June 30. Represents estimated direct benefits to persons below the poverty line through federal expenditures and direct loan programs.

† Includes programs that actively promote education, the development of work skills, and community and economic development.

‡ Programs that provide income support and certain essential noncash support and services to meet the basic needs of persons with low income.

§ Includes data not shown separately.

‖ Department of Housing and Urban Development, Department of the Interior, Railroad Retirement Board, Department of Commerce, Civil Service Commission, and Small Business Administration.

Source: U.S. Department of Commerce (1972), p. 335.

security retirement benefits. Of this total, 40 percent was paid to people who would **not** be poor even if they received no payments under the programs.[7] In spite of these programs, a good many people remain poor. What's more, about half the poor, chiefly families of low-wage workers, aren't eligible to receive any benefits under the traditional antipoverty laws.

Perhaps the best way to analyze the impact of the War on Poverty and the legislation that preceded it is to understand the pathology of poverty. Poverty in some of its manifestations has an ethos of its own that tends to perpetuate itself in particular families generation after generation. The corollary to this rule is that it is far more difficult for general growth and prosperity to enhance the economic position of at least some of the poor than of middle-income individuals.

This, in turn, suggests that although monetary and fiscal policy may be the vanguard of the attack on poverty, supplementary programs are necessary—programs which deal with poverty's specific causes and symptoms (which are causes one poverty generation hence), including programs which aid the labor force to adjust to changing patterns of demand. This applies both to those who are born poor and could spend their lives in poverty and to those who are likely to fall into poverty when they become old. By raising their productivity, people in the latter group will have a greater ability to accumulate a basis for retirement income during their working life.

Note that in this context we are not referring to all of the poor, only to that segment of the poor population that is caught up in a vicious circle in which poverty begets poverty. The aged who are poor, young people in low-wage jobs who are on their way up, low-income farmers whose children can and will migrate to better opportunities, and families experiencing hard times on a temporary basis were not target groups of the War on Poverty. Just what portion of the total who are classed as poor these groups constitute is unknown.

Why does poverty have an ethos of its own? Let's review what scholars have learned about the forces that explain the life-style of the poor. Sociologists were studying poverty during the many years in which the problem was ignored in other quarters. Their findings have come as a shock to many who speak of a "culture of poverty" and attribute a unique set of poverty-biased aspirations to the poor or, in the extreme, assert that the able-bodied poor are poor by choice, that they prefer their life-style and are willing to pay for it by remaining poor.

In fact, the great majority of the poor long for exactly those things that are the goals of the so-called middle class—home ownership, college for the kids, and a respected place in the community. There is nothing

---

[7] Batchelder, pp. 145–46.

about their basic drives and desires that makes the poor particularly vulnerable to poverty.[8]

However, the poor recognize the futility of adopting these desires as the day-to-day goals on which they base a strategy for living. For the most part, they feel walled in by the factors in their environment that are responsible for their low-income position—chiefly poor education, frail health, housing restrictions, and employer discrimination with respect to age, race, and sex. Thus, they maximize their position behind the poverty wall by adopting a life-style that consists of setting and meeting goals that are different from their "middle-class aspirations"— and this involves behavior that often reinforces the tendency for poverty to infect successive generations.

> There is no denying that children brought up in poverty experience life in ways that make the journey out of poverty a difficult one from almost every point of view; *this is what hard-core poverty is all about.*
>
> What it comes down to is that among those who have long lived in poverty without hope, where poverty has meant persistent failure and human indignities, family life is eroded, expectations of failure are cumulatively reinforced, and men react both by devaluing and by protecting themselves. So do children.[9] [Italics supplied.]

Among other things, a good deal of escapism involving drugs, including alcohol, is built into the behavior patterns of the poor. In general, the urban and the rural poor live lives of not so quiet desperation, in which TV persistently reminds them of their positions as have-nots by bringing middle-class America into their living rooms on a daily basis. Little wonder that drug addiction, alcoholism, and mental disease are disproportionately diseases of the poor.

However, some say the poor need not be desperate: if the poor bought very wisely, scrimped and scraped, they could get along on $3,000 a year, even with six in the family. U.S. Department of Labor studies have, in fact, proved something like this. But keeping the regimen prescribed requires a Bachelor of Science degree in home economics and the fortitude of a Trappist monk.

In sum, what the culture of poverty argument states is that basically the poor are poor because they behave in ways that make them poor—its antithesis, a counterargument for which there is supporting evidence, states that the poor act in certain ways because they have low incomes. Both schools of thought view poverty as a closed circle, but what is identified as the force that closes the circle has a great deal to do with choosing an optimum antipoverty strategy.

The view that appears consistent with the evidence is the assertion that the frustrations of poverty produce an attitude which mortars the

---

[8] See, for example, Lewis.

[9] Bowman, p. 85; for a contrasting point of view see Gallaway, chap. 5.

walls of poverty; but if some force comes along to make it realistic to think of vaulting that wall, the actual behavior of low-income people changes markedly. As one student of poverty has summarized it, "A large proportion of those able-bodied adults who are classified as poor by our income definitions would respond to a chance for a regular job, and . . . until poverty and the conditions of life associated with living in poverty have beaten them down, children of even the poorest of the poor will respond to opportunities to learn and to work . . . just as children born into other strata of our society."[10]

The question arises, What kinds of programs, public or private, are best suited to breaking the poverty cycle, to inducing behavior changes?

Our experience with the welfare legislation of the 1930s has been instructive in a negative sense; in fact, much of the legislation may have evolved to become causes of poverty. The Social Security Act, including the Medicare and Medical amendments, leaves many uncovered, especially those employed in industries where labor is paid the least, such as agriculture. The same observation applies to unemployment compensation and minimum wage laws. Further, there is evidence to support the assertion that our minimum wage laws, selective as they are in their coverage, cause unemployment and push wages to poverty levels in uncovered industries. Teen-agers with few skills seem especially vulnerable to the disemployment effects of minimum wages.[11] And, ironically, the minimum wage doesn't provide an income above the poverty line for a family of four in which there is only one income earner.

Public housing puts a premium on remaining poor so as to maintain eligibility for quarters. Urban renewal, a postwar baby of 1930s parentage, has pushed part of the poor out of their quarters and crowded them into the remaining low-income neighborhoods. This, as we will describe in chapter 16, has driven up rents per cubic foot while the cleared space has gone into high- or middle-income housing or business uses instead of low-income housing.

The public assistance programs which are lumped together under the popular label *welfare* and are typified by the Aid to Dependent Children (ADC) program were structured with the intention of helping people over some rough weeks and preventing chiseling. But they have the side effects of becoming a cause of the conditions they were designed to treat symptomatically—e.g., in most states every additional dollar earned by welfare recipients results in the deduction of 67 cents from their welfare checks, certainly a strong incentive not to bother working. (Such programs as aid to the blind and the disabled are exceptions to this observation.) Further, these public assistance programs fail to raise their recipients out of poverty—fully 50 percent of welfare re-

---

[10] Bowman, p. 85.

[11] See Adie for a statistical analysis and citations of the literature on teen-age unemployment and minimum wages.

cipients remain poor after receiving public assistance. And half the poor do not qualify for public assistance because they don't fall into one of the eligibility categories; these are primarily the working poor.

The school lunch program which subsidizes public school cafeterias and the surplus food distribution and food stamp plans—both were designed as part of the farm program—get better grades. The first often constitutes the difference between a health-sustaining diet and malnutrition for some youngsters, while the other two have prevented starvation for whole families. But the balance of the farm program amounts to welfare payments for the middle class, since most poor farmers benefit little or not at all from the support programs.

The entire package adds up to what one student has called the "paradox of the welfare state." Harrington has described it as "socialism for the rich and free enterprise for the poor."[12]

Policy alternatives

What are the alternatives to a paradoxical welfare state? One line of attack involves redesigning those aspects of the current system which fall within the general approach called *categorical assistance.* Another frequently cited approach advocates *income supplements* based solely upon an income criterion.

Categorical assistance involves programs of services and financial aid for the poor in certain categories, such as the blind, the disabled, the poorly educated, the unemployed without unemployment compensation, dependent children, and so on. Advocates of this approach suggest adding to the types of programs that came out of the New Deal. The causes and symptoms of poverty would be identified and programs designed for those afflicted by poverty, *but* with adequate guarantees that incentives to self-sufficiency will be kept intact or stimulated. In other words, those who favor categorical assistance would not only continue the War on Poverty, they would step it up.

Those who advocate the income supplement approach deny that a sufficient number of public and private programs can be designed to deal with all the causes of poverty that are open to change through social action. The most pessimistic of the people in this camp cite the fact that the working poor are largely ignored by categorical assistance programs; they deny that category and income eligibility criteria can be combined so as to maintain work incentives; they feel that more programs mean more red tape, not more help for the poor; and they see no evidence that we know enough about the psychology of poverty to really enable the poor to help themselves. In short, they feel that the War on Poverty was lost before it started.

Rather, those who advocate supplementing incomes feel that such

---

[12] See McConnell, pp. 673–74; Harrington, p. 157.

payments should be large enough to bring low-income people up to a level that assures economic security at what society defines as decent income levels. Those who cannot participate in the labor force owing to disabilities would be assured a decent standard of living. For those who can work, incentive would be maintained by reducing income supplements by considerably less than any increases in after-tax earned income, so that it would always pay to raise one's earning power and income.

In the current debate over how to end poverty the income supplement approach usually referred to is the **negative income tax.** It calls for a transfer payment to all individuals and families and a special tax that is levied in such a way that taxpayers with sufficient incomes from other sources receive no income supplement; the usual rate suggested is 50 percent on earned income until the special tax reaches the value of the transfer payment.

The least optimistic advocates of a negative income tax feel that while we can't cure poverty in a basic sense, we can eliminate it in a superficial sense by adding to the incomes of the poor on a sustained basis. The most optimistic adherents of the negative income tax see income supplements as providing a ladder to scale the poverty wall. In other words, they assert that assuring a family a given income level makes possible adequate housing, clothing, and diet plus access to good schools and cultural advantages. In turn, the children in such a family will grow up with both the will and the ability to "succeed," to make middle-class aspirations a basis for day-to-day decisions.

Those who advocate categorical assistance programs in which income supplements and services come in a package doubt that the poor will take advantage of the opportunities that a negative income tax would make financially possible. Theirs is a variation on the cliché that in the next generation after the redistribution of income the cream will again rise to the top.

Again we have a case in which discussion has turned into polemics, and advocates have polarized their positions. Yet a review of the causes of poverty makes it apparent that a synthetic approach is called for. For example, consider the family in which the head of the household fits the stereotype of the shiftless poor—lazy, drunken, sex-crazed, prolific, and illiterate. In terms of the traditional goals of antipoverty legislation, income supplements would be wasted unless some sort of categorical assistance went with them to channel the funds into a permanent escape route from poverty for at least the children of the household.

As a second example, take a middle-aged, black, female head of a household with four children who works as a "domestic." Obviously, she cannot find the time, income supplement or not, to enter a training program in order to enhance her productivity. Yet a training program that pays a salary and provides day care facilities for her children would accomplish this end. Of course, compared to an income supplement, the costs would be higher during the training period, but they would terminate, whereas an income supplement would have to continue indefinitely.

The War on Poverty was represented as just such a synthetic approach. Yet, as of this date, its programs constituted only a token recognition of the income supplement approach. On the other hand, President Nixon's *Family Assistance Plan,* which was defeated by Congress, combined a negative income tax with a modified version of ADC.

We can perhaps speculate as to the future of antipoverty legislation. Given our aspirations and impatience, it is not unlikely that a negative income tax will be enacted and complemented by a superstructure of specific programs which bolster productivity for particular categories of individuals. Such a system would enable those who are capable of raising their productivity to do so while those who cannot or will not would at least have sufficient income for other members of the family to extend their choices beyond those lying within the perimeter of the closed circle of poverty.

The budget outlays for any concentrated attack on poverty will be large, much larger than the OEO funds allocated and spent to date. But if the programs they support do in fact reduce poverty to minimal levels, they will be self-limiting and so will the ancillary costs associated with poverty, such as crime. Further, the higher productivity of those assisted would increase GNP. On the other hand, the self-regenerating nature of untreated poverty promises to perpetuate the costs of poverty.

Education and poverty

This brings us to the question of education as it relates to the process of combating poverty. The Nation has an educational system that has served the majority very well, if various studies linking educational attainment, economic success, and economic growth are a guide. But poor rural youngsters who have been forced to migrate to an urban-industrial environment, and children locked into the inner-city ghettos have not been served well by the educational system. In recent decades, the failure of our educational system to serve these minorities has taken a heavy toll in civil strife and lost productivity. Functional illiterates with high school diplomas and dropouts are symptoms of this failure—the effects are, usually, lifetimes of drudgery in dead-end, low-pay jobs with no skill requirements, or lifetimes spent on the streets.

If we are really serious about eradicating poverty, the experience of the last few years indicates that our system of public education must be tailored to that end. And this does not mean just more conventional schooling—it means programs capable of doing what is accomplished in both the school and the home in middle-class neighborhoods.

It means communicating to adults who have lost hope that education and job training can help them to become independent and fulfilled. It means demonstrating to young people that there is a road that leads out of the ghetto or its rural equivalent. And it means incorporating into the curriculum subject matter that specifically prepares young people to adapt to life outside a poverty environment.

Powerful a tool as education is, it is not a panacea for poverty. Educators can now only point to a winding, narrow, hazard-strewn path out of poverty. That path must be widened and paved with income maintenance programs and the elimination of racial discrimination in housing, schooling, and the labor market. In turn, our monetary and fiscal policies must keep the growth rate of demand for labor in line with the expansion of the labor force.

The War on Poverty with its Title I education funds, Job Corps, Neighborhood Youth Corps, and Head Start for young people plus training programs for adults constituted steps in the directions indicated above. Yet the appropriations for these programs were modest compared with the task, and current indications are that most of them won't get larger in the near future even if they aren't completely emasculated. Beyond expenditure of Title I funds, which were specifically aimed at financing compensatory programs for the "disadvantaged," school boards haven't faced the problems posed by the urban and rural poor; and, given the current fiscal problems of almost every school district in the Nation, they aren't likely to in the near term.

On the antidiscrimination front, important strides have been made, and perhaps the civil rights movement has gained sufficient momentum to have become a part of our institutional fabric. Monetary and fiscal policies have been our most effective weapons in the War on Poverty and are likely to remain so—but countercyclical policies can't win the war alone.

Our survey of the incidence of poverty and the special roles played by age and illness shows how particular characteristics of households make for low earning power of the individuals within them. It also suggests that there is a vicious cycle of poverty: low income means an environment in which the preconditions for another generation of poverty are present. Our earlier observation that poverty is self-regenerating along lines of race and sex can be extended to include almost all of the attributes of low-income households. Now let's look more generally at the various ways in which individual security and opportunity have been increased for the great majority of Americans.

Assuring individual security

From the foregoing, it is obvious that it has become increasingly important for individuals in an urban, industrial society to save, to accumulate financial reserves in order to protect themselves in times of need. While times of illness and death are unpredictable, the proportion of people likely to be sick (or to die) at any one time can be predicted from social experience; thus, the risks of individuals can be spread by the insurance principle, and, therefore, saving for a rainy day can be a meaningful hedge against death or catastrophic illness.

Fortunately, our rising incomes have been accompanied by a rise in real wealth per capita. The development of banks, savings and loan associations, insurance companies, and stock and bond markets not only helped finance the capital needs of industry but also helped many individuals to accumulate small holdings of assets in a diversified form. 14–11 shows how important these assets can be in relation to personal

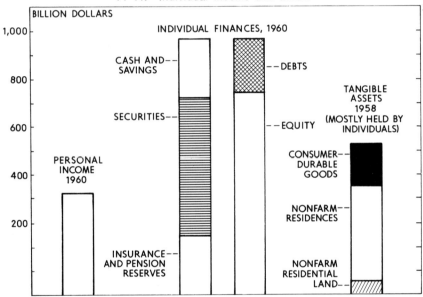

14–11.   Individual income and assets

SOURCE: U.S. Department of Commerce (1962), pp. 328, 338.

incomes for the Nation as a whole. With all cash and savings more than offsetting debts (both consumer credits and mortgages), individual financial equity consists mostly of securities (stocks and bonds, both public and private) and the accumulated cash reserve values of insurance and pension funds. In addition, individuals own considerable tangible assets in the form of consumer durable goods, homes, and land. In total, the financial and physical assets of individuals, clear of debt, amount to over four times one year's personal income.

While ownership of assets or wealth may be more unequally distributed than income, there is some tendency for it to be distributed in favor of older persons, farmers, and the self-employed. For those who can remain employed, income-earning power tends to rise with age (until a later age, in fact, for the higher income occupations), and older people have had more time to accumulate savings.

At the same time that rising incomes have enabled individuals to accumulate more wealth to protect themselves, rising incomes have also enabled our economy to have the luxury of devoting a larger share of resources toward public insurance and forced-savings programs. The biggest single change in our national income distribution since the 1930s was, no doubt, the public pension program instituted under the Social Security Act. Since 1920, one of the largest increases in government expenditures, after the defense and interest items, has been for what is termed, often incorrectly, social insurance. In the last group, pension payments are the largest single item, and nearly all of this expenditure is by the federal government.

In 1970, social insurance benefits under federal, state, and local programs came to $55 billion, or 7 percent of total personal income. Of this total almost three fifths was accounted for by federal Old Age and Survivors Insurance (social security in everday terms), including Medicare. Other social insurance programs include unemployment compensation and disability insurance.

Since employees, as well as employers, are taxed to contribute to the buildup of a pension fund, the individual receiving a social security pension does not feel that he is receiving charity. Actually, of course, the program was started by giving pensions to individuals who had not fully paid in advance for their benefits; and today the program is still not fully "funded"—that is, people of this generation of beneficiaries will draw more in benefits than they have contributed during their working lives. Thus, as more people have started drawing their pensions, workers have had to pay higher social security taxes to cover part of the costs. Young workers in the next few decades, in fact, are going to be supporting a larger generation of old people than perhaps any previous generations. But rising productivity and income levels will ease this burden.

Among other items, disability compensation is paid for by employer taxes whose rates are set on an insurance principle. Although unemployment is not properly an insurable risk, except during good times, the unemployment compensation program is operated as if unemployment were subject to the laws of probability. However, during depressions a great many people draw compensation at the same time, which is counter to the insurance principle. (Of course, this has the useful feature of providing an automatic countercyclical spending flow by government when private spending tends to slow down.)

14–12 indicates the large role now played by private pension and insurance plans. In 1970, almost $35 billion was set aside by employers

14–12.   Private employee benefit plans, 1970

Coverage of wage and salary workers by type of employment and benefit plan	Covered workers as percent of all workers	Employer-employee contributions (in millions)
Workers in public and private employment		
Life insurance and death benefits.	69	$ 3,523
Accidental death and dismemberment	52	224
Hospitalization	80	7,569
Surgical	79	3,998
Regular medical.	71	
Major medical	36	2,310
Workers in private employment		
Temporary disability	51	2,922
Long-term disability	12	417
Supplemental unemployment benefits.	4	130
Retirement	48	14,000
Total	–	34,672

SOURCE: U.S. Department of Labor (1971), p. 273.

and employees to provide for retirement, disability, and expenses incurred during illness; these are amounts over and above government-operated programs for the same purposes, such as social security. This figure was nearly 6 percent of total employee compensation in 1970. Note that total health benefits and retirement are the largest two categories; at about $14 billion each, they account for about 80 percent of all the contributions listed in 14–12.

Whether the employer contributes all or only part of these costs, economic theory suggests that it is really the worker who pays in the end; payroll taxes and employee contributions are labor costs to the employer, and increased fringe benefits tend to take the place of increased wage payments. This involves, of course, an element of forced savings which may make sense given the tendency of people to underassess their future financial needs. As most insurance salesmen will agree, most people do not make sufficient provision for known future needs, let alone unpredictable calamities. By forcing everyone to make more provision for predictable social needs, the social security legislation of the 1930s has meant that there is less need for charity and welfare expenditures to take care of those who failed to take adequate precautions.

Unemployment and displacement

As we have said, unemployment associated with recessions and depressions is not simply an insurable risk of individuals. As 14–13 shows, almost one fourth of the labor force was unemployed in 1933. Unemployment of this magnitude is not predictable and thus not subject to the actuary's calculations; it is a problem not for an insurance company, public or private, but for monetary and fiscal policy. During the postwar years, we have succeeded in avoiding astronomically high unemployment levels. However, in recent years there has been increasing concern over gradually rising levels of unemployment, even during periods of prosperity. During the recession recoveries of 1953, 1956, and 1958, the unemployment rate was reduced successively less each time. In the 1960s unemployment was brought down to 3.5 percent of the labor force, but inflation at more than 5 percent per year came with it. This trend, which has been referred to as the *secular rise in unemployment*, has been alternatively attributed to the changing structure of demand for labor and to an insufficiency in aggregate demand.

On the structural side, economists have pointed to the elements of change in the industrial structure of the economy and to the consequent change in the structure of labor force demand as the cause of the secular rise in unemployment. Their view is that the *full-employment range* pictured in 14–13 is creeping up as the qualitative mismatch between

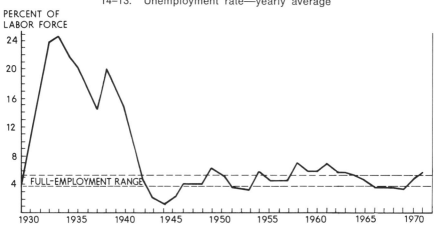

14–13.   Unemployment rate—yearly average

SOURCE: *Economic Report of the President*, p. 220.

the supply and the demand for labor increases over time. Their policy prescription is to enact manpower programs that increase the mobility and productivity of labor.

Some studies have analyzed rising unemployment in terms of the characteristics of unemployed persons; they have been found to have the same characteristics as the low-income persons we discussed previously. Blacks and young people who account for far more than their proportionate share of unemployment have been found to experience frequent short spells of unemployment, usually having been laid off from dead-end jobs in highly seasonal industries. Other studies have pointed to the persistently high unemployment levels in particular industries and communities. Textile towns, coal mining towns, and rural southern counties have been identified as *depressed areas.*

There has also been some speculation that our efforts to protect workers has tended to aggravate the unemployment problem. Seniority rules and pension rights on the job with a particular company make a worker less ready to change jobs or to seek work elsewhere when laid off. Present unemployment compensation rules may make workers less willing to accept lesser paying jobs; and unemployment compensation is an important part of the annual income of some seasonal or irregular workers. In short, some argue that our efforts to protect workers against the hardships of rapid change may hinder or slow down the adjustments needed. Our whole experience with the unemployment compensation system is relatively new, and there is much that we do not yet fully understand about its impact on the mobility of labor.

A recent variation of the structuralist view holds that there is a "natural" rate of unemployment—about 5 percent in the eyes of many—which is a joint product of workers' attitudes about shifting jobs and changes in the economy's industrial structure. According to this view, monetary and fiscal policy can always influence the unemployment rate temporarily, but, nevertheless, unemployment will work its way back to its natural rate.

On the aggregate demand side of the argument, some public leaders believe that persistently high unemployment merely reflects our *fiscal drag* and the problem of keeping national growth rates at high and stable levels. In other words, the aggregate demand argument denies that the full-employment range is creeping up owing to structural changes, but asserts that total spending and the aggregate demand for labor did not grow rapidly enough in the 1950s. 14–14 shows that our labor force is constantly rising, and unless employment increases at the same rate, we will have a widening gap of unemployment.

With employment on farms and in certain nonfarm industries declining, nonfarm jobs in expanding industries must be increased to provide jobs for both the new workers entering the labor force and for workers who must leave declining industries. 14–15 breaks down nonfarm employment by major industry groups. It shows that mining employment has been declining throughout the postwar period while manufacturing employment did not exceed its 1953 peak until the mid-1960s. On the other hand, trade, finance, services, and government are industries with rapidly rising employment. It is in these industries that the bulk of job increases from the expansion of aggregate demand will come.

The implication of our discussion so far is that the structural and aggregate demand explanations for the secular rise in unemployment are not mutually exclusive. The tax cut of 1964, a recovery year, and

14–14.   Labor force and employment, 1947–70

MILLIONS OF PERSONS

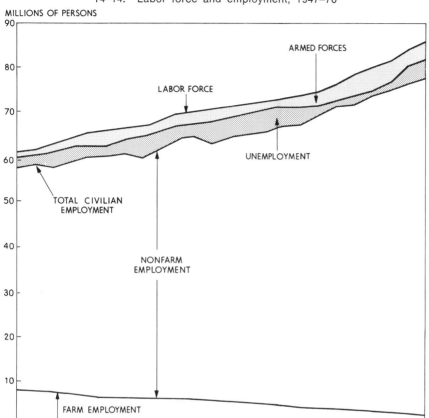

SOURCE: U.S. Department of Labor (1972), p. 26.

the continued reduction of unemployment that followed it are consistent with the aggregate demand argument. And, at times of unemployment in the range of 4 to 6 percent, the coexistence of inflation and shortages of labor in certain high-demand areas with high unemployment in particular industries, occupations, and population classifications is consistent with the structural point of view. The overall experience shows that to achieve full employment, total spending must grow as fast as the labor force, and the labor force must be able to conform to new patterns of industrial demand as they emerge in a full-employment economy.

This should reinforce the lesson that our ability to protect individuals from unemployment depends heavily upon the ability of our labor force to adjust to changing job requirements. New products and new methods need not bring undue hardships to individuals from prolonged unemployment provided that we maintain the capacity of workers to shift among industries and areas as the structure of labor demand changes.

14–15.   Employment by industry

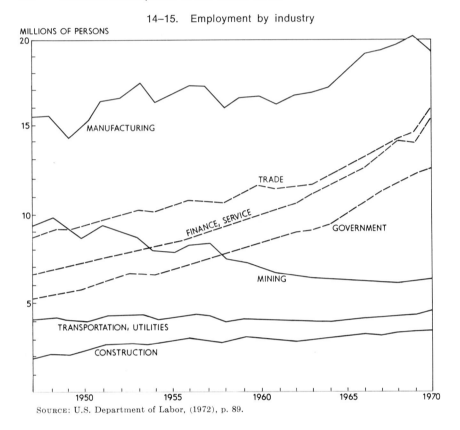

SOURCE: U.S. Department of Labor, (1972), p. 89.

At present, we may not have adequate job information, placement, or training services to do this. Nor is our system of formal education attuned to the problem of preparing young people to enter a labor market in which demands are continually shifting and skill requirements are constantly rising.

SUMMARY

Economic development produces structural shifts that pose a threat to the economic security of various individuals. In turn, some individuals have reacted by organizing politically and by forming unions in order to protect their job security and gain higher real incomes. Others, however, have not been able to use group action as a way of protecting their economic security and have had to face economic adversity as individuals.

1.   The American labor union movement was insignificant as measured against the total labor force until the eve of World War I, when the principal legal restraint against organization was lifted. It then grew

in fits and starts in the face of heavy employer opposition until the 1930s, when New Deal legislation outlawed various unfair labor practices by management. Recently, union membership has been growing at about the same rate as the labor force and seems to have peaked out as a percentage of total workers.

2. Whether the collective bargaining process has produced significant income gains for labor as a whole cannot be stated unambiguously. Real wage rates have followed productivity changes very closely, rather than varying with the expansion rate of union membership. Labor's share of aggregate income has increased since 1920, but much of this change is attributable to the decline in the number of self-employed farmers. It is clear, though, that unionized workers have been successful in redirecting income flows in their favor.

3. Although working conditions have improved markedly since the 19th century, the labor front is not without its serious problems. Boredom on production-line jobs has produced grave antisocial results. And discrimination by organized labor against minority groups and women remains a blot on organized labor's record.

4. The distribution of personal income among households has moved in favor of the lower income groups since 1920. However, as rising per capita incomes have pulled all income classes up, our conception of what constitutes poverty has escalated. Consequently, the poor are still with us, and there is national concern about their plight.

5. According to the Social Security Administration's criteria, in 1970 the poverty line was drawn at almost $4,000 per year for a family of four. Those who fall below the poverty line are disproportionately black, rural, poorly educated, old, and from households headed by women.

6. The War on Poverty was declared shortly after President Johnson came into office and was in the process of being terminated in 1973. It consisted of a host of programs designed to raise the productivity of the poor so that they might raise themselves out of poverty. Many, including President Nixon, feel that the War on Poverty failed, whereas others feel that it wasn't waged long enough to determine whether its approach was valid. Some attribute failure to a lack of sufficient techniques and knowledge to assist the poor; others feel that not enough was spent; and still others feel that being poor just goes along with a lifestyle many prefer.

7. Currently, there is a division of attitudes regarding antipoverty strategy. Some advocate expanding the categorical assistance programs inaugurated in the 1930s as well as reviving the War on Poverty. Others prefer an income supplement approach, such as the negative income tax. Under any conditions, education is a very important policy variable in determining economic opportunity. Although the Nation's educational system has served the majority well, the rural and ghetto poor have been served badly.

8. Economic growth has made it possible for individuals to amass personal savings to hedge against the hazards of age and illness. In addition, the federal government has instituted forced-savings programs, the most important of which is the social security system.

9. Potential unemployment is such a serious threat to economic security that the federal government has provided a cushion against it through the unemployment compensation program. However, unemployment compensation can't assist the worker who has been laid off because the industry or firm in which he was employed is in decline. Monetary and fiscal policy can maintain a brisk demand for labor in general, but workers must be able to meet the shifting job requirements that are results of the economic development process.

REFERENCES

D. K. Adie, "Teen-age Unemployment and Real Federal Minimum Wages," *JPE*, March/April 1973.

A. B. Batchelder, *The Economics of Poverty* (New York: John Wiley & Sons, Inc., 1971).

G. F. Bloom and H. R. Northrup, *Economics of Labor Relations* (Homewood, Ill.: Richard D. Irwin, Inc., 1973).

M. J. Bowman, "Poverty in an Affluent Society," in *Contemporary Economic Issues*, ed. N. W. Chamberlain (Homewood, Ill.: Richard D. Irwin, Inc., 1973).

H. M. Douty, "Collective Bargaining Coverage in Factory Employment, 1958," *MLR*, April 1960.

Economic Report of the President (Washington, D.C.: U.S. Government Printing Office, 1972).

L. E. Gallaway, *Poverty in America* (Columbus, Ohio: Grid Inc., 1973).

M. Harrington, *The Other America* (Baltimore: Penguin Books, Inc., 1962).

R. L. Heilbroner, "The Future of Capitalism," *Commentary*, April 1966.

R. J. Lampman, *The Low Income Population and Economic Growth* (U.S. Congress, Joint Economic Committee, 86th Cong., 1st sess. (Washington, D.C.: U.S. Government Printing Office, 1959).

H. Lewis, *Culture, Class, and Poverty* (Washington, D.C.: Cross-Tell, 1967).

C. R. McConnell, *Economics*, 3d ed. (New York: McGraw-Hill Book Co., 1966).

R. Marshall, "The Development of Organized Labor in the South," *MLR*, March 1968.

O. Ornati, *Poverty Amid Affluence* (New York: The Twentieth Century Fund, 1966).

A. Rees, "Patterns of Wages, Prices and Productivity," in *Wages, Prices, Profits and Productivity* (New York: The American Assembly, 1959).

A. Strasser, "Factory Workers Under Bargaining Agreements," *MLR*, February 1965.

U.S. Department of Commerce, *Historical Statistics of the United States* (Washington, D.C.: U.S. Government Printing Office, 1960).

———, *Statistical Abstract of the United States* (Washington, D.C.: U.S. Government Printing Office, 1972, 1970).

U.S. Department of Labor, *Handbook of Labor Statistics* (Washington, D.C.: U.S. Government Printing Office, 1972).

S. L. Wolfbein, ed., *Emerging Sectors of Collective Bargaining* (Morristown, N.J.: General Learning Corp., 1970).

15 INTERREGIONAL AND INTERNATIONAL ADJUSTMENTS

Economic growth and development have important geographic dimensions. Particular areas flourish or decline as places in which to live and produce according to the changes in demand and technology that go along with the growth process. In turn, the growth rate of any national economy depends to some degree upon the way in which it meshes with the world economy. At this point, we should review and expand upon the companion principles of specialization and exchange according to comparative advantage which were introduced in Part I.

A process which is vital to economic growth is the *division* of the economy's work among specialists who in a relative sense excel at particular tasks. Specialization increases productivity. And the economy that is able to increase the degree to which it follows this maxim is able to increase its growth rate. But application of this principle is not as straightforward as it might seem at first blush. Complications arise because we find specialization *among* economies, *within* economies, and both *among* and *within* producing units within an economy.

Let us first look at this phenomenon as it occurs *among* economies. To use a trite but clear example, Brazil and the United States could each grow both coffee and soybeans. For the United States, coffee culture would be highly artificial, requiring what amounts to giant hothouses. Thus, we specialize in soybeans and through the market mechanism trade them for coffee beans. Why? The first response is to say, "Coffee growing would require too many men and materials per ton of coffee produced." That is a correct but partial answer. A more complete explanation is, "Compared with soybeans, coffee growing here would require so many men and so much material that to produce each dollar's worth of coffee would force us to reduce soybean production by, say, ten dollars."

In essence, the cost of any product is the alternative products the

542

economy sacrifices to allocate resources to the product in question. So the best pattern of specialization and division of labor among national economic units requires that each trading nation minimize the value of products sacrificed in order to produce its actual array of outputs. We produce soybeans rather than coffee because our coffee production wouldn't be worth much per man-hour, whereas the Brazilians do the opposite because of the same cost considerations.

Do both Brazil and the United States benefit by this arrangement? Yes, of course! Both specialize at what they do best, produce a surplus, and trade off that surplus for what they do least well. For the United States, an acre of land will produce much more coffee by the indirect route of planting soybeans and trading the beans for coffee than by planting coffee directly. The reverse is, of course, true for Brazil.

The principle of specialization demonstrates why national economies produce surpluses and swap them off to each other in *inter*national trade. The trading patterns that evolve are those dictated by the law of comparative advantage which we have just reviewed in our Brazil–United States example. Now let us turn to *intra*national trade and see if these principles apply.

Within each national economy there is a wide variety of resources of greatly varying productivities. From this it follows that the production jobs the economy wishes to perform should be divided among its human and material resources so that overall productivity can be maximized. In short, the rule that productivity is increased by specialization applies to resources within an economy as well as among economies.

Specialization within national economies leads to regional differences within nations. Resource mixes vary from region to region, so quite naturally cost structures and, therefore, output mixes vary from region to region. Some examples may prove helpful at this point.

Cotton can be grown in both the Old South and the New South and so can tobacco. But cost considerations arising from differences in resource endowment make the Middle or New South a cotton economy, while tobacco dominates in the southern coastal states.

Clothing can be manufactured in both major metropolitan areas and remote rural areas. High-fashion clothing is made almost wholly in New York City, and the industry is one of the city's most important employers because a New York location offers certain vital inputs at very low cost— so low that high labor costs are overcome. On the other hand, inexpensive ready-to-wear clothing can be most efficiently manufactured in the remote hamlets of the southern agricultural states because labor costs are the most strategic input variable to that industry. Consequently, mass-produced garments are a specialty of the low-wage South.

In an engineering sense, both sawmilling and aerospace instruments can be produced at either rural or urban locations. But cost considerations dictate that sawmilling be performed very near forests, whereas the precision instrument industry is found in cities that have large universities. This pattern of specialization has emerged from the same cost consideration: trees and highly trained technical personnel are both very expensive to move.

Once again, it should be easy to see how the notion of specialization applies in the third way we mentioned above—among and within producing units within an economy. Firms and plants specialize in particular products according to their comparative advantages. Within firms, employees specialize according to the employer's assessment of comparative skill advantages.

Now let us see what kinds of general observations the above discussion leads us to.

First, nations and regions within nations are more productive when they specialize rather than when they attempt to produce the entire array of products desired. The same principle applies to production *among* and *within* business firms. The other side of this coin is that specialization and division of labor require large markets in order to spread high plant and equipment costs over a large sales volume.

Second, this requires a trade pattern *among* and *within* nations in which each nation and region trades the surplus it produces in its specialty for the specialty surpluses of other nations and regions. In other words, the export-base products of nations and regions are traded against each other.

Third, international and interregional trade require a universal means of payment. Within the United States dollars are such a means, and internationally gold and certain national currencies serve as a means of payment.

Fourth, the productivity of the export base depends on the quality of productive resources and the world demand for the product mix of the export base. The higher the productivity of the export base, the greater will be the power to import and thus the more prosperous will be the economy, whether it be a city, a state, a region, or a nation.

Fifth, changes in the structure of world demand and technological innovations are capable of increasing or decreasing the productivity of the export base. Consequently, the prosperity and growth rate of an economy will often depend upon the nature of such changes.

When we apply this fifth principle to the relationship between a national economy and its regions, we find that when the nature of a nation's export base changes, the productivity of the export bases of each of its regions will change also. Consequently, when a nation's export-base mix changes, within that nation a reallocation of resources and a change in the distribution of income among regions will take place.

Sixth, the larger an economy is, the more diversified it can be and the less dependent will it need to be upon imports to satisfy its demands.

Thus, a state such as Arkansas devotes almost half of its resources to several agricultural mainstays, garment manufacture, and timber products, and exports about half of its total production, while the United States spreads its resources among a vastly wider variety of industries and exports less than 10 percent of its production.

Consequently, the larger an economy is, the less will its growth rate and prosperity depend upon other economies. A corollary to this principle is that the larger an economy is, the greater is the number of variables that are susceptible to manipulation by public policy and the less is the degree to which a nation's economic fate is determined outside the economy and out of the reach of the policy-makers.

Seventh, as we shall see, the conclusion we reached immediately above does not apply to problems relating to international payments. In the United States, trade imbalances have become the tail that wags the dog in the sense that our adjustments to international payments difficulties have an impact upon all sectors of the economy.

With these observations regarding specialization and a nation's degree of prosperity and economic growth rate, we can look first at the varying development of regions within the U.S. economy and then at the relationship of the U.S. economy to the world economy.

REGIONAL DEVELOPMENT OF THE U.S. ECONOMY

The topic regional development returns us to consideration of another broad aspect of the national economy: its geographic structure. We have surveyed U.S. regional development prior to and after the Civil War. In this chapter we will consider some of the changes in the modern period, especially in the decade of the 1950s.

We will be interested in more than just how regional specialization contributed to national productivity and growth. We also want to turn particular attention to the adjustments that regions have had to make as a result of changes in the national economy. In a very real sense, then, this topic concerns one more of the adjustment problems of our high-income growth economy.

Let us start by considering the factors behind the regional specialization pattern of our national economy. It will help, to begin with, if we look at a map that is most representative of the regional structure of the economy (see 15–1). Since we are concerned with the resulting levels of individual welfare more than with the size of total output, it is appropriate to make per capita income our basic measure of regional differences. 15–1 shows per capita income levels by state in 1970 expressed as a percentage of the national average, which in 1970 was $3,920.

Above average income levels are generally found in the industrial states and in the Far West. Below average income levels (except for

15–1.   State per capita incomes, 1970
(percent of U.S. average)*

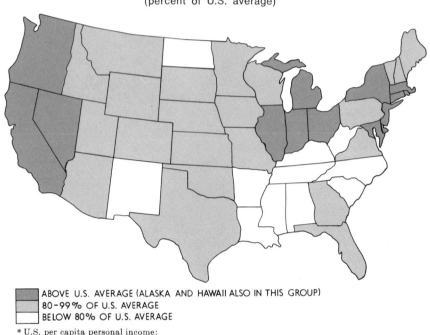

ABOVE U.S. AVERAGE (ALASKA AND HAWAII ALSO IN THIS GROUP)
80–99% OF U.S. AVERAGE
BELOW 80% OF U.S. AVERAGE

* U.S. per capita personal income:
SOURCE: U.S. Department of Commerce (1972), p. 321.

North Dakota and New Mexico) are concentrated in the Southeast. Now turn to 15–2 and note that the regional income disparities shown adhere to the same basic pattern established by 1880 (refer to 9–13). However, as you can see, the differentials have been narrowing as differences in regional output mixes have been reduced over the years.

Now, how did this configuration emerge? The answer lies in our pattern of regional specialization. 15–3 notes some of the basic influences on regional specialization and, therefore, productivity. In order to bring our discussion into historical focus, let us review the development of regional specialization that we presented in several earlier chapters, then consider the operation since 1920 of the factors presented in 15–3.

At least until the 1880s, agriculture was our principal source of export income and the economic base of most American communities. External changes in world food and fiber demand and internal changes in agricultural technology and transportation determined the relative prosperity of the various regions. The colonies developed around ports and rivers. Then, with the rising importance of cotton and better inland transportation, the East, West, and South developed the interdependent pattern of specialization that we reviewed earlier.

After farm productivity had increased sufficiently to release significant

15–2. Per capita incomes by regions, 1920–70

| | *Percent of U.S. average* | | | |
	1920	1940	1960	1970
Northeast				
New England	125	127	111	109
Middle Atlantic	136	132	117	114
North Central				
East North Central	109	112	107	104
West North Central	87	81	93	94
South				
South Atlantic	64	77	84	91
East South Central	53	49	66	74
West South Central	72	64	81	85
West				
Mountain	101	87	94	90
Pacific	136	132	118	110

SOURCE: U.S. Department of Commerce, p. 321.

15–3. Influences on regional specialization and productivity

1. Competitive resource advantages
2. Access costs (transportation)
3. Plant and market size
4. Relative prices of items in output mix
5. Proximity advantages
6. Local market demands

numbers of workers to manufacturing, regional income patterns changed in response to changes in regional specialization. Manufactured exports gained supremacy over agriculture. The manufacturing heartland developed and stretched westward to the Middle West. At the same time, the rest of the Nation became a raw materials (especially minerals) and agricultural hinterland for the Northeast and Great Lakes regions which had become the heartland of our export base. Income patterns followed the redeployment of the export base.

The heartland-hinterland relationship continued in this pattern until around 1920, by which time the movement of manufacturing into the hinterland had begun to blur the distinction between the two types of areas. With this change came the narrowing of regional income differences that we referred to above. Labor-intensive industries continued their movement South, while the West, especially California, and certain key cities in the Southwest were the recipients of capital-intensive, high-wage industries.

The South continued to specialize in cotton and, more recently, soybeans. Around the turn of the century, it also had a boom in lumber production, which continued until the building slump of the 1930s, when its virgin forests also began to be depleted and competition was faced from western lumber areas. The Southwest benefited from a boom in oil, while the Gulf area benefited from the growth of both the petroleum and chemical industries.

As the Nation continued to grow, certain nonresource influences continued to favor manufacturing expansion in the manufacturing belt and in large cities in particular. These are indicated as the last two points in 15–3. First, there was the advantage of proximity to other firms—both in the same type of production and in other fields—which yielded external economies of scale in the form of agglomeration economies. That is, the growing size of all industry in an area makes possible the specialization of certain types of supplier and service industries and minimizes certain marketing costs. An apparel manufacturer, for example, finds that a large city with many apparel plants has a large supply of experienced workers, nearby suppliers of machinery and cloth, and nearby centers of finance and marketing. He can show his wares at annual shows and personally contact both customers and suppliers. And it's easy to keep tabs on his competitors.

Agglomeration economies are responsible for making our historically large urban areas even larger. Improvements in city transportation—streetcars, then buses and commuter trains—as well as technological improvements in the construction of tall buildings made possible the concentration of more and more manufacturing, commercial, and financial businesses in close proximity to one another in our major metropolitan areas.

A second influence on the growth of major cities was the last item shown in 15–3—the growth of local markets. As more industrial firms located near one another in cities, more jobs in other industries were required to serve not only those industries themselves but also the worker population of the area. City planners have described this multiplication of locale-serving jobs by using a base industry–service industry scheme of analysis. In line with the analysis at the beginning of this chapter, they point out that the basic industries of a community exist largely to serve a regional or national market—that is, they export their goods and services from the local community. Manufacturing is a very important example. The locale-serving, or residentiary, industries, however, depend upon the size and productivity of the local work force or population. They expand or contract with the local work force—especially the portion that is employed in export industries—but are not primarily responsible for causing a metropolitan area to expand or contract. Thus, community leaders are well aware that the development of new manufacturing jobs is critical to the growth of their community. Of course, recreation, finance, and other industries may also be part of a community's export base.

Influences on regional change

The basic structure of regional specialization in the Nation was established before the Civil War. By 1900, the economy had reached a peak in the degree of regional specialization it had achieved. Let's now turn to consider some of the influences that produced different kinds and different rates of change in the various regions. 15–4 lists some of these influences.

15–4.   Influences on regional
change

1. Technological change
2. Income elasticity of demand
3. Changes in consumer preferences
   and, thus, structure of demand
4. Sunk costs
5. Changes in amenities
6. Growth of local markets

We have already shown how technological change caused different rates of growth in various industries. Changes in consumer preferences have had, of course, a similar impact on the structure of total demand. We have also stressed the importance of different rates of growth in demand as incomes rose—that is, differing income elasticities of demand. It should be easy to understand, therefore, that regional specialization in different products generated different rates of growth among regions because of what was happening to their major industries. For example, the competition of aluminum has cut into the production of steel, and thus affected the steelmaking cities. Western lumber expanded at the expense of southern lumber; and southern textiles and apparel displaced some New England textiles and apparel. Also farming and many consumer goods industries have experienced smaller increases in demand for their output than have other industries.

Changes between 1950 and 1970 in employment among the major nonfarm industries are shown in 15–5. Mining experienced a decrease in employment, while transportation, communications, utilities, and manufacturing increased at less than the average rate for all nonfarm industry. The highest rates of increase were in finance, real estate, and insurance; services; and government (primarily state and local government, incidentally).

Within manufacturing, also, different rates of change have occurred in different industries; and these changes have also affected regions differently. Between 1950 and 1970, decreases in employment occurred in tobacco, textiles, leather, lumber, and miscellaneous—which are low-wage industries—and also in petroleum refining and primary metals. Employment also decreased in auto vehicles and parts as well as in railroad equipment, although the transportation equipment group in-

15–5.   Nonfarm employment in the United States, 1950 and 1970

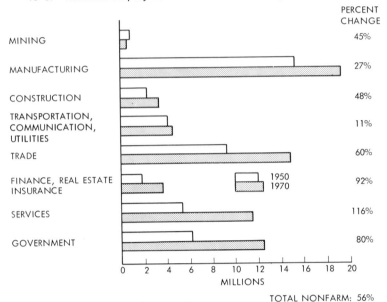

SOURCE: U.S. Department of Labor (1972), p. 26.

creased due to increases in aircraft (and missiles) and in boats. Otherwise, the increases continued to be led by chemicals, electrical machinery, and instruments; and growth continued in ordnance, machinery, fabricated metals, and paper and printing.

Different regions tended to fare well or poorly depending on which industries were concentrated there. Nevertheless, the biggest differences among regions arose out of different rates of growth within industry groups (although some of the group averages in the data merely result from different product concentrations).

New regional patterns

In the post–World War II period, the economy was generally prosperous and, in the main, employment grew in line with the growth of the labor force. However, national growth rates disguised regional trends that were in many instances quite unlike the national averages. Some regions grew much faster than the Nation as a whole, as income growth and demand shifts favored their industrial bases; other regions lagged behind the U.S. average; and within both prosperous and lagging regions pockets of unemployment and localized economic distress persisted. The slow-growth regions and *depressed areas* are explained by the industrial trends we have just cited—in general, such regions and areas host the industries which have been declining in relative or absolute amounts since the end of World War II. On the other side of the coin, the flourishing areas are, for the most part, the sites of the Nation's most rapidly growing industries.

Notable among the urban depressed areas are New England textile towns, coal mining areas, railroad equipment or repair centers, and automobile or household machinery centers. In the 1960s, conditions in such areas improved somewhat in response to out-migration and national expansion. However, these areas are still characterized by comparatively high unemployment rates and stagnation or relatively low growth rates. The rural depressed areas are, of course, concentrated in the South, in farming, lumbering, and textile areas. Nevertheless, in spite of its islands of depression, the South as a whole has been growing faster than the Nation as a whole in terms of per capita income.

At this point, we might ask why some industries and people do not move out of old areas more rapidly. Much of the steel industry, for example, is in older, high-cost locations. Here, the existence of fixed capital investment in plant and equipment acts as a dampening influence on the rate of change. With their capital already sunk in equipment that cannot be sold or used up quickly, the owners continue to operate the equipment even though it is no longer very profitable. In the same sense, many farmers and homeowners in depressed industrial cities are reluctant to move away from the homes, schools, and churches in which they already have a large capital investment. Some so-called depressed areas have managed to adjust to loss of demand for their export industry output by converting their export base to new products or by retraining their labor for other work. Some of the New England towns, in particular, have been successful in using old textile mills for new and diversified types of industry.

Now let's look at broader regional trends. 15–6 gives a very rough idea of how different rates of industrial changes affected total nonfarm employment in different regions. Not shown is farm employment, which, of course, was declining nearly everywhere. The map shows that the industrial areas in the Northeast tended to lag most behind the national average in nonfarm employment growth, while states along the southern and western rim of the Nation experienced greater than average rates of growth.

What forces explain this pattern of regional change? A first source of insight is the different degrees of geographic mobility that exist among industries. In addition, different amenity endowments and the rapid expansion of trade and service employment also help to explain why some states grew much faster than others.

Industries with lower capital requirements and independence from bulky mineral raw materials are able to locate almost anywhere. These so-called *footloose* industries are able to move to depressed areas where

15–6.   Post-World War II state nonfarm employment changes

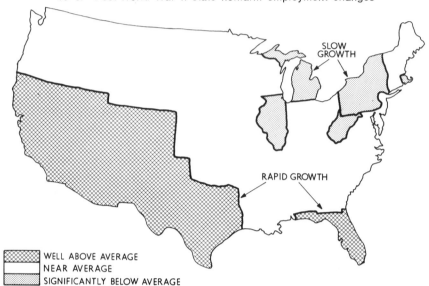

WELL ABOVE AVERAGE
NEAR AVERAGE
SIGNIFICANTLY BELOW AVERAGE

SOURCE: U.S. Department of Labor (1972), pp. 103–4.

labor supply is in surplus, provided that the labor surplus also means lower wages and lower labor costs for them.

Southern rural areas especially have attracted such industries on the basis of their ample labor supply, low wages, and, often, financial inducements in the form of low-interest loans or low taxes. Recently, some of the depressed industrial areas have been competing for these footloose industries; and the U.S. Department of Commerce (Economic Development Administration) aims to aid both urban and rural depressed areas in obtaining such industries. The competition, however, is keen; and the number of jobs in footloose industries is limited in relation to the supply of surplus workers in depressed areas. Thus, significant out-migration will have to continue in these areas. At any rate, in spite of the fact that manufacturing has not grown very fast nationally over the past generation, its relative relocation explains the rapid growth of the South.

Two other influences have been favoring the South and the West. One is the fact that communities that have a warm or moderate climate and favorable recreational, cultural, and medical facilities exert a strong pull on people and industry. Southern and western cities are attracting older people, an important factor in this era of a rapidly growing retirement generation. And some of the footloose industries are attracted on this count, especially if they have a relatively smaller requirement for unskilled labor and a greater need for professionals and skilled technicians. They find it easier to lure key personnel to desirable living areas. Florida, southern California, and the Southwest have social and climatic amenities that have helped them pull in both people and industry.

Another influence favoring the South and West has been the growing size of regional markets. The limits of economies from large plants and from concentration in industrial centers have apparently been reached in many industries. Now many of them are locating branch plants in regions outside of the manufacturing belt in order to reduce transportation costs and provide quicker service. That is, as regions and regional centers grow larger, more and more industries find it advantageous to locate plants in such growth centers rather than to expand in traditional locations. Thus, the size of local markets has been a factor in encouraging regional decentralization of industry in the postwar period. This is in line with our earlier observation that the larger an economy, the more diversified and the less dependent upon other economies it will be.

A related phenomenon is the rapid national growth of trade and service employment. Given the relatively rapid growth of manufacturing employment in the South, it follows that southern cities have been booming in spite of the decline in farm employment. The same kind of observation applies to the West—for example, between 1960 and 1970 Los Angeles moved from third rank to second rank in population largely as a reflection of the growth of manufacturing activity attracted to the California area by its climate.

Expanding metropolitan areas

Urban growth and regional decentralization have taken on a new pattern since the 1920s. Regional decentralization is not a move back to rural areas, and it is not a move toward ever larger central cities. Rather, something has been happening to our metropolitan area that is causing them to suffer major problems of readjustment. That something is the final culmination of the revolution in motorized transportation, an automobile for eight out of every ten households in the Nation. Instead of causing our cities to get larger, this has been causing them to spread out.

Within metropolitan areas (which are defined in census statistics to include a whole county or very often several counties), the percentage of the population in the central cities has declined since the 1920–30 decade, especially since 1950, so that currently less than 45 percent of metropolitan area populations live in the central cities. The population has used the automobile and better highways to move out to suburbs or rural nonfarm areas surrounding the cities. The resulting urban sprawl has caused rising costs of sewers, water, streets, police, fire protection, and other public services, plus the rising costs of smog from an increased number of autos and industrial plants in each metropolitan area. It has also resulted in a decline in property values in the central cities as downtown stores have felt the loss of business. And as poorer income groups have crowded into the older dwellings abandoned by the middle classes, the social costs associated with high population density have been intensified.

Industry has also tended to move out of older multistory plants in crowded city centers because of the transportation revolution. Trucks make the movement of goods less dependent upon railroad marshaling yards; and workers are able to commute in private cars to outlying plants or even to plants in nearby cities. But the burden on transportation facilities at rush hours has partially offset any advantages of moving industry out, especially because crisscross traffic patterns are harder to provide for. (We will have more to say about urban trends in chapter 16.)

However, it would be misleading for rural areas to pin their hopes on the trend toward regional decentralization and movement out of the center of major cities. For the most part, industry has moved only as far as the suburbs, so manufacturing employment is still concentrated in metropolitan areas. Nationally, metropolitan areas have gained an increased share of all manufacturing employment. Only in the East South Central region have nonmetropolitan areas gained a larger share of manufacturing employment in the postwar period. Small apparel, shoe, and light assembly plants do locate in small cities or rural areas; but industrialization in rural regions is largely a process of growth of the medium and large cities in those regions.

Population and income changes

As we have already noted, one way that regions have reacted to the changing rates of employment growth has been to organize industrial development programs to improve their resource advantages and provide information services and/or inducements to attract more industry. Some states and cities have succeeded remarkably in inducing more manufacturing industry to locate or expand plants in their communities. And as the new export-base industries have supported more workers and a larger population, these communities have expanded their residentiary industries.

Looking at regional trends quite broadly, the major way that regions have adjusted to different rates of employment growth has been by migration of people. Migration is a rather unpopular subject among local community leaders when out-migration is taking place. Yet a major characteristic of our time, as throughout the history of the Nation, has been the mobility of our people. In continuation of past trends, the U.S. population center is moving westward as the cities of the West

Coast and the Southwest continue to grow faster than the rest of the Nation. (The population center of the U.S. has moved from western Indiana to within hailing distance of East St. Louis since 1920.)

15–7. Migration rates, 1950–60
(percent of 1950 population)

	Total	Urban	Rural		Total	Urban	Rural
New England				East South Central			
Maine	−12	−12	−11	Kentucky	−15	6	−27
New Hampshire	− 4	− 2	− 6	Tennessee	−11	9	−26
Vermont	−14	− 9	−18	Alabama	−14	13	−35
Massachusetts	− 8	− 9	− 2	Mississippi	−22	14	−36
Rhode Island	− 9	− 6	−24				
Connecticut	9	10	5	West South Central			
				Arkansas	−26	2	−40
Middle Atlantic				Louisiana	·· 1	20	−22
New York	− 5	− 5	− 4	Oklahoma	−14	10	−39
New Jersey	7	10	−11	Texas	5	30	−35
Pennsylvania	−10	− 9	−14				
				Mountain			
East North Central				Montana	− 4	14	−17
Ohio	4	9	− 9	Idaho	− 4	8	−14
Indiana	1	5	− 7	Wyoming	− 4	12	−20
Illinois	− 3	2	−18	Colorado	15	38	−24
Michigan	5	9	− 6	New Mexico	21	65	−23
Wisconsin	− 3	9	−19	Arizona	55	115	−20
				Utah	12	31	−24
West North Central				Nevada	60	101	5
Minnesota	− 3	13	−23				
Iowa	−12	− 1	−23	Pacific			
Missouri	− 9	0	−23	Washington	2	11	−14
North Dakota	−16	18	−28	Oregon	− 1	17	−22
South Dakota	−14	6	−23	California	30	41	−13
Nebraska	−11	5	−26				
Kansas	− 4	16	−25				
South Atlantic							
Delaware	22	28	10				
Maryland	13	20	− 3				
District of							
Columbia	−26	−26	None				
Virginia	0	22	−20				
West Virginia	−25	−16	−30				
North Carolina	− 8	12	−18				
South Carolina	− 9	6	−17				
Georgia	− 6	19	−27				
Florida	59	82	15				

SOURCE: Henderson, p. 176.

15–7 shows migration rates by states for the period 1950–60; the figures shown are typical of the kinds of long-term regional population shifts that have characterized the post-1920 period. The 1950–60 period, however, is of special interest because it was a period of especially heavy farm employment decreases. In 15–6, positive figures reflect in-migration, usually into cities, expressed as a percentage of the area they moved into. Negative figures reflect out-migration, primarily from the rural areas.

The net migration figures are not the same as total population changes, because the excess of births over deaths would normally cause population to grow in each area. In the United States between 1950 and 1960, total population increased by about 19 percent; so any state that grew by less than 19 percent experienced out-migration, and any state whose net out-migration exceeded 19 percent chalked up a net population loss.[1]

The data in 15–7 provide several useful insights about migration as it relates to changing economic opportunity. First, note that in only 4 states were migration rates positive for rural areas. Second, in 38 of the 44 cases of rural out-migration, the states involved experienced urban in-migration because their cities grew to offset rural decline. Third, from 1950 to 1960 only 17 states recorded in-migration rates, whereas 31 states posted out-migration rates; in the main this reflected a continued movement of the population westward. Fourth, in 9 states, most of them in the Northeast, urban areas were characterized by out-migration. And fifth, in only 2 states, Arkansas and West Virginia, was out-migration heavy enough to cause total population to decline.

The foregoing shows that the American labor force is highly mobile and is willing to move in response to changes in the demand for labor as industry shifts its location. It also indicates that the growth of urban-oriented industry made major contributions toward offsetting the decline in farm employment in rural states. However, in all but a handful of states, the decline of rural job opportunities was too great to be offset by the growth of urban industrial job opportunities.

The relationship of migration as a means of adjusting to shifts in industrial location and income growth can be seen by looking at 15–8. This graph shows changes from 1950 to 1960 as index numbers (1950 = 100) plotted against a log scale on each axis. The vertical scale shows percent changes in personal income. The horizontal scale shows percent changes in population. The horizontal and vertical lines at 100 reflect the 1950 levels of population and income; any point on one of these lines indicates zero change in either income or population.

In 15–8, the dashed diagonal line drawn through the intersection of 100 on the vertical scale and 100 on the horizontal scale reflects equal changes in both income and population. Any point on that line indicates that the state's per capita income remained unchanged; any point above

---

[1] This is an oversimplification in that birthrates and death rates vary among states; e.g., Mississippi had a 22 percent net out-migration rate from 1950 to 1960, but its high natural population increase offset its heavy out-migration rate so that its population remained unchanged.

15–8.   State income and population changes, 1950–60

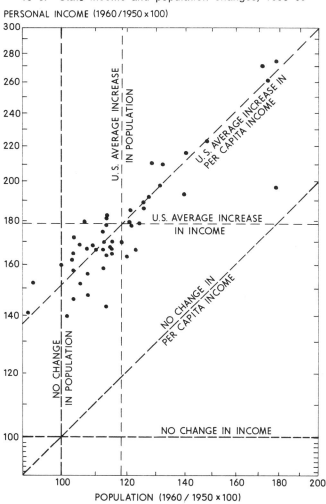

PERSONAL INCOME (1960/1950 x 100)

POPULATION (1960 / 1950 x 100)

Source: U.S. Department of Commerce (1962), pp. 11, 322.

that line indicates that the state's per capita income increased between 1950 and 1960.

On the dashed line drawn above and parallel to the "no change" line, any point indicates that per capita income in the state in question grew at exactly the same rate as in the United States as a whole. For example, one state's income grew to 165 percent of the 1950 value while the population grew to 110 percent of the 1950 level so it just matched the U.S. increase in per capita income. Of course, some states fell below and some above this line, although all increased their per capita incomes substantially over the decade.

One thing that 15–7 illustrates is that there are several ways in which a state's income and population can change in such a way as to produce economic growth. Thus, states which failed to have very large increases in total income still had large per capita income increases if their population grew slowly. Consequently, a farm state which experienced a disappointingly slow rise in demand for its products and, therefore, in its income may have been able to achieve an above average increase in per capita income by heavy out-migration and, correspondingly, a slower growth in population. This is exemplified by Arkansas and West Virginia, which were the two states that lost population (plotted at the extreme left of the graph) and which were among the lowest in overall gain in total personal income. However, *primarily because of heavy out-migration* they were among the states that experienced above average rates of per capita income gain.

It is chiefly because of the heavy in-migration to the West and the heavy out-migration from the South, in fact, that regional per capita incomes have persisted in converging on the national average. Thus, while particular areas may not be able to expand their populations at the U.S. rate, there is no reason why a given area cannot grow faster than the rest of the Nation in the individual incomes and living standards of its people—after all, it's the people, not the place, for whom prosperity is important. That's exactly what happened in the case of the 14 states clustered above and to the left of the U.S. per capita income and population increase lines.

AMERICA IN A GROWING WORLD

In the introduction to this chapter we pointed out that the larger a national economy becomes, the less will be its reliance upon exports to achieve efficiency and rapid growth. The development of the American economy exemplifies this principle. In the post-Revolutionary period the ascension of King Cotton raised the value of our export base and generated unprecedented gains in total and per capita income. In the period prior to the Civil War, the foreign sector was as high as 13 percent of total GNP and a much more important part of the market sector.

But the very growth of cotton and its companion exports generated a series of secondary effects which caused the foreign sector to decline in importance. The sequence was something like this: Export-base growth raised profits and wages which, in turn, attracted capital and labor. The inflow of capital and labor produced an extremely rapid absolute growth rate in the total economy. Extensive and intensive growth increased the size and geographic density of our markets. Bigger and geographically more concentrated consumer and industrial markets made investment in the most modern and efficient transportation facilities practical. The combination of bigger markets and better transportation made it possible to capture the economies of specialization and division of labor which had given European and British manufacturers a competitive advantage over Americans. So manufacturing investment was encouraged at home and, thus, our dependence upon the rest of the world for manufactured products was reduced. In short, over the long pull, we persisted in a pattern of import substitution.

This chain of events, which began with Eli Whitney's cotton gin, set in motion a trend toward a steadily declining importance of exports. This trend was well established by the Civil War. And by the post–World War II period, the foreign sector had fallen to less than 10 percent of GNP, and currently it is only about 5 to 7 percent of total GNP.

U.S. balance of payments

Let us begin by bringing to a recent date the kind of balance of payments data that we have shown for previous historic periods. 15–9

15–9. U.S. balance of payments—balances of trade and specie and other official reserves, 1915–71

BILLIONS OF DOLLARS

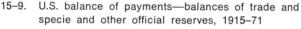
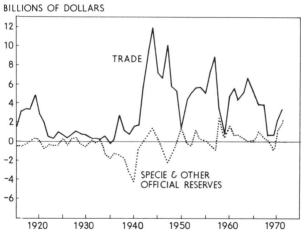

Note: For 1960–71 all military expenditures are included in invisible items; capital includes errors and omissions and changes in U.S. liquid liabilities; and specie and other official reserves includes gold flows and changes in special drawing rights, convertible currencies, and the International Monetary Fund gold tranche position.
SOURCES: For 1915–57, U.S. Department of Commerce (1960), pp. 537–64; for 1958 and 1959, U.S. Department of Commerce (1966), p. 814; for 1960–71, U.S. Department of Commerce (June 1972), pp. 28–30.

and 15–10 show these data, this time in billions of dollars, for the period 1915 through 1971.

During the 1915–71 period the United States maintained a positive trade balance until 1971, when our thirst for imports outpaced the

15–10. U.S. balance of payments—balances of invisible
items and capital, 1915–71

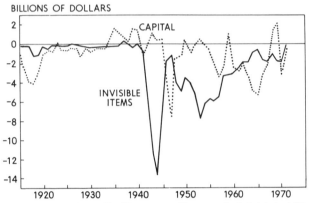

BILLIONS OF DOLLARS

Note: For 1960–71 all military expenditures are included in invisible
items; capital includes errors and omissions and changes in U.S. liquid
liabilities; and specie and other official reserves includes gold flows and
changes in special drawing rights, convertible currencies, and the International Monetary Fund gold tranche position.
SOURCES: See 15–9.

growth of exports and pushed our trade balance into the deficit column.
Invisible items were of little net consequence until World War II; since
the war our expenditures overseas for services have been very large
and have often required more foreign exchange than our positive merchandise trade balance earned for us. Outward capital flows continued
in the pattern established at the turn of the century, when Americans
became net overseas investors on a persistent basis; the only exceptions
to this are two periods of international chaos, the Great Depression
and World War II. Specie (gold) flows were of little importance prior
to the 1930s. During the Great Depression and for a while after World
War II, gold flowed into the United States. However, for the past two
decades gold has been sold abroad to earn foreign exchange to finance
our overseas purchases of merchandise and services.

We can use these payments data to review our international relations
as they developed historically. First, it is important to understand that
World War I brought a sharp break in international trading relations
as well as in the balance of political power. The war was a great drain
on the production of the industrial nations of Europe. No longer could
the rest of the world pay for its excess of imports over exports from
the United States with earnings from its investments in American business
and securities. During World War I and for a while in the 1920s, our
surplus exports were made possible by the flow abroad of American
loan and investment capital. For example, during World War I, European nations financed their purchases of food and war materials from
the United States with the funds Americans loaned or invested in

Europe. After the war, Europe financed its imports of American food and of American machinery and equipment required for recovery in a similar manner.

Our Nation, however, continued a policy of raising tariffs to exclude imports. As a part of the "return to normalcy" program of President Harding, the Emergency Tariff Act of 1921 increased duties and the Fordney-McCumber Act of 1922 raised them even higher. In 1930, under President Hoover, the Hawley-Smoot Tariff Act was passed in the midst of the Depression decline. (See 15–11 for average duties over the 1921–70 period.)

15–11.   Ratios of duties to values of imports

Yearly average	Total imports (percent)	Dutiable imports (percent)
1921–25	14	36
1926–30	14	40
1931–35	18	50
1936–40	19	38
1941–45	11	32
1946–50	7	16
1951–55	5	12
1956–60	7	11
1961–65	7	12
1966–70	7	11

SOURCE: U.S. Department of Commerce (1972), p. 788.

America's Great Depression was part of a worldwide depression, and America's Great Contraction had a severe impact on the rest of the world. With the end of the 1921 boom, American investment abroad was reduced. Along with higher American tariffs, this made it increasingly difficult for other countries to pay for American goods. Other nations followed our example by pushing tariffs even higher. Just when our economy suffered a cumulative slowdown in the flow of income and production and when everyone became pessimistic and tried to reduce investments and hold cash, the nations of the world fell into a vicious circle of reducing their imports and trying to expand their exports. World trade declined, and capital and specie flowed back into the United States.

The depression was a shock to our confidence and led to reform measures. Europeans were equally shaken by the depression. With this calamity following so soon after the destruction of World War I, and with the ominous example of the Russian Revolution, the European industrial nations were ready for measures more desperate than social reforms. As the Communist and Socialist parties became stronger, the traditional upper classes were frightened into supporting military dictatorships. Where the fascists came to power, they instituted a policy aimed at economic self-sufficiency which further restricted world trade.

The 1930s decade was one of conflicting actions on the international economic scene. Although President Roosevelt initially followed an isolationist line, in the late 1930s he used the Reciprocal Trade Act to reduce tariffs and restore trade somewhat (note the blip in the trade plot for the 30s). But the dictatorships and impending war in Europe caused a flight of capital to America, mostly in the form of continued gold flows to this country. Such capital movements were a source of embarrassment and a spur to financial restrictions among nations.

Thus, after more than a century of world peace, industrial expansion, and free trade, the international economy was smashed. It broke on the rocks of war and depression. The aftermath consisted of dictatorships, attempts at self-sufficiency, rivalry for exclusive trade rights and access to resources, and a second world war.

During World War II, America had a very large volume of exports to its Allies. These were offset by large current payments in the form of spending on supplies and payrolls for our military forces abroad which appear as part of the huge dip in the invisible items plotted in 15–9. Our lend-lease program also supplied both military and civilian goods to support our allies.

In the first few postwar years, foreigners withdrew funds held in the United States, and American investors supplied a large volume of capital funds to Europe and Japan to help them buy American machinery and materials to repair and restore their own productive capacity. Under the Marshall Plan, public loans and financial grants were made by our government to help the European nations, including Greece, Turkey, and, a little later, Yugoslavia. An Organization for European Economic Cooperation was established to help direct the use of these aid funds. Japan received similar assistance, but on a smaller scale. Accordingly, from 1945 to 1950, trade remained very high, while specie and capital flows and invisible items increased to finance European imports from the United States.

The United States was one of the leaders in establishing international organizations whose objectives included the restoration of world trade. Chief among them was the United Nations. The International Bank for Reconstruction and Development (World Bank), which lends money for development purposes, and the International Monetary Fund, which assists the balance of payments flows between nations, were also founded in this period.

Early in the 1950s, during the Korean War, America's invisible items deficit and export surplus grew even larger. Not only increased expenditures on military forces abroad but also a very large increase in foreign investment were mainly responsible for supporting a further increase in our export surplus. After 1960, our foreign aid for development rather than military purposes increased moderately, but in recent years the course of foreign aid has been reversed, and foreign aid remains in constant jeopardy as a consequence of congressional and public dissatisfaction.

From dollar shortage to dollar glut

The decade or so after World War II was known as the period of the *dollar shortage.* European nations and Japan found it difficult to amass enough foreign exchange to purchase all the U.S. imports they required for rebuilding, then expanding, their economies. They incurred chronic and large *balance of payments deficits.* Europe's and Japan's merchandise imports from the United States vastly exceeded their sales of goods and services to Americans in spite of large U.S. military expenditures in both Europe and Japan. U.S. aid, such as the Marshall Plan, World Bank loans, sales of gold for U.S. dollars, and private American investment, helped to offset their unfavorable trade balances. In addition, our trading partners imposed stringent exchange controls on their citizens. In effect, American dollars were rationed, and permission to buy dollars was granted to those who would import products considered vital to their country's national interest.

Over the years, the dollar shortage grew less and less serious as Europe and Japan regained prosperity and U.S. trade barriers were lowered. West Germany's "economic miracle" has been singled out as phenomenal—and it was, considering the condition of West Germany at the end of the war—but at least to some degree every Western European nation had its economic miracle, and Japan outstripped them all. As the power of Europe and Asia to produce and export grew, U.S. tariffs were lowered, thus increasing the access of foreign producers to U.S. markets. Currently, U.S. tariffs are lower than ever and vastly below their historical average (see 15–11). However, in recent years, quotas on particular exports to the United States urged on foreign governments by the United States have somewhat offset the impact of lower tariffs.

By the late 1950s a *dollar glut* had developed. The United States was finding it difficult to earn enough foreign exchange to accommodate importers, investors, and tourists and to continue financing our overseas military expenditures and foreign economic aid programs. Of course, Europeans and Asians continued to purchase U.S. products, but American producers who had previously found it easy to market a portion of their output in Europe and Asia increasingly found themselves coming up against European and Japanese competitors with brand-new, highly efficient plants whose forays into U.S. markets were often aided by export subsidies.

The figures for the years 1958 and 1971 tell the story: U.S. merchandise exports grew by a factor of 2.6, whereas merchandise imports increased to almost 3.5 times their 1958 level; and net U.S. travel and transportation expenditures increased to more than 3 times the 1958 figure as did private overseas investment. By 1971, our merchandise exports had fallen below imports for the first time in 100 years. The figures are summarized below in millions of dollars for 1958 and 1971. (See 15–12.)

15–12.   U.S. balance of payments, 1958 and 1971
(millions of dollars)

	1958	1971
Merchandise balance	3,462	−2,689
Exports	(16,414)	(42,770)
Imports	(−12,952)	(−45,459)
Military transactions	−3,135	−2,894
Net investment income.	2,584	7,995
Net travel and transport	−633	−1,684
Gifts and grants	−2,361	−3,574
Balance on current account	−5	−2,846

SOURCE: See 15–9.

We financed our balance of payments deficits in too ways: the United States sold gold for foreign currencies, and foreign banks agreed to hold ever-increasing amounts of dollars in what are in effect their American bank accounts. From 1958 on, our gold stock declined without interruption until 1971, when it fell below $10 billion, less than half its 1958 level. A world monetary crisis ensued which led to a partial restructuring of the system for making international payments and stemmed the outflow of U.S. gold.

The factors that led to the 1971 world monetary crisis were genuine enough. The United States began the postwar period unrivaled in productive capacity, but, naturally, as Europe and Japan rebuilt, their industry supplanted American producers in various markets. But this fully predictable economic evolution did not have to generate a worldwide crisis. Rather, the chaotic events of 1971 were brought on by the inability of the United States and its trading partners to adjust on a month-to-month basis to both the realignment of the world's productive capacity and differential domestic inflation rates. The world monetary system and international payments mechanism adopted after World War II did not allow for that kind of flexibility.

In July 1944, representatives of 40 of the world's largest nations met at Bretton Woods, New Hampshire, with the aim of establishing a system for solving short-run currency and exchange problems in an "orderly" manner and of planning solutions to the long-run problems of reconstruction and development. The Bretton Woods agreement was, alas, internally inconsistent. By providing for the World Bank and, in spirit, laying the groundwork for the Marshall Plan, it set in motion a process that led to massive long-term shifts in the distribution of the world's productive capacity. But the Bretton Woods agreement didn't allow for timely adjustments to the scores of changes that world trade underwent over the quarter century after World War II.

Under the Bretton Woods agreement, signatory nations agreed to maintain, or *peg*, their exchange rates, i.e., the market price of their currencies, within 1 percent of their par value as expressed in U.S. dollars or gold by buying and selling its currency whenever market exchange rates reached their plus or minus 1 percent limit of par. In turn, the United States promised to peg the price of gold at $35 an ounce by buying and selling gold at the pegged rate.

The International Monetary Fund (IMF) was established to assist nations in maintaining their currency values at par, to provide for changes in exchange rates, and to assist nations with balance of payments deficits. Were a given country to run a temporary balance of payments deficit, it was to be allowed to borrow from the IMF with the expectation that it would repay the loan when it experienced a balance of payments surplus. Whenever a nation suffered a "fundamental disequilibrium" in its trade relations, it could raise the price of gold in terms of its currency. This is the equivalent of lowering the price at which its currency would be pegged, i.e., it could devalue. In essence, devaluation would mean that its products would sell at lower prices in the world market and that its exports would increase while its imports decreased, thereby eliminating its deficit.

Unfortunately, the Bretton Woods agreement did not define "fundamental disequilibrium"; however, consensus arose to the effect that "fundamental" meant large and sustained as well as basic. As a consequence, any nation choosing to devalue its currency had to wait until its balance of payments difficulties reached crisis proportions. For the United States, this meant that the dollar remained overpriced while we incurred persistent and increasing balance of payments deficits for almost two decades, with gold losses beginning in 1958.

By 1971, foreign holders of dollars were in panic. The year began with the U.S. balance of payments deficit jumping from $9.8 billion to an annual rate of $22 billion in the first quarter. Then, in the second quarter, we ran a deficit in our merchandise trade balance. In the 1960s we had tried a variety of stopgap measures: an interest equilization tax on foreign borrowing in the United States (1963); "voluntary" controls on overseas investment (1965); mandatory controls over U.S. investment abroad and the establishment of a two-tier gold market which ended central bank sales of gold outside the official gold market (1968); and upward revaluation of the West German mark (1961 and 1969). They hadn't worked.

Our demand for foreign currencies exceeded our supply, and dollars continued to pile up in European and Japanese banks. The inflation that had come with the war in Vietnam exacerbated our problems by reducing the attractiveness of our products overseas and eroding our excess of merchandise exports over imports. Foreign investors recognized that we couldn't continue to hold the value of the dollar at 0.889 grams of gold and began shifting their assets into other currencies.

By 1971, our monetary gold stock had fallen to about $10 billion, which was less than the additional dollars foreigners accumulated in the first half of 1971. Foreign bankers made it very clear that they were drawing the line and that the United States must act. So in August 1971 President Nixon:

1. halted gold redemption of dollars held by foreign central banks, thereby removing the peg from the dollar and allowing it to "float" downward;
2. levied a 10 percent surcharge on U.S. imports; (now expired); and
3. ordered a wage and price freeze.

In December 1971 the dollar was again pegged, not at a gold price of $35 an ounce but at $38, while the Japanese yen and the West German mark were revalued upward. The result was a lowering of about 11 percent in the price of the dollar as compared with the mark and the yen. In addition, the range within which exchange rates might vary was increased to $2\frac{1}{4}$ percent.

Although President Nixon cited the 1971 international financial agreement as "the most significant monetary achievement in the history of the world," it turned out to be considerably less than that. In 1972 we ran an even larger trade deficit, $6.4 billion versus less than $2 billion in 1971, and the overall balance of payments deficit was $10 billion. Consequently, in February 1973, the dollar was again devalued, this time to a gold price of $42.22 per ounce.

It is doubtful that the February 1973 devaluation constituted an end to the international monetary muddle. For one thing, the system remained inflexible although less so than under the original IMF *Articles of Agreement.* Crisis situations following long periods over which some nations run balance of payments deficits and others surpluses are not conducive to the growth of world trade. If recurrent breakdowns in international money markets are to be avoided, a means must be found to adjust exchange rates in a truly "orderly" manner. If this is achieved, adjustments to shifts in the world's trade relations can be made without long periods of disequilibrium.

In addition, the international payments media, of which gold is ultimately the most acceptable, have not grown in a nice, neat pattern fashioned after the growth of world trade. Gold mining adds to the world's gold stock at about 2 percent per year, whereas world trade has been growing at 8 percent. That's how the dollar became a key currency, that is, a currency which nations use in settling accounts with each other. In other words, there hasn't been enough international money (gold) to facilitate the growth of world trade, so nations have for many years used national money (dollars, pounds, and West German marks) to settle international claims. (The dollar's role as a key currency explains why we could incur a balance of payments deficit for so many years without experiencing gold losses until 1958. The rest of the world was willing to hold dollars to facilitate international exchanges. This also explains why the negative figures in the capital account are modest for the period 1960–71—our export of dollars to foreign banks largely offset our annual investments overseas.)

What is unsatisfactory about the use of key currencies is that a given nation will accept them only as long as it feels it can trade them at no less than the price at which it bought them originally. Consequently, as U.S. deficits grew and the U.S. trade balance turned negative, foreign central banks, fearing devaluation, sent dollars back to the United States and demanded gold. The result, of course, was devaluation.

In recognition of the need for additional international money, the IMF nations agreed in 1967 on the use of *paper gold* as a means of settling international accounts (the official name is *special drawing rights,* or SDRs). In 1970, 1971, and 1972 SDRs were issued to IMF nations in proportion to the size of their respective economies. Because paper gold can be used to buy foreign currencies in the same way that real gold can be used, its creation has added to the stock of international money. However, it is not clear that SDRs will eliminate the disadvantages associated with the use of particular national currencies as key currencies; much depends upon the quantity relative to world trade in which they are issued.

The growth and evolution of the economies of other nations and of the U.S. economy have put us in a paradoxical position in that foreign trade is a small part of our GNP but a very large part of world trade. This paradox has been intensified by the post–World War II expansion of trade among nations.

Our merchandise exports are only 4 percent of our GNP, but they account for 25 percent of the rest of the world's imports, and about the same is true of our imports. We are also the largest single supplier of investment capital in the world. Our income from overseas is the world's largest, totaling six times that of Britain, the occupant of the number two slot. Therefore, whatever happens to the American economy has a major impact on the economies of most other nations. With an increase in our prosperity, our imports rise, so demand for the production of other countries rises, and vice versa. Similarly, the changes in our trade policy over the postwar years have had significant effects upon our trading partners. While our lowering of tariffs has tended to increase international specialization and trade and to benefit nations exporting to us, our use of import quotas has had opposite effects.

Less developed nations

In the postwar period there has been an effort among the governments of the less developed countries (LDCs) to develop their economies. World War II started the breakup of the European colonial empires, and in the postwar period many nations were granted or won their freedom. These nations, however, have faced severe problems and obstacles to the development of their economies at the same time that their people have acquired overoptimistic hopes that their per capita incomes could be suddenly raised.

On the one hand, the governments of the new countries are unstable, and the people are poorly prepared for self-government. Thus, many LDCs are controlled by military dictators, and there is continual danger of revolt. On the other hand, these countries are very poor and have very unequal income distributions, relatively little capital, and few capable business leaders to build private industry. Thus, they seek to solve their problems through central planning and direct government production. Although this approach is no doubt more productive than unrestrained laissez-faire, central planning per se is not a substitute for the organizational class, the counterpart of the entrepreneur, that is typically absent in the LDCs.

Since the end of World War II, the United States has extended loans, outright grants, and technical assistance to the LDCs. The motivations behind our foreign aid are diverse: in the Cold War paradigm, foreign economic aid is a paramilitary strategy; to those who feel that developed capitalist nations can't maintain full employment without exporting their surplus, foreign aid is a full-employment strategy; others view it as a concomitant of U.S. leadership in world affairs; and some see aiding the LDCs as the charitable, honorable thing to do.

The amount of foreign aid extended by the United States to the LDCs has been relatively small compared with the aid it gave to Europe during and after World War II. Yet the needs of the less developed nations are much greater than were those of Europe. Europe lost its capital and much of its manpower during the war, but in its people it retained the knowledge necessary to operate a modern industrial economy—the LDCs have never had this human capital endowment.

The pattern of our military and nonmilitary foreign aid since World War II is summarized in 15–3. First, the most striking factor is the modest value of foreign aid as compared with the size of the U.S. economy—$133.4 billion, the total for the 27-year period from 1945 through 1971, is less than 15 percent of U.S. GNP in 1971. What's more, both as a percent of GNP and after adjustment for price changes, our aid has been declining. Those who have attacked foreign aid as a device for squandering our plenty on the world's masses just haven't looked at the record.

Second, the military portion of our aid has increased significantly since the late 1940s, both in absolute terms and as a proportion of all aid (although the rise in the price of military hardware probably hides an actual decline in military aid in recent years).

Third, loans have shifted in importance compared with grants—in the 1945–50 period, loans were about one third of nonmilitary aid, whereas in recent years loans have accounted for over half of nonmilitary aid. The geographic pattern has also changed markedly. As Western Europe regained its economic strength, the flow of nonmilitary aid to Europe diminished to a trickle, then shifted to a negative value as loans were repaid. Currently, military aid is the only significant assistance extended to European countries. On the other hand, the LDCs now receive large amounts of U.S. military and nonmilitary aid.

15–13.   U.S. government foreign aid, 1945–71
(in billions of dollars)

Type of aid	Total aid 1945–71	Average annual aid				
		1945–50	1951–56	1957–62	1962–68	1969–71
Net nonmilitary grants						
West Europe	17.4	1.81	0.90	0.16	0.00	0.03
Asia, Africa, Near East	29.6	0.76	0.83	1.38	1.26	1.36
Rest of world	6.7	0.26	0.10	0.31	0.26	0.33
Total	53.7	2.83	1.83	1.85	1.52	1.72
Net loans						
West Europe	6.1	1.35	0.03	−0.35	0.02	0.06
Asia, Africa, Near East	17.2	0.01	0.13	0.47	1.40	1.43
Rest of world	7.0	0.10	0.08	0.30	0.41	0.53
Total	30.3	1.46	0.24	0.42	1.83	2.02
Net military grants						
West Europe	17.6	0.05	1.83	0.70	0.21	0.27
Asia, Africa, Near East	30.1	0.23	0.85	1.21	1.43	2.56
Rest of world	1.7	0.01	0.10	0.01	0.05	0.03
Total	49.4	0.29	2.78	1.92	1.69	2.86
Net total, grants and loans	133.4	4.58	4.85	4.19	5.04	6.60

SOURCE: U.S. Department of Commerce data cited in Samuelson, p. 708.

Aid from developed nations may be strategic in getting development underway, but what is most crucial to sustained economic growth in the LDCs in their ability to increase exports and to attract foreign private capital on a continuing basis. The LDCs have the opportunity to transplant the most advanced technology in developing their economies. But to do so they must be in a position to import the machinery in which modern technology is embodied. Unless foreign aid is sustained at unrealistically high levels, LDCs must pay for machinery and other capital imports by increasing exports and attracting investment funds from other nations.

The new nations retain an attitude of hostility and suspicion toward Europeans and toward owners of capital because their outlook has been conditioned by the excesses of colonial rule. In fact, many people both in and out of the LDCs view both foreign aid and private investment in LDCs as a variation on 19th century imperialism. By design, colonial policy was aimed at furthering the interests of the large plantation and mining firms. Such progress came at the expense, real or imagined, of the "host" nations or colonies. Consequently, foreign private investment is strictly controlled in most LDCs; and foreigners are wary of such control, fearing expropriation or curbs on the removal of profits. Further domestic savings can only be a minor source of capital accumulation given the typical LDCs low per capita income, thirst for consumer goods, and rapid population growth. Even where export earnings are quite substantial, as they are in some LDCs, they are quickly exhausted by the demand for imported consumer goods.

Transplanting advanced technology is hampered beyond foreign exchange problems. The traditional economies of the LDCs do not boast the institutional setting in which development flourishes. Modern machinery requires skilled labor, competent managers, social overhead capital, well-organized markets, and a population with an aggressive, acquisitive mind-set. Thus, rendering technical and material assistance to the less developed countries cannot simply consist of shipping some machinery with a man from the factory to demonstrate its operation. The LDCs must revolutionize their economic organization so that the modern industrial method can function within their borders. Although the nations which extend aid know a great deal about technology, they are dismally ignorant when it comes to the social engineering necessary to modernize a nation's economic organization. So those who are willing to extend aid can't be of much help in building an environment conducive to economic development.

Whatever the motivations behind the extension of aid, development assistance is vital to the modernization of the nations of Latin America, Asia, and Africa. But given the often well-founded suspicions of formerly colonized peoples, the lack of cultural empathy that often characterizes the aiding nations, and the institutional setting of the typical LDC, the aid process has not been without its frustrations. And the results have not been rewarding. The economic progress achieved by the LDCs has been minimal; income gains have generally been absorbed by population growth. In short, it's easy to give, but very difficult to give effectively.

SUMMARY

As measured by GNP, the United States constitutes the largest free trade area in the world. Accordingly, the economic advantages of particular states and regions have produced a distinct pattern of geographic specialization which has enhanced the economy's income and growth rate. In turn, in spite of artificial trade barriers, the United States is part of a world division of labor which has operated to the mutual benefit of the world's trading nations.

1. Since 1920, the historical differences in state per capita income have narrowed, although most of the manufacturing states remain significantly above the U.S. average, while the southeastern states, which are still predominantly agricultural, remain well below the U.S. average. The changes in per capita income experienced by individual states over the period largely reflect national industrial trends.

2. After World War II, nonfarm employment grew most rapidly in the Southwest and the West, whereas in the manufacturing states nonfarm jobs expanded at rates significantly lower than the overall U.S. rate. This pattern is explained by the movement of footloose industries which have been pulled to the rural areas of the South by surplus labor and to the cities of the South and West by the superior amenities they offer. In addition, growing regional markets have attracted branch plants which have been established to supply multistate areas.

3. The decline of agricultural employment and the concomitant rise in manufacturing and residentiary employment have caused urban areas to grow much faster than the total population. Within urbanized areas, automobiles and trucks have made possible a movement of economic activity to suburban areas where more efficient, huge single-story plants can be built. As a consequence, our central cities have fallen into a pattern of long-term decline.

4. Population migration is the major way in which regions have adjusted to changes in economic opportunity, especially declines in farm employment. In all but a very few states rural areas lost population, whereas out-migration from urban areas occurred largely in the Northeast. In net terms, the migrating population moved out of eastern states to the West. Because people have been willing to move in response to changes in economic opportunities, many areas which have experienced very slow extensive growth have grown faster than the United States as a whole in terms of per capita income.

5. As U.S. markets continued their expansion in the 20th century, the Nation's dependence on foreign trade declined significantly, to between 5 to 7 percent of GNP. This reflects the fact that internal (regional) specialization partially replaced international specialization as a means of gaining scale economies.

6. Prior to 1946, our balance of payments accounts shifted with the alternating winds of war and peace, prosperity and depression. In the post–World War II period, our traditional positive trade balance was gradually eroded, and, finally, in 1971 our merchandise imports exceeded our merchandise exports for the first time in a century. Since the end

of the war, the invisible items deficits and our overseas investment flows have been greater than our foreign exchange earnings. The result has been a persistent outflow of gold and dollars to foreign central banks.

7.   In the late 1940s and early 1950s a dollar shortage overseas resulted inexorably from the efforts of war-torn economies to rebuild by importing American machinery and materials. But once rebuilt, Europe and Asia exported huge volumes of goods and services to the United States, dollars piled up in foreign central banks, and the dollar shortage was replaced by a dollar glut.

The International Monetary Fund agreement was not sufficiently flexible to accommodate the massive shifts that took place in world trade patterns over the past generation. In spite of a variety of stop-gap measures, the dollar glut reached crisis proportions in 1971. Consequently, the dollar was devalued (from a price in gold of $35/ounce to a price of $42.22/ounce) in 1972. What is now required is a new institutional arrangement, one that permits timely adjustments to changes in trade relations before such changes become cumulative in their effects on a nation's balance of payments.

8.   Acting on the basis of a variety of motivations, the United States and other developed nations have attempted to assist the less developed countries in their attempts to modernize their economies. However, a variety of factors have prevented foreign aid from sparking sustained economic growth in most LDCs.

The LDCs are characterized by traditional economic organization and attitudes, very low capacities to save and to export, and acute shortages of human and physical capital. On the other hand, the nations that extend aid don't know enough about the economics of development to give in such a way that a self-sustained development process gets underway. Thus, extensive economic growth in the LDCs has generally been accompanied by a parallel population growth and, consequently, static per capita income.

REFERENCES

J. M. Henderson,   "Some General Aspects of Recent Regional Development," in *Essays in Southern Economic Development*, eds. M. L. Greenhut and W. T. Whitman (Chapel Hill, N.C.: University of North Carolina Press, 1964).

P. A. Samuelson,   *Economics* (New York: McGraw-Hill Book Company, 1973).

U.S. Department of Commerce,   *Statistical Abstract of the United States* (Washington, D.C.: U.S. Government Printing Office, 1960, 1962, 1966, 1972).

————,   *Survey of Current Business* (June 1972).

U.S. Department of Labor,   *Handbook of Labor Statistics* (Washington, D.C.: U.S. Government Printing Office, 1972).

16 ECONOMIC POLICY AND THE QUALITY OF LIFE

Americans live in a nation torn by strife, a nation in crisis. Or, at least, they see the contemporary scene that way. Newspaper headlines and newscasters refer to the urban crisis, clogged transportation arteries, lethal waters, and noxious air, all seemingly linked to the processes by which we provide our goods and services output. In spite of affluence, economic problems seem to confront us in unprecedented variety and magnitude—in fact, we view some of our problems as by-products of affluence.

Of course, some of our perceptions of our economic ills are illusory—we aren't passing from a terrestrial heaven to a hell on earth. Each generation must learn certain old and hard truths for itself. But many of the economic problems that command our attention are in some respects unique to this generation, if not because they are new, then because they have grown in importance or because they plague us at a time when our capacity to generate solutions is greater than ever. In earlier chapters of Part IV, we have already dealt with several of these bona fide sources of consternation—poverty, inflation, regional imbalance, concentration of economic power, and international balance of payments disequilibrium all represent persistent, important economic maladjustments. In this chapter we will analyze several additional problem areas especially as they relate to the growth and change in the economic role of government.

THE CHANGING ROLE OF GOVERNMENT

War, depression, and the structural changes we have discussed have all contributed to a very rapid rise in the scope of governmental activity. The economy has grown fivefold since 1920. Population, real income, and per capita real income have all increased; so we would expect government to have grown as well. More people carrying on more transactions require more government services. But what is especially important about the past five decades is the relative growth of government. While the economy grew by a factor of five and population by a factor of less than two, government at all three levels—local, state, and national—grew by a factor of eight.

Much of this remarkable growth has been related to wars—past, present, and future. But international conflict does not entirely explain the acceleration in governmental economic activity since the 20s—economic growth and transition have also promoted the expansion of government. Let's look at some of the details of government's growth and then appraise the facts in the light of some of the basic factors that determine the importance of government in the total economy.

The growth of the government sector

A glance at 16–1 indicates the very rapid growth that has characterized government expenditures and revenues since the 1920s. Expenditures are now over 30 percent of GNP as contrasted with less than 10 percent

16–1.   Direct government expenditure, 1922–70
(in billions of dollars)

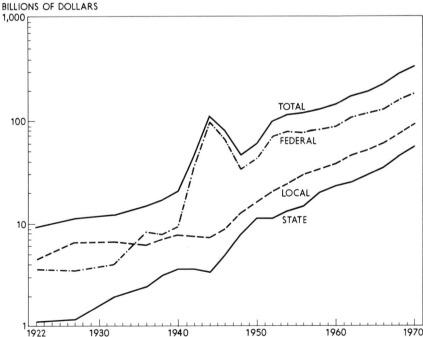

BILLIONS OF DOLLARS

Sources: U.S. Bureau of the Census (1969, 1st citation), tables 2, 3, 5, 6; (1969, 2d citation), table 5; (1971), table 5.

in 1920. In the 1930s, low income and expanded governmental responsibilities combined to bring the public sector to about 20 percent of GNP. Then, during World War II, the war effort not only absorbed all excess capacity, but forced us to expand government expenditures to just under half of the gross national product. Since then, continued international involvement has been the most important force maintaining the goverment sector at 25 to 30 percent of the aggregate economy.

In absolute terms the rapid growth of government spending is attributable to three main factors: (1) population increases, (2) rising prices, and (3) increased per capita demand for defense and nondefense spending. 16–2 shows the per capita growth of government expenditures over the period. The fact that the per capita trend is far less steep than the trend of aggregate expenditures is a reflection of the population explosion's impact on the government sector since World War II. Much

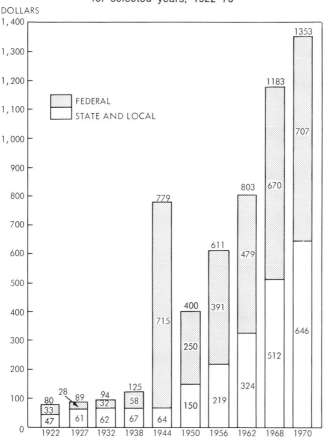

16–2. Per capita direct general government expenditures
for selected years, 1922–70

SOURCES: U.S. Bureau of the Census (1971), table 7; (1969, 2d citation), table 7.

of the growth of government is attributable to population increase, so
when we place the figures on a per capita basis, the rise in expenditures
appears less imposing.

The prices which federal, state, and local governments have to pay
have more than tripled since the early depression years. Consequently,
a large portion of the growth of government expenditures and receipts
is a result of inflation.

In 16–3, the effects of price increases have been removed from the

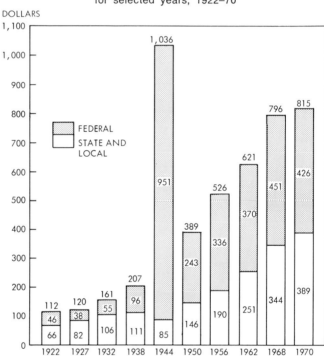

16–3.   Real per capita direct general government expenditures
for selected years, 1922–70

SOURCES: See 16–2.

per capita data to show the trend of real expenditures per person. This
upward trend is in essence an index of the rising demand per person
for governmental services, especially defense. Note that per capita real
expenditures reached a peak in 1944, the year of our most intensive
war production, declined after the war, then climbed again because
of the Korean War and expanded defense and nondefense outlays after
Korea. Another surge in federal spending in the mid-1960s, associated
with our Vietnam involvement plus the rapid expansion of state and

local spending, brought total expenditures to 80 percent of their 1944 high mark.

The federal expenditure trend was reinforced by activity in the state and local government sector which reflected the bulk of the rise in nondefense public service demands. During World War II, state and local needs had to be deferred, so that the combined expenditures of the two levels declined from well over half to less than 10 percent of the total government sector. Thus, the state-local sector built up a backlog of needs. After the war, this backlog was magnified by the rise in demand for state and local government services. Especially important in this regard was the postdepression baby boom which lowered the average age of the population and correspondingly raised per capita requirements for schools and residential services. Note in 16–3 that the growth of the state-local sector matched that of the federal government from 1948 to 1956, but that since then growth of state and local spending has outpaced that of direct federal spending.

Much of the increase in state and local government operations has been concentrated among functions in which the federal government encourages activity through grants-in-aid (note the large increases in education, welfare, and health since 1957 in 16–4). Consequently, federal intergovernmental expenditures have become a larger and larger part of total general government expenditures (see the last line in 16–4).

On the revenue side, the growth of government has been equally impressive. The expansion of demand for services has not only required raising the real tax burden but has forced the national, state, and local

16–4.   Percent distribution of general expenditure by function for all governments for selected years, 1922–70

	1922	1927	1934	1938	1944	1948	1957	1962	1970
All functions.	100.0	100.0	100.0	100.0	100.0	100.0	100.0	100.0	100.0
National defense and international relations	9.9	5.8	4.6	6.4	79.3	32.1	41.7	35.7	34.4
Postal service	6.2	6.7	5.4	4.8	1.0	3.4	2.8	2.7	2.9
Education	19.3	21.2	16.6	16.3	2.6	15.4	13.8	15.3	18.5
Highways	14.6	17.2	15.1	13.2	1.1	6.1	7.2	7.0	6.5
Public welfare	1.4	1.5	8.1	7.6	1.1	4.3	3.2	3.5	4.4
Health and hospitals	4.0	4.1	4.4	4.2	0.8	3.9	3.8	4.1	4.4
Natural resources	1.6	1.9	10.3	12.8	2.5	4.4	6.9	8.2	4.7
Financial administration and general control	5.0	5.0	4.4	4.5	1.0	2.6	2.2	2.1	2.1
Interest on general debt	15.5	12.7	12.2	9.3	2.5	9.4	6.0	6.1	6.2
All other	22.5	23.9	18.9	21.0	8.1	18.3	12.4	15.2	15.9
Exhibit: federal intergovernmental expenditure as percentage of total state and local general revenue	2.5	1.7	12.7	8.3	9.8	10.3	10.1	13.3	16.9

SOURCE: U.S. Bureau of the Census (1971).

governments to introduce countless innovations in their revenue systems.

At the federal level, World War II brought increased reliance upon individual and corporate income taxes, a reliance that continues. In the 1920s and early 1930s, income taxes comprised 35 to 45 percent of the total revenues of the federal government, while taxes on sales, including import duties, hovered at around 25 percent of total revenues. By 1944, individual income taxes were 44 percent of total revenues, corporate income taxes 30 percent, and the various sales taxes only 10 percent. More recently, the figures have been as follows: individual income, 55 percent; corporate income, 20 percent; and sales, 11 percent.

The pattern of increases for state and local governments has also produced dramatic shifts within the revenue structure. Sales taxes rose during the depression and the war from less than 5 percent to more than 20 percent of general revenues, while property taxes declined from over 70 percent to only a little more than 30 percent. Income taxes almost doubled in their importance during the war but are still less than 15 percent of total revenues. In particular states, though, they account for as much as 35 percent of state government revenues. Federal grants to the states and localities have grown faster than any revenue source so that currently they are about seven times more important in the budget than they were in the 1920s and account for almost 17 percent of all revenues.

The separate patterns of change for state and local governments have been very similar; however, the resulting revenue structures are still quite diverse because property taxes were such a large part of local budgets at the beginning of the period. In spite of new revenue sources, the property tax remains the dominant levy of local governments in contrast to the state governments, in which sales taxes have come up from obscurity to assume a leading role.

Recently, growing popular despair over the inequities of local property taxation and its administration has generated demands for "property tax relief." Increased reliance on other tax sources and aid from the states and/or the federal government are the usual alternatives proposed. Historically, a great deal of the growth in federal aid to local governments is attributable to the inflexibility of local revenue sources at times of rapid increases in demand. The recent federal revenue sharing program is clearly a response to the shortcomings of the local property tax.

Taxes have not fully covered expenditures over the years; governmental indebtedness has increased at all levels of government (see 16–5). As we have noted, during the Great Depression sliding income and rising governmental responsibilities pushed the federal government into a deficit position. Then, during World War II, the "disequilibrium system," our option for financing the war, caused the debt to skyrocket. At the end of the war, the debt had reached some $250 billion, about 120 percent of GNP and close to twice the value of private debt.

16–5.   Net public and private debt, compared with GNP,
for selected years, 1930–70
(billions of dollars)

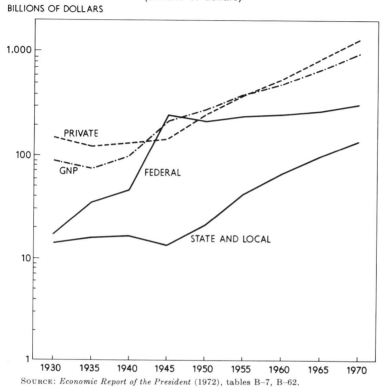

BILLIONS OF DOLLARS

SOURCE: *Economic Report of the President* (1972), tables B–7, B–62.

Since World War II, intermittent deficits have more than offset surpluses. The federal debt held by the public has grown slowly to over $300 billion in absolute terms. In the same period it has declined to less than one third of the value of GNP and to less than one fourth of the value of private debt.

The postwar rise in the debt can be attributed to three factors. First, built-in stabilizers pushed the federal budget toward a deficit in times of recession. Second, a latent sluggishness in private demand would have caused total spending to fall below the level required by full employment except that prodding from a federal deficit pushed the private economy along. In general, the federal government spurred aggregate demand over this period by cutting private spending (through taxes) by less than it added to total spending through its outlays for goods, services, and transfer payments. Third, we financed the Vietnam War without increasing taxes sufficiently to avoid inflation and the concomitant growth of the debt.

On a per capita basis, the net federal debt has actually declined from its 1945 peak of $1,800; in 1970 the figure was $1,470. And when adjusted for price level increases, the comparative figures are $3,340 for 1945 and $1,267 for 1970.

From a debt standpoint, the state-local sector presents a marked contrast with the federal government. A rising need for long-term capital investment, principally in schools and roadways, has encouraged the flotation of bond issues. The combined state and local debt has increased steadily at a significantly faster rate than the federal debt. Yet, like the federal debt, it has expanded much less rapidly since World War II than has the debt of the private sector. In per capita terms, the state-local debt has expanded modestly, while after adjustment for price level increases it is apparent that the real burden of government debt has actually declined since World War II. Over a longer period (1922–71), the real interest burden of the debt for all levels of government has increased on a per capita basis. However, interest charges have declined as a percentage of total nondefense spending (see 16–6).[1]

16–6.   Distribution of real per capita general nondefense expenditures by function for all governments, 1922 and 1970

	1922	1970	Percent change*
Total expenditures	$120.85	$786.57	469
Health, education, and welfare	36.08	399.27	562
Education	(25.93)	(239.76)	(824)
Welfare	(1.93)	(74.11)	(†)
Housing and urban renewal	(0.02)	(13.49)	(†)
Health and other	(8.22)	(71.91)	(774)
Transportation	24.20	88.31	265
Public safety	5.48	36.53	567
Natural resources, including parks and recreation	3.40	56.25	†
General and financial administration	6.65	34.52	419
Postal service	8.37	32.67	290
Interest on the debt	20.75	77.89	275
Other	15.92	61.12	284

Note: All dollar amounts are given in 1957–59 dollars of purchasing power.
* GNP per capita rose 160 percent from 1922 to 1970.
† More than 1000 percent.
Sources: U.S. Bureau of the Census (1969, 1st citation), vol. 6, no. 5, table 1; (1971), table 1.

Why has nonmilitary government spending grown?

In reviewing the chronology of government's expansion, we have pointed to three very general explanations for the growth of government expenditures and revenues. Now it seems appropriate to regard the effects of war and price increases as self-explanatory and approach the

---

[1] It is important to note that when the real burden of the debt is reduced by inflation, the taxpayer who must service the debt gains, but the bondholder loses correspondingly.

"why" of government growth by examining the catalog of reasons for government spending and control.

Note that we are broadening the discussion beyond government spending to include the qualitative role government plays in influencing economic behavior and spending in the private sector. Our discussion will reveal that the process of growth and the rising level of income associated with economic growth have caused the nondefense portion of the government sector to expand faster than population and income per person (see 16–6).

In the most general terms, government economic activity is aimed at three kinds of goals: (1) to adjust the allocation of the economy's productive resources, (2) to alter the distribution of income among households, and (3) to stabilize the economy.

We have already seen how both automatic and discretionary fiscal and monetary policies have been employed to flatten out the business cycle. Since 1920, government's growth as a percentage of the economy has increased its ability to serve its stabilizing role. Further, our survey of fiscal policy performance revealed that especially since World War II the federal government has shown a growing sophistication in the matter of countercyclical policy. Over the same period, state and local expenditures have had stabilizing side effects. The great relative and absolute growth of nonfederal expenditures has provided an offsetting force for any tendency toward secular stagnation.

As to income distribution policy, the growth of income taxes at all levels of government has tended to redistribute income *after taxes* slightly in favor of the lower income brackets. This tendency has been reinforced by expenditures for education, health, welfare, public housing, and other programs whose value to the recipient tends to be a higher percentage of income the lower the recipient's position on the income distribution ladder. In fact, as we have discussed, our traditional approach to correcting inequality has been to give aid according to certain categories of need and to escalate that aid as the economy has grown. Thus, as 16–6 indicates, education, housing, urban renewal, and public welfare expenditures have grown very rapidly relative to total per capita nondefense expenditures.

Important as stabilization and distribution policies have made government's role, the public sector's economic influence has grown chiefly through its direct and indirect effects upon resource allocation. The term economics, you'll recall, connotes the process by which a society divides its scarce resources, its factors of production, among the limitless number of goods and services it finds desirable. In the American economy, we depend most heavily upon the decisions of individuals made in market exchanges to guide the allocations of factors. This is because we feel that the operation of *competitive* markets generally tends to be compatible with one of our central economic goals—getting the most value out of our scarce productive factors. Often this proposition is put as follows: the **competitive market solution** is compatible with **optimum resource allocation.** However, the market often fails, for one reason or another, to generate a solution compatible with an optimum resource allocation pattern.

What we shall now look at are the often overlapping situations in which government, through spending, taxing, or direct control, influences resource allocation, usually to counteract instances of market failure.

As the discussion will make evident, government has been called upon to adjust the pattern of resource allocation either because the services required would not be provided at all by the private sector or would be privately provided but in insufficient amounts. Further, government has found it necessary to intervene in the private economy when regulation or other controls have been agitated for because the public has been dissatisfied with the operation of private markets.

Unfortunately, government has also interposed its influence in the private sector in instances in which doing so has meant a distortion of resource allocation because special interest groups have been successful in placing their narrowly defined objectives above those of the consumer at large. Historical examples include the following: chain store taxes that penalized large, efficient, and low-price retailers to protect inefficient "momma and poppa" stores; minimum wage laws which tend to generate unemployment and to depress wages in uncovered industries; and percentage depletion allowances that subsidize oil consumers at the taxpayer's expense. It is only just to add that many legislators back such legislation because, in error, they feel its effects will be wholesome for the public at large, not because they are beholden to vested interests.

Since 1920, the growth of the economy has made the United States **more industrial, more urban,** and **more affluent.** The consequence has been an increase in government's influence over the allocation of productive resources quite apart from military commitments. In other words, the demand for government services has continued to display a high income elasticity. Higher per capita incomes have increased consumer incomes to a point at which households want and can afford more public services. Further, the changes that have taken place in the economy as part of the development process have required more public resource allocation activity, especially at the local level.

The productivity increases which have generated growth have also raised educational and training requirements; the postdepression population explosion has increased the proportion of the population which is of school age; and higher income levels have increased the number of people who can afford to stay out of the labor force long enough to finish high school or college. Although education could be—in fact, is—produced and sold privately, we choose to encourage education beyond levels that would result from a wholly private system. Thus, we have mandatory school attendance laws and publicly subsidize education at all levels. And we have elected to meet the increased demand for education by expanding public outlays. Per capita education expenditures increased in excess of 800 percent in the 1922–70 period and accounted for almost one third of the growth in total nondefense expenditures. (See 16–6.)

Urban growth is very much a function of intensive economic growth. As family incomes grew, household expenditure patterns increasingly favored the production of manufactured goods and personal services, urban economic activities. Consequently, the urbanization trend that became so important after the Civil War continued to be a dominant feature of the economy after World War I. In turn, urbanization meant that the demand for government services grew faster than the aggregate economy for several reasons. First, the government renders certain functions in urban areas that are performed by the household in rural areas; sewage and trash disposal, fire protection, and local transportation are examples. And, second, high population densities intensify demands for traditional government services, such as police protection and public health services. If you glance at 16–6, you'll see that the 160 percent increase in GNP per capita for the period 1922 to 1970 is overwhelmed by the increases in expenditure categories that involve rendering services to people on a local basis.

Population growth in the cities has exacerbated their traditional problems. What is worse, the problems of the cities have taken on new dimensions. The flight to the suburbs which began in the 1920s has left the central cities of America with a seriously eroded tax base. Black migration from the rural South to the urban slums has copied past ethnic migration patterns except in one vital respect: deep-seated prejudices and the Negro's visibility have all but blocked Negro assimilation. For blacks the city has not proved to be the frontier that it was for European immigrants. As a consequence, the old term ghetto has taken on a new meaning. It now connotes a concentration of poverty enclosed by walls built of artificial barriers to economic opportunity.

Thus, the city has found itself with problems that grow faster than its population and a tax base that grows slower than its problems. The expenditure pattern which has emerged from the city's travails consists of rising per capita public safety outlays and very rapidly increasing welfare, housing, and urban renewal expenditures. (See 16–6.) In fact, most of the noneducation items included in the "health, education, and welfare" category of 16–6—such as sanitation, public health, and recreation—have had growth rates that exceed the average for nondefense expenditures.

Governments have traditionally subsidized transportation for two reasons—good transportation facilities enhance economic growth, and the high cost of collecting tolls on local streets and intrastate highways prohibits private provision in most cases. The development of the automobile and the airplane as widely used vehicles began in the 1920s. Accordingly, governments have been called upon to provide highways at unprecedented levels and to subsidize the airlines in various ways. As compared with 1922, real per capita transportation expenditures has more than doubled by 1970. (See 16–6.)[2]

Economic growth, and especially industrial growth, is not without its cost. Most of these costs are borne directly by the private sector, e.g., households forgo present consumption in order to save, making possible capital investment and, therefore, higher future consumption. But some of the costs of industrial expansion are very public, in the sense that they do not fall upon producers and/or consumers of the products in question. Rather, they are shifted to the general public—such effects are termed *neighborhood effects, third party costs,* or *spillover costs.*

Stream pollution is an example. When a paper mill is constructed which subsequently pollutes the river on which it is located, downstream communities that must install additional water treatment facilities are forced to bear part of the cost of increased paper output. Cases of this kind have multiplied as the Nation has become more crowded and industrial. So government has been called upon both to control the sources of some neighborhood effects and to spend to compensate for other such effects. In recent years, this kind of government activity has influenced the overall growth of per capita government expenditures by speeding the expansion of many agencies whose outlays are summarized in 16–6.

The size and complexity that the private sector has achieved have added to the size and complexity of the public sector. In other words, the growth of the industrial establishment has exacted tolls in addition to the spillover costs discussed above.

On the one hand, government must provide a legal environment that facilitates private market exchanges; as industrial and financial organizations have increased in complexity, the range of required government services has been extended. On the other hand, government has been called upon to protect or assist those who are especially vulnerable to the costs of industrial transformation. In addition, government has had to act when competition gave way to collusion in concentration markets or when competitive markets have produced results with which the public was not happy.

The Justice Department's antitrust activities, the various regulatory agencies, expenditures to assist small business, and the costs of the agri-

---

[2] The failure to collect tolls on federal interstate highways and major intrastate roads as well as on major urban commuter arteries is an example of government resource allocation activity that generates unwanted side effects—in this case, congestion.

cultural stabilization programs are all attributable to the industrialization process and the adjustments it requires. Tariffs constitute a system of negative incentives which change domestic resource allocation in favor of certain industries, and import quotas have about the same effects. Subsidies to the merchant marine are also designed to foster home industry. With the exception of agriculture, expenditures for these functions do not and have not accounted for a very large part of the budget. Nevertheless, such expenditures have grown. But what is most significant, they affect the pattern of resource allocation well beyond their importance in the consolidated budget.

By producing affluence in the majority of American households, growth has changed the pattern of final demand in favor of a larger relative role for government. Increased capacity makes production of a greater variety of final products possible. As an individual's income grows, he expands somewhat his consumption of food, clothing, and shelter, but the bulk of his increased purchasing power will be devoted to other items, some of which will be new to his budget. By the same token, when national income grows, the public opts both for more private goods and for more public goods, with an emphasis on the latter. The reason for this is the complementary nature of the public and private sectors. In some ways, the two sectors are intimately complementary—automobiles require streets. In other respects, the connection is less direct, but nevertheless very important—the enjoyment of a nice house is increased by easy access to good public recreation facilities; so once adequate shelter has been provided for, the public sector is called upon to create parks, pools, playgrounds, and tennis courts. Thus, beyond those reasons we have cited above, government's role has grown faster than the national economy because the best allocation of our resources pointed in the direction of per capita government growth.

The affluent society

Whether the relative growth of civilian government activity has been adequate, too great, or not great enough has been debated for almost two decades. In the mid-1950s, critics of the social scene looked around at what they termed public poverty amid private affluence—an alleged situation of social imbalance. The spectacle of luxurious automobiles running on potholed roadways was accepted as evidence of general privation in the public sector. In the wake of the debate that ensued, the growth of the public sector's nondefense activities was accelerated.[3]

What impact has this spurt in spending had? Whether social imbalance has been alleviated (if there was a deficit in the public column) or intensified (if the public sector was in fact too large at mid-century),

---

[3] For an early statement of the notion of public poverty amid private affluence and the source of the debate's jargon, see Galbraith.

no one can say with precision. The *public will* is difficult to interpret
and equally hard to translate into legislation. And the statistical measures
we have at hand are of little use because we do not have any reliable
criteria that indicate what ratio of public to private activity is desired
by the electorate.

We are left then with a dilemma in summarizing developments in
the public sector since 1920. The growth of prices, population, per capita
and total income, international involvement, urbanization, and industrialization have generated increases in government expenditure. Collectively,
these forces have caused government to grow as a percentage of the
economy. But whether government has grown enough to provide an
optimum allocation of resources cannot be answered. Economic growth
has been sufficient in its cumulative effects to allow a vast range of
public-private combinations in resource allocation. But the social
machinery does not exist to guarantee the achievement of what we would
as a Nation consider the *best* combination.

ECONOMIC GROWTH AND ENVIRONMENTAL DECAY

Over the past 20 years or so, public concern about the future of
our natural environment has mounted steadily. By 1970, Americans considered the future of the environment to be an issue of crisis proportions,
so much so that Earth Day was declared in the spring of that year
as a formal sign of our intent to win the ecological battle. It's not
hard to explain the anxiety of the average American over his physical
surroundings and the quality of his life-support systems. Increasingly,
the news media have reported that:

> smog from automobile exhaust fumes daily takes its toll in human
> lives;
> industrial organic and inorganic discharges place unbearable assimila-
> tive burdens on our waterways and fill the air with a grand variety
> of noxious chemicals and particulate matter;
> daily, electrical power generation from fossil fuels discharges thousands
> of tons of particulate matter and sulfur and nitrogen oxides into the
> atmosphere, while the discharge of power-plant cooling water produces
> thermal pollution by reducing the assimilative capacity of our streams;
> "incidents" at nuclear power installations result in radioactive dis-
> charges into surrounding lakes, producing "mortality responses in fish";
> in this age of scientific agriculture, pesticide and fertilizer runoff
> pours into our streams, while silting from eroded farmlands continues
> unabated;
> the American countryside is disappearing as the cornucopia of pro-
> gress pours forth more highways, more billboards, and more tract housing
> developments, while simultaneously generating a flow of solid waste
> that threatens to bury us alive;

airport noise pollution deafens nearby inhabitants and erodes property values; and

clear-cutting forests and strip-mining not only reduce our precious natural resources but result in vast amounts of soil erosion.

In short, we read and hear that the American (human) lust for *more* generates a heavy toll in air, land, and water pollution which makes every dollar of additional GNP increasingly expensive.[4]

If we cut through the rhetoric, what can we conclude about the status and future of our environment? First, the scare headlines and apocalyptic news stories do refer to genuine, scientifically documented ecological problems.[5] Second, those problems have received a great deal of legislative and judicial attention in the post–World War II period.[6] But, third, legislation and government expenditure apparently have not succeeded in shunting us off the track to ecological suicide. Analysis of our progress to date presents a gloomy prospect.

Indices of environmental quality show that the waste loads imposed on environmental resources have been growing continuously . . . . The recent report of the Council on Environmental Quality [1970], for example, indicates that emissions of all the major air pollutants have increased at an overall rate of over three per cent per year and that, in recent years, "the overall quality of the nation's water probably has deteriorated because of accelerated eutrophication, increased discharges of toxic materials, greater loads of sediment, and other factors." The legislation of past decades has, in fact, failed to deliver on its promises.[7]

When you contrast the last two decades with the late 19th century, this seems a perplexing history. Most detailed accounts of city life in the 1870s, 80s, and 90s document the heavy burden of unhealthy, polluted conditions borne by the average city dweller. What's more, the conservation movement of the early 20th century gained its impetus from the rapacious practices of the turn-of-the-century lumber and mining companies. Although we can't document it, the period from 1900 to 1945 was apparently one in which, on balance, the quality of the environment improved. Then the trend changed direction; e.g., sulfur oxide discharges from electric utilities are now seven times their 1940 level.[8] Why the reversal?

The superficial answer is to say that economic expansion has placed increasingly heavy demands on the environment as a receptacle for production's waste by-products. Environmental degradation need not travel side by side with production, yet it does. Why? The answer lies in

---

[4] The title of this section is borrowed from Barkley and Seckler.

[5] The literature is vast, but a good starting point from an economist's point of view is provided by Freeman et al. and their bibliography.

[6] For an evaluation see Freeman et al. and Eyestone, chap. 9.

[7] Freeman and Haveman, pp. 51–52.

[8] Freeman et al., p. 51.

the interrelationship of our ecosystem, production processes, and property rights.

Spaceship earth

Years ago we lived in what has been described as a cowboy economy. Now we live on spaceship earth. When the planet was less crowded, the waste products associated with production could be "thrown away" with no perceived damage because so little of the environment's assimilative capacity was in use—in effect, the environment was a free good because *in*creased utilization by one party didn't require *de*creased utilization by a second party. But today, spaceship earth is the proper metaphore because the environment is no longer a free good: the earth, like a spaceship, is a closed system without unlimited supplies of anything, including the services provided by the environment. For example, more miles driven in our cities mean reduced access to clean air for those who wish to breathe it, and vice versa.[9]

What this adds up to is as follows. Production and consumption consist of assembling and processing inputs that yield two outputs, products which are useful for the services they render and residuals (refuse) which are not useful. We call upon the environment to absorb the unwanted gases, liquids, solids, and energy (heat and noise) which are by-products of production. And there is a cost associated with discharging these residuals into the environment. In the economic sense, the environment is damaged; that is, its ability to render services is reduced when it is used as a waste receptacle. More refuse means less environment to serve as a habitat, to provide such amenities as recreation, or to supply production inputs.

At this point, you might say that everything has its costs and that *fewer* environmental services are merely society's price for *more* products. This is true, but it overlooks two crucial considerations: (1) in many instances, the costs associated with reducing the flow of environmental services are greater than the benefits that result from increasing GNP, and (2) in most such cases, those who bear the burden of a reduced flow of environmental services are not those who gain the benefits of increased production.

The basic reason these two problems crop up is that no individual owns the environment, so everybody gets to use it free on a first-come, first-served basis. But for society as a whole, the environment is not free: somebody must pay for its use as a waste receptacle by sacrificing environmental services. On the other hand, if individuals and/or governments held title to the environment, those who chose to use the environment for discharging residuals would have to compensate the owners

---

[9] Boulding gets the credit for the two metaphors "spaceship earth" and "cowboy economy."

for the reduction in its capacity to provide environmental services. Thus, in cases in which environmental services render benefits which are more valuable than the production activity that generates residuals, more production would yield to preservation of the environment.

Paradoxically, we are drowning, suffocating, and poisoning ourselves as a consequence of rational actions taken by individuals in responding to the rational demands of other individuals for the production of goods and services. Neither individual consumers nor individual producers have any incentive to reduce the burdens they place on the environment because they would bear the costs of abatement individually with only insignificant gains to them personally simply because others would continue to pollute.[10]

How close to exhausting spaceship earth's assimilative capacity are we? A satisfactory general index of environmental destruction is impossible to come by. There is no way to assess the cost associated with each instance of air, water, and land pollution. We just can't monitor each instance of destruction. And where we can observe destructive actions, we can't assess costs beyond guesswork—some pollutants are more harmful per pound to life and property than others, and the geography, climatic conditions, and population density of an affected area are important determinants of the actual costs of pollution.[11] Consequently, we cannot put a figure on the current cost of environmental damage, let alone say whether the per capita rate of environmental destruction is more or less than it was in 1870, 1900, or 1920. And we certainly can't indicate how close we have come to "using up" the environment.

With this word of caution in mind, read over 16–7 through 16–9. Incomplete as the data in these tables are—they summarize only certain kinds of air and water pollution—they give us some rough ideas about the status and trend of environmental destruction. The following generalizations appear to be relevant.

First, the automobile contributes about half the weight of air pollutants, but with emission-control devices the emission trend (not necessarily the damage trend) may be downward. Second, although the emission of solid waste and automobile pollutants declined in 1969, emissions of air pollutants increased overall, with particulates showing the largest increase. Third, the concentration of air pollution is greatest in the major metropolitan areas, although there is some evidence that the trend is negative in some of the larger cities.[12] And fourth, chemicals, paper,

---

[10] On the other hand, even if an individual felt certain that all others would cut back their use of the environment, he would have no incentive to cut back himself knowing that his pollution would be insignificant.

[11] See Dorfman and Dorfman, p. 426, for a bibliography on measuring the costs of environmental destruction.

[12] See Freeman et al., p. 51.

16–7.   Emissions of air pollutants by source, 1969
(in millions of tons per year)

Source	Carbon monoxide	Partic- ulates	Sulfur oxides	Hydro- carbons	Nitrogen oxides	Total	Percent change 1968-69
Transportation	111.5	0.8	1.1	19.8	11.2	144.4	−1.0
Fuel combustion in sta- tionary sources	1.8	7.2	24.4	0.9	10.0	44.3	+2.5
Industrial processes	12.0	14.4	7.5	5.5	0.2	39.6	+7.3
Solid waste disposal. . . .	7.9	1.4	0.2	2.0	0.4	11.9	−1.0
Miscellaneous	18.2	11.4	0.2	9.2	2.0	41.0	+18.5
Total	151.4	35.2	33.4	37.4	23.8	281.2	+3.2
Percent change 1968-69	+1.3	+10.7	+5.7	+1.1	+4.8	+3.2	

SOURCE: Freeman et al., p. 49.

16–8.   Pollution concentration by population size, annual
averages
(micrograms per cubic meter)

Population	Total suspended particulates	Sulfur dioxide	Nitrogen oxides
Nonurban	25	10	33
Less than 10,000	57	35	116
10,000–25,000	81	18	64
25,000–50,000	87	14	63
50,000–100,000	118	29	127
100,000–400,000	95	26	114
400,000–700,000	100	28	127
700,000 to 1 million	101	29	146
1 to 3 million	134	69	163
More than 3 million	120	85	153

SOURCE: Freeman et al., p. 50.

and food products manufacturing are the most important sources of industrial water pollution, which accounts for about 80 percent of water pollution from organic sources, the remaining 20 percent being contributed by domestic sewage from areas served by sewers.

Avoiding doomsday

Using up the environment is not an irreversible process. In fact, it is possible to increase the services of the environment. What is required is to achieve political and economic reorganization which results

16–9.   Estimated waste loads before treatment in the
United States—1968
(in millions of pounds per year)

Biochemical oxygen demand

Manufacturing

Food and kindred products	4,600
Textile mill products.	1,100
Paper and allied products	7,800
Chemical and allied products . . .	14,200
Petroleum and coal.	550
Rubber and plastics	60
Primary metals	550
Transportation equipment.	160
All other manufacturing	470
Machinery	180
Total manufacturing.	29,670
Domestic	
Served by sewers	8,500
Total	38,170

SOURCE: Freeman et al., p. 57.

in giving consumers and producers the incentive to use available technology to reduce the burdens they place on the economy.

Four kinds of tactics are appropriate: avoidance, the treatment of residuals, changing the place and timing of residuals discharges, and increasing the assimilative capacity of the environment.

Avoidance calls for reducing the flow of materials and energy through the production process and can be achieved in a variety of ways—reducing production with or without restricting population increase; altering the composition of output in favor of products that require low levels of environmental inputs; recycling; and altering production processes to get more output per unit of environmental input. Waste treatment processes can render residuals harmless to the environment and often useful as product inputs. The ability of the environment to assimilate residuals can be increased by changing both the place and timing of discharges or by altering its basic assimilative capacity (e.g., by impounding water to dilute streams during low-flow periods).

Environmental control strategies fall into three main categories: government regulation and enforcement, reliance upon bargaining or legal proceedings between polluters and injured third parties, and the use of economic incentives operating through the price system.

Historically, regulation-enforcement has been the most common control device employed and remains so long before London's Clean Air Act, the British Parliament tried to cope with the air pollution problem by banning low-quality fuels. Although direct regulation may be simple to impose, its performance record is bleak. Once standards are complied with, there is no incentive to improve performance even if a superior antipollution technology is developed. It also can prove expensive for the taxpayer when, as has often been the case in this Nation, subsidies are provided to enable polluters to make the capital investments required to meet certain standards. Further, control bodies charged with imposing standards and enforcement are traditionally understaffed, politically vulnerable, and often become advocates of the polluter's cause. The classic case illustrating the last is the Atomic Energy Commission, which is charged by law with both promoting the use of atomic energy and regulating its use to avoid radioactive contamination.[13]

Bargaining between affected parties is of limited potential simply because polluters and/or injured third parties are usually so numerous that the logistics of negotiations are too difficult to permit reaching an enforceable agreement. Reliance upon the courts on the basis of the *nuisance doctrine* or the *public nuisance doctrine* presents similar logistic problems, but in recent years has been made less difficult by new laws and legal precedents.[14]

Controls that impose economic incentives through the price system hold the greatest promise for reducing environmental damage, although in the United States legislators have been slow to see their advantages. Ways to build antipollution incentives into the operating markets abound, but possibly the easiest to put in operation is an effluent charge, i.e., an emission-control fee or tax levied on each unit residual discharged into the environment.

The principle involved in an effluent charge is that in a corporate sense everyone owns the environment, and the government as the owners' representative sells rights to use the environment for the discharge of residuals. The use of the environment as a discharge medium would thereby become a systematic element in the cost structure of firms and households. Ideally, the fee paid for these rights should be as high as the damage that the pollutants in question would ordinarily cause so as to discourage their purchase whenever alternatives such as waste treatment or emission controls are possible and less expensive and thus to encourage the search for better pollution abatement techniques.

Since almost no devices reduce pollutants by 100 percent, the effluent fees collected would become an automatic source of revenues for the pollution control authority—a clear advantage in cases where polluters find lobbying expenses cheaper than antipollution devices.

U.S. environmental policy

In spite of a great deal of recent concern about the environment, the volume of our rhetoric has exceeded our actual attempts to come

---

[13] See Eyestone, pp. 201–207.
[14] See Freeman et al., p. 163.

to grips with the problem of preserving the environment.[15] In the first place, we have **not** firmly established the principle that the rights to the environment reside with those who would use it without damaging it and that those who would use it to assimilate residuals should pay to do so.

Second, our approach to date has been piecemeal. The environment has been legislated upon as if it stopped at our national boundaries. Within the Nation, pollution and the environment have been viewed as identical subjects, whereas pollution is in fact only an element within the aggregate complex that makes up our environmental control problem; this is one reason why population control has been all but ignored as a strategy for reducing pressure on the environment. In the water pollution category, we have singled out organic substances and discharges from sewer pipes while slighting both nonorganic pollutants (such as heavy metals, plant nutrients, toxic materials, and heat) and pollution from nonpoint sources (such as erosion, fertilizer, pesticides, and irrigation water).

Our water pollution strategy has been to combine regulation, enforcement, and subsidies to spur the treatment of effluents before discharge into our waterways. Within each state, the typical approach has been to issue permits to use waterways as discharge media subject to certain regulations. At the federal level, the Water Pollution Control Act of 1956 provided for federal subsidies for building municipal waste treatment plants, while the Tax Reform Act of 1969 made possible $120 million in annual tax reductions for firms investing in waste water treatment facilities. The federal enforcement provisions of the 1956 act were generally inadequate. Consequently, the Water Quality Act of 1965 charged states with implementing pollution control plans and now makes it possible for the federal Environmental Protection Agency (established in 1970) to bring court action against violators.

In 1969 the comptroller general of the United States reported to Congress on the effectiveness of our regulation-enforcement-subsidy strategy in combating water pollution.[16] The consensus of experts in the field was that the system had failed: lagging federal appropriations had pushed the program behind schedule; local governments had sat on their hands while awaiting federal funds; some of the waste treatment plants that had been built had been inappropriate for their tasks; enforcement had been hindered by the exercise of political power by large corporations; and the enforcement process had proved both time-consuming and expensive.

Federal air pollution policy has been based on a regulation-enforcement strategy, but because gaseous and particulate matter can't

---

[15] See Freeman et al., chaps. 5–7, for an expanded discussion of U.S. policy; the capsule version presented owes much to this source.

[16] U.S. General Accounting Office.

be collected and treated on an area-wide basis, no subsidies to finance building treatment facilities have been authorized. Local governments have traditionally attempted to check air pollution by specifying emission levels or the use of antipollution equipment.

Until 1963, federal legislation was limited to providing funds to study the effects of air pollution. In 1963, the Clean Air Act authorized grants to states and localities to initiate air pollution control programs and allowed federal action in cases involving air pollution that crossed state lines. Like those of its water counterpart, the Clean Air Act's enforcement provisions were ineffective, so additional legislation followed in 1965, 1967, and 1970. As a result, each state has promulgated air quality standards which are currently under federal review. In addition, new stationary facilities and new automobiles must adhere to federal, not state, emission standards.

In 1969, Congress established the President's Council on Environmental Quality. Then, in 1970, the Environmental Protection Agency (EPA) was established to enforce newly legislated pollution control acts and to combine all the antipollution regulation and research functions that had been assigned to various federal agencies.

In 1972, Congress passed, over President Nixon's veto, the 1972 amendments to the Federal Water Pollution Control Act. The amendments provided 18 billion dollars in federal grants to the states for waste treatment facilities and set as a national goal the elimination of all polluting discharges into U.S. waters by 1985. As an interim goal, the amendments required making rivers, lakes, and streams safe for people and aquatic life by 1983. The 1972 amendments called for two types of enforcement: the EPA was to establish a pollutant discharge permit program; and citizens' suits against polluters, the federal government, or the EPA were permitted in cases in which citizens' economic or recreational opportunities might be impaired. Although these measures are the strongest on record, they still leave enforcement to the discretion of the EPA or the courts as opposed to making it automatic, as would be the case with an effluent charge.

As we noted at the outset of this section, in spite of 15 years of legislation and billions of dollars in treatment and control expenditures, the assimilation load placed on the environment has continued to grow. Why? The proximate answer lies in our failure to utilize effluent charges or similar devices designed to incorporate the cost of using the environment into the cost structure of firms and households. The sole instance of an effluent charge finding its way into federal law is a recent stipulation that federally subsidized municipal sewage treatment systems must charge industrial customers according to both the volume and the "potency" of their discharges. On the other hand, taxes on lead in gasoline and on sulfur oxide emissions have been proposed but not passed by Congress.

The ultimate reason for our failure is political and arises out of the fact that really doing something about pollution would be costly (according to the President's Council on Environmental Quality, the cost would be $105 billion over the period 1970 to 1975). Fundamentally, we are engaged in a struggle over who shall pay for survival, a struggle that can only be settled in the political arena. In the words of Freeman and Haveman:

> It is not entirely facetious to suggest that the reason an economic-incentives approach has not been tried in this country is that it would work. In the absence of effective pollution-control policies, polluters are able to expropriate the environment for their own use by the act of discharging wastes. A system of pollution charges, on the other hand, would establish the principle that the environment is owned by the people as a whole and that the polluters must pay for the privilege of using part of the environment for waste disposal. Such massive transfers of property rights and the wealth they represent seldom occur without political upheaval. Viewed in this light, the most formidable barrier to controlling pollution is probably not technology, population, or public attitudes, but rather the politics of power in our pluralistic democracy.[17]

URBAN PROBLEMS

"The mess our cities are in" represents a problem as old as urbanization. The Black Death was largely an urban phenomenon; Elizabethan England had to regulate the use of soft coal because of air pollution; Jefferson judged colonial cities as agglomerations that made beasts out of humankind; the New York of O. Henry teemed with crime and its sanitary facilities were so poor that basements and privy vaults were indistinguishable in wet weather. Although the precise mix of our urban problems has changed, urban problems are certainly not unique to the late 20th century.

What does appear to be new is a growing conviction that our major cities don't seem to work anymore. To many, the big city has evolved from an imperfect but advantageous site to a place in which, at great monetary and psychic cost, one must work in order to survive. Whether life in major metropolitan areas is really more costly in economic and emotional terms than it was 100 years ago can't be calculated. We can say, though, that the major socioeconomic problems of our day are chiefly urban. Traffic congestion, air pollution, crime in the streets, dope

---

[17] Freeman and Haveman, p. 65. It is entirely possible that effluent charges have not been tried because the public doesn't understand how prices operate to allocate resources and how government policy can alter prices by affecting producers' costs in order to improve the allocation of resources. However, Freeman and Haveman's point is that any effective antipollution strategy will face very rough political sledding because it means higher costs for producers who have a great deal of political insight and power.

addiction, decaying housing, and racial violence are centered in cities and compounded by the fiscal problems which tie the hands of municipal governments. So even if urban problems aren't worse than they were in grandfather's day, we can be pardoned for thinking that they are, as indeed they may be!

If the American public views cities as worsening by the hour, why do the statistics presented in 16–10 accurately reflect urban history? Why

16–10.   Changes in urban and rural population, 1960–70

		1970		Change 1960–70	
	Places	Population (thousands)	Percent	Population (thousands)	Percent
Total population	20,768	203,212	100	+23,889	+13.3
Urbanized areas*	248	118,446	59	+22,598	+23.4
Greater than 1 million	25	70,828	35	+19,044	+36.5
Less than 1 million	223	47,617	24	+3,554	+8.1
Urban outside urbanized areas	3,840	30,878	15	+1,458	+4.9
Rural	13,706	53,887	26	−167	−0.3

* The Bureau of the Census defines an "urbanized area" as a central city of 50,000 plus its urbanized fringe.
SOURCE: U.S. Bureau of the Census (1972), table 4.

did the population of "urbanized areas" grow by 23 percent between 1960 and 1970, whereas rural areas declined by 167,000 people, and cities of less than 50,000 and their environs grew by only 5 percent?

Our discussion of 19th century urbanization provided, in essence, the answers to these questions. The economies of urban agglomeration dictate the location pattern of industry as it expands. From the standpoints of markets and production costs, our larger urban areas have proved superior operating sites, so population growth has followed the pattern of expanding job opportunities. To put it in a slightly different way, in spite of the host of urban problems that add monetary costs and frustrations to the lives of workers and executives, the largest metropolitan areas, urban places with populations of over 1 million, have proved to be the most profitable operating sites for most expanding industries. But for society as a whole, this expansion pattern may not represent the best allocation of resources.

Why are the big cities sick?

In one sense, there is nothing unique about the problems of our largest metropolitan areas. High population density and a high rate of population growth present problems to any urbanized area, especially when much of that growth represents farm-to-city migration.

However, in a second sense, the size of our major metropolitan areas and their combined rapid growth may present unique management problems, and such areas may have grown well beyond their economically optimum sizes. In other words, our hypothesis is that the recent history of American urban growth has been characterized by market failure. Our largest cities have been growing at such a pace that their growth-related problems have outstripped the ability of urban managers to cope with them.

Why has the market failed? Why have cities grown too fast, become too big? The answer, we feel, lies in the same phenomenon that explains why pollution has been carried to uneconomic levels: those who generate expansion, chiefly business firms that create jobs by investing in additional facilities, don't bear the full costs associated with expansion. The firm that adds to its capacity pays for the labor it hires, the interest on its capital investment, and additional local taxes, but the rise in its tax burden doesn't pay for a host of costs that are directly attributable to its operations or to the population growth its new investment has generated.

Examples are extra smog damage, a higher incidence of crime, greater traffic congestion, overcrowded classrooms, and increases in the population density of already overcrowded slums. These are costs borne by the general public or by specific target groups within the public, not by the investing firm. Each firm taken independently may add only a little bit to these problems, but collectively the industries of an urban area generate a backlog of needs that city management hasn't the funds or the facilities to meet.

To recapitulate our hypothesis: Over the past several generations the problems of the Nation's metropolitan areas have been those which characterize any urban place. However, in the largest metropolitan areas they have arisen with such intensity that the costs of additional expansion have outweighed the benefits derived therefrom.[18]

Urban pathology

At this point, it seems useful to examine the economics of several of society's current problems in their urban context. And the place to start is the big city slum, the acres upon acres of what small-town Americans call the wrong side of the tracks, the places which shelter over 10 million low-income Americans, half of whom are black.

What creates a slum? In the ultimate sense, the existence of poor people and their economic and psychological need to congregate produce

---

[18] See Hansen for discussion and bibliography related to the alleged overexpansion of urban places over 750,000 in population.

a slum—the word ghetto is aptly used when applied to our urban slums. Perhaps an expansion of the dictionary definition of a city slum will validate this explanation to your satisfaction.

City slums are islands of urban poverty. They are populated by the entrapped poor: the unskilled; the low-wage workers; the chronically unemployed; those who can't work because they are too old, over-burdened with children, or disabled; the self-employed who manage only a minimal existence from their enterprises; and the children of large families, children who are predominantly slated to grow up and remain in their ghettos as tomorrow's low-income, low-productivity urban population. They crowd together in older housing units where rents per unit, if not per cubic foot, are low and landlords will accommo-date them regardless of their race or ethnic origin.

On these islands, the poor derive an element of security from their proximity to people in the same circumstances, with similar backgrounds, and from largely the same racial, ethnic, or religious group. From these islands, the poor who can work and who have jobs commute athwart the current of rush hour traffic, often at great expense in time and money. They commute to low-paying jobs in the outlying industrial districts, in the central business districts, or in the last vestiges of the original manufacturing center in the city's core. One of the saddest paradoxes of our recent urban history is the conflict between industrial and human migration. In the 1920s, just as the truck released factories from the grip of the central city railyard, southern blacks migrated to the older residen-tial neighborhoods. And where were those neighborhoods? They were adjacent to the very factory districts that were emptying out.[19]

In the slum, city services are rudimentary. Just why isn't clear. Per-haps it's because the poor don't have political punch, or because a geographically even distribution of services isn't ample for dense aggre-gations of low-income people, or both. If not worse, the quality of ghetto schools isn't much better than the quality of other city services. Sub-urbanization has eroded the tax bases of central city school districts, and the urban poor must compete for tax dollars against neighborhoods of well-organized middle-class school patrons who are politically active and articulate. Even where funds per pupil are equalized throughout the city, some educators feel that they are inadequate to provide services that compensate for the environment in which ghetto children must grow up.

Taken together, substandard housing and the congregation of the poor constitute the slum's hallmark. A complicated set of interacting economic and social forces explain both phenomena. Housing makes its way to the poor through a process economists call *filtering*. Neighbor-hoods made up of structures of about the same age command lower

---

[19] See Kain and Persky.

and lower rents as they get older. Consequently, in three or four generations they are within the financial reach of the poor. By that time, they are all so dilapidated that no landlord can afford to make more than the minimum renovations necessary to keep them from crashing to the ground. The landlord can't afford more because any rental increase he could get for the improvements wouldn't cover the additional interest and depreciation charges. Because surrounding properties would remain substandard, they would hold down the attractiveness of the general neighborhood and, therefore, place a ceiling on the rent that could be charged for a single above average unit.

Why must neighborhoods depreciate in this manner? Why aren't sound but modest housing units built for the poor in middle-class neighborhoods when such neighborhoods are first developed? Local building codes plus ethnic and racial discrimination go a long way toward explaining the uniformity of structures in newly created neighborhoods. Historically, local governments, developers, builders, realtors, and middle-income house buyers have adopted policies designed to herd the poor together.[20] And at this writing, attitudes don't seem to have changed—almost everywhere, efforts to effectuate a federal program aimed at creating housing for low-income families in middle-income suburban communities have been scuttled by local resistance.

Generally, governmental programs to deal with the slum have been place- rather than people-oriented. In the 1930s, federally subsidized public housing was built to house the poor, and the program was renewed after World War II. The result was modern, structurally sound slums—the inhabitants of public housing remained poor and had the same social problems that they had in the ghettos of ancient tenements and decaying brownstones. What's more, the public housing program has been a minuscule contributor to the housing supply. In 1960, for example, only 7 percent of eligible families had been able to find places in public housing units.[21]

After World War II, the federal urban renewal program was enacted. Its intention was to improve housing conditions, but, oddly enough, its method was to reduce the supply of housing. Slums were bulldozed, making their sites attractive locations again. But the poor were displaced and crowded into other already decaying neighborhoods, thus driving up rents while intensifying social frictions. And the bulldozed areas were often developed as upper- or middle-income housing areas or sites for public buildings, such as sports arenas. Sardonically, blacks renamed urban renewal Negro removal.

---

[20] Nonwhites comprised 10 percent of 1960's metropolitan area population but accounted for 31 percent of those living in substandard housing, most of it in the slums; see Downs, p. 121.

[21] James R. Prescott, "The Economics of Public Housing: A Normative Analysis" (Ph.D. dissertation, Harvard University, 1964), p. 120, quoted in Schreiber et al., p. 79.

In at least partial recognition of its folly, Congress turned to interest and rent subsidies aimed at letting low-income individuals purchase or rent housing in the open market. The notion underlying this program is that adding *directly to demand* for housing by increasing the housing expenditures of the poor will stimulate increases in supply. So far, these programs have not been enacted on a sufficient scale to allow judging whether this approach will prove to be a panacea for slums.

Paradoxically, the most powerful government stimulus to the provision of better housing for the poor has been the federal income tax provision that allows house buyers to deduct interest payments from their taxable income. This is a subsidy to middle- and upper-income recipients because low-income people don't have incomes high enough to itemize deductions when computing their income tax liabilities. By making housing less expensive for the middle- and upper-income brackets, the filtering process has been speeded up so that the rate at which additional housing comes into the poor man's price bracket has accelerated.[22]

In sum, federal housing policies have probably contributed significantly to the improvement in housing for the poor, with the deductibility of interest payments being the chief factor at work. At any rate, the housing stock has been upgraded—substandard units dropped from 17 million in 1950, or 37 percent of the housing stock, to 7 million units in 1970, or only 10 percent of total housing.[23] How much of this upgrading is attributable to federal housing programs and how much is the result of rising incomes no one has determined. Nevertheless, the slum remains a part of urban life and will as long as people are poor and as long as the nonpoor choose to live apart from the poor.

The other side of the slum coin is urban sprawl, which has arisen from the tendency of urban populations to move out from the city's residential ring to suburban and exurban locations from which they commute to work by auto or train. As poor blacks, Chicanos, and Puerto Ricans have moved into the central city in search of improved economic conditions, middle-class whites, often from the poor immigrant groups of several generations ago, have fled to the suburbs in search of space, fresh air, and isolation from other races and ethnic groups. What makes sprawl a problem? "If the new residential subdivisions are too extravagant in their use of land—house lots too large—or if much usable land is skipped over in the march of urbanization outward, the urban area grows 'unnecessarily large' and transportation, communication, utility services, local public services all become 'unnecessarily' inefficient and uneconomical."[24]

A horror story of unfortunate veracity is the one frequently told in

----

[22] See Schreiber et al., pp. 72–80, for an evaluation of U.S. housing policy.

[23] Downs, p. 117.

[24] Thompson, pp. 320–21.

middle-class circles about the couple with four youngsters who moved to an acre lot surrounded by cornfields in the 1950s. To their dismay, they found that the property tax quadrupled in the 1960s when the farmland was built on by other couples, also with four heirs, and new schools, roads, a sewer system, and a waterworks all had to be built overnight.

Traffic congestion is a thread that has come to tie the central business districts, the ghetto, and suburbia in a common package. Since World War II, the expression "rush hour traffic" has ceased to connote a mild source of aggravation. The journey to work and back has come to be viewed as one of the most expensive and unpleasant aspects of urban life. As you might suspect, this postwar development is largely a consequence of market failure.

By the 1920s, the truck and automobile made a suburban location for factories and residences a feasible alternative to downtown locations. After World War II, rising per capita incomes generated huge increases in the demand for suburban housing. At the same time, changes in production technology made the single-story, rambling factory building imperative. Urban sprawl accelerated in no small part because transportation pricing policies were weighted in favor of the suburbanization of the American city.

The automobile has proved the cheapest and most convenient conveyance for accommodating all of a family's transportation needs, or at least so it appears to the individual suburban family. However, no single motorist pays commuting prices that reflect the full cost associated with his daily journey to work.

Although registration fees and motor fuel taxes are earmarked for highway construction, they do not vary with the time or place in which automobiles are driven. On a per mile basis, the provision of highway services is much more expensive in an urban area, particularly at peak hours, than in the open country, especially when the costs of air pollution and congestion are taken into account. Consequently, commuters have been consistently subsidized by off-peak drivers and those who drive outside commuter patterns. Naturally, suburbanization received a shot in the arm from this pricing policy, and, logically, suburbanites reacted by passing up mass transit alternatives. The strength of this reaction is testified to by a recent study which showed that motorists would actually have to be paid in addition to being granted free fares to utilize Chicago's existing rail facilities at their peak-hour capacity.[25]

As people moved to the suburbs in the early postwar period, managers of bus, streetcar, and commuter trainlines reacted to lower volume by curtailing service and reducing maintenance, often by cutting back service during shopping hours. City dwellers reacted, in turn, by moving

---

[25] See Moses and Williamson.

to the suburbs at a faster rate, since worsening public transit meant that they needed a car to shop and visit anyhow. City governments were forced to take over bankrupt transit companies, and service continued to be cut back in response to declining revenues. The downhill slide of mass transit accelerated, and the attractiveness of suburbs increased accordingly.

Thus, today, one of the most irksome, paradoxical, and costly urban problems is traffic congestion. While railroad trackage is underutilized and attempts to intitiate commuter buses fail, motorists fight traffic snarls to get to work at speeds averaging 25–35 miles an hour on speedways that were built to accommodate lower volumes at 55–65 miles an hour— all because the private automobile has proved the cheapest means of commutation for the suburbanite.

While the upper- and middle-income suburban commuter is fighting traffic on his way downtown, ghetto workers are on their way to the industrial suburbs by auto or public transport. The reverse commuter experiences the realities of market failure to an even greater degree than his suburban counterpart. Commuter trains don't connect the ghetto with the industrial park. Bus routes between the two often require several transfers and up to two hours' travel each way. In many cases, car pools have proved the easiest and cheapest way to get from the inner city to outlying factory jobs, but the required routes frequently don't permit taking advantage of the expressways, on which reverse flow traffic is characteristically light. In short, in today's American city, getting to work is a genuine hassle regardless of the commuter's race, ethnic origin, or income status; but if you are black and poor, your commutation problems are likely to be worse than those of middle-income suburbanites.

It must seem obvious to you that only a small degree of foresight was needed to establish better metropolitan transport systems. It is possible to have roadways, commuter trains, and bus service that avoid the kind of congestion that requires many if not most transit commuters to stand, and holds traffic on freeways to second-gear speeds. However, an atomized governmental structure has made consolidated metropolitan transportation planning a pipe dream. On top of this, federal motor fuel taxes and federal highway policies have been the chief forces behind distortion of the prices that the commuter faces when deciding between driving his car and using public transportation.

It's also true that at the local level overall transportation facilities could be altered to eliminate congestion through capital investment in mass transit, especially buses, and extensive use of variable tolls whose peak charges come at rush hours. But intergovernmental bickering has frustrated most such attempts. Consequently, although local traffic is not a federal matter in the usual American political tradition, Congress has recognized the inability of metropolitan governments to act in concert and has voted funds to aid mass transit systems. However, to this date the highway lobby has blocked efforts to channel funds from the highway trust fund for building mass transit facilities—it seems that relieving highway congestion by adding to roadways is a justified expenditure but that relieving congestion by reducing the number of vehicles on the highways is unjustifiable even if the latter proves cheaper.

A second problem that knits the history of suburb and city together is the metropolitan area's fiscal dilemma. Postwar urban sprawl is a continuation of a trend that reaches back into the 19th century. Today, the typical urbanized area has grown to consist of a downtown business and shopping district, the old industrial district in or near the heart of the central city, the decaying slum districts, older middle-income residential districts within the original city limits, plus the suburban residential, industrial, and shopping districts. All these entities are economically interdependent. The functioning of one unit depends on the operation of the others, and public services are vital to all. But history has imposed a political grid on the metropolis which in some instances divides local government into a hundred or more separate governments, with drastic results from the standpoint of public finance.

An atomized governmental structure would pose few problems if public services were most efficiently rendered on a small-area basis. But, in fact, traffic control, metropolitan highways, public transportation, police protection, zoos, research libraries, and pollution control are services that are rendered most effectively on a metropolitan scale. And taxing power and local needs don't necessarily match—the factory suburb with its rich tax base and few children to educate standing beside the bedroom community that averages 1.5 children per residence is an anomaly generated by the automotive revolution. What's more, given that most children move out of a district after being educated suggests that the larger society that benefits from their education ought to help finance their schools. Similarly, a central city made up increasingly of welfare recipients can't finance its own welfare program indefinitely—income redistribution programs require donors as well as recipients.

In recent years, metropolitan areas have experimented with a variety of devices for solving the intergovernmental fiscal dilemma. Financial responsibility for income redistribution policies, i.e., welfare programs, has been moved to the country level in some metropolitan areas. In some instances, services whose quality is of area-wide significance have been provided by a county-wide department—police protection in Los Angeles is an example. In many pollution control cases, states or multi-county districts have designed area-wide programs to combat pollution. The local property tax as a basis for school finance is under attack in the federal courts, which could result in area-wide financing for public education.

In Dade County, Florida (the greater-Miami area), a new county government was formed in the late 1950s which made possible the transfer of some government functions to the county level. And if minimum performance standards aren't met in separate municipalities, the county government has the right to take over operation of those functions. In Los Angeles County, the Lakewood Plan cities operate as if they were consumer cooperatives by purchasing all their city services from the county, other cities, and private vendors.

Where these various experiments in government organization will lead is not clear at this point. However, it is clear that so far they are just experiments. In no sense can it be said that metropolitan areas are well on the way to solving their fiscal problems. As yet, no institutions exist to guarantee that the groups benefiting from particular public services will in fact pay for them or that the level of government that is most efficient in producing various services will be charged with doing so.

Local reliance on the taxation of property has grown to be the most important source of fiscal mismatching. The property tax became the most important local tax when land and improvements approximately measured the value one received from local government services, including the education of an essentially local labor force. But over the decades, local governments have multiplied in each urban area, labor has become more mobile, and individual taxing units, i.e., individual municipalities, have become increasingly specialized. Consequently, the value of local land and improvements no longer mirrors the tasks the local government must perform. To make matters worse, those who might add to property values by improving structures in declining areas are discouraged from doing so by the knowledge that this would cause their property taxes to rise.

Across the nation, affluent suburbs have been able to maintain relatively low property tax rates while central cities have had to escalate levies in order to cope with problems associated with mounting traffic congestion, crime, and pollution. The same kinds of observations apply to school districts: in recent years, some inner-city school districts have been faced with the possibility of having to close their schools for lack of operating funds, and some districts have had to terminate all but the core of their educational programs.

Alternative local taxes have been adopted over the past generation, especially local income and sales taxes. However, conflict with state governments and the reluctance of suburbs to levy comparable taxes have hampered central cities in their attempts to adopt other forms of taxes. Fees and user charges which can be applied to certain public services in much the same manner as prices apply to ordinary private-sector transactions have been more widely used in recent years. But students of public finance feel that much ground remains unbroken in this area.

The history of the major American city in the 20th century certainly doesn't constitute an unblemished record of human accomplishment and flexibility—quite the contrary. On the one hand, our big cities have become titans of industrial might, and as transportation and production technology have changed urban configurations, they have adapted accordingly. On the other hand, the major metropolitan areas have not only mirrored society's social and economic problems, but, largely because of their high densities and gigantic scales, have intensified those problems. Of course, continued per capita income growth can increase our ability to cope with contemporary problems—to wage war on poverty, to reduce pollution and traffic congestion, and to eliminate slums. Whether we will resolve to do so and find the required organizational techniques is another question—one to which the postwar record does not suggest an encouraging answer.

MAINTAINING GROWTH: A POSTSCRIPT

Our subject has been economic growth—more specifically, American economic growth. We have discussed the history of a process in operation, specifically, the process of economic development. This concluding section will face the question: How do we maintain or, if it is our choice, speed the rate of economic growth? But first it seems appropriate for us to raise the question, Why is growth important?

Economic growth is a means to an end. That end is a higher level of economic welfare per capita. This means that growth is capable of bringing more goods, more services (including the services of the environment), and more leisure to the citizens of an economy. In the discussion that follows, bear in mind that by economic growth we mean more than growth in GNP per person—rather, we mean growth in individual economic well-being. This concept goes well beyond the GNP accounts to include changes in leisure time, variations in the distribution of income, and the ebb and flow of environmental services.

But greater economic welfare also serves other ends—it provides the material basis and the time required for men to achieve more meaningful lives, to raise the quality of life. Historically, it was felt that the good life would be at hand once man had easy access to food, shelter, and clothing, so that he no longer had to spend every waking hour grubbing for a livelihood. But as we have become more and more affluent, we have learned that achieving the good life is not quite so simple.

Man's material aspirations have escalated along with the productivity of his economy. And, as we have remarked, both within and among economies, as some have become increasingly rich, others have been left behind in poverty, relatively untouched by the fruits of economic growth and higher per capita income. As a consequence, warfare of one kind or another has been carried on continuously between the haves and have-nots. Yet continued growth, we feel, will allow us to catch up with our rising aspirations and to bring high levels of economic welfare to all nations and their citizens—or will if growth as recorded in the GNP accounts doesn't come at so great a cost to the environment that a growing GNP per person actually masks a reduced level of personal welfare.

Thus, as a policy matter, we are interested in at least maintaining growth and, if possible, in raising the growth rate, both here in the United States and in the world as a whole. This, we caution, is not the economist's judgment—the Nation has made the value judgment that the growth rate is a concern of national policy. Further, recent legislative history demonstrates that gains from growth in GNP per person should not be overwhelmed by associated losses in the services rendered by the environment. Let us now review our knowledge of the growth process by summarizing its important variables and then face the questions of how to maintain and accelerate the rate of economic development.

The variables of growth

Recall that the key variables which actively determine or modify the course of economic growth in a market economy are technology, resource inputs, methods of organizing production, and social goals, including ways of sharing economic benefits. 16–11 is an outline of these

16–11. Maintaining or accelerating economic
growth in a market economy

1. Advance knowledge
    a. research
    b. innovating enterprise
    c. education
2. Expand inputs
    a. use of resources
    b. quality of labor
    c. incentives to invest
3. Organize efficiently
    a. full use of resources
    b. flexible adjustment of resource allocation pattern
    c. resource allocation guided by free choice
4. Distribute fairly
    a. broad participation
    b. security and opportunity

variables and their most important subelements. With this outline in mind, let us review the results of a study which analyzes the expansion of GNP in the United States between 1929 and 1957.[26] Note, however, that al-

---

[26] Denison (1962).

though the figures presented give an air of precision, this and similar studies rely on a great deal of educated guesswork in making estimates and weighting specific variables. Tentative though such studies are, they are a great source of insight.

Over the 1929–57 period:

1. Increases in employment and rising average labor productivity resulting from shorter working hours accounted for 27 percent of the total increase in output.
2. Increases in the educational level of the labor force so increased productivity that 23 percent of total expansion is attributable to this factor.
3. The increased percentage of women in the labor force and the more efficient utilization of women accounted for 4 percent of total extensive growth.
4. Increases in capital inputs contributed 15 percent toward the total increment in output.
5. Increased knowledge and its application to production, marketing, and transportation and communication accounted for 20 percent of total expansion.
6. Economies of scale realized through the extensive growth of the economy produced 9 percent of the increase in total product.

Note that increases in the quality of the labor force and the application of new knowledge to production accounted for 43 percent of the rise in the annual rate of production over the 1929–57 period. In contrast, increased physical capital yielded only 15 percent of the rise in GNP. This shows that, having become the leading nation economically, we no longer can depend, as in the 19th century, upon extensive growth bringing with it the importation of capital and people that embody the latest technology and knowledge. Growth must now come from learning more, developing new technologies, and building the capital and teaching the people that will embody new knowledge. With this in mind, let's investigate the problems of maintaining and accelerating expansion and intensive growth in our market economy.

Influencing growth rates

Modern industrial society has been made possible by revolutionary advances in our knowledge of methods for controlling our environment (physical and social) to serve our goals. Thus, if growth is our interim goal, primary attention should be given to ways to advance our knowledge. This requires more research and perhaps more emphasis on re-research in business administration and methods of organizing our economic institutions. We need to find better ways to encourage invention, and we need to encourage new and expanding business enterprise that is resourceful in putting better methods into operation. Expanded education is an aid both to research into new areas of knowledge and to faster application of existing knowledge.

Greater output is in part a matter of expanded inputs, as we have seen; but the inputs need not be in the same proportions or of the same quality. With our limited existing physical resources, we need to find better ways to utilize resources efficiently and to utilize a greater variety of nature's resources, especially the more plentiful ones, to serve our purposes. And we need to learn how to increase our utilization of various resources in ways that don't decrease our use of other resources in a more than offsetting manner. Unless we learn how to speed up our growth of output in ways that don't drown us in pollutants, the population growth of both our nation and our planet will have to be limited within the next few generations.[27]

Part of our higher standard of living has resulted from reducing our labor input per person, especially the hard muscle effort and the long hours. As we have seen, this has been made possible through laborsaving machinery plus education and improved skills. Thus, greater attention needs to be given to ways to make workers more productive. Our capital per worker is still increasing, but net capital formation has been slowing down. If we are to maintain full employment and maintain or speed our growth rate, we must not only encourage investment but also find additional ways to increase the amount of capital each workingman can control.

Productive inputs also need to be organized efficiently to serve social goals. The first principle of efficiency is to fully utilize available resources; so every effort must be made to check and minimize recessions during which workers and equipment are partly idle.

At the same time, we must recognize the need for continual adjustments to change. There can be no guarantee to particular industries or producer groups that demand for their services or their income levels will be maintained without adjustment or change on their part. We must reexamine our economic institutions to see how flexibly they adjust to change and how well they contribute to encouraging more mobility of capital and labor resources.

We should also resist the incessant and often successful pressure of various producer and labor groups to use government agencies to force a resource allocation pattern that protects narrow vested interests rather than the public interest. Our market economy is consumer-oriented, and its efficient operation requires a decentralization of production decisions

---

[27] The exact date of Armageddon is hotly debated, but most students of ecology in both the social and biological sciences are agreed that it is in the foreseeable future. For a bold forecasting attempt, see Meadows et al.

among a multitude of individuals and firms. This preserves a maximum freedom of individual choice in reaching a social consensus as to priorities among social goals.

We also need to devise machinery that will bring to bear the interests of third parties who are affected by resource allocation decisions. The spillover costs of pollution and the spillover benefits of education are only examples of the external effects of private decisions. In this interdependent economy, many private contracts have widespread public ramifications.

Finally, our growth depends ultimately upon the consensus of American citizens as to how our resources are allocated and used; and this consensus, in turn, depends upon a feeling that the benefits of growth are being distributed fairly. If we understand current American public opinion, equity in the distribution of income is defined as a more equal distribution of benefits than now characterizes the Nation, notwithstanding the prevailing discontent over our "welfare mess." Fairness also involves protection against sudden or undue hardship, especially when the causes are beyond individual control. And fairness is not consistent with discrimination in economic affairs along lines of race, religion, ethnic background, or sex. But, as we interpret the American frame of mind, fairness does not require equality of income. Rather, it involves an expectation of equal opportunity to serve individual goals by saving, education, effort, and ability.

One of the driving forces in our economic history has been the range of opportunities afforded to the hardworking and unusual individual to try out ideas and to advance himself. Our market organization has provided a framework in which the freedom of individuals has been relatively great in spite of anticompetitive concentrations of business, professional, and labor groups. On the other hand, racial, religious, ethnic, and sexual attitudes have circumscribed the economic freedom of some people in spite of their unusual assets and their willingness to work hard.

Perhaps the best way to bring our study of growth into broad perspective is to address directly the problem of raising our long-term growth rate. Denison whose work was cited above, has calculated the specific changes necessary to raise his projected growth rate of total income by one percentage point per year over a 20 year period.[28] In other words, he has determined what must be done to cause total income to grow at an average yearly rate of $4\frac{1}{3}$ percent rather than the $3\frac{1}{3}$ percent he projected for the 20-year span. Modest as 1 percent sounds, note that it is more than 25 percent of the projected $3\frac{1}{3}$ percent growth rate. To see just how formidable the job of spurring growth is, we need only take a cursory look at his catalog of required changes. The most remarkable characteristic of his list is the very small gains that

---

[28] Denison (May 1962).

come from drastic changes in each of the growth variables. Again we stress, Denison's work is groping and tentative, impressionistic in many respects; but it does highlight the fact that growth comes from many specific sources, each of which makes a modest contribution to overall expansion.

To raise the extensive growth rate by one percentage point per year, Denison suggests the changes listed below.

Increase inputs by:

1. doubling immigration—a gain of 0.10 percent;
2. adding three hours to the projected average workweek—a gain of 0.28 percent;
3. adding one year to the average length of schooling—a gain of 0.07 percent;
4. cutting structural unemployment and underemployment by one half—a gain of 0.03 percent; and
5. raising the increment in the capital stock by 10 percent—a gain of 0.20 percent.

And increase output per unit of input by:

1. abolishing racial discrimination—a gain of 0.04 percent;
2. removing international trade barriers—a gain of 0.07 percent;
3. repealing "fair trade" laws—a gain of 0.05 percent;
4. eliminating union-enforced rigidities in the labor market—a gain of 0.02 percent;
5. adopting more widespread use of incentive pay systems—a gain of 0.05 percent
6. consolidating the regulated industries, such as railroads—a gain of 0.02 percent;
7. reducing the lag between the development of new business methods and their adoption—a gain of 0.03 percent; and
8. increasing research and development outlays—a gain of 0.04 percent.

To Denison's list we would add effective antipollution controls that would increase the flow of environmental services. We would also add elimination of the conditions in our urban ghettos that make life a dead-end experience for millions of Americans.

Certainly, the above proposals do not constitute unachievable modifications of our system—each of the kinds of changes listed has taken place in the past. How realistic it is to assume that all of them will be adopted is another question—especially in view of the fact that many of the proposals are not directly subject to policy variation. Denison's exercise is perhaps less a guide to accelerating growth than a point-by-point enumeration of the difficulty of increasing the growth rate. This seems a fitting note on which to conclude this text.

SUMMARY

Affluence is not an unmixed blessing. Americans find themselves vexed by a host of problems that seem to be corollaries to economic growth and high per capita income.

1. Many of the problems that characterize the American economy are susceptible to control through governmental intervention. Consequently, federal, state, and local governments have all increased the size and scope of their operations since 1920. In addition, civilian government expenditures have grown simply because the demand for government services exhibits a high income elasticity; for example, affluence has brought a tremendous increase in automobile ownership and has generated a concomitant growth in highway building, maintenance, and patrolling.

In recent years, concern that the United States was characterized by public privation in the presence of private affluence led to significant increases in civilian government outlays. However, whether the mix of private and public economic activity is now at a socially optimum level is not clear because the public will in this regard is not easily quantified.

2. Over the past generation, increases in economic activity have taken an increasingly heavy toll in environmental degradation. Governments have reacted to "the environmental crisis" by adopting a regulation-enforcement strategy which has often been combined with subsidies to aid polluters in their purchases of antipollution devices. Generally, this approach has been adopted in a piecemeal fashion and has failed to reverse the course of environmental decay. Most economists agree that our antipollution efforts have been ineffectual because we have not adopted a strategy that places a sufficiently high price on each act of pollution (in the form of fines, fees, or taxes) so that polluters would avoid pollution.

3. America's largest metropolitan areas are beset with the usual array of urban problems; however, the great intensity of their problems suggests that our municipal giants have grown well beyond economic limits. Slums, urban sprawl, traffic congestion, crime, fiscal ills, and an atomized governmental structure which nearly paralyzes decision-making all imply that the market mechanism has failed to stop metropolitan area growth at|optimum population levels.

Various attempts to reorganize the structure of metropolitan area government, to introduce new sources of revenue, and to increase the flow of federal funds to the cities have made some headway toward solving our many urban problems. However, life in most large cities is inferior to what it was a generation ago—many are convinced that our biggest cities have all but collapsed—and recent trends give no clear indication that the downward course is going to be reversed in the near future.

4. Economic growth is a means by which men can free themselves from material preoccupations and elevate the quality of life. However, increasing the growth rate is not easy to accomplish. The sources of growth are tremendous in number, and their susceptibility to control through public policy is limited. Nevertheless, given the socially desired ends that increased economic capacity can accomplish, continued or accelerated growth is well worth pursuing.

REFERENCES

P. W. Barkley and D. W. Seckler, *Economic Growth and Environmental Decay: the Solution Becomes the Problem* (New York: Harcourt Brace Jovanovich, Inc., 1972).

K. E. Boulding, "The Economics of the Coming Spaceship Earth," reprinted in Garret DeBell, *The Environmental Handbook* (New York: Ballantine Books, Inc., 1970).

E. F. Denison, "How to Raise the High-Employment Growth Rate by One Percentage Point," *AER*, May 1962.

——, *The Sources of Economic Growth in the United States and the Alternatives Before Us* (New York: Committee for Economic Development, 1962).

R. Dorfman and N. S. Dorfman, eds., *Economics of the Environment,* (New York: W. W. Norton & Co., Inc., 1972).

A. Downs, *Urban Problems and Prospects* (Chicago: Markham Publishing Co., 1970).

Economic Report of the President (Washington, D.C.: U.S. Government Printing Office, 1972).

R. Eyestone, *Political Economy: Politics and Policy Analysis* (Chicago: Markham Publishing Co., 1971).

A. M. Freeman and R. H. Haveman, "Clean Rhetoric, Dirty Water," *PI*, Summer 1972.

——, R. H. Haveman and A. V. Kneese, *The Economics of Environmental Policy* (New York: John Wiley & Sons, Inc., 1973).

J. K. Galbraith, *The Affluent Society* (Boston: Houghton Mifflin Co., 1958).

N. M. Hansen, *Intermediate-Size Cities as Growth Centers* (New York: Praeger Publishers, 1971).

J. F. Kain and J. J. Persky, "The North's Stake in Southern Rural Poverty," in *Rural Poverty in the United States* (Washington, D.C.: U.S. Government Printing Office, 1968).

D. H. Meadows et al., *The Limits to Growth* (New York: Universe Books, 1972).

L. Moses and H. Williamson, Jr., "Value of Time, Choice of Mode, and the Subsidy Issue in Urban Transportation," *JPE*, June 1963.

A. F. Schreiber, P. K. Gatons, and R. B. Clemmer, *Economics of Urban Problems: An Introduction* (Boston: Houghton Mifflin Co., 1971).

W. R. Thompson, *A Preface to Urban Economics* (Baltimore: Johns Hopkins University Press, 1968).

U.S. Bureau of the Census, *1970 Census of Population: Number of Inhabitants, United States Summary* (Washington, D.C.: U.S. Government Printing Office, 1972).

————, *Governmental Finances in 1969–70* (Washington, D.C.: U.S. Government Printing Office, 1971).

————, *1967 Census of Governments*, vol. 6, no. 5 (Washington, D.C.: U.S. Government Printing Office, 1969).

————, *Governmental Finances 1967–68* (Washington, D.C.: U.S. Government Printing Office, 1969).

U.S. General Accounting Office, *Examination into the Effectiveness of the Construction Grant Program for Abating, Controlling, and Preventing Water Pollution, Report to the Congress by the Comptroller General of the United States, No. B-16650* (November 1969).

Index

INDEX

This book has been set in 10 and 9 point Caledonia, leaded 2 points. Part and chapter numbers are set in 36 and 48 point Baskerville, and chapter and part titles are in 24 point Baskerville. The size of the type page is 27 x 46½ picas.